Women's Realities, Women's Choices

Canadian Edition

Women's Realities, Women's Choices

An Introduction to Women's and Gender Studies

Hunter College Women's and Gender Studies Collective
and Joan Simalchik

Oxford University Press is a department of the University of Oxford.
It furthers the University's objective of excellence in research, scholarship,
and education by publishing worldwide. Oxford is a registered trade mark of
Oxford University Press in the UK and in certain other countries.

Published in Canada by
Oxford University Press
8 Sampson Mews, Suite 204,
Don Mills, Ontario M3C 0H5 Canada

www.oupcanada.com

Copyright © Oxford University Press Canada 2017

The moral rights of the authors have been asserted

Database right Oxford University Press (maker)

Women's Realities, Women's Choices was originally published in English in 2005.
This edition is published by arrangement with Oxford University Press.
198 Madison Avenue, New York, N.Y. 10016-4314, USA.
Copyright © 1983, 1995, 2005 by Oxford University Press, Inc.

All rights reserved. No part of this publication may be reproduced, stored in
a retrieval system, or transmitted, in any form or by any means, without the
prior permission in writing of Oxford University Press, or as expressly permitted
by law, by licence, or under terms agreed with the appropriate reprographics
rights organization. Enquiries concerning reproduction outside the scope of the
above should be sent to the Permissions Department at the address above
or through the following url: www.oupcanada.com/permission/permission_request.php

Every effort has been made to determine and contact copyright holders.
In the case of any omissions, the publisher will be pleased to make
suitable acknowledgement in future editions.

Library and Archives Canada Cataloguing in Publication

Women's realities, women's choices : an introduction
to women's and gender studies / The Hunter College Women's
and Gender Studies Collective; Joan Simalchik.— Canadian edition.

Includes bibliographical references and index.
ISBN 978-0-19-543023-3 (paperback)

1. Women's studies—Textbooks. 2. Women's studies—Canada—
Textbooks. I. Simalchik, Joan, 1951-, editor II. Hunter College.
Women's and Gender Studies Collective, editor

HQ1180.W63 2016   305.4   C2016-905045-9

Cover image: © Delphine Renou. Kabul 2013. Shamsia Hassani, an Afghan Graffiti Artist.

Oxford University Press is committed to our environment.
This book is printed on Forest Stewardship Council® certified paper
and comes from responsible sources.

Printed and bound in the United States of America

1 2 3 4 — 20 19 18 17

To our teachers, colleagues, and students
Our parents and children
Our spouses, partners, and friends
And our sisters and brothers both literal and metaphorical
We dedicate this book in the spirit of collaboration, intellectual engagement, political commitment, lively debate, and love in which it was written.

—Hunter College Women's and Gender Studies Collective, 2015

The Canadian edition is dedicated to the feminist community of learners from coast to coast to coast who are working to create a more just world.

—Joan Simalchik, 2017

Brief Overview

Tables and Boxes xiii
Preface xv
The Authors xvii
Introduction 1

Part I | Defining Women and Gender
1 Cultural Representations of Women 5
2 Historical Ideas and Theories about Women and Gender 31
3 Intersectionality 58
4 Learning, Making, and Doing Gender 80
5 Gender and the Politics of the Body 107

Part II | Women's Relationships, Women's Selves
6 Families and Their Configurations 126
7 Women over the Life Course 155
8 Women's Health 182

Part III | Women in Society
9 Women and Education 215
10 Women and Religion 245
11 Women and Work 270
12 Women and Politics 299

Glossary 328
References 331
Index 365

Contents

Tables and Boxes xiii
Preface xv
The Authors xvii
Introduction 1

Part I | Defining Women and Gender

1 Cultural Representations of Women

Culture, Representation, and Gender 6
- Experience, Perception, and the Construction of Reality 6
- The Construction of Gender in Culture and Individuals 6

Language as a Cultural System 8
- The Relationship between Language and Culture 8
- Changes in Language 9

Enduring Symbols of Women 9
- Selected Images of Women in Mythical and Religious Stories 9

Changing Representations of Women's Sexuality 10
- The "Sexual Revolution" and Its Legacies 10
- Women's Sexuality in Recent Popular Culture 12

Consuming the Body Beautiful 15
Can Reality Be Changed by Changing Images? 18
- Reshaping Representation 18
- Women's Search for Self through Art 19

Women's Search for Self through Literature 20
- Women as Heroic 21
- Telling Other Stories 22
- Writing as Political Activism 23

Representation in the Internet Age 23
Gender in Film: A Case Study 24
Summary 28
Discussion Questions 29
Recommended Resources 29

2 Historical Ideas and Theories about Women and Gender

Why Ideas and Theories Are Important 32
The "Waves" of Feminism 34
Ancient and Early Modern Ideas about Women and Gender 35
Classical Liberalism and Feminism 37
- Wollstonecraft 38
- Mill and Taylor 39
- Contemporary Liberal Feminism 40

Socialism and Feminism 40
- Marx and Engels 41
- Zetkin and Kollontai 41
- Utopian Socialism and Social Gospel 42
- Goldman 43
- Contemporary Socialist Feminism and Marxist Feminism 43

Simone de Beauvoir 44
- Woman as "Object" 44
- Woman as "Other" 44

Contemporary Feminist Debates 45
- Radical Feminism and Cultural Feminism 45
- Black Feminism 48
- Post-modern Feminism 49
- Psychoanalytic Feminism 50
- Ecofeminism 50
- Transnational Feminism 51

Contemporary Feminist Philosophies 52
- Rethinking "Knowledge" and Values of Inquiry 53

Summary 55
Notes 56
Discussion Questions 56
Recommended Resources 57

3 Intersectionality

Intersections of Oppression 60
Heteronormativity and Heterosexism 63
Historical Foundations of Intersectionality 65

Sojourner Truth 65
Anna Julia Cooper 66
Angela Davis 66
Audre Lorde 67
Intersectional Approaches to Feminist Activism 68
Shifting Policy Demands 69
Global Intersections 70
Intersectional Approaches to Feminist Scholarship 72
Intersectional Identities 72
Research Methods 73
Debates over Intersectionality 75
Summary 77
Discussion Questions 78
Recommended Readings 78

4 Learning, Making, and Doing Gender

What Is Gender? 81
Sex versus Gender 82
Gender Expression 83
Traditional Explanations for Gender Differences 84
Anatomical and Evolutionary Differences 84
Psychoanalytic Theory 86
Neurobiological and Hormonal Explanations 88
Feminist Critiques of Theories of Gender 90
Feminist Psychoanalysis 90
The Importance of Culture 91
The Importance of Relatedness 91
Rethinking Biology 92
How Is Gender Learned? 93
Cognitive-Developmental Theory 93
Social Learning Theory 94
Gender Schema Theory 95
Social Interactions and Gender Roles 99
Performativity Theory 100
How Gender Is Enforced 101
Alternative Gender Arrangements 101
Historical Challenges to Gender 101
Gender outside the Binary 103

Summary 104
Discussion Questions 105
Recommended Resources 105

5 Gender and the Politics of the Body

Feminism and the Body 108
Mind/Body Dualism 109
Naturalizing the Body 109
The Nature of Sex Differences 111
The Gendered Brain 111
The Sexed Body: Hormones, Chromosomes, and Genitalia 113
The Politics of "Nature" 114
Discourse/Knowledge/Power 114
Discourses of Sexuality 115
Feminists Rethink the Body 118
Summary 121
Discussion Questions 122
Recommended Resources 122

Part II | Women's Relationships, Women's Selves

6 Families and Their Configuration

The Family as an Evolving Social Organization 127
The Nuclear and Extended Family 129
Conventional Marriage: Why Marry? 130
Whom to Marry? 131
Diverse Marital Households 132
The Incorporated Wife 133
Children in the Family 135
Elders in the Family 137
Marriage and Gender Roles in North America in Historical Perspective 138
Extramarital Experiences 141
Divorce 141
Alternatives to Conventional Marriage in the Past 142
Religious Communities 142
Labouring Communities 142
Utopian and Experimental Communities 143

Families in the Early Twenty-First
    Century   145
   Changes in the Global South   145
   Changes in the Global North   145
"New" Family Configurations   146
   Blended Families   146
   Single-Parent Families   146
   *Consensual Unions: Cohabitation, Domestic
        Partners   147*
   Power, Domination, and Rape   148
   Multiracial Unions and Families   148
   Families We Choose   149
   Same-Sex Families   149
   Visiting Unions—Living Apart Together   150
   Transnational Families   150
   Role Reversals   151
   Choosing Not to Mother   151
   Women on Their Own   151
Summary   152
Discussion Questions   153
Recommended Resources   154

7   Women over the Life Course

Girlhood   156
Daughter in the Family   157
   Female Infanticide   157
   The Value of Daughters   158
   Naming the Daughter   160
   Daughters' Work   160
   Parental Relationships   161
   Sibling Relationships   161
   Inheritance   163
Motherhood   164
   Images of Mothers   164
   Parental Behaviour: "Instinct" and Culture   168
   *The Assignment of Motherhood: Whose Interest
        Does It Serve?   170*
   *The Cultural Shaping of Biological Events Related to
        Motherhood   170*
   Women Other Than Birth Mothers Who Mother   172
Women Growing Older: The Double Standard
    of Aging   173
Life Events and Role Transitions   174
   Mid-life to Later Adulthood   174
   Divorce   174
   Widowhood   174
   Singlehood   176
   Motherhood   176
   Grandparenthood   176
   Housing Transitions   176
   Workforce Changes   177
   Retirement   177
The Sisterhood of Women   178
Summary   178
Discussion Questions   179
Recommended Resources   179

8   Women's Health

The Women's Health Movement   183
   Redefining and Reframing Health   184
   Why "Women's" Health?   185
   Health, Gender, and Human Rights   186
   Health-Care Systems   186
Uncovering the Gender Dynamics of Western
    Medicine   188
   Woman as Deviant   188
   Woman as "the Weaker Sex"   189
   The Gendered Profession of Medicine   189
The Medicalization of Life Processes   190
   Menstruation to Menopause   191
   Reproductive Rights   192
   Childbirth   194
   Sexuality   195
Gendered Violence   196
   Intimate-Partner Violence   196
   Rape and Its Impact   196
   Bodies as Battlegrounds   197
   Female Genital Cutting   199
Impact of Social and Cultural Disparities on
    Women's Health   201
   Health Status and Risks   201
   Poverty   202
   Racial and Ethnic Discrimination   203
   Occupational Health Risks   203
Women and Physical Health: Some Specific
    Concerns   203
   Heart Disease   203
   Cancer   204
   *Sexually Transmitted Disease Infections, Including
        HIV/AIDS   204*

Hysterectomy   206
Osteoporosis   206
Alzheimer's Disease   206
Women and Mental Health   206
Gendered Differences   206
Homophobic and Transphobic Bias   207
Women as Special-Risk/Vulnerable Populations   207
Depression   208
Women as Refugees   209
Women with Disabilities   209
Older Women   209
Women Who Are Incarcerated   210
Summary   210
Note   211
Discussion Questions   211
Recommended Resources   212

Part III | Women in Society

9   Women and Education

Why Education Matters   216
A Matter of Life or Death   216
The Politics of Knowledge   216
Education as a Contested Arena: What Should Be Taught?   217
Women's Traditional Knowledge   217
Men as the Measure of Knowledge   217
The Rise of Feminist Scholarship   217
Contemporary Constraints   218
Education as a Contested Arena: Who Should Be Taught?   218
Gender, Educational Participation, and Illiteracy Globally   218
Women's Struggles for Formal Education in the Past   220
European Struggles for Women's Education   222
European Colonization and Women's Education   223
The Debate in Canada   224
Women's Struggles for Education in the World Today   225
Broadening Canadian Educational Participation   226

Schools as Socializers of Gender Inequities   227
Elementary Schools   227
Secondary Schools   227
Post-secondary Education   228
Educational Institutions as Gendered Workplaces   231
Educational Barriers of Girls/Women in Diverse Communities in the Global North   233
Gender and Cultural Assimilation   233
Indigenous Experiences   233
Black Canadian Experiences   233
Immigrant Experiences   234
Multicultural Education/Ethnic Studies as Resistance   234
The Contemporary Struggle for Equal Access to Knowledge   235
Re-entry/Adult Women   236
Women: The New Post-secondary Majority?   236
Is There a Male Crisis in Educational Access?   236
Transforming the Curriculum   237
Empowering Women Learners   238
Educational Achievements of Girls and Womens Schools Debated   238
Womens Struggles to Become Scientists   238
Women and Gender Studies   241
Summary   241
Discussion Questions   243
Recommended Resources   243

10   Women and Religion

Religious Beliefs   246
What Is Religion?   246
Religion and Social Reform   247
World Religions   248
Females in the Supernatural World   248
Beyond the Gender Binary in Religions   252
The Non-religious   252
Religion and Social Controls   253
Religion and the Family   253
Beyond the Family   255
Women as Religious Leaders   259
Healers   260
Missionaries and Martyrs   260

Women's Impact on Religious
  Movements   261
  Protestant Denominations   261
  Jewish Denominations   264
  Roman Catholicism   264
  Hinduism   265
  Islam: Piety Movement   265
  Feminist Contributions to Religious Change   266
Summary   267
Discussion Questions   268
Recommended Resources   268

11 Women and Work

The Labour of Women   272
  Division of Labour by Gender   272
  Maintenance of the Domestic Unit   273
  Women's Work in the Marketplace   273
  The Contribution of Women to Economic Development   273
The Domestic Mode of Production   275
  Food Production   275
  Maintenance   276
  Exchange and Marketing   276
The Capitalist Mode of Production   276
  Urbanization and Class Distinctions   276
  Working for Wages: Its Organizational Prerequisites   277
  Women's Work   277
  Globalization and the Transformation of Work   288
  Self-Employment   290
  Unemployment   291
The Politics of Work: Barriers and
  Strategies   291
  Sexual and Gender Harassment   291
  Social Support for Working Women   293

  Laws against Sexist Job Discrimination   294
  Equal Pay–Comparable Worth   295
The Impact of Feminist Activism   295
Summary   295
Discussion Questions   297
Recommended Resources   297

12 Women and Politics

Political Power   301
  What Is Power?   301
  Power and Authority   302
  Types of Government   305
  Women's Political Power in the Past   305
  Patterns of Patriarchy   306
Women as Political Leaders   307
  Political Gains of Women in Office around the Globe   308
  Do Women in Office Make a Difference?   310
  Right-Wing Women   311
  Obstacles Facing Women in Politics   312
Women as Citizens   316
  Royal Commission on the Status of Women   318
  Women and the Law   318
Women's Political Participation   320
  Women and Peace Movements   321
  Global Feminism and Human Rights   322
Summary   324
Discussion Questions   325
Recommended Resources   326

Glossary   328
References   331
Index   365

Tables and Boxes

Tables

Table 6.1 Births and Total Fertility Rate, by Province and Territory   137

Table 9.1 Female University Presidents in Canada, 1998–Present   232

Table 11.1 The Eight Most Typical Occupations for Women and Men Globally and the Percentage of the Dominant Sex in the Occupation   272

Table 11.2 How Much of a Woman's Income Goes to Child Care?   274

Table 11.3 Labour Force Characteristics by Sex and Age Group   280

Table 11.4 Average Public and Private Worker Wages, Full-time, Full-year Work, for Workers Aged 40–54, Various Demographics   283

Boxes

In Her Own Words

Emily Carr   20
De Beauvoir Looks Back   45
Gloria Steinem on Feminist Labels   54
Black Feminist Thought in the "Matrix of
    Domination"   72
Margaret Mead on Sex and Temperament   87
Uses of the Erotic: The Erotic as Power   118
Public Says Children Better Off When Unhappy
    Parents Divorce, and Single Moms
    Suck   136
Sappho's Daughter and Mother   165

National Aboriginal Council of Midwives   190
The Right Education of the Female Sex   223
The Ritual Bath: Positive and Negative   254
Phillis Wheatley: "Thoughts on the Works
    of Providence"   262
Maquila Leaders: Yannick Etienne,
    October 2012   289
Donna Dasko: Getting Women Elected in
    Canada   313
Why Organize?   319

Key Issues

Deformed Feet: Bunions, Corns, and Arch Pain 16
What Is Feminism? 38
DAWN Executive Summary: Legislation, Policy and Service Responses to Violence Against Women with Disabilities and Deaf Women in Canada 63
Intersex 83
The Conflation of Gender and Sexuality 117
Changes in Family Structure in Canada 129
Same-Sex Couples across Canada 147
Bacha Posh: Girls Masquerading as Boys 159
Tips on Searching for Health Information on the Web 195
Research on Equality and AIDS 205
Teaching Women 227
Feminist Goddess Worship Today 251
Equal Pay 271
Levels of Sexual Harassment 292
Women Do Not Belong in the Public Sphere: "Nice Women Don't Want to Vote" 303

Women in Media

Making Feminist Sense of Lady Gaga: Two Views 13
Sunera Thobani 47
Lee Maracle 68
Gender-Neutral Clothing Goes Mainstream with New Department Store Campaign 95
Ellen Page 115
Sophie Grégoire Trudeau 134
Bonnie Sherr Klein and Naomi Klein 161
Henrietta Lacks 188
Lidia Casas 194
The Teenage Girl Who Wanted to Go to School 221
The Trial of Joan of Arc 258
"Flowers and Threads": The FAST Campaign 281
The Struggle for the Vote 317

Time to Reflect

Women, Writing, and Language 21
Men's Ideas about Women 33
Dorothy Smith and Standpoint Theory 55
Simon Fraser's Institute for Intersectionality Research and Policy 61
"Mapping Transnational Feminist Engagements: Neoliberalism and the Politics of Solidarity" 71
Doing Gender: An Early Theoretical Perspective 90
"Imagine Gender as a Planet": *The Gender Book* Map 93
Baby Storm Five Years Later: Preschooler on Top of the World 96
Is There a Female Brain? Two Scientists Review *The Female Brain* by Louann Brizendine 112
Monogamous Marriage as Economic Exploitation 133
The Loving Family Story 150
The 60s Scoop 162
DES in Canada 191
"Gender Parity and Equality in Education—What's the Difference?" 219
Female University Presidents in Canada 232
The Montreal Massacre 239
The Varied Creation Stories of Indigenous North Americans 249
Women at the Top 288
"Sultana's Dream" (1905) 304

Preface

From the American Fourth Edition

In the three decades since the first publication of this introductory textbook in women's studies, there has been an extraordinary transformation in scholarship. Consideration of gender as it interacts with race, ethnicity, class, and sexuality has become an essential factor of analysis in every field, while the issues raised by the modern women's movement have reshaped much of public discourse around the world.

The authors have shared with each other and share with the reader the multiple perspectives they bring to this examination of women's lives and experiences, treating women as subjects rather than objects, looking at the world through women's eyes. Our examination of the workings of gender relate to many more aspects of women's everyday lives as well as across the globe.

Rethinking the world through women's eyes has affected the very basis of knowledge in our universities. Until this revolution in scholarship, only men's experiences, and especially those of privileged men, were seriously studied, with the assumption that to understand them was to understand all that was worth knowing. Over 40 years of research focused on women has not only added new information about their lives historically and cross-culturally but also changed our understanding of what happened in the past and how our world works today across cultures.

The writing of this book has continued to be a collaborative effort, with each author contributing to all chapters. The organization of the book, as set out in the introductions to each of its three parts, deals with women as individuals, as family members, and as members of society. In every chapter we point out the contradictions between social or cultural "givens" that generally have been structured by men in their own interest and what we perceive to be women's realities. At each point we consider what changes would be required to ensure better choices for women. The title of the book acknowledges our awareness of the gap between women's realities and women's choices, and the book sets out to analyze that gap and to find ways of bridging it.

The history of this book goes back to 1978–79. The founding co-authors were Ülkü Ü. Bates, Florence L. Denmark, Virginia Held, Dorothy O. Helly, Susan H. Lees, Sarah B. Pomeroy, E. Dorsey Smith, and Sue Rosenberg Zalk. The second edition was published in 1995 without Dorsey Smith and with the addition of Shirley Hune and Carolyn M. Somerville as authors. For the third edition in 2005, dedicated to our late co-author Sue Rosenberg Zalk, we added as author Frances E. Mascia-Lees. Changes in this fourth edition, which has nine co-authors, include as new authors Hunter College faculty Linda Martín Alcoff, Jacqueline Nassy Brown, Sarah Chinn, and Rupal Oza, while those choosing to retire from the project included founding authors Ülkü Ü. Bates, Virginia Held, and Susan H. Lees and third-edition author Mascia-Lees. In this book we can at times still recognize the voices of past authors, making it also collaboration between past and present.

Acknowledgements for the US Edition

From the beginning, a great many people have been generous to us with their support, time, and expertise. At Hunter College, Provost Jerome Schneewind, in 1978–79, funded the seminar that launched this project from overhead monies from a Mellon grant obtained by the Humanities Dean, Gerald Freund. Donna Shalala, president of Hunter in the 1980s, encouraged its completion and wrote the Foreword to its first three editions. We are still grateful to our earliest reviewers who helped shaped the book when it was a project funded by NEH—Nancy Hartsock, Joyce Ladner, and Catherine Stimpson.

Our labours on the fourth edition have also been aided by Dr Emily Fairey, who helped us prepare the manuscript for the press, including merging all references into a single bibliography. At Oxford University Press, we are grateful to our fourth-edition editor Sherith Pankratz and to her assistants at various times, Richard Beck, Cari Heicklen, Caitlin Greene, and Katy Albis. We are also delighted to note that Niko Pfund, whom we first met years ago as an editorial assistant, is now president of Oxford University Press (USA).

We would also like to thank the following reviewers:
Christina S. Brophy, Triton College
Teresa Collard, University of Tennessee at Martin
Patricia Hill Collins, University of Maryland, College Park
Mary Duarte, Cardinal Stritch University
Wendy K. Kolmar, Drew University
Robin Powers, Gannon University
Anita Storck, Chapman University

Acknowledgements for the Canadian Adaptation

I acknowledge that what is called Canada in this text is in fact the ceded and unceded land of the Indigenous peoples of this territory and I am grateful to have the opportunity to work on this land.

I am enormously grateful for the research support provided by University of Toronto Mississauga Women and Gender Studies alumnae Sandra Danial, Pamela Kramer Estoril, Mercy Lillian Gichuki, Harsimer Singh, and Bethel Woldemichael. Special appreciation is extended to UTM WGS faculty Victoria Tahmasebi, Cassandra Lord, and Beverly Bain, whose research, teaching, and thoughtful encouragement served as inspiration for my effort here.

This text owes much to the insight and clarity of Oxford University Press editor Amy Gordon. Her expertise greatly enhanced the final version and I remain indebted to her contribution. I would like to say thank you to copy editor, Leslie Saffrey, whose suggestions and attention to detail has been invaluable. Finally, particular recognition is extended to Katherine Skene, who saw the need for Canadian-based content and championed this edition from the start.

I would like to thank the following reviewers, as well as those who chose to remain anonymous:
Katharine Bausch, Trent University
Lisa Bednar, University of Manitoba
Michelle Meagher, University of Alberta
Andrea Peloso, George Brown College
Norman Smith, University of Guelph
Kimberly A. Williams, Mount Royal University

The Authors

Linda Martín Alcoff is Professor of Philosophy at Hunter College and the Graduate Center, CUNY. She is a past President of the American Philosophical Association, Eastern Division. Her writings have focused on social identity, race, gender, knowledge, sexual violence, and Latino issues. She has written two books: *Visible Identities: Race, Gender and the Self* (Oxford, 2006), which won the Frantz Fanon Award in 2009, and *Real Knowing: New Versions of the Coherence Theory* (Cornell, 1996). And she has edited 10 books, including several important collections on feminist topics. She is currently at work on two projects, one on the future of white identity and one on effective resistance to rape. She was named the Distinguished Woman in Philosophy for 2005 by the Society for Women in Philosophy, in 2006 she was named one of the 100 Most Influential Hispanics in the United States by *Hispanic Business* magazine, and in 2011 she was awarded an honorary doctorate from the University of Oslo. She is a high school dropout and a college dropout who had children early but managed to go back and get her degrees. She is originally from Panama, but lives today happily in Brooklyn.

Jacqueline Nassy Brown is Associate Professor of Anthropology at Hunter College and the Graduate Center, CUNY. Her academic passions concern the intersection of race, place, and nation; diasporic formations of black culture and identity; and feminist geography. She is the author of *Dropping Anchor, Setting Sail: Geographies of Race in Black Liverpool* (Princeton University Press, 2005). She has published in *American Anthropologist, American Ethnologist, Cultural Anthropology*, and *Social Text*. She earned an Excellence in Teaching Award from the University of California, Santa Cruz. With her contribution to the present book, Jackie pays tribute to her beautiful late mother, who was her first feminist role model. She also taught Jackie most of what she knows about writing—and about life.

Sarah E. Chinn teaches in the English Department at Hunter College, CUNY. She is the author of two books, *Technology and the Logic of American Racism: A Cultural History of the Body as Evidence* (2000) and *Inventing Modern Adolescence: The Children of Immigrants in Turn-of-the-Century America* (2008). She's currently working on a book on the representation of masculinity in early American drama. She has published widely in American literature and culture, LGBTQ studies, and disability studies. From 2007 to 2011 she was the Executive Director of the Center for Lesbian and Gay Studies (CLAGS) at the CUNY Graduate Center. She lives in Brooklyn with her partner and two children and is finally learning to play the guitar.

Florence L. Denmark is the Robert Scott Pace Distinguished Research Professor at Pace University in New York, where she has served as chair of the Psychology Department for 13 years. She previously taught at Hunter College for 26 years. A social psychologist who received her doctorate from the University of Pennsylvania, she has published extensively on the psychology of women and gender. She is a fellow of the American Psychological Association (APA) and served as its eighty-eighth president in 1980. In addition, she was president of the International Council of Psychologists, the Eastern Psychological Association, the New York State Psychological Association, and Psi Chi. She was vice president of the New York Academy of Sciences. She has six honorary doctorates and is the recipient of many awards including APA's Distinguished Contributions to Education and Training, Public Interest, and the Advancement of International Psychology. Professor Denmark is currently an APA non-governmental organization representative to the United Nations and continues to teach graduate courses at Pace University. She has one surviving child, three stepchildren, four grandchildren, and one great-grandchild. She is also a frustrated sports writer.

Dorothy O. Helly is Professor Emerita of History and Women's Studies at Hunter College and the Graduate School at the City University of New York. She is associated with St. Antony's College and the Institute for Gender Studies (Lady Margaret Hall) at Oxford University, has been a scholar in residence at the Rockefeller Foundation Study Center at Bellagio, Italy, and on the boards of the Feminist Press, the *Journal of Women's History*, and *Women's Studies Quarterly*. She co-chaired the program committee of the Seventh Berkshire Conference on the History of Women (1987) and the Fourth International Interdisciplinary Congress on Women (1990). The author of *Livingstone's Legacy: Horace Waller and Victorian Mythmaking* (1987) and coeditor of *Gendered Domains: Rethinking the Public and Private in Women's History* (1992), she has published in the fields of history, women's studies, and higher education, including curriculum transformation. She is finishing a biography of Flora Shaw, Lady Lugard (1852–1929), the first woman on the staff of *The Times* of London in the 1890s, serving as its colonial editor. Her articles on Shaw appear in four anthologies and in the *Oxford Dictionary of National Biography* (2004). She enjoys Pilates, playing Scrabble, and reading mysteries.

Shirley Hune is Professor Emerita of Urban Planning at UCLA where she also served as Associate Dean of the Graduate Division and PI of several NSF grants to increase graduate diversity in science, technology, engineering, and mathematics (STEM) and social sciences doctoral programs. Previously, she was an Associate Provost at Hunter College and Professor of Social Foundations of Education. She has authored many publications on nonaligned countries (Global South), the human rights of international migrant workers, and on Asian Americans, notably their historiography and race and gender issues in higher education. She has been involved in the development of ethnic studies for more than three decades and is a past president of the Association for Asian American Studies. Her writings on Asian American women include *Teaching Asian American Women's History* (1997), *Asian Pacific American Women in Higher Education: Claiming Visibility & Voice* (1998), and *Asian/Pacific Islander American Women: A Historical Anthology* (2003). Her recent publications focus on the experiences of women students, faculty, and administrators of color. She lives with her husband in Seattle, where she teaches at the University of Washington and enjoys gardening, travelling, walking her dog, and visits with her large extended and blended family.

Rupal Oza is the Director of the Women's and Gender Studies program at Hunter College, CUNY. Her work focuses on political economic transformations in the Global South, the geography of right-wing politics, and the conjuncture between development and security. Her first book, *The Making of Neoliberal India: Nationalism, Gender, and the Paradoxes of Globalization*, was published in 2006 by Routledge, New York, and by Women Unlimited, India. She has several articles in peer-reviewed journals. She is currently working on three projects: the first examines the mobilizing of particular human rights and feminist discourses against "Muslim extremism" in an age of terror and empire; the second explores security beyond its conventional mooring in law and order to examine its deployment at different scales in south Asia; and the third examines the link between special economic zones, the discourse of security, and Hindutva politics in Gujarat, India. She is on the Board of the Brecht Forum and has been involved in South Asian political organizing in New York for 10 years.

Carolyn M. Somerville is Associate Professor of Political Science at Hunter College. Her research, writing, and teaching interests include African politics, international relations, and international human rights. She has published in the *International Journal of Middle East Studies*; *Sex Roles: A Journal of Research*; *PS: Political Science and Politics*; *The Oxford Companion to Politics of the World*; and *Globalization and Survival in the Black Diaspora*. She has also served as acting director of the Women's Studies Program at Hunter College. Somerville practices Nichiren Buddhism. She has a daughter and a son.

Kathryn Rolland, who contributed Chapter 9 on women's health, is now an Associate Professor Emerita of Public Health/Community Health Education whose fields of concentration are women's health, sexuality, and curriculum development and is proud to have created one of the first multidisciplinary courses for undergraduates on HIV/AIDS in the United States. She also enjoys reading poetry and mysteries and thinks that in an alternative life she would have been a swimming instructor who "never left the water."

Joan Simalchik, who undertook the immense job of Canadian adapter, is the coordinator for the interdisciplinary Women and Gender Studies Program at University of Toronto Mississauga, and teaches courses on women and social change, history, memory and human rights, and transnational perspectives on gender and cultural difference. In 2012 she received the University of Toronto's Ludwik and Estelle Jus Memorial Human Rights Prize and in 2016 she was recognized with Chile's Presidential Award for Humanitarian Service to the People of Chile. She has delivered and published many papers dealing with diasporic refugee communities and human rights.

Introduction

The field of women and gender studies has emerged over the past number of decades as a site for transcultural and transdisciplinary study. Traditionally most introductory courses in this discipline provide students with an overview of women's movements for equality and offer an emphasis on the relationship between theory and social practice. These texts foreground the development of women and gender studies as an academic program designed for critical engagement with feminist inquiry. How this is understood and taught has continued to develop.

The milieu that birthed women's studies was part of the social upheaval of the 1960s, when feminism in North America declared an undifferentiated sisterhood to be universal. The work then was to add women, their experiences, and their achievements into the curriculum. The aim was to right the wrong of their absence and write women into academic disciplines across the academy: through the humanities, social sciences, and science. Beyond inclusivity, women's studies began to change the academy. Just the notion of keeping an eye on "gender" deepened the scope of research and worked to provide a more complete approach to scholarship.

Since that earlier time, as the political and academic context was changing/changed, feminist theorists developed more deeply the concept of gender. The refashioned women and gender studies programs complicated and "problematized" the earlier analysis. Beyond gender, intersectional analysis identified how additional identity markers and power relations affect the complexity of people's lives and experiences. Intersectionality as a research, policy, and action paradigm has become fundamental to feminist studies. Intersectionality focuses its attention on a variety of multi-level intersecting social locations, forces, factors, and power structures that shape and influence life. It has a long and rich history in black feminism, Indigenous feminism, Third World feminism, and queer and post-colonial theory.

These theoretical developments create pedagogical challenges. How can a women and gender studies textbook reflect a contemporary national terroir while simultaneously offering transcultural insight beyond Canadian borders? How can it reflect a contemporary understanding of Canada as a settler state on Indigenous land? Despite the significance of globalization and a transnational analytical gaze, there remains a pedagogical need to reflect people's own experience and context. Many times, this is missing for Canada and thus, the need for "Canadianizing" a foundational US textbook, providing a framework grounded in Canadian history and experience. *Women's Realities, Women's Choices* was an ideal choice given the organization, breadth, and scope of its curricular content.

But since it is almost a national preoccupation for Canadians to ponder what it means to be Canadian, a challenge underlies the question: what *is* Canadian? What is this process? Who is included: francophone-Canadians; Indigenous peoples; immigrants; racialized peoples; LGBTQ communities? Who has been historically rendered absent and silent?

Clearly this is a challenge that extends beyond the incorporation of Canadian examples. Penny Van Esterik, in her own editing of a US anthropology textbook "rejected the model of creating 'beaver moments' or of 'maple-leaf' flagging" (Van Esterik 2006, 255). Canadianizing involves more than replacing US suffragettes with ours, or substituting our heroines for theirs, such as Viola Desmond for Rosa Parks.

The task entails an interpretation of past and present and surrounds the significance and signification of "Canadianization." Concepts critical to the study of women and gender, including (but not limited to) multiculturalism, indigeneity, diaspora, racialization, and bi-nationalism relating to Quebec, hold the possibility of offering transcultural insight beyond Canadian borders. How these issues are expressed, their contexts determined, and their meaning explained take up pedagogical challenges. What is the impact of institutional context on how the history of race, class, religion, sexuality, and indigeneity is taught?

Still, it is instructive to heed University of Toronto historian Jan Noel's caution to avoid parochialism in nationalist debates. Canadian—and other—feminists owe much insight to our US colleagues for their theoretical contributions. The concept of "pivoting the centre" has particular application in this effort.[1] Pivoting the centre of any issue exposes new concepts, analyses, and quandaries and holds potential for Canadian historical experience to be placed transculturally and transnationally.

And there remains the need to recognize Canada's privileged global position while taking up Chandra Mohanty's challenge in her *Feminism without Borders: To Decolonize Theory, to Practice Solidarity* (2003). As Mohanty writes in the Foreword to the fourth edition of the US version of *Women's Realities, Women's Choices*, "We do, however, need productive analytical tools and gender-just visions that allow us to acknowledge both the inheritance of colonial legacies, and of movements for emancipation—to hold onto the contradictions in our lives and act with accountability to improve the lives of people in our own neighborhood as well as across the world in communities thousands of miles away" (Hunter College Women's and Gender Studies Collective 2015, xxiv).

What remains for us as teachers and as learners are the opportunities involved in determining *Women's Realities*, and prompting *Women's Choices*.

Note

1. Patricia Hill Collins, "Gender, Black Feminism, and Black Political Economy," *Annals of the American Academy of Political and Social Science*, 568 (March 2000), 543. For another work that uses the concept of "pivoting the centre," see Bettina Aptheker, *Tapestries of Life: Women's Work, Women's Consciousness, and the Meaning of Daily Experience* (Amherst: University of Massachusetts Press, 1989), esp. 12, 20. For an even earlier use of the notion, see Benjamin Brawley, *Social History of the American Negro, Being a History of the Negro Problem in the United States, Including a History and Study of the Republic of Liberia* (New York: MacMillan 1921). See also Earl Lewis, "To Turn as on a Pivot: Writing African Americans into a History of Overlapping Diasporas," *American Historical Review*, 100 (June 1995), 765–87.

Part I

Defining Women and Gender

Women and Gender Studies today is committed to understanding the social, political, economic, historical, and cultural factors that give rise to different conceptualizations and differential practices concerning women, men, and gender both across cultures and within the same society. The first task is to understand how women and gender have been perceived and how the dominant ideas and practices concerning women and gender are reproduced from place to place and from one generation to the next. This perspective helps in understanding both how the past influences the present, and how current thinking, and how it is enacted today, can influence the future. Understanding context, recognizing power relations, and seeing how agency can be used are fundamental to feminist thought and action.

The long history of ideas about women and gender demonstrates the ways power can infuse philosophy and scholarship in general. Until very recently, women's own ideas and experiences were overlooked and omitted within academic disciplines. Privileged men, with the power and authority to control ideas and their dissemination, were the main producers of knowledge about the world and about how gender identities should operate. One important consequence of this control of knowledge is that in nearly every society the male was viewed as the "ideal," and thus characteristics associated with men were more highly valued than those associated with women.

Women as a category long were defined as "not men" or as the "other" to men. Because women were viewed as defective or incomplete males, inherently inferior, and even less than human, their characteristics, their work, and their contributions to society were devalued, rendered invisible, or ignored altogether. In Western thinking, for example, women were seen as less rational, more frivolous, closer to nature, more emotional, and less aggressive than men. The conceptualization of women as "other" led to an emphasis in much thinking and research on the *differences* between women and men rather than the *similarities* shared by all humans. In many cases, there are more differences within genders than between genders; yet gender differences continue to be emphasized. Since the most obvious differences between women and men are anatomical, it is not unusual for women to be defined in terms of their reproductive systems and for these biological differences to be taken as the explanation and rationalization for women's social subordination.

Thus, women were understood and studied as the "other" for centuries; only recently, with the advent of the contemporary women's movement and women's and gender studies, has there been a sustained effort to understand women from the perspective of women themselves, to put the elements of women's daily lives at the centre of analysis, to value women's contributions to ideas, to acknowledge their creativity, and to document the central role women play in the maintenance, reproduction, and development of their society, wherever they may live. There is also a growing scholarship on the actual historical and cultural varieties of social ideas and practices of gender and the many different formations gender has taken. Gender arrangements and gender-based divisions of labour have been varied, and not all societies have assumed that there are only two genders.

Today there are lively debates among feminist scholars, especially in the humanities and social sciences, over how the history of gender identities, expressions, and roles is understood and what sort of future to work toward. These debates show that just as gender can differentially privilege men over women, heterosexuals over lesbians and gay-identified persons, and cisgender persons over members of the trans community, so too can social structures involving race and ethnicity, class, ability, age, religion, national origin, and culture differentially privilege some women over others and even some women over some men.

These insights have led to the development of intersectional approaches to scholarship where multiple categories of analysis are understood to be necessary for any explanation. The experience of sexism, for example, differs not just in degree—or how much of it one might have to bear—but also in the kind or form that it takes. There is no lowest common denominator of sexism or any other form of discrimination. Thus, feminist scholars today study and analyze how ideas about "woman" and gender maintain and reproduce power relations and how ideas about race, ethnicity, disability, indigeneity, and other forms of difference intersect with ideas about gender to produce social stratification.

Women, from whatever social group, need not read the scholarly literature on women to know how they have been seen and understood. Definitions of women, ideas about women's bodies and the biological basis of gender categories, and assumptions about race, ethnicity, sexuality, citizenship, and differential ability are communicated in multiple ways in all countries of the world. They are communicated through images, language, and non-linguistic symbols in myths, rituals, folklore, and the media. In the course of socialization and education, whether in a household, a classroom, or a movie theatre, people learn how to act, what and who to desire, who to strive to be, and how to be valued. The implications and consequences of such definitions affect daily lives, moulding identities and sense of self from childhood to old age. Such definitions impose on women and men the expectations of society and provide a framework within which to censor those who do not, or will not, conform to those expectations.

The chapters in Part I investigate how the questions about women and gender have traditionally been answered and how these answers have changed over time. They focus on how these beliefs have been constructed through images and ideas about women's "nature," their bodies, and "proper" social roles. They assess how these images and ideas vary across cultures and how they differentially affect lives and choices.

1 Cultural Representations of Women

Chapter Outline

- Culture, Representation, and Gender
- Language as a Cultural System
- Enduring Symbols of Women
- Changing Representations of Women's Sexuality
- Can Reality Be Changed by Changing Images?
- Women's Search for Self through Literature
- Representation in the Internet Age
- Gender in Film: A Case Study

This chapter will help you
- Discern the nature of *culture* and how it operates in constructing ideas
- Recognize how language works to shape culture, and how it can reinforce or disrupt it
- Learn how power and context influence the construction of cultural paradigms and how agency can subvert them
- Comprehend how representations of gender, race, class, and sexuality affect dominant social structures

> *Identity is not as unproblematic as we might think. Perhaps instead of thinking of identity as an already accomplished fact . . . we should think, instead, of identity as a "production" which is never complete, always in process, and always constituted within, not outside representation.*
>
> —STUART HALL (1990)

Culture, Representation, and Gender

Experience, Perception, and the Construction of Reality

Think about what is known about gender. What is it that makes a woman a woman or a man a man? What physical, psychological, emotional, professional, and other characteristics combine to create what is understood as "woman" or "man"? Now think about *how* one knows about gender. Is there a moment when an adult tells a child that a behaviour, toy, or article of clothing is not for boys or for girls? Or a classmate makes fun of one's clothes, appearance, or taste in books or music as not appropriate for one's gender? What children's books describe what girls should do? What boys should do? Do television programs show girls as central, active participants in the action, or are they mostly hanging around in the background? In video games, how many of the protagonists are girls or women? How about in music videos: How are women represented either at the forefront or in the background? What kind of clothes are they wearing?

Much of this book explores where ideas of gender come from, how they play out in Canada and elsewhere, and how they change over time and vary across cultures. **Culture** is a concept that embraces the behaviours and attitudes that are learned from communities, systems of symbols like language and religious practices, and complex social organizations such as families, friendship groups, and voluntary associations (Tomasello 1999). This chapter discusses how these ideas are communicated and absorbed through *cultural representation*: through myths, books, music, television, movies, magazines, the Internet, fashion, and other cultural phenomena. While representation can seem trivial compared to nuts-and-bolts politics and policies affecting women's lives, in fact, it pervades lives in a way unparalleled in history. Almost from birth, people are surrounded by images from a variety of media, and none of those images is free from assumptions about appropriate gender behaviours and self-presentation.

Earliest learning comes through imitation: babies watch and imitate parents and other children, a pattern that continues throughout childhood. In order to make sense of the world people absorb their culture's literal and figurative languages: not just the words *woman* and *girl*, but the *concepts* of womanhood, girlhood, and femininity, and not just the words *man* and *boy*, but the *concepts* of manhood, boyhood, and masculinity.

The Construction of Gender in Culture and Individuals

Many of the images that are seen today have deep roots in North American culture; some are of more recent vintage. Cultural representation is tricky to negotiate, particularly when it comes to gender, because of ongoing debates about cause and effect: Do the images of women simply reflect women's experiences in the world, or do they also actively construct what is believed to be known about women and men? While it is clear that representation provides a mirror, however distorted, of how gender is understood, it is also true that the images shape expectations of how the world *should* be, how women *should* look, behave, and interact with each other and with men and children. Representation is also culturally specific—for example, in North America skirts and dresses are represented and worn as female clothing, something that might come as a surprise to an Egyptian man wearing a *djellaba*, an Indonesian boy wearing a sarong, or a Scotsman wearing a kilt.

While representations of gender may feel self-evident and natural, they are on the whole constructed and sometimes even arbitrary. For example, it seems obvious that children wear specific colours depending on gender, with blue being assigned to boys and pink to girls. This seemingly inevitable colour-coding is an invention of the twentieth century. In fact, before World War I, pink was associated more with boys; one newspaper in 1914 suggested: "If you like the color note on the little one's garments, use pink for the boy and blue for the girl, if you are a follower of convention." Even as late as 1918, the *Ladies Home Journal* declared: "There has been a great diversity of opinion on the subject, but the generally accepted rule is pink for the boy and blue for the girl. The reason is that pink being a more decided and stronger color is more suitable for the boy, while blue, which is more delicate and dainty, is seen as prettier for the girl" (Historical Boys' Clothing 1999).

There is no logical reason that men should be more adept at repairing cars or solving mathematical equations than women or that women should be responsible for keeping homes clean or worrying about their children's academic achievement. Yet, it is uncommon to find media representations of men cleaning houses or women fixing cars. And it is a short step from not seeing these images to believing that a woman should not want to fix cars or a man should see cleaning house as not his responsibility.

As important as the external effect of images of women and men, representation shapes inner lives as well. The images of women's lives: their work, love, sexuality, and relationships with others; their mothering; and their overall place in society shape the ways women understand their own lives. From the earliest stories—such as Cinderella and Sleeping Beauty, who are each rescued by a prince and live "happily ever after"—to romantic comedies in which the happy ending is the pairing up of male and female protagonists, people learn that women's satisfaction in life depends upon love and marriage. As will be seen, even (or especially) the ways in which women experience their bodies are powerfully shaped by the images of female beauty and attractiveness, in that idealized bodies—slim, curvaceous, hairless, able bodies—are represented not just as the ideal but as the norm. For decades, almost all images of idealized women and men were of white people: film producers, television writers, and advertisers could not even imagine that people of colour should be represented. It was only in the wake of the civil rights movement that the popular media represented people of colour in any meaningful way, and this lack of representation is still a major problem. When a variety of images of masculinity and femininity across class and race is not seen, it is difficult—although not impossible—to generate those concepts.

The problem with the stereotyped images is not that they exist. After all, there is nothing objectively wrong with a man fixing a car or a woman mopping a floor. The problem is that these images act as *norms*: sets of social and cultural rules that "normalize" behaviours and that everyone is expected to follow. Norms are so powerful that they are enforced internally through self-discipline to replicate what is seen. A **norm** defines an activity and erases the possibility of other definitions, so that mopping a floor becomes an activity identified only with women and femininity. Cultural representations then reinforce that norm: advertising for floor cleaners features women who are thrilled with their sparkling floors; women's blogs complain about men who do not understand how important clean floors are; male comedians make fun of women's seeming obsession with keeping their kitchen floor clean, and so on. In addition, since housekeeping is seen as a private matter, rather than one of political and global importance, the norm that women are concerned about clean floors reinforces the norm that women are not serious enough to participate on the same level as men in public life. The norm becomes the only possible reality.

Language as a Cultural System

The Relationship between Language and Culture

Language is one of the most basic systems of representation. In fact, language is pretty much *only* representation: a set of sounds and written shapes that take the place of actual things and ideas in the world. As with most cultural forms, there is no necessary relationship between most words and the things or ideas they represent: no reason that C-A-T means a furry four-legged creature (any more than C-H-A-T or G-A-T-O or Q-I-T-T-A does), or that these particular shapes are used to represent their associated sounds. And like other systems of representation, language is both descriptive and normative. Since people live in a male-dominated society where English is the dominant language, *man* has meant all people, rather than just male people, whereas *woman* means only female people. One *masters* material; one does not *mistress* it. *Patrons* support the arts; *matrons* serve as prison custodians or washroom attendants. *Patrimony* describes an inheritance from one's ancestors (who include women), while *matrimony* refers to marriage. The phrase "a farmer and his wife," is used commonly but it might sound odd to hear "a farmer and her husband." Until recently, there was no gender-neutral way to describe people who fought fires, chaired meetings, policed communities, or spoke for others: they were firemen, chairmen, policemen, and spokesmen. The word *maid*, which originally meant a young woman, has come to mean someone who cleans other people's houses. Even non-gendered words have gendered connotations: since nurses, babysitters, fashion models, and housekeepers are assumed to be female, these are modified with the word *male* when describing men in those roles. Similarly, in the recent past, the term *lady* was added to the occupation title when women were still an anomaly in male-dominated professions. For example, *lady doctor*, *lady lawyer*, and *lady politician* were all used to describe women who practised these professions. These gendered references persist today, as in *woman comic* or *female rapper*.

When language operates in this way, the messages about gender and its norms are clear: men are doers and producers; women are watchers, caretakers, and consumers. Men act in the public world while women are relegated to the private and domestic sphere. When there are only postmen and firemen and spokesmen, the cultural assumption is that only men "man" these posts. This assumption stretches from adults down to children, reproduced in children's games. Girls play house, looking after children, cooking, and cleaning, and boys pretend to be policemen and firemen. Boys who want to play house or dress-up are quickly told by adults or by other children that this kind of play is not appropriate for boys, and representation of a norm becomes a reality.

Not all languages spoken in Canada are based on patriarchal assumptions. In Indigenous languages such as Cree and Ojibway, there is no gender and the male-female-neuter schema does not exist.

And what about trans or intersex persons? Languages that reflect an exclusive gender binary based on male and female are exclusionary. To remedy this, some propose a new pronoun that would not refer to an essentialized notion of a constructed male or female gender. The Swedish Academy's dictionary includes the new pronoun *hen*, in addition to *han* ("he") and *hon* ("she"). The pronoun does not linguistically assign gender—either the person is transgender or intersex, or the gender simply does not matter. In English, some propose using the gender-neutral plural *they* and *them* to replace *he* and *she* as the preferred pronoun, and many already do use these when the gender is unknown or unimportant.

The prevalence of **cisgender language** (language based on individuals' experiences of their own gender that agrees with the sex they were assigned at birth) poses important challenges for an inclusive society. This binary can be resisted by having people designate their "preferred pronoun." Increasingly, the assignment of gender in many situations is considered superfluous.

Inequalities in language extend to concepts of masculinity and femininity, and can be seen in the asymmetry between cultural representations of the masculine versus the feminine. Concepts attached to women are more often negative, particularly when used to describe men, but concepts attached to men can be positive not just for men but also for women. *Effeminate* is always a "bad" word, meaning weak, flaccid, irresolute. Women can *emasculate* men by undermining their power, but there is no equivalent term for a process by which women are rendered more powerful. *Feminine* is a "nice" word as applied to women, but applied to anything else it is likely to be uncomplimentary. Masculinity in little girls is tolerated when they are *tomboys* (as long as they grow out of it), but femininity in boys is always represented negatively—*sissy* is always pejorative. And doing anything "like a girl"—throwing, screaming, running—is problematic for both boys and girls.

Changes in Language

In recent years the gendering of the English language has changed, as terms like *firefighter, police officer*, and *councillor* have entered the public discourse. Often these changes in language accompany actual social change, as more women join police forces or become political representatives. However, most of these changes involve women joining traditionally male fields of action, rather than vice versa. The phrase "stay-at-home father" has entered the cultural vocabulary, but integrating men into traditionally female roles has moved more slowly than the as associated changes in language. The title *Ms*, which, like *Mr*, refers to an adult regardless of marital status, is gradually replacing *Miss* and *Mrs* in public life to the extent that the exceptions stand out.

As some parts of language become more egalitarian, other parts have become more gendered. Specifically gendered insults have become more common. calling someone a *pussy* to indicate that he is weak or cowardly turns what has long been slang for *vagina* into a slur that attributes negative femininity to men. Similarly, the term *douchebag*, a device for washing out the vagina, has become increasingly popular to mean a despicable person, usually male.

Enduring Symbols of Women

Stereotypical images of women have existed since the beginnings of human communication, particularly since women have rarely had the same levels of literacy, and literary and artistic opportunity as men. If only men, not women, are the artists, writers, historians, and performers, then the images of women depicted in visual arts, literature, historical accounts, and performance will be men's. More importantly, if male experience is believed to be universal for all people and women's experience specific only to women, then even when women do create art, it will have a narrower audience and even be trivialized as "folk art," "women's art," or "women's writing." If women have access to the products of this creativity only as "consumers"—if, for example, they listen and read but do not speak or write—then their perceptions will be shaped by a one-sided view of reality. While there have been some cultures in which women have been valued as the creators of stories, songs, art, and performance, most cultures that have left significant legacies of artistic production have been dominated by privileged men and present male perspectives.

Selected Images of Women in Mythical and Religious Stories

Normative images of women did not come into being only in the age of mass media. Every culture has myths and legends representing ideal or "typical" female behaviour from which women and men are supposed to learn how womanhood works and what it means. In one version of the story of Adam and Eve, an origin myth for many of the world's religions, man is created by God "in his own image." Here, it is taught that man came first and that God is like man (because man is like God). Eve was made as a companion to Adam and constructed from his rib, deriving from him rather than directly from divine origins, and designed as his "helpmeet" or assistant. The next event in this creation myth is that Eve, defying God, eats the fruit from the forbidden tree of knowledge and convinces Adam to do the same, bringing evil into the world. From this, women learn that they are morally weak, that they cannot resist temptation, and that their weakness leads men into trouble. In this case, the trouble is great: Adam and Eve are expelled from paradise and cursed. The curses themselves are interesting: Adam's curse is that he shall have to work for a living, and Eve's is that she shall bear children in pain.

Similarly, in Greek mythology, Pandora cannot resist opening her box of gifts from the gods, which she was explicitly commanded not to open. The box contains all the evils that afflict humanity, and the story thus attributes the troubles of the world to a woman who could not control her curiosity. Other Greek myths and Roman ones as well, are full of stories of women (e.g. Leda, Europa, Selene) abducted and impregnated by male gods to fulfill the gods' desires and of women (e.g. Clytemnestra, Deianira, Medea) motivated by jealousy or infidelity to murder their husbands or children.

Ancient mythology rarely has a single origin, since much of it emerged in cultures that were preliterate. However, such myths reflect the assumptions about male dominance and the role of women of the time when they originated and were written down. The Hebrew bible makes clear that women are predominantly men's property, useful for cementing connections between tribes by marriage, and that their sexuality is men's possession. Chapter 19 of Leviticus, which lays out forbidden sexual practices, for example, takes for granted that it is *men's* sexuality that is being regulated, since it speaks only to men, forbidding a man from having sex with various relatives or from putting other men in the sexual position to which women are relegated. The messages that these ancient stories and laws convey are complex; there may be contradictions and multiple aspects and many levels of communication. Moreover, these beliefs are played out in more than written texts or explicit doctrines: they find their way into sculpture, painting, literature, dance, drama, ritual, clothing, gesture, words (spoken and written), and other ways in which humans use their imaginations to express ideas.

Yet in many Indigenous cultures, legends can be read without a gender attribution. The omnipresent "trickster" figure is an important example. Canadian playwright Tomson Highway explains "the central hero figure from our mythology—theology if you will—is theoretically neither exclusively male nor exclusively female, or is both simultaneously" (Highway 1998, iv).

More recent religions that came into being in literate societies are more easily traced to the person or people who wrote their holy books and the historical moment and geographic location from which the religion emerged. The Quran, the holy book of Islam, does not indicate the order in which the first couple was created. However, in Islamic traditionalist literature inscribed in the period following the Muslim conquests of lands inhabited by Jews and Christians, Eve is once again referred to as created from a rib. This is an example, among others, of how Islam worked with religions that were already established in adjoining regions and in which segregation of the sexes and use of the veil were already common practices (Ahmed 1992).

Changing Representations of Women's Sexuality

The "Sexual Revolution" and Its Legacies

Representations of women's sexuality have changed significantly since the middle of the twentieth century with the discovery of antibiotics that could easily cure sexually transmitted infections and birth control pills that could more effectively disconnect heterosexual intercourse from pregnancy. Pioneers in sex research like Alfred Kinsey and the team of William Masters and Virginia E. Johnson studied women's sexual response in detail and demonstrated not only that women were not less interested in sex than men, but also that women's sexual response was far more varied and intense than the divide between asexual "good girls" and voracious "bad girls" allowed for. Kinsey's 1953 study *Sexual Behavior in the Human Female*, which was based on thousands of interviews with US women, made a huge splash in popular culture with its findings about women's diverse sexual activities inside and outside marriage and with other women. Similarly, Masters and Johnson's 1966 book *Human Sexual Response*, which gave detailed descriptions of women's orgasms, turned the conventional wisdom about women's sexuality upside down in its focus on the clitoris as the source of women's sexual pleasure.

These developments contributed to what was called the "sexual revolution" of the late 1960s and 1970s. As a result, the belief that only "bad women" were sexually active before, outside of, or in the absence of marriage faded. Feminists embraced sexual self-determination as an important goal, and women began producing sexually explicit materials that put women's desires at the centre, rather than focusing on men's fantasies about women. *Our Bodies, Ourselves*, a groundbreaking self-help and informational book about women's health first published by the Boston Women's Health Collective in 1973, advised women to claim their sexualities for their own pleasure and featured chapters about lesbian sexuality, reproductive health and rights, and sexual independence (including a section teaching women about masturbation).

The change in cultural values was not wholly positive for women's sexuality, however. Representations of women in mass media became increasingly sexualized. The American Psychological Association defines **sexualization** as occurring when

a person's value comes only from his or her sexual appeal or behavior, to the exclusion of other characteristics; a person is held to a standard that equates physical attractiveness (narrowly defined) with being sexy; a person is sexually objectified—that is, made into a thing for others' sexual use, rather than seen as a person with the capacity for independent action and decision making; and/or sexuality is inappropriately imposed upon a person. (2007, 1)

These processes were clearly in effect in the 1970s and beyond: images that were usually found only in pornography made their way into the mainstream. On the one hand, women were shown initiating and enjoying sex. On the other hand, the growing explicitness of sexual representations suffused the culture, reducing complex feelings about sexual desire and practice into a depersonalized social mandate to have sex.

Feminist responses to the sexualization of representations of women and the popularization of pornography varied considerably in these years. A significant group of feminists opposed pornography, arguing that it is degrading to women, encourages violence, and perpetuates sexist images of women in general (Russell 1993). Some antipornography feminists (notably Andrea Dworkin [1979] and Catharine MacKinnon [1993]) promoted legislation against images deemed to be degrading to women. Others took a position based on their belief in free speech and images that protected even offensive representations of women (Burstyn 1985; Ellis et al. 1986; Vance 1990) and argued for social policies that promote non-sexist education and the protection of women from sexual violence or its effects (by establishing rape crisis centres, battered women's shelters, and abortion services). An enduring legacy of this debate is the emergence of "pro-sex" feminists, who argued that rather than limiting the production of sexually explicit images, women should create their own sexual materials and claim their sexuality for themselves (Califia 1988; Bright 1992; Duggan and Hunter 1995).

Others advocated for a better understanding of eroticism that could enhance women's lives (Lorde 1984).

Enter the category of "feminist porn." The (assumed) privacy of the Internet has shaped how women engage in sex, for now there are myriad websites dedicated to feminist pornography to help them along. Any rigid definition of what counts as either "feminist" or "porn" would defeat the radically open nature of the category itself. Yet according to the website "Feministe," some of the highlights include an openness to all body types and to queer- and trans-friendly sexuality; consensual sex that might include rape fantasies; women engaging in sexual acts that involve active menstruation; and the eroticization of safer sex (creative use of dental dams, for example). Although some feminists such as Gayle Rubin (1993) argue brilliantly against narrow ideas about what counts as appropriate, non-degrading sex acts, and although sex expert Annie Sprinkle (2005) has been doing pro-sex feminist educational performances for decades, the category of feminist porn is still emerging. Popular texts, such as *Jane Sexes It Up: True Confessions of Feminist Desire* (Johnson 2002), address the question of how to reconcile one's sexual fantasies with one's feminism. What may indeed be an innovation, however, are the Good for Her Feminist Porn Awards, the Emmas. The brainchild of a women-run sex-toy store in Toronto, the award was inaugurated in 2006 to honour women directors of erotic films for particularly revolutionary work for women and trans folk. The namesake of the award, Emma Goldman, the late nineteenth- to early twentieth-century anarchist, championed the cause of free love decades before it became a 1960s rallying cry.

Women's Sexuality in Recent Popular Culture

One of the most powerful mass-media instruments of this sexualization has been cable TV, especially the channels MuchMusic and MTV, among the few places in the 1980s and 1990s to show music videos, which had barely existed before then. Music videos produced and reproduced sexualized images of women, particularly very young women, and reinforced the idea that women's sexuality existed for men's benefit. As music videos expanded to the Internet in the 1990s and into the twenty-first century, this trend of representing women as sexualized accessories to men has not abated.

At the same time, female musicians laid claim to the power of representation of women's sexuality. An early influential figure in this phenomenon was Madonna, who rose to fame in the early 1980s. Madonna pushed the limits of how women's sexuality could be represented on television, mixing erotic imagery with images that challenged religion, race, and class; bringing previously marginalized sexual practices like sadomasochism into the mainstream; and claiming ownership of her sexual desires. In response to rock-and-roll musicians who traded in images of pliable, receptive sex objects, Madonna insisted on her own independence, sexual and commercial.

In the same period, Janet Jackson asserted herself as a sexual being who was fully in control, as her first breakthrough album emphasized. Yet even as she celebrated the pleasure principle and reimagined the sexual body by putting "abs" (abdominal muscles) on the map, her songs also alluded to issues of sexual responsibility in the age of AIDS.

Women singers in Canada often combined their talent with their politics. Pauline Julien (1928–1998), actress, singer, feminist, and sovereigntist, was celebrated for her artistry and political commitment to Quebec independence. She played a critical role in the cultivation of Quebec nationalism and popularized pro-independence songs. She was arrested during the 1970 October Crisis but was never charged with a crime. Buffy Sainte-Marie, a member of the Cree nation born in Saskatchewan, significantly influenced the 1960s folk scene with her songs that were covered by many international artists including Donavan, Roberta Flack, and Janis Joplin. Her song "Universal Soldier" became an anthem of the 1960s peace movement. During a period of being **blacklisted** in the United States for her anti-war work and for her participation and support for Indigenous rights, she became a regular on *Sesame Street*. Later relocating to Hawaii, Sainte-Marie established the Cradleboard Teaching Project for Native North American children that she has operated since 1969.

Born in Calgary, identical twins Tegan Rain Quin and Sara Keirsten Quin became internationally famous for their indie rock band Tegan and Sara. Neither has ever hidden their sexuality (though their lyrics are intentionally universal), and following the success of their hit single "Closer," they have both opened up about their awareness of the necessity of gay role models in music, particularly for women. They headlined the WorldPride Toronto 2014 closing ceremonies. Canadian female singers continue to break into the international music market: Alanis Morissette with "Jagged Little Pill," Avril Lavigne with "Complicated," Nelly Furtado with "Like a Bird," and Carly Rae Jepsen with "Call Me Maybe."

These singers have crafted places for themselves in the popular imagination despite the fact that they have never done so with complete freedom. First, their messages, no matter how creative, always engage on some level with the predominant view of women as being the other. And second, they craft their self-images so as to succeed in a highly corporatized male-dominated arena that is attuned to the market—that is, to the need to sell records.

Box 1.1 Women in Media

Making Feminist Sense of Lady Gaga: Two Views

. . . Gaga is explicit in her insistence that, since feminine sexuality is a social construct, anyone, even a man who's willing to buck gender norms, can wield it.

Gaga wants us to understand her self-presentation as a kind of deconstruction of femininity, not to mention celebrity. . . . "Me embodying the position that I'm analyzing is the very thing that makes it so powerful." Of course, the more successful the embodiment, the less obvious the analytic part is. And since Gaga herself literally embodies the norms that she claims to be putting pressure on (she's pretty, she's thin, she's well-proportioned), the message, even when it comes through, is not exactly stable. It's easy to construe Gaga as suggesting that frank self-objectification is a form of real power.

Real young women, who, as has been well documented, are pressured to make themselves into boy toys at younger and younger ages, feel torn. They tell themselves a Gaga-esque story about what they're doing.

Source: Nancy Bauer (2010).

Lady Gaga is a symbol for a new kind of feminism . . . Gaga Feminism, or the feminism (pheminism?) of the phony, the unreal, and the speculative, is . . . a monstrous outgrowth of the unstable concept of "woman" in feminist theory, a celebration of the joining of femininity to artifice. . . . Gaga feminism is not totally new, it does not emerge from nowhere, but it certainly strives to wrap itself around performances of excess; crazy, unreadable appearances of wild genders; and social experimentation. . . . This version of feminism looks into the shadows of history for its heroes and finds them loudly refusing the categories that have been assigned to them:

continued

these feminists are not "becoming women" in the sense of coming to consciousness, they are unbecoming women in every sense—they undo the category rather than rounding it out, they dress it up and down, take it apart like a car engine and then rebuild it so that it is louder and faster. This pheminist takes it upon herself to "occupy gender" as the new terminology of our political moment might phrase it.

Source: J. Jack Halberstam (2012, xii–xiv).

Lady Gaga in 2015 (left) and 2016 (right). While there's no feminist consensus on whether Lady Gaga's image challenges or reinforces norms about femininity, she certainly makes her viewers think about the limits of acceptable femininity.

The achievement of female sexual empowerment in hip hop is also ambiguous. Black women have worked hard to establish their place within a problematic sexualized culture. However, there has always been a critical female presence in that world. In the 1980s, artists such as Salt-N-Pepa, Queen Latifah, and MC Lyte both criticized **misogyny**, or **anti-women sentiment**, in rap music and advanced their own female-centred views of society, including more affirmative expressions of their own sexuality. This struggle has continued into the twenty-first century. Certainly, more black women such as L'il Kim, Missy Elliot, Nicki Minaj (who gunned down the male gaze in the music video for her song "Lookin Ass") and Canadians Michie Mee and Eternia have become extremely successful rap artists—for women. Even though they often go toe-to-toe with men in expressing their sexual bravado, and they rap just as well, they often garner less label support and lower record sales than male rappers. As one record producer explains: "males just don't want to hear hard things from women" (quoted in Rivera 2012, 428). Becoming businesswomen in the rap industry might be a boon to female artists—unfortunately, while there are many excellent "femcees," there is, as of yet, no female equivalent to the rap-star-turned-mogul Jay Z.

People today live in a media-saturated culture, surrounded by television, movies, the Internet, music, magazines, and billboards. For that reason, the trend of sexualization around the world seems to be expanding instead of receding. In addition, the processes of sexualization are trickling down to younger and younger women and girls: a report by the American Psychological Association (2007) found a disturbing upswing in sexualized representations of young girls or the use of images associated with childhood in sexualized contexts, and other research supports this finding. Toy manufacturers produce dolls wearing black leather miniskirts, feather boas, and thigh-high boots and market them to 8- to 12-year-old girls (La Ferla 2003). Clothing stores sell thongs with sexually suggestive slogans printed on them, sized for 7- to 10-year-old girls (Cook and Kaiser 2004; Brooks 2006), while thongs sized for women and late adolescent girls are printed with characters from Dr Seuss and the Muppets (Pollet and Hurwitz 2004; Levy 2005). A whole subculture of child beauty pageants encourages young girls to wear extensive makeup and imitate their adult counterparts with sexualized costumes and gestures (Cookson 2001). This excessive sexualization can have negative effects on girls and adolescents, particularly teenagers, who are in the process of working out what sexual desire and sexual behaviour mean (Tolman 2002). And the sexualization of girls encourages adults to see children as appropriate objects of sexual desire well before girls themselves may understand how sexuality operates.

Consuming the Body Beautiful

In 1792, Mary Wollstonecraft wrote wryly of women's mind/body predicament: "Taught from their infancy that beauty is woman's sceptre, the mind shapes itself to the body and, roaming round its gilt cage, only seeks to adorn its prison" (Wollstonecraft 2012 [1792], 37). One hundred years later, with the rise of industrial society and consumer society in the Global North, women were fashioned into the ideal consumer. Department stores appeared offering commodities that provided fantasies of more desirable self-titillated elite women. With the increasing "democratization of consumption" throughout the twentieth century, working-class women were offered compensation and respite from the bodily drudgery of their daily lives through purchasing products. Although women were enticed to buy newer and better commodities to improve the home, their "proper" domain, a woman's primary act of consumption was aimed at making herself into an object of desire, sometimes with serious medical consequences.

Currently, consumption is fundamental to many women's lives, and shopping is a major leisure activity for women of all classes and cultures; their diverse bodily wants are largely filtered through mass-produced images in commercial ads found in magazines, on TV, and on the Web. Through such images, women are offered more than simply products; they are promised a more beautiful body, a more gratifying life, and a more gratified self (Rosenblatt 1999, 8). Today around the world, the marketplace is central to women's pursuit of beauty as well as to the construction of women's other bodily needs and desires. Globally, the market in fragrances, cosmetics, and toiletries is worth $330 billion per year (Jones 2010, 1). Yet a cursory visit to beauty industry websites such as *GCI Magazine*'s www.gcimagazine.com reveals the growing global importance of men's bodily desires to the beauty industry's growth. For example, South Asian men are apparently seeking "male-specific skin care," owing to India's own increasing importance in the global economy.

Indian businessmen are in greater contact with their peers in the West, and as a result "Indian men are feeling the pressure" (Bhattacharya 2008). That same website offers a superlative glimpse into the ways that the globalized beauty industry is constructing new markets through old, orientalist stereotypes, as in the headline of another article, "The Mystique of Mainstream Middle Eastern Beauty" (Grubow 2010).

Jean Kilbourne produces work that explores how media images affect women's health, especially with regard to eating disorders and addiction. Her cutting-edge documentary *Killing Us Softly 4: Advertising's Image of Women* (2010) exposes how the media can negatively influence girls' and women's self-image. Kilbourne links the notion of the **male gaze**, the objectification of females, with media images to demonstrate how girls and women are constructed as "subjects" and the "other." The **gaze** is a concept that depicts the power relations between viewer and viewed.

Carla Rice uncovers a "culture of contradiction" where increases in individual body acceptance are matched by even more restrictive feminine image ideals and norms. With insider insights from the Dove Campaign for Real Beauty, Rice's *Becoming Women* exposes the beauty industry's colonization of women's bodies and examines why "the beauty myth" has yet to be resolved (Rice 2014).

Women's consumption continues to be critical to the success of a capitalist economy. Canada has become the number-one prestige beauty market globally with growth of 8 per cent in dollar value in 2014, well surpassing the 5 per cent growth in the US (NPD Group 2014). Much of this expenditure is directed at the body and, in particular, at the pursuit of beauty. Yet do cosmetics and fashion merely situate women visibly in their oppression? The history of the cosmetics industry shows that even as women felt increasingly compelled by social pressures to use cosmetics, they also claimed them for their own purposes (Peiss 1999).

Moreover, the cosmetics industry included few racialized women entrepreneurs and even, as in the case of Madame C.J. Walker early in the twentieth century, millionaires at a time when black women were among the most economically disadvantaged. To simply see fashion as a "moral feminist problem" is to miss the richness of various forms of self-expression or self-enhancement,

---

Box 1.2 Key Issues

Deformed Feet: Bunions, Corns, and Arch Pain

Bunions are a common problem experienced mostly by women. The deformity can develop from an abnormality in foot function, or arthritis, but is more commonly caused by wearing improperly fitting footwear. Tight, narrow dress shoes . . . can cause the foot to begin to take the shape of the shoe, leading to the formation of a bunion. [Bunions] can worsen to the point where surgery is necessary.

Corns . . . develop from an accumulation of dead skin cells on the foot, forming thick, hardened areas. They contain a cone-shaped core with a point that can press on a nerve below, causing pain. Complications that can arise from corns include bursitis and the development of an ulcer.

Arch pain can be caused from a structural imbalance . . . most frequently the cause is a common condition called plantar fasciitis . . . [in] tissue located along the bottom surface of the foot that runs from the heel to forefoot. The inflammation often leads to pain in the heel and arch areas. . . . If left untreated, a bony protrusion (heel spur) may develop.

Source: www.foot.com/site/foot-conditions/bunions

some of which might signal one's affiliation with a subcultural group, often with a strong political orientation. The punk fashion of the 1970s, for example, with its torn and slashed clothing, vinyl, bondage gear, and outrageously dyed, spiked, and sculpted hair, mocked traditional style. Punk style and other "anti-fashion aesthetics," such as the slacker styles of the 1980s and the cyberpunk styles of the 1990s, were attempts to resist standard encodings of beauty, femininity, female sexuality, and class.

Women's processes of self-creation, resistance, and transgression through the body and fashion exist within capitalist consumerist formations and gendered power relations and, thus, are necessarily influenced, mediated, and constrained by them. However, women are active creators and, as such, can use the resources offered by these formations, if not to escape or transcend them then to negotiate, protest, and resist them. To understand shopping and fashion only as frivolous, empty-headed feminine activities reproduces the denigration of the body with which women have so long been associated. It devalues a historical sphere of women's activities and concerns, and it does not allow for the diverse ways in which women can use these activities to improve their lives. Some women might starve themselves to death in the pursuit of impossible images of beauty and perfection, but others will playfully adorn themselves and seek pleasure in their own bodies (Mascia-Lees et al. 1990). The manipulation of the body and its adornment can also result in the tangible accumulation of both symbolic and economic capital (Brydon and Niessen 1998). That said, a disturbing trend lies in the growth of anorexia and bulimia among men, in particular gay men. In a British study, an estimated 10 per cent of people with eating disorders were men, and 20 per cent of those men were gay. The degree of bodily dissatisfaction among gay men stems from a norm that often puts a high premium on attractiveness and bodily musculature (Petersen 2007, 68). And it is hard to separate the pleasure found in adorning bodies from the multibillion dollar industries producing fashion, makeup, and diet products, whose goal is not to help women—and increasingly men—feel beautiful but to enrich their CEOs and shareholders.

Pop culture icons who happen to be women of colour can revise the standards of beauty in ways that are at once liberating but also problematic. Jennifer Lopez's celebrated "Booty" has allowed black and Latina women to see reflected in the mainstream the body shapes that many of them have as the thinness that is exalted in the world of high fashion and mainstream culture is not universally valued.

While some women seek out cosmetic surgery, others find empowerment in the strong and sculpted body they build at the gym. Such is very much the case with the US first lady. Michelle Obama's body is, in a word, buff. In magazine interviews, she has described her workout routine (for which she wakes up at 4:30 a.m.) and some of her favourite exercises (including squat thrusts). In all the pomp of the 2009 inauguration and in the months following, she often wore sleeveless dresses that showed off her biceps. Journalists could not get enough, and headlines declared her "right to bare arms." Yet not everyone was pleased. On the occasion of the president's first state of the union address, the political commentator David Brooks of the *New York Times* remarked on air that she should cover her arms. Michelle Obama's official portrait, taken in a sleeveless dress, was critiqued on the same grounds. Once again, there is intense inspection of a black woman's body; surely, such abundant discourse on a woman's arms is unprecedented in US culture. It was improper for a first lady to show her arms, apparently, because they were so beautiful. Rather than allowing those arms to serve as a clarion call for physical fitness, especially in view of the country's obesity crisis, critics sexualized them. Her arms became such a subject of controversy that one would think she were flaunting cleavage.

It bears noting in this context that athleticism is one of the activities that have historically served to differentiate men and women. Femininity and visible musculature have been mutually opposed, and women are often reluctant to lift weights because doing so might make them "bulk up" and look masculine. When Venus and Serena Williams emerged on the tennis scene some years ago, proudly describing their game as "power tennis," they too were criticized for being too muscular, a code word for masculine. One of their competitors, Martina Hingis, was heard to liken playing against one of them to playing against a man. Whether intentionally or not, the Williams sisters work against the masculinization of their athletic bodies by portraying feminine sexuality through bodily displays on the tennis court.

Can Reality Be Changed by Changing Images?

If self-image and the ways people feel and act are shaped by predominant social images of gender, then presumably perceptions, feelings, and behaviour can be changed in part by a change in representation. In the 1980s and 1990s, feminists focused on contesting images perceived to represent women negatively, often by creating diverse alternatives in academia, art, literature, and the media (Rakow 1992). A short-lived but influential movement of the 1990s, Riot Grrrl focused on the similarities between feminist and punk rock values: rebellion and resistance to mainstream standards of beauty, do-it-yourself aesthetics, collective action and collaborative creativity, sexual self-determination, and self-expression of all kinds (Monem 2007). Through zines and live shows, Riot Grrrl bands like Team Dresch, Bikini Kill, and Bratmobile created confrontational, explicitly feminist and pro-lesbian music and culture. They reclaimed misogynistic terms like *bitch*, *dyke*, and *slut* as empowering labels and challenged the male-dominated music scene of the era. While their radical message was soon co-opted by less political musicians and by the music industry in general and watered down into "girl power," Riot Grrrl relaunched radical feminism for a new generation.

Another powerful example of how women can and do overturn conventional, media-driven standards of beauty lies in the realm of body politics. Despite the "thin ideal" that is prevalent in North American society writ large and despite the rise of eating disorders among young racialized women (National Eating Disorders Association 2005), these women have historically responded to a different set of aesthetic pressures. They, along with an increasing number of other women, cultivate the "thick" and "bootylicious" look of such stars as Jennifer Lopez, Beyoncé, and Nicki Minaj. While that look offers a liberating alternative to thinness, it also establishes yet another difficult ideal, one dictating that women be "phat" (meaning "plenty hips, ass, and tits") without being fat; it is no coincidence that *phat* is slang for *good*.

Hence, as the need to produce alternative images became a goal in the 1980s and 1990s, a new consideration came to the fore. What, in fact, constitutes an alternative? Are alternatives de facto "positive"? And who gets to decide? After all, "the production of meaning is inseparable from the production of power" (Chadwick 1990, 216).

Reshaping Representation

Despite the significant challenges discussed above, important changes have occurred in the years since feminism began exerting its influence on public discourse. In part, these changes in representation have followed political and economic change, but in some cases remaking representation itself has led to larger cultural shifts both in the mainstream and in subcultures.

Television provides a case in point. It is undoubtedly the most powerful and influential medium of communication in the world, cutting across national and class barriers. The number of women who work as news anchors and correspondents has been steadily rising and includes some of the best paid, most successful people in the business (Marlane 1999; Gutgold 2008). Women have been reporting from the front lines of wars and upheavals, showing how women are no longer confined to "soft" topics. Women also serve as political pundits and as hosts of mainstream political talk shows. *The Social* and *The View*, popular daytime programs featuring female co-hosts, have become important vehicles for conversations about major social issues and current events. Openly lesbian news commentator Rachel Maddow began helming her own news analysis show in the US in 2008.

Such developments have undoubtedly made a difference to millions of viewers who can now watch and hear women in positions of authority speaking about business, international politics, and sports. Even so, women in the media still have to contend with gendered expectations about what signifies seriousness. Interviewing Katie Couric about her historic selection as the first woman to anchor the CBS Evening News, CNN's Larry King said: "We've got to begin with the most important question that all, everybody wants to know: your hair. What have you done with your hair?" (Gutgold 2008, 16). And Canadian female reporters have repeatedly been harassed, insulted, and heckled online with obscene taunts, and even when broadcasting live. In 2015, CityNews reporter Shauna Hunt directly confronted two hecklers outside a sporting event who were yelling a crude phrase made popular by an online hashtag (#fhritp). She had endured close to a year of such harassment and said it was time to say something. (CBC News 2015). Her action drew much attention to "everyday" workplace harassment and scorn for the two particular harassers, one of whom was fired from his public-sector job (and later reinstated).

While there have been advances in the representation of (mostly white, middle-class, able-bodied, and straight) women on television, the advent of "reality" programming shows such as the Real Housewives franchise and *The Bachelor* and *The Bachelorette* reinforce negative gender stereotypes.

Very few changes have been made to the representation of racialized, disabled, or poor women, or LGBTQ folk; this may be because of their virtual absence from the point of production power. Stereotypical images remain embedded in social and economic structures.

Women's Search for Self through Art

Historical Perspective. In the past, the designation of much of women's work as mere "craft" or "folk art" rather than "high art" caused their creations to be devalued. Consider needlepoint, quilt making, and painting on porcelain. These have been termed crafts or arts, as in "arts and crafts," rather than art. Such terms demonstrate that political power dictates the assignment of labels and categories. Some contemporary women are reviving such skills as weaving and quilting and finding a special pleasure in the collaborative nature of much of their creative work. Fibre arts like knitting, crocheting, and embroidery are being adapted into the world of "fine art" by organizations like the Fiber Artists' Collective.

Art historians have recently brought women's works into the mainstream of art history, making it no longer possible for critics to ask, "Why were there no great women artists?" (Harris and Nochlin 1977). Though much frustration remains, some contemporary women artists have seen their works installed in prestigious museums like the National Gallery of Canada in Ottawa. The National Museum of Women in the Arts in Washington, DC, founded in 1981, displays works exclusively by women artists from the Renaissance to the present. Not only painters but also silversmiths, textile makers, potters, and others are given due attention (Heller et al. 1980, 158–9).

In the mid-twentieth century, modern Inuit art became an established art form in Canada and internationally. Kenojuak Ashevak (1927–2013) was a dynamic force in the development of the genre and created carvings, drawings, and stained glass. Her 1960 print *Enchanted Owl* became a classic, and the original is in the National Gallery of Canada. As part of the Cape Dorset community, she has been honoured with a Governor General's Award, the Order of Canada, and honorary degrees, and her work has been replicated on a Canadian stamp and coin.

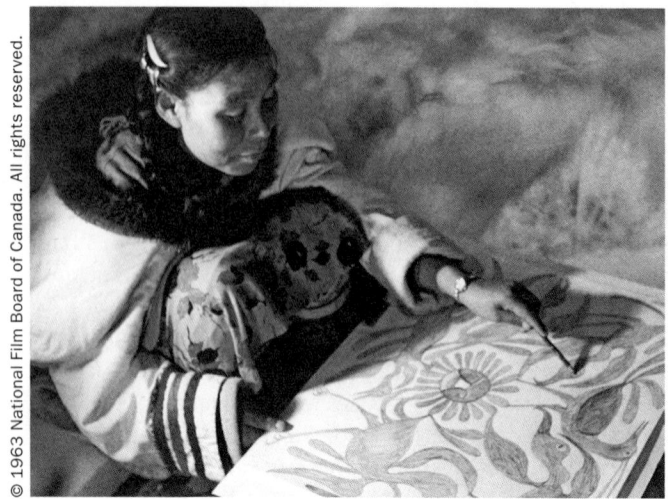

"There is no word for art. We say it is to transfer something from the real to the unreal. I am an owl, and I am a happy owl. I like to make people happy and everything happy. I am the light of happiness and I am a dancing owl."—Kenojuak Ashevak (in Feeney 1963)

Contemporary Feminist Imagery. Feminism has created a new context within which women artists may work, with feminist and mainstream critics commenting on their work. Feminist artists now flourish. The multiplicity of their work demonstrates that there is no single form of expression that must be labelled "feminist."

Women's Search for Self through Literature

The earliest woman writer in Western literature whose works are extant is Sappho, who lived on the Greek island of Lesbos in the sixth century BCE. She wrote poetry for and about a group of younger women who spent time with her before they departed for marriage. The emotions expressed by Sappho run the gamut from love to jealousy to hate, and they were all inspired by women. Although she lived in a male-dominated culture, Sappho asserted woman-centred values. She would not trade her daughter for limitless treasure, she appreciated the beauty of other

Box 1.3 In Her Own Words

Emily Carr

Born in Victoria, BC, Emily Carr (1871–1945) was a Canadian writer and pioneer Modernist post-Impressionist artist. Her early works were inspired by the Indigenous peoples of the Pacific Northwest Coast, but she later became better known for her landscapes.

> I went no more then to the far villages [of the Indigenous peoples of the Pacific Northwest], but to the deep, quiet woods near home where I sat staring, staring, staring—half lost, learning a new language or rather the same language in a different dialect. So still were the big woods where I sat, sound might not yet have been born. Slowly, slowly I began to put feeble scratchings and smudges of paint onto my paper, returning home disheartened, wondering, waiting for the woods to say something to me personally.

Source: Emily Carr (1946, 238).

Associated with Canada's (all male) Group of Seven artists, Carr did not receive the acclamation they did until late in her life when she became a "Canadian icon." The Virtual Museum of Canada (run by the Art Gallery of Greater Victoria) has paired quotations from Carr with her art: www.virtualmuseum.ca/edu/ViewLoitCollection.do?method=preview&lang=EN&id=72.

Box 1.4 Time to Reflect

Women, Writing, and Language

I shall speak about women's writing: about *what it will do*. Woman must write her self: must write about women and bring women to writing, from which they have been driven away as violently as from their bodies—for the same reasons, by the same law, with the same fatal goal. Woman must put herself into the text—as into the world and into history—by her own movement.

Every woman has known the torment of getting up to speak. Her heart racing, at times entirely lost for words, ground and language slipping away—that's how daring a feat, how great a transgression it is for a woman to speak—even just open her mouth—in public. A double distress, for even if she transgresses, her words fall almost always upon the deaf male ear, which hears in language only that which speaks in the masculine.

It is by writing, from and toward women, and by taking up the challenge of speech which has been governed by the phallus, that women will confirm women in a place other than that which is reserved in and by the symbolic, that is, in a place other than silence. Women should break out of the snare of silence. They shouldn't be conned into accepting a domain which is the margin or the harem.

Source: Hélène Cixous (1981[1976], 245, 251).

---

women, and she preferred love to war. Despite her focus on women's culture, Sappho was admitted into the mainstream of classical literature because of her technical versatility. Male poets would adopt her erotic imagery for their own purposes.

Sappho's poetry is an artistic rearrangement and interpretation of reality, though it appears to be frank and personal. In fact, most women's literature is personal to such a degree that the confessional style of writing has been labelled "feminine" even when men employ it. Because of the circumstances of their lives, women writers have often turned inward to explore the private sphere.

Women as Heroic

In male-dominated societies, heroism is often identified by actions that are specific to men: battles, hunts, quests, and long journeys. For women, long limited in their mobility by social mandates to care for home and children, it has been harder to identify (and identify with) heroes in literature. Is Penelope in *The Odyssey* heroic because she waits for her warrior husband Odysseus and resists demands to remarry? Is Cordelia in *King Lear* heroic because she is honest about her love for her father and suffers death because of her sisters' treachery? Is Bella Swan in the *Twilight* series heroic for putting her life at risk in order to be able to see visions of her absent lover and again to bear her child to term? While men's heroism is associated with action, women's heroism is often hard to distinguish from suffering. At the same time, historically, few women have been able to participate in the kinds of activities that mark men as heroic. Many women writers, as a result, have had to create new and woman-centred ways of thinking about heroism.

M. NourbeSe Philip, in her novel *Harriet's Daughter* (1988), does exactly this. By focusing on a young black woman who wants to be called Harriet in honour of Harriet Tubman, leader of the **Underground Railroad**, Philip rethinks how heroism is defined, in both the past and the present. Harriet creates a game that replicates the struggle for freedom under slavery and that has relevance for contemporary racialized communities. In this and other novels, heroines are girls and women who do not accept their fate passively. They think, choose, and act.

It is not surprising that all these girls and women are marginalized in some way—through race, sexuality, class, and/or national origin. If, as has already been seen, myths are powerful tools to transmit cultural messages, then so too are the marginalized histories that lesbian writers and women writers of colour draw upon in their effort to craft new ways of situating themselves in the world.

Telling Other Stories

Many women writers have been more inclined to reject the model of heroism and mythmaking altogether. As the novel—a genre that focuses much of its attention on the domestic sphere and ordinary lives—became the dominant literary genre in the Global North in the nineteenth century, women characters moved into greater focus. Unlike epic poems, myths, and legends, which primarily focus on the acts of men, the novel often features women in central roles. This did not mean that women writers were welcomed, however: Jane Austen, one of the great novelists of the early nineteenth century, initially published her books anonymously; the Brontë sisters published under male names; and Mary Anne Evans, one of the best-regarded novelists in the English language, is still most commonly known by her male pen name, George Eliot. Harriet Beecher Stowe claimed that her bestselling antislavery novel *Uncle Tom's Cabin* was written by God, and the popular novelist Fanny Fern argued that women writers were forced into publication by economic need, not artistic drive.

Women did find increasing opportunities as writers beginning in the nineteenth century. A role model for many of these emerging writers was Aphra Behn (1640?–1689). Behn, born in England, was one of the first women who could pursue her craft professionally, even though she wrote under the pen name Astrea. She was well known for her plays and poetry, and her work *Oroonoko or the Royal Slave* (1688), which is sometimes credited as being the first novel in the English language. It took up themes of colonialism and the horrors of slavery while *The History of the Nun or the Fair Vow Breaker* (1688) is an example of romantic torment.

In the twentieth century, women writers were among the most adventurous and experimental, seeing literary self-expression as the way to represent the many varieties of women's lives (Dickie and Travisano 1996). Virginia Woolf, writing from the 1920s to the 1940s, focused on the everyday experience of particularly situated women's lives through a stream-of-consciousness technique that put women's thoughts and feelings at the centre. Nella Larsen's novels *Quicksand* (1928) and *Passing* (1929) explored urban black women's lives in similar ways as did Zora Neale Hurston in *Their Eyes Were Watching God* (1937). In poetry in particular, women writers were intensely experimental: Gertrude Stein, Hilda Doolittle (also known as H.D.), Laura (Riding) Jackson, and Angelina Weld Grimké embraced complex poetry to represent the particularity of their lives as lesbians (Stein and H.D.), women of colour (Grimké), and feminists ([Riding] Jackson).

While women continued writing throughout the twentieth century, the growing anti-feminism following World War II dismissed the representation of women's experiences as "trivial" or "boring." It is not surprising, then, that the second wave of feminism brought with it an explosion of writing by women about women. Women of colour were especially productive, creating magazines, journals, poetry, novels, essays, and journalism to represent their experiences and create community. Women writers have won the Nobel Prize for literature seven times in the past two decades—certainly not equal to male writers but considerably better than the previous 90 years when only five women won or the period between 1955 and 1990, when none did. Alice Monroe, author of numerous short story collections, including *The Lives of Girls and Women* cycle, wrote about the lives of females in rural Canada. She won the Nobel Prize for literature in 2013, and is the only woman among 23 Canadian Nobel recipients.

The latter part of the twentieth century and the beginning of the twenty-first saw a resurgence of diverse women writers telling stories and creating new modes of cultural production. Indigenous writers, including Lee Maracle,

Eden Robinson, Leanne Simpson, and Lisa Bird-Wilson, created a new genre of literature centring on Indigenous lives and cultures. Dionne Brand, Jen Sookfong Lee, Gurjinder Basran, and Farzana Doctor are a few of the writers giving expression to the immigrant experience. Marina Nemat's *Prisoner of Tehran* is a testimony of her torture in Iran, and Chilean-born Carmen Aguirre's *Something Fierce* gives voice to a childhood spent in exile and revolution.

Writing as Political Activism

Women writers around the world have used literature as a form of political activism. Under apartheid in South Africa, Nadine Gordimer used her novels to protest the cruel and unequal treatment of racialized people. In Egypt, Nawal El Saadawi's novels dramatize the abuse of women and the ways in which they fight back. Women writers have often explored the genres of science fiction and fantasy to imagine better (or dramatically worse) worlds in which gender difference either has been eradicated or has become even more unequal. Marge Piercy's *Woman on the Edge of Time* (1976) uses the science-fiction genre to suggest two opposing possible futures, one sexist and one non-sexist. Her vision is conveyed in part through terms that underscore social inequality and equality. In *The Handmaid's Tale* (1986), Canadian Margaret Atwood describes a feminist dystopia called Gilead in which a totalitarian regime imposes roles on women that are extensions of what some people have always believed women should be.

In more recent years, women writers have also engaged political issues through their writing. Arundhati Roy, an Indian writer, explored class and sexual castes in her 1997 novel *The God of Small Things* and has taken a leading role in writing about the degradation of the natural world, neo-imperialism, and nuclear proliferation. Isabel Allende, cousin of Chile's assassinated president Salvador Allende, wrote of her country's destruction under military rule in *House of the Spirits* (1982), *Eva Luna* (1987), and *Stories of Eva Luna* (1989). Mi'kmaq poet Rita Joe published six books, including her autobiographical *Song of Rita Joe* (1996), in which she describes her traumatic experience in a residential school.

Many women writers have now integrated into their writing issues that were controversial in the early years of feminist and liberation movements in the 1960s and 1970s. Zadie Smith, a leading British novelist of European and African-Caribbean descent, represents a multinational, multilingual England grappling with the changes wrought by the end of the British Empire and immigration of Caribbean and Asian people to Britain in *White Teeth* (2000). Alison Bechdel's graphic memoir *Fun Home* (2006) uses the insights of lesbian politics to meditate on her father's life and death as a closeted gay man. And in a rare move, Bechdel produced a follow-up memoir, *Are You My Mother?* (2012), in which she incorporates her mother's comments upon the evolving text. "I don't know why everyone has to write about themselves," her mother remarks at one point.

Representation in the Internet Age

Each generation has its defining medium that has both been shaped by and transformed the representation of gender. Visual art, literature, movies, radio, and television have all been deeply implicated in representations of gender and sexuality and made mass distribution of images of dominant models of masculinity and femininity more easy and widespread. At the same time, feminists have been able to take hold of these different technologies to generate alternative and resistant representations of women and gender and then spread these representations to a larger public. However, as has already been seen, cultural representation, particularly that of mass culture, has historically been transmitted from the top down—that is, from dominant cultural groups. The production and distribution of cultural products is usually separated from the people who consume those products; most people listening to music, watching movies or television, reading books, and looking at art are consumers, not musicians, filmmakers or actors, writers, or artists themselves.

The Internet has changed this balance between producers and consumers of culture. While someone would need significant money, influence, and connections to produce a TV show and actually have it appear, anyone with access to a computer can create a website or blog; anyone with a smartphone can make and post a YouTube video; anyone with a digital camera and access to a computer can upload photographs and make them public to billions of viewers. Indeed, the Internet has proven a significant challenge to authoritarian political regimes, which struggle to control the proliferation of information and images that can spread worldwide in hours. The Internet is not unique in its do-it-yourself format: resistant political movements from anti-colonial struggles to Quebec nationalist groups to Riot Grrrl punk rockers have created their own cultural products and distribution networks. However, what distinguishes the Internet is that an image created by one person is accessible to everyone with an Internet connection. Distribution is effortless and immense. And fast.

What effect will the Internet have on cultural representations of women and gender? It is hard to predict. There are some promising signs, however, particularly the emergence of organizations that focus on media literacy and awareness of the messaging of gender in the media and online. The Girls, Women + Media Project (n.d.) is "a 21st century, nonprofit initiative and network working to increase awareness of how pop culture and media represent, affect, employ, and serve girls and women—and to advocate for improvement in those areas." Young women, who are most familiar with new media technologies, are creating blogs and e-zines such as *Feministing*, *What about Our Daughters*, and *Velvet Park*. Feminist non-profit organizations such as Ontario's Dames Making Games are part of a larger network that aims to create opportunities "for making, playing, changing games" (Dames Making Games, n.d.). Canadian-born Anita Sarkeesian created the video web forum *Feminist Frequency* in 2009 to critique the representation of women in popular culture and create educational resources. Sarkeesian has been the target of intense cyber-harassment that escalated into death threats and ultimately led her to cancel public appearances.

But as mentioned above, cultural representations are produced by larger social systems, and the Internet has become a place not just for bottom-up culture making but also for cybermisogyny, cyberbullying, sex trafficking, and demeaning images of women. Feminists have their work cut out to make spaces on the Internet that resist male dominance, racism, and heterosexism.

Gender in Film: A Case Study

In considering cultural representations of gender in film, presented here is an extended case study of a single genre rather than presenting a survey. This section examines gender in the context of a global phenomenon of cultural representation: Bollywood cinema. In so doing, it emphasizes that "gender is always already constituted by other forms of difference" (Sinha 2004, 233), especially, when used as a cultural representation of the nation.

Bollywood is a term coined in the late 1970s to refer to the Hindi film industry centred in Mumbai (formerly Bombay), India. As the world's largest film industry, Bollywood produces some 900 films per year and reaches millions of people, not only in India but also in the South Asian diaspora, the millions of people of South Asian descent (the term *South Asia* generally includes India, Sri Lanka, Pakistan, and Bangladesh) living in the Middle East, the Caribbean, Africa, the United Kingdom, Canada, Australia, the United States, and other parts of Asia. Since the 1950s—long before the current era of globalization—Indian films have enjoyed an impressive global reach (Gokulsing and Dissanayake 2004, 3).

Not all Indian films are products of Bollywood. Rather, certain conventions define the genre. Chief among these is the use of melodrama and grand spectacle. Sumptuous visuals abound, famous Indian locales often serve as backdrops, and every film features several song-and-dance sequences that contribute to the film's fantastical effect. For its themes and plot lines, Bollywood draws widely from a variety of sources: from ancient Indian epics (*The Ramayana* and *The Mahabharata*) and Parsi theatre to recent North American films and classics of Western literature. For example, *The Ramayana* provided the religious basis of one of the most popular Bollywood films of all time, *Hum Aapke Hain Koun!* (Barjatya 1994), a film celebrating traditions of marriage and family. Ten years later, *Bride and Prejudice* (Chadha 2004) took up the theme of the patriotic family romance in a cheeky send-up of Jane Austen's classic novel. No matter its inspiration, though, the essence of a Bollywood film lies in its gloriously larger-than-life representation of India itself.

Popular Hindi film has long associated the Indian woman with the Indian nation, drawing on a symbolic relation dating at least as far back as the mid-nineteenth century (Chatterjee 1993). In the mid-twentieth century, the first generation of Hindi filmmakers reinvigorated that association in critical response to the politics of culture under British colonialism. The British justified their rule over India in part by representing certain rare though oppressive practices such as *sati* (the immolation of widows) as if they were the cornerstones of Hindu tradition (Chatterjee 1993). In support of British rule, a US woman, Katherine Mayo, a member of the Society of Mayflower Descendants, wrote a book called *Mother India* (2000 [1927]), in which she provided sensationalist details of the oppression of Indian women. Child marriage, early sexuality, early motherhood, and unsafe midwifery practices were all, in her view, signs that India lacked the fundamentals of civilization (Sinha 2004).

Mayo's book became a cause célèbre within India and in international circles. In India, the text gave impetus to a nascent women's movement around such issues as child marriage, even as Indian women activists denounced Mayo's diatribe against India. In Britain, it was proclaimed "the most powerful defense of the British raj that has ever been written" (Mishra 2002, 67) and has even found its way into more recent books by feminists—yet with no reference to its imperialist origins (Sinha 2004). In sum, books about women in non-Western contexts written for popular Western audiences are powerful forms of cultural representation in their own right. The example of *Mother India* shows that knowledge produced about women in colonial contexts often derive less from ideologies of gender difference per se than from powerful politically motivated representations of cultural difference in service of empire.

With India's gaining independence from British rule in 1947, Indian nationalists promoted ideas of Indian culture as if there were a single, pure, authentic form of it—one that was spiritual (and Hindu) to the core and hence distinct from and superior to materially oriented Western culture (Chatterjee 1993). And given the gendered and highly damning criticism of Indian culture that sought to justify British imperialism, post-colonial nationalism in India became powerfully gendered in kind. There was a premium on exalted images not simply of Indian womanhood, but of motherhood. Mothers were represented as paragons of Indian values, keepers of Indian traditions, and protectors of the nation.

Diaspora provides a crucial context for understanding the production of patriarchal themes and narratives. Whereas the South Asian world beyond India was previously an afterthought for Bollywood filmmakers, this huge, worldwide audience is currently their primary target, providing at least 65 per cent of the industry's revenues (Ninian 2003). Filmmakers play to their viewers' desires for depictions of India, but they do so in ways that refer to diasporic life as culturally inauthentic. Whether the films are set in India or, say, England, the films portray diasporic families as in need of cultural education. And here again, the burden of maintaining Indian tradition falls exclusively to the female

These movie posters capture the stark contrast between the chaste Indian woman, who is represented as the very personification of the nation in *Mother India*, and the more sultry diasporic Indian woman of *London Dreams*, who invites fantasy and desire.

characters (Hirji 2011). Men's burden, meanwhile, is to support India's pocketbook. Both in their global travels and in their messages, films depicting diasporic Indian life participate in a largely successful Hindu nationalist agenda within India aimed at attracting capital investment among "non-resident Indians." In light of the millions of dollars that successful Indian North American corporate elites have invested in Indian enterprises, some Bollywood films have recast the image of immigrant men from disloyal sons to heroes coming to the rescue of Mother India (Mankekar 1999).

To the degree that Bollywood satisfies a desire for cultural connection, one might expect its conservative representations of women and gender relations to be readily embraced and perhaps emulated by its viewers. However, the opposite is often true. In one study of South Asians in Canada, young women expressed "annoyance with sexist plot lines and portrayals," reporting that they used such depictions "as a starting point for discussion and debate with parents, relatives and peers" and that the films inspired them to identify as feminists (Hirji 2011, 160). And as an antidote to the presentation of ostensibly authentic Indian culture in ways that normalize heterosexuality, Bollywood's queer diasporic viewers subject the films to transgressive interpretations, reading female homosexual desire into scenes and songs that might otherwise pass as straightforwardly heterosexual (Gopinath 2005b). Diasporic filmmakers, working well outside of the Bollywood machine, more freely resist its most powerful norms. Deepa Mehta's *Fire* (1996) famously represented the "traditionally" female space of the middle-class Indian home as a site of homosexual desire—a move that was met with complete outrage from both the nationalist right wing and the political left within India. Together, then, the practices of diasporic queer viewers and diasporic filmmakers transform the significance of "India" from its would-be status as an object of nostalgic longing and source of authentic originary culture to a touchstone of alternative sexuality for South Asians (Gopinath 2005b).

Bollywood has recently been "discovered" by the North American mainstream. Andrew Lloyd Weber's Bollywood-themed musical *Bombay Dreams* appeared on Broadway in 2004 following its London premiere in 2002. It appropriated and readjusted Bollywood conventions to fit the narrative expectations of white audiences. Yet this happy attempt to mainstream South Asian people, rendering theirs one among many "ethnic" diasporic stories, belies the unique reality they face. In post-9/11 US society, South Asian men have been subjected to intense surveillance and detention in another poignant example of the ways that gender and nation intersect—in this case, through race (Gopinath 2005b).

Despite the degree of historical, political, economic, cultural, and social contextualization that is necessary to understand the dynamics of such globally popular genres as Bollywood films—and here one could add hip hop and Latin American telenovelas—they bear studying precisely because they shape and reflect the ever-shifting experience of gender in so many parts of the interconnected world.

The crowning example of this phenomenon lies in a film titled, ever so strategically, *Mother India* (Khan 1957), which was a remake of the same director's *Aurat* (1940), or "Woman." *Mother India* centres on Radha, a woman raising four sons in extremely adverse circumstances. The film dramatizes her heroism by quickly dispensing with her husband, who leaves the family in shame after an accident renders him dependent on his wife. (As the loyal wife, though, she pines for him throughout the film.) Radha is left to work the land, a task made all the more difficult by the floods that ravage her home and her harvest, killing two of her sons. An evil moneylender offers to erase her considerable debts if she marries him. In the name of her chastity, she declines. When one of her son grows up, he avenges the earlier insult against his mother's honour by killing the moneylender and threatening to abduct his daughter. Instead, Radha kills her son, again to preserve her honour, which collapses with that of the village, its women, and the nation. Indeed, the actress who played Radha, Nargis, was effectively rendered one and the same with her film character. As Salman Rushdie writes of Nargis, "she became, until Indira-Mata supplanted her, the living mother-goddess of us all" (Rushdie 1995, 138–9). More than 50 years after its release, *Mother India* remains "the quintessential Indian film" (Gokulsing and Dissanayake 2004, 79), influencing Bollywood cinema for decades. It is shown somewhere in India every day of the year (Mishra 2002, 66).

Bollywood has long portrayed the ideal Indian woman as a loyal wife and self-sacrificing mother. Her moral stature was also enabled by constrained representations of her sexuality. Until the early 1990s, filmmakers were bound by censorship codes prohibiting the depiction of "excessively passionate love scenes" or "scenes suggestive of immorality" (Prasad 1998, 88). On-screen kissing, sex, and nudity were associated with low Western morals and were hence constituted as a threat to the nation (Prasad 1998, 91). Filmmakers commonly circumvented these codes by, for example, featuring titillating "wet-sari scenes." In large measure, the films trafficked in dichotomous depictions of women as sexual beings: the appearance of an occasional vamp (a Westernized woman) functioned to throw into stark relief the real (that is, culturally pure) Indian woman's virtue (Gangoli 2005).

The liberalization of the Indian economy in the 1990s and the advent of satellite television—a harbinger of globalization—ushered in a new era for Bollywood films. As heavily sexualized images from abroad began circulating within India, filmmakers of the "new Bollywood" (Durham 2007) were licensed and inspired to revise their images of women. Now they are far less demure than in the past—even to the point of having a profession and a premarital sex life. But the old association of women and tradition persists. Where she is made into a doctor, an Indian woman must still manifest exceptional beauty while cooking classic Indian dishes and being a consummate caregiver (Hirji 2011). Where she is made to share men's lust for money and power, shamelessly using her body as a means to achieve those, she becomes an anti-heroine and meets with a violent end (Durham 2007). The continuing conflation of women with tradition affects the female actors who now choose between what they themselves call "admirable" or "trashy" roles; those who choose the latter often disavow the personas they create on film, publicly claiming to be quite different in real life (Govindan and Dutta 2008). Critics of Bollywood's turn to sex and nudity decry these as "Western assaults on Indian culture," while directors (male) defend these moves as feminist and modern (Durham 2007, 47). Meanwhile, it is largely in India's "parallel cinema" where women directors do their work, raising difficult social issues such as surrogacy (when a woman gestates another's baby to birth, often paid) or otherwise critiquing the gendered status quo as well as the Indian political system writ large (Chakravarty 1993; Pudasaini 2009).

Summary

The ideas that women and men have had about who they are, how they relate to one another, and their potential are the products of their cultures. An important part of any culture is its representation of reality. Individuals (or their cultures) shape perception of what is "out there" based on the ways in which they have learned to interpret reality. These perceptions, or images, are social creations whose shape and origin need to be examined rather than accepted at face value.

Notions of what women are have been shaped by representation. Society conveys imagery through ordinary language and social and creative works. The images themselves have served to set women aside from humanity by reducing them to one or a few essentialist aspects of their personalities, physiologies, or behaviours. The sexualization of women and girls transforms women into vessels for sexuality rather than people with complex human desires. The image of woman in singular, stereotypical terms reduces all women to something less than whole, individual human beings. Conversely, the use of woman to represent an entire group—whether a nation or an ethnic, racial, or religious group—places an inordinate burden on the women of that group. Popular media both produce and reflect these dynamics.

Most cultural representations have been created by dominant groups and disseminated through established networks. This means that women, particularly marginalized women (women of colour, working-class women, colonized women, and lesbians, bisexual, and trans women, to name a few), have rarely been fairly or accurately represented. However, women have always been writers, artists, and cultural participants, and as they have claimed opportunities to share their work, ideas about women and gender have expanded. In such realms as popular music and feminist erotica, women lay claim to expressing their sexuality on their own terms. Yet women's agency and their claims to free expression are not necessarily devoid of political implications or repercussions. While feminists have been analyzing and critiquing all forms of cultural representation for generations, the Internet presents new challenges: it is highly democratic, meaning that it can be used effectively toward progressive ends as well as to advance many harmful agendas.

Discussion Questions

1. Choose a popular song, television show, or film and describe its representations of gender, including the language and imagery used. Do you think your description would match that of its creator? Why or why not?
2. Can you provide an example of a particular group being represented through the image of its female members? In what form(s) (music, art, television) do such representations come?
3. Images of sexualization are everywhere. In what ways are women depicted in order to be "sexy" compared to the ways men are depicted as "sexy"? Who is depicted in media without being sexualized?
4. What opportunities exist for the Internet to expand different kinds of representations of women and gender? What are its limitations? What are its problems?

Recommended Resources

The Achilles Effect. www.achilleseffect.com/2011/03/word-cloud-how-toy-ad-vocabulary-reinforces-gender-stereotypes/. Shows cloud maps of vocabulary used to describe girls' and boys' toys.

Bannerji, Himani. 1993. *Returning the Gaze: Essays on Racism, Feminism and Politics.* Toronto: Sister Vision Press. This volume is a foundational analysis of the structural barriers that limit and pervert the representation of racialized women in mainstream Canadian culture. Bannerji constructs a strong critique of how race, class, and gender intersect in patterns of systemic exploitation.

The Canadian Women Artists History Initiative. http://cwahi.concordia.ca/. Based within the art history department at Concordia University, the Canadian Women Artists History Initiative's mission is to enhance research and scholarship on pre-1967 historical women artists in Canada and their contributions to the cultural and material history of Canada.

Fleras, Augie. 2011. *The Media Gaze: Representations of Diversities in Canada.* Vancouver: UBC Press. Drawing on a variety of thought-provoking case studies, Fleras explores the implications of the media's framing of women, young men, the elderly, racialized and new Canadians, Indigenous peoples, the working class and poor, gays and lesbians, and religious minorities and presents readers with alternative ways of creating, understanding, and analyzing mainstream media.

Media Smarts, Canada's Centre for Digital and Media Literacy. *Queer Representation in Film and Television.* http://mediasmarts.ca/digital-media-literacy/media-issues/diversity-media/queer-representation/queer-representation-film-television. This website is a comprehensive repository of material concerned with film and television on how "queer" has been culturally presented. It also offers key prompts to assist in independent analysis.

Nicholas, Jane. 2015. *The Modern Girl: Feminine Modernities, the Body, and Commodities in the 1920s.* Toronto: University of Toronto Press. Nicholas traces the transition of Canada into a consumer society through the construction of images of modern women. She emphasizes the agency of women themselves in self-presenting the modern image even when faced with social and familial sanction.

Rice, Carla. 2014. *Becoming Women: The Embodied Self in Image Culture.* Toronto: University of Toronto Press. This text explores popular imagery by means of individual narratives from marginalized and misrepresented groups. Rice exposes the beauty industry's colonization of women's bodies, and examines why "the beauty myth" has yet to be resolved.

Walcott, Rinaldo. 2003. *Black Like Who?: Writing Black Canada*. Toronto: Insomniac Press. Walcott examines the role of black Canadians in defining Canada while arguing against essentialist notions.

2 Historical Ideas and Theories about Women and Gender

Chapter Outline

- Why Ideas and Theories Are Important
- The "Waves" of Feminism
- Ancient and Early Modern Ideas about Women and Gender
- Classical Liberalism and Feminism
- Socialism and Feminism
- Simone de Beauvoir
- Contemporary Feminist Debates
- Contemporary Feminist Philosophies

This chapter will help you
- Learn some of the key developments in feminist theory
- Appreciate the context of the historical foundation of women's and gender studies
- Recognize the multiple and varied strands of feminist thought and how these lead to a consideration of "feminisms"
- Reflect upon the complexities of feminist theories and challenges for future work
- Perceive the rationale for contemporary feminist debates

> *(You Make Me Feel Like) A Natural Woman*
> —HIT SINGLE BY ARETHA FRANKLIN, 1967

What does it mean to be, as in the famous Aretha Franklin song, a "natural woman"? Do women and men have naturally different characteristics, styles of parenting, ways of relating to others, or values? Or are men and women essentially the same? Is sexism the idea that women *are not the same as men*, or is it sexist to demand that women *have to act and think the same as men do* if they want to be treated equally? Many philosophers and other thinkers have addressed these questions over the centuries, and their ideas about women, gender, and difference continue to be debated today. Although many thinkers in the past supported male dominance, some opposed it even over 2000 years ago. The eighteenth- and nineteenth-century revolutions and liberatory movements began a more systematic challenge to the subordination of women. In this chapter, both historical ideas and theories about women and gender and newer analyses from the perspectives of feminist philosophers and thinkers are considered. The focus is on the critical analysis of sexism while emphasizing the many varied positions feminists writers have held.

Why Ideas and Theories Are Important

Why read about old ideas and theories concerning the nature of women and gender differences in the face of the rapid changes in the understanding of gender and women's social roles globally? It is important to study these because (1) they represent not just the beliefs of the thinkers who developed them but also the widely held beliefs in their societies at those times, and (2) they still influence current debates. Although most people today agree that women should have control over their lives, many continue to believe, as in the past, that men and women have different roles to play in the family, in society, and in the workplace and that these roles are justified by the essential nature of gender differences. Old ideas and theories about women and gender have been around for a very long time and may still have influence.

The question of whether there are natural facts about women and gender is a scientific question, but scientific inquiry has to begin with *concepts and definitions* so that one knows what one is studying. These change over time as usage changes and social ideas change. *Fathering* used to mean begetting a child by impregnating a woman; today it means something comparable to *mothering*, involving the actual care of a child. *Marriage* used to signify more of an economic unit than a romantic partnership. New concepts can also emerge in language, such as violence against women, to indicate new ways of interpreting events and experiences. While violence against women is not a new phenomenon, Canada only named it as a crime in recent decades. A shared way of speaking reflects a society's values and how it understands the world. Using more inclusive gender terms, such as *firefighter* rather than *fireman*, indicates that society has begun to believe that this occupation can be performed by any qualified person. Fighting over language is not trivial, since language indicates belief systems and can sometimes reveal that old ideas about gender are still influential. Children who are learning the language of their communities are also learning about social roles, expectations, and beliefs. Many of the commonly accepted ways to talk about women and gender have contained hidden, implicit sexism (Daly 1978; Vetterling-Braggin 1981). See Chapter 1 for more on how language reflects and perpetuates gender stereotypes.

There is also a need to distinguish between *descriptive* and *prescriptive* aspects of the way concepts and definitions are used. In developing theories, the aim is not merely to understand the way human beings have generally done things (descriptive) but also to consider how things *should* be done (prescriptive). Human beings are always striving to improve, from decreasing violent tendencies to overcoming disease. Just because something is called natural does not prove that it is good or even inevitable. Humans are intensely imaginative and creative animals with innovative capacities to change, adapt, and learn.

Box 2.1 Time to Reflect

Men's Ideas about Women

The glory of a man is knowledge, but the glory of a woman is to renounce knowledge. —CHINESE PROVERB

Whenever a woman dies there is one less quarrel on earth. —GERMAN PROVERB

Women are sisters nowhere. —WEST AFRICAN PROVERB

I thank thee, O Lord, that thou hast not created me a woman. —DAILY ORTHODOX JEWISH PRAYER

There is a good principle which created order, light, and man, and an evil principle which created chaos, darkness, and woman. —PYTHAGORAS (GREECE, C. 570 BCE–c. 495 BCE)

When a woman thinks, she thinks evil. —SENECA (ROME, C. 4 BC–65 CE)

Wives, submit yourselves unto your husbands for the husband is the head of the wife, even as Christ is the head of the church. —EPHESIANS 5:23–24

In childhood a woman must be subject to her father; in youth, to her husband; when her husband is dead, to her sons. A woman must never be free of subjugation. —HINDU CODE OF MANU, V (C. 200 BCE–C. 200 CE)

A man in general is better pleased when he has a good dinner than when his wife talks Greek. —SAMUEL JOHNSON (ENGLAND, 1790–1784)

The difference between men and women is like that between animals and plants. —G.W.F. HEGEL (GERMANY, 1770–1831)

Nature intended women to be our slaves. —NAPOLEON BONAPARTE (FRANCE, 1769–1821)

Women have great talent, but no genius, for they always remain subjective. —ARTHUR SCHOPENHAUER (GERMANY, 1788–1860)

Regard the society of women as a necessary unpleasantness of social life, and avoid it as much as possible. —LEO TOLSTOY (RUSSIA, 1828–1910)

Women, in general, want to be loved for what they are and men for what they accomplish. The first for their looks and charm, the latter for their actions. —THEODOR REIK (AUSTRIA/US, 1888–1969)

Therefore, it is important to consider how language is used since this may actually inhibit change or conceal aspects of something to be understood. Much of written "women's history" in the Global North has actually been white women's history. This acknowledgement makes clear what work still needs to be done to have a more complete story. Anthropologists once assumed that it was perfectly justifiable to study a culture by talking only to the men. They believed that women's lives are determined by nature rather than culture and that women do essentially the same sorts of things in every society. Feminist anthropologists questioned this assumption and argued that interviewing only men would produce a skewed theory about the community, about how harmonious it really is, or how power relations operate. And anthropologists could only discover whether their assumptions about "natural women" were true by actually talking to the women. Similarly, critical race feminists (discussed below and in the next chapter) have argued that the stories of white women do not encapsulate all of "women's history," and, in fact, produce skewed theories about power relations, the universality of the female experience, and the success of feminism as a movement.

Definitions of *woman* and *gender* have often reflected faulty theories; however, these ideas were and continue to be constantly challenged.

The "Waves" of Feminism

North American feminism has traditionally used the metaphor of waves to describe the movement. In this portrayal, waves depict the ebb and flow of women's rights activism and are linked to particular historical eras.[1] When women's liberation emerged in the 1960s, many in that movement designated an earlier period of feminism the first wave. The 1960s movement thus was called the second wave. Later developments in feminist theory and practice became a third wave. And some maintain that there is now a fourth wave. This wave metaphor has been used to make clear distinctions and explicit categories between and within the temporally based feminist movements. This is but one problem that the wave model presents.

This model begins with the first wave, in the nineteenth and early twentieth centuries. The first wave of feminism was concerned with gaining civil and political rights for women with much emphasis on suffrage—the right to vote. It was embedded in liberal notions of democracy and European Enlightenment ideas (see later in this chapter for more).

After the right to vote was gained by many—but not all—women, the feminist movement seemed to recede. It appeared to make a comeback in the widespread grassroots peace and "liberation" movements of the 1960s. This second wave was characterized by slogans such as "the personal is political" and "sisterhood is universal." It included campaigns against domestic violence and for reproductive rights and equal pay. The second wave continued in the liberal traditions of inclusion in the public sphere while also taking on issues that had traditionally been considered part of the private domain, especially those related to the family unit.

The beginning of the third wave is often located in the early 1990s, and the movement appeared to respond to second-wave issues. Theories based on the assumptions of universality were challenged by the third wave, especially by women of colour, LGBTQ activists, and academics. For example, the family was viewed differently by white middle- or upper-class women, for whom it was a site of oppression, than it was by many black women, who saw the family as a unit of solidarity and support against racist systems of oppression. If first and second-wave feminist objectives were to have women included in "the system," then third-wave feminists sought to change the system. Audre Lorde's maxim "The master's tools will never dismantle the master's house" (1983) most clearly expresses this sentiment. The third wave advanced concepts of inclusivity that went beyond binary systems and problematized the notion of gender. Intersectionality was introduced as a fundamental theory along with the politics of difference. It engaged a transnational, post-colonial, and cultural framework for feminism (see Chapter 3).

The fourth wave is frequently described as twenty-first century feminism. While it picks up from the third wave, it operates within and amid social media and new information technologies and is opposed to feminism that excludes transgender women. It employs an intersectional analysis to achieve solidarity and social justice and is continuing to develop while embracing more and more strands of lived experience.

As noted above, one problem with the wave analogy is that it creates exclusive time frames for each wave in chronologically captive frames. But the reality of feminist activism is often blurred by these exclusionary categories. For example, where does Simone de Beauvoir fit? Her landmark book, *The Second Sex*, falls clearly outside of the wave timelines. Also, overlapping issues have been carried along the waves. Sojourner Truth's *Ain't I a Women?* was reintroduced by bell hooks in her book of the same name (1981) in the second wave, but Truth spoke during the first wave. Both raised the issue of racism within feminism that isolated, erased, and rendered invisible women of colour (see Chapter 3).

The wave metaphor limits how the multiple ideas that are contained in feminist theory and activism can be appreciated and taken up. In its place, many now embrace the contemporary understanding of *feminisms* rather than a single framework. In this way, many approaches can be encompassed and expressed, including Indigenous feminism, ecofeminism, critical race feminism, post-colonial feminism, socialist feminism, black feminism, and transnational feminism, all of which are discussed in this chapter.

The notion that the waves express a history of feminism replicates a colonial approach to theory by which it excludes the history and contemporary voices of different peoples in the global community. As Mohamad Tavakoli-Targhi (2015) explains, "waves only hit one shore."

Ancient and Early Modern Ideas about Women and Gender

Like many ancient thinkers, Confucius (551–479 BCE) held that women's proper place was in the home and that their proper attitude was one of obedience. Women must be obedient first to their fathers, then to their husbands, and then to their grown sons. Confucius believed in maintaining a clear division between the private—or domestic—and public spheres, which continues to shape much thought about women: "the woman's correct place is within; the man's correct place is outside." On the other hand, the public sphere was modelled on the private sphere: the family was seen as a microcosm of the state, and just as the state was ruled by a divinely mandated male emperor, so too the father's authority was seen as part of the natural order.

By contrast, the founder of Buddhism, Gautama Buddha (c. 563–c. 483 BCE), supported women joining monastic sects as teachers alongside men and even believed women could achieve enlightenment. Buddhism taught that the highest state of *nirvana* was achieved through gender neutrality, or transcending one's **gender identity**. However, it was thought to be harder for women to achieve nirvana than men, indicating what many scholars believe today was a rather ambivalent attitude toward women in early Buddhism.

Although the Greek philosopher Plato (427–347 BCE) was a well-known critic of democracy, he held remarkably egalitarian views about women. He believed that the natural capacities of individuals were not determined by their gender and that women could become rulers or physicians or philosophers. In *The Republic* he says, ". . . if it appears that [the male and the female sex] differ only in just this respect, that the female bears and the male begets . . . no proof has yet been produced that the woman differs from the man for our purposes, but we shall continue to think that our guardians and their wives ought to follow the same pursuits" (Plato 2005, 454). Equality of education followed from this: if women are to be assigned similar duties as men, Plato said, "We must also teach them the same things" (453).

Aristotle (384–322 BCE) was Plato's pupil, yet he developed some of the most notoriously sexist views about women in the history of philosophy. He believed that the "female is as it were a deformed male," meaning that females have male features but in impure and undeveloped form. Aristotle believed women to be intellectually and morally inferior to men, but much of his account was based in mistaken biological claims, the most important of which was that the pregnant female is simply a vessel or incubator for the human form that has been implanted by the man's seed. A woman, he thought, makes no formative contribution to the child but only provides its sustenance (Aristotle 1943; Bell 1983, 63).

Western philosophical definitions of "woman" have been based on faulty theories and biased cultural assumptions. This is also true of biological definitions of the sexes focused on the body, but while today it may be easy to see that Aristotle's view of women as "imperfect men" was an ideological construct that served political ends, it is more difficult to conclude the same for definitions of the sexes grounded in scientific research. Is science not, after all, the unbiased, objective pursuit of truth? Are scientific definitions of the sexes not based on biological facts that can be observed and measured with precise and accurate instruments?

Many of the most important Christian theologians viewed sexuality as sinful and women as unclean. According to the North African bishop Saint Augustine (354–430), given the depraved nature of women and human sexuality, the best form of life would be absolute chastity, with marital sex only for the purposes of reproduction a second-best alternative. Maimonides (1135–1204), philosopher and Jewish theologian, provides an interesting alternative view.

Hypatia: 370–415 CE philosopher, astronomer, and mathematician, in Alexandria, Egypt. In the early sixteenth century, the famous Italian painter Raphael (1483–1520) wanted to honour Hypatia by including her image among the famous philosophers of the past in his *The School of Athens*. When the Bishop of Rome disapproved of including her, since she had been killed by Christian monks of Alexandria for heretical teachings, Raphael was unwilling to give her up, "disguising" her by lightening her skin colour and painting her face to resemble a favoured nephew of the Pope.

He held that the conjugal rights of wives are so important that "a wife may restrict her husband in his business journeys to nearby places only, so that he would not otherwise deprive her of her conjugal rights." Neither can a husband change his occupation to one involving a less "frequent conjugal schedule . . . as for example, if an ass-driver seeks to become a camel-driver, or if a camel-driver seeks to become a sailor" (Maimonides 1972; Bell 1983, 95). No mention is made of reproduction, indicating that it is sexual fulfillment that is the wife's right. Despite this acknowledgement of female sexual needs,

Maimonides supported a husband's right to all his wife's earnings and to restrict her public movements, and he held that in cases of rape, compensation should be paid to the woman's father in an amount based on her beauty.

In the eighteenth century, a lively debate arose concerning women and rationality. Most intellectuals, such as David Hume (1711–1776) and Immanuel Kant (1724–1804), believed that women reason very differently than men. They thought that women's rationality is "related to the finer feeling" of sentiment and delicate discernments, such as the capacity to distinguish jealousy from envy. Others, such as Denis Diderot (1713–1784) and Jean-Jacques Rousseau (1712–1778), held that women have little rationality of any sort and are driven more by visions and hysteria. Others in the eighteenth century disagreed with both these types of view and argued that women's different capacities were the result of being treated and educated differently, rather than the result of innate, natural differences.

This anti-naturalist view about gender differences began to influence the wider revolutionary movements that were developing in Europe and throughout the Americas against the landed aristocracy, colonialism, and monarchy. Feminism, as the new ideas about women came to be called, became an integral part of the two main political philosophies that emerged during this period of ferment: liberalism and socialism.

Classical Liberalism and Feminism

Enlightenment philosophers of the eighteenth century began to criticize the idea that the male hierarchy that had dominated Western thought since the ancient slavery-based Greek societies was a natural phenomenon. They also dismissed much of the religious teachings that, based on the doctrine of original sin, rejected the idea that human beings can improve themselves. They emphasized instead the essential equality of all men, the importance of liberty, the right of self-governance, and the possibility of social change. If men were essentially equal and each deserves liberty, then it followed that feudal systems of governance dominated by crown and church would not suffice. Liberals thus began to argue for free elections, an independent judiciary, laws that respect the right of citizens to be treated fairly, and government that is accountable to the will of its citizens as expressed through the political process. These tenets are the basis of classical liberal political thought.

Feminists often take for granted the principles that liberalism first espoused, such as that people have the right to be free and to be treated as equals and that social arrangements ought to be based on the consent of all. Yet these ideas were not applied to women until recently. Women struggled to claim their political and civil rights until the vote—the absolute minimum of political equality—was won for some at the end of the nineteenth century: first in New Zealand in 1893, and then slowly in most countries around the world through the twentieth century. Not until 1990 were women allowed to vote in all of Switzerland's cantons, and women's suffrage was granted in the United Arab Emirates only in 2006. In Canada, racialized women and Indigenous peoples were not granted the franchise until mid-twentieth century. (See Chapter 3 for a history of Canadian voting rights.)

Despite this slow progress, liberal ideas are still considered by many in the Global North to be the foundation upon which feminism is built, since they stress freedom and equality. But many liberal theorists acknowledge the need to reconsider how these concepts are understood in order to make them more effective forces for women's equality. Women cannot live freely if they are sexually, physically, or economically dominated in the "private" sphere of either the home or the workplace. How the private sphere is treated, as well as how its boundaries are defined, is a political issue.

Most classical liberal thinkers assumed that the family was *necessarily and naturally*

> **Box 2.2 Key Issues**
>
> ### What Is Feminism?
>
> In the most basic sense, feminism is exactly what the dictionary says it is: the movement for social, political, and economic equality of men and women. Public-opinion polls confirm that when women are given this definition, 71 per cent say they agree with feminism, along with 61 per cent of men. We prefer to add to that seemingly uncontroversial statement the following: Feminism means that women have the right to enough information to make informed choices about their lives.
>
> Source: Baumgardner and Richards (2000).

hierarchical. They did not consider the possibility of women acting in the political realm as free and equal citizens, nor did they consider that relations within the family needed to become more egalitarian and consensual, even though they argued for such changes in society. As Susan Moller Okin (1979, 202) writes, "Whereas the liberal tradition appears to be talking about individuals as components of political systems, it is in fact talking about male-headed families.... Women disappear from the subject of politics."

Some of the architects of liberalism and social equality for men vigorously opposed gender equality. Jean-Jacques Rousseau (1712–1778), one of the most important figures of the Enlightenment, argued that women are simply unfit for self-governance or political participation. In *Émile* (1966 [1762]), he maintains that women should be educated in such a way that they will learn that their happiness requires submitting to men's will.

Along with many others, Rousseau invoked nature to justify democracy, arguing that social hierarchies are man-made, not ordained by God. Yet he also used nature to justify women's subordination: "Nature herself has decreed that woman, both for herself and her children, should be at the mercy of man's judgment.... When the Greek women married, they disappeared from public life; . . . [and] devoted themselves to the care of their households and family. This is the mode of life prescribed for women alike by nature and reason" (Rousseau 1966 [1762], 328–30).

Since, for Rousseau, the essence of being human is being free, it follows that he believed women to be less than fully human. He argued, like Confucius, that the father must be the dominant authority within the family, and without this "proper order" both the family and society would fall apart.[2] But if Rousseau was right that not even two persons who have common concerns and ties of affection can reach decisions on the basis of mutuality rather than of domination and submission, there is little hope for the democratic, consensual decision making in the larger society that he so passionately advocated. On the other hand, if governments should be based not on tradition or force but on consent between free and equal individuals, then this liberal and democratic approach must be extended to women inside families as well (Okin 1989).

Wollstonecraft

Mary Wollstonecraft (1759–1797), an Enlightenment philosopher writing in England in the late eighteenth century, disputed Rousseau's views on women and gender relations. A journalist and author who struggled to live on her own earnings, Wollstonecraft criticized the social conventions that created barriers to women's ability to achieve economic independence. She developed philosophical counter-arguments against the widespread beliefs about women's "natural" idleness, weakness, and irrationality (Eisenstein 1981).

Wollstonecraft pointed out that women had been *taught* to be creatures of emotion rather than of reason. Even if one accepted Rousseau's belief that women were responsible for the raising of children, women needed an education to raise children well. Wollstonecraft further reasoned that if women's childlike status were truly innate and women truly incapable of being educated, why did professional education for women have to be prohibited by law? Why were laws needed to ensure what traditional thinkers believed to be natural?

> Men, indeed, appear to me to act in a very unphilosophical manner when they try to secure the good conduct of women by attempting to keep them always in a state of childhood. . . . It is a farce to call any being virtuous whose virtues do not result from the exercise of its own reason. This was Rousseau's opinion respecting men: I extend it to women. (Wollstonecraft 1967 [1792], 50, 52)

Wollstonecraft was not discouraged by the magnitude of the changes needed in her society; along with other Enlightenment thinkers, she was optimistic about social change. Unfortunately, traditional ideas about gender such as Rousseau's appealed more to the male elites in power. Although the French Revolution of 1789 opened up a debate about gender equality, Olympe de Gouges, author of *Declaration of the Rights of Woman*, went to the guillotine in 1793, and whatever gains women had made in the political turmoil of the eighteenth century were soon lost in the subsequent conservative reaction to the revolution. Mary Wollstonecraft died at the young age of 38 giving birth to her daughter Mary Shelley (the author of *Frankenstein*).

Her death was part of an epidemic of deaths in childbirth across Europe caused when obstetrics was wrested away from midwives in favour of doctors who unknowingly carried the germs of their ill hospital patients to the bedsides of women in labour. Midwives were seen as unprofessional, ignorant, and dirty despite their high level of skill, and their replacement by trained male physicians led to the loss of generations of women due to septicemia (Ehrenreich and English 2010; see also Chapter 8).

Mill and Taylor

Almost all the main figures of the liberal tradition excluded women from the political realm, but there were a few exceptions. In his treatise *On the Subjection of Women* (Mill 1970 [1869]), John Stuart Mill (1806–1873) took the radical position that equal rights and opportunities should be extended to women. He argued that women ought to be able to own property, vote, attend schools and colleges, and enter into any profession for which they were qualified. Such ideas went against the beliefs of his day and, as a result, were until recently often omitted from philosophy textbooks covering Mill's views. His lifelong companion, collaborator, and eventual wife, Harriet Taylor (1807–1858), helped him develop his feminist arguments.

Mill's arguments ran counter to those of the French philosopher Auguste Comte (1798–1857), who is often considered the "father of sociology." Comte believed that biology was already "able to establish the hierarchy of the sexes, by demonstrating both anatomically and physiologically that, in almost the entire animal kingdom, and especially in our species, the female is formed for a state of essential childhood" (Okin 1979, 220). Mill took Comte on, arguing, like Wollstonecraft, that observable deficiencies found among women cannot be attributed to innate inferiority when their life circumstance is so different from men's. Until women are given a chance to have the same education as men, Mill reasoned that no one can claim to know what their real capacities are. Harriet Taylor demanded equality for women even more forcefully than Mill. She derided the faulty arguments through which men tried to justify their dominance:

> The world were once persuaded that the supreme virtue of subjects was loyalty to kings,

and are still persuaded that the paramount virtue of womanhood is loyalty to men.... Self-will and self-assertion form the type of what are designated as manly virtues, while abnegation of self, patience, resignation, and submission to power... have been stamped by general consent as preeminently the duties and graces required of women ... power makes itself the center of moral obligation ... a man likes to have his own will, but does not like that his domestic companion should have a will different from his. (Taylor Mill 1970 [1851], 97)

Contemporary Liberal Feminism

Liberal feminists, past and present, view biological differences as irrelevant to the question of women's rights (Jaggar 1983; Littleton 1987). They continue the task begun by Wollstonecraft, Taylor, and J.S. Mill to extend liberal principles of self-governance and equality to women and family relations. Equality can never be realized for most women if the primary responsibility for household tasks, child care, and eldercare falls on them while the opportunities for economic independence are much greater for men (Okin 1989). Liberal feminists hold that women have a right to choose whether or not to have children, and that if they choose to become parents they should have adequate social supports for their mental health and self-development. Contemporary liberals realize that making legal rights effective requires regulation of the private sphere, whether this involves private enterprise or family relations, in order to ensure that it is both fair and equal for all.

For example, to make equality of opportunity a reality, liberals supported policies of "affirmative action" as a proactive way to force employers to give access to qualified women as well as qualified men from racialized groups who have experienced patterns of discrimination. Advocates of affirmative action argue that (1) white males have long benefited from an unacknowledged preference in hiring, and affirmative action is a way of levelling the playing field; and (2) people's attitudes about who can perform what type of job can most effectively be changed when they see the jobs performed well. Yet affirmative action has been strongly opposed by some of those who previously enjoyed employment privilege based on racism and sexism. Despite some progress in opening up opportunities previously closed, most types of work remain highly segregated by gender and race.

Those who do housework and who care for children and the elderly perform long hours of hard work that is vital to the functioning of the economy. Yet often neither the value nor the difficulty of this work is recognized (Folbre 2001). Starting in the nineteenth century, some feminists began to argue that the oppression of women, especially the devaluing of women's work, could not be sufficiently explained or solved in the terms of classical liberal theory. They argued for a more systematic analysis that links the political sphere to the economic sphere. Thus began the development of socialist feminism.

Socialism and Feminism

Socialist feminists aim for a society with a more rational, just, and democratic system of economic production. Socialism developed differently in each country depending on its different social and political context. Yet it must not be forgotten that, although former socialist societies in the USSR and Eastern Europe had their problems, current capitalist societies are causing environmental destruction, encouraging wars for profit, derailing democracy through the influx and influence of money in electoral campaigns, and continuing to wantonly exploit vulnerable populations in the labour market, which includes large numbers of women. Surely, socialist feminists argue, humanity can do better than this.

Socialist feminists believe that the feminism that develops in liberal capitalist societies simply encourages women to scramble for self-advancement up the corporate hierarchy, leaving most women out. Because liberal feminists focus on individualism and individual *legal rights*, their reforms leave most women *economically* disadvantaged. Liberal feminism does not even aim to address the oppressive structure of a global economy dominated by corporate power. Liberal feminism wants inclusion in the existing capitalist system, not a change to the system.

The situation of women worldwide is centrally connected to their labour. Women's labour in the home is unpaid and often undervalued (for example, it is never included in a country's gross domestic product [GDP]), while women's labour outside the home is routinely underpaid. The large majority of women work in a gender-segregated workforce, as office workers, retail employees, garment workers teachers, nurses and nursing aids, hotel maids, wait staff, and so on, with low wages and benefits and fewer unions. The focus on individual liberties for women provides neither an adequate analysis of nor an effective solution to this problem.

Marx and Engels

Karl Marx (1818–1883) and Friedrich Engels (1820–1895) argued that relations between men and women under capitalism are similar to relations between the bourgeoisie (corporate business owners) and the proletariat (workers): one side always negotiates from a position of weakness (Marx and Engels 1848). They held that women's economic dependence on men is neither natural nor inevitable. In *The Origin of the Family, Private Property and the State* (1972 [1884]), Engels argues that the particular institutions, laws, and ideas of a given historical period—including forms of the family and gender relations—arise as a by-product to the particular form of its economic relations. Moreover, men became dominant not through any natural superiority but through historical happenstance. Although some of the anthropological data Engels drew from is outdated, he was right that women were not always unequal but lost power as social change advantaged men who controlled the tools of economic production. Men's subsequent material dominance then led to their cultural dominance, or their ability to create belief systems that served their interests. Engels described the bourgeois wives of the nineteenth century as little more than legally sanctioned prostitutes, bought and sold in marriages that legally ceded all power and property to their husbands. With no right to seek a job or education, travel freely, have their own bank account, or go to the authorities when they were raped or beaten by their husbands, wives were essentially a form of property themselves, and their husbands, as the owners of that property, could do with them what they wished.

Women of the working classes were economically exploited at a rate even greater than that of male workers during the Industrial Revolution. Marxists argued that the capitalist class had no interest in overturning sexist views about women's worth: they could reap greater profits from women's labour as well as commodify their sexuality and profit from their unpaid reproductive labour (not just bearing and raising children but all the domestic work necessary to sustain workers). Capitalism's profit motive ensured that women would remain underpaid and oppressed. Socialism would liberate women by reorganizing the system of production to make it more rational and more just, basing wages, for example, on the difficulty of a job and its value to society. Sexism and racism would disappear in the future classless society because there would no longer be an economic advantage.

Zetkin and Kollontai

Clara Zetkin (1857–1933), leader of the German socialist movement, wrote in 1896 that the struggle of proletarian women was very different from the struggle of bourgeois women: the former, unlike the latter, were not struggling *against* the men of their class. Because the vast majority of women were workers, Zetkin thought the struggle for women's liberation should aim to bring about a political rule of the proletariat in which men's and women's interests would be aligned. She agreed with the reforms demanded by the bourgeois women's movement, but for her, these reforms would mainly help working-class women in their battle alongside working-class men for shared goals of social justice (Zetkin 1984).

Other Marxist feminists such as Alexandra Kollontai (1872–1952), a leader of the 1917 Russian Revolution, added the component of women's sexual liberation. Kollontai argued that the "moral codes" that govern sexual relationships, including monogamy, should be rethought. She chastised socialist leaders who neglected the issue of sex as a "private matter" unworthy of "the effort and the attention of the collective" (Kollontai 1972 [1911]). She wrote that the state of personal, sexual relationships always has a significant effect on social struggle, sometimes disabling social movements. Socialists were sometimes guilty of assuming values of individualism and possessiveness in sexual relationships, she believed, and needed to think more expansively about how to maximize freedom, equality, and genuine friendship between the genders. Her novel, *Love of the Worker Bees*, depicts three generations of women's love lives, pre-revolution, revolutionary, and post-revolution, to project how she saw female sexual freedom incrementally expand under communism.

Kollontai founded the Women's Department after the Russian Revolution and became the People's Commissar for Social Welfare, making her the most senior woman in the new Soviet government. She created new programs for women's literacy, working conditions, and health care. She opposed liberal feminism while maintaining that the full emancipation of women could only occur after full socialism was achieved. In the repressive turn of the revolution, she was one of the few opponents of Stalin who avoided imprisonment and execution. Relegated to the diplomatic corps, she wrote *The Autobiography of a Sexually Emancipated Communist Woman* in 1926 and several more works before her death in 1952.

Zetkin and Kollontai founded International Women's Day in 1911 to bring attention to the needs and strengths of women workers.

Utopian Socialism and Social Gospel

Although Marxism or **"scientific socialism"** was the dominant strain of socialist thought in the nineteenth century, there were also other versions, including "utopian socialism," Christian communism, market socialism, and others.

In the late nineteenth century, Canadian utopian socialists organized associations such as the Canadian Socialist League (CSL) with many members espousing Christian-based utopian-oriented socialism. Women often held multiple memberships in socialist groups, the Woman's Christian Temperance Union, and in organizations dedicated to women's suffrage. In 1902 Margaret Haile was the CSL candidate in the Ontario provincial election: the first woman candidate in a political election in the British Empire (Newton 1995). (See Chapter 12 in this volume.)

The Social Gospel was an important Canadian movement from the 1890s through the 1930s. It espoused a progressive biblical response to contemporary social problems caused by rapid industrialization. Ideas of morality and social justice formed the foundation for their work, and the movement achieved a degree of influence within churches and the political establishment. Even though women's suffrage was not among its priorities, many women reformists found the Social Gospel movement an important place from which to organize (Allen 2006).

During this time, women in these movements often acted from ideas found in maternal feminism, an ideology that became especially strong throughout the British Empire, including Canada, which linked women's role as mothers to a wider understanding of social welfare. They believed that women, through their biological reproductive and domestic role, had a deeper insight into how society should be reformed (Reisenwitz 2013). Maternal feminism often was class based, where middle- and upper-class women sought to reform the "lower classes" with a charity-based approach. They often shared the views and membership of the temperance movement, which saw alcohol consumption as the root of much of society's ills.

Edith Wrigley (1879–1964) was a journalist for the Canadian Socialist League's *Citizen and Country* and wrote its "Kingdom of the Home" column. She was also active in the Woman's Christian Temperance Union. Her themes centred on the positive maternal values that could overhaul the corruption of the political arena. Lucy Maud Montgomery (1874–1942), best known as the author of *Anne of Green Gables* (1908), is said to have portrayed maternal feminist views in her books (Rothwell 1999).

Goldman

Emma Goldman (1869–1940), a Russian Jew who emigrated to New York when she was 16, began work in a clothing factory and quickly became involved in trade union organizing. She became one of the most influential anarchist writers and leaders of all time. Like Kollontai, Goldman believed that sexual freedom was central to women's liberation. Like Marx and Engels, she believed that most women were forced to provide sexual favours in exchange for their livelihood. "To the moralist, prostitution does not consist so much in the fact that the woman sells her body, but rather that she sells it out of wedlock" (Goldman 1996 [1911], 181).

Yet, Goldman pointed out, despite women's need to sell their sex, they were kept systematically ignorant about sex. As a result, their own desires were usually thwarted. Anticipating theories of sexual liberation that came much later, Goldman wrote in 1911 that people's capacity to freely pursue their sexual desires was linked to their capacity to resist oppression and imagine a more just world: "If the world is ever to give birth to true companionship and oneness, not marriage, but love will be the parent" (1996 [1911], 213).

The idea of a woman condemning marriage and espousing free love and anarchism struck terror in the hearts of conventional society. When Goldman travelled to small towns to give a lecture, sometimes riots would erupt and she was often arrested, but thousands of people continued to flock to hear her speak. In her early twenties, Goldman was imprisoned for a year for advocating that the starving poor should steal food, and during World War I she was imprisoned again for organizing against the military draft. After the war, the US government deported her to Russia, where she soon became a critic of the Soviet suppression of open debate. By 1921, she and her longtime lover Alexander Berkman left Russia. On three separate occasions, Goldman spent time in Canada, and she died in Toronto in 1940. She lived her life in a way that was consistent with her ideals, continuing to write no matter what it cost her. She predicted that the greatest obstacles to women's freedom would prove to be not man-made laws, but "internal tyrants": women's internalization of the social conventions that oppress them.

Contemporary Socialist Feminism and Marxist Feminism

In the 1970s, dissatisfaction with corporate capitalism, as well as the gender conservatism of much orthodox Marxism, led to an explosion of new socialist feminist organizations and theoretical writings (Eisenstein 1981; Jaggar 1983; Hartsock 1998; Holmstrom 2002). Socialist feminists wanted a theory that could integrate race and class oppression alongside the gender concerns of liberal feminists. Feminists began to debate whether patriarchy, white supremacy, and capitalism constituted *independent* systems of oppression, or whether racism and sexism were always caused by economic forces and the profit motive. Socialist feminism came to represent the idea that both Marxism and feminism were insufficient on their own: Marxism provided a class analysis, but, as Heidi Hartmann (1981) argues, it was "blind" to gender- and race-based forms of discrimination. And classical Marxism underplayed cultural forces that were independent of the profit motive.

But liberal feminism was also stunted in its focus on individual preferences and rational choices. Socialist philosophy espoused the idea that human beings are historical creatures, the product of the collective economic labour of their time. On this view, current preferences (for example, excessive consumerism) may not express "real" gendered natures or their highest potential. Collective action is needed to create the social conditions for new desires and new capacities for equality.

Simone de Beauvoir

The philosopher Simone de Beauvoir (1908–1986) developed an innovative feminist theory in the 1940s that incorporated insights from both liberalism and socialism. Her book *The Second Sex* (de Beauvoir 2011 [1949]) began with the socialist idea that human nature *changes* through history, at least in part. If human nature can change, she reasoned that people should be wary of ideas about natural femininity or natural masculinity.

Woman as "Object"

De Beauvoir postulated that being human means being subjects: humans choose what has value and what is meaningful, whether in art, ideas, or ways of living. But women are viewed as more object-like than subject: women's lives are determined by their biology; that is, by their bodies more than their minds. According to this theory, men alone have escaped being objects by creating culture and deciding how to live their lives.

This sharp distinction between men and women serves men well. It is easy for men to feel secure in their rationality when contrasted with an inferior female, just as a man self-conscious about his height might prefer to be with a much shorter woman. Thus de Beauvoir suggested that ideas about "woman" are really motivated by the desire to construct man as comfortably superior and justifiably dominant. She believed that men resist feminism because changing ideas about women necessarily changes ideas about men.

Women, de Beauvoir argued, are encouraged to embrace their object-like status and to follow their male partners' life plans rather than making their own. They are discouraged from thwarting gender conventions by the threat of family disapproval and the possibility of a life lived alone. Women are not biologically determined to be obsessed with their appearance, de Beauvoir argued, but it makes sense to be so when that is the primary source of one's desirability and worth.

Woman as "Other"

De Beauvoir argued that male-dominant cultures have also conceptualized women as the "other," or the second sex. Women are never taken to be central to a society's history and formation, and their lives are never taken to be paradigmatic of the human condition; rather, women are seen as a supporting cast to men who are the real protagonists. The norm of human psychology, biology, and so on, is the male experience; women are an afterthought.

When women grow up in cultures that take the male as the norm, they learn to take the man's point of view. Thus women come to accept the idea that history is the unfolding of male activity, to value men's opinions above women's, and to have a generally negative assessment of women. "The representation of the world as the world itself is the work of men; they describe it from a point of view that is their own and that they confound with the absolute truth" (de Beauvoir 2011 [1949], 162).

On the other hand, de Beauvoir believed women have long seen through the contradictions of conventional gender practices, such as the hypocrisy of men who publicly espouse a high-minded morality while privately pursuing sexual adventure and infidelity. So she believed that the more women interpret their experiences themselves, the less likely they will be to accept the misconceptions that have prevailed throughout history about "woman" and "women's nature." Women can then begin to truly make their own lives.

> **Box 2.3 In Her Own Words**
>
> ### De Beauvoir Looks Back
>
> This book was first conceived . . . almost by chance. Wanting to talk about myself, I became aware that to do so I should first have to describe the condition of woman in general; first I considered the myths that men have forged about her. . . . In every case, man put himself forward as the Subject and considered the woman as an object, as the Other.
>
> . . . I began to look at women with new eyes and found surprise after surprise lying in wait for me. It is both strange and stimulating to discover suddenly, after forty, an aspect of the world that has been staring you in the face all the time which somehow you have never noticed. One of the misunderstandings created by my book is that people thought I was denying there was any difference between men and women. On the contrary, writing this book made me even more aware of those things that separate them; what I contended was that these dissimilarities are of a cultural and not of a natural order.
>
> Source: de Beauvoir (1964, 185–7).

For de Beauvoir (see In Her Own Words, Box 2.3) this process requires women to seek meaningful work outside the home in order both to develop their capacities and to gain social recognition free from their social relations to others. She viewed the life of the housewife as too cloistered and monotonous to be truly rewarding. She also believed a social transformation was needed to make jobs outside the home truly meaningful, jobs in which women can be subjects and not mere objects.

Contemporary Feminist Debates

Socialist feminism and liberal feminism continue to influence thought and inspire action today, but since the 1960s there have been numerous other theoretical and political trends within feminism.

Radical Feminism and Cultural Feminism

Radical feminists sought an analysis focused on misogyny or the systematic derogation of everything associated with women and the feminine. In their view, the problem is not simply discrimination against women, but an all-out war on women including their very rights to bodily autonomy, to live free from violence, and in some cases just to live.

Radical feminists began to use the concept of patriarchy to define societies, broadening this term from its traditional anthropological usage of "father-right" to mean male dominance in general. Kate Millett's important book *Sexual Politics*, published in 1970, introduced this idea: ". . . our society, like all other historical civilizations, is a patriarchy . . . the military, industry, technology, universities, science, political office, and finance—in short, every avenue of power within the society, including the coercive force of the police, is entirely in male hands" (1970, 25). Patriarchy may vary greatly across time and cultures, but Millett insisted male dominance is global, and males as a group, no matter their class, benefit from the oppression of women.

Millett advocated **androgyny** as central to the liberation of women. If sexism exaggerates gender differences, and in some cases creates differences where there are none, feminism should aim to overcome gender differences.

Though many feminists agreed with Millett, some radical feminists began to develop a critique of androgyny in the 1970s. Mary Daly (1978) and Adrienne Rich (1976; 1980) argue that patriarchy mischaracterized and unfairly devalued feminine traits and that feminism should be wary of rejecting traditions associated with women such as the domestic arts and crafts, empathetic relationships, and valuing peace over violence.

Radical feminists find two cultures within societies: the visible and documented world of male culture, which is divided by national boundaries, and the invisible world of women's culture, which exists universally "within every culture" (Jaggar 1983, 249). Dominant male culture portrays a picture of social reality in which men are and should be aggressive, dominant, objective, strong, and intellectual, while women are valued as passive, emotional, intuitive, dependent, and submissive. Many liberal and socialist feminists view such differences as socially constructed rather than natural and believe that in an egalitarian future men and women will be viewed as basically the same and that women have as much potential for autonomy and rationality as men.

Some radical feminists, by contrast, began to develop a form of "cultural feminism," arguing that while male culture honours competition and aggression even to the point of killing, "woman culture" celebrates birth, connection, and peace. They pointed out that feminists who espoused androgyny rarely aimed for a true mix of traits but generally aimed to make women more like men. In *The Second Sex*, for example, de Beauvoir takes meaningful work outside the home as the only route to becoming truly human. By contrast, cultural feminists promoted a woman-centred approach for women that would value relationships with the women in one's life and create new forms of culture that affirm women.

Radical feminists also coined the slogan "the personal is political" (Jaggar 1983, 255). It was meant to criticize leftist and anti-racist men with whom women were engaged in shared political

Dionne Brand, poet, writer, filmmaker, educator, and activist, moved to Toronto from Trinidad in 1970 to attend the University of Toronto. She has published prize-winning poetry, fiction, and essays and taught literature, creative writing, and women's studies at universities across North America. Her work creates a nexus between past and present and draws a diasporic map charting the lives of women of colour as they cross borders and eclipse boundaries. A human rights activist, Brand is University Research Chair in English and Creative Writing at the University of Guelph. She was made a Fellow of the Royal Society of Canada in 2006 and appointed Poet Laureate of Toronto in 2009.

struggle but whose personal lives continued to be sexist. The slogan encouraged activists to analyze the politics of housework, child rearing, and sexual relationships alongside war, racism, and capitalism, rather than viewing the former as trivial or irrelevant to the important work of revolutionary change.

Canadian-born Shulamith Firestone (1945–2012) was a leading figure of radical feminism and a founding member of New York's Redstockings collective. Her 1970 book, *The Dialectic of Sex: The Case for a Feminist Revolution*, became a classic of second-wave feminism.

In it she argues that women could never achieve equality because of the biological necessity of childbirth. Instead, she proposes to liberate women from reproduction by in vitro fertilization and **cybernetics**. She also proposes the abolition of the nuclear family and the creation of socialist communities where traditional gender roles would be abrogated.

Radical feminists viewed patriarchy as a system of pervasive domination most clearly expressed in the efforts to control women's bodies. Conservative attitudes about contraception or abortion aim at maintaining a system of compulsory motherhood. Pervasive sexual harassment, rape, prostitution, and pornography are other ways by which men dominate women and channel their sexuality for their own needs or profit (MacKinnon 1987).

For some radical feminists, heterosexual relationships are always in danger of becoming oppressive to women. They suggest separatism may be an answer and can take the form of celibacy or lesbianism. In this way, lesbianism came to be associated with a political stand, as when Charlotte Bunch argues that

> being a Lesbian means ending identification with, allegiance to, dependence on, and support of heterosexuality. It means ending your personal stake in the male world so that you join women, individually and collectively, in the struggle to end your oppression. Lesbianism is the key to liberation and only women who cut their ties to male privilege can be trusted to remain serious in the struggle against male dominance. (Bunch 1975, 36)

Box 2.4 Women in Media

Sunera Thobani

Dr Sunera Thobani is associate professor at the Institute for Gender, Race, Sexuality and Social Justice at the University of British Columbia. She is an accomplished academic who has advanced research in the areas of critical race, post-colonial, and feminist theory. Her 2007 book, *Exalted Subjects: Studies in the Making of Race and Nation in Canada*, examines how the national subject has been conceptualized in Canada in distinct historical contexts and how the power of the state has exalted certain subjects over others.

As an activist-scholar, Thobani is a founding member of the Researchers and Academics of Colour for Equity (RACE), a Canadian network that promotes the scholarship of academics of colour and of Indigenous ancestry, and is past president of the National Action Committee on the Status of Women (NAC), Canada's then-largest feminist organization (1993–1996).

Sunera Thobani

Some feminists also argued that the hatred and fear of lesbians is politically motivated in a way that distinguishes it from a general homophobia, as indicated by the fact that "uppity" women were often called "dykes." As Adrienne Rich (1980, 648) expresses it: "Lesbianism is a threat to the ideological, political, personal, and economic basis of male supremacy. The Lesbian threatens the ideology of male supremacy by destroying the lie about female inferiority, weakness, passivity, and by denying women's 'innate need for men.'"

Some radical feminists also came to believe that racial and class oppression is derived from gender domination. As the oldest form of social domination, gender oppression was seen by them to be the model and organizational structure on which all others were developed.

Black Feminism

Many women of colour were actively writing theory and influencing the development of liberal feminism, socialist feminism, radical feminism, and other trends. By the 1970s, some began to name specific forms of feminism that were based on the experiences and conditions of women of colour. "Black feminism" is one of the most influential of these theories, and there has been also the emergence of Latina feminism, Asian feminism, Arab feminism, Indigenous feminism, and "women of colour feminism." Given the different conditions of women's lives, these feminists argue for the need for specific theories to understand specific groups, as well as to develop realistic strategies for change.

Conventional gender practices have very different histories in different contexts. Enslaved persons were not allowed to marry or to form or maintain familial relationships. As a result, many racialized women have cherished the right to have families and children and have experienced this sphere as, at least potentially, a domain of freedom rather than the domain of oppression and monotony that de Beauvoir described.

Moreover, black feminists pointed out that the form of femininity conventional to elite women was largely denied black women, who were rarely put on a pedestal or "protected" from long hours of gruelling labour. Cheryl Clarke (1983), Audre Lorde (1984), and others also argue that homophobia and **lesbophobia** took on specific forms based on the false claim by some black nationalists that homosexuality was a European invention. But because of the oppression of racialized heterosexual families, those who wanted to defend gay rights needed to address the specific history of specific groups of people.

Black feminists differed over whether they should pursue organizational autonomy from other feminist groups. Some, such as Barbara Smith (1983), argue that the specific conditions of black women's oppression required a period of organizational independence so that they could develop and deepen their theoretical and political analysis. For others, like bell hooks (1984) and Angela Davis (1998), having separate groups would prolong the struggle and might wrongly imply that the oppression of black women has different causes from other forms of social oppression.

Black feminists generally agreed, however, on the importance of an intersectional analysis that could make visible the interconnections of multiple oppressions of social identities including race, gender, class, sexuality, and so on. In 1983's *Women, Race and Class*, Angela Davis demonstrates how interlocking oppressions created difference among women as a constructed social category. Kimberlé Crenshaw develops her legal analysis of multiple forms of oppression as an intersectional traffic metaphor (see Chapter 3). Patricia Hill Collins's *Black Feminist Thought: Knowledge, Consciousness, and the Politics of Empowerment* (2000a) is only one of her many theoretical contributions to an understanding of how oppression operates and how justice can be achieved.

Intersectionality has become an important trend in feminist theory and is discussed throughout this text.

Post-modern Feminism

Post-modern and psychoanalytic trends in feminist theory were motivated by a sense that existing theoretical analyses were too shallow. Many of the formal legal reforms that liberal feminists had fought for were beginning to be won by the late 1970s: women were legally guaranteed equal employment free from sexual harassment; abortion in the first trimester of pregnancy was made legal; and many women benefited from employment equity programs. Yet sexual violence, economic disparity, and a general cultural sexism persisted. Racialized groups of women found even less change to their status. As some feminists argued, a post-structuralist analysis of how a culture is organized by gender relations reveals that the roots of misogyny are not in explicit beliefs that can be legislatively addressed, but in deep structural formations of language and belief systems.

Post-modern feminists looked to the work of European post-structuralist philosophers like Jacques Derrida (1978) and Michel Foucault (1978) as a way to analyze the persistence of gender divisions. Post-structuralists shared the structuralist view that some social dynamics cannot be explained by the aggregated conscious choices of individuals; rather, as Marx and other structuralists argued, individuals are caught up in structures over which they have little control. Structuralism was thus able to provide better explanations of many social phenomena like war, environmental destruction, and gender hierarchies without relying on evil intentions or conspiracies. Sometimes dominant groups pursue actions that are against their own best interests, and sometimes outcomes are unintended consequences; structuralism explained how this is possible.

The great structuralists like Marx (see above), Sigmund Freud, and Claude Lévi-Strauss (1908–2009) believed that structures represent deep mechanisms that operate like laws of history: they cannot be changed, although people can become aware of them and perhaps subvert their damaging effects. Post-structuralists disagreed on just this point: they saw structures as changeable rather than absolute. Structures represent not stable patterns of human behaviour but variable systems of meaning and ways of producing meaning and what is taken to be truth (Lévi-Strauss 1963).

According to post-structuralists, conventional ideas and ways of life are not the natural developments of human nature or experience but the effect of what Foucault called "discourses": systems of meaning that connect language and practice such that people come to experience things differently through different discourses. He rejected the idea of false consciousness, since this assumes there is a true consciousness beneath the veil of social convention. Rather, discourses fully determine experience and are not simply a means of concealing reality. To understand experience as socially constructed—constituted by specific discourses—is to understand that experience is neither natural nor inevitable. Discourses are the variable manifestations of power structures and relations and thus can be critically evaluated, not on the grounds of whether or not they express the "truth" about human experience, but on the grounds of *how* they produce experience, and with what effects. Post-structuralism took the feminist critique of naturalist approaches to gender to the next level.

Other feminists in this trend argued that deconstructing existing discourses is not a guarantee of decreasing oppression and that the post-structuralist view generally, like Marxism, is blind to gender and race. These feminists turned to psychoanalysis for a deeper explanation of sexism and a more fully developed plan for subversion.

Psychoanalytic Feminism

Psychoanalysis, feminists argued, is a sexist theory. Freud believed women naturally have penis envy, are naturally sexually submissive, "evolve" (if they are normal) from clitoral to vaginal orgasms, and are naturally less rational than men. But feminists like Juliet Mitchell (1973) argue that, as a theory, psychoanalysis helpfully describes the effects of patriarchy, even if Freud himself did not understand his theory in this way. She believed that Freud beautifully captured what male dominance does to the psyche of both men and women.

Nancy Chodorow took up this approach and used Freud to develop an account of why males can be irrationally afraid of commitment and monogamy and why they fear being swallowed by female power even when in most cases males have greater ability than females to leave their relationships. Growing up with mothers who are socialized to make parenting the central focus of their life, males often struggle to achieve independence. When a tight connection with obsessive mothers leaves little room for separate development, and when masculinity is defined as the *opposite* of femininity, males are indeed psychically threatened. This effect is not inevitable in mother–son relationships but is caused by societies with oppositional concepts of gender and parenting practices that make mothers the exclusive caregivers of young children. Chodorow (1978) thus concludes that these dynamics are changeable.

Feminists working with psychoanalysis in Europe, notably Luce Irigaray (1985 [1974]), Hélène Cixous (1981 [1976]), and Julia Kristeva (1980), developed further ways to analyze the implicit sexism in language and culture. They traced the erasure of mothers throughout societies that worship male deities and inscribe males as the givers of life: the (male) God giving life to Adam, Zeus giving birth to Athena (from his head), and Aristotle's influential view that mothers are merely the vessels of male seed. Defining sex as intercourse includes male orgasm as part of sex but not women's: whether or not a woman has an orgasm is irrelevant to how sex is defined. The experiences of women and mothers are not only objectified; they are erased.

Psychoanalysis provided a way to understand this widespread erasure of women as well as irrational fears about what the female represents. Cixous (1981 [1976]) argues that the antidote to such social patterns is for women to begin to write themselves back into language, not through following the style of male writers, but by freeing themselves to develop their own *écriture feminine*.

Ecofeminism

Also in the 1970s, feminists began to make connections between the oppression of women and the disregard for the environment based on the historical associations between women and nature, both of which were viewed as unruly, unpredictable, and irrational forces that need to be tamed and controlled. Carolyn Merchant (1980) traces this attitude to the rise of industrialization in Europe between the fourteenth and seventeenth centuries. Whereas in medieval times, Europeans believed nature was given to humanity by God as a kind of sacred trust, the emerging capitalist societies viewed nature as either a dangerous nuisance or an exploitable resource. Merchant also links the witch-hunt craze that swept Europe—that put tens of thousands of women to death—to ideas of both women and nature as dangerous and diabolical forces needing to be controlled. Many so-called witches were in fact healers who relied on natural herbs and midwives who assisted women in a full range of reproductive needs. During this period women suffered a significant loss of social status and economic power in European societies, losing their ability to join guilds or own land. Overturning the view of nature as divine and mysterious and worthy of reverence was correlated to a similar demotion of women.

Ecofeminists sought to understand the connections between feminism and ecology and to develop a unified vision of social change. Some argued, like maternal feminists and cultural feminists, that women have a stronger connection to life-affirming values because of their reproductive experiences, such as childbirth. Organizations like Mothers against Nuclear Disarmament made explicit reference to motherhood as a motivation for disarmament.

Other ecofeminists avoided reinforcing the association between women and nature. Ynestra King argues that the goal of ecofeminism should be to create a more integrative culture that combines "intuitive, spiritual and rational forms of knowledge" accessible to all (1995, 19). The obstacle to this is not men per se, but a particular way of defining gender identity. Dorothy Dinnerstein (1923–1992) argues similarly that the current system of gender is a threat to the planet. By defining masculinity in terms of violent aggression and by restricting nurturance and emotional caregiving to femininity, expressions of nurturance for the earth are viewed as feminine, rather than human or even rational (Dinnerstein 1977).

Ecofeminists agreed, however, that treatment of wombs and female bodies as generally subject to state control and exchange for profit is connected to a contemporary view of nature. They espouse the need to learn to respect both women and nature, to recognize the sacred rhythms and harmonies of life, and to respect and *work with* these natural processes rather than always trying to control or alter them.

Ecofeminist theorists like Vandana Shiva emphasized the connections between the oppression of women, global imperialism, and the ideology of development. Development along a capitalist model that emphasizes excessive materialism and consumerism is neither possible nor desirable on a global scale. Shiva argues that there is a

> ... mistaken identification of the growth of commodity production as better satisfaction of basic needs. In actual fact, there is less water, less fertile soil, less genetic wealth as a result of the development process. Since these natural resources [e.g. water, soil] are the basis of nature's economy and women's survival economy, their scarcity is impoverishing women and marginalized peoples in an unprecedented manner. (Shiva 1988, 89)

Women hold the key to a sustainable agricultural model, Shiva argues. Women across the world practise a form of subsistence economics in which they provide basic needs through self-provisioning, including making their own houses, clothing, and seed supplies, without having to participate in the market for everything they need. Sometimes women are perceived as poor only because they participate less in the market economy. Ecofeminism must combine its critique of gender ideology with a critique of capitalism and imperialism and learn from the struggles of rural women who have fought to protect natural resources like water, seeds, and herbal remedies as communally shared rather than as private property or subject to patents so that corporations can make profits.

Transnational Feminism

Along these lines, transnational feminist theory seeks to develop a feminism "without borders," as Chandra Talpade Mohanty puts it (2003). This requires addressing the challenges of creating global feminist solidarity so that there can be unity around international issues such as sex trafficking or women's sweatshop labour. It can be a challenge to identify sexism across differences of religion and values. For example, is it possible to argue that polygamy may be good for women? Is there one universalizable model for achieving women's equality or many different ones? How are power relations implicated within feminism?

Before transnational feminist solidarity can be built, Mohanty and others argue the necessity of understanding the ways in which feminism can be used to promote colonialism and imperialism. Some leading Western feminists have viewed women of the Global South as powerless victims who need help from the North, implying that those women are the vanguard of the movement for women's equality. Thus, they have judged women's lives from the perspective of their own cultural values, associating feminism with individualism, for example, and in opposition to family or community-centred identities and ignoring the ongoing legacy of colonialism and imperialism.

Uma Narayan (1997) identifies a tendency to downplay the way in which sexism in the West is *culturally* mediated. While, for example, women in India are portrayed as victimized by their culture, the epidemic of male violence against women in the North America is not seen as connected to the commodification of women's bodies in market societies. Therefore, the first task for transnational feminism is to analyze the assumptions of Western feminism that may inhibit solidarity.

Yet transnational feminists remain optimistic that solidarity is possible. Mohanty (2003) argues that it is vital to develop a global analysis of the conditions of women's lives that can explain the connections between the diverse structures and institutions that oppress women. Understanding is needed, for example, of how the global assembly line—or division of labour in commodity production—takes advantage of women's social vulnerability in many societies to increase profits and how birth control devices intended for North American markets have been tested on poor women in the Global South before they were deemed safe.

Another proposal to achieve solidarity is Nira Yuval-Davis's concept of transversal feminist politics in her 1997 *Gender and Nation*. Here she offers the idea of "rooting and shifting" as a means of addressing differences created by state borders and cultural privilege. One "roots" by reflexively identifying and acknowledging one's intersectional identity and "shifts" to imagine and acknowledge the difference of others' realities.

Transnational feminism is especially urgent in a period where military interventions are justified on the basis of protecting women or improving their lives. Many women in war-torn countries point out that war destroys communities and infrastructure and increases sexual violence. Most importantly, the effort to advance the cause of women in any part of the world must rely on *their* leadership and *their* knowledge of local conditions. Transnational alliances can only be built through communicative networks with equal and meaningful participation. True feminism cannot be imposed unilaterally, and a strategy of women's liberation must work for all and not just some women.

Contemporary Feminist Philosophies

Feminist philosophers argue that feminist analyses are relevant to every sphere of inquiry. Historically, moral theories started from the idea that people have to find a way to justify the claim that independent individuals have moral obligations to others. These theories ignored the obligations that exist within families and communities in which there are relations of interdependence. Theories of knowledge had similar blind spots, defining "reason" in such a way that it mirrored conventional ideas about masculinity and femininity. Reason came to be defined in such a way that it excluded the realm of the emotional and the intuitive. Philosophers today are trying to formulate broader notions of rationality that are less distorted by social ideologies of gender and more realistic about what it means to reason well.

One common idea about reasoning is that it should ideally be value-free, interested only in the facts. But many "facts" advanced about women and gender purport to show that gender hierarchies are natural and therefore normal and right. Defining reason as neutral assessments of facts can obscure the ways in which values and goals structure projects of inquiry, influence assessment of what evidence is relevant, and provide support for conclusions.

As seen in this chapter, there is a long tradition of thinking that women's subordination is natural and inevitable. Today, there are new versions of this argument. For example, some claim that because women are sometimes said to be biologically disposed to be less aggressive than men, it is therefore natural that men should be the dominant leaders in societies. Even if it were true that men are innately more aggressive, however, society might be organized so as to restrain and discourage the aggressiveness of men rather than to reinforce and reward it.

Because women are the ones who can give birth, it has often been supposed that this is their primary function, and therefore it is fitting that they be confined to the role of mother, nurturer, or homemaker. Yet, again, no such conclusion follows from the biological facts. There is no reason to believe that the person who gives birth must be the person who spends the following 20 years doing the primary parenting or that giving birth automatically provides knowledge about how to parent effectively. Nor does being a dedicated parent exclude a person from pursuing other interests and activities.

Sexual organs are obviously functional for reproduction, but is reproduction their singular or primary purpose? Sexual organs have at least three possible functions: to reproduce, to give pleasure, and to express love. Most human beings use their sexual organs most of the time for the latter two functions, not the former, which means that LGBTQ sexual activity is coherent with the proper functions of human sexual organs. Reasoning about matters such as sexuality and gender roles, therefore, requires reasoning about what is valued and why. Without attending to values, reasoned arguments may well go off course.

Rethinking "Knowledge" and Values of Inquiry

Feminist theorists have shown that there is a need to rethink how knowledge is attained to overcome the gender biases built into what has been taken to be "knowledge." Moreover, traditional fields of study will have to be rethought if they are to reflect the perspectives of women as fully as they reflect those of men (Harding 1987; Zalk and Gordon-Kelter 1992; Alcoff and Potter 1993; Fausto-Sterling 2000). Not only have many topics been neglected that are of interest to women, but the very concepts and assumptions that inform inquiry have often reflected a male point of view. Bringing in perspectives on race, gender, class, and global issues requires radical rethinking of what has been thought of as impartial and objective knowledge (Williams 1991; Narayan 1997; Collins 2000a).

As it turns out, not all values are equal when it comes to the search for truth. Remember the earlier example in this chapter about the anthropologist who only interviewed men in his effort to study a foreign cultural system. Feminist philosophers of science like Elizabeth Anderson (2004) argue that anti-sexist or feminist values would have improved his research. Anti-sexist values would have led the anthropologist to talk to the women, even if the men had told him that the women were unimportant and uninformed. And anti-sexist values would have led him to develop a more complete database of information that included women's perspectives and experiences for a comprehensive analysis.

Helen Longino (1990) argues that values enter at multiple stages in the pursuit of scientific knowledge. Each stage of inquiry—formulating questions, developing plausible hypotheses, developing methods of testing, and deciding when the evidence is conclusive—involves a judgment call. Sexist values may hinder research at any of these stages, whereas anti-sexist values may enhance the likelihood of reaching more reliable conclusions. People need to rethink the assumption that knowledge is best attained through impartial or politically neutral methods.

Feminists are increasingly concerned with the ways in which mainstream practices around knowledge and science are exclusionary. Everyday people have knowledge and often a thoughtful analysis, but both are underappreciated and underutilized. With this in mind, feminists began looking for ways to include as part of the process those groups often excluded not only by gender but also by race, class, and sexuality (Spelman 1988; Anzaldúa 1990; Card 1995).

From the beginning, feminist theorists and social scientists used women's experiences to question received wisdom and develop new hypotheses. Sandra Harding develops this approach into a "feminist standpoint epistemology," based on the idea of starting inquiry from women's actual experience, lives and work (Harding 1987; 1991). Harding reasons that understanding and overcoming social oppression of all sorts would be much higher on the agenda of inquiry given women's material labour in most societies and women's presence in every oppressed group, from the disabled to the working class. She also argues that women's "outsider status" in many social positions of power and dominance would give them an epistemic privilege: outsiders can often detect the unfounded assumptions that insiders may be too immersed in to see. University of Toronto OISE's Dorothy Smith expanded the notion of standpoint theory by incorporating an intersectional lens taking account of gender, race, class, and sexuality.

Post-structuralist feminist theorists voiced concern at this approach, however. They argue that women's experiences are socially constructed, influenced by culture, and are repositories of ideology and therefore cannot be taken as reliable knowledge (Scott 1992). Other feminist epistemologists defended the importance of taking women's experience into account, no matter how it is constructed. Experience need not be a timeless universal or completely pure of social influences to have value for inquiry. And some experiences, especially bodily ones such as rape and pregnancy, can be socially constructed only so far. It remains important to take women's experiences seriously, even if approached with a critical analysis (Alcoff 1997; Wylie 2004b).

The concept of positionality allows for a determinate though fluid identity of woman . . . woman is a position from which a feminist politics can emerge rather than a set of attributes that are "objectively identifiable." Seen in this way, being a "woman" is to take up a position within a moving historical context. (Alcoff 1988, 435)

Even as a problematized category, those who are classified as women have a distinct experience of society the world over, and there is much shared sexism in the history of multiple cultures. Beyond the legacy of ideas, there is also a real

---

Box 2.5 In Her Own Words

Gloria Steinem on Feminist Labels

In the label department . . . I would prefer to be called simply "a feminist." After all, the belief in the full humanity of women leads to the necessity of totally changing all male-supremacist structures, thus removing the model and continuing support for other systems of birth-determined privilege. That should be radical enough. However, because there are feminists who believe that women can integrate or imitate existing structures (or conversely; that class or race structures must be transformed first, as a precondition to eliminating sexual caste), I feel I should identify myself as a "radical feminist." "Radical" means "going to the root," and I think that sexism is the root, whether or not it developed as the chronologically first dominance model in prehistory. . . . The tolerance of a habit as pervasive as male-dominance not only creates an intimate model for oppression as "natural," but builds a callousness to other dominations—whether based on race, age, class, sexuality, or anything else.

Source: Steinem (1978, 92–3).

Box 2.6 Time to Reflect

Dorothy Smith and Standpoint Theory

Standpoint theory is a feminist theoretical perspective developed by US feminist theorist Sandra Harding that posits that knowledge stems from where one stands in society. A person's knowledge is based on her own experience therefore it calls into question the objectivity or centrality of science and the scientific method.

Canadian sociologist Dorothy Smith further developed standpoint theory. In her book *The Everyday World as Problematic: A Feminist Sociology* (1989), Smith argues that "relations of power" govern where people are positioned. Since women have historically had little power, their knowledge has been ignored. Smith believes that including women's experiences add value to knowledge, for without it, the picture is incomplete.

---

material difference in embodied experience concerning the division of labour in reproduction, menstruation, and menopause. Thus, gender categories continue to help make sense of historical, experiential, and material differences. The future of gender may yet change radically as new social practices unfold that accept more various ways to be in the world and new technologies transform the practices of human reproduction. Feminist theoretical analyses will be needed every step of the way to question assumptions and to develop concepts and values that make sense for the people of the future.

Summary

Definitions of *woman* have often reflected faulty theories about the "nature" of women. Distorted definitions result from seeing women as more biologically determined than and inferior to men, especially in their capacity to reason. Women are deemed less like active subjects who make their own lives, and more like passive objects.

Enlightenment philosophers rejected hierarchical traditions of Western political thought—but not for women. The liberal principles of equality and freedom that helped to shape democracy applied to men and to male heads of households. Many liberal thinkers were silent on the subject of women or, like Jean-Jacques Rousseau, operated with a double standard of condemning social hierarchies everywhere but in relations between women and men.

The Enlightenment philosopher Mary Wollstonecraft argued that women's rational capacities would be increased if they had an education comparable to men's. Contemporary liberal feminists favour equality in the home as well as in the public realm, advocating that women and men share equally in child care and household tasks. Employment equity programs may be needed to provide women and racialized groups with equal job opportunities.

Socialist feminists argue that while liberal feminists underemphasize the role of the economy in creating sexism, traditional Marxists underestimate the role of sexism in society. Socialist feminists argue that there needs to be a focus on the oppression of women both as women and as workers, paying special attention to the economic structures around the world that continue to create conditions of gender and class oppression.

Radical feminism emphasizes patriarchy as a fundamental structure organizing every aspect of society. Cultural feminism advocates for valuing the strengths of women's traditional practices and interrelationships.

Black feminism contends that the specific conditions of racialized women's lives require a specific analysis and set of solutions. Davis, Crenshaw, and Collins each developed aspects of intersectional analysis that became fundamental to feminist theory.

Post-structuralist and psychoanalytic feminisms stress the implicit deep structures of gender that operate to produce misogyny without people's intentions. Ecofeminism looks at the relationship between the domination of women and the domination of nature. Transnational feminism seeks the basis for a global solidarity of women and a global analysis of all women's oppression.

What has been thought to be impartial and objective "knowledge" has often represented the views and values of men only. Feminist theorists call for radical reconceptualizations of both knowledge and the values of inquiry to address gender biases.

Feminist standpoint theory advocates starting theory from women's lives to value women's experience and marginalized status as epistemically useful.

Although feminists frequently disagree, all share one goal: to overcome the oppression of women and the creation of gender equality. They are interested in work that meets human needs, with the work fairly divided and cooperatively organized, and believe society should be governed with a minimum of domination and subordination.

Women need to be able to reject the concepts that others have had about them and about society. They can choose for themselves what ideas to accept and what their goals should be.

Notes

1. Some date the beginning of the wave metaphor to Martha Weinman Lear's 1968 *New York Times* article. See the entry on Martha Weinman Lear at http://womenshistory.about.com/od/feminism-second-wave/a/Martha-Weinman-Lear-Second-Feminist-Wave.htm.

2. Rousseau's views on protecting the family have always been taken with a grain of salt by readers of his autobiography, who learn that he ordered his mistress to take all five the children she bore with him to the steps of the local orphanage.

Discussion Questions

1. Do women have a "choice"? Discuss the ways in which women can or cannot choose to "accept" subordinate roles. What do you think are the barriers to independence and autonomy?
2. Are you a feminist? Do you identify with a particular feminism?
3. In what major areas do you think feminist theory needs to change and develop?
4. What would be needed for women to have equal opportunities in the home and in the workplace?
5. Discuss the importance of feminist theory in your own experience. Has it helped you to understand, to choose, to act? If so, how?

Recommended Resources

Archer Mann, Susan, and Ashly Suzanne Patterson. 2016. *Reading Feminist Theory: From Modernity to Postmodernity*. New York: Oxford University Press. The authors present concise introductions to sections that include a wide range of primary source writings by leading theorists.

Atlantis: Critical Studies in Gender, Culture and Social Justice. http://journals.msvu.ca/index.php/atlantis/index. Canadian scholarly research journal that reflects current approaches to the field of women and gender studies.

Bakan, Abigail B., and Enakshi Dua. 2014. *Theorizing Anti-racism: Linkages in Marxism and Critical Race Theories*. Toronto: University of Toronto Press. Bakan and Dua provide a comprehensive conversation that bridges multiple theories in contemporary contexts.

Bromley, Victoria L. (2012). *Feminisms Matter: Debates, Theories, Activism*. Toronto: University of Toronto Press. Bromley offers Canadian academics and activists feminist critical engagement within a transnational context. She demystifies the complexities of theory and emphasizes the centrality of intersectionality.

Canadian Women's Studies. http://cws.journals.yorku.ca/index.php/cws. A feminist quarterly that was founded 29 years ago to make widely accessible current writing and research on a variety of feminist topics.

Cannon, M., and L. Sunseri, eds. 2014. *Racism, Colonialism and Indigeneity in Canada: A Reader*. Toronto: Oxford University Press. The authors provide an important analysis for feminism by locating the historic roots of the Canadian colonial settler project and its present day manifestations.

Davis, Angela Y. 1981. *Women, Race, and Class*. London: The Women's Press. Davis provides a theoretical bridge from second-wave feminism to a more inclusive feminism that recognizes difference. She presents a comprehensive view of socialist feminism through her examination of women's work and family structures.

de Beauvoir, Simone. 2011 (1949). *The Second Sex*, translated by Constance Borde and Sheila Malovany-Chevallier. New York: Vintage. A classic book about how the ideas and social conditions of women have affected women and how they can begin to think for themselves about themselves.

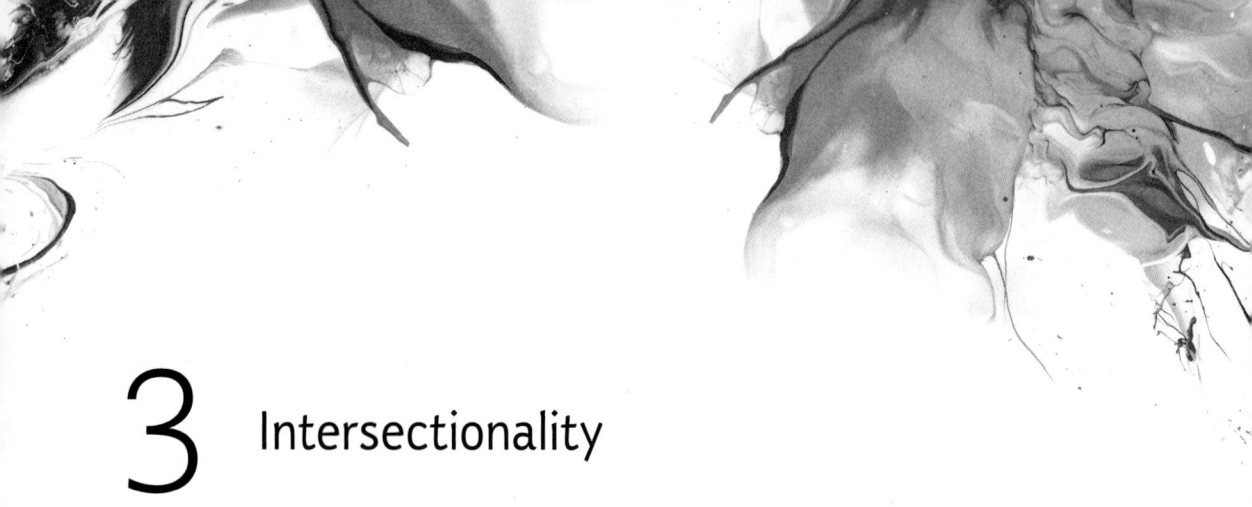

3 Intersectionality

Chapter Outline

- Intersections of Oppression
- Heteronormativity and Heterosexism
- Historical Foundations of Intersectionality
- Intersectional Approaches to Feminist Activism
- Intersectional Approaches to Feminist Scholarship
- Debates over Intersectionality

This chapter will help you
- Appreciate the centrality of *difference* in feminist analysis
- Comprehend how race, class, ethnicity, age, ableism, and sexuality, among other identity markers, influence the construction of gender
- Understand how a particular context will affect how an intersectional analysis operates
- Realize that intersectionality is not a fixed concept and its theoretical application is not mechanistic

I find I am constantly being encouraged to pluck out some one aspect of myself and present this as the meaningful whole, eclipsing or denying the other parts of self. But this is a destructive and fragmenting way to live. My fullest concentration of energy is available to me only when I integrate all the parts of who I am, openly . . .

—AUDRE LORDE (1984, 120)

Intersectionality is a critical theoretical approach that is fundamental to women and gender studies, feminist analysis, and feminist activism. It acknowledges that there are more components to one's individual identity, to social analysis, and to activist demands than gender and gender alone. It is one way for feminist studies to approach a more whole "truth" in knowledge and knowledge production.

Consider, for example, how history is often taken up. It is commonly understood and taught that women in Canada won the right to vote during the second decade of the twentieth century. Yet, this does not relate the whole story. Where in Canada? Which women? Were voting rights applicable to all levels of government? In the nineteenth century, female property holders were legally allowed to demand municipal voting rights. Propertied women in Quebec were able to vote between 1809 and 1849, when the word *male* was inserted into the province's franchise act. However, starting in 1850, women with property, married or single, could vote for school trustees in Ontario. By 1900, propertied women had gained municipal voting privileges throughout Canada (Jackel 2013). Even then, not all women in Quebec and Ontario, not even all female property owners, were allowed to vote, because citizens, male and female, who had immigrated were disenfranchised.

In the early twentieth century, **suffrage laws**—regulations about who could vote—were enacted in more provinces. They still contained many provisos, mostly including property ownership or "British" ethnicity. Some provinces, such as British Columbia, allowed women to vote if they were related to men in the military. And these laws were not geographically inclusive of what is now Canada. Newfoundland's 1925 Electoral Act came later and included the age requirement of 25 years. Still later, women in Quebec gained the right to run for office in 1940 while it was 1951 for the Northwest Territories. And it was only in 1960 that Indigenous men and women could vote without giving up their treaty rights or status under the federal Indian Act.

Many of these gendered suffrage acts were also racialized. Canada's 1920 Electoral Act made the franchise universal except for Indigenous peoples and other designated racialized groups. Indeed, throughout the twentieth century, various provinces took away the right to vote for Canadians of Hindu, Chinese, and Japanese descent. For example, British Columbia's 1947 Election Act gave the franchise to every age-eligible Canadian with the explicit exclusion of Japanese and Indigenous peoples. It also removed the right to vote from the Doukhobor, Hutterite, and Mennonite religious minorities except for those individuals who had served in the armed forces (Canadian Human Rights Commission, n.d.). Today, poverty continues to affect people's right to vote; one cannot vote without a permanent address, so the homeless are often excluded. And people who are disabled can find it difficult to access polling stations.

So when it is said, "women in Canada," who exactly constitutes the category? Who are included and excluded? An intersectional analysis that takes up race, ethnicity, sexuality, immigration status, religion, age, class, and different abilities ensures that the category of "women" is more closely examined with difference noted. An intersectional analysis provides a vehicle to probe beyond the dominant discourse and can reveal the contemporary power relations of a **colonial settler state.**

Beyond specifications of identity markers, intersectional analysis probes conditions of power and context. Race, class, sexuality, and so on each intersects with each other and creates simultaneous conditions of privilege and oppression. These conditions are produced according to the power dynamics embedded in particular contexts. In one context, gender can accord privilege when combined with class and racial advantage. At the same time, there can be discrimination and marginalization based on gender,

Intersectionality demands interpretation and reinterpretation of power and domination according to the specific cultural and social position of individuals and groups of individuals. One's location within society in a distinct time and place determines how the position is understood and lived. Intersectionality is the foundation to understanding how difference operates within and outside of particular groups.

Ideas about identity and difference were openly debated in Canada. Marlene Dixon argued in 1970 that race and class were too great a divide, preventing a unified women's movement. The national Indian Rights for Indian Women organization was founded in 1971. The first Canadian conferences of lesbians in 1973 debated whether to form a separate organization of their own or join forces with the existing women's movement or the LGBTQ movement. Feminism was integral to the growing Quebec sovereignty/nationalist movement. As union activist Monique Simard recalls: "The slogan of the women's liberation movement was: 'There can be no liberation of Québec without women's liberation, and no women's liberation without the liberation of Québec'" (Robbins 2010). Simultaneously, others formed organizations such as the Congress of Black Women of Canada, the Disabled Women's Network, the Native Women's Association of Canada, and Pauktuutit (an Inuit association) to concentrate on their own priorities. As Wendy Robbins points out, it was several years later that post-colonial theorist Gavatri Chakravorty Spivak coined the term *strategic essentialism*—the idea that sometimes it is in women's best interests to temporarily adopt a simplified group identity in a strategic move to achieve certain goals (Robbins 2010).

Intersectional analysis creates an opportunity to acknowledge Canada's colonial past and present. In 2004, Amnesty International published *Stolen Sisters: A Human Rights Response to Discrimination and Violence against Native Women in Canada*, which documented the cases of missing and murdered Indigenous women in Canada. The report detailed nine specific cases, and *Stolen Sisters* established a context in which to understand them. In lieu of government statistics, it relied on information collected by the Native Women's Association, which had compiled a database of names of the missing and murdered women. This report was followed by 2009's *No More Stolen Sisters*, which enumerated 520 cases from the past three decades. Ongoing Indigenous women's campaigns were joined by human rights groups in raising these concerns by means of petitions, vigils, marches, and testimonies presented in parliaments and at the United Nations. A demand for the federal government to commission an independent inquiry has been a consistent component of the movement. Yet even when the RCMP concluded in 2013 that 1017 Indigenous women and girls were murdered in Canada between 1980 and 2012 (a homicide rate 4.5 times greater than that for the general female population), the federal government refused to hold a public inquiry. Thus an intersectional approach reveals that such violence is fundamentally gendered and racialized. (The Government of Canada launched an independent National Inquiry into Missing and Murdered Indigenous Women and Girls in September 2016.)

Intersections of Oppression

Feminist professors argue that feminist theory and women's and gender studies scholarship should adopt an *intersectional approach*. Such an approach holds that "ideologies of race, gender ... class, and sexuality are *reciprocally constitutive categories* of experience and analysis" (Smith 1998, xiii; emphasis added). In other words, how racism is experienced will differ depending on whether it is targeting a male or female, a working-class or a middle-class group. Both gender discrimination

Box 3.1 Time to Reflect

Simon Fraser's Institute for Intersectionality Research and Policy

The Institute was first launched in 2005 as the Institute for Critical Studies in Gender and Health at Simon Fraser University (SFU). At this time our overall goal was to integrate and support health and natural sciences, social sciences, and humanities research utilizing the paradigm of intersectionality to better understand how gender relates with other axis of discrimination and disadvantage in multiple contexts. Throughout the subsequent years of doing this work, there has developed an increased awareness of the role played by multiple relational factors when trying to understand and respond to the complexities of health inequities. As we have grown, the Institute has moved to the forefront of intersectional scholarship in Canada, and is now able to provide opportunities to collaborate with other organizations, Centres, and Institutes at SFU and beyond who are developing intersectionality as a framework for research and policy. In January 2011 we changed our name to the Institute for Intersectionality Research and Policy (IIRP). This change occurred in order to better reflect the current debates, methods, and perspectives related to this paradigm and to support emerging opportunities for collaboration across Canada and internationally.

Source: IIRP (n.d.).

and racial oppression take different forms when these occur in different configurations. An intersectional approach takes into account these multiple dimensions of identity and experience operating in a given context and the ways in which these dimensions *interact*.

Academics are realizing the importance of an intersectional approach for all fields, including humanities, social sciences, and sciences. (See Box 3.1.)

Without an intersectional approach, the experiences of women of colour cannot be adequately understood, as writers such as Audre Lorde (1984) and bell hooks (1984) and the philosopher Elizabeth Spelman (1988) argue, and as the legal theorist Kimberlé Crenshaw (1989, 1991) shows in her work on domestic violence: "The experiences of women of color are frequently the product of intersecting patterns of racism and sexism, and . . . these experiences tend not to be represented within the discourses either of feminism or antiracism." As a result, "women of color are marginalized within both" (Crenshaw 1991, 1243–4). Without an intersectional approach, Crenshaw argues, neither feminism nor anti-racism will be able to address adequately the specific obstacles that women of colour face. A distinguished scholar of race and gender issues, she is one of the earliest contemporary analysts of intersectionality as a valuable tool for making visible and addressing the needs and concerns of women of colour:

> Discrimination, like traffic through an intersection, may flow in one direction, and it may flow in another. If an accident happens in an intersection, it can be caused by cars traveling from any number of directions and, sometimes, from all of them. Similarly, if a Black woman is harmed because she is in the intersection, her injury could result from sex discrimination or race discrimination. (Crenshaw 1989, 149)

University of New Brunswick Professor Wendy Robbins was guest contributor for the 2010 Canadian Federation for the Humanities and Social Sciences' Equity Portfolio's "Equality

Kimberlé Crenshaw

Then and Now" blog series, marking 40 years since the Royal Commission on the Status of Women. She noted the intersectional oppression of racialized women within the academy and how racialized Canadian academics have researched and documented their own multiplied marginalized experience. Dionne Brand, Himani Bannerji, Arun Mukherjee, Patricia Monture, Shahrzad Mojab, and Sunera Thobani are among those who have advanced the field of study (Robbins 2010). Other notable figures include University of Ottawa law professor Joanne St Lewis, the first black woman to be elected as a Bencher of the Law Society of Upper Canada, who addressed systemic barriers to justice in Canada as author of *Virtual Justice: Systemic Racism in the Canadian Legal Profession*. As Executive Director of LEAF (Women's Legal and Education Fund), St Lewis argues how both a racial and a gender analysis of Canadian law needs to be combined intersectionally for real progress to be made. As well, Malinda S. Smith of the University of Alberta, and Fatima Jaffer of the University of British Columbia edited an important theoretical contribution, *Beyond The Queer Alphabet: Conversations on Gender, Sexuality and Intersectionality*, which re-emphasized the primacy of solidarity across difference. Their collection speaks to the necessity of engaging in critical diversity praxis in a variety of sites with much discussion of how this could be undertaken in academia.

Intersectional approaches are just as important in understanding the situation of any group of women, or any group at all, even those from the perspective of a society's dominant social groups. Their particular experiences of sexism are also affected by the multiple aspects of their identity, albeit accompanied by the privilege accorded their more elite status. While working-class black women were long treated as "mule[s] of the world," as the Harlem Renaissance writer Zora Neale Hurston puts it, upper-class white women were put on a pedestal and viewed as delicate flowers in need of male protection (Wallace 1978). But both are forms of sexism: being "protected" from the world of work and politics was hardly liberation since it denied this group of women both their autonomy and their right of self-determination. The ideology of the pedestal infuses patriarchal protection and interference into the decisions a woman makes about her own life, while being treated as a mule means one is mercilessly exploited. Intersectional approaches allow for the recognition of how race and class differentiate gender discrimination among and between different groups of women. It provides a means to recognize power relations both between groups of women and between women and men. In the one case, there is class exploitation and a brutal neglect of well-being, and in the other, excessive and paternalistic oversight. This is not a difference in degree, but in kind. Intersectionality demonstrates how under certain conditions, oppression and privilege can be simultaneously experienced. There is no generic sexism meted out to women in varying degrees depending on their specific status and identity. Rather, there are different *forms* of sexism depending on one's race, class, sexuality, religion, able-bodiedness, nationality, ethnicity, age, and legal or citizenship status. This is what is meant by calling these categories **co-constitutive**. One's racial identity can constitute how one's gender identity and expression is understood and experienced, whether as a form of fragility or as an excuse for mistreatment. And these categories are fluid, changing within and over different contexts.

Taking an intersectional approach does not dilute or disable the possibility of making gender-based discrimination a political priority. But developing a woman-centred policy requires an intersectional approach. Otherwise, the full dimensions of the problem cannot be understood or addressed and systems of oppression will not be affected. As Audre Lorde maintained in "The Master's Tools Will Never Dismantle the Master's House" (Lorde 1983), new theoretical approaches need to be applied to systemic problems.

Considerations of race and class were not the only motivators behind the development of an intersectional approach in feminist theory and activism. Women working against the concept of ableism see the value of taking an intersectional approach.

Heteronormativity and Heterosexism

Considerations of race and class were not the only motivators behind the development of an intersectional approach in feminist theory and activism. And, as with all identity markers, sexuality is contextually understood as part of a larger matter of social location. Lesbian feminists began to argue throughout the 1970s and 1980s that the oppression of lesbians takes a different form than the oppression of cisbodied straight women. Heterosexual women who express a desire for children or who demonstrate a loving devotion to their partners are praised; the same behaviour in lesbians

Box 3.2 Key Issues

DAWN Executive Summary: Legislation, Policy and Service Responses to Violence against Women with Disabilities and Deaf Women in Canada

The Criminal Code and Family Laws throughout Canada prohibit violence against women. Human Rights legislation, including international treaties such as the CEDAW and the CRPD further prohibit systemic discrimination. However the lived experiences of women with disabilities and Deaf women tell a different story.

Women with disabilities and Deaf women, through the intersectional lens/multiple identity positions they hold, are the largest, poorest minority group in Canada with the highest rates of physical, systemic, financial, psychological and interpersonal/family violence. The rate of violence for this cohort is 2 to 3 times that of non-disabled women. . . . A key to the success of the IN FOCUS project was the establishment of networks at the community level that included important stakeholders such as women with disabilities and Deaf women and service providers (Police, VAW and Victims Services, Disability organizations, Social and Health Services). Together, they identified the issues and recommended solutions at the local level. A clear message that has emerged from this community research is that beyond the urgent need to create a national network of resources including accessible shelters and transition houses, there is a *need to address the alarming rates of secondary systemic violence experienced by women with disabilities and Deaf women due to gaps in service provision.*

Source: DisAbled Women's Network Canada (2015).

has been reinterpreted as perverse and makes them subject to homophobic attack. Such double standards indicate that a society is **heterosexist**; that is, it considers only heterosexual relationships and heterosexual love or desire acceptable. Heterosexism is a construction that **normalizes** heterosexuality. US poet Adrienne Rich wrote an important essay "Compulsory Heterosexuality and Lesbian Existence" in 1980 that delineated how male power in society operates and how this creates a dominant culture in which heterosexuality becomes the imperative. Rich contends that all women's sexuality and desires are constrained and denied within this paradigm, which renders lesbians as the invisible other. Rich further argues that compulsory heterosexuality is a mechanism that restricts all aspects of women's freedom. Stevi Jackson explains that "institutionalized, normative heterosexuality regulates those kept within its boundaries as well as marginalizing and sanctioning those outside them" (Jackson 2006).

Heterosexuality is related to **heteronormativity**, a concept that assumes and enforces the view that there are only two essentialized genders—male and female—and therefore, only heterosexuality is "natural." Heterosexuality fails to recognize that ideas of male and female are culturally and socially constructed and are not fixed categories. Nor does it accept that socially constructed conceptions of gender vary through time and across cultures. Jackson explains

> There is no consensus on the question of definition, in large part because gender, sexuality and heterosexuality are approached from a variety of perspectives focusing on different dimensions of the social. It is not a case of some having a clearer view than others, but rather that the social is many-faceted and what is seen from one angle may be obscured from another. Sexuality, gender and heterosexuality intersect in variable ways within and between different dimensions of the social – and these intersections are also, of course, subject to historical change along with cultural and contextual variability. (Jackson 2006)

For more on sexuality, see Chapter 5, Gender and the Politics of the Body.

More recently, theorists have been exploring the intersections of heterosexism and the state itself. M. Jacqui Alexander's groundbreaking work (2006) demonstrates how globalization, sexuality, racialization, and desire intersect in the formation of neo-colonial states. She challenges North American feminism and queer studies to take up transnational frameworks that foreground questions of **colonialism**, political economy, and racial formation. To challenge colonialism requires understanding it as a system that violently imposed political, economic, social, and cultural domination by European powers of the American, Asian, and African continents for over 500 years. Alexander describes how the European ideological legacies of colonialism linger in modernity, but more, how modernity needs to be reconceptualized to account for the heteronormative regulatory practices embedded in modern state formations (Alexander 2006).

Heteropatriarchy and **heteronationalism** ensure and enforce male supremacy and heterosexual white privilege in private and public jurisdictions. Ideas embedded in state formation reinforce and conflate heteronormative understandings of patriarchy and nationalism and the persistence of colonial legacies. How these processes work can be clearly seen in immigration policy as well as nationalist discourses. Many of the immigration policies that affect the ability to obtain working permits and residency status, attend public school, and so on favour heterosexual family relationships. Gay and lesbian family relationships are generally excluded by most national policies. On the other hand, an ostensible commitment to anti-homophobia has been used by some countries to justify immigration policies that prevent whole ethnic or religious groups, such as Muslims, from entering a country. Feminist theorists have argued that the struggle to reduce homophobic violence and heterosexist government policies needs to operate in an intersectional way so that considerations include immigrants, refugees, and the undocumented, as well as communities that may be targeted with Islamophobic or other forms of prejudice. Just as heterosexism must be understood in an intersectional way, so too must the fight against heterosexism so that the movement is not used to support policies that inflict other kinds of discrimination.

What unites these diverse accounts about heterosexism is the idea that an intersectional approach is needed that takes into account both gender and sexuality, that is, whether one is lesbian, gay, straight, bisexual, or **transgender** (someone who holds or expresses a gender identity that differs from the one assigned at birth). The oppression of heterosexual women, lesbians, and transgender people cannot be collapsed into a single account. Heterosexual women do not hide their sexuality for fear of violence, family rejection, or discrimination in the job market. Their relationships can be public and are supported by a variety of social, legal, and economic mechanisms. Their legal and social privilege to form families is taken for granted, socially sanctioned, and factored into immigration and other public policy. None of this can be taken for granted by lesbians or bisexual or transgender persons. Here, then, is another example where the forms of oppression differ in kind and not merely in degree.

Historical Foundations of Intersectionality

The intersections of race, class, sexuality, ethnicity, ability, age, and gender were widely recognized among the more radical and socialist trends of the women's liberation movement that emerged in the 1960s and 1970s in North America. Feminism in this period had multiple sites of development as women were beginning to articulate their own demands within labour organizations such as Organized Working Women Ontario (OWW), the Equal Pay Coalition, and Canadian Women in Trades. The freedom and liberation movements, various anti-imperialist, peace and anti-colonial groups, and student organizations all saw women play major roles in theorizing and organizing, even if they were not admitted into leadership positions. Many of the women active in these organizations took the links between gender oppression and other forms of oppression as an obvious starting point and began trying to formulate a way to understand the connections between identities and oppressions. Organizations of women of colour took the lead in this direction out of the necessity to address multiple and interlocking systems of discrimination. Debates emerged over whether multiple systems of oppression were interdependent or distinct, or whether they could all be traced to capitalism, to patriarchy, or to both.

Historically, an intersectional approach to the oppression of women began with the influential writings and speeches of African American women in the nineteenth century arising from the interplay between abolitionist groups and women's suffrage groups, where race and gender oppression intersected. These women include Sojourner Truth (1797–1883), Ida Wells-Barnett (1862–1931), and Anna Julia Cooper (1858–1964) (Guy-Sheftall 1995; May 2007).

Sojourner Truth

Sojourner Truth's 1851 speech "Ain't I a Woman?" became famous for her challenge to women's rights organizations to include abolitionist perspectives and the demands of racialized and enslaved persons. Truth ably countered the assumption that white elite organizations did or could represent all women by arguing that racialized women's interests needed to be included in the movement. "Ain't I a Woman" addressed the multiple issues of structural oppression and exposed how white middle- and upper-class women's organizations interests did not extend to all women. "Woman" as a social category is not universally constituted. bell hooks took up Truth's claim more than a hundred years later in her 1981 book *Ain't I a Woman: Black Women and Feminism* critiquing mainstream feminism's tendency to universalize gender experience.

Anna Julia Cooper

The principal source of the concept of intersectionality is generally agreed to be Anna Julia Cooper. Born to an enslaved mother, Cooper (1858–1964) lived a remarkable life as a leader in education and politics. In 1892, she published a collection of her essays entitled *A Voice from the South*, which examined racism, sexism, and colonialism. Instead of addressing racism and sexism as general problems throughout society, Cooper made specific criticisms of sexism within the African American communities she inhabited, as well as specific analyses of racism as she observed it in the white women she worked with. She noted how the various social reform campaigns that different groups advanced to undermine racial and sexual oppression systematically ignored some of the most egregiously injured parties. She showed, for example, how the campaign to improve the working conditions of women was really only concerned with white women:

> One often hears in the North an earnest plea from some lecturer for "our working girls" (of course this means white working girls). . . . how many have ever given a thought to the pinched and down-trodden colored women bending over wash-tubs and ironing boards. . . . Will you call it narrowness and selfishness, then, that I find it impossible to catch the fire of sympathy and enthusiasm for most of these labor movements at the North? (Cooper 1988 [1892], 254–5)

From this perspective, Cooper began to give voice to the idea that a particular subgroup of women should not characterize their cause as "the" cause of women, especially when their demands were put forward as more important than the demands of other groups who have also experienced enslavement or colonialism (the latter, for example, through the annexation of Indigenous lands):

> Is not woman's cause broader, and deeper, and grander, than a blue stocking debate or an aristocratic pink tea? Why should woman become plaintiff in a suit versus the Indian, or the Negro or any other race or class who have been crushed under the heel of Anglo-Saxon power and selfishness? (1998 [1892], 123)

Cooper's arguments in *A Voice from the South* ultimately supported a version of the feminist standpoint theory through her argument that black women's social position has important political and epistemic implications. Just as Sandra Harding (2004) argued a century later, Cooper held that addressing the oppression of African American women would require understanding racism, sexism, class exploitation, and the history of colonialism. Developing a political project from the starting point of racialized women's lives would produce an intersectional analysis.

Still, these concerted efforts to make the conditions of racialized women's lives visible and to complicate the oversimplified pictures of racial and sexual oppression that were written by the theorists of the day had surprisingly little influence. Individuals and organizations advancing women's rights remained focused on white middle-class women and their concerns. It would take another several decades and the sustained efforts of the rights movements of the 1960s to push an intersectional approach further.

Angela Davis

The influential work of Angela Davis, Audre Lorde, and bell hooks developed intersectional approaches in important respects. Philosopher and political activist Angela Davis wrote her first essays in 1970–71 while in prison on a charge of conspiracy involving her support for the Soledad brothers, three African American men accused of murder. She was acquitted and went on to become an influential theorist on the specificity of the oppression of black women. Davis (1971) provides critical historical and sociological analyses of black women's lives under slavery, arguing that their treatment will not be understood unless it is seen as the result of how class intersected with sexism and racism. Within the discourses of the 1960s, histories of slavery often viewed enslaved women as suspect for consorting with the enemy by having babies by their white masters. Davis showed how this analysis was misguided precisely because it did not take into account the role of rape and sexual violence under slavery. Rather than "reproducing with the enemy," women under slavery were treated as conduits for reproducing the enslaved population. Through these kinds of examples and many others, Davis inaugurated the methodology of taking race, class, and gender into account in the study of any group of women. Her 1981 text, *Women, Race, and Class*, provides important critiques of the ways in which some of the mainstream feminist theories of the time ignored issues of race and class, undermining the legitimacy of their analyses of issues such as domesticity, rape, and reproductive technologies. For many African American women, Davis argues, the ability to nurture and provide domestic labour for their own families was experienced as liberatory rather than oppressive, given the generations who had had to serve and care for white children and white families instead of their own. The demand to increase criminal penalties for sexual violence also needed to be analyzed in relationship to racist court systems that were biased against black defendants. Davis's work (1983) shows that every feminist topic and policy proposal needs to be analyzed in a context sensitive to the historical and sociological dimensions of race, class, and gender.

Audre Lorde

Audre Lorde (1934–1992) was a Caribbean-American poet, writer, and activist and one of the earliest out lesbian black activists. Both her poetry and her theoretical writing consistently drew from elements of her experience in the LGBTQ community as well as in anti-racist and feminist communities (De Veaux 2006). During a period in the 1960s and 1970s when many feminist groups wanted to put the differences among women aside in order to articulate a unified women's politics and culture, Lorde insisted on the critical importance of acknowledging the differences among women: "It is not those differences [of race, age and sex] between us that are separating us. It is rather our refusal to recognize those differences, and to examine the distortions that result from our misnaming them . . ." (1984, 115).

Lorde argues that movements for social justice and transformation will be derailed not by acknowledging and exploring the different experiences and interests of the persons engaged in struggle, but in trying to pretend that these differences have no significance. This pretense leads to misunderstanding others and misinterpreting their actions and motives. It also leads to a poor theoretical and political analysis. Those on the margins of power, she said, "often identify one way in which we are different, and we assume that to be the primary cause of all oppression, forgetting other distortions around difference, some of which we ourselves may be practicing" (1984, 116). The project of an organization or group to render some differences as less important than others may be motivated by the desire of some of its members to de-emphasize the way they are privileged. Whether this comes from white women who de-emphasize race, or African American women who de-emphasize homophobia, or African American men who refuse to engage with gender oppression, Lorde declares that the result is the same: trust and understanding are reduced, and solidarity is broken.

As Anna Julia Cooper had done decades before, Lorde explains the personal impossibility of separating out the multiple aspects of her identity by explaining that, for women of colour, no such separation is even conceivable:

> I find I am constantly being encouraged to pluck out some one aspect of myself and

present this as the meaningful whole, eclipsing or denying the other parts of self. But this is a destructive and fragmenting way to live. My fullest concentration of energy is available to me only when I integrate all the parts of who I am, openly, allowing power from particular sources of my living to flow back and forth freely through all my different selves, without the restrictions of externally imposed definition. (1984, 120–1)

The intersectional approach to understanding and addressing gender and sexual hierarchies is itself an attempt to uproot dualistic or binary types of thinking. As racialized feminists emphasized, racialized men are themselves the object of social, cultural, and economic oppression. Even in situations of violence against women, there are often strong ties of love and solidarity with male abusers because of these shared, complex histories. Binary thinking either would put the "community's" interest above women, as if the community has a unified set of needs and interests without internal conflict, or, as a feminist dualism, would put all women on one side, including women of all groups, and all men on the other, no matter their social condition. Intersectionality is a demand for an acknowledgement of the harm and abuse women have suffered, for acts of support and solidarity, and for equal power in the struggle to change society.

Intersectional Approaches to Feminist Activism

Much North American feminist activism in the 1960s and 1970s focused on the following sorts of demands: equal pay for equal work, making abortion and contraception accessible and/or legal, opening up educational opportunities and professions to women, and creating more childcare centres. Even though some gains were made, many women's lives did not appreciably change. Today there is still at least a 20 per cent (and often higher) wage gap between men and women doing comparable work, many women do not have effective access to abortion because of geographical or financial obstacles, and although there are many more women in the professions, the ranks of the poor are disproportionately filled by women. Racialized, Indigenous, lesbian, and transgender women predominantly experience these inequalities. Why?

One contributing factor may be that early feminist demands did not operate in an

---

Box 3.3 Women in Media

Lee Maracle

Lee Maracle, a member of the Sto:lo Nation, was born in Vancouver and grew up on the North Shore. She is professor, author, poet, activist, and theorist. Her 1996 *I Am Woman: A Native Perspective on Sociology and Feminism* is most often described as visionary. She explains

> *I Am Woman* represents my personal struggle with womanhood, culture, traditional spiritual beliefs and political sovereignty, written during a time when that struggle was not over. My original intention was to empower Native women to take to heart their own personal struggle for Native feminist being.

Columpa Carmen Bobb

Source: Maracle (1996, vii)

intersectional way. Consider, for example, how the second-wave slogan "Sisterhood is Universal" collapses difference. They were looking at gender issues and women's rights as if these are universals, unaffected by whether one works as an executive or a maid, lives in a rural or urban area, has the money to attend a professional school, is racialized, or is an immigrant or refugee.

Shifting Policy Demands

By taking an intersectional approach to the problem of gender equity in the labour force, connecting class, race, and gender, comparable worth could reach many more women from the working class who work in the service sector, health care, hospitality industry, and other gender-segregated areas of the labour force. Rather than pushing women to change professions if they wanted higher pay, this movement argued that the work most working-class women do is highly valuable to society and much more difficult than traditionally acknowledged.

Although it was important to open the higher-status and higher-paid professions, such as medicine, engineering, and law, to women, this also proved difficult for most working women and women of colour, few of whom could effectively take advantage of the newly opened opportunities to attend university or professional schools. An important effort with the potential to change more women's lives was unionization. Teachers, health-care workers, and office workers became unionized throughout the 1980s and 1990s, often with women union organizers leading the way, vastly improving their wages, benefits, and working conditions as well as their ability to participate in democratic governance structures at their work sites. The efforts to unionize these types of jobs were often opposed by those who held gender-related stereotypes about the skill level these required or women's motivations to pursue this work. Organizers had to develop new analyses of work to show that being a nursery-school teacher was a highly skilled and demanding profession. Today teachers and nurses earn much more in real wages than a generation ago, with the top strata earning annual salaries of more than $100,000.

Perhaps a clear example of intersectional changes in feminist activism has been in the sphere of reproductive rights. The legal right to an abortion, after mass protests, did not result in accessible abortion services for all women. Abortion is unavailable in most rural communities and provinces (it has been entirely unavailable in Prince Edward Island but a proposal to remedy this is underway), which adds the cost of travel (not covered by provincial health-care insurance) to the cost of the procedure. Moreover, many poor women and women of colour argued that their communities were in desperate need of a full range of reproductive services, including contraception, assistance in childbirth, prenatal care, and health services for infants and children, as well as abortion. Poor women, disabled women, Indigenous women, immigrants, and women of colour were violated when they were sterilized in government-mandated programs without their informed consent. (For more on compulsory sterilization in Canada, see Dyck 2013.) Lesbian advocacy groups advocated for the right to adoption as well as reproductive technologies. Thus, an intersectional approach indicated that much more than legal abortion was required to ensure women's autonomy in their reproductive lives and that the overall demand should be for reproductive rights as a whole—the right to *have* children as well as to *not have* children. Moreover, women needed not merely *legal* rights but *effective* rights, or rights that they could actually enact, to a full range of reproductive health care in order to have agency in their reproductive and sexual lives.

Rosalind P. Petchesky, one of the leading analysts of reproductive issues, argues that separating out the struggles around violence, sexuality, development, work, education, and reproductive needs in the lives of girls and women eliminates the possibility of effective solutions. "The most important operational principle of a human rights framework" is, Petchesky claims, "the principle of *indivisibility*," which requires integrating "civil and political, economic, social and cultural and so-called solidarity rights (such as sustainable human development and environmental safety)." She explains that

> ... a woman cannot avail herself of her right "to decide freely and responsibly the number, spacing, and timing of her children" if she lacks the financial resources to pay for reproductive health services or the transport to reach them; if she cannot read package inserts or clinic wall posters; if her workplace is contaminated with pesticides or pollutants that have an adverse effect on pregnancy; or if she is harassed by a husband or in-laws who will scorn her or beat her up if she uses birth control. (Petchesky 2002, 75)

Effective activism that actually changes the conditions of women's lives must be integrative and intersectional. Actual effective policies must take into account the different contexts and the structural oppression in which women live.

Global Intersections

Another set of implications for activism concerns the intersectional ways in which structures of discrimination operate. Governments may respond positively to the activism of one part of the community but in a way that exacerbates the problems in another part. Jasbir Puar, Zillah Eisenstein, and others have shown that if they do not take intersectional issues into account, anti-homophobic and anti-sexist activism can exacerbate Islamophobia and the oppression of Muslim women and become an alibi for imperial military aggressions (Eisenstein 2004; Puar 2007). The treatment of gays and lesbians has become a key issue in Canadian, US, and European nationalist discourses, used to hypocritically bolster claims that the West is modern, enlightened, and protective of human rights while Muslim majority nations are culturally backward with no right to be part of international dialogues and treaties. This hierarchy has been used to justify unilateral military invasions that result in negative impacts for women's lives and the abrogation of basic human rights for millions.

Puar argues that the fight against homophobia cannot operate through a single-issue lens or ignore the movement's intersections with nationalist rhetoric. In some cases, LGBTQ rights provides a cover for other agendas or an alibi that paints a moral face on what is actually an immoral motivation for war—such as profit or power. Eisenstein argues that if feminism is truly concerned with all oppressed groups, it must work against racism and against military or economic empires.

Intersectional analyses need to be applied within every movement and every constituency. Just as there are important differences among women—with implications for their interests—so too are there important differences among gay, lesbian, and transgender people, among all religious communities, among people of colour, and within every group. Some within a given group may even benefit from their particular privilege by their oppression and discrimination of others, such as when rich white women benefit from the typically low wages of domestic workers. This does not doom the possibility of coalition, since alliances may continue to be possible across broad differences if privilege and power differentials can be acknowledged. But it does call for a clear-eyed, intersectional approach to the complex challenges social movements must face.

Kimberlé Crenshaw conducted a policy analysis of feminist-led organizations. She describes how a Latina woman in desperate need of help was denied entry to a battered women's shelter because she spoke only Spanish, since the rules of this shelter required that every resident be able to participate in support group meetings deemed vital to their psychological empowerment and mental health. Because the meetings were only held in English, some of the most vulnerable sectors of the population were denied services. Crenshaw (1991) argues that this shelter was operating with a "single yardstick" model for assisting women fleeing abuse.

As this example showed, intersectional analyses are vital not merely in how movement goals and demands are formulated, but also in how feminist-led organizations operate. Shelters for abused women and children, rape crisis centres, feminist health centres, women's bookstores, women's and gender studies programs, and women's political organizations all need an intersectional approach in setting their policies and priorities and ensuring that the process of decision making is truly representative. An organization designed to meet the needs of women will not succeed if it does not fully understand the varied conditions of women's lives, much less if it requires women, as did the shelter Crenshaw describes, to conform to a white Anglo norm before they can take advantage of its services. bell hooks (1984) argues that this does not mean that every organization must have a representative diversity in its leadership (this may not be possible), but it can still take an intersectional approach to its work.

Many organizations today have adopted such an intersectional approach. Planned Parenthood in Canada is a good example with its expanded and appropriate programming. The Service Employees International Union is another: it has adopted multilingual communications, sets aside designated places to ensure gender and racial composition at conventions, and conducts training workshops on discrimination against transgender people in the workplace.

The widespread influence of intersectionality yields new questions about how to understand the complexity of social identities as well as new questions about research methods.

Box 3.4 Time to Reflect

"Mapping Transnational Feminist Engagements: Neoliberalism and the Politics of Solidarity"

In the above-titled article, Linda Carty and Chandra Talpade Mohanty reflect on their survey conducted among 33 feminist scholar-activists in Asia, South America, the Caribbean, North Africa, Europe, and North America in their forties to eighties. The testimonies reflect on lessons learned, victories savoured, and losses mourned. They probe and problematize the possibility of feminist solidarity across place, time, and difference in the context of neo-liberalism and conclude that an intersectional analysis could assist.

Professor and activist Beverly Bain's contribution speaks to the complexity of making change:

> As part of a group of feminists of color working on the ground to end violence against women, we were struggling simultaneously inside the black and color patriarchal communities to recognize gender and in the white feminist movement to recognize the intersections of gender and race. As black women and women of color, in struggle we have always occupied the insider–outsider position in the Canadian women's movement and in the nation. This position has been placed upon us but is often embraced as a way to mediate the deleterious effects of black and other forms of nationalism, racism, patriarchy, and sexism. In the struggle to make known the differing impacts of sexual and physical violence in the lives of women of color, we saw these experiences culturalized in institutions and treated as extraneous to the experiences of violence and sexual assault of white women. In fact, while we as black women and women of color were successful in bringing an intersectional analysis based on gender, race, and class to the antiviolence movement, the discourse of the black, brown, and native rapists continue to drive the antiviolence agenda within the women's movement and institutionally.

Source: Carty and Mohanty (2014).

Intersectional Approaches to Feminist Scholarship

Intersectionality poses new challenges to feminist scholarship and, in particular, to the formulation of projects of inquiry and research. Some question whether it is possible to take one category of analysis—such as disability or heterosexism—as an object of inquiry for a given study or to prioritize one element of a complex social reality in order to study it in a sustained manner (Carby 1987; Saldivar-Hull 1998). Others argue that the causality of multiple strands of identity-based oppression can be traced to a single source such as capitalism or to ideas about what is normal (Davis 1983; Pharr 1997; McWhorter 2009). But the first question that intersectionality raises for feminist scholarship is a simple one: What does it mean to say that one has a gender identity in the first place?

Intersectional Identities

As has been discussed throughout this chapter, the concept of intersectionality is meant to be applied both to the varied forms that gender oppression can take as well as to identities.

Intersectional approaches to social categories of identity are often posed as an alternative to additive approaches that assume one can simply add race and gender and other categories together to develop an adequate analysis. Additive approaches do not work because they assume that one can take a singular or non-intersectional approach to understanding any one category and then simply add

---

Box 3.5 In Her Own Words

Black Feminist Thought in the "Matrix of Domination"

Patricia Hill Collins's "matrix of domination" inscribes the importance of recognizing one's own location within social and cultural systems. She urges the application of agency to resist oppression and create change:

> In addition to being structured along axes such as race, gender, and social class, the matrix of domination is structured on several levels. People experience and resist oppression on three levels: the level of personal biography; the group or community level of the cultural context created by race, class, and gender; and the systemic level of social institutions. Black feminist thought emphasizes all three levels as sites of domination and as potential sites of resistance....
>
> This level of individual consciousness is a fundamental area where new knowledge can generate change. Traditional accounts assume that power as domination operates from the top down by forcing and controlling unwilling victims to bend to the will of more powerful superiors. But these accounts fail to account for questions concerning why, for example, women stay with abusive men even with ample opportunity to leave or why slaves did not kill their owners more often. The willingness of the victim to collude in her or his own victimization becomes lost. They also fail to account for sustained resistance by victims, even when chances for victory appear remote. By emphasizing the power of self-definition and the necessity of a free mind, Black feminist thought speaks to the importance African American women thinkers place on consciousness as a sphere of freedom. Black women intellectuals realize that domination operates not only by structuring power from the top down but by simultaneously annexing the power as energy of those on the bottom for its own ends.

Source: Collins (1990, 221–38).

these up. This assumes that racial identity or sexual identity can be described and explained prior to its intersection with other categories. Through the additive approach, Elizabeth Spelman explains,

> . . . we may get the impression that a woman's identity consists of a sum of parts neatly divisible from one another. . . . This is a version of personal identity we might call tootsie roll metaphysics: each part of my identity is separable from every other part, and the significance of each part is unaffected by other parts. (Spelman 1988, 136)

Such an additive approach conflicts with the way Audre Lorde described her life as a black lesbian. Recall that Lorde (1984) responded to those who asked her to "simply speak as a woman" by explaining that her life makes up a whole that cannot be subdivided into racial, sexual, and gendered parts. It also contradicts Valerie Smith's definition of intersectionality, in which one's race and gender are co-constituting, with every aspect of one's identity affected by the others (1998).

The idea that various factors co-constitute any given identity leads to new ways of thinking about identity as both historical and relational. Identities change in relation to specific contexts and are in fact in constant flux. The actual mediation of factors influencing a given social identity varies constantly depending on context. One may be viewed as a budding intellectual among friends, as a potential thief in stores, as still a child when at home, or as a primarily sexual being when walking down the street. These diverse treatments affect how people actually act and perform in given situations—with easy assurance or pained self-consciousness, or with an expectation to fail.

Identities are dependent on relational contexts, and as these contexts change, identities can undergo important transformations. Surely these can add up to a set of experiences and options that are different, one from another. Yet what it means to be marked by any one of these categories is both contextually variable and historically evolving. As Monique Wittig argues, to be designated a "man" in patriarchal societies was to be designated as someone who had the right of access to women's services, and thus even the identity "man" is a relational one. As feminist movements expand women's rights and freedoms and alter their behaviour and sense of themselves so that they no longer accept subordinate status, the relations between men and women are changed in workplaces as well as domestic spaces with a subsequent impact on what it means to be a man today. There will undoubtedly continue to be historical shifts in the meanings and practices associated with every element of identities. It makes no sense to ask who people "truly" are in some final, stable sense. How might the meanings of social identity categories be changed, and are there some that might be eliminated entirely?

Research Methods

Since the 1990s the intersectional approach to gender analysis has become the cornerstone of new research methods in the social sciences and some sciences as well as in the development of post-colonial and transnational feminism. Intersectional approaches have transformed research in women's and gender studies, bringing about a new epistemological framework for understanding the object of inquiry. Whether a researcher is studying gender, race, class, or sexuality, or whether the project is focused on work, citizenship, families, disability, or health, a multidimensional approach is increasingly understood to be required.

One way to think about gender, race, sexuality, and class is that they are social structures that organize individual practices and construct systems of meaning. Racial and gender systems operate as structures in this sense. There are "gender frames" that predispose people to perform different roles, develop different skills, interact in specific ways, and interpret the actions of others differently (Valian 1998). For example, in some communities women may be encouraged to engage in a lot of emotional caregiving of others, such as listening to friends' stories, providing encouragement, advice, and gestures of support. Because this activity has a "gender frame," women who neglect these social expectations may be judged negatively. Men who engage in emotional caregiving, in contrast, may be negatively judged as less than masculine. Before a conclusion is made that women are naturally better at caregiving, there is a need to consider the gender structures that cultivate or discourage these skills.

But are women expected to provide emotional caregiving to everyone? Not really. It is expected within the community of one's peers, a grouping that may be defined by religion, age, race, class, and so on. A young woman who provides emotional caregiving for a rich older man may be subject to suspicion for having less than altruistic motives. A wealthy woman who offers a lot of encouragement and advice to her servants may be viewed as patronizing and interfering. Conventions of gender expectations are modulated by intersecting structures. Thus, the analysis of structures in academia needs to take an intersectional approach.

The relational and contextual nature of social identities has also brought home the idea that dominant identities are just as much in need of analysis as non-dominant or marginal ones. Dominant identities such as whiteness or maleness or cisbodies or heterosexuality are relational, context dependent, and subject to historical shifts and operate to mediate other elements of identity in complex ways. In the past, these dominant identities were generally considered norms of neutrality that required no historicization or political genealogy to understand. One could call a book "women's history" if it covered only white women, but would have to call it "Chinese women's history" if it covered only Chinese women, while a book covering mainly men's history could be called simply "history." Unlike non-dominant identities, dominant identities were thought to be the normative, rational way all human beings should be understood and treated. However, once people begin to understand dominant identities as relational and contextual—as taking the specific form that they do because of their relation to other identities—it can be seen that they cannot provide a standard that can be universally applied. The entitlements of dominant identities to be the centre of attention, to control the discussion, to secure the most resources, to have their language enforced on all, to represent what is "normal," and so on, are not universalizable.

Analyses of gender, therefore, require foregrounding the ways in which masculinity is expressed as much as femininity. Analyses of sexuality require making the structure of heterosexual expressions of gender and familial formations more visible. An inquiry into race and ethnicity must include whiteness as well as other identity categories.

One way in which researchers respond to the fact that identities are relational, contextual, and fluid is to reframe their study to focus not on "men," for example, as if this is a natural category, but on *masculinity* (Blount and Cunningham 1989; Murphy 2004). How is masculinity operating in this specific domain, in this specific work site? What characteristics are assumed, and what behaviour is enabled for whom? By reframing it in this way, researchers can recognize that some women may participate in masculine privilege by performing as managers, bosses, or leaders, radically changing their relations to others and their position within structures of gender. Workplaces are conceptualized as highly specific constellations of space–time, affecting the way people interact and understand the relation of the work site to other parts of their lives. High-status health-care workers, such as surgeons, may bring their sense of self-importance at work to bear on their familial relationships at home, while police work may transform gender identities in non-work settings. Identities and structures are not simply brought to the workplace but emanate from the specific possibilities that workplaces produce.

While Thornton Dill, and Kohlman laud the growing social justice impact of intersectionality within and outside the academy, they also urge caution to avoid misapplication of the theory. They distinguish between what they call "strong intersectionality" and "weak intersectionality." Weak intersectionality can be dangerous when it merely describes difference without history, context, or how difference came to be. It fails to recognize the *evolving* nature of difference. In these cases, it is limited to acknowledgement of separation and contributes no analysis. Alternatively, "strong intersectionality" analyzes institutions, systems, and identities in relation to each other and recognizes how the individual is implicated in the systems, it describes. It examines how these phenomena are interdependent, mutually constituted, and fluid. It does not leave social oppression unchallenged but analyzes in order to act (Thornton, Dill, and Kohlman 2012).

Finally, even as scholars and researchers explore difference using the concept of intersectionality, they find it important to note commonalities. As Margo Wilson and Martin Daly argue in their 1998 study of family violence, men beat their wives in many societies while the reverse happens only rarely, and men are by far the main perpetrators of sexual violence around the globe. Legal theorists Lynn Welchman and Sara Hossain (2005, 13) similarly argue in their analysis of the concept of "honour crimes" that "it is important to identify commonalities as well as differences in the structure of violence."

These efforts to develop intersectional research methods can be summarized in the following points: (1) specify the object of inquiry as finely tuned as the project requires, rather than assuming broad and undifferentiated categories like "women"; (2) do not assume that any one subcategory of a group can serve as the paradigm of the whole or be positioned at the centre of the analysis; (3) consider the relational nature of both privilege and oppression; (4) recognize the historically changeable nature of oppression and human agency; (5) account for the fluid nature of identities across contexts and time periods and the possibility that socially recognized categories of identity can come into and pass out of existence; (6) avoid the practice of simply averaging the data from representative samples of informants as if this can form a picture of the whole: the median or mean is sometimes meaningless; and (7) while acknowledging the importance of difference, avoid assuming that commonalities across difference never occur.

Taking these points into account could lead researchers to realize M. Jacqui Alexander's challenge to "those in the academic factory to teach for social justice" (2006).

Debates over Intersectionality

Recently, some feminist theorists have debated the concept of intersectionality. Few dispute the fact that multiple structures of oppression and identity formation are operating in every context, requiring a multi-strand analysis, but some are concerned whether the term *intersectionality* itself can cover this complexity. The term, after all, implies that single lines of identity meet at a certain point, like roads meeting at an intersection under a stoplight, as Crenshaw suggested in her original metaphor (1989). This might wrongly imply that race, gender, class, sexuality, and so on, can operate independently before they intersect. Thus some find *intersectionality* misleading and suggest alternative terms, such as *interstitiality* or *assemblages*, that cause fewer problems.

The philosopher Maria Lugones, for example, argues that intersectionality implies a logic of purity that values unity, homogeneity, and control over multiplicity, fragmentation, and impurity (2003; 2007). The idea of clearly demarcated lines that only intersect at certain points reveals this problem, she asserts. Moreover, a theoretical approach is needed that will show that it is impossible to disconnect gender oppression, capitalism, heterosexism, racism, and colonialism, rather than assume these simply "intersect." In a different line of argument, philosopher Naomi Zack is concerned that the adherence to intersectionality causes too much fragmentation and disables feminist solidarity. Intersectionality implies, Zack argues, that women of different ethnicities will have different genders, obscuring the common ground women share. Still other theorists are concerned that intersectionality puts too much emphasis on identities that have themselves been socially constructed under conditions of oppression. While the second-wave feminist movement often obscured identity beyond gender, these critics charge that it is necessary to deconstruct identities, reveal their fluidity and vulnerable contingency, and find forms of political solidarity and motivation that are not predicated on identity ascriptions (Phelan 1994).

Feminists have also debated whether intersectionality has mistakenly implied that it is mainly black women who are intersectional subjects (Nash 2008). For philosopher Kathryn Gines, while "Black women loom large in the literature on intersectionality, this has more to do with the concept coming out of Black feminist scholarship than an effort to make Black women prototypical intersectional subjects" (2011, 280). It is probably no accident that the most far-reaching work on the concept of intersectionality has come from women who have experienced their own specific forms of oppression as relatively invisible, such as lesbians of colour.

Other feminists argue that the concept of intersectionality itself is only a metaphor and should not be taken too far. Ann Garry argues that intersectionality is "the best strategy we have at the moment for developing truly pluralistic and inclusive" feminist theory and politics (2011, 844). Unity can arise, she argues, via a concept of "family resemblances," taken from Ludwig Wittgenstein, to signal the idea of the ways in which members of a biological family may be recognizably related even though there is no single trait that each one shares. Moreover, Garry argues, intersectionality is a more modest idea, in reality, than the critics charge: it is not a fully developed theory of identity formation or a theory of oppression, but a framework or "'method checker' that provides standards that a method or methodology should meet" (2011, 830). Identity categories are not abolished, that is true, but in an intersectional approach their inherent complexity, ambiguity, and fluidity is revealed (Gines 2011).

Other theorists such as Jasbir Puar who emphasize the multiplicity and fragmentation of identity categories continue to argue that "intersectionality as a heuristic may well be indispensable" (2007, 125). An approach that views the oppression of sexuality through a single-axis lens, Puar holds, creates binaries between oppressor and oppressed that are overly simplistic as well as politically dangerous. The desire for a single-axis approach may well come from those who experience discrimination in only one part of their lives, who have uninterrupted access to public space, who see themselves reflected in the media, and who are not faced with racial profiling or the demand to prove their citizenship. For these reasons Puar holds that intersectionality remains a critically important guiding framework for every arena of social inquiry.

Chandra Talpade Mohanty argues that intersectional analyses, rather than inhibiting solidarity, are vital to the very possibility of transnational feminist solidarity, but that there is a need to go even further to analyze interwoven histories. Rather than studying women in terms of "discrete and disconnected cultures and nations," they should "frame agency and resistance across the borders of nation and culture" and look for "points of connection and distance among and between communities of women marginalized and privileged along numerous local and global dimensions" (Mohanty 2003, 243). This means that there is a need to take a macro analysis that considers the interdependent relationships between groups and structures in different parts of the globe, rather than assuming that they can be studied as one small, discrete unit and ignore the way that it is affected—positively and/or negatively—by its relations with others. Mohanty stresses that solidarity can happen when lines of commonality and shared interest emerge between specific communities or constituencies, whether or not they are geographically contiguous. Solidarity can occur in local contexts or across vast distances over issues of intellectual property rights, the policies of global financial institutions, sexual violence, or occupational health hazards. But to develop strong lines of solidarity, there is a critical need to remain attentive to power, to differences, to mutual interdependencies, and to the intersectionality of identities and structures in every location.

Summary

Intersectionality is a way of approaching both identities and structures of oppression. Its basic premise is that to understand anyone's identity or social position, one needs to take into account more than a single axis, more than gender—for example, race, class, and sexuality.

Feminist theorist Valerie Smith shows that the mainstream media rarely provide an adequate analysis of current events because they do not take an intersectional approach. Legal theorist Kimberlé Crenshaw argues that without an intersectional approach neither feminism nor anti-racism will effectively address the specific obstacles experienced by women of colour. Sexism must also be interrogated for its heterosexist bias that has excluded lesbians, gay men, and transgender persons.

The history of intersectionality emerges primarily from African American women. In the nineteenth century, Sojourner Truth and Anna Julia Cooper argued that campaigns to improve the conditions of women only addressed the situation of white women. Many women of colour and lesbians have built on this approach in recent decades. In the 1970s, Angela Davis adopted a methodology of incorporating race, class, and gender to assess the lives of any group of women. Without recognizing differences of race, age, and sex, bell hooks and Audre Lorde argue, trust and solidarity cannot be built across groups.

Feminist activists have adopted intersectional approaches. For example, the comparable worth movement, by connecting race and gender, could enhance the well-being of many more working-class women in gender-segregated workplaces. In reproductive rights struggles, intersectionality has uncovered the limited type and lack of services made available to low-income women, women of colour, disabled women, rural women, lesbians, and trans women given their particular circumstances. Rosalind Petchesky argues that reproductive rights must operate within a principle of indivisibility whereby effective solutions for girls and women in their reproductive needs must also address violence, sexuality, work, education, and so forth.

Activists working at the global level must also consider intersectional methods but recognize biases that promote the Global North as modern and superior in its ways. For example, one dimensional anti-homophobic and anti-sexist activism can exacerbate Islamophobia and the oppression of Muslim and LGBTQ women while justifying imperialistic military interventions.

Intersectionality also creates new challenges when applied to the notion of identities. Scholars have begun to consider multiple identities as not being additive, linear, or binary, but historical, relational, fluid, and contextual.

Research methods in women's and gender studies have been transformed as intersectional approaches are commonly applied to their wide range of projects. Nonetheless, women's commonalities as well as differences need to be taken into consideration.

Today intersectionality is a widespread approach throughout feminist theory, gender scholarship, and feminist organizing but remains an emerging framework of analysis. While some scholars argue that the term does not explain the full complexity of the multiple structures of oppression and identity formation in every context, others suggest it is an indispensable tool of analysis. Chandra Talpade Mohanty, for example, finds this approach vital if people are to begin to develop solidarity among feminists transnationally.

Discussion Questions

1. Analyze yourself in terms of intersectionality. What are the multiple parts of your identity? Identify one situation in which a different aspect of yourself plays the predominant role and privileges you. Name another situation when a different identity aspect works against your interests.
2. How should researchers use the concept of intersectionality to design empirical studies? In a survey, for example, is it sufficient to draw from a diverse sample of participants, or is more needed?
3. Is it ever useful or appropriate to focus on a singular category of analysis, such as sexuality or race or gender, without an intersectional approach?
4. The theory of intersectionality complicates linear-binary thinking. Do you find it a useful tool to understand difference? Why?
5. Locate a historical example of women advocating for women's rights and apply an intersectional analysis.

Recommended Readings

Canadian Research Institute for the Advancement of Women. 2006. *Intersectional Feminist Frameworks: An Emerging Vision.* (www.oaith.ca/assets/files/Publications/Intersectional%20Feminist%20Frameworks_CRIAW_e.pdf). CRIAW provides a tool to assist with intersectional analysis for policy and advocacy initiatives.

Carty, Linda, and Chandra Talpade Mohanty. 2014. "Mapping Transnational Feminist Engagements: Neoliberalism and the Politics of Solidarity." In *The Oxford Handbook of Transnational Feminist Movements*, edited by Rawwida Baksh and Wendy Harcourt. This work reflects on a survey conducted among 33 feminist scholar–activists from Asia, South America, the Caribbean, North Africa, Europe, and North America in their forties to eighties and constructs a dialogue that foregrounds the similarities and the differences in collective thinking and praxis as it has evolved through the decades. It provides insight into how the concept of intersectionality has evolved through activist practice.

Collins, Patricia Hill and Sirma Bilge. *Intersectionality.* Cambridge UK: Polity Press, 2016. The authors produce a clear yet complex revisiting of how the theory of intersectionality has been defined and applied, inside the academy and in the wider community. It takes up current debates about the theory and its use and highlights its potential for bringing about social justice change. It is most instruction in its sections discussing praxis.

Crenshaw, Kimberlé. 1991. "Mapping the Margins: Intersectionality, Identity Politics, and Violence against Women of Color." *Stanford Law Review* 43 (6): 1241–99. Crenshaw explores race and gender dimensions of violence against women of colour and the failure of scholars to examine the intersections of racism and patriarchy. This work was one of the first to define intersectionality and how it operates within the law and society.

Davis, Angela. 1983. *Women, Race, and Class.* New York: Random House. In this groundbreaking text, Davis uses an intersectional analysis to expose the racist and classist biases of some activists within the second-wave women's movement, which contributed to divisions within the membership. Her examples provide a cogent rationale for how difference operates within gender relations.

Dua, Enakshi, and Angela Robertson, eds. 1999. *Scratching the Surface: Canadian Anti-racist Feminist Thought.* Toronto: Women's Press.

This foundational text comprehensively sets out a historical background to the contemporary legacy of colonialism and empire in Canada and how race and gender are situated within state law, policy, and practice. Dua's chapter "Beyond Diversity: Exploring the Ways in Which the Discourse of Race has Shaped the Institution of the Nuclear Family" analyzes gender, race, and class in the construction of the family within the Canadian colonial settler state.

May, Vivian M. 2015. *Pursuing Intersectionality, Unsettling Dominant Imaginaries.* New York: Routledge. May analyzes how, while intersectionality is widely known, acclaimed, and applied, it is often construed in ways that depoliticize, undercut, or even violate its most basic premises.

Smith, Malinda S., and Fatima Jaffer, eds. 2012. *Beyond the Queer Alphabet: Conversations on Gender, Sexuality and Intersectionality.* Ottawa: Canadian Federation for the Humanities and Social Sciences. www.academia.edu/3717749/Beyond_the_Queer_Alphabet_Conversations_on_Gender_Sexuality_and_Intersectionality. This text emerged from a series of blogs around the issue of homophobic and transphobic violence and extended the conversation to education and praxis.

4 Learning, Making, and Doing Gender

Chapter Outline

- What Is Gender?
- Traditional Explanations for Gender Differences
- Feminist Critiques of Theories of Gender
- How Is Gender Learned?
- How Gender Is Enforced
- Alternative Gender Arrangements

This chapter will help you
- Comprehend the difference between biology and social constructions of gender
- Learn how culture influences gender definitions
- Appreciate the problematics involved with gender binaries
- Recognize the key theories that purport to explain gender
- Understand feminist contributions to gender theory and debate

One is not born a woman, one becomes one.
—SIMONE DE BEAUVOIR (1949)

If the rigid social constructions of the masculine have resulted in political and cultural forces of oppression, repression, and denial, can masculinity be rehearsed in a way that alters its ideological boundaries? In other words, can masculinity be performed so as to render it less repressive, less tyrannical?
—MAURICE BERGER, BRIAN WALLIS, AND SIMON WATSON (2012, 5)

One of the most powerful effects of oppression and marginalization is that it represents dominant groups as neutral and unremarkable. For example, before the emergence in the mid-twentieth century of political movements fighting for the rights of people of colour; women; lesbian, gay, bisexual, intersex, and transgender people; people with disabilities; and others, social inequality was defined as the problem of the oppressed group. What would now be called racism and sexism were identified as "the Negro Question," or "the Indian Question," or "the Woman Problem." In other words, discrimination against women was not the result of male dominance, but a "problem" with and of "women." A major contribution of the liberation movements of the twentieth century was to redefine these social issues as the responsibility of the dominating elite: racial segregation was not caused by "the Negro Problem," but was the result of white racism. Gender inequality was not caused by "the Women Problem," but was the result of patriarchy.

This conceptual change has had far-reaching influence. One consequence has been the rethinking of how race, gender, sexuality, and other categories of social existence are imagined. From their beginnings, women's studies programs have recognized that not only women but also men are shaped by cultural mandates about gendered behaviour. All people are equally defined, contained, and controlled by social expectations of how they should look, act, speak, move, desire, interact with others, affect their surroundings, and think about themselves. Indeed, many women's studies programs in colleges and universities have made this explicit by including the word *gender* in their names to acknowledge that not only women have gender and that gender as a category of identity is non-binary and constructs everyone, albeit within socially unequal contexts.

In this chapter, gender is explored: how it operates in different temporal, cultural, and geographical contexts; how it is enforced; and how it is resisted and subverted. It is examined through the ways in which the differences between women and men have been constructed, naturalized, and normalized.

What Is Gender?

The term *gender* comes from the Latin root *genus*, which originally meant "birth, family, or nation"—that is, where something or someone is born from (a meaning that evolved into words like *generate* and *generation*). Over time *genus* came to be more generally defined as "a kind or type of thing," and the words that derive from it share that sense, such as *genre*, meaning a kind or type of music or literature. *Gender* came to mean "a kind of thing defined by sex difference," both biologically, like people and animals, and grammatically (so, for example, Spanish nouns can have either masculine or feminine gender, like *el gato* or *la playa*).

Gender is embodied by more than just physical characteristics. In contemporary society, gender also represents a broad network of behaviours, attitudes, activities, prohibitions, mandates, relationships, identities, and beliefs. For example, the English language has only two options in describing someone's gender: male or female (inanimate objects have no gender). Other languages, such as Finnish, Persian, and Japanese, do not distinguish gender. And some Indigenous languages have up to 16 genders (Boroditsky 2009). Many in the transgender community propose using plural pronouns: *they* and *them* can replace gender-specific *he* and *she*, and *her* and *him*. Some propose new neutral pronouns (e.g. *ve, xe, ze*) to avoid gender binaries. Increasingly, meetings, classes, and public events open with attendees stating their gender pronouns preference.

When gendered activities are defined as either masculine or feminine, this restricted classification of gender into feminine or masculine qualities or behaviours is prone to damaging stereotypes and constructs an unnatural binary. Not only is the vocabulary of gender impoverished, but cultural imagination around gender is constrained. At the same time that it is limited, it is also immensely powerful. Not everyone may agree on every single quality that constitutes masculinity or femininity, but when people break the rules of gender it is clear exactly what those qualities are. Though the extent to which gender stereotypes reflect actual gender comparisons between men and women is debatable, gender-associated processes are often so deeply engrained and subtle that most people not even realize how strongly they affect behaviour, thoughts, feelings, language, desires, and interpersonal interactions, and the structure of social interactions (Denmark, Rabinowitz, and Sechzer 2005).

When behaviour or gender expression by an individual differs from existing cultural masculine and feminine gender norms, it is gender variable or gender non-conformist. While **gender non-conformity** may be tolerated in girls more and for longer than it is for boys—girls can be tomboys until puberty, whereas boys beyond toddlerhood who express stereotypically feminine characteristics are often harshly reined in—there is no doubt which qualities "belong" to boys or girls, and which are inappropriate for gender conformity.

As long as there have been rules about gender, however, people have been breaking those rules. Some cultures make room for gender non-conformity by creating specific social roles for people who step outside the binary or want to occupy a role that is not prescribed for their gender. Other cultures try to relegate gender bending to the sphere of performance: drag queens and androgynous pop stars, for example. But in every society people push against the strictures of gender assignment.

Sex versus Gender

Until the late twentieth century, differences between women and men were defined through the word *sex*. Women were called "the fairer sex"; in English-speaking countries in the nineteenth century, women were referred to simply as "the sex" (again reinforcing the idea that women are a sex, and men are just people). However, as feminists have pointed out for centuries, the differences between women and men are created at least as much by social and cultural norms as they are by biology.

Gender entered the cultural vocabulary in several ways. Psychologist John Money adopted the word *gender* to describe societal notions of masculinity and femininity. His practice and research identified people whose bodies were not wholly male or female and he ascribed the term **intersex** to them. Money and Ehrhardt (1972) argue that gender was imprinted on the brain at a very young age, and so intersex children, especially those who had undergone medical reassignment surgery to "correct" their ambiguous genitalia, had to be intensely schooled in their assigned gender. These scholars did not challenge how gender was arranged or why certain behaviours and feelings were appropriate to men or women; their principal concern was that children be provided with the "right" gender messages. This biomedical approach did not take into account individuals' own feelings and identity. Since Money's time, intersex has been defined as a socially constructed category that reflects real biological variation (Intersex Society of North America, n.d.).

In the 1960s, psychoanalyst Robert Stoller coined the phrase *gender identity* to mean a person's awareness of being male or female. Unlike John Money, Stoller did not see a necessary relationship between an internal gender identity and conformity to social expectations of that role (Germon 2009, 66). At the same time, Stoller had

Box 4.1 Key Issues

Intersex

Intersex is a general term used for a variety of conditions in which a person is born with a reproductive or sexual anatomy that doesn't seem to fit the typical definitions of female or male. For example, a person might be born appearing to be female on the outside, but having mostly male-typical anatomy on the inside. Or a person may be born with genitals that seem to be in-between the usual male and female types. . . . Or a person may be born with mosaic genetics, so that some of her cells have XX chromosomes and some of them have XY.

Though we speak of intersex as an inborn condition, intersex anatomy doesn't always show up at birth. Sometimes a person isn't found to have intersex anatomy until she or he reaches the age of puberty, or finds himself an infertile adult, or dies of old age and is autopsied. Some people live and die with intersex anatomy without anyone (including themselves) ever knowing.

Which variations of sexual anatomy count as intersex? In practice, different people have different answers to that question. That is not surprising, because intersex is not a discrete or natural category.

Source: Intersex Society of North America (n.d.).

---

a clear and uncomplicated sense of what constituted appropriate behaviours and activities for girls and boys and women and men.

With the emergence of second-wave feminism in North America, the concept of gender came under intense scrutiny. In 1975, Gayle Rubin offered a new way of thinking about these differences: a mechanism she called the "sex/gender system," which she defined as "the set of arrangements by which a society transforms biological sexuality into products of human activity, and in which these transformed sexual needs are satisfied" (Rubin 1975, 159). Through the sex/gender system, biological women are turned into commodities that can be traded by men through kinship transactions. (Vestiges of this persist today in the Global North, in which fathers hand over their daughters to husbands-to-be in many wedding ceremonies, and women exchange their fathers' last names for their husbands'.)

During this time, the belief was adopted that the social construction of gender was separate from the biological material of sex; many feminists took on the project of reducing gendered difference as much as possible and embraced androgyny. The Gay Liberation movement was at the forefront of these efforts: some politically engaged gay men grew their hair and rejected the confines of masculinity in their actions, dress, and relationships, while some lesbians cut their hair short and strove against conventional notions of femininity (Jay and Young 1992). The influence of transgender activists during the early years of Gay Liberation also challenged assumptions within the movement about any inevitable connections between biology and gender.

Gender Expression

Over the past two decades, feminists have developed a nuanced and sophisticated vocabulary about gender, especially in reference to questions of gender expression. **Gender expression** refers to how a person enacts gender, regardless of their biological sex: rather than talking about men and women, or male and female, gender expression discourse deals with ideas of masculinity and femininity and complicates notions of a gender binary.

This focus on the expression of gender comes in part from the work of transgender theorists, although it also has roots in early Gay Liberation and feminist and lesbian writers such as Joan Nestle. Just as Gayle Rubin differentiated sex (biology) from gender (culture), theories of gender expression separate gender (behaviour, appearance, identification) from **sexuality** (desire and partner-choice). Heternormativity, the assumption that heterosexual desire is the most natural and inevitable kind of sexuality, assumes not just that men desire women and vice versa, but that masculine people desire feminine people or, at the very least, that masculine women must be lesbians and feminine men must be gay. Theories of gender expression challenge these assumptions.

Gendered identities and expressions take different shapes around the world. Sometimes they fulfill formal social roles like the *hijras* of South Asia. Hijras are born with male bodies but take on feminine identities in dress and social status; while they are often marginalized and impoverished, hijras are also a crucial part of life-cycle ceremonies like weddings and baby blessings (Nanda 1986). In Thailand, *Toms* are masculine women who, while they identify and are seen as women, have strongly masculine gender expression and partner with feminine women (Sinnott 2004). In the Global North, the identities *butch* and *femme* have long had currency in lesbian (and some gay male) communities for masculine and feminine gender expression.

Before European colonization, many North American Indigenous people integrated the idea of a third gender into their social arrangements. These "two-spirit" people (so-called because they were thought to contain both male and female spirits) often had specific roles, such as healers, matchmakers, craftspeople, and communicators of traditional songs and wisdom (Jacobs, Thomas, and Lang 1997). Two-spirits become so by vision, with advisement from parents and elders, not solely through an individual decision based on anatomical ambiguity.

It is rare to see authentic representations of gender non-conformity in popular culture, although this is slowly changing. Canadian poet Coyote uses gender-neutral pronouns, and their work includes the 2012 collaboration with Rae Spoon, *Gender Failure*, a touring multimedia show in which they performed music and spoken-word pieces about their failed attempts at fitting into the gender binary.

While a number of movies portray men taking on female identities, they are usually comedies that work to reinforce assumptions of gender difference by showing the impossibility of actually giving up one's own gendered identity. A spate of these films in the 1980s and early 1990s—*Tootsie* (1982), *Mr. Mom* (1983), *Mrs. Doubtfire* (1993)—played with gender reversal mostly to show that men could take on and excel in realms previously assigned to women and that women ultimately could never compete with men's superiority.

Traditional Explanations for Gender Differences

Anatomical and Evolutionary Differences

The oldest explanations for the differences between women and men look to women's and men's different anatomies as the source. In the second chapter of the book of Genesis in the Judeo-Christian bible, God creates the first woman from

An elderly hijra with a younger member of their community. hijras are born as male but identify as female in their dress, behaviour, and roles. While often marginalized in their societies and discriminated against, they play important roles in life-cycle ceremonies such as weddings and the birth of a male child.

a rib of the first man. Other creation myths, of peoples ranging from the Yoruba in what is now Nigeria, to the Menominee in northern Wisconsin, to the inhabitants of ancient Egypt, represent their gods as male and female, taking gender differences for granted in both divine and human life (see, for example, Hoffman 1890; Anderson/Sankofa 1991; and Ions 1991).

In the European tradition, anatomical explanations for gender difference were popularized by the ancient Greek philosopher Aristotle (384–322 BCE). Aristotle held two interrelated beliefs about gender: first, that women were defective versions of men; and second, that women's and men's innate characteristics complemented each other. He argued that in both animals and humans, females were not just generally smaller and less muscular, but they were more easily trained and controlled, more emotional, more nurturing, and less brave. Men, on the other hand, were naturally stronger and more impulsive, protective, and controlling.

According to Aristotle, men's bodies were hot, and their blood was thin and clear, which made them more noble and valiant. Women's bodies were cool and their blood was viscous, which made them less intelligent and less courageous. However, since men's heat could lead them into excessive acts of impulse and violence, and women's cool blood could render them passive and overprotective of children, the two sexes could complement and regulate each other. This complementarity could never raise women to equality with men, though; for Aristotle, women were mutilated, impotent men, whose biology relegated them to inferior status (Matthews 1986).

Aristotle's theories were powerfully influential on European thought for centuries. The second-century Greco-Roman physician Galen (c. 130–200 CE) reinterpreted the complementary theory of gender to mean that women's reproductive organs were men's organs turned inside out (so the testicles became the ovaries, the penis became the vagina, and so on). According to Galen, women did not have sufficient heat in their bodies to push these organs outside, and instead provided a cool, protected space first for semen and then for fetuses. These essential, biological differences between women and men's reproductive systems created a whole analysis of sexual difference more generally that lasted in Europe and its colonies until the late eighteenth century, so that whenever women challenged male dominance, their "anatomical inversion" and "cooler system" were used as irrefutable arguments for women's subordination (Gallagher and Laqueur 1987).

Ideas about women's and men's bodies changed in the nineteenth century, shifting from the belief that women were inside-out men to the assumption that women and men were essentially different both biologically and psychologically. Women's bodies were reimagined not as deficient male bodies, but as wholly different and physically fragile. Routine parts of women's biological life cycles such as menstruation, pregnancy, childbirth, and menopause were redefined by doctors as dangerous and draining for women. This fragility also generated moral and psychological purity: women's delicacy meant that they could devote themselves to the nurturing of their children and husbands. Out of this rose what historian Barbara Welter has called the "Cult of True Womanhood," in which North American women were expected to embody the qualities of "piety, purity, submissiveness, and domesticity" (Welter 1966, 152). Women who strayed from these values were deemed unnatural and depraved, doomed to a bad end or to a life of poverty and shame. Achieving these standards, which was challenging for white middle-class women, was impossible for working-class, Indigenous, and enslaved women. Since their survival depended on their ability to perform physical labour, they could not embody the delicate, leisured "True Woman." As a result, working women were constructed as the opposite of the middle-class white woman: sexually uncontrolled, coarse, and undeserving of respect from men of all classes.

While the Cult of True Womanhood was most powerful during the middle of the nineteenth century, the belief that women were ruled by their bodies retained its explanatory power.

Opponents to women's education argued that women were too feeble for the rigours of higher education; in 1873, the US physician Edward Clarke (1820–1877) published *Sex and Education; Or a Fair Chance for the Girls*, which claimed that women who engaged in sustained vigorous mental activity, studying in a "boy's way," risked atrophy of the uterus and ovaries, masculinization, sterility, insanity, even death (Palmieri 1987). Women of colour and working-class, Indigenous, and immigrant women were defined not just by sex, but also by race, class, and national origin—by **eugenics**, the scientific racism of the era that insisted that all people outside the dominant class of white, middle- and upper-class men were biologically and intellectually inferior.

After the horrors of World War II, which were motivated in large part by the extreme Nazi belief based on eugenics that some populations (such as Jews, Roma and Sinti, Slavs, the aged, and people with disabilities) were biologically inferior, anatomical and biological arguments for social subordination lost their appeal. However, more recently, evolutionary psychology, a new form of socio-biology, has gained popularity as an approach to explaining gender differences. Socio-biology was first formulated by E.O. Wilson (1975), who argues that psychological traits are selected in a population because they are adaptive and help maintain that population.

As socio-biologist Richard Dawkins explains, male and female gender behaviour is motivated by "selfish genes." That is, males and females can be thought of as trying to exploit the other, trying to force the individual of the other sex to invest more in their offspring in order to optimize the chances that their own genes will be passed down to future generations (Dawkins 1976, 150). To increase this "genetic fitness," males need to impregnate as many females as possible. Males, according to evolutionary psychologists, are thus genetically programmed for behaviours and psychological traits such as hypersexuality and philandering that will ensure this result. According to this theory, these traits propel them to have frequent sex with multiple partners.

Females, however, in this hypothetical scenario, must be chaste to increase the chances of passing on the male's genes. Once she does become pregnant and gives birth, a female increases the chances of her initial investment paying off by investing even more time and energy in the rearing of her child. To relieve some of this burden, a woman encourages a man to help her care for her dependent child. It is in the female's interest to find a man who is willing to remain after the birth of a child and help her with child-care responsibilities rather than a man who wants sex without commitment.

Evolutionary psychologists discount cultural variation in personality traits and behaviours, even though evidence for this variation has been available for decades. For example, Margaret Mead (1901–1978), an anthropologist and pioneer in research on the cultural and social context of personality development, studied men and women in a number of societies around the world in the early part of the twentieth century. She began with the question: Do universals of personality development exist? She empirically tested propositions about universals by comparing people in different cultural settings. Comparing men and women in several South Pacific societies with those in her own society, the United States, Mead discovered that what many people think of as feminine and masculine traits are culturally produced, not inherent biological differences (Mead 1949) (see Box 4.2).

Psychoanalytic Theory

Traditional psychoanalytic theory was founded by Viennese neurologist Sigmund Freud (1856–1939). Freud became intrigued by the number of patients he saw, especially women, whose symptoms appeared to be the result of sexual conflicts and repressions. Based on case studies of these patients, Freud developed a theory of personality development called "psychosexual development," which explained what he saw as fundamental characteristics of the female personality: dependence, passivity, masochism, and an inferior sense of justice.

Box 4.2 In Her Own Words

Margaret Mead on Sex and Temperament

We have now considered in detail the approved personalities of each sex among three primitive peoples. We found the Arapesh—both men and women—displaying a personality that, out of our historically limited preoccupation, we would call maternal in its parental aspects, and feminine in its sexual aspects. We found men, as well as women, trained to be co-operative, unaggressive, responsive to the needs and demands of others. We found no idea that sex was a powerful driving force either for men or for women. In marked contrast to these attitudes, we found among the Mundugumor that both men and women developed as ruthless, aggressive, positively sexed individuals, with the maternal cherishing aspects of personality at a minimum. Both men and women approximated to a personality type that we in our culture would find only in an undisciplined and very violent male. Neither the Arapesh nor the Mundugumor profit by a contrast between the sexes. . . . In the third tribe, the Tchambuli, we found a genuine reversal of the sex-attitudes of our own culture with the woman the dominant, impersonal, managing partner, the man the less responsible and the emotionally dependent person. These three situations suggest, then, a very definite conclusion. If those temperamental attitudes which we have traditionally regarded as feminine—such as passivity, responsiveness, and a willingness to cherish children—can so easily be set up as the masculine pattern in one tribe, and in another be outlawed for the majority of women as well as for the majority of men, we no longer have any bias for regarding such aspects of behavior as sex-linked. And this conclusion becomes even stronger when we consider the actual reversal in Tchambuli of the position of dominance of the two sexes . . .

. . . Only to the impact of the whole of the integrated culture upon the growing child can we lay the formation of the contrasting types. There is no other explanation. . . . We are forced to conclude that human nature is almost unbelievably malleable, responding accurately and contrastingly to contrasting cultural conditions. The differences between individuals who are members of different cultures, like the differences between individuals within a culture, are almost entirely to be laid to differences in conditioning, especially during early childhood, and the form of this conditioning is culturally determined. Standardized personality differences between the sexes are of this order, cultural creations to which each generation, male and female, is trained to conform.

Source: Excerpt from pp. 261–2 from *Sex and Temperament in Three Primitive Societies* by Margaret Mead. Copyright © 1935, 1950, 1963 by Margaret Mead. Reprinted by permission of HarperCollins Publishers.

For Freud, sexual drives underlie all personality development and arise from a fundamental difference in anatomy that differentiates males from females: the presence or absence of a penis. Thus, for Freud "anatomy is destiny" (Freud 1925).

Freudian theory stipulates that the significant turning point in the formation of gender identity occurs at about the age of three. Before this time, sensual pleasure is centred first on oral, then on anal, gratification. During the subsequent genital stage, the sexual organs become the source of pleasure. It is then that girls notice that boys and men have penises. According to Freud, this recognition leads girls to develop a sense of inferiority and the desire for a penis, a wish he called "penis envy." Women's supposed tendency to be masochistic was thought to arise from their self-loathing due to this lack. At the same time, boys notice that girls and women do not have penises, and this leads boys to suspect that girls' penises were somehow denied or taken away by the main source of power, the father. Freud concluded that this produces anxiety in boys that their own fathers will take away their penises. Freud called this "castration anxiety." He argued that girls blame their "inferior anatomy" on the mother. Girls then turn affections toward the father, hoping to get the desired object (a penis) or a substitute (a baby) from him. Girls later learn that the father cannot provide either and must replace him with another man to provide gratification. Boys, on the other hand, possess a desire to have sex with their mothers and replace their fathers but fear that their fathers will retaliate for this desire by castrating them (Freud called this the Oedipal conflict, based on the classical Greek story of Oedipus, who unwittingly murdered his father and married his mother). A resolution of this conflict is generally achieved by relinquishing the mother as love object while identifying with the father. This identification with the father removes a boy from the realm of competitor, thus reducing castration fears. As a result of this identification, the boy develops a male identity and internalizes dominant moral standards. By contrast, girls must identify with their mothers, a mixed result, since the mother clearly cannot supply a girl with her desired object, a penis. Girls' own moral standards are weaker and less developed than those of boys because they evolve not in response to castration fears but, rather, to counteract the shame of having been castrated. Because internalization of moral standards is essential to maturity, girls are seen as having more difficulty maturing than boys. So, according to this theory, gender identity and the foundation of all later personality development is established in the first six years of life and indirectly derived from anatomy.

Neurobiological and Hormonal Explanations

Under pressure from feminist critics (discussed below) and an increased focus on chemical and hormonal influences on personality and behaviour, psychoanalytic and anatomical rationales for gender differences have lost their explanatory power in the past few decades. That is not to say that theories about the innate differences have disappeared: far from it. But they have been supplanted in large part by arguments grounded in neurobiology and endocrinology. Numerous scientists who study the brain and hormones have offered arguments for essential differences between women and men that look to brain chemistry, during both gestation and everyday life, to support their claims.

The central thread to neurobiological arguments for the brain as the source of gender identity is that humans are "hard-wired" for gender differences by exposure to various hormones in the uterus. Sex differences exist not just in reproductive organs but also in brains, a result of hormones that make men and women desire each other and want gender-specific things. Neuroscientists claim that prenatal hormones "organize" the human brain, imprinting it with preferences and behaviours that align with anatomical sex (Jordan-Young 2010). Psychologist Simon Baron-Cohen pointed to prenatal testosterone as the reason that men are "systemizers," good at mathematical and scientific pursuits, which require systematic thinking, whereas prenatal estrogen causes women to be "empathizers," who rely more on intuition and emotion than scientific method (Baron-Cohen 2003). Some scientists see their research on brain organization as having direct policy implications: Richard Udry argues that since "males and females have different and biologically influenced behavioral dispositions . . . if we depart too far from the underlying sex-dimorphism of biological predispositions, they will generate social malaise" (Udry 2000, 454). But Stephen Jay Gould, evolutionary biologist and paleontologist, countered biologically based arguments with his view that scientists themselves have their own inherent bias that influence how they analyze research findings. In the chapter "Women's Brains" in *The Panda's Thumb* (1980), he states, "One may affirm the validity of biological distinctions but argue that the data have been misinterpreted by prejudiced men with a stake in the outcome, and that disadvantaged groups are truly superior" (158). Gould concludes, "I would rather label the whole enterprise of setting a biological value upon groups for what it is: irrelevant and highly injurious" (159).

The belief in a "gendered brain" has extended to speculations about hormonal and neurochemical sources for sexuality and transgender identification. In the middle of the twentieth century, the idea that gay men and lesbians had an excess of the "wrong" hormone led to experiments in which men were injected with testosterone to lead them toward the "correct" sexual orientation. Although these efforts failed, neuroscientists continued to look to the brain as the cause of gender and sexual non-conformity. The most prominent study was by Simon LeVay in 1991, who analyzed the different sizes of the hypothalamus (a gland that in part controls sexual activity and desire) in gay and straight men. One shortcoming of this work is that just as it assumes a normative gender arrangement of two "opposite" sexes—men and women—neurological research into sexual desire takes for granted that there are just two kinds of sexual orientation—gay and straight. The research is grounded in the belief that male and female, gay and straight, transgender and **cisgender** constitute distinct, opposite groups that remain stable across geography and history and over the course of a person's life, something that many people's experiences contradict (Jordan-Young 2010).

However, as molecular biologist Anne Fausto-Sterling has detailed in her book *Sexing the Body* (2000), this research is not as straightforward as one might suppose. For example, "the corpus callosum is a structure that is difficult to separate from the rest of the brain, and so complex in its irregular three dimensions as to be unmeasurable" (Fausto-Sterling 2000, 120–1).

Again, the problem lies with the biases scientists bring to their studies of hormones and gender. Fausto-Sterling (2000) shows that the history of hormone research has been no less burdened with unproven assumptions and misinterpretations than the history of brain research, which she has also studied. She painstakingly shows how endocrinologists' choices about what to name a particular hormone, how to measure it, and how to interpret its effects have been so greatly influenced by cultural ideas about gender as to render questionable the assumption that "sex hormones" exist.

In fact, the primary role of hormones in the bodies of both women and men is not to control behaviour but to work at the cellular level to govern cell growth, cell differentiation, cell physiology, and cell death. Hormones may be present in different quantities in males and females and might affect the same tissues differently, but all hormones operate throughout the bodies of both women and men. There is, in other words, no hormone specific to either men or women. Despite this, scientists have labelled some of these chemical secretions "male" hormones (*androgen*, meaning "to create a man") and others "female" hormones (*estrogen*, meaning "to create estrus," which itself means "crazy," "wild," or "insane" and which also refers in animals to the period when females are "in heat"), thus gendering them and infusing them with cultural assumptions about women and men. The results of research on the activities of these substances in the bodies of women and men have been similarly affected by pre-existing gendered assumptions, leading Fausto-Sterling and other biologists to call for abandoning the organizing metaphor of the sex hormone in endocrinology studies altogether.

Needless to say, the actual science is much more complicated than this. First, both women and men have a variety of "sex hormones" in their bodies, and even the archetypal hormones—testosterone and estrogen—exist in proportionally low quantities compared to amounts found in other mammals. Moreover, testosterone and estrogen are chemically very similar to each other and have a number of different functions beyond controlling secondary sex characteristics like breast development, body hair, menstruation, and testicular development (Jordan-Young 2010).

Theories of prenatal hormonal formation cannot explain how sexual desire changes over time or even how people may feel differently about their gender at different moments in their lives.

And of course, gendered behaviour is strongly linked to cultural and historical context: while in twenty-first-century Canada men dressing in women's clothes are sometimes identified with homosexuality or femininity, in seventeenth-century England that same behaviour was regarded as hypermasculine, since only a man who powerfully desired women would want to dress like them.

Feminist Critiques of Theories of Gender

Feminist Psychoanalysis

Some psychoanalysts have pointed out the lack of empirical evidence for Freud's theories, noting that findings from both direct-observational studies of children and clinical reports lend little support to Freud's formulation of female psychosexual development. Fliegel (1980), for example, rebukes those analysts who rigidly adhere to this dynamic in the face of contradictory information and notes

Box 4.3 Time to Reflect

Doing Gender: An Early Theoretical Perspective

When we view gender as an accomplishment, an achieved property of situated conduct, our attention shifts from matters internal to the individual and focuses on interactional and, ultimately, institutional arenas. In one sense, of course, it is individuals who "do" gender. But it is a situated doing, carried out in the virtual or real presence of others who are presumed to be oriented to its production. Rather than as a property of individuals, we conceive of gender as an emergent feature of social situations: both as an outcome of and a rationale for various social arrangements and as a means of legitimating one of the most fundamental divisions of society . . .

To elaborate our proposal, we suggest at the outset that important but often overlooked distinctions be observed among sex, sex category, and gender. Sex is a determination made through the application of socially agreed upon biological criteria for classifying persons as females or males. . . . Placement in a sex category is achieved through application of the sex criteria, but in everyday life, categorization is established and sustained by the socially required identificatory displays that proclaim one's membership in one or the other category. In this sense, one's sex category presumes one's sex and stands as proxy for it in many situations, but sex and sex category can vary independently; that is, it is possible to claim membership in a sex category even when the sex criteria are lacking. Gender, in contrast, is the activity of managing situated conduct in light of normative conceptions of attitudes and activities appropriate for one's sex category. Gender activities emerge from and bolster claims to membership in a sex category.

. . . Doing gender also renders the social arrangements based on sex category accountable as normal and natural, that is, legitimate ways of organizing social life. Differences between men and women that are created by this process can then be portrayed as fundamental and enduring dispositions. . . . Thus if, in doing gender, men are also doing dominance and women are doing deference . . . the resultant social order, which supposedly reflects "natural differences," is a powerful reinforcer and legitimator of hierarchical arrangements.

Source: *Gender & Society* by Sociologists for Women in Society. Reproduced with permission of SAGE Publications Ltd. in the format Book via Copyright Clearance Centre.

that a belief in penis envy has "almost become a test of doctrinaire loyalty." Freud's findings were based on universalist assumptions that the Viennese patients he studied were the same as people everywhere without taking into consideration difference in culture and context. However, this has not caused all feminists to reject Freud entirely.

A number of feminists have drawn on some aspects of Freudian theory while questioning others. Many reject the **androcentric**, male-focused, Freudian premise that "anatomy is destiny" but share with traditional psychoanalytical models the belief that individuals form a core gender identity based on early childhood experiences. They argue that psychological development must be understood within the cultural context within which girls and boys develop.

The Importance of Culture

Karen Horney (1885–1952) and Clara Thompson (1893–1958) were among the first women psychoanalysts to diverge from the classical Freudian theory of female psychology and to elaborate on the cultural constraints that contribute to the formation of the feminine personality. Horney suggested that psychological traits, such as women's dependence on men and female masochism, were products of male social dominance, not anatomical difference. Horney argued that the fact that women with little power of their own gained status through fathers and husbands explained why they may seem to be more afraid of losing love than men are. Similarly, she saw masochism as an attempt on the part of women to achieve personal safety and satisfaction by appearing inconspicuous and dependent, not as a reaction to the recognition of the lack of a penis.

Horney (1973 [1922]) also suggests that anatomical envy could work in both directions, since men lack women's ability to bear children. She argues that men's envy of women's reproductive capacities is at the root of misogyny and male oppression of females; in fact, research suggests that males in many societies experience feelings of breast and womb envy (Mead 1949; Zalk 1980, 1987).

Thompson challenged the classic assumption that discovery of the penis invariably causes psychic trauma for a girl, arguing that what appeared to be penis envy was actually women's awareness of their lower status and fewer privileges within the family, which has historically been the case in many Western societies (Thompson 1942, 1943). Rather than attribute the adolescent female's renunciation of the "active" role in life to the resolution of penis envy, Thompson attributed it to external social pressures. In his collection of short stories *Tales of Nevèrÿon* (1993), Samuel R. Delany parodies theories of penis envy and points out the social construction of the centrality of the penis in male-dominated cultures by inventing a societal hierarchy organized around the "rult," a wooden carving that boys and men wear around their stomachs. Like the penis, the rult is seen as powerful but rarely referred to by its actual name; it is the domain of men only and explicitly excludes women and girls. In the story, a father comes up with a theory of "rult envy" that exactly mimics Freud's idea of penis envy. In this culture, in which people are naked most of the time, genitals have no symbolic power. But as the dominant class, men have created the rult as a sign of their importance.

The Importance of Relatedness

Attempts by feminists to understand gendered psychological development within a psychoanalytical or psychodynamic framework have led many theorists to explore the mother–daughter relationship and the differential impact on girls and boys of being raised by a female caretaker. These writers focus not on genitals but on the impact on early identity formation of having a same-sex or an other-sex caretaker. The fact that the female child is cared for and raised primarily by a parent or a parent-surrogate of the same sex may engender feelings and conflicts that differ from those elicited in the mother–son relationship (Denmark 1977).

In the 1980s and beyond, a number of psychoanalytical feminists looked beyond anatomy to understand those aspects of the female psyche often overlooked in mainstream psychological theory and studies: women's pleasures, desires, and fantasies. These theorists have tended to draw on the work of French psychoanalyst Jacques Lacan (1901–1981), who reinterpreted aspects of Freud's theory, focusing specifically on how a child comes to be either one sex or the other. Lacan's conceptualization of this process centres on how a child becomes a "subject," or an "I" (like the subject of a sentence). In other words, Lacan asks how children come to have a conscious understanding of themselves as distinct from the mother, possessing their own identity, and suggests that it is through entry into the symbolic realm of culture, through the acquisition of language. This entry, based on the recognition of oneself as distinct, however, splits the child from its mother, producing a sense of loss and a constant desire for this unattainable lost object (see Wright 2000). To disavow this lack and to make up for the lost object, the male projects fantasies onto the female: she becomes the desired *object*. However, this has different consequences for women because of their differing relationship to language.

Unlike Freud, who saw male and female genital anatomy as the basis of sexual identity and sex difference, Lacan sees no predetermined nature to sex difference; instead, sex difference is a "construction in culture." For him, it is not the penis (the biological organ) or lack of one associated with one's actual father that is significant in the development of gender identity but the "phallus," the cultural sign or symbol of the father, a metaphor for society's rules and laws and their imposition. The symbolic order, according to Lacan, is organized around the phallus, meaning that in language the male is taken as the norm (e.g. the word *man* subsumes both men and women) and the female is defined as "lack of maleness." Since coming into language produces subjectivity, however, there is no subject position in language for the female; the female subject is constituted as an exclusion. Constituted by lack and defined by men as an object onto which their fantasies are projected, "woman" does not exist.

Rethinking Biology

Evolutionary biologists have found several weaknesses in traditional evolutionary explanations for gender differences. Perhaps the most important is the role of environment in the broadest sense: not just the physical environment of altitude, temperature, and water sources but also psychological environments of comfort, trauma, separation, and so on (Jordan-Young 2010). For a developing fetus, environment comprises not only prenatal hormone levels, but also the pregnant woman's nutrition levels, her sleep patterns, and her rate of activity. Organisms react to a host of environmental factors. In one study of rhesus monkeys, scientists found that females took on male-linked spatial skills in a new environment, while in another study, female rats who had never encountered rat pups before seemed not to know how to care for their own children, even though maternal behaviour is one of the key characteristics that neuroscientists identify as conditioned by hormones (Leboucher 1989; Herman and Wallen 2007).

Recent studies in brain chemistry reveal that the brain is actually fairly malleable. Studies of people with serious brain injury, for example, have shown that the brain has the capacity to adjust and adapt, to shift the function of a damaged part to an intact section. Even activities like playing the piano or doing word puzzles can affect the brain's functioning (Zuger 2007). In light of these findings, it is hard to believe that prenatal hormones have the last word about experiences and expressions of gender.

The field of **epigenetics** has arisen in the early twenty-first century to examine how the nature-versus-nurture debate not only has the wrong answers but is asking the wrong questions. Evelyn Fox Keller (2010) uses the analogy of two children filling a bucket with water. If Billy puts 40 litres of water in a bucket and

Box 4.4 Time to Reflect

"Imagine Gender as a Planet": *The Gender Book* Map

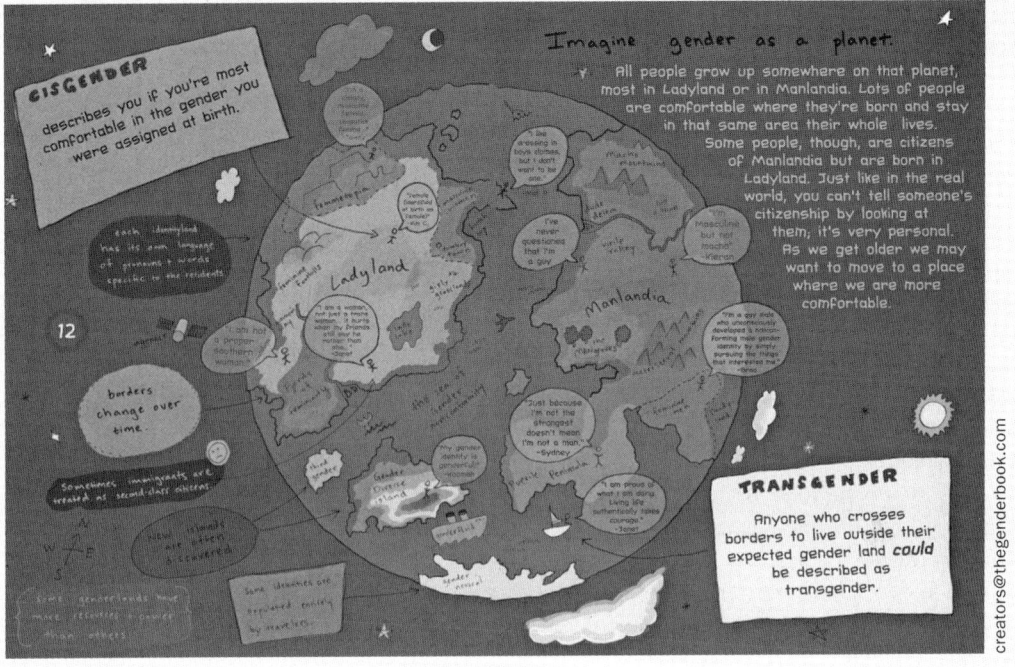

The Gender Book graphically explains the nuances of gender identity and gender expression.

Suzy puts in 60 litres, one can clearly say that 60 litres of the water in the bucket was caused by Suzy. But if Billy turns on the tap and Suzy holds the hose over the bucket, then this kind of calculation no longer makes sense. One cannot even ask how much water was put in by Billy compared to Suzy; one can only know that both children co-operated to fill the bucket. Likewise, although various genes can be identified and located inside specific people, there is rarely a direct causal relationship between a single gene and a single outcome. Just as brain chemistry interacts with experience to create new neural pathways, genes function only when they are expressed, and the conditions under which that expression happens vary widely with environment.

How Is Gender Learned?

Cognitive-Developmental Theory

One approach to thinking about how gender is learned is cognitive-developmental theory; that is, ideas about how brains develop from childhood onward. Cognitive psychologists are interested in how people organize and understand their perceptions of physical and social reality and how these perceptions change at different developmental stages. They argue that the human brain needs to make order out of what it perceives and focus on the individual's internal need to fulfill a learned gender identity in order to categorize different kinds of people coherently (Kohlberg 1966; Kohlberg and Ullian 1974). Studies in cognitive psychology suggest that at age two girls and boys begin to learn and reproduce gender categories based on experiences with representatives of each gender, although they are not initially aware of anatomical distinctions and do not conceive them to be unchangeable characteristics. These categories, or gender schemas, are structures that allow a person to organize information related to gender by linking gender labels to objects, traits, and behaviours. Children learn to categorize information based on gender at a young age and demonstrate this knowledge in their preferences for play, toys, and playmates (Denmark, Rabinowitz, and Sechzer 2005). During this period, young children might "try on" different kinds of gender expression or imitate the gendered behaviour of their primary caregiver(s). Once children have classified themselves as female or male and recognize that their gender does not change (at about age five), they are motivated to approximate to the best of their ability the social definitions of this identity. In the case of female children, the motivation to fulfill their gender identity presses them toward the ideal of femininity (as socially defined), independent of externally mediated rewards or punishments for attaining such a goal. This explanation for gender-role acquisition may account for the fact that often girls and boys will conform to stereotypic gender roles and police the gendered behaviour of other children even when their parents or other socializing agents do not differentially reinforce feminine and masculine behaviour in them (Kohlberg and Zigler 1967).

Social Learning Theory

All societies teach their young culturally prescribed gender roles. This gender socialization often begins at the moment of birth. Socialization theories focus attention on the social context of this learning of gender roles that gives rise to characteristically female and male personality traits and behaviours. They are particularly interested in the messages a child receives from others in the social environment and how these messages are conveyed. Parents and peers are powerful socializing agents, informing children that certain activities and toys are not for girls/boys, but gender expectations are communicated in many different ways. The organization and transmission of cultural prompts such as television, school, books, clothing, toys, and even fairy tales operate as socializing agents.

Social learning theory argues that conformity to gender is policed by a series of external reinforcements, either rewards or punishments. This theory holds that individuals learn female and male behaviour by observing others and the world around them. However, which behaviour they actually perform depends on whether it is rewarded or punished. Social learning theorist and experimental psychologist Albert Bandura (1965) suggests that the introduction of rewards for cross-sex behaviour will enable girls and boys to expand their behavioural repertoires with little difficulty.

One of the most powerful socializing messages in modern Western culture is that men are central to any story worth telling. This is especially true of the mainstream movie industry, which churns out one male-focused narrative after another. Recently, feminist commentators have begun to use a metric by which to identify movies that are not focused on its male characters, the "Bechdel test," named for its creator, lesbian-identified cartoonist Alison Bechdel. The test makes three requirements of a movie: that it feature (1) two or more female characters who (2) talk to each other (3) about something other than a man. While this test is not perfect, it does reveal how few Hollywood movies feature meaningful and self-sustaining relationships between women. More importantly, male-focused movies teach girls and boys that relationships between women are necessarily centred on their connections to men, rather than having value in themselves, and that women are rewarded for organizing their emotional lives around men. Similarly, the "racial Bechdel test" questions whether there are characters of colour in a film and whether they speak to each other outside of a dominant white plot. While these tests are not proof of bias, they are genuine indications of how oppressions are constructed and replicated through popular culture.

Theories of socialization have long been popular among feminist writers, especially those

Box 4.5 Women in Media

Gender-Neutral Clothing Goes Mainstream with New Department Store Campaign

Gender-neutral fashions have popped up on the runways of Paris and in the shops of Toronto in recent years, but a new shopping experience at a major London department store suggests unisex fashions may be entering mainstream consciousness.

Starting in mid-March, the flagship Selfridges store—a British chain owned by Canada's Galen Weston since 2003—will feature non-gender-specific fashion collections in a concept space spanning three floors.

"Moving away from the tradition of a societal and sartorial binary gender definition, we will take our customers on a journey where they can choose to shop and dress without limitations or stereotypes," reads Selfridges' announcement of "Agender."

One of the designers featured among the collections is Canadian Rad Hourani, whose eye-catching unisex fashions have turned heads in the world of haute couture.

Ben Barry, a fashion researcher and assistant professor at Ryerson University's school of fashion, says Selfridges' new campaign suggests they've noticed a change in how consumers see gender, amid broader cultural shifts like the social and political acceptance of the LGBTQ communities and the rise of anti-bullying campaigns . . .

Natalia Manzocco, who operates Toronto-based gender-neutral vintage store Future is the Future, says there's definitely a demand for unisex apparel. "I've received emails of support from as far away as Portland," she says.

Source: Pelley (2015). From Toronto Star, 2015-03-03, © 2015 Toronto Star Newspapers Limited. All rights reserved. Used by permission and protected by the Copyright Laws of the United States. The printing, copying, redistribution, or retransmission of this Content without express written permission is prohibited.

who are interested in imagining alternative ways of being. Feminist science fiction and fantasy writers have created new worlds in which gender is arranged very differently as a way to consider that what are imagined to be natural qualities attached to gender are actually created by social conditions. Joanna Russ's 1975 novel *The Female Man* follows the lives of four women living in parallel worlds that differ in time and place. When they cross over to each other's worlds, their different views on gender roles challenge each other's pre-existing notions of womanhood. In the end, their encounters influence them to evaluate their lives and shape their ideas of what it means to be a woman. Octavia Butler took on the intertwined systems of race and gender in her *Lilith's Brood* series of novels, which features a female human protagonist kidnapped by an alien species to sustain them through reproduction. Through these and other books, Butler examines the legacies of slavery, racism, and sexism by transporting them to unfamiliar environments.

Gender Schema Theory

Sandra Bem (1981, 1983, 1985) proposes a *gender schema* theory, which incorporates cognitive, child-rearing, and cultural factors to explain the development of gender identity and personality traits. According to this theory, people have mental categories that are a network of associations. In order to understand or make sense of information, individuals try to place it into these categories, which form a sort of blueprint in the mind. A schema is descriptive and consists of associations and assumptions. For example, schemas for

Box 4.6 Time to Reflect

Baby Storm Five Years Later: Preschooler on Top of the World

As a baby, Storm Stocker-Witterick drew attention from around the world.

Now, as a 5-year-old, she's more likely to be getting attention from her parents and siblings.

When the Star first profiled Storm and her family in 2011, they turned heads the world over. Parents Kathy Witterick and David Stocker had decided not to publicly reveal the sex of their third child.

And nearly everyone had an opinion as to why that was right or wrong.

The family endured "vitriolic" criticism, as Kathy puts it, but also gained a much stronger network of support.

The Toronto-based couple wanted to let Storm decide in her own time what gender she wanted to identify with. They didn't want anyone to assume the sex designated by doctors would match the gender their baby would identify with later.

Their eldest child Jazz, 10, explains the difference.

"Sex is what is between your legs, and gender is what you think of yourself as a person," says Jazz. All three of the Stocker-Witterick children were given a choice of gender identity.

Now 5-and-a-half years old, Storm confidently says her preferred pronoun is "she."

Storm, her two siblings and parents spoke to the Star in their first interview as a family in years.

She sports a shock of pink hair shorn in a pixie cut, her wide blue eyes constantly darting to explore the hustle and bustle in Barbara Hall Park, behind the 519 Community Centre.

On a dime, she climbs a nearby lamp post—which appears to be at least three metres tall—to get a better view.

At least six times over the course of an hour, Storm nearly reaches the lamp post's light bulb. Others milling in the park stop when they notice someone among the tree branches. Some point and say: "Oh, look at her!"

In an email in 2011, Kathy and David told their friends and family they wouldn't be announcing Storm's sex.

"A tribute to freedom and choice in place of limitation, a stand up to what the world could become in Storm's lifetime (a more progressive place? ...)," the email read.

When the Star first covered their decision, public outcry was fast and furious. People delivered angry letters to the family's door. Drivers slowed to shout "Boy!" from their windows at Storm, as the family was en route to the pool or the library.

Interview requests poured in from around the world—from NBC, *National Geographic*, *60 Minutes Australia*, Anderson Cooper, Dr. Phil and the Oprah Winfrey Network.

After the flood of attention, Kathy and David are still confident in their parenting choices. Along with the harsh words sent their way came hordes of supportive ones.

They've found camaraderie among a like-minded community at the 519, where Kathy works in education and training and supports queer and transgender family programs. David still teaches Grades 7 and 8 at the City View Alternative Senior School during the year.

"The people who were angry moved away from us, and the people who were affirming moved closer to us," Kathy says.

"So both sides of the response were helpful to us overall, although at the time, of course, it was hard..." they trail off.

Kathy and David haven't strayed from their democratic parenting style and their openness to discussing gender and its fluidity. They taught their kids about gender and its many nuances with help from a map in *The Gender Book*.

The map locates gender identities—from male and female, to transgender, non-binary and beyond—in a global drawing. Each member of the family has a colour copy of the page where they map their own gender journey.

The couple continues to unschool their kids, a version of homeschooling where the young ones direct lessons based on what they hope to learn.

All three of the Stocker-Witterick children let it be known which pronoun they prefer.

Jazz prefers the pronouns "she" and "her." She identifies as a transgender girl, having begun her transition three days before she turned 7. Her birthday is Dec. 27, and she announced the change right around Christmas, after spending a year grappling with the decision on her own.

Kio, 7, identifies as non-binary and uses the pronoun "they." Kathy also opts for "they," while David uses "he or they."

In the five years since the family's story became public, mainstream recognition of gender diversity has come a long way.

In 2012, the Ontario government passed Bill 33, also known as Toby's Law, to update the human rights code to include protection against discrimination for gender identity and gender expression.

continued

In May, Bill C-16—federal legislation similar to Toby's Law—got a second reading in the House of Commons.

These days, the Stocker-Witterick family's gender diversity is more understood, they say, but other components of their life still draw ire.

"The core issues of democratic parenting and how much we fail to share power with young people (in society) I think are still really entrenched and draw fire," David says.

In the Stocker-Witterick home, everyone has a say and family decisions can come down to a vote.

That was the case last year when the family debated enrolling the children in public school three days a week.

They filled out the paperwork, which was a "valuable experience," Kathy says.

"We wanted to be able to present documentation where the sex designation assigned at birth was blotted out by stickers," they say. And the school, which is part of Toronto's Public School Board, tried to be accommodating.

"They wanted to be an affirming space and a safe space. They're really trying to work within the system they've been put in, but the system doesn't work in a very inclusive way," Kathy says.

Last August, the family congregated around the dining table, after the kids had drawn up a long list of the pros and cons for going to school.

The age segregation between grades and the sex separation between washrooms were some of the cons they considered. A pro and a con? Spending time away from their siblings.

Ultimately the family voted against going to public school, preferring to stay home and unschool for at least one more year.

Some of their favourite things to do at home are math problems and sports (Jazz), reading and Sudoku puzzles (Kio) and playing with stuffed animals (Storm). (She likes naming the toys after her favourite types of candy and flowers.)

The whole family loves going on adventures together, from navigating forests to rafting down the Grand River, as they did earlier this month.

The only drawback to river rafting was it rubbed off nearly all the kids' temporary tattoos they got at Pride.

The water didn't wash away their bright hair colours, however, which were dyed just in time for Pride. David, Jazz and Storm rock sections of pink strands, while Kio has a blue-ish pink combo. Kathy keeps their hair its natural red, shaved to a near buzz cut on one side.

The Stocker-Witterick family's story isn't "radically different" than it was in 2011, Kathy says. But the social environment has changed.

Jazz says she considers her family different and that same quality is one she values most in herself.

"I like being different from everybody else. It's just awesome being trans. I'm really good at a lot of stuff, like sports," she says.

Storm hesitates to answer when asked what she likes best about herself.

Instead, she climbs the lamp post again and grins, calling out: "Kathy, look at me!"

Storm is on top of the world.

Source: Botelho-Urbanski (2016). From Toronto Star, 2016-07-01 © 2016 Toronto Star Newspapers Limited. All rights reserved. Used by permission and protected by the Copyright Laws of the United States. The printing, copying, redistribution, or retransmission of this Content without express written permission is prohibited.

"teacher" and "student" include the descriptors "one who teaches" and "one who learns," respectively, as well as myriad associations about authority, judgment, power, expertise, interdependence, and more.

One of the most culturally salient categories in which people are grouped is gender, with the development of a gender schema beginning early in childhood. Children learn quickly to categorize people by gender and develop a gender schema that incorporates cultural gender roles, norms, attributes, and definitions of *feminine* and *masculine*. Bem proposes that gender schemas become part of an individual's self-concept.

As children learn the contents of the society's gender schema, they learn which attributes are to be linked with their own gender and, hence, with themselves. This does not simply entail learning where each is supposed to stand on each dimension or attribute—that boys are to be strong and girls weak, for example—but involves the deeper lesson that the dimensions themselves are differentially applicable to the two (Bem 1981, 355).

Bem does not consider gender typing as inevitable; she suggests that raising children in gender-aschematic homes and school environments, in which *sex* refers only to anatomy, results in fewer gender-typed behaviours, traits, and expectations. Bem, however, continues to analyze gender as a binary,

Social Interactions and Gender Roles

The above theories attempt to explain how individuals develop gender identities and personality traits and the relationship between gender identity and gender roles. Other theories place greater emphasis on social roles; rather than view gender-typed traits and behaviours as primarily a function of internalized gender identities, they understand them as the result of how gender is assigned and maintained and the unequal distribution of power between females and males. These theories hold that gender-typed personality traits or behaviours are, at least in part, behavioural displays that are shaped by, or result from, social demands, interactions, or oppression, rather than necessarily representing internal or stable characteristics.

Alice Eagly (1987), for example, explains gender-typed traits as compliance to gender-role expectations. Her social/role theory suggests that women and men demonstrate different personality characteristics because the family and occupational roles to which they are assigned require them. Thus, women are communal because of their roles in the family as caretakers and nurturers, and men are more active in the world because of their roles in the workplace. Although roles may be changing in much of the world, women and men continue to assume different family and workplace responsibilities and roles (for example, see Ruble 1983). Women are more likely to assume the child-care and domestic work in the home, and many employed women are in service-related jobs (Levine and Neft 1997).

Candace West and Don Zimmerman (1987) present a thoughtful argument for conceiving of gender as a verb rather than a noun. In other words, they view gender as something people *do*, not as something they *are*. Other researchers have presented a model that explains the display of gender-typed traits and behaviour rather than their acquisition. They propose that the enactment of gender takes place within the context of social interactions, is highly flexible, and is context dependent (Deaux and Major 1987). In other words, gender-related traits and behaviours are an outcome of the individual's self-perception, expectations of others, and the context of ongoing social interactions.

That such behaviours are related to the characteristics of social interactions rather than to those of particular individuals is borne out by research on non-elite individuals, both male and female. Henley (1977), for example, found that when females relate to males and subordinate males relate to more dominant males, they touch less, smile more, make less frequent eye contact, and are more tentative. The effect of male dominance on women may be a direct and powerful influence on gender-related traits and behaviours in other ways as well. MacKinnon (1987), for example, suggests that women behave differently from men because they grow up and live under the constant threat of physical violence and sexual exploitation. It is understandable that women may behave in ways that minimize a challenge to male dominance and the possibility of being victimized (Zalk 1987). These theories relate to particular contexts and with particular groups in North American society. Making universalist claims, they do not account for intersectional views for non-dominant persons.

Performativity Theory

The theories discussed above identify either cognitive processes inside the body or social pressures outside the self as determinants of gendered identity and behaviour. Theories of performativity take a different approach. Largely based in the work of Judith Butler (1990 1993, 2004), performative theories of gender critique the idea of "identity" as a single or knowable thing. But if gender is not an identity—that is, a set of attributes and behaviours that belong to a certain kind of person, whether by nature or by training—what is it?

In her 1990 book *Gender Trouble*, Butler took on two basic but not quite identical issues. The first was Gayle Rubin's idea of the sex/gender system, the assumption that biological sex is the raw material that social forces shape into gender. The second was how gender—which for Butler meant everything produced by discourse under the binary, opposed pairs of signs "man" and "woman," "masculine" and "feminine," and so on—operates at all. At the foundation of her discussion is the claim that "there is no gender identity behind the expressions of gender;" that identity is performatively constituted by the very "'expressions' that are said to be its results" (Butler 1990, 25).

Butler moved the argument that gender was produced by social relations into a new arena, claiming that gender

ought not to be conceived merely as the cultural inscription of meaning on a pregiven sex . . . gender must also designate the very apparatus of production whereby the sexes themselves are established. As a result, gender is not to culture as sex is to nature; gender is the discursive/cultural means by which "sexed nature" or "a natural sex" is produced and established as "prediscursive." (Butler 1990, 7)

Bodies are not beings in and of themselves. They are understood through the constructs of binary sex: without the ideas "man" and "woman" bodies would not make sense. Butler argues that sex is a mechanism that makes otherwise incomprehensible biological material coherent as male and female bodies.

For Butler, biological sex is not only not a fact of nature; its production through discourse is coercive and prescriptive. Sex itself is "a regulatory ideal, a forcible and differential materialization of bodies" (Butler 1993, 22), not a self-evident explanation for why various bodies look certain ways. Sex makes sense of bodies through a regime of binarized difference, and any bodies that do not exactly fit into the binary are denied, rejected, surgically altered, or reassigned (Butler 2004).

In Butler's view, sex and gender are produced by and perpetuate norms of behaviour, feeling, action, and psyche. Part of this process is to repudiate everything that does not conform to this compulsory heterosexuality. At this point, then, Butler makes her most radical move, an analysis that distances her from previous feminist scholars. Rather than seeing gender as extending from sex, Butler argues that *sex* is produced by *gender*. That is, the construction of masculinity and femininity requires the belief in a naturally bifurcated structure of biological sex. In order for gender to seem inevitable, sex (that is, the ways in which are bodies are made intelligible by being assigned as male or female, never neither, never both, and never just something else) must appear self-evident. *Of course* everyone is biologically either male or female. *Of course* anatomy, sex, and gender are mapped directly onto each other. And *of course* sexuality is motivated by gendered desires.

For Butler, there is no "of course" about it. People are conscripted—press-ganged—into gender even before conscious of it. Gender is forced from birth—the words "it's a girl" are in fact a command and a threat: "be a girl; if you want to be a real person with a real identity, act out girlness." Most of the ways to "be a girl" are implicit within discourse, and others must be explicitly enforced by parents, educational institutions, magazines, and so on. And of course, the most effective way in which gender is enforced is the fact that it is made to feel natural to behave in certain ways, "as a girl."

Butler's central point is that gender performativity is neither optional nor natural. Once a child has been "girled," for example, with the words "it's a girl," she is compelled to perform girlness and (or perhaps because) she does not even recognize this compulsion. Gender is performed reiteratively through an array of "acts, gestures and desires" (the girl really *wants* to be a girl) that imply an essential gendered self. But for Butler, these "acts and gestures, articulated and enacted desires create the illusion of an interior and organizing gender core" (Butler 1990, 136, my emphasis). There is no subject underneath the gender, no universal self. Rather, the self is constructed through its strenuous performance of gender.

How Gender Is Enforced

Many people feel that their gender is the most intrinsic part of them, deeply rooted in their beings. According to Butler, though, nothing could be further from the truth. Gender is "a construction that conceals its genesis; the tacit collective agreement to perform, produce, and sustain discrete and polar genders as cultural fictions is obscured by the credibility of those productions—and the punishments that attend to not agreeing to believe in them" (Butler 1990, 140). Considering that gender is often represented as a natural outgrowth of biological sex, it is surprising how intense the penalties can be for subverting the gendered order of things.

Gender is enforced in many ways, from the subtle to the violent. From the earliest ages, children's clothes are divided into "boys" and "girls"; there are few options that are not explicitly gendered. Divergence from the norms of gender are often met with a range of responses from gentle correction to shaming and humiliation. As children learn gender, they are often eager to police gender conformity in others: non-conforming children are asked, "Are you a girl or a boy?"

Gender-non-conforming youth are among the most victimized in Canada and represent a disproportionate number of homeless young people, often because they have run away, have been thrown out by family members, or have been forced out of school by the violence of schoolmates. Some reports indicate that one in five transgender individuals need or are at risk of needing homeless shelter assistance for these reasons (Ray 2006). However, since shelters are gender segregated, transgender and gender-non-conforming people are often refused housing or are placed in a hostile environment because they are not read as "really" women or men.

Alternative Gender Arrangements

Historical Challenges to Gender

Although the gender-binary divide exists in some form in every culture, it has hardly been the only way to define how gender operates. Many cultures have names and social roles for women and men who occupy gender outside the norm. Looking back through history, numerous examples of individuals and classes of people who have challenged the gender binary can be found. The Greek myth of Hermaphroditus, Jewish legal debates in the Talmud, and early modern English legal reference books (Greenberg 2006) are a few examples.

While still using the conventional signs for male and female, many restrooms are now all-sex, allowing people of a variety of genders to use them.

In societies that have been strictly defined by the gender binary, there have been women and men who could not conform to these rules. One of the most famous examples in European history was Joan of Arc, a young woman who grew up in fifteenth-century France. Inspired by religious visions, she dressed in soldier's armour to join the French struggle against English occupation (Warner 1981). When she was captured by English troops, Joan was condemned for her cross-dressing as much as for her military efforts; church officials were outraged by her short haircut and male attire, and she was burned at the stake at the age of 19. Joan was not the only woman to see military service as a way to escape the strictures of femininity. Angolan "King" Nzinga ruled in the mid-seventeenth century and led her troops against Portuguese colonizers. Indeed, times of upheaval and social change often provide gender-non-conforming women with the ideal environment to slip out of femininity. As the documentary film *She Even Chewed Tobacco* (1983) chronicles, the westward expansion of the United States allowed many women to take on male personae and live out much freer lives than they could have as women back East.

Given the higher social status of men and masculinity in many societies, men who challenge the gender binary often suffer significant marginalization. In seventeenth-century England, men who wore women's clothing were subject to hanging. But men at the top of the social hierarchy were freer to express their gender nonconformity: for example, the Chevalier Charles D'Eon, an eighteenth-century French nobleman, wore women's clothes almost exclusively, and Edward Hyde, the governor of New York and New Jersey in the first decade of the eighteenth century, was famous for dressing in ornate women's clothes at ceremonial occasions, including his wife's funeral (Bonomi 2000).

Celebrations and performance have made space for the stretching and bending of gender boundaries, however. In all-male theatrical traditions from Greek tragedy, to the early modern British stage, to Japanese kabuki, men played female roles. Several of Shakespeare's comedies feature female characters who disguise themselves as men, which must have been quite a challenge for the young male actors in those roles, since they were men playing women playing men. The Jewish holiday of Purim is celebrated by parties, drinking, and dressing up, which often includes cross-gendered costumes, and Halloween and Mardi Gras have a strong element of drag performances for women and men.

Expectations of gendered behaviour have always been historically and politically specific. During World War II, for example, many adult men Canada were away fighting, so women were encouraged to take their places in farms, factories, and shops. The government launched propaganda campaigns to convince women that heavy industrial work, which was essential to the war effort, was not in conflict with gendered expectations and that patriotism should trump femininity. However, as soon as the men returned home from war, an equally powerful campaign was initiated to persuade women that the very same work was inappropriate for them and that their patriotic impulses should be channelled into housework and child rearing. While many women lost their jobs, the rates of women working outside the home never fell back to pre-war numbers (Field 1980).

Following World War II, gender was policed especially strictly. At the same time, lesbian and gay life flourished, and gender-non-conforming people often found a safe place in gay environments. Especially in working-class communities, butch lesbians and feminine men established footholds, women working in the building trades, in factories, as bartenders, or men in the beauty industry (D'Emilio 1983; Kennedy and Davis 1993).

Since the rise of contemporary feminism and the LGBTQ rights movement, attitudes about gender have oscillated, but a return to the rigidity of earlier years is unlikely. Although culture in the twenty-first century seems in some ways more inflexible about the gender binary, especially for children and young adults, there are many more venues for experimenting with gender expression than there were even a few decades ago.

The medicalization of bodies—the view that the human condition can be limited or reduced to a biological problem—also impacts negatively on intersex individuals, who are often subjected to profound and invasive forms of medicalization; yet for them, it largely occurs soon after birth, when they have no ability to protest. Intersex people have genitalia, chromosomes, and/or gonads in a combination that differs from the most common configuration for either boys or girls. It has been estimated that approximately 1.7 per cent of all births are intersex (Fausto-Sterling 2000, 53–4). But birth statistics do not represent the full situation since many times intersex conditions manifest during puberty and later life.

Despite the fact that nature presents society with a perfect opportunity to challenge dichotomized gender categories, physicians and parents usually insist on assigning one of two dichotomized categories to intersex infants. They may even undergo "clarifying" surgery to bring their external appearance in line with social expectations about masculinity and femininity. Genital surgery is most often conducted on infant girls who are perceived to have an overly large clitoris and on infants who have XY chromosomes and/or male gonads but whose penises are perceived as too small for sexual function. Overwhelmingly, then, the cultural assumptions and expectations that motivate such surgery revolve around heterosexual intercourse (vaginal penetration by a penis) and reproduction (Karkazais 2008).

A further motivation is to enhance what the medical establishment calls "psycho-social functioning," or one's sense of being normal. Over the last 20 years, an intersex movement has emerged, composed of individuals who protest such surgery, claiming that it is a form of genital mutilation that ruins future sexual pleasure (Lorber 2001, 228). Despite that movement, genital surgeries are still a common "solution" to the perceived problem of being intersex. Often the surgery is performed not only at the recommendation of doctors, but at the insistence of the parents, who need to "see" the evidence of unambiguous gender in the genitals of their infant child so as to be able to convincingly socialize it accordingly.

Gender outside the Binary

Transgender performer and activist Kate Bornstein has written of her own experiences with gender, "I know I'm not a man—about that much I'm very clear—and I've come to the conclusion that I'm probably not a woman either, at least not according to a lot of people's rules on this sort of thing. The trouble is, we're living in a world that insists we be one thing or the other" (Bornstein 1994, 8). Bornstein uses the metaphor of a cult to think about gender: like cults, gender has to defend its boundaries, requires continual demonstrations of allegiance to its rules, demands attacks on its enemies, and makes clear hierarchical distinctions between leaders and followers, insiders and outsiders. Instead of the coercive tactics of gender conformity, Bornstein asks what it would be like if gender was thought of as a voluntary organization, like a bridge club or a political party, or a charitable organization: a group that people choose to join, whose rules they can choose to follow or decide to challenge and change, a group that can be left in favour of an alternative.

Of course, this is much easier said than done. But people all over the world, in a variety of settings, are working to make gender less like a cult. In Sweden, the University of Umeå has initiated a project called "Challenging Gender," in which a group of international scholars "contribute to more complex and reflexive gender theory" (Umeå Center for Gender Studies 2011). AIDS activists in the southern African country of Namibia are using a gender analysis to reduce new HIV infections by questioning gender hierarchies and binaries and opening up honest conversations about how expectations of gendered behaviour can increase sexual transmission of HIV and about how women, men, and transgender people can reduce their risk of HIV infection (Clifton and Feldman-Jacobs 2011).

The Trans Murder Monitoring Project reports that 1123 transgender people were murdered in 57 countries between 2008 and 2012. To assist in ending transphobic violence in Canada, legislators have been at work since June 2011 to expand the Criminal Code to include gender identity and gender expression on the list of characteristics protected by hate crime law. Bill C-279 was passed in the House of Commons in 2013 by a vote of 149–137, but the bill was stalled in the Senate for over two years, and died on the order paper when the 2015 federal election was called. In the current Parliament, An Act to amend the Canadian Human Rights Act and the Criminal Code (gender identity and gender expression) has been introduced in the House of Commons.

Most Canadian governmental registries have fallen behind other private and institutional groups and other countries, that have changed statistical categories to reflect one or more non-gender-binary designations (Ontario was the first province to adopt a non-binary system). Australia, New Zealand, Germany, Nepal, and India have adopted demographic systems that recognize third genders (British Columbia Law Institute 2014). Statistics Canada has announced a series of public consultations to be held prior to the development of the 2021 census that could lead to more fair and accurate changes to data collection.

Challenges to gender conformity happen in informal and individual contexts as well. The growing visibility and politicization of transgender communities is an encouraging sign that gender boundaries are more elastic than they seem.

Summary

Gender represents a broad network of behaviours, attitudes, activities, prohibitions, mandates, relationships, identities, and beliefs about how men and women should behave and relate to each other. However, feminist theorists have argued that gender is a social and cultural construction, different from biological and anatomical sex. This can be seen in varieties of gender expression.

For centuries, explanations of gender differences were rooted in the physical differences between women and men, both real and imagined. Freudian psychoanalysis locates the origins of gender in girls' desire for a penis and boys' need to identify with their fathers to avoid castration—the fate of girls and women. Ideas about the importance of biology found new life in the late twentieth century from evolutionary biologists, who saw gender as part of the evolutionary mandate to pass along genes. Similarly, some neurobiologists argue that hormonal differences create gender.

A central concept in feminist thought is that gender cannot be separated from social and cultural conditions. Feminist psychoanalysts argue that women's psychology is formed by gendered power relations and by the socially assigned nurturing role played by mothers, rather than by the absence of the penis. Feminist psychologists more generally have shown that culture teaches people how to inhabit gender. In addition, they have argued that female-identified values of relatedness and care must be integrated into understanding how gender works.

Other critics have challenged the focus on biology, showing the importance of environment and context for human development. Judith Butler's performative theories of gender critique the idea of "identity" as a single or knowable thing. For Butler, biological sex is not only not a fact of nature; its production through discourse is coercive and prescriptive.

Gender is learned, reproduced, and disciplined in a variety of ways.

Discussion Questions

1. List three differences between girls/women and boys/men that have been reported in traditionally based research. These can be differences in personality, skills, or conduct. What kinds of contrasting explanation can you give for them? Which do you find most convincing and why?
2. Imagine what it would be like to live in a world in which gender was voluntary rather than mandatory. How would your life experiences be different?
3. Theories of personality development offer different explanations for gender identity and expression and gender roles. What experiences did you have as a child that shaped your gender-role behaviours and attitudes? Explain these from two or three different theoretical positions. Are they consistent with the research on gender-role socialization, or do they contradict it?
4. Apply the Bechdel test to the films you have seen this year. Do any of them pass the test? Beyond Bechdel, apply an intersectional analysis to these same films. How are race, sexuality, class, and so on structured? What does this analysis suggest about how the movie industry constructs a sense of who is or is not important in Western culture?
5. On Tumblr, locate a few examples of gender performance and examine the ways in which gender prescriptions are used. Examine how gender-binary and non-gender-binary illustrations are employed.

Recommended Resources

Alexander, M. Jacqui. 2006. *Pedagogies of Crossing: Meditations on Feminism, Sexual Politics, Memory, and the Sacred*. Durham, NC: Duke University Press. Alexander makes a compelling case for North American feminism and queer studies to take up transnational frameworks that foreground questions of colonialism, political economy, and racial formation. She focuses on the criminalization of queer communities in both the United States and the Caribbean in ways that prompt rethinking of how modernity invents its own traditions.

de Beauvoir, Simone. 2011 (1949). *The Second Sex*. New York: Vintage. A classic discussion of male and female identities as social constructions rather than products of nature.

Butler, Judith. 1990, 2007. *Gender Trouble: Feminism and the Subversion of Identity*. New York: Routledge. Butler's foundational work interrogates the categories of masculinity and femininity and how they are constituted.

Butler, Judith. 2001, 2015. *Undoing Gender* New York: Routledge. Butler reconsiders gender performativity and writes on the "New Gender Politics" including trans and intersex movements and how they impact feminist and queer theory.

Dryden, OmiSoore H., and Suzanne Lenon, eds. 2015. *Disrupting Queer Inclusion: Canadian Homonationalisms and the Politics of Belonging*. Vancouver: UBC Press. This text makes an important contribution to theoretical understanding by unsettling the notion that inclusion means justice. Multiple and wide-ranging examples demonstrate how inclusion into a system built on foundational inequality can only fortify and advance complicity with injustice.

Fitzgerald, Maureen, and Scott Rayter, eds. 2012. *Queerly Canadian: An Introductory Reader in Sexuality Studies*. Toronto: Canadian Scholars Press. In this collection, many of Canada's leading sexuality studies scholars examine the fundamental role that sexuality plays in Canadian narratives, myths, and anxieties about identity while integrating race, class, and gender.

Laqueur, Thomas. 1992. *Making Sex: Body and Gender from the Greeks to Freud*. Cambridge, MA: Harvard University Press. A historical examination of how ideas about the biological differences between women and men changed over time and were products of their era.

Lorde, Audre. 1984, 2007. *Sister Outsider*. New York: The Crossing Press. A landmark volume of essays about the intersections of race, gender, and sexuality. Lorde inspired a generation of feminists of all races to think deeply about the meanings of identity.

Naugler, Diane, ed. 2012. *Canadian Perspectives in Sexualities Studies: Identities, Experiences, and the Contexts of Change*. Toronto: Oxford University Press. This anthology reveals the Canadian experience as well as international examples of the evolution of views on sexuality. It engages contemporary debates and encourages critical thinking on emerging concepts.

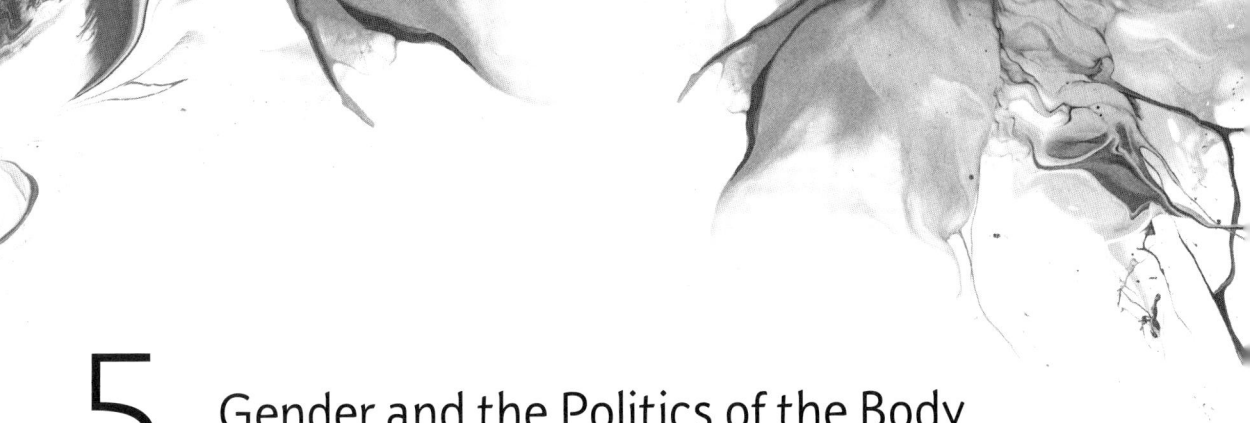

5 Gender and the Politics of the Body

Chapter Outline

- Feminism and the Body
- The Nature of Sex Differences
- Discourse/Knowledge/Power
- Discourses of Sexuality
- Feminists Rethink the Body

This chapter will help you
- Comprehend how bodies are socially and culturally constructed and how this pattern varies according to time and place and intersectionality
- Understand what *embodiment* means
- Learn the role biology has historically played and how it differentiated sex and gender
- Reflect on how anatomy is not destiny
- Recognize some of the cultural prompts that construct "beauty"
- Understand sexuality as distinct from sex and gender

There are a great many people in the world—I dare say most of 'em—who would say I'm a pervert and a bad person because I'm a transsexual woman. I was born male and now I've got medical and government documents that say I'm female, but I don't call myself a woman, and I know I'm not a man. That's the part that upsets the pope—he's worried that talk like that—not male, not female—will shatter the natural order of men and women. I look forward to the day it does.

— KATE BORNSTEIN (2012, X)

The human body is not merely flesh and bones; it is also constructed by culture. This means that while bodies feel natural and self-evident, they are not purely biological entities: the body's meaning and significance are shaped by cultural ideas that vary tremendously across time and space.

It is almost impossible, too, to separate how a culture aesthetically values different kinds of bodies and the ways in which those bodies are gendered, racialized, and sexed. For example, everyone ages, but aging as a cultural construct has profound consequences for how women experience their senses of self, especially their sexuality. In a culture that values youth, particularly in women, what makes a body desirable is not a trivial question. Not only are the cosmetic, fashion, and fitness industries built on women's desires to meet an often unattainable ideal, but in large part those industries *create* those desires. And even though these industries make billions of dollars from the women whose desires they manufacture, some women gain pleasure and even power from using makeup, shopping, and working out.

These contradictions originate in the fact that women are disproportionately judged on physical appearance and that women's bodies are *objectified*; that is, made into things to be inspected and evaluated. Objectification shapes the ways in which women (and indeed, all gendered beings) inhabit their bodies and their worlds. But, women also actively participate in processes of **embodiment**. This chapter is focused, then, on some highly specific forms of power that have effectively—if differently across times and places—produced the gendered body as a social, political, and cultural phenomenon, while also attending to the ways that women are differently implicated in and by those very processes.

Feminism and the Body

Since the first organized women's movement during the late nineteenth and early twentieth centuries, North American feminists have recognized the body as a site of political domination. They have protested cultural constraints placed on women's bodies and argued for women's rightful control of their own bodies. Feminists in 1968 threw their bras into "a freedom trash can" outside the Miss America Pageant to symbolically protest how women's bodies are controlled, whether through codes of fashion, ideal notions of femininity and beauty, forced sterilization, abuse, or rape (Bordo 1993, 15–23). In many countries today, maintaining a woman's reproductive freedom remains a centrepiece of feminist political struggle.

The body is a complex construction: it is a physical thing whose movements can be controlled explicitly by force and implicitly by social pressures; a place onto which gender and race are written and from which they are expressed; and a symbolic space in which selfhood, identity, and self-worth are worked through. Understanding how the body is variously constructed and the impact of these constructions on women's lives, experiences, and choices has been essential to feminist scholarship since its beginnings. Yet it was in the late 1980s that the most exciting and theoretically challenging research on the body began to emerge in feminist studies (Conboy et al. 1997, 7–8). Much of this research was premised on the view of the body as a site of struggle on which battles for competing ideologies are waged. The following sections show how some of this work has been interdisciplinary, although much of it has come out of particular fields such as biology, philosophy, sociology, and anthropology.

Bodies are constructed through language, practices, and representations. Each of these can produce different ways of understanding the body and its relationship to the self, often producing intersecting, overlapping, and contradictory images. Feminists have been at the forefront of research on the way bodies become gendered—or written over with meanings and ideologies concerning masculinity and femininity—and become lived, or experienced. Feminist work has further produced new models of gender that push past the binary and speak to intersex and transgender bodies. The discussion below focuses on both the constraints placed on women by various constructions of the body and how women have creatively resisted such conceptualizations and altered their bodies in protest against them.

Mind/Body Dualism

In Western thought, at least since Plato, the body has been juxtaposed with the mind and seen as inferior to it. This distinction between mind and body is an aspect of what is often referred to as "Cartesian dualism," named for the Western philosopher René Descartes. Descartes's famous dictum "I think, therefore I am" vividly encapsulates the widespread association in Western culture of the mind and its reasoning processes with the self. The body places limitations on the self, according to this view, and must, therefore, be transcended. Everyday language encodes this understanding of the body as an entity distinct from the self: a person is likely to say, "I have a body," not "I am a body" (Mairs 1997, 298). Cartesian dualism is so taken for granted that it can be understood as an unwritten, official doctrine of Western societies.

This mind/body dualism is also part of the Christian tradition that has influenced Western thinking: the body is seen in opposition not only to the mind and the self but also to the "soul" and the "spirit." The body, in this view, represents the animal side of human existence, possessing unruly appetites and desires that must be controlled and suppressed for salvation.

What is most significant for women about this conceptualization is that "woman" has been associated with the body, while "man" has been linked with the mind. "Woman" equated with the body is, therefore, not mind and not self. She is not a self or subject but an object, not spirit but flesh. She is aligned against reason (a woman is more emotional, intuitive, and irrational than a man, sentiments still heard today) and against spiritual salvation (woman, it is still widely believed, is naturally a temptress and seductress). According to these beliefs, then, she must be controlled.

This logic has had profound significance for how women have been valued, treated, and constrained in their opportunities and choices. As Simone de Beauvoir argues in *The Second Sex*, the entrapment of women in their bodies means that women have been made "the second sex," defined by a lack of masculine qualities and traits that men assume stem from a natural defectiveness (Conboy et al. 1997). As Susan Bordo argues,

> The cost for such projections to women is obvious. For if, whatever the historical content of the duality, the body is the negative term, and if woman is the body, then women are that negativity, whatever it may be: distraction from knowledge, seduction away from God, capitulation to sexual desire . . . failure of will, even death. (Bordo 1993, 5)

Naturalizing the Body

The association of women with the body also allies femaleness with the negative term in another set of associations: nature/culture. The body has been seen as natural and the mind as the source of human cultural control over nature's destructive forces. The association of women with nature arises from the function of woman's body in giving birth and nurturing children, but de Beauvoir's (2011[1949]) insights are again instructive: she argues that if women's bodies have constrained them, it is not because this is natural or inevitable but because women have been interpreted through the lens of culture, thought of as "natural" by men who have created the very category of "nature" to serve their own aims. Evidence from around the world indicates that women have combined motherhood with almost every task imaginable. This suggests the cultural, rather than the natural, character of such limitations in Western culture where "woman" has been defined by her body and seen as trapped in nature because of it. This not only has rendered her as object not as subject, as other not as self, but also has served as a rationalization for her domination and subordination. In contemporary society, science plays a particularly important role in this subordination because scientific theory and practice are concerned with knowledge of, and mastery over, nature (Jardanova 1993). In nineteenth-century science, nature was often even conceptualized as a woman "to be unveiled, unclothed, and penetrated by masculine science" (Jardanova 1993, 376).

The construction of the female as natural has had particular consequences for women in the Global South and women of colour, who have been seen as doubly natural and "other" due to the intersection of their gender and race. In Western racial discourse, the "naturalness" of bodies of colour has been equated with animality, in particular with an animal-like sexuality. This belief was perhaps nowhere clearer than in Victorian England, where, under the guise of scientific interest, the African woman Saartjie Baartman, known as the "Hottentot Venus," was displayed nude in a public pornographic exhibition disguised as science. Baartman was probed at by anatomists and stared at by a repulsed but fascinated white public audience. Her distinctive bodily traits—enlarged vaginal lips and protruding buttocks—were taken as signs of a rampant and animalistic sexuality (Gilman 1985). This conclusion reinforced the notion at the time that African women were savages, devoid of the sexual modesty necessary for achieving "true" femininity. The ethics of creating a spectacle of a woman's body, and dehumanizing her, was not recognized as savagery.

The bodies of Asian women have also been represented as particularly erotic and exotic, but in contrast to the bodies of black women, they have been associated with smallness, timidity, and subservience, traits that have made them seem desirable to many men in Western societies. This perception has led to the development of a highly profitable mail-order business in which Asian women are sold to Western male consumers as brides. The sensationalist attention that activists and journalists have paid to this industry and the stereotypes on which it is built elide the variety of strategies that Asian women themselves enact in seeking husbands in the West (Constable 2005).

This image is from the art collection "Yellow Fever Vol. 1," in which Canadians artists Yi-Chieh (Alisha) Weng and Chieh Huang explore the subject of "Yellow Fever," or the fetishization of Asian women, through photography.

One instance of resistance to essentialist constructions of Asian womanhood is found in the plays of David Hwang. In *M. Butterfly*, he brilliantly critiques the orientalist view contained in Puccini's opera *Madama Butterfly* that an Asian woman's highest goal in life would be to marry a white man. In Hwang's play, the exquisitely demure Asian woman turns out to be a man.

In Western thought, then, the body has been understood not only as the physical ground of gender differences, but also as the gendered ground of racialized differences. Because the body has conventionally been understood as a natural, relatively unchangeable entity and gender differences are thought to arise from the body, gender is also seen as natural and, thus, inevitable. The differences between the bodies of women and men have been taken as the justification for treating women and men differently. Yet feminist scholarship on the body in the last 30 years reveals that the body is far from being a stable ground of sex differences, as will be seen below. Indeed, the very instability of the body as a ground for gender difference allows people to use their bodies to resist constraining definitions of femininity—and masculinity.

The Nature of Sex Differences

Historians of science have documented repeatedly how the gender, race, and class assumptions of scientists influence their supposedly objective, scientific experiments and the conclusions drawn from them (see, for example, Keller 1985; Longino and Doell 1987; Martin 1987, 1994; Haraway 1989; Fausto-Sterling 2000; Jordan-Young 2010). Thus, although science is framed in a language of rationality and objectivity (e.g. the scientific method), the apparent neutrality with which it speaks and through which it gains authority conceals its cultural assumptions (Jackson et al. 1993, 363). Because science has until recently been dominated by men and was so often seen to "prove" male superiority, revealing its cultural biases has been an important feminist project.

Cultural factors affect the very questions scientists deem important enough to ask and which studies are deemed important enough to fund. That many researchers choose to focus on identifying, indeed often creating, the differences between women and men, rather than the similarities, is itself a product of their history, as well as their social and political agendas. This interest in difference is so deeply embedded, for example, that suggesting that the study of gender differences might be misguided and that research on gender similarities might be unproductive tends to strike most people as absurd. Why? Today, most scientists believe it is wrongheaded to look for biological explanations of many other kinds of difference. Yet, it was not that long ago that learned cultural differences between Jews and non-Jews were attributed to biological causes, an assumption that found its most hideous expression in the notion in Nazi Germany that Jews were so different from non-Jews that they were actually "life unworthy of life" and therefore in need of extermination. Today, most scientists find claims that vast biological differences exist between groups of people to be unwarranted, and the idea that biological factors best explain ethnic and cultural differences between people rightfully strikes many people as ludicrous. Might this not be true for gender as well?

The Gendered Brain

Cultural assumptions affect scientific investigations not only at the level of the questions asked but at every stage of the research process as well. The history of brain research into gender and racial differences clearly indicates this. The claim that women and men have differing brains, and therefore necessarily think differently, has been a long-standing one in Western society. Such supposed natural "brain differences" have been used historically to rationalize and further systems of oppression and to determine social policy. For example, toward the end of the nineteenth century, it was erroneously concluded that white men were naturally superior to women in intelligence because of their larger brains (Fabian 2010; Gould 1980). This assumption was used to justify women's exclusion from higher education. Brain measurements were also taken of racialized groups assumed to have intelligence levels inferior to those of white men, and a similar "conclusion" was reached: smaller brain size was taken as evidence of lower intelligence. It is well known now, however, that the size differential noted by these scientists was based on measurement techniques affected by pre-existing cultural assumptions about the supposed inferior intelligence of white women and of women and men of colour. Craniometrists (the scientists who measured skull sizes) consistently underestimated the cranial capacity of these groups, which biased their results. Even if such measurements had been correct, they would hold no significance today since it has been repeatedly shown that human brain size is not related to intelligence. Facts are one thing; how they are interpreted is another.

In the 1980s and 1990s, differences in brain structure and in the way women and men use their brains became the basis for theories of innate gender differences. In the wake of one study conducted in 1982, which reported a difference in size of the corpus callosum (the band of white matter connecting the left and right hemispheres of the brain) in nine men and five women, a virtual industry of brain lateralization research arose. The popular press was soon awash in feature articles about gender differences in the brain, claiming that they were responsible for everything from women's intuition and difficulties with physics to

Box 5.1 Time to Reflect

Is There a Female Brain? Two Scientists Review *The Female Brain* by Louann Brizendine

Despite the author's extensive academic credentials, *The Female Brain* disappointingly fails to meet even the most basic standards of scientific accuracy and balance. The book is riddled with scientific errors and is misleading about the processes of brain development, the neuroendocrine system, and the nature of sex differences in general. At the "big picture" level, three errors stand out. First, human sex differences are elevated almost to the point of creating different species, yet virtually all differences in brain structure, and most differences in behaviour, are characterized by small average differences and a great deal of male–female overlap at the individual level. Second, data on structural and functional differences in the brain are routinely framed as if they must precede all sex differences in behaviour. Finally, the focus on hormone levels to the virtual exclusion of the systems that interpret them (and the mutual regulatory interactions between receptor and secretion systems) is especially lamentable, given the book's clinical emphasis on hormone therapies.

Source: Young and Balaban (2006).

The fact that *The Female Brain* was written by a woman should serve as a crucial reminder that women are often guilty of the scientific phenomenon called "neurosexism" (Fine 2010). That term refers to the underlying gender bias in the scientific study of so-called "sex differences." The most popular version of neurosexism currently lies in the arena of brain organization research, which hypothesizes that the surge of prenatal hormones delivered to male fetuses in utero explains the ostensibly distinct emotional, intellectual, and sexual characteristics associated with male and female persons. One psychologist argues that men and women are "hardwired" for systemized thinking and empathic feeling, respectively.

Source: Baron-Cohen (2003).

women's stronger verbal skills and more holistic way of thinking. Despite the fanfare that accompanies the publication of each new piece of scientific "proof" of binary gender characteristics, the scientific evidence supporting counter-arguments generally fail to get the same publicity. The case of the bestselling book *The Female Brain* provides a perfect example (Brizendine 2006). When it was published, it caused a sensation in the popular media, garnering a lot of very positive press. Yet it was actually severely critiqued in scientific journals such as *Nature* (see Box 5.1 for two other reviews).

Perhaps because of the cultural value that has been placed on the high-tech and thoroughly computerized dimensions of lives, the term *hard-wired* has now entered the popular lexicon to refer to the underlying design features of differently gendered brains. In connoting a blueprint and a function, that term renders supposed male/female brain differences not only natural but also good, and probably permanent. Again, however, there are several serious limitations of this body of work.

Decades of research on brain organization in humans were inspired initially by research on rats, and even there researchers have found links only between differences in hormones and differences in brain size, but never between differential brain size and behaviour (Fine 2010, 104). Moreover, drawing a clear line from rats to humans is hardly unproblematic. Because studies of hormone delivery cannot be done on pregnant women (for obvious ethical reasons), and because researchers cannot construct controlled experiments on human subjects—administering the hormone and watching its effects, as they do with rats—the only option left is to examine gender-differentiated experiences, personalities, and attitudes that develop in childhood, long after the initial infusion of the hormones that are said to be their cause. Other problems with this research abound. In a close examination of over 300 peer-reviewed scientific articles published between 1967 and 2000 concerning the relationship between brain organization and the development of gender identity and roles among humans, one researcher found a series of patterned flaws in scientific method, reasoning, and use of evidence (Jordan-Young 2010). Most notably, these studies assume an impossible-to-prove linear path from the initial delivery of hormones to human fetuses, on the one hand, to the development of such complex structures as behaviours, desires, and identities, on the other. These studies often cite each other's data, bolstering the number of experiments from which they can draw conclusions. And in the interest of advancing their views about gender difference being rooted in the brain, these studies fail to account for the fact that invariably the majority of research subjects—male and female—occupy the middle ground rather than the two poles on any particular measure of gender (Jordan-Young 2010).

Recent studies point to differences found in transgender brains that show distinct variance from both male and female brains (Russo 2016). Researchers cite this evidence as preliminary but substantial enough to complicate the gender binary.

So are there any foolproof biological signs of the physical differences between women, men, and transgender? Do differences in genital anatomy, hormones, or chromosomes allow women and men to be defined as biologically distinct? At first glance, this might seem the case, but a closer look at the range of variation among females and males in basic bodily traits suggests otherwise.

The Sexed Body: Hormones, Chromosomes, and Genitalia

The contemporary biological definition of a man and a woman is a genetic one: an individual with two X chromosomes is designated a female and an individual with one X and one Y chromosome, a male. But even this seemingly incontrovertible distinction has its exceptions. For example, some "genetic males" with XY chromosomes have a rare mutation of the Y chromosome that results in a lack of male genitalia. These individuals look typically female, including having fully developed breasts at puberty, but do not have female reproductive organs. Other people have a variety of chromosomal combinations—XO,

XXY, XXX, and XYY—making their clear assignment as "male" or "female" difficult.

Even in people with standardized chromosomal distribution of XX and XY, hormones do not predict identity. The common scientific view that differences in women's and men's behaviour are explicable in terms of the presence of differing "sex hormones" in their bodies is a popularly accepted one, often difficult to dislodge. It has, for example, become commonplace to blame complex human behaviours, such as male aggression, on the supposed "male" hormone testosterone or women's unhappiness on fluctuating levels of the supposed "female" hormone estrogen. Some critics of women's participation in politics have even argued that female hormonal fluctuations might cause erratic behaviour, which would preclude responsible decision making. Ideas that attributed biologically based erratic thinking to women may be one factor that has kept them from attaining political leadership.

How hormones are invoked to explain behaviour is also gendered:

> Although male hormones are used to account for general masculine proclivities (such as aggression) only rarely is any individual man's behaviour explained in these terms. When a man loses his temper we seldom hear anyone say, "It's just an excess of androgen," yet how often women's anger is explained in terms of the "time of the month." (Jackson et al. 1993, 364)

Such ideas reinforce the image of woman as more trapped in her body than man, even though studies of these hormonal effects have produced contradictory and inconclusive results, and all humans have both estrogen *and* testosterone in their bodies, although at different levels.

The Politics of "Nature"

The previous discussion shows that defining males and females biologically, that is, determining their "sex," is a complicated business. This is so not just because biology is complex, but also because "our debates about the body's biology are always simultaneously moral, ethical, and political debates about social and political equality and the possibilities for change" (Fausto-Sterling 2000, 255). The stakes are high in such debates: If women and men can be shown to be different, then it is an easy next step to conclude that such differences, and the benefits and drawbacks associated with them, are natural, and nothing can be done to change them. No better example exists than the statement made in 2005 by Harvard University president Lawrence Summers. At an academic conference about increasing diversity in the fields of science and engineering, Summers suggested that innate differences may explain why women do not succeed in math and science careers at the same rate as men, and why women may be under-represented in the math and engineering departments of top research universities. That kind of statement turns a social and cultural phenomenon—the fact that women are discouraged from pursuing careers in science and are not offered opportunities equal to their male counterparts—into a biological one—women are inherently not as good. Biology thus can be enlisted to make arguments (no matter how dubious the claim) about public policy.

Discourse/Knowledge/Power

In the last few decades, feminist scholarship has focused on how the female body is created through *discourse*: cultural phenomena that include representations, commodification, reproduction, and technology. The role of language in the body's construction has been a particularly fruitful area of feminist inquiry.

Language is a system through which reality is constructed and ordered. Through interaction in the lived world, language transforms social existence. It is also a system tied to how power is distributed both socially and materially in any given society. Language is tied to power through *discourse*; that is, systems of knowledge supported by institutions and practices that create a picture of what is true and what is not. Historically, various institutions, such as the medical, psychological, and religious establishments, have produced images of women as frail, helpless, dependent, passive, submissive, childlike, and emotional creatures, defining these traits as inevitable, natural, and normal. This "discourse of femininity" not only circumscribes women's lives and choices but also brings them into "the norm," in line with the standardized ideas and behaviours desired by adherents with the power to construct and disseminate discourses. In contemporary Western societies, science is a privileged discourse, one that is widely believed to "speak the truth" about sex differences and women's bodies. Individuals who diverge from what science claims is natural, normal, or healthy are labelled "deviant," "abnormal," or "sick" and often feel themselves to be just that.

Discourses of Sexuality

Since the nineteenth century the discourses of science and medicine have increasingly gained hold over women's sexuality. This process has had significant consequences for how women experience their bodies and their selves. Susan Bordo, following philosopher Michel Foucault (1980), describes how, during this time period, the incessant probing of the patient's body and mind for knowledge about sexual practices paradoxically forced sexuality inward. What were understood as sexual *acts* before being subjected to science's scrutinizing eye were transformed into sexual *identities*, which were then represented as immoral and/or diseased:

> The medicalization of sexuality in the nineteenth century . . . recast sex from a family matter into a private, dark, bodily secret that was appropriately investigated by such specialists as doctors, psychiatrists, and school educators. The constant probing and interrogation . . . ferreted out, eroticized and solidified all sorts of sexual types and perversions, which people then experienced (although they had not done so originally) as defining their bodily possibilities and pleasures. The practice of the medical confessional, in other words, in its constant foraging for sexual secrets and hidden stories, actually created new sexual secrets. (Bordo 1993, 142–3)

Medical and psychiatric researchers produced "knowledge" of women's bodies and sexual behaviours and declared, based on standardized assumptions of ideal femininity, that some of

---

Box 5.2 Women in Media

Ellen Page

Ellen Page, from Halifax, told the world she was a lesbian in 2014, several years after her Academy Award nomination for the film *Juno*. She said that she came out because she was tired of "lying by omission" (Mungin 2014)—a reference to the fact that in North America (and indeed most of the world) a person is assumed to be heterosexual unless otherwise communicated. She notes that this results in an erasure of lesbian role models, and says she "felt guilty for not being a visible person for the community, and for having the privilege that I had and not using it" (Haewood 2016).

Page also connects the anxiety of keeping this secret (in order to maintain her career, since Hollywood is notorious for keeping LGBTQ actors on the back bench) with her experience of her physical body. She says that after she told the public that she was a lesbian, "I *was* totally different! Just the immediacy of how much better I felt. I felt it in every cell of my body" (Haewood 2016).

those behaviours were natural and others were deviant. In general, those women with little or no sexual desire but who complied to satisfy their husbands' sexual needs and to have children were deemed "good" women. The sexual woman was viewed as sick, dangerous, and promiscuous. Sigmund Freud, perhaps the most significant sex researcher of the day, dissented from this view. He saw women as sexual beings and identified the repression of their sexual desires as a major cause of neurosis. He nonetheless had his own notions of what constituted normal female sexuality: he believed, for example, that women's sexual fulfillment could come about only through vaginal orgasm (as distinct from clitoral orgasm, which Freud considered "masculine" and childish) and the subsequent bearing and nurturing of children. Lesbian sexuality, according to Freud, was a neurosis based on lesbian women's inability to give over their early masculine identification with the clitoris, the "inferior penis," to the vagina, thereby rejecting their true feminine role as passive receptacles in heterosexual vaginal intercourse.

Through such "normalizing discourses," women's sexual appetites and behaviours were tamed and new identities created. Nowhere was this more evident than in the creation of the category of "homosexuality" at the end of the nineteenth century. As people's sexuality became an important focus of study, medical and psychiatric researchers and practitioners sought and gained information about same-sex sexual behaviours, organizing it into a "discourse of homosexuality," deeming desire between members of the opposite sex normal and same-sex desire abnormal. This medicalizing moved beyond mere sexual activity, defining "the homosexual" as a certain kind of person defined not just by sexual desires and behaviours that had always existed, but also by personality traits, physical characteristics, and moral qualities (Foucault 1980). Medicine and psychiatry created this category of identity through organizing information about same-sex sexual relations under the heading "homosexuality."

What is particularly significant about this and other discourses is that people have great difficulty constructing identities outside of them. Indeed, just the opposite occurs: meaning and identity is found in them. Discourses create categories of identity to sustain power relations and patterns of domination by speaking the supposed truth about an individual's normality. These are then internalized and these norms reproduced: their power works from within. If people understand themselves and their desires in terms of these normalizing discourses, they will recognize themselves in talk about normality and abnormality. If their behaviour diverges from the norm, they will most likely feel aberrant or deviant and may even secretly believe something is wrong with them, rather than seeing the norms themselves as a form of social control.

Psychoanalytical theories such as Freud's dominated Western beliefs about sexuality for many decades and represented a set of assumptions about "normal" sexual behaviour and roles for women. In the 1940s and 1950s, Alfred Kinsey conducted an extensive survey of the sexual behaviour of women and men in the United States (1948, 1953). His findings, based on interviews, astonished his contemporaries. He found that many people engaged in a range of sexual behaviours considered deviant by standards of that time. In fact, the majority of Americans participated in at least one of these supposedly aberrant behaviours, such as masturbation, same-sex sex, and oral–genital sex.

Beginning in the 1960s, sex researchers William Masters and Virginia Johnson continued to produce unexpected results (1966). Their research was an influential corrective to long-held heterosexist and androcentric beliefs about female sexuality. They realized that female orgasms result from clitoral stimulation and that the phases of female sexual response are the same regardless of the source of stimulation, a direct rejection of the notion that a woman's full sexual satisfaction requires sexual intercourse with a man. Their studies indicated that women generally reach orgasm more quickly and with greater intensity from manual stimulation of the clitoris, especially when they stimulate themselves. This finding suggests that delays in achieving or failure to achieve orgasm during intercourse may be a result of techniques that are incompatible with women's physiological responsiveness.

Of course, although laboratory studies of sexuality and physiological sexual responses have discredited many old assumptions and raised new possibilities, sexual desire involves more than just simple physical response. Sexuality is also a complex *social* construction; many feminists have pointed out that focusing solely on biology in attempts to study and understand sexuality limits comprehension of the multiple factors that combine to create sexual desire and sexual satisfaction.

Box 5.3 Key Issues

The Conflation of Gender and Sexuality

What is the best way to refer to those who are non-heteronormative in their sexuality, or non-cisnormative in their gender identity or expression? You may have heard the terms "the queer community," "the gay community," LGBT, LGBTQ, or one of the longer attempts at inclusivity: For example, in 2014, Pride Toronto listed their event as celebrating LGBTTIQQ2SA: lesbian, gay, bisexual, transsexual, transgender, intersex, queer, questioning, two-spirited, and allies (Armstrong 2014). These attempts at inclusivity are not always considered positive; One criticism is that these "alphabet soups" highlight exclusivity rather than inclusivity—a person can look at these acronyms and, if none of the terms relate to them, feel excluded. Another criticism is that these acronyms reflect a gender binary that, as discussed in this chapter, is socially constructed. Finally, critics note that these groupings of terms encourage the conflation of gender and sexuality. Some argue that the lesbian, gay, and bisexual part of the term should be split from the transgender, transsexual, two-spirit, and intersex parts. Both transgender community members and lesbian, gay, and bisexual members have argued for this split, though for perhaps different reasons (Roberts 2016). However, most agree that while the conflation between gender and sexuality can be tiresome, the strength of the community as a whole is worth the risk. In fact, some argue that other people's conflation of gender and sexuality is why those with non-heteronormative sexualities and with non-cisgender identities should stick together: "there's people out there, they don't make a differentiation between whether you're gay or trans, you're just a queer to them" (Paris Lees, quoted in Roberts 2016). In 2016, Pride Toronto responded to criticisms and changed its branding to say that Pride celebrates "the history, courage and diversity of our community," with the goal to "unite and empower people with diverse sexual orientations, gender identities, and gender expressions" (Pride Toronto, n.d.).

And for those still confused, here is a brief break down of Pride Toronto's categories: gender identity is the gender to which a person feels they belong; gender expression is the way a person presents (whether or not it reflects their identity); and sexuality refers to the sex (or sexes) a person is attracted to, sexually and/or romantically. If one was suddenly to wear an article of clothing socially associated with a gender that does not match the gender identity (e.g. high heels, if gender identity is male in Canada), that would affect gender expression (people might read the person as embodying aspects of the female gender), but not gender identity (one still feels that one belonged to the male gender) or sexuality (the shoes would not affect who is desired for sexual or romantic relationship).

> **Box 5.4   In Her Own Words**
>
> **Uses of the Erotic: The Erotic as Power**
>
> The erotic is a measure between our sense of self and the chaos of our strongest feelings. It is an internal sense of satisfaction to which, once we have experienced it, we know we can aspire. For having experienced the fullness of this depth of feeling and recognizing its power, in honor and self-respect we can require no less of ourselves.
>
> Source: Reprinted with permission from *Sister Outsider* by Audre Lorde, 53–4. Copyright © 1984 by Audre Lorde, The Crossing Press, a division of Ten Speed Press, Berkeley, CA 94707, www.tenspeed.com.

Feminists Rethink the Body

Perhaps it is because Western philosophy has constructed so many dualisms that subjugate women that feminist philosophers have set about to wholly rethink the body. They have done so in ways that speak not just to philosophy but also to politics. And since, as philosophers, they tend to operate in a highly abstract and conceptual realm, this section will try to ground their work by putting it in conversation with feminist and queer anthropology.

In the late 1970s and early 1980s, French feminists such as Hélène Cixous and Luce Irigaray theorized that because women's difference from men is located in the body, it is the female body and female sexuality to which women must turn for a source of female creativity that is both authentic and disruptive. Cixous has referred to this as *l'écriture féminine*, "writing in the feminine." In her article "The Laugh of the Medusa," she exhorts women to "write yourself. Your body must be heard. Only then will the immense resources of unconscious spring forth" (Cixous 1981, 250). Many contemporary women have begun to take this exhortation literally: through tattooing and piercing, they inscribe their own bodies and use them to "write their own stories." Women often explain their body modifications in terms of exerting control over meaning, as a means of replacing the predetermined scripts of what women do with their bodies with their own signifying marks. As Margo DeMello (2000, 173) writes, for women, the tattoo is often "an important step in reclaiming their bodies, and the narrative in which they describe this process is equally important." Frances Mascia-Lees and Patricia Sharpe (1994) have found that women speak of piercing and tattooing as enabling them to control pain, which they could not do in situations where they felt victimized, to dictate some of their own terms in the sexualizing and eroticizing of their bodies, to accept their bodies as desirable, and to resist external control, using the body as a canvas for their own self-expression. As one anonymous woman writes,

> Tattoos are an important part of who I am. They let me take control of my own body and appearance. They make me feel better about myself, and they improve my self-image. They let me express who I am and what I believe, and they will always be a part of me. (Tattoo rant, 2004)

Tattooing provides an example of the view that without new ways to imagine the body, there can be no vantage point from which to transform culture (Bordo 1993, 41). Yet taking control over bodies may not always be so liberating. Studies of anorexic women show that they, too, see themselves as reclaiming their bodies.

Feminists have critiqued the inherent if unacknowledged maleness that undergirds Western philosophical approaches to "the body" as if it were a single entity, as if *bodies* were not multiple

Venus and Serena Williams work against the masculinization of their athletic bodies by portraying feminine sexuality through bodily displays (and feminine clothing) on the tennis court.

and specific. Philosopher Elizabeth Grosz (1994) argues for a theory of corporeal feminism that looks to the politics of experience and a sense of self that emerges from the physical and social construction of sexed bodies. Rather than totally rejecting sex difference as a complete social construction, she analyzes the bodily effects of the way sex is made specific and the ways that subject positions are rooted in the sexed body. She does not limit her analysis to female bodies, but rather examines the specificity—as opposed to the presumed universality—of male bodies as well. For example, Grosz hypothesizes that heterosexual men experience their sexed bodies in terms that are based on a perceived differentiation from women's bodies, which are defined sexually by passivity and biologically by fluids and flows. She writes that "part of the process of phallicizing the male body, of subordinating the rest of the body to the valorized functioning of the penis, with the culmination of sexual activities occurring, ideally at least, in sexual penetration and male orgasm, involves the constitution of the sealed-up, impermeable body." Unlike women's bodies, which receive penetration and emit fluids and babies, male bodies are constructed as closed circuits, hermetically sealed. Grosz credits gay men for deriving a different kind of sexual subjectivity through their embrace of an open male body: "A body that is permeable, that transmits in a circuit, that opens itself up rather than seals itself off, that is prepared to respond as well as to initiate" is capable of very different kinds of pleasures from the stereotypical heterosexual male body (1994, 200–1). She hopes that straight cisbodied men will follow suit.

Grosz's analysis of masculinity "phallicized," that is, defined through the penetrating power of the penis, helpfully implies that men's relationship to their sexed bodies is socially produced—and could thus be altered. There is hope here: men's sexual subjectivity might transgress expected boundaries of bodily experience. And equally importantly, while the cultural construction of men as sexually active, non-penetrated, and closed off is a crucial part of the discourse of male power, it also closes off all kinds of sexual and cultural possibilities that men might explore.

Judith Butler presents a different view of the body as a site of political transformation. Butler argues that bodies implicitly marked as "normal" have come into being through everyday practices, specifically the acts performed every day in order to occupy gendered places. She suggests that bodies are made to seem material and unchangeable through the work that is done to inhabit and enforce norms. Yet, she continues, bodies can also be remade by performing those norms in very different contexts. This is particularly relevant to those gendered bodies that exist on the social margins enforced by structures of race, gender, and sexuality. Her model famously rests on the example of black and Latino gay men who appeared in Jennie Livingston's documentary film *Paris Is Burning* (1991). In that film, gay men of colour are seen competing in drag shows in which they perform various, minutely defined aspects of masculine and feminine dress and bodily comportment. In a prelude to her reading of the film, Butler suggests, first, that these men's "contentious practices of 'queerness' might be understood not only as an example of citational politics, but as a specific reworking of abjection into political agency, thereby explaining why 'citationality' has contemporary political promise" (1993, 21). Second, she proposes that drag is subversive "to the extent that it reflects on the imitative structure by which hegemonic gender is itself produced and disputes heterosexuality's claim on naturalness and originality" (1993, 125). In other words, drag reveals that not only might men perform femininity; indeed, women perform it all the time, just less self-consciously.

By arguing that gender is the result of repeated performances of "male" and "female"—that is, that gender is created through the processes that claim to define it—Butler opened up significant theoretical space to think about gender as both enforced and alterable, as written onto a body but also extricable from it. These insights are very useful for thinking about categories of gender outside the male/female binary, especially transgender identities.

Like "male" and "female," "transgender" is not a single idea or identity. For some transgender people, such identification opens up the space for more fluid understandings and expressions of gender, ones that intersect with but operate separately from anatomy. At the same time, this argument could return the debate to the mind/body split and suggest that the body is something that gender can transcend through rejected binarized sex.

Many anthropologists emphasize the cultural basis of binary sex distinctions—but not without difficulty or contradiction. In Jakarta, Indonesia, "tombois" are born-females who live as males. They define themselves as such based on their sexual desires: they define men as people who are attracted to women. In that way, tombois see themselves as practising normative gender insofar as they explicitly seek to enact dominant forms of masculinity. But when tombois travel from the urban milieu of Jakarta back to their rural villages, their practice of gender shifts. They find that the pull of family commitments is so intense that they relent to the pressures of being not simply women but daughters, fulfilling the normative obligations associated with that role (Blackwood 2010). Also, anthropologists themselves, despite their best efforts at deconstructing appeals to biological signifiers in gender studies, sometimes give in to their terms. One anthropologist who conducted an ethnographic study of transgender persons in New York City uses the term *male-bodied* to refer to some of his informants (Valentine 2007). Another anthropologist who did similar work in Brazil refers to his own research subjects as *not-men*, a destabilizing term that only works by referring to—and hence reinforcing—a stable biological category (Kulick 1998). What comes across so clearly in such works is that even the most earnest attempts to destabilize appeals to biology sometimes fail, raising the question of whether people are trapped by language, biological reference points, or both.

Ultimately, transgender activists argue, the questions of language and of the variety of ways in which transgender people conceive of themselves may be less crucial than the singular need to develop strategies for attaining social justice. Toward that end, "'transgender' refers to a collective political identity. Whether we have psychological features in common or share a particular twist in our genetic codes is less important than the more pressing search for justice and equality" (Currah et al. 2006).

Much of this chapter has emphasized the work of feminist philosophers, anthropologists, and even biologists who have laboured to unsettle biology-based understandings of the categories male and female. But still the question remains of how to think about the body as a material, physical entity in relation to the politics of gender. Is there a way of thinking about maleness and femaleness materially—that is, in terms of flesh—without making those categories inevitably just the outcome of cultural construction? On the other hand, can bodies be thought of as bodies while at the same time not falling into biological determinism, and without excluding bodies, both abled and disabled, that do not match whatever physical or biological characteristics are arbitrarily placed in categories? Linda Alcoff has sought a way out of this conundrum by arguing for a "possible objective basis" for sexed identity: "Women and men are differentiated by virtue of their different relationship of possibility to biological reproduction, with biological reproduction referring to conceiving, giving birth, and breast-feeding, involving one's own body" (2006, 172). What is crucial here is the *potential* for reproduction, not actual reproductive acts, abilities, or even desires, and the differences in consciousness that potential produces. Alcoff's proposition differs from Grosz's, cited above, in positing the potential to reproduce as the primary marker of sexual difference, as opposed to a larger set of individual markers such as fluids, permeability, and particular body parts. In terms of politics, Alcoff is critical of what she sees as the unhelpful abstractions of much theorizing about the body that offers no stable ground from which one can speak and act politically as a woman about women's experiences and concerns. For example, Alcoff argues that approaches that rely so heavily on Foucault—who has been well cited in this chapter—are, in the end, frustrating because they tend to conclude that "it's turtles all the way down." That is, such approaches essentially present a bottomless pit of discourses about "woman" without ever arriving at "women." Much of Alcoff's work is geared toward redeeming identity politics, which have been maligned in mainstream, progressive, and right-wing political spheres alike. Likewise, Alcoff is very attuned to the multiple sets of power relations (such as race, compulsory heterosexuality, transphobia, able-bodiedness, age) that differentially shape the lived experience of sex difference, as defined.

Summary

The human body is a cultural construct; its meaning and significance are shaped by differing cultural ideas. Historically, women have been associated with the body and nature and men with "self," "soul," and culture, profoundly affecting how women have been valued, treated, and constrained in their opportunities and choices. The body has also been understood as the physical ground of gender differences, which science has been charged with uncovering. Today it is a subject of continual debate whether there are clear-cut biological sex differences. The debate itself is so politicized that it might make more sense to scrutinize the uses to which biological categories are put, rather than try to definitively assess biology's role in the production of gender.

The female body (and, indeed, all bodies) is created through discourse; that is, through practices, representations, commodification, reproduction, and technology. Medical discourse, in particular, has constructed negative notions of the female body and sexuality, representing women's bodies and the natural processes they go through as diseased.

The integrity of the female body—and by extension, the status of women and girls—has been a frequent concern in world politics, with forms of feminist activism having different and sometimes contradictory effects. Women, especially those in the Global South, should be seen not as only victims and objects in these arenas, but as active agents and subjects.

Bodily needs and desires today are constructed in and inextricable from the marketplace. Through mass-media images, women and men of various sexualities around the world are differently promised a more beautiful body through buying products and maintaining time-consuming daily beauty regimens. People have found places to use their bodies and fashion for self-expression and self-enhancement and to signal political commitments.

Discussion Questions

1. The body can be experienced as a site of control, contestation, and empowerment. Compare and contrast times when you felt cultural pressures controlling your body, when you felt yourself challenging and resisting cultural definitions of your body, and when your body acted as a source of power. What does this analysis reveal about the relationship of the body to culture?
2. Locate a scientific article that claims that women and men are biologically different and analyze it for any cultural assumption about masculinity and femininity that may affect its "objectivity." Does it reinforce a gender binary? How, for example, do such assumptions influence the question asked, research methodology employed, or conclusions reached?
3. Locate and analyze a description of one of women's biological or physiological processes in a popular magazine. How does the language affect the interpretation of that process?
4. Choose a Hollywood film and pay close attention to how it constructs a viewing position for you as spectator, especially in relationship to the women's bodies on the screen. In particular, note how factors such as race, class, sexuality, and ethnicity affect them. Compare your analyses of the film based on these two approaches for their strengths and weaknesses regarding the "visibility politics of the female body."
5. Examine the coverage of sports events on television or in a newspaper. Are men and women athletes described in the same way? Does the question of appropriate masculinity arise in regard to male athletes as often as the issue of appropriate femininity arises for female ones?

Recommended Resources

Bordo, Susan. 1993. *Unbearable Weight: Feminism, Western Culture, and the Body.* Berkeley: University of California Press. A foundational work on the cultural analysis of the contemporary female body and the myths, ideologies, and practices that construct, manipulate, and constrain it. It focuses on the commodification of the female body, analyzing how consumption "normalizes" women's bodies and leads some to discipline their bodies so rigorously that it produces dangerous extremes in behaviour that might harm or even kill them.

Fausto-Sterling, Anne. 2000. *Sexing the Body: Gender Politics and the Construction of Sexuality.* New York: Basic Books. An in-depth analysis of the role of science in constructing "truths" about sexuality, sex differences, and sexual identity. It focuses specifically on past and current research on intersex individuals, sex-based brain differences, and "sex hormones," showing how the gender politics have been, and continue to be, at work in each of these areas.

Kimmel, Michael, Amy Aronson, and Amy Koler. 2015. *The Gendered Society Reader, third Canadian edition.* Toronto: Oxford University Press. This text examines the role of gender and the construction of bodies in a Canadian context. It looks at the process of racialization and colonial practices in shaping how bodies are read and inscribed in contemporary Canada.

Malacrida, Claudia, and Jacqueline Low. 2016. *Sociology of the Body,* 2nd edn. Toronto: Oxford University Press. This volume provides a broad overview of the theoretical foundations of embodiment and highlights the relationship between categories of identity and gender expression using an intersectional lens of analysis.

Namaste, Vivien. 2016. *Oversight: Critical Reflections on Feminist Research and Politics.* Toronto: Women's Press. This volume makes an important contribution to feminism by engaging what has been overlooked and rendered invisible in theory and practice. Exploring the lived experience of trans women in diverse case studies, the author creates a context for understanding how particular bodies are elided in Canadian scholarship.

Rice, Carla. 2014. *Becoming Women: The Embodied Self in Image Culture.* Toronto: University of Toronto Press. *Becoming Women* examines the search for identity told through the experiences of a diverse group of young women. It exposes the beauty industry's colonization of women's bodies and analyzes why and how "the beauty myth" continues its powerful influence.

Stienstra, Deborah. 2012. *About Canada: Disability Rights.* Halifax, NS.: Fernwood. This volume puts forward an analysis that disability is not about "faulty" bodies that need to be fixed but about the institutional, cultural, and attitudinal reactions to certain kinds of bodies, contending that neo-liberal ideas of independence and individualism are at the heart of the continuing discrimination against "disabled" people. It urges a social transformation of Canadian society that would be inclusive and supportive for all.

Transgender Archive, University of Victoria, www.uvic.ca/transgenderarchives/. The world's largest repository of material on the history of transgender activists and research issues, under the direction of Professor Aaron Devor, chair of Transgender Studies at the University of Victoria.

Part II

Women's Relationships, Women's Selves

In Part II the focus is on women's relationships within family configurations, traditional and fictive. In doing so, the text also deals with women in roles they inherit and those they create for themselves. The section concludes with a focus on women's ability to lead healthy lives.

Throughout time and around the globe, the socially accepted roles and relationships for young females, those deemed best suited for her within her household, community, and society have been to become first a wife and then a mother. Moreover, these roles were to be established through a conventional heterosexual marriage of a woman and a man and assumed within a nuclear family or an extended family household. Such beliefs still exist and continue to be idealized and pursued. Yet readers may be surprised to learn how much has changed over time for women and men, young and old, in their family roles through their life course. At the same time what has not changed in terms of women's domestic and familial responsibilities is considered.

Chapter 6 examines different types of family configurations worldwide, the changing notions of an ideal marriage, and how individuals' choices and roles and relationships within families have evolved. Chapter 7 gives attention to other components of a woman's life. It examines women's experiences as they grow older and the role of transitions that occur in their familial and work lives. Finally, Chapter 8 considers gender disparities in women's physical and mental health in the context of life processes, including the ways in which women have been all too often disempowered by the professional medical community.

Part II therefore explores women's roles and relationships as wives, mothers, grandmothers, daughters, lovers, and sisters and the widening options available to them as they negotiate their lives from girlhood to late adulthood. Throughout, the text considers the persistence of women's inequalities in these roles while highlighting their struggle globally for gender equity and enhanced well-being within family contexts and throughout their lifetime.

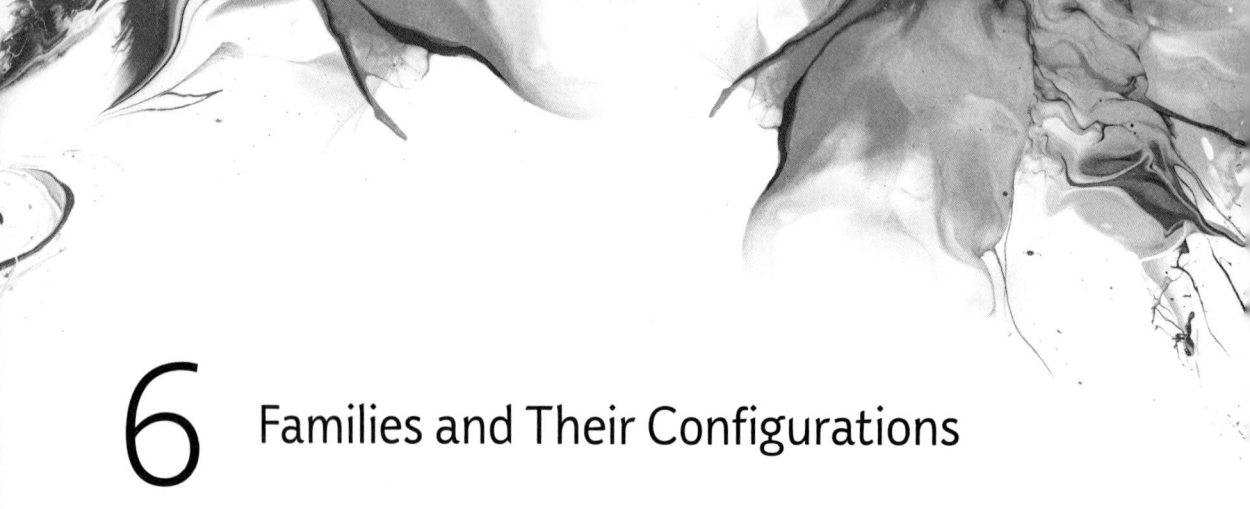

6 Families and Their Configurations

Chapter Outline

- The Family as an Evolving Social Organization
- Alternatives to Conventional Marriage in the Past
- Families in the Early Twenty-First Century
- "New" Family Configurations

This chapter will help you
- Learn how the family is socially constructed
- Appreciate how the family unit differs across cultures and through diverse time periods
- Recognize how family roles are gendered
- Comprehend how an intersectional analysis discerns difference with diverse family settings
- Understand different family formations in their own temporal and contextual space

familia: All persons subject to the control of one man, whether relations, freedmen, or slaves, a household.

—OXFORD LATIN DICTIONARY, 1971

The Family as an Evolving Social Organization

The family is the most ancient and universal unit of social organization. Until recently, it has generally been seen as comprising people related to one another by marriage or "blood." In the past, in small-scale societies, all social life took place within or between families: child rearing, food production, exchange of goods, religion and rituals, and power struggles. A woman's place within the family as wife, daughter, sister, and mother has defined her role in most societies. Although women participate outside the home in paid work and in public activities, adult women worldwide still bear the primary responsibility for their family's daily routine and maintenance. Fulfilling these obligations influences what else women might do with their lives.

This chapter on family configurations begins with broad historical trends and a focus on the nuclear and extended family. Then, alternative communities to the family for women are explored. The last section discusses how families in the early twenty-first century have changed from previous eras, especially in terms of their forms and gendered division of labour. Other common family types found today are identified. Throughout, women's choices in forming families, including remaining single or becoming unmarried because of divorce or widowhood, and how gender roles have been affected by changing social, economic, and political conditions are considered.

The term **nuclear family** was first used in the 1950s and has been assumed to be the most common family type in human history, but it is not universally so. The family is often based upon the union or marriage, commonly recognized through societal custom, religion, law, or blood kinship of a couple and their offspring. In some societies the nuclear family is part of a larger entity, sometimes called the **extended family**, consisting of one or more nuclear families and other relatives, often living in the same household as a multigenerational unit. Marriage is only one way by which people create families.

Feminists have been ambivalent about the family but more often have been critical of it. One of the more enduring criticisms has been the loss of personhood that a woman faces when she marries; not just to society or to those around her, but in the eyes of the law. Until Bill C-127 in 1983, rape could only exist outside of marriage; Canadian husbands could not be charged with raping their wives (Koshan 2010). The marriage vows were seen as a contractual obligation for a wife to provide for her husband's needs, with no consideration for her own needs or interest. Viewing the heterosexual family as a political institution—a site of power, sexual inequality, and constricted gender roles where women are subordinated in the home and in the larger society—feminists also call attention to variations in family forms and situations, some of which provide opportunities for more equitable roles for women (Satz 2011).

Looking at structures without an intersectional analysis obscures how differently constituted families are. bell hooks (1981) challenged the critical and universalist view of the family for women of colour holding that a European model does not fit all families. For racialized persons, families can be a source of support and sustenance in a racist, classed society. Enakshi Dua explains how the state played a major role, along with bourgeois notions of morality, in the construction of the nuclear family. In Canada this occurred through legislation and social programs that reinforced the male role of breadwinner and tied the female to domesticity (Dua 1999). While proclaiming the virtues of "family," Canadian immigration policies had the effect of keeping families apart. Racist legislation that defined immigrant workers of colour as temporary sojourners had the effect of preventing women from accompanying their labouring spouses.

Racialized female domestic workers were also seen as temporary workers, thus keeping families separated across borders. For more than 20 years, Citizenship and Immigration Canada offered a Live-in Caregiver Program, whereby workers from outside Canada were admitted to the country to provide child and senior care for families. A controversial component of this program was the stipulation that the worker (more than 90 per cent of them women) must live in the employer's home, where conditions were not monitored. Despite the many drawbacks, the promise of the opportunity to apply for permanent residence after two years in the program ensured a sizable supply of workers. Many of these workers were mothers who had left their own children in their homeland to earn money to assist them. The majority of the workers came from the Philippines and the Caribbean with increasing numbers from Eastern Europe. A participatory action research project called *Caregivers Break the Silence* revealed the hardships of many in the program (Arat-Kroc and Villasin 2001). In 2014, it was renamed the Caregiver Program as the live-in regulation was withdrawn, as was the universal ability to apply for Canadian permanent residence. While the policies of the Canadian state often support white middle- and upper-class women in nuclear families, these same policies restrict women of colour from living in nuclear families (Dua 1999).

Families are fluid, flexible, and socially constructed by individuals, circumstances, state policies, and cultural practices. They vary around the globe and have changed over time. In contemporary industrialized societies, what constitutes a family has expanded beyond marriage, biology, and adoption to include those who are

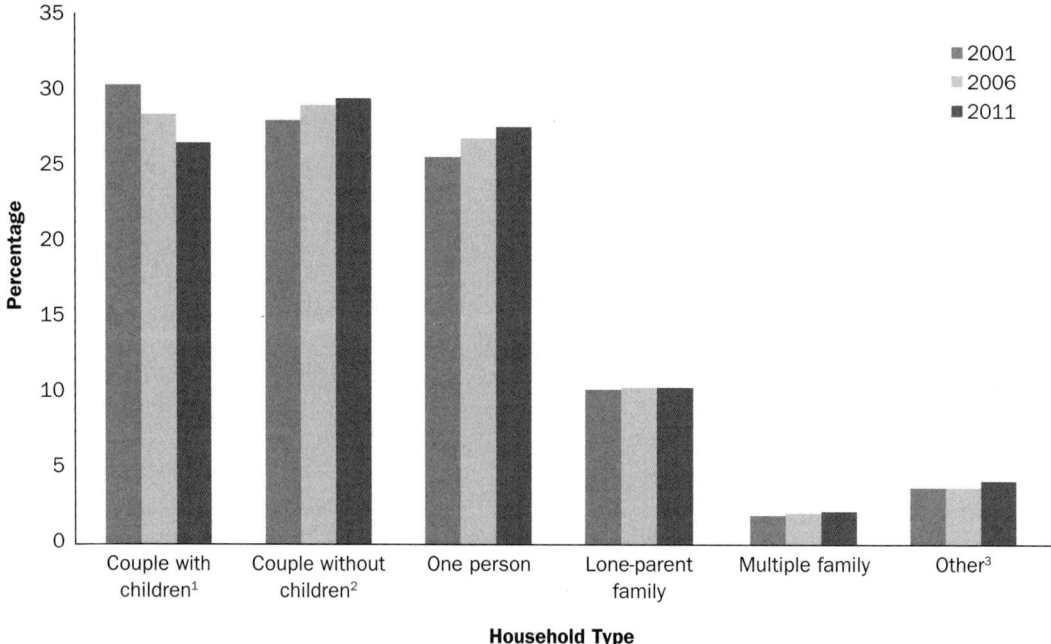

Figure 6.1 Distribution (in Percentage) of Private Households by Household Type, 2001 to 2011

Notes: "Couple" households and "lone-parent family" households refer to one-family households.
1. Refers to one-family households with children aged 24 and under.
2. Refers to one-family households without children aged 24 and under.
3. Refers to two or more people who share a private dwelling, but who do not constitute a census family.

Source: Statistics Canada, censuses of population, 2001 to 2011.

related emotionally, that is, who share affection and commitment, as well as those who are legally related.

In Canada, according to the 2011 census, "traditional" nuclear families make up barely more than a third of all families, 31.9 per cent, down from 37.4 per cent in the 2001 census (Den Tandt 2012). Current public opinion reflects the new reality of multiple household types (see Box 6.1).

The Nuclear and Extended Family

The nuclear family for the most part was founded upon a marriage between a woman and man who become wife and husband. Marriage, then, has served to legitimate heterosexual relationships and often was an economic arrangement between larger family units (Hunter 2011). Such a marriage is so customary that it is seen as conventional and natural.

Historically and intersectionally, the nuclear family was differently constituted in diverse communities. Colonialism created **settler states** that radically and violently usurped the land and culture of Indigenous peoples. Both the French and English colonists imposed a European patriarchal notion of family on Indigenous peoples in Canada that replaced the traditional roles of women in families and community. Moreover, the 1876 Indian Act established and defined a category of "Indian" and stipulated how this government-created status could be lost. If a First Nations woman married a non-Native, she and her children lost all claims to land and status as defined by the Indian Act. The converse was not true for a First Nations man, who could marry a non-Native but retain status for himself and his family. The Native Women's Association of Canada and others lobbied, advocated, and marched to end this legal discrimination but long failed to gain support from Canadian courts or legislatures. It was only after Sandra Lovelace (now a senator) took their case to the United Nations Human Rights Committee in 1979, which found that the Indian Act violated First Nations women's rights to their culture, was Parliament

Box 6.1 Key Issues

Changes in Family Structure in Canada

From 2006 to 2011 changes in family structure in Canada include:
- Married couples remained the most common family structure (67 per cent), although it has decreased.
- Common-law couples were the most rapidly increasing family structure (increase of 13.9 per cent).
- Single-parent households increased by 8 per cent, with the greatest increase seen among single-parent households headed by men. Despite this, women still head 8 out of 10 single-parent families.
- Same-sex married couples almost tripled, and the number of same-sex-common-law couples grew 15 per cent, which was higher than for opposite-sex-common-law couples.
- The gap continues to widen between couples with children at home (39.2 per cent) and couples without children (44.5 per cent).
- Mothers' participation rate in the Canadian workforce has nearly doubled. The participation rate of working mothers has increased from 39 per cent in 1976 to almost 73 per cent in 2009.
- The percentage of mothers working with children under three years old has increased 133 per cent from 1976 (27.6 per cent) to 2009 (64.4 per cent).
- Single mothers are less likely to be employed than mothers living in a two-parent household.

Source: Adapted from the Catalyst Research Center for Equity in Business Leadership, Catalyst.org.

prompted to amend the Indian Act in 1985 and revoke this clause.

State-sanctioned residential schools violently separated Indigenous children from parents and communities in an attempt to assimilate them into settler culture. The wounds of this policy remain today as evidenced by the testimonies of residential school survivors and their families told to the Truth and Reconciliation Commission of Canada. Family ties that were severed over prolonged periods created painful ruptures with multiple traumatic impact. (See Chapter 9 for an examination of the role of residential schools in damaging Indigenous families, communities, and cultures.)

Conventional Marriage: Why Marry?

For most of human history, marriage was economically necessary; women and men needed what the other provided in terms of work to form a stable family. In general, men provided food in the form of large game and protection against marauders, while women gathered nearby plants, tended small animals for food, and cared for children. To a certain extent, this pattern remains even in today's societies. Some people, however, can purchase household services traditionally performed by one gender or another (a woman can hire a plumber to do what husbands used to be expected to do; a man can hire a cook or buy pre-cooked meals to do what wives used to be expected to do), and of course they can learn to perform these tasks themselves. Regulating sexuality is another important reason why people marry. In every known society there is a prohibition against incest, generally defined as sexual relations among close kin: parents and children, siblings, and other family members. In order to have sexual relations and bear children, people must seek a mate outside the family circle. In earlier times and in small-scale societies, this often meant marrying outside the local community, where people were likely to be closely related. As most societies have been patrilineal, typically daughters were sent away and the young bride would begin her married life in the home of her husband's family. Less commonly, in a few matrilineal groups, the groom went to live with his wife's family. One can imagine how the dynamics of these households would differ.

In such situations, parents decided where to send their daughters or sons based not only on the expected compatibility between their children and those of the other family but also on what was anticipated in an alliance between the two families brought together by their children's marriage. The bride and groom had little to say about the arranged match and could only hope that it would be tolerable. The families of the bride and the groom generally exchanged gifts; sometimes, the much larger gift would be given by the groom's family, especially when the bride was leaving her birth family to join his parents' household. The gift (sometimes known as *brideprice* or *bridewealth*) compensated for the loss of her economic contribution to her natal family and would be used to help her brothers acquire wives. It was also a kind of marriage insurance for the husband's family: the bride's own family, having accepted a substantial gift, would be reluctant to return it, and thus would discourage her from leaving her husband if she felt inclined to do so. In some societies, notably in historical Europe among elite families but also elsewhere, it is the bride's family that is expected to give the groom or the groom's family a gift, known as *dowry*. Families without sufficient funds to provide a dowry despair of finding a good marital match for their daughters. Some daughters might spend years creating handicrafts to sell for a dowry. In contemporary times, young women in many parts of the world are strongly motivated to find work in factories to make money to contribute toward their dowry so that they can marry.

Whether in arranged marriages or not, couples who marry usually anticipate having children. Many people think this is the purpose of marriage. Marriage generally legalizes a man's claim to his children, a woman's claim to support for her children by a man, and the children's claim to some part of their family's income or property. Childlessness is often seen as tragic for both men and women and frequently regarded as justification for divorce or, in **polygynous** societies (see page 132) for taking another wife on the assumption that it is she who is infertile.

Sexual intimacy is also desired, and until recently marriage was commonly seen as the only legitimate realm for this activity. Not all societies confine sex to marriage, and in practice, even in societies where sex for women outside marriage is strictly forbidden, premarital and extramarital sex do occur. Nevertheless, infidelity is generally prohibited, particularly for women (who might bear another man's child), and is often a cause of strife. In some societies, the punishment for women's adultery is severe, ranging from gang rape to death by stoning. Sometimes a woman accused of infidelity will prefer death by suicide to social ostracism and the other sanctions that will result from this accusation. A double standard in sexual conduct usually prevails, however, and most societies are more lenient to male adulterers.

In the past, therefore, people were expected to marry for mutual economic support, to make alliances between families, to have children, and to engage in socially approved sexual intimacy. These social functions of marriage have been superseded in industrial, urban society by other social, political, and economic institutions, which have undermined many of the earlier reasons for marriage. Arranged marriages for family alliances are no longer common in Western societies (ultra-Orthodox Jewish communities are one exception); but in Asia, the Middle East, Africa, and elsewhere, they persist, as they do to a certain extent among immigrant communities from these regions. Especially in large urban centres, sexual relations and having children without being married are more acceptable, but in most regions, the sanction of marriage is preferred for both sexual unions and parenthood. Still, just because unmarried sex and parenthood are more common in some societies does not mean that there is no longer pressure to marry.

Whom to Marry?

Girls and young women globally are still educated in anticipation of their assuming the roles of wife and mother, regardless of what else they might do. In a heteronormative society, women who do not (or have not yet) become wives and then mothers can be seen to be anomalous (unless they assume other socially esteemed roles, such as being a nun) and, as a result, can feel a sense of inadequacy or deprivation. Consequently, most families strive to ensure that their daughters become married, and many women do marry. Though there have always been women who did not marry, only in recent decades have a significant number of women in the world had the option not to be married and not to be mothers as a matter of personal choice.

In some societies, parents turned to professional matchmakers to pair up their children with an appropriate mate and to smooth the path from betrothal to the wedding itself. In some cases, children are betrothed in infancy or childhood; in others, the prospective couple is allowed to meet before betrothal. When marriage concerns whole families, the suitability of the individuals to be married as a couple is considered less important than the appropriateness of the tie between the families. Families are chosen for their wealth, stability, and social standing. Often, a family is obliged to marry their daughter to an appropriate kinsman—say, the father's sister's son—if one is available (*cross-cousin marriage*); in other societies, cousin marriages are forbidden. Sometimes, a family has the right or obligation to provide a close kinsman as a husband to a young widow (*levirate marriage*). In societies where such marriage forms are practised, individual choice is simply not an issue. It is hoped that the bride and groom will become fond of one another over time so that the marriage will be stable and even happy (Potash 1986).

In industrialized societies, individual preference has become a primary factor in the choice of a spouse. Young adults, especially in the Global North, seek their own partners, though matchmaking may continue through friends and Internet dating services. Even so, people marry largely within certain socially acceptable boundaries and may be encouraged or compelled to choose somebody within a similar social class, race, caste, religion, or ethnic community and other commonalities, such as their own age group, educational background, and even geographic origin.

Where marriage has come to be understood as a romantic commitment rather than a pragmatic arrangement, much is made of falling in love, getting engaged, preparing for a wedding, and having the wedding itself. Expectations about marriage can often leave couples disappointed when, and if, the romance has faded. Divorce has become frequent in societies where it is permitted, sometimes because of this disappointment and, more importantly, because often women have more ability to choose how they live. Today, more women are able to support themselves and live independently of a spouse. The practical consequences of divorce for women are complex, something that will be discussed below.

Diverse Marital Households

As noted above, in some marriage formations the bride moves into the household of her husband's parents, or, less often, the groom moves into the household of his wife's parents, though there are many variants of each of these practices. The household might comprise several generations of couples and their children and various unmarried adult siblings of different ages. The experience for a young married woman, and the way this experience evolves as she matures, depends on the configuration of her household. If she is alone with her husband when she starts out, she might have much to learn about managing the household and might have little or no help. If she is in a large household, while she will have teachers and helpers, she might suffer the criticism of older women, particularly her mother-in-law (Hrdy 2009). Alternatively, her life as a wife alone might be yet more difficult when she has children, unless she can afford to hire help. In a larger household she will have help at hand and her status may rise with motherhood.

Some societies allow **polygamy**, the practice in which an individual may have more than one spouse at the same time. For example, Muslim religious law permits a man to have up to four wives at once. The ideal of **polygyny** (marriage to more than one wife) is more possible for the minority of men who have the wealth to support multiple wives: at the time of his death in 2014, Saudi King Abdullah had 30 wives. In other situations, however, a man might seek multiple wives to enhance his economic advantage because women do most the work of farming and herding along with child care. The converse, **polyandry**, in which a woman marries more than one man, is truly rare—a well-known example comes from the Himalayas, where in land-scarce areas several brothers might be married to one wife rather than splitting up their land holdings to provide for several families (Levine and Silk 1997).

Polygyny, however, is found on every continent. In Canada polygyny, although now outlawed, continues to be practised—for example, among some religious fundamentalist groups such as the Mormon sect in Bountiful, BC. Some women argue that there are advantages in having co-wives in a large household, particularly in the pooling of wealth and labour. In East Africa, for example, it takes teamwork among a number of wives to cultivate land, care for livestock, and raise children. Beyond the constructed notion that plural marriage is inherently harmful for women, some contemporary feminist scholars challenge this assumption. They explore how these type of family units can break down patriarchal power relations and create self-determining spaces for the women who embody them (Calder and Beaman 2014).

Polygyny, however, is not necessarily a happy state for women. There can be jealousy and bitterness among the wives, a subject of poetry and literature in works from the Hebrew bible to contemporary novels and essays. Human rights activist and lawyer Rafia Zakaria's book *The Upstairs Wife* (2015) chronicles the family discord precipitated by the introduction of a new wife. Another example is the portrayal of the four wives of a Mormon man, their differences, and negotiations with their husband and each other in the US reality television series *Sister Wives*. Even when husbands are limited by law to only one wife, in many parts of the world it is common for them to make second and even third families, and such practices are not limited to the wealthy and powerful. While the husband might try to keep his other family secret from his first wife, often she and her children know of them and vice versa.

These examples reflect the traditional subordination of wives to husbands. Although marriage presumably guarantees a wife certain rights and entitlements, generally, in most parts of the world, these have been secondary to those of her husband (see Box 6.2). She often becomes his dependent, owning very little or no property of her own, lacking in inheritance rights or control over finances except those of immediate household management. In such cases, a wife may have virtually no identity of her own. It is her job to provide her husband with sexual satisfaction when he wishes it, physical comfort in his home, and food for their children, his family, and guests. Living away from her family, she is often without support. She is judged by him, his family, and her own family, as well as the neighbours and society at large, according to how well she performs as a homemaker and mother, for these are seen to be the primary roles of a wife. A young bride is often deprived of future schooling that could improve her own and her family's future and can be the target of an abusive husband. She is more likely to bear children early, which places her and her offspring at risk (United Nations 2010).

This asymmetry in traditional marriage is reflected in myriad ways, from the frequent practice of changing a woman's name to that of her husband upon marriage in many Western societies to the unequal household tasks allocated wives and husbands today. Wives continue to put in more time daily than husbands do in domestic activities, even when both have full-time jobs outside of the home.

The Incorporated Wife

Many careers and occupations involve not one person but two, and sometimes the whole family. Traditional heteronormative relationships establish that whatever a man does for a living, his wife is to be his supportive junior partner. If a man is a farmer, his wife is called a farmer's wife. In industrial societies, where most people are employees, the incorporation of a wife (more often than a husband) into a spouse's job is less explicit. Wives are expected to support their husbands' activities

Box 6.2 Time to Reflect

Monogamous Marriage as Economic Exploitation

The first class opposition that appears in history coincides with the development of the antagonism between man and woman in monogamous marriage, and the first class oppression with that of the female sex by the male. Monogamy was a great historical step forward; nevertheless, together with slavery and private wealth, it opens the period that has lasted until today in which every step forward is also relatively a step backward, in which prosperity and development for some is won through the misery and frustration of others. It is the cellular form of civilized society in which the nature of the oppositions and contradictions fully active in that society can already be studied.

Source: Engels, Friedrich. *The Origin of the Family, Private Property and the State*, translated by Alec West, edited by Eleanor Burke Leacock, New York: International Publishers, [1884] 1972. Page 129.

by taking care of all their domestic needs and also by taking an active interest in company functions as well. They are expected to entertain (depending on the husband's rank in the company) and to appear with their husband at all social functions run by the company (Callan and Ardener 1984).

Until recently, the wives of professors, doctors, and clergymen had important roles to play in the conduct of their husbands' work—both assisting with the work itself and making a social life for the husband's work community. The work of a politician's wife is very apparent in today's world, especially at the higher levels. This poses something of a dilemma for professional women married to politicians. Only after her husband became the prime minister of Canada did Laureen Teskey ask to be identified as Laureen Harper. She went on to support several important causes, including animal welfare organizations and the National Arts Centre. Sophie Grégoire Trudeau, who also added her husband's name to her own once he began his political career (see Box 6.3), has so far carved out her wife-of-the-prime-minister role advocating for girl's self-esteem issues, preventing violence against women, and supporting the National Inquiry into Missing and Murdered Indigenous Women and Girls.

In recent years, because many wives also have careers, some companies posting their employees to different locations or recruiting new personnel have assisted in finding a new job for the wife or, if the employee is a wife herself and her rank is high enough, for the husband. Some organizations have adopted this practice for same-sex couples. Still, a female "trailing spouse" is often made to feel less important. As the number of dual-career couples grows, many wives are reluctant to give up their careers and, in some cases, are the primary breadwinners. Husbands then must adjust their roles and careers, as did the husband of British prime minister Margaret Thatcher or the spouses of other political women. Moreover, among highly public political and celebrity marriages, not all wives are choosing to "stand by their man," for example, in the face of revelations of their husband's infidelity.

Box 6.3 Women in Media

Sophie Grégoire Trudeau

Sophie Grégoire Trudeau is the first wife of a Canadian prime minister to have a double surname. (Until March 2016 she spelled it with a hyphen.) Quebec provincial law prevents married people from adopting the name of their spouse in legal documents, and, as a Quebec resident, she was known by her birth name, Grégoire, for most of her career as a television journalist. Only when her husband ran for office in 2007 did she begin to use the hyphenated name, and it was not used regularly until 2015, when Justin Trudeau's campaign office gave the hyphenated name as her preference.

Part of the reason for her decision is likely political—Maureen McTeer, wife of Prime Minister Joe Clark, received severe criticism for not changing her name when her husband was in office in 1979. Clark was criticized for not being able to control the country because he did not exert control over his wife.

When Grégoire married Justin Trudeau in 2005, her choice to keep her name was commented on with some derision. In the October 2006 issue of *Chatelaine*, an article observed: "After they were married, Sophie held on to her surname, even though the mark she's made with it professionally has been modest" (quoted in Kingston 2015).

It is unknown whether Grégoire's choice to hyphenate her name had any effect on her husband's political career, but the fact that it was even considered a possibility—that the concerns of 1980 are the concerns of 2015—is instructive.

Despite these changes, women with paid employment outside the home often experience a "double day" or "second shift." Homemaking, cooking, cleaning, laundry, and child and eldercare default to them after they finish work as they carry a "double burden" of labour. This problem is described in *The Second Shift: Working Parents and the Revolution at Home* by Arlie Russell Hochschild with Anne Machung. First published in 1989, it was reissued in 2012 and exposes a continuing gendered "leisure gap" as working mothers were found to put in an extra month of work a year compared to fathers. (See Chapter 11, Women and Work.)

Increasingly, in divorce settlements some wives who have given up their careers to support a spouse have obtained a share of their husbands' earnings and pensions because of the role they have played in their husbands' careers or businesses. Courts have also awarded "palimony" or compensation similar to alimony to unmarried women who have made similar sacrifices. Such recognition is a further indication of the value of women's economic and social role in families.

Children in the Family

While having children is one of the expected consequences of a marriage, in Canada the rise in the number of children born to single mothers (discussed later in this chapter) is a profound change. This trend in many developed countries has been politicized and reduced to a debate on the acceptable form of "family." In Canada, "for the sake of the children," two-parent marriages are thought to be preferable by political conservatives and by some social scientists as well. For example, Linda Waite and Maggie Gallagher (2000) defend even bad marriages, which, they believe, with enough determination and work from both spouses can improve and become quite satisfactory. Marriage, they argue, benefits a woman and her children financially. Consequently, as divorce economically punishes the wife and her children, they counsel women to work out a marital partnership. Others argue that a bad marriage does not benefit either wife or children, and, if the husband is physically abusive, preserving the marriage can endanger all of them. While some researchers (Wallerstein et al. 2000) fear for the long-term damage that is inflicted on children by divorce, others find that the vast majority of children of divorce are resilient and become well-adjusted adults (Hetherington and Kelly 2002) (see Box 6.4). Children who experience a single parental divorce are much like the children of continuously married parents in their psychological well-being. The children who may suffer more are those who undergo multiple family transitions (parents divorcing, remarrying, and divorcing again) and the inevitable parental conflict involved (Amato 2010). Children may suffer equally from the conflict involved with parents remaining in unhappy marriages (see Box 6.4).

Changes in cultural traditions, more education, being in the paid workforce, better health care, and higher standards of living have had

The Arnolfini Portrait (1434) in Flanders, oil painting by Jan Van Eyck. Giovanni di Nicolao Arnolfini, a wealthy merchant, and his wife are depicted here. His wife gathers up her skirt to her waist, giving the appearance of pregnancy and alluding to the promise of future motherhood.

Box 6.4 In Her Own Words

Public Says Children Better off When Unhappy Parents Divorce, and Single Moms Suck

Posted by Talyaa Liera, as Karen Murphy, 20 September 2007:

My oh my, the public (whoever they are) certainly is opinionated! Blah-de-blah, we like to shoot off our mouths, apparently, about *anything*. Especially when we can spout off about someone else's business. And the Pew Research Center recently asked a whole bunch of people their very opinionated opinions about a whole bunch of things like marriage and parenting, and this is what they said:

1. **Unmarried moms = bad.** Almost half the Judgy McJudgerpants "public" (whoever they are) says you and your spawn are bad, bad, bad if you're not married, and a full two-thirds says it's bad for society! But only if you're a mom. There's no word on the dads, so I guess they're in the clear.
2. **Premarital sex = bad.** Well, the one goes with the other, I suppose. Though fewer people said premarital sex was the beginning of a long and slippery downward slope to the Land of Evil than got all judgmental about unmarried moms, so I guess the real moral of the story is: *don't get caught*. Oh, and cohabitation is also bad, bad, bad.
3. **Children are your path to happiness.** 85% of the people gave "having a relationship with my minor children" a "10" in Importance in Personal Satisfaction and Fulfillment. Take that, non-breeders!
4. **If you're unhappy in marriage, get a fucking divorce already.** Especially when there's kids involved. Kinda ironic, though, isn't it? It's okay to divorce (and thus become a single parent) if you're *already married*, but it's NOT okay if you were never married to begin with. Have I got that right?

Freakin' public. Who *are* these people, anyway?

Source: Liera (2007). "Public Says Children Better Off When Unhappy Parents Divorce, and Single Moms Suck". Babble [blog].

---

an impact on the total fertility rate (TFR) or the number of children that a woman will have over her child-bearing years. Women are choosing to delay marriage and childbirth and to have fewer children. Worldwide, the TFR was 2.5 children in 2010, half of what it was in 1950, though this varies by region. The TFR was highest in 2010 in a number of African states where women had 5 or more children. In most countries, the TFR is 1.5–2.1. In Canada, the 2013 TFR was 1.61 children with a wide provincial difference (Statistics Canada, 2015c). In a few developed states such as Germany, Japan, and Switzerland and in developing states in Eastern Europe and elsewhere, women were having 1.5 or fewer children, well below the population-replacement level. Small family size in the People's Republic of China was reflected in the government's one-child policy, which from 1980 to 2016 penalized parents for having more than 1 child. In other countries, uncertain economic and political times, strict gender roles, and the lack of child care for women who work outside the home

Table 6.1 Births and Total Fertility Rate, by Province and Territory (Fertility Rate)

	2007	2008	2009	2010	2011
	Total Fertility Rate				
Canada	1.66	1.68	1.67	1.63	1.61
Newfoundland and Labrador	1.46	1.58	1.59	1.58	1.45
Prince Edward Island	1.63	1.73	1.69	1.62	1.62
Nova Scotia	1.48	1.54	1.50	1.47	1.47
New Brunswick	1.52	1.59	1.59	1.58	1.54
Quebec	1.69	1.74	1.74	1.71	1.69
Ontario	1.57	1.58	1.56	1.53	1.52
Manitoba	1.96	1.96	1.98	1.92	1.86
Saskatchewan	2.03	2.05	2.06	2.03	1.99
Alberta	1.90	1.92	1.89	1.83	1.81
British Columbia	1.52	1.51	1.50	1.43	1.42
Yukon	1.58	1.64	1.66	1.60	1.73
Northwest Territories	2.11	2.08	2.06	1.98	1.97
Nunavut	2.97	2.98	3.24	3.00	2.97

Note: Total fertility rate is the average number of children per woman.

Source: Statistics Canada, CANSIM Table 102–4505.

also leads them to limit their offspring. Maternity leave with pay before and after childbirth and institutions that provide quality child care and the possibility of free or inexpensive health care and medicine for mothers and their children would benefit working mothers (United Nations 2010).

Elders in the Family

Extended families have always included elders, such as older siblings, parents, and grandparents in their living arrangements. In many cultures, elders, including elder female relatives, play an important role within the family unit. Their wisdom and advice assists in replicating culture and values. In Indigenous cultures female elders serve to maintain community and resist cultural and political incursions from settler colonialism.

In non-industrial societies, a woman has traditionally assumed the role and responsibility of taking care of elders, typically her husband's parents, in conjunction with child care, although an older woman in the household often would assist with child care. Today, with longer life expectancy and the high cost of living and health care, many nuclear families in the Global North are becoming multigenerational as aging parents of the wife, the husband, or both move in with their adult children. For some cases, these caregivers are referred to as "the sandwich generation," supporting both younger and elder family members. Studies show that female family members undertake the majority of caregiving tasks even when they are employed full-time. This causes stress in personal and professional lives, especially when social services are limited or non-existent (Williams 2004).

As women tend to live longer, it is likely that women are taking care of more senior women. For many families, caring for elders is an adjustment, whether a women does it in her own home, in the home of elders, or in visits to assisted-living facilities, and is an addition to her daily workload, although she often does it with loving care and concern. Because women tend to provide most of the basic physical and emotional care for elders, like child care, those in the paid workforce may reduce their hours or leave it, while men retain their work hours and contribute more financially. Historically, caregivers have been disproportionally women (Cranswick and Dosman 2008); an estimated 54 per cent of caregivers were women in 2012 (Sinha 2012). In Canada, mothers are a significant part of the workforce: 73 per cent of women with children under the age of 16 living at home were employed as of 2009, compared to 39 per cent three decades ago.

> According to the 2010–2011 Statistics Canada survey of women's economic and employment status, women earned only 75 per cent of what men did in 2009, and the wage gap was even greater if all employed men and women—and not just full-year, full-time workers—were considered: in that larger grouping, women earned only 69 per cent of what men did. Women who had children earned between 12 and 20 per cent less than women without children (Stastna 2012).

These inequalities are exacerbated further when intersectionalities like race or Indigenous status come into play.

Times may be changing though: "About 80 per cent of Quebec fathers take paternity leave compared to about 15 per cent in the rest of Canada," according to Diane-Gabrielle Tremblay, a professor of labour economics, innovation, and human resources management at the University of Quebec in Montreal (quoted in Stastna 2012). This discrepancy is at least partly due to the fact that Quebec offers non-transferable paternity leave (either the father takes leave or it is lost) as opposed to the leave time shared between mothers and fathers offered to families in the rest of Canada. Policies such as Quebec's have been shown to increase paternity leave taken, which in turn has been shown to improve the quality of life for families (O'Brien 2009).

Marriage and Gender Roles in North America in Historical Perspective

In colonial North America and later, the status of the wife was determined by the husband's occupation and place in society. In a 1792 critique of this inequity, British philosopher Mary Wollstonecraft called for *A Vindication of the Rights of Woman*, advocating education for young women so they would not be subject to the "slavery of marriage" (see Wollstonecraft 2012 [1792]). Property, family, and social status remained important criteria for selecting a mate. Until the twentieth century, poor women were more likely to have unformalized or common-law marriages with the men with whom they lived, and they continued to work both at home and outside it, caring for their men and children and marrying only when and if there were enough leisure time and extra money for a ceremony. The ideal for middle- and upper-class white women was to stay in the privacy of their home. In these classes, the husband was expected to be the sole provider, and his world was in the public arena.

Many societies have had alternatives to conventional marriage, but often these have been hidden because of social stigma and because researchers have paid more attention to the dominant forms. More equal relationships between husbands and wives have coexisted with the more common patriarchal family. In colonial Canada, in the early nineteenth century, marital models often deviated from religious and cultural norms with established legal precedents for divorce allowing for more female say in domestic relations (Backhouse 1986). In most cases, however, "his" marriage continued to be better than "hers," as when marriage ended in divorce and the woman suffered from loss of earnings and insufficient (if any) child support.

By the late nineteenth century, women in Europe and North America were making some gains toward equality. In 1848, feminist reformers including Elizabeth Cady Stanton (1815–1902), who would be a wife for almost 50 years (and a mother of seven), and Quaker Lucretia Coffin

Mott (1793–1880) met at Seneca Falls, New York, and proclaimed a *Declaration of Sentiments*, which demanded redress for many inequalities in the legal code. In their view, "the only acceptable marriage was based on love, sympathy, and equality between the sexes" (Stanton 1971 [1898]; Hartog 2000, Chapters 8, 11, and 13). In 1871, Stanton declared

> From a woman's stand-point I see that marriage, as an individual tie, is slavery for woman, because law, religion and public sentiment all combine, under this idea, to hold her true to this relation, whatever it may be, and there is no other human slavery that knows such depths of degradation as a wife chained to a man whom she neither loves nor respects no other slavery so disastrous in its consequence on the race, or to individual respect, growth and development. (Stanton 1871)

Reforms concerning equality, however, were slow to come. By the 1890s, some wives had acquired some new legal rights: they could keep their property and earnings in their own names when married, and if separated or divorced, they could claim custody over their children. So long as she was legally a "wife," however, the state expected a woman's husband to provide for her.

Marriage for women in the southern United States was a different story. Before the Civil War (1860–65), only free women, black and white, could legally marry; enslaved people, as the property of their owners, could not. After the US Civil War, when slavery was ended and all black people could marry, interracial marriage was forbidden by state laws. Some of these laws remained in place until very recently (in Alabama until 2000), despite being overturned by the US Supreme Court in 1967 (see Box 6.6). As discussed above, at this time in history Indigenous women in Canada were also "discouraged" from interracial marriage (through the real and present threat of losing their legal status).

From the 1920s through World War II, women's increased public participation through their right to vote and in the paid workforce contributed to a change in the traditional form of marriage in which the husband was the undisputed head of the household and women were deemed sexually ignorant. The "companionate marriage" became a new ideal where spouses shared emotional bonds and intimacies, while maintaining their gendered roles in the workplace, in the home, and as parents. With men in military service during World War I (1914–18) and World War II (1939–45), large numbers of unmarried and married women filled in the ranks at factories, offices, and shops. Especially after World War II, when the returning servicemen demanded their old jobs, women were forced out of them and married women were told to return home, a message justified by a "new" image of the wife. As depicted in the popular media in the 1950s, the young middle-class wife was idealized as one who cleaned her house, shopped and cooked, put her children to bed, and prettied herself, waiting for her (corporately employed) husband to return from work to drink the cocktail she had prepared for him. This gendered division of labour was supported in the policies and practices of other Western societies as well (Cooke and Baxter 2010). The decade of the 1950s in North America was when the term *nuclear family* (discussed earlier in this chapter) first came into being; the goal being to idealize and reinforce the family structure that had existed in North America for the entirety of colonization. The 1950s was the high point of the male-breadwinner and female homemaker family with two, three, even four children (Cherlin 2005; Simmons 2009). These offspring grew up to become the "baby-boomer" generation. The US television series *Mad Men* depicts the strivings and anguish of corporate men and women, single working women, and married women with children in their gendered environments in the late 1950s to the early 1970s.

This devoted homemaker image cloaked the intersectional reality that many women worked at sex-segregated and lower-paid jobs. Mirra Komarovsky's 1962 study *Blue-Collar Marriage* depicted the struggles of working-class women who had to work both at low-paying jobs and at home with little appreciation by their husbands, describing how children added to the strains of marriage. Betty Friedan's *The Feminine Mystique*, published in 1963, laid bare what she saw as the monotony, drudgery, and isolation of the suburban wife. The book struck a chord in the lives of discontented middle-class wives, many of whom had college degrees and wished to use them and pursue careers. Many women began to rethink their situations as a new women's liberation movement, now sometimes referred to as the second wave of feminism, gained momentum by the late 1960s. One outcome was a sharp rise in the divorce rate (see Figure 6.2). The decriminalization of abortion, along with the development of a contraceptive pill, provided a degree of sexual liberation for women (see Chapter 8.)

After a period of acceptance, the legalization of abortion came under attack by conservative religious and political groups and their largely male spokespersons. Because pregnancy and child-bearing were no longer the inevitable outcome of heterosexual intercourse, a woman had more options available, including having sex without getting married.

Through this growing resistance to their past subordination, women's choices in relationships, marriage, and family life expanded after the 1970s. There were new trends: women as well as men living on their own, women staying single longer and cohabiting without marrying, a further increase in divorce, women choosing later motherhood, single parenting, and more women completing post-graduate studies and working outside the home, including after marriage and motherhood. There was also a public recognition of same-sex non-binary gendered partnerships. Consequently, a more egalitarian form of marriage that was flexible and negotiable, the

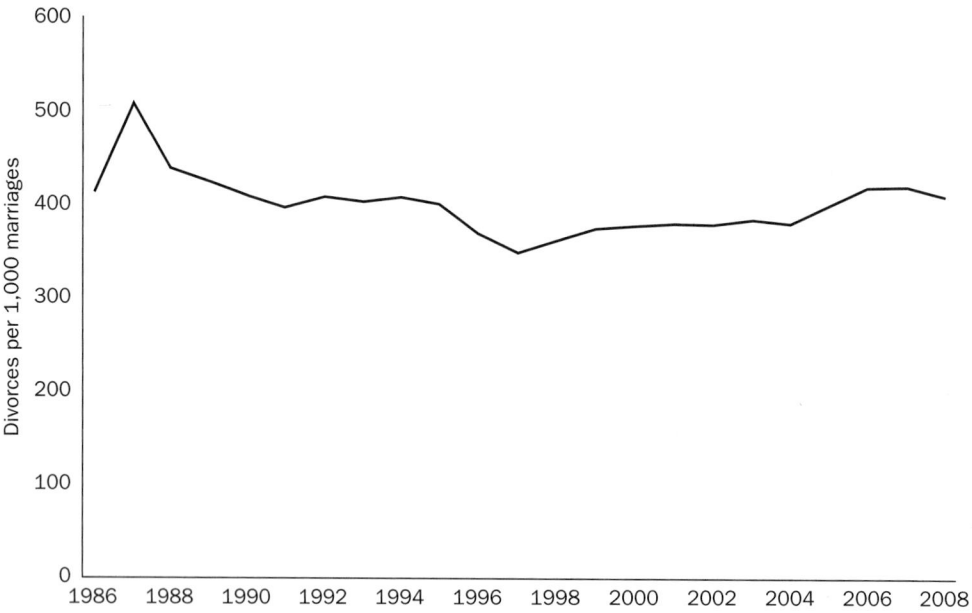

Figure 6.2 Incidence of Divorce in Canada 1986–2008

Source: Employment and Social Development Canada (2016).

"individualized marriage," emerged as an ideal, in which wives and husbands began to consider their own self-development and personal satisfaction with each other as more or equally important as raising children. Such a partnership means that both spouses contribute to the economic and physical maintenance of the home, and both have the opportunity and the responsibility to pursue other interests (Held 1979; Cherlin 2005).

Extramarital Experiences

Whether love develops before marriage or grows between spouses later, many wives and husbands have sought love in extramarital relations. In medieval Europe, for example, among the elite, love was thought to be found only outside marriage, or so it was suggested in many songs of the thirteenth-century French troubadours (Amt 1993). After the 1450s, the European upper classes put renewed emphasis on a wife's role in upholding the family honour by being chaste, attentive to decorum, and absolutely faithful to her husband and by producing heirs to bear the family name. If wedlock was primarily expected to produce legitimate offspring, love need not have anything to do with it. In the nineteenth century a wife, especially a mother, was not meant to stray away from the nuptial bed. Gustave Flaubert and Leo Tolstoy wrote novels, *Madame Bovary* (2003 [1857]) and *Anna Karenina* (2000 [1873–77]) respectively, to remind their readers of the terrible end that awaits married women who search for fulfillment and self-definition through adultery.

Definitions of infidelity vary across and within cultures and types of relationships, and over time, but such actions generally involve violating an expected bond of exclusive intimacy and sexual relations with another person. In Canada, the dramatic changes in family life and culture since the late 1960s, combined with the availability of contraception, have contributed to the rise in extramarital experiences. The meaning of sexual fidelity has changed and is a more complicated personal issue than it was in the past.

Divorce

Not all societies treat divorce the same way. In one anthropologist's sample, women and men had approximately equal rights to initiate divorce in 75 per cent of societies, while men enjoyed superior rights in only 15 per cent. In 10 per cent, women had superior rights. For example, in a **matrilocal** society, such as the Iroquois Nation in North America, wives could divorce husbands by dumping their belongings outside the door (Murdock 1950). The majority of societies disapprove of divorce, and Western society is no exception—as testified to by the many legal obstacles to divorce in both religious and state laws. In ethnically diverse societies, family law (in which generally divorce is dealt with) is complex. Some countries assign responsibility for legal decisions about marriage and divorce to special courts from each ethnic or religious group, with no civil law on these matters, while others struggle to devise ways to accommodate religious/ethnic diversity, with varying degrees of success.

Divorce is a primary contributor to an increased number of impoverished women and children. Most of the families in Canada living in poverty are female-headed households, although not all are the consequence of divorce (Eichler 2012). In 2008, female lone-parent families in Canada earned an average of $42,300, while male lone-parent families earned an average of $60,400 and two-parent families with children earned an average of $100,200 (Statistics Canada 2012b). Gender roles in marriage and the gender gap in the workplace help explain these differences. Married women contribute domestic labour to the household. Though many are stay-at-home wives, others also earn an income working full- or part-time. Despite a wife's increased earning power in recent years, husbands in general contribute the greater amount to the household because of their larger income (DeNavas-Walt, Proctor, and Smith 2011). When a marriage or similar union ends, a woman generally loses access to the financial resources and other supports that were available through a spouse. As women continue to be discriminated against in the job market and bear a major responsibility for the care of children, divorce can severely reduce their standard of living, just at the moment when they and their children may be emotionally vulnerable.

While the law requires former husbands to pay child support in most cases, in 2014, nearly two-thirds of all support orders in Canada in 2014 were in arrears (Moore 2014). Divorce may involve a bitter struggle over the division of property and money.

It is relatively easy for opposite-sex couples to marry in Canada, but more difficult, although not as difficult as in the past, to get divorced. To get divorced, couples usually require lawyers, legal documents, one or more court hearings, and often a considerable amount of time, even when both parties are in agreement. If the couple disagrees about the terms of divorce, and there are children and property rights in dispute, the legal cost of settlement can be high.

Alternatives to Conventional Marriage in the Past

The alternative configurations to conventional family roles and lives are diverse. Some have been devised without women's input or consent, and some have evolved as a "last resort" because women lacked the option not to marry and have children. Different types of community for women in the past are considered—religious, educative, work-oriented, and supportive. At times, women could join ideological communities based on religious or political convictions rather than be traditionally married. The few described here are mainly the options that women have shaped for themselves, the ways of living that they have chosen, designed, or imagined.

Religious Communities

Buddhist and Christian orders of nuns have enabled women to live outside the boundaries of the family circle for centuries. Christian convents originated in the fourth and fifth centuries in the Mediterranean area and, like the churches to which they belong, have had a complex history (McNamara 1996). Buddhism also has a long history of monasticism for women in Asia and a comparable complexity (Falk 1980). See Chapter 10 for more on women in religious communities throughout history.

Today, nuns (both Christian and Buddhist) vary widely in work, dress, and social relationships. What has not changed are a dedication to spiritual life, a decision not to marry or engage in any sexual relationships, and a commitment to a community of like-minded women organized in convents and orders. Members of these orders may be committed to teaching, nursing, helping the poor, providing shelter for orphans or single mothers, working with drug addicts, or fighting for human rights. Indeed, some nuns have been in the forefront of the struggle for social justice around the world. The number of women seeking to become nuns is declining.

Labouring Communities

Social pressure in the form of low wages, abuse of unprotected women, and outright coercion has sometimes led working women to organize into collectives. In Belgium and the Netherlands, for example, unmarried women, including widows, formed quasi-religious communities called *beguinages* based on collective housekeeping and economic enterprise. The religious element in their organizations during the late twelfth and thirteenth centuries ensured their social respectability and enabled members to claim the protection of local ecclesiastical authorities. Nevertheless, women met with hostility and even violence from the men in craft guilds, who would neither admit women to their craft "brotherhoods" nor allow them to compete by working for lower wages or longer hours (Neel 1989; Gilchrist 1994).

Industrialization in the nineteenth century in western Europe and North America caused a major social shift away from the organization of production by the individual artisan to factories owned by industrial capitalists. A feature of early factory communities was the supervision and control of unmarried girls and young women who had left home to work in the mills. The most famous experiment of a protected mill community was in Lowell, Massachusetts, in the 1820s. The young rural women recruited into the textile factories there lived in company boarding houses, where their morals and physical needs were carefully monitored. They enjoyed the benefits of urban life; lectures and other culturally enriching events were scheduled in the few leisure hours. Several young women produced a magazine, *The Lowell Offering*, and some were inspired to go on to more rewarding careers (Eisler 1977). The Lowell experiment lasted fewer than two decades and was not repeated. In *North and South* (2008 [1855]), British novelist Elizabeth Gaskell (1810–1865) describes the independence of the factory girls in Manchester, England, who used a bit of their earnings to dress themselves better. For most women, the experience of the factory system was not an idyll but a disciplined life of hard labour, tuberculosis and other diseases, and sexual exploitation. Nevertheless, for some women in Europe and North America, industrialization made possible a new image and a new kind of role, an alternative to those of "wife" and "mother."

Utopian and Experimental Communities

Utopia was first used by philosopher Thomas More (1478–1535) as the name of an imaginary community whose design eliminated social ills such as injustice and moral degeneracy. The elements of the design reveal the author's critique of his own society as well as providing a proposal for correcting society's flaws, however fanciful or unrealistic that construction might be. Many imagined or attempted utopias focus on the conventional family and its assigned roles as the root of many social problems and propose radical alternatives. Some attack marriage itself, while others target the nuclear family.

The "solutions" envisioned are diverse and often inventive: elimination of sexual intercourse, keeping sex but eliminating sexual exclusivity, communal child rearing, and, the most fanciful, eliminating men altogether and/or altering the body so that reproduction does not rely on coupling. While the last of these has not occurred with humans so far, the others have been both attempted experimentally and described in writing. Some of these literary and real utopian (or "intentional") communities can be described as feminist, and some explicitly so. Two examples from the early days of the second-wave women's movement are Joanna Russ's *The Female Man* (1975) and Marge Piercy's *Woman on the Edge of Time* (1976).

The most influential utopian writer of antiquity is the Greek philosopher Plato. His *Republic*, written in the fourth century BCE, is perhaps the prototype of anti-family utopias. He imagined a state governed by an elite group, the "guardians," in which women and men would participate on equal terms. Reproduction would be carefully regulated. When children were born, they would be taken from the mother and put under the supervision of special caretakers, a group that included both women and men. New mothers would breastfeed at random and would be prevented from knowing which infant was theirs. Women would thus participate in the job of governing and develop concern and affection for all the society's children (Plato 1998). Plato's *Republic* has sometimes been seen as feminist because it challenges male supremacy, educates women equally with men, and frees women from the constraints of child care.

There are no known utopian constructs written by women in antiquity, but a number of modern utopias have been conceived by women. "Ladyland" is such a place described by the Bengali author Rokeya Sakhawat Hossain in her story *Sultana's Dream* (1905; see Hossain 1988). It is a land where the private and public roles of women and men have been reversed. Women take control of Ladyland after men prove incapable of defending the country through conventional warfare. Men are relegated to seclusion, thus eliminating both crime and sin. Women take over all public and political functions, while men are assigned the job of child care. Women rule in Ladyland not through the traditional male manner of domination and oppression but through more co-operative means and working with nature, for example, to extract the sun's energy. As a result of a less exploitative approach to nature, many disasters, such as drought, are eliminated.

Herland, written by Charlotte Perkins Gilman (1979 [1915]) a decade later, solves the problem of women's inequality through the simple device of eliminating men from society altogether. In her utopia, women find a way to conceive children by *parthenogenesis* (nonsexual reproduction) and motherhood is a venerated achievement. All of society is oriented toward nurturance of human beings as well as of nature. The women see themselves as potential mothers who are not obliged to become wives (see also Chapters 2, 4, and 7). These utopias are a product of their time, and so do not take into account the intersectional experiences of women (and therefore the idea that different women might have different needs from a utopia).

Utopias and *dystopias* (the disturbing opposite of utopias) have been imagined by many modern feminist writers in the guise of fantasy and science fiction. Many utopian writers rely on radically modifying not only marriage and the family but also the process of reproduction. This suggests that while social inequality is the "problem," the root of inequality is the biology of reproduction (Lees 1984). Change this and everything changes; without changing this, they suggest, there is little chance of changing anything else.

Celibacy seems to be the central rule for many communities based on religious conviction. Celibacy, communitarians argue, reorders the priorities of a community over those of the individual (Muncy 1973). For the community of Shakers, celibacy was a theological issue; its founder, Ann Lee (1736–1784) preached equality of women with men, deemed possible only by eliminating sexual relations, which would distract women and men from their religious duties, and motherhood, which would create inequality. There were communities which approved sex but not marriage. The most famous and longest-lasting such community (c. 1848–1881) were the "Perfectionists" in Oneida, New York, who practised "complex marriage," in which each member was married to every other person of the opposite sex, and exclusive attachments between couples were forbidden. Young women who were chosen to bear children had to give them up to specialists to raise them. In this community, as in many others, the rights of women were still limited, although equality among the members was advocated. Contrary to its theory, friction arose between the mothers and the rest of the community over the control of the children. Feminists have sometimes advocated celibacy as a strategic method to disrupt the patriarchal family. Breanne Fahs' work (2010) provides insight into 1960s– and 1970s–radical feminist efforts to destabilize traditional mores about gender, sex, and power by choosing asexuality.

Since the nineteenth century, experimental communities have attempted to create societies with unconventional marriage and child-rearing practices. Few of these have been led by feminists, and few have succeeded for very long. The early Israeli kibbutz was viewed as a success in the tradition of communes based on socialist ideals of equality and shared effort. Everyone worked, and all economic conditions, profits, and debts, were shared communally. During that period (from the 1920s to the 1970s), children were raised in "children's houses," seeing their parents at the end of the work day but sleeping apart from them with other children of their age group. Housework was done communally, although mostly by women. The ideology of women's equality with men and the subordination of private interests to those of the collective were fundamental to the kibbutz movement. Over the years, the nuclear family, traditional gender roles, and privatization have re-emerged and replaced communal living and shared work. Most kibbutz women now tend to the home and their own children, and fewer of them attend college or university than kibbutz men (Peres 1998). Other communal social arrangements have been more short-lived for a variety of reasons, but utopian communities are not the only alternative to conventional family life.

Families in the Early Twenty-First Century

Over the past five decades, societal changes have transformed the ways people live, love, work, play, and conduct political change. When small and remote communities are linked to major centres worldwide by cellphones and the Internet, traditional ways, including family life, are affected. Also, global economic restructuring has altered how most women and men earn a living. International efforts to improve individual rights, labour, education, and health care, for example, along with demands for equality by women and other members of subordinated racialized, ethnic, religious, and Indigenous groups, have brought new national policies and cultural shifts with implications for families, their structures, and their values.

Changes in the Global South

Many multigenerational families in Africa, Asia, and the Americas are becoming nuclear families. Family members may no longer live in the same household, and having relatives who work in Europe and elsewhere is common. Some Malian women are pleased with the end of polygyny but miss being part of a large household of wives and children, although they do not want to have many children themselves. Other women in Egypt, El Salvador, and Thailand, for example, express enthusiasm for opportunities with new jobs that take them away from their families and communities to urban centres and other nations, sometimes not fully aware of the challenges that await them (Huston 2001). Some single women in Sri Lanka who left their villages to work in the global assembly line in Colombo have to defend themselves as "good girls" and hence appropriate marriage partners (Lynch 2007). Globalized economies often divide families with one parent or the other crossing borders for employment.

Changes in the Global North

Differences in culture and national policies concerning child welfare, parental leave, and employment benefits, for example, have contributed to variances in family life in industrialized societies over the past five decades, but there are also commonalities. In regard to household duties, for example, women's increased participation in paid employment and in political representation has brought only a modest gain in the time men commit to housework. Moreover, as women's earnings increase, both partners do less housework (though it is important to note that as with all things, these benefits are experienced or not based on one's intersectional inequalities). Many couples who can afford the cost turn to restaurant or store-prepared meals and use time-saving appliances. More affluent dual-career households hire domestic labour, often immigrant women, some of whom are undocumented and thus open to exploitation. German couples, for example, depend upon an Eastern European *Bügelfrau* "ironing-board woman" or *Putzfrau* "cleaning woman" (Cooke and Baxter 2010, 523). Instead of forming new gender roles and a more equal division of labour in household tasks, families with employed women in Western societies are outsourcing much of the unpaid labour in the home to women of a different national origin, race, ethnicity, and class, thereby converting housework to low-paying labour.

New trends in family formation have emerged. These include delaying marriage, a decline in marriage, and fewer children, along with an increase in cohabitation, non-marital child-bearing, and the legalization of same-sex marriage or domestic partnerships. Wide variations do exist. In countries where the male-breadwinner family is still dominant, such as Italy, women are more likely to marry than to cohabit. In countries such as Sweden where national policies in health benefits and child-care support more female equality, the rate of cohabiting is higher. In Sweden and North America, which have high rates of female employment, as women increase their earning power they have more choices in partnering and are seen as more desirable marriage partners. In Japan, however, where the male-breadwinner family prevails, women's higher earnings decrease the likelihood of marriage for Japanese women (Cherlin 2005; Cooke and Baxter 2010).

In Canada, as women's education and incomes have increased, the incidence of dual-earner families in which the wife earns more than the husband has also grown. Between 1976 and 2008, wives in dual-earner families earning more than their husbands increased from about 12 per cent to 29 per cent (Williams 2013). Additionally, marriage between people of the same level of educational attainment increased from 1971 to 2001. Educational homogamy has occurred over and above what would be expected based on the increase in women graduating university (Hou and Miles 2007), which means that people are intentionally choosing to marry someone of similar educational attainment (whereas they might not have in the past). This rise in selecting a marriage partner based on educational attainment has contributed to inequality in earnings between lower-income families and higher-income families. Research has also shown a "marriage gap" between the top quartile of income earners and the bottom three quartiles, and that this gap has widened since 1976 (Cross and Mitchell 2014). That means that the highest-earning Canadians are the most likely to reap the economic and social benefits of marriage.

"New" Family Configurations

Blended Families

Blended families likely have always existed in human history when women might die in childbirth and men in warfare, and life expectancy generally was shorter. A new union would be sought for mutual support. In some societies it was the duty of family members to make such an arrangement. Today, blended families, sometimes known as stepfamilies, are formed through remarriage or cohabitation after a divorce or a death but also may involve a partner who was unmarried with children. Some seek to replace the term *step* with *bonus* because being a stepmother/parent or a stepsister/sibling connotes, historically, a lesser or negative status, when in practice additional adults and children in the family can be positive and welcome additions. Regarding this family form that is based on love as much as economics, women speak of the challenges of merging lifestyles, housing, and child custody and visiting arrangements while developing new traditions that reflect their being a blended family (Morello 2011; Strong, DeVault, and Cohen 2011).

Single-Parent Families

Single-parent families, in which children are raised by one parent, usually the mother, are more common and are increasingly common worldwide. Female-headed single-parent families are too often negatively depicted because they are assumed to be the result of out-of-wedlock or cohabiting relations, or they are pitied if they are an outcome of divorce or widowhood rather than by choice. Globally, single mothers are likely to be both poorer than mothers who live with a partner and even poorer in comparison to single fathers. In the United States, which provides fewer social services and less social support for human needs than almost any other advanced industrial country, single mothers and their children have long faced difficult hurdles unless the women are high-income earners themselves (United Nations 2010; Strong, De Vault, and Cohen 2011).

Consensual Unions: Cohabitation, Domestic Partners

Cohabiting couples form consensual unions based on an intimate relationship, and many of these families include children. Today women and men living as domestic partners are more acceptable and normal in many parts of the world, without the stigma attached to such relationships in the past. Couples may cohabit because they cannot marry for financial reasons, because one or both partners may not be free to marry, or because it is simply made difficult or is not permitted by their society. As well, couples may simply prefer cohabiting as a lifestyle or choose it because it is common practice in their social group. In some cases, cohabitation is long term or permanent; in other cases, it may be relatively short term; such couples may be testing their relationship before marrying or may not desire to make a long-term commitment (Cherlin 2010). Some observers suggest a relationship between the increase in consensual unions in various forms in Europe and

---

Box 6.5 Key Issues

Same-Sex Couples across Canada

As same-sex marriages were legalized in Canada in 2005, census data on legally married and same-sex couples are available for 2006 and 2011 only.

According to the census, the number of same-sex married couples nearly tripled between 2006 and 2011, while the number of same-sex common-law couples rose 15.0 per cent.

As a result, married couples represented about 3 in 10 same-sex couples in 2011, nearly twice the share of 16.5 per cent in 2006.

- **64,575**: The number of same-sex couple families in 2011, up 42.4 per cent from 2006
- **21,015**: The number of same-sex married couples
- **43,560**: The number of same-sex common-law couples
- **0.8 per cent**: The proportion of all couples in 2011 who were same-sex couples
- **54.5 per cent**: The proportion of same-sex couples who were male
- **45.5 per cent**: The proportion of same-sex couples who were female
- **25.3 per cent**: The proportion of same-sex married spouses and common-law partners aged 15 to 34
- **17.5 per cent**: The proportion of opposite-sex married spouses and common-law partners aged 15 to 34
- **6.2 per cent**: The proportion of same-sex married spouses and common-law partners aged 65 and over
- **17.8 per cent**: The proportion of opposite-sex married spouses and common-law partners aged 65 and over
- **45.6 per cent**: The proportion of all same-sex couples in Canada living in Toronto, Montreal, and Vancouver
- **33.4 per cent**: The proportion of all opposite-sex couples in Canada living in Toronto, Montreal, and Vancouver

Sources: Statistics Canada (2012a; 2015b).

North America and the weakening of the institution of marriage. The acceptance of children born out of wedlock in most regions of the world is another contributing factor. Some countries provide some legal rights for consensual unions, deemed domestic partners, such as health benefits. In a few countries, however, cohabitation may be punishable by imprisonment.

It is interesting to note the provincial differences in rates of cohabitation in Canada, as recorded by the 2011 census: 31.5 per cent of couples were in common-law relationships in Quebec; the next-highest provincial rate is 16.0 per cent in New Brunswick. The lowest is in Ontario, at only 10.9 per cent. The territories, on the other hand, average 28.8 per cent of households being made up of cohabiting couples (Nunavut is the only province or territory where cohabiting couples make up a larger percentage of families than married couples).

Power, Domination, and Rape

Historically worldwide, warriors and colonizers, for example, "took" conquered women. Chandra Mohanty's groundbreaking work, *Feminism without Borders: Decolonizing Theory, Practicing Solidarity* (2003) reveals how the colonial process worked to conflate gender and race as a strategy for subordination. She cites the example of the 1909 confidential circular by Lord Crewe to British colonists in Africa (often referred to as the "Concubinage Circular") as a "sanctioned mode of colonial rule" that officially discouraged "relationships with 'native women.'" Mohanty argues "The effect of the consolidation of this bureaucratic masculinity was of course not necessarily restraint. Sexual encounters between white men and native women often took the form of rape. This racialized, violent masculinity was the underside of the sanctioned mode of colonial rule." (Mohanty 2003, 60). While publicly acknowledged relationships, either marital or commonlaw, were subject to colonial disapproval, rape was not precluded.

During and after conflict, rape of the conquered population was commonly practised as part of "the spoils of war." It was accepted as legitimate and not designated a war crime nor was it subject to prosecution. Children born from these actions often were not acknowledged by their fathers and, along with their mothers, were subject to poverty and isolation. It was only after the genocidal wars in the former Yugoslavia and in Rwanda that gendered violence including rape, sexual slavery, and sexual violence was recognized as a war crime.

Multiracial Unions and Families

People of different races have fallen in love and sought to have their union recognized by custom, religion, or law only to face stern opposition from families and officials and even ostracism, imprisonment, or death. In Canada, policy and social prohibitions sought to separate races. The first generation of Métis in the Canadian Prairie provinces were the children of colonizing French fur traders who married First Nations women, despite resistance from the Hudson's Bay Company (their employer), resulting in a distinct culture and Indigenous nation. To prevent further intermarriage, the infamous 1876 Indian Act contained clauses that penalized Indigenous women for marrying white men (see above in this chapter). During this same period, laws were passed in parts of Canada that forbade Asian employers from hiring white women. Many of these restrictions continued for many years. In her memoir, *Incorrigible* (2003), Velma Demerson relates how in 1939 she was sentenced to 10 months in a reformatory under Ontario's Women's Refuge Act and subjected to weeks of solitary confinement, forced labour, and painful medical experiments. Pregnant when incarcerated, her child was taken from her by the state. Her only "crime" was being in love with a Chinese man. Upon her release, they were married, after which she lost her Canadian citizenship because her husband was born in China. Jean Lumb, a Canadian-born entrepreneur and humanitarian, also lost her citizenship in 1939 after marrying her husband, Doyle, who had been born in China.

mixed-race couples in Canada representing 4.6 per cent of all unions, almost double the 1991 level of 2.6 per cent.

Families We Choose

Often LGBTQ people suffer both economically and emotionally from being rejected by biological families and have created alternative family networks (Schulman 2009). In *Families We Choose* (1991), sociologist Kath Weston examined how lesbian, gay, and transgender people formed families of unrelated adults to provide emotional and financial support when their families of origin had abandoned them because of their sexual and gender identities. These relationships were especially important during the height of the AIDS crisis (c. 1982–1995), when gay men and lesbians cared for their ailing friends and lovers, taking on the responsibilities family members usually fulfill. Other families are formed by women and trans friends who may live together, celebrate holidays, and support each other in good times and bad.

Velma Demerson's memoir *Incorrigible*. Other countries also have histories of trying to prevent interracial relationships. In South Africa under the state policy of **apartheid**, two Immorality Acts and the Prohibition of Inter-race Marriage Law made sexual relations between races a crime, stipulating penalties of four to five years imprisonment. Athol Fugard's 1974 play *Statements After an Arrest under the Immorality Act* depicted the human cost of state racism. Family and societal fears of **miscegenation** are found in literature, theatre, and film and have been critiqued by feminist scholars (for example, Marchetti 1993).

Today multiracial families are more common globally as people of different races and ethnicities interact on more equal terms at school, at work, and in public spaces. In the United States, it took a 1967 Supreme Court decision, *Loving v. Virginia*, to overturn Virginia's law against racial intermarriage and to recognize marriage between a man and woman as an individual and not a state matter (see Box 6.6). Statistics Canada found in its 2011 National Household Survey that there were more than 360,000

Same-Sex Families

Although couples and groups of women and of men have formed families with each other for centuries, only in the past 150 years as lesbian and gay identities emerged have these families become more structured. The law usually defines a family in terms of blood relationships, heterosexual marriage, shared property, and the legitimization of children. This limited and conventional definition often excludes same-sex unions, especially in places in which same-sex marriage and legal co-parenting of children and even LGBTQ sexuality is prohibited. Same-sex marriage has been legalized in a number of countries in Europe, Africa, and the Americas, including Canada, the Netherlands, South Africa, Argentina, and Norway. These changes have not taken place without opposition, but political organizing among LGBTQ people and their allies has been a powerful force.

Box 6.6 Time to Reflect

The Loving Family Story

The 2016 film *Loving* depicts the story of Mildred Jeter and Richard Loving, working-class people in a small town in Virginia, who wanted to marry and raise their children where they grew up, but she was "coloured" (half black and half Indigenous) and he was white. It was 1958 and Virginia had passed a Racial Integrity Act in 1924 that banned interracial marriage not only between whites and blacks, the primary focus of bans in other states, but also between whites and Asians and Indigenous peoples. In June, Jeter and Loving were married in Washington, DC, where it was permitted, and returned to Virginia only to be arrested in their own home weeks later; the Act also forbade interracial couples married elsewhere to live as husband and wife in the state. The Lovings were given one-year jail sentences, which would be suspended if they left Virginia and promised not to return as a couple for 25 years. They moved to Washington, DC, and had three children, occasionally returning secretly to visit family members. They were not activists, but simply in love. In 1963, working through the American Civil Liberties Union upon Mildred's initiative, they sought to end what they experienced as exile and appealed to the Supreme Court of Virginia for the right to live in the state as a married couple. The appeal was denied in 1966, and their case went to the US Supreme Court. In a unanimous 1967 ruling, *Loving v. Virginia*, the Supreme Court overturned Virginia's anti-miscegenation law, declaring marriage between any man and any woman to be an individual right and that no state could deny the "fundamental freedom" of marriage based on race. This landmark civil rights case also invalidated racial intermarriage bans in 16 other states, and has since been cited as precedent in Canadian case law as an analogy and argument for the legalization of same-sex marriage.

Sources: Newbeck (2012); Schwender (2002); Buirski (2011); Bird (2008).

Visiting Unions—Living Apart Together

The movement of large numbers of people globally has never been so great. Workers, refugees, immigrants, or students may enter into informal unions while retaining a marital union in their original residence. Some informal unions are formalized with or without the knowledge and consent of one or more other partners, thus ending up as polygamous marriages. Holding a higher status or income and being unhindered by pregnancy and small children, men are more likely than women to form more than one union and may pay regular or occasional visits to their various "families." Women in "visiting" unions may be disadvantaged relative to women in legal marriages with respect to financial commitments in case of separation; but, of course, the opposite is true when a woman is wealthier than her partner. Nevertheless, since informal unions are usually more common among poor women, the social and financial consequences of their dissolution are even more severe.

A variation of visiting unions is the "living apart together" family in developed countries. The reasons for couples in an intimate relationship maintaining separate residences include employment factors (for example, one having a job in a different location), state welfare regulations, complications of merging other family members into a single household, and personal lifestyles, such as the desire for private space, and are not limited to young adults prior to deciding to cohabit or to marry (Schwartz 2011).

Transnational Families

International migration for employment, family reunification, and physical safety from ethnic, religious, and civil conflicts has contributed to the growth in transnational families where family members may live in different countries for an extended period of time. In their new adopted country, higher-income immigrants have the financial capability of maintaining regular contact with family in their country of origin. For the working poor, increasingly it has been women who have emigrated to support their families and left their children and spouses/partners behind (in some cases, the marital or cohabitation relationship has ended). This is another example of the intersectional nature of inequalities. Today, for example, some Turkish women in Germany, Colombian women in Spain, Filipinas and Jamaicans in Canada, Hong Kong, Italy, and the United States, and Mexican women in the United States support their families by sending remittances home and mothering from afar. Low-income transnational families suffer from split-family relations that contribute to anguish on the part of absentee mothers, increased responsibilities for other womenfolk, including daughters, who now manage the household, and children's resentment for the minimal physical contact with their parent. Despite the sacrifices, many women feel they gain from these new gender roles and opportunities (Parreñas 2005; Dreby 2009). In such situations, being in a transnational family is not a choice but is imposed out of economic conditions, with mixed results for family relations.

Role Reversals

Crossing gender roles, though not widespread, has been accepted in some societies. A typical example is that of "women marriage" among the Igbo of southeast Nigeria, where women could marry other women by paying a bride price. This Igbo institution provided an opportunity for women who had skills and economic resources to operate as men did, within socially sanctioned patterns (Uchendu 1965). Role reversal may be available to men, too, as in the case of the *two-spirit people* of the Cheyenne in the United States, men who adopt the clothing and behaviour of women and become "wives" (Hoebel 1960).

The view that men in general would not willingly take on "housewifely" roles and take care of children has weakened considerably. Some men choose to be more involved with parenthood; others are led to be so through unemployment. The traditional low regard conferred on domestic jobs to which women have traditionally been relegated is hard to change, but associations between kinds of work or activity and gender are becoming less rigid.

Choosing Not to Mother

Until recently wives achieved "adult status" primarily by becoming mothers. While the mandate to mother is still strong, it is fading a little. As has always been true, some women cannot bear children, and some choose not to. A growing movement of women "child-free by choice" argues that child-centric culture limits women's lives and puts enormous stress on the environment.

Queen's University philosophy professor Christine Overall wrote *Why Have Children: The Ethical Debate* (2013) as a backdrop to the choice to procreate or not. She turns the argument on its head: Rather than asking why a women does not have children, Overall insists that the ethical way forward is to consider the moral, psychological, and social rationale for choosing to do so.

Women on Their Own

The proportion of women who choose to live alone and to not have children has increased in recent years. Being single is not the same as being alone or feeling lonely; in many cases, it is a lifestyle choice (Klinenberg 2012). Some researchers have argued that discrimination exists against single people. Not only are single women often deemed less worthy and pressured to marry, they are penalized in policy and practice. Many employers, for example, do not give a single woman time off to care for a relative or close friend. Single women with or without children often devote more time and energy to community work and maintaining ties to neighbours and other family than do married couples, who focus on each other. One study showed that 84 per cent of never-married women provide routine assistance to their parents, compared to 68 per cent of married women. Never-married women also are more likely to be community volunteers, collecting signatures for petitions and attending political gatherings, for example, than their married female counterparts (Parker-Pope 2011).

Today, young women are marrying at a later age than their mothers did, if at all. Economic, educational, and job opportunities have relieved many women from the dependent wifely role. Many married (and divorced or widowed) women who were "housewives" are returning to school or the workplace or are establishing businesses, some performed at home. With improved financial standing, the need to marry or stay married or be coupled for economic security has become less compelling to women. The opportunities for lesbians to partner, marry, or be single and to be public about their relationships are greater than ever before. The first requirement for women's emancipation, and for a larger range of choices, is a source of income—for most, a job that pays enough to live independently.

Freedom to find love and emotional sustenance outside of conventional marriage and family and the opportunity to be self-supporting are prerequisites to choosing an alternative arrangement to the marital union. This choice is not universally available to women around the world in societies that do not readily condone the unmarried status of a woman and that continue to censure the independent and autonomous woman. The search for personal autonomy may be difficult and costly even for women with economic means. The reality of the modern world, however, is that families in their multiple forms persist but are less dependent upon a marital union.

Summary

The family is an ancient and universal form of social organization. In most societies people have formed families based on marital heterosexual households. Marriage is often explained as an economic necessity. Its gendered division of labour implies that women and men are interdependent. Regulating sexuality and having children are other reasons for marriage. After marriage, couples may reside with the wife's natal family, with the husband's, in a new household of their own, or according to some other pattern. Every society has customary rules and expectations about the formation of households.

Parents and families have in the past usually selected mates for their children, often according to traits desired by the family and according to the economic, social, and political interests of the family. In developed countries today most people expect to make their own choices; in these cases, ideas about personal attraction and love play a greater role.

Marital households usually include a husband, wife, and children and often elders, but some societies allow and even encourage more than one spouse (*polygamy*). Having multiple husbands (*polyandry*) is extremely rare, but having multiple wives (*polygyny*) is prohibitive due to the cost of providing for such. Whether single or multiple, wives in traditional marriages in most societies are deemed to be subordinate to husbands. In contemporary industrial societies, this subordination is illustrated by the concept of the "incorporated wife."

The question of the role of marriage in the welfare of children is controversial. Most societies, like many social scientists, regard a two-parent household as ideal but do not necessarily agree about the effects of single-parent homes on children. Traditionally, women were expected to marry and stay married for the sake of the children. Today, many women have the option of birth control, which reduces the necessity to marry or stay married. Nevertheless, social pressures on women to marry persist.

Women have always assumed, or been socially and culturally assigned, primary responsibilities for care for elders and ill family members. With increased longevity, more women are caring for elders longer, causing some to jeopardize their own health and their future welfare by leaving the paid workforce.

By the end of the twentieth century, many people were choosing not to marry, many couples were choosing cohabitation without marriage, and many couples were choosing to delay parenthood, to limit the number of children they have, or to not become parents at all. The new status of women—individual rights, more education, higher income, and maintaining careers—has changed the character of unions (married or not) and of household organization.

Historically women have been punished for extramarital experiences (as well as premarital ones), while men tend to be excused. This too has changed, especially in the Global North. Divorce for marriages that do not work out is an option in many societies; in North America it tends to result in unfavourable economic consequences for women. Widowhood remains an often tragic circumstance for women.

Alternatives to conventional marriage have existed in earlier times and in the present. Some couples, for example, reject unegalitarian marriages, in which women are subordinates, for true parity. Larger non-marital communities, such as the convent, have been an option for Buddhist and Christian women for centuries. These religious communities provide opportunities for some women to develop their skills and talents and to serve their societies in ways unrealized as wives and mothers. Utopian communities constructed by male and female writers critique the conventional family and imagine alternative roles for women and men, though often by means of celibacy and eliminating reproduction. Actual "utopian" communities have experimented with similar methods to produce ideal societies, though these have proven very difficult to sustain for any length of time.

Multiple new family forms include blended families; single parenthood; same-sex families; domestic partners; role reversals for women and men; families that cross races, ethnicities, and continents; the choice to remain childless; and the choice to live alone. However, choice is highly limited for most women in the world, and in fact, many women continue to wish for the ideal conventional marriage and family.

Discussion Questions

1. Calder and Beaman's *Polygamy's Rights and Wrongs* complicates the issue of plural marriage. What have you seen in film or television about the lives of women in polygamous marriages? Consider the possible positive and negative implications of this family formation and whether it should be legal in Canada.
2. Review current popular journal publications, TV shows, or films on married life, brides and weddings, gender roles in housekeeping, home life, and babies/children. What is the image of the woman's role that emerges? In your opinion, do these media representations affect the definition and formation of the *wifely roles* in Canada, in your own family, in your circles?
3. Draw your own family tree, including the birthplace and dates of as many people as possible. What does it tell you about the patterns followed in your family?
4. What, in your view, would be an ideal family configuration? What social conditions would be necessary for this kind of family form to be possible?
5. Think about the role of Canadian law in regard to family formations. How does it regulate who may live together or love together? What changes are needed to prevent families from being separated?

Recommended Resources

Ahmed, Leila. 1999. *A Border Passage.* New York: Farrar, Straus, and Giroux. A memoir by an Egyptian feminist and one of the foremost scholars on women and Islam. In the chapter titled "Harem" she reflects on her experience of Islam in the family as complicated but not necessarily oppressive. She examines the everyday Islam of women that gives them some autonomy and power to interpret their own lives.

Calder, Gillian, and Lori G. Beaman, eds. 2014. *Polygamy's Rights and Wrongs: Perspectives on Harm, Family and Law.* Vancouver: UBC Press. This text is a valuable and provocative contribution to the conversation on plural marriage. It opens with the question: "Is Polygamy Inherently Harmful?" and continues to probe how this particular family form can exist within contemporary legal frameworks and social and cultural mores.

Cheal, David, and Patrizia Albanese, eds. 2014. *Canadian Families Today.* Toronto: Oxford University Press. This text provides a rich overview and historical context of the terrain concerning contemporary Canadian families.

Dua, Enakshi. "Beyond Diversity: Exploring the Ways in Which the Discourse of Race has Shaped the Institution of the Nuclear Family" in Dua and Robertson, eds. *Scratching the Surface: Canadian, Antiracist Feminist Thought.* Toronto: Canadian Scholars Press, 1999. Dua's analysis of the historic economic and cultural factors that shaped the formation of Canadian and other families remains fundamental to an intersectional anti-colonial understanding.

Huston, Perdita. 2001. *Families as We Are: Conversations from around the World.* New York: The Feminist Press. Using interviews with multigenerational families of all socioeconomic backgrounds in 11 countries, the author describes how the concept of family worldwide is being expanded and how women's and men's roles are being transformed. Women share their strengths, worries, and hopes about the impact of urbanization, economic changes, immigration, and global culture and information on their family structures and relationships in the twenty-first century.

Mandell, Nancy, and Ann Duffy. 2011. *Canadian Families: Diversity, Conflict, and Change.* Toronto: Thompson Nelson. The family is explored in its multiple and varied formations and analyzed through a feminist lens.

Moore, Holly. 2014. "Family Support Arrears across Canada: Deadbeats Owe $3.7 Billion across the Country." CBC News, 1 October. www.cbc.ca/beta/news/family-support-arrears-across-canada-1.2782421. The interactive map in this article shows the data for people in arrears on their support payments in each province.

Zakaria, Rafia. 2015. *The Upstairs Wife.* Toronto: Beacon Press. Zakaria creates a world in which public and private lives are conflated, in a compelling drama of women's roles when a second wife joins a family in the time surrounding Pakistani prime minister Benazir Bhutto's assassination.

7 Women over the Life Course

Chapter Outline

- Girlhood
- Daughter in the Family
- Motherhood
- Women Growing Older: The Double Standard of Aging
- Life Events and Role Transitions
- The Sisterhood of Women

This chapter will help you

- Learn about the distinct gender differences that occur in families
- Understand how the particular construction of gender relegates the assignment of women's roles in families and society
- Appreciate how age, race, sexuality, and class interact with gender to produce difference in the construction of "girls" and "women" throughout their lives
- Recognize the constructed nature of women's social position versus the notion of "natural" or biological determinism

*A son's a son until he gets him a wife.
A daughter's a daughter all the days of her life.*
—OLD ENGLISH PROVERB

I attribute my energy to post-menopausal zest!
—MARGARET MEAD, ANTHROPOLOGIST, 1971

Women's and gender studies have focused largely on young and middle adulthood. Growing up and growing older are formative experiences but less studied components of women's lives. This is changing with more research conducted more and courses offered on girlhood in post-secondary institutions. Girlhood in most parts of the world today has changed greatly over the centuries. Over the past five decades as part of the global community's efforts to advance the human rights of women and children, states and organizations have sought to end the labour and sexual exploitation of girls. More daughters in the Global South, for example, are attending school and for longer periods of time. In industrialized states, depending on their economic class, girls now generally experience an extended period of relatively carefree youth before assuming adult responsibilities.

Womanhood also has changed with increased longevity. The quality of those later adult years depends in large part on a woman's health, finances, interests, familial and other relationships, and government policies and societal customs pertaining to gender roles and the elderly. This chapter examines girlhood and adolescence, adulthood, and later adulthood for women within the context of family or family-like households.

Girlhood

Although girls generally hold a subordinate position in their families and societies compared to boys, their experiences, past and present, vary widely across the globe and within communities given differences in backgrounds, cultures, and family dynamics in specific historical eras. In Canada, for example, girlhood as a daughter of migrant farm workers differs significantly from girlhood as a daughter of professional parents in a predominantly white middle-class suburb (Forman-Brunell 2001). Moreover, around the world girls are negotiating changing and often-competing notions of what it means to be a woman from within their own societies and under the external influence of the globalization of Western culture in media, advertisements, and consumer goods (Leach 2010).

In the early 1990s, feminist studies of Euro-North American middle-class girlhood emphasized girls' vulnerability, including problems of body image and eating disorders, loss of confidence as they increasingly encountered the dominant male culture during adolescence, neglect by schools, and the pressures of consumer culture with its sexualized representations of girls (Brown and Gilligan 1992; Brown 2008; Driscoll 2008). Working-class girls, on the other hand, were deemed to be at risk of teen pregnancy, drug abuse, and gang involvement (Kehily 2008).

Essentialist ideas that all girls are the same everywhere and throughout all time fail to recognize that context matters. Not all girls are sweet, passive, and "good" at all times, in every situation. They can be "mean" to other girls, bullies, and cliquish (Simmons 2002). In movies like the 2004 *Mean Girls*, these kinds of behaviour are played for laughs, although they can be damaging for both perpetrators and victims. Such verbal and physical acting out may also be a form of opposition to having to conform to expectations of how girls should be (Lamb 2001). Studies on girls' aggression have been balanced by others that give attention to girls who are emotionally and socially confident, do well in school, are active in sports and clubs, have close relationships with their families and friends, and feel no need to strive to be popular (Meadows and Carmichael 2002).

Currently, the discourse of girls as disadvantaged and "in crisis" is being countered by the discourse of girls as proactive. "Girl power" recognizes girls' agency as they express their goals, navigate their pathways, and work collaboratively for safe spaces for themselves to develop (Brown 2008; Driscoll 2008; Kehily 2008), although "girl-power" rhetoric can often be appropriated in ways that are hardly empowering. Moreover, the marketing of pink "princess" outfits and products to preschoolers is a challenge for many modern parents seeking to raise their daughters with models other than Cinderella waiting for her prince (Orenstein 2011). Girlhood, then, is a more complex period than formerly understood.

In the following sections, the ways in which daughters, past and present, have been treated differently from sons are considered. Also discussed are why strategies and programs to support and enhance girls' empowerment are necessary and part of the global effort to end discrimination against females.

Daughter in the Family

The conception and birth of a child is usually a welcome event in a family. Sometimes, however, it is inconvenient or even disastrous to a household's economic survival. A new infant may threaten the health of the mother and older children, especially an unweaned child. Other times, when the child has been conceived in rape, incest, or another form of unsanctioned relationship, or when the mother is very young or single, its arrival may complicate family relations and harm the new mother's future prospects. Where contraceptive and abortive methods are unknown, unavailable, or undependable, infanticide, abandonment, giving the baby to others to raise, or simply neglecting a newborn have been options in the past for an unwanted child. Reflecting women's inequality worldwide, the death rate of infant girls far exceeds that of infant boys today as in the past. Male preference, which is almost universal, is manifested in parental and societal discrimination, family resource allocations, and government policy (Kristof and WuDunn 2009; Rosenberg 2009). Why and how have daughters been seen as more expendable than sons?

Female Infanticide

Infanticide has existed since ancient times as a method of population control and sex selection of children, but female infanticide is more widespread. In 1 BCE, for example, a husband in Alexandria wrote to his wife in the Egyptian countryside: "I beg you and urge you . . . if by chance you bear a child—if it is a boy, let it be; if it is a girl, cast it out" (Hunt and Edgar 1932). The Greeks abandoned many more girls to die than boys, and the Romans had a law requiring fathers to raise all healthy sons but only one daughter (Pomeroy 1975). In medieval Christian society, where church law strictly forbade infanticide, it was still carried out extensively. Girls were the most common victims of "accidents" where women claim to have "overlaid" (smothered) children at night. When foundling homes were established, as in Florence in the fourteenth century, the records revealed that parents discarded many more females than males (Trexler 1973).

Those readers who believe in a "maternal instinct" that causes mothers to protect their children must wonder what could prompt women to kill them instead. Inability to care for a child, particularly if it is deemed "illegitimate" by a society's norms or if the other parent or other members of the society are not available for assistance, may be a motive. In some situations, a mother may suffer from postpartum depression or a debilitating physical or mental illness. Where infanticide is a socially recognized option, it may be the father alone who makes the decision and it may be the midwife or another party who carries it out.

Today, when new technologies can reveal the sex of the fetus in early pregnancy, they have been used, for example, by families in patrilineal societies to abort fetuses identified as female. In such households, one daughter may be considered ideal to help in the home, and additional ones may be seen as a burden. The "missing girls" in such families contribute to a disparate male–female sex ratio (Das Gupta 2009; Rosenberg 2009).

Social practices that allot girls less food and medical care and overwork or abuse them physically help explain why more girls than boys die in infancy and early childhood (Rosenberg 2009). The neglect of daughters is masked almost everywhere by the assertion that girls require less food than boys. When protein has been scarce, women have customarily stinted themselves and their daughters in favour of the husband and sons. This has prejudiced the daughters' well-being and socialized them to do the same later in their own households. This belief might account more for the differences in the size and physical strength of girls and boys than is generally acknowledged. In other cases, daughters are simply abandoned, put up for adoption, or even sold, often into a life of servitude or prostitution (Kristof and WuDunn 2009).

Worldwide, more couples still prefer to have a son than a daughter, particularly if it is the first child, and many couples continue having children until they have a son. There is virtually no society that positively prefers girl babies to boys.

The Value of Daughters

The selective destruction and neglect of female babies by individual families throughout history would not have been possible unless society as a whole condoned it. Many of the answers lie in the social patterns that define women's place and value to their society.

When and where high social value is placed on males engaged in chronic warfare, sons must be raised with "masculine" qualities stressed. Because investment in daughters detracts from investment in sons, daughters are sacrificed. The evidence supporting this argument shows a systematic correlation between female infanticide, chronic warfare, and male supremacist cultural values (Divale and Harris 1976). Marital strategies of individual families are often political and economic decisions. In some cultures, the most common way in which a family gets a daughter-in-law is in exchange for a daughter. Some societies operate on a rigid one-to-one basis, exchanging cousins, for example. In many societies, a bride must be accompanied by wealth when leaving her father's house, a costly endeavour. In others, a daughter represents potential wealth that will be paid to her parents in exchange for her and can be used to secure a bride for a son, pay off debts, or accumulate wealth. Where the potential marital pool is known and limited, parents may sacrifice daughters for whom there is no possibility of a profitable future marriage settlement (Coleman 1976). Hence, while daughters are valuable directly or indirectly as producers of grandchildren, the possibilities of enhancing family wealth and power or impoverishing the household play an important role in families' decision making about the value of girls.

In countries that do not provide publicly funded social support, especially for child or eldercare, the work of female members is crucial for the running of the household. Daughters' own interests and desires are often made subservient to the needs of the family.

Still another theory emphasizes gender ideologies. Particularly in patrilineal societies, where daughters are considered temporary members of a family—while sons generally and historically have inherited property, carried on the family line, fulfilled cultural rituals, and had responsibilities for parents and female members of the household—son preference is reinforced (Das Gupta 2009). In Afghanistan, so great is the social pressure to have a son that some families of girls may have one daughter masquerade as a boy to keep up appearances (see Box 7.1). In other societies, subtle family choices can still disadvantage daughters. For example, one study found that US parents invested more of their resources in improving their housing when they had a son (Leonhardt 2003).

Decisions that favour women seem to exist only in the realm of fantasy. Ancient Greek myths about Amazons tell of women warriors who preferred girl babies to boys. Sons were maimed, killed, or immediately sent to their fathers. Feminists have adopted this myth about strong women but have modified its ugly features. In

Box 7.1 Key Issues

Bacha Posh: Girls Masquerading as Boys

Afghans of several generations report knowing a female relation, acquaintance, neighbour, or co-worker who spent her childhood and sometimes her early adulthood dressed up in boy's clothing and participating in activities such as attending school and going to the market as a male. In the Dari language, these girls are called *bacha posh* or "dressed up as a boy," a phenomenon that generally occurs in families of many daughters. Why do parents create a "fake son" of one daughter, who is then returned to a woman's dress, role, and place, usually upon puberty? The many reasons reflect the greater value and privileges of boys. Societal pressures for male children are so great that having a pretend son offsets expressions of pity and enhances a family's standing even if only for a brief time. Also, some families may hold to a superstition that by so doing a real son will be conceived. Moreover, because a *bacha posh* can work in a shop, run errands after school to places females are not permitted without a male escort, and in her male attire accompany sisters on their outings as is the custom, this daughter plays a vital role in the family's economic and social well-being as a son. She may be replaced by a younger sister when she grows out of her son role.

How do "fake sons" feel about their experiences? For some, living as a boy gave them greater freedom to play sports and be educated, making them more determined to change gender inequities in their society. Others had a more difficult time "changing back" and had to learn to socialize as women. Azita Rafaat, who spent some years as a boy and whose third daughter is a *bacha posh* (see photo), found the experience enhanced her ability to communicate with men. Formerly a health worker, she became a politician and women's rights advocate and was one of 68 women in the 249-member Parliament in 2010. She hopes her own daughter will have a positive experience, but like other women wishes the practice did not have to exist in Afghanistan.

Source: Nordberg (2010).

The Female Man (1975), for example, Joanna Russ created a fictional utopia where women live without men and have only girls. Reproduction is accomplished by the merging of ova, and children are raised communally. More recently, fiction for young adults tells of girls who compete with and outdo their male counterparts: in the *Hunger Games* trilogy (2008), Suzanne Collins created in Katniss Everdeen a daughter who provides for her mother and sister, protects her male peers, and ultimately spearheads a revolution against a totalitarian government.

Naming the Daughter

The (low) status of women in different societies is revealed in naming patterns. A name generally designates the gender of a child. The more emphasis a society places on the difference between girls and boys, the more it distinguishes their names. Medieval Europeans usually got through life with a single name, which often repeated the father's name or embroidered on it, such as *Charles, Charlotte,* or *Charlene*. When named for fathers, daughters were given a close feminine form of his name: for example, *John/Joan, Robert/Roberta*. Boys are almost never given names identified with girls, but the reverse can occur, perhaps reflecting the greater worth attached to male associations. Sons are frequently named for their fathers. Daughters are far more rarely named for their mothers. Today, some daughters are given gender-neutral names (*Alex, Lee, Jessie,* or *Nicky*) or are named for places (*Jordan* or *Dakota*) and other novelties, which may suggest the desire of parents to reduce gender stereotyping in naming.

The importance of children for the continuity of a lineage is reflected in the use of *patronymics* (fathers' names). For example, the ancient Romans did not give their daughters individual names: they were automatically called by the feminine form of the father's name. Thus, all the daughters of a Claudius were called Claudia and referred to informally in numerical order: *Claudia prima, Claudia secunda, Claudia tertulla*. In some areas, patronymics continue into modern times. The Russian heroine of Tolstoy's novel *Anna Karenina* (first published in 1873–77) was named *Anna Arkadyevna* ("daughter of Arkady") *Karenina* ("wife of Karenin").

Traditionally in Korea, Confucian custom deemed female status too low for married women to be permitted to use the family name of their husbands. In contrast, Myanmar/Burma, with its Buddhist tradition and a matrilineal past, did not have a family name system. Both females and males were registered using their own individual names, and historically women did not change their names after marriage (Matsui 1989). In Spanish-speaking societies, women retain their father's name by adding it (sometimes with *y*) to the husband's name. In other societies, children will perpetuate the name of their mother's family as a first or middle name.

In North America, a daughter generally changed her surname to that of her husband's upon marriage. The exception to this rule is in Quebec, where it is legally forbidden for a woman to change her surname to that of her spouse upon marriage. Many women have reported feelings of a loss of identity when they became Mrs.———. A woman's married name designates a position rather than a person, and a first Mrs. ——— may be replaced by a second or third with the same surname. Nowadays women may keep their family name when they marry, as they are legally entitled to do, and some do so for their professional lives. Many couples experiment with combining or hyphenating both names as a family name. It is still most common for children to have the surnames of their fathers. Some women reject the surnames of both fathers and husbands and choose their own for themselves and their children.

Daughters' Work

Despite their lower status worldwide, girls can occupy an important position within their natal families based on the work they perform. In most households daughters are expected to care for younger siblings and assist in food preparation and other domestic chores. In developing societies, where child labour is more common, girls fetch water and firewood, feed chickens, go to the market, wash clothes, help with the dairying and agricultural work, and undertake income-producing tasks like garment work. In some societies women cannot get paid work unless they pretend to be boys. Despite a daughter's lack of paid options, daughters provide important unpaid labour for the family including sibling and eldercare, as well as household tasks (see Chapter 11 for more on unpaid work).

Parental Relationships

From the moment she is born and named, a girl is started on a track that will take her through her whole life as a daughter. Historically, social conventions tend to prescribe parents' behaviour. Although gender roles remain rigid in many parts of the world, the changing structure of families worldwide in the twenty-first century has created more flexibility in how mothers, fathers, and other relations are raising daughters and sons. Nonetheless, the family remains a political system comprising parents, siblings, and others. Daughters struggle for identity and material advantage within a pattern imposed by chance and social convention.

Daughters and Mothers. Mother–daughter relationships are varied and complex. Mothers may try to mould daughters in their own images; they may also consciously set out to create daughters who will not repeat their experiences. Mothers are often strong allies in helping daughters to realize their dreams. French author Sidonie-Gabrielle Colette (1953 [1930]) wrote of the encouragement she received as a child in her mother's house. The leader of the militant British suffrage movement, Emmeline Pankhurst (1858–1928), raised her daughters Christabel Pankhurst (1880–1958), Sylvia Pankhurst (1882–1960), and Adela Pankhurst (1885–1961) to live independent

---

Box 7.2 Women in Media

Bonnie Sherr Klein and Naomi Klein

Bonnie Sherr Klein's 40-plus years as a documentarian included 1982's *Not a Love Story: A Film about Pornography*, which was one of the most celebrated works from Studio D, the women's studio of the National Film Board of Canada. Sherr Klein suffered a catastrophic stroke when she was 46 years old that left her a quadriplegic. She subsequently wrote *Slow Dance: A Story of Stroke, Love and Disability*, with writer and artist Persimmon Blackbridge (1997) and directed the film *Shameless: the Art of Disability* (2006). Sherr Klein's daughter, Naomi Klein, is an author, activist, and also a filmmaker (*The Take*, 2004). Her book *No Logo* (1999) was the first of a series of critiques of globalization that includes *The Shock Doctrine: The Rise of Disaster Capitalism* (2007), and *This Changes Everything: Capitalism vs. the Environment* (2014).

Bonnie Sherr Klein (left) and her daughter, Naomi Klein

and creative lives. Each daughter distinguished herself in her own way as a leader of women's rights and social reformer. Part of their story is related in the film *Suffragette* (2015), starring Meryl Streep as Emmeline.

Daughters in Varied Family Configurations. Not all girls grow up in two-parent households. Because different kinds of family structures often open up non-traditional gender roles, daughters may grow up differently. One study found that daughters in divorced mother-only households exercised more power and were given more responsibilities than girls in non-divorced two-parent families. As noted, daughters of colour have long experienced non-traditional gender-role divisions of labour and household decision making, where their mothers were prominent. Daughters of lesbians also demonstrate higher rates of leadership and a greater sense of adventure than their counterparts in heterosexual families (Bronstein 2006).

Women of colour, such as Patricia Hill Collins (2000b) and Gloria Joseph (1981, 1991), have identified the importance of other female figures in mothering, such as grandmothers, siblings, aunts, cousins, and women who are not biologically related, as well as men who "mother." Joseph writes of the respect and affection of daughters for their mothers and mother surrogates in recognition of the obstacles the women (and occasionally men) confront in holding households together under conditions of racism and economic constraints, in addition to gender discrimination, that often require them to work long hours outside the home. Many racialized mothers have purposely raised girls to be strong and independent for themselves and their households.

Globalization, especially in terms of transnational migration, may disrupt parent–daughter relations but may also work to cement gender roles in the families left behind by migrant worker parents. A study of Filipino transnational families where one parent migrated overseas for work found that traditional assumptions about the appropriate roles for the mothers and fathers who remained prevailed in both mother-away

Box 7.3 Time to Reflect

The 60s Scoop

The term "60s Scoop" refers to events in Canada between 1960 and 1990 when 11,132 status Indian children and unknown numbers of non-status Indigenous people were adopted by mostly non-Indigenous families (Sinclair 2007). It was called a scoop because, in many cases, children were taken from their homes and communities without the knowledge or consent of their birth families or bands. In many cases, when consent was requested but not given, Canadian authorities and social workers acted under the assumption that Indigenous people were culturally inferior and were inadequately providing for their children. This colonial assumption was often made without investigation or recourse for the families whose children were forcibly taken (ibid). The forced removal of the children from their families (as in the residential school system) is seen as an attempt at cultural genocide.

Of the children who were adopted, 70 per cent went to non-Indigenous homes. Of those who went to non-Indigenous homes, the breakdown rate of adoptions was also 70 per cent (ibid).

A substantial portion of those who were adopted faced cultural and identity confusion issues, particularly for those who were transracially adopted. There is an effort now to reunite adoptees with their birth families, bands, and communities, though this experience has also resulted in further identity issues for some (ibid).

and father-away households. Moreover, the eldest daughter assumed major domestic responsibilities that often enhanced empathy between mothers and daughters but also could intensify the daughters' feelings of abandonment (Parreñas 2005).

Sibling Relationships

Girlhood is defined by sibling relationships as well as relationships with parents and other adults. Sex and age ranking are the most common means of discriminating among siblings. Many societies reserve specific privileges for older children. The upper ranks of British society and feudal Japan long held a tradition of passing the family wealth and property to the oldest male offspring. Parents also discouraged younger daughters from marrying until an older sister was settled. The first-born female child will tend to be given more responsibility for the care of younger children. The older child will generally go to school first and break the path in obtaining privileges from the parents. Fairy tales are replete with stories like Cinderella and Hansel and Gretel that tell of the plight of younger children making their way in a hostile world controlled by elders.

Inheritance

A daughter's possibilities from birth through girlhood to adulthood are defined by custom, law, and social institutions. The family, however defined, is the recognized unit that bestows status, class, property rights, privilege, or position upon its members. If the sexual relationships of one's parents have followed a prescribed pattern of propriety or if they have fulfilled a socially approved set of rituals governing formal adoption, daughters will usually be given that approved place.

The inheritance of social status may include legacies from both parents. Women may derive their citizenship in a modern state from either mother or father or from both, depending on the laws set by the state. Jews, for example, inherit Jewish affiliation and, therefore, the right to claim Israeli citizenship through the mother's line. In Canada, children of an unmarried female citizen inherit the mother's position. Often, lower status or dependent status (slavery, serfdom, or non-citizenship) comes through the mother. Thus, in Canada in the era of slavery, daughters and sons of enslaved women were born enslaved, even if fathered by a freeman or slaveholder.

Gender affects inheritance among sisters and brothers. Patrilineal societies pass authority, property, and descent directly through the male line from father to son. Matrilineal societies sometimes pass authority and property through males, but descent passes through females; property, like tools for producing clothing and food, often passes from mothers to daughters. Although matrilineal societies, such as the North American Iroquois and the African Bemba, tend to confer greater authority upon women than do patrilineal societies, these societies have a less rigid system of authority in general. Where extensive trade or manufacturing exists, matrilineal systems appear to vanish and even patrilineal systems are modified in favour of a bilateral system, allowing a child to inherit from both parents. One exception to this pattern is the Minangkabau of Indonesia, who are highly educated and integrated into Indonesian society. They pass property exclusively through the mother, and women wield significant power (Blackwood 2006).

Historically, a household head in Japan without children would often adopt a boy to be raised as the successor to manage the family's economic matters, inherit property, and worship the ancestors. If the household head had only daughters, he would adopt a son-in-law as his successor, who would also assume the head's surname (Yanagisako 1985). Even in less complex societies, where personal property is restricted to a few effects that are buried with their possessor, the inheritance of parental skills or privileges will generally be apportioned according to a child's gender. In capitalist societies, patterns of inheritance of property and position have favoured sons over daughters. In socialist societies, which typically aim at reducing disparities of private property, it remains possible to inherit status or position informally. There, too, discrimination still favours the male.

Commonly, a system that allows the passage of property to and through women is accompanied by the development of class and caste hierarchies with strict rules for controlling individual heirs, particularly females. Generally, women are admitted to the inheritance of their fathers and/or brothers only when strong measures exist to control their marriages and sex lives in general. These societies are careful to enforce adultery laws against women, to link "honour" with virginity before marriage and fidelity after, and to endow fathers and brothers with strong coercive powers over the female members of their families (Goody 1976).

Many societies have laws that restrict the leaving of property. These laws may recognize *primogeniture* (passage of the patrimony to the first-born son), *entail* (a legal device which establishes a strict line of succession to property, which then cannot be sold off, through the oldest related male), and *coverture* (a husband's legal control over his wife's property). The more wealthy and productive a society, the more likely it is to have a social hierarchy of class that causes women to lose status in a variety of ways.

Inheritance laws and practices are another area in which girls and women are disadvantaged and through which gender discrimination persists. In the twenty-first century, many individual families seek a more equitable distribution of inheritance between daughters and sons. Societies, likewise, must do the same.

Motherhood

Among the social roles that a woman fills, motherhood is difficult to define: being a mother is multifaceted and multidimensional. It is one of the hardest roles a woman may play, whether she is the biological (natural/birth) mother or an adoptive or foster mother, mother-in-law, grandmother, stepmother, godmother, or unrelated surrogate mother. While mothers' relationships with their children are often complex and ambivalent, fictional mothers loom large: loved and hated, loving and vengeful, nurturing and destructive, all-giving and completely withholding. What makes a "mother" so significant in people's stories and lives?

Since for the most part society has agreed that the most important function of a woman's body is to bear a child, motherhood is subject to regulations in all its aspects, biological and social. In the twenty-first century, in an overpopulated world with dwindling resources, to focus on women's bodies as reproductive machines may seem misguided, yet it cannot be denied that the biological aspect of the female body is intimately intertwined with political, social, cultural, and economic realities.

The starting point for understanding motherhood is to investigate how it is constructed, that is, how in any society motherhood is defined by belief systems and visual images, because ideas about motherhood are reflected in and shaped by social processes. Attitudes toward the biological aspects of motherhood are also informative, such as ideas about a "maternal instinct" (Hrdy 1999). These biological events are also shaped by society at large. Motherhood is such a critical role assignment that many people, particularly men, have been determined to design it according to their own convictions and the cultural mores of the day. Girls in every society learn what it means to be a "good" or "bad" mother: at home from their own parents and from community gossip and unspoken rules; from religious traditions and texts; from media such as television, movies, and the Internet.

Images of Mothers

Mother is a multi-layered term, implying many concepts depending on the context. It may be a metaphor, as in "the mother of all evil," an adjective denoting the superlative. It appears as a

Box 7.4 In Her Own Words

Sappho's Daughter and Mother

The poet Sappho lived in Mytilene, Lesbos, in the seventh century BCE. Lesbos is a Greek island off the coast of Turkey where Lydia and its capital Sardis were located. Both her daughter, who is addressed in the first poem, and her mother, who is the subject of the second, were named Kleïs. Most of Sappho's poetry survives only in fragments.

> I have a beautiful child, her form
>
> Like golden flowers, beloved Kleïs
>
> Whom I would not trade for all of Lydia
>
> Or lovely . . .
>
> . . . My mother . . .
>
> In her youth it was a great
>
> Adornment if someone had her hair
>
> Wrapped round with a purple [braid]
>
> It really was.
>
> But for the one with hair
>
> More golden than a pinetorch
>
> . . . fitted with garlands
>
> Of blooming flowers.
>
> Recently a hairband of many hues
>
> From Sardis . . .
>
> . . . cities . . .
>
> But for you, Kleïs, I have no colorful
>
> Hairband—where will it come from—
>
> But the Mytilenean . . .

Source: *Sappho's lyre: Archaic lyric and women poets of ancient Greece* by Rayor, Diane Reproduced with permission of University of California Press in the format: Republish in a book via Copyright Clearance Center.

prefix, as in *motherland*, meaning the country one identifies as one's home. Even when the term is limited to its most common and stereotypical usage, the woman who undertakes that role can evoke multiple images, such as a pretty woman embracing a child, a complaining mother-in-law, or an evil stepmother. Images of mothers, as depicted in mythology, religious texts, and the visual arts, as well as in written and oral literature and the performing arts, are usually of central importance. These images, on the one hand, instruct people about the currently acceptable role ascribed to mothers and, on the other, inform them about the notions of motherhood that prevail in a particular culture. From its beginnings, feminism has turned an analytical eye on motherhood as both an institution and an experience central to women's lives, whether they choose to be mothers or not.

"The Happy Mother": A Western Image as Political Ideology. For centuries, the predominant representation of motherhood in the Christian world was of the Virgin Mary (the Madonna) and the baby Jesus. From the early Christian era, the image of the Madonna looking adoringly at her divine offspring was defined as the ideal relationship of a mother and her (male) child. Non-religious depictions of a mother and her child(ren) are relatively rare before the sixteenth century in Europe. Most paintings depicting specific mothers were commissioned by the members of various courts as propaganda for a prince to show off his private riches. Representations of ordinary mothers and their children, both inside and outside their homes, became popular in seventeenth-century Netherlands, where the Calvinist Dutch eschewed traditional depictions of the Virgin and child. The interiors of houses were represented as places where all the human virtues were combined and cleanliness was next to godliness. More often than fathers, it was mothers who figured in Dutch paintings and prints as the protectors of the pure household. One of the most affecting family scenes in Dutch genre painting are of children submitting to their mother's inspection of their heads for nits and lice.

Images portraying mothers in blissful ecstasy proliferated in western Europe as wealth spread to the expanding middle class in the eighteenth century (Duncan 1973). There was a new emphasis on domesticity and the elevation of maternity to an exalted state. This type of genre painting in Europe accompanied a shift in attitudes that reflected intellectual, economic, and social changes beginning in seventeenth-century maritime and mercantile Holland and slightly later among the bourgeoisie of France. Heredity had less to do with one's success in life than previously, and the home environment took on increasing importance in the education and formation of children for society. Though many mothers and children were subsequently forced to work for pitiful wages in horrendous conditions as the world industrialized, the aspirational image was that of woman as joyful guardian of the peaceful home. The paintings of this idealized home life convey a clear moral message: a woman's place is in her clean home, a symbol of purity, where she cares for her children. This early form of media representation continued to change along with social and cultural conditions, but the core remained unaltered. The image was increasingly popularized with the mass-media development of women's magazines, advertising, motion pictures, and television. This was the encouraging image that accompanied the burgeoning generation of "baby boomers," who were born during and after World War II and whose mothers were urged to eschew the workplace and devote themselves to raising their children. But other ambitions had been unleashed when women entered the workforce during World War II, and that genie was hard to put back in the bottle: these contradictory goals led to real ambivalence and conflict related to the balance between work and home life.

The Intersectional Impact of Class, Race, and Ethnicity on Images of Motherhood. Of course, idealized (or villainous) representations of motherhood hardly tell the whole story. While dominant images of mothers have primarily represented white, middle-class women, motherhood is an experience that cuts across lines of race, class, and ethnicity, even as the specifics of that experience are profoundly affected by social hierarchies.

Under slavery (roughly 1500–1837 in Canada), women of African descent had a very different experience of motherhood from that of their white and free counterparts. Seen primarily as labourers, black women were expected to integrate pregnancy, childbirth, and motherhood into their working lives. Mothers were crucial to the economy of slavery. Since children "followed the condition of the mother," enslaved mothers had financial value as reproducers of the workforce. Parents who were enslaved had no rights to their own children, who could be sold away from them. In fact, much of the rhetoric of the political movement against slavery focused on the destruction of families and the heartbreak of mothers (see, for a Canadian example, the Ward Chipman slavery brief from 1800 [University of New Brunswick Libraries, n.d.]).

Immigrant narratives often represent friction between mothers and children, especially daughters, over sexual freedom, financial independence, and marriage. During periods of increased immigration, the immigrant mother has sometimes been represented as a vestige of the "old country." Mothers and grandmothers have been represented as the repositories of old customs and values. This can be a positive, loving image, but just as often, immigrant mothers come off as out of touch with the new reality, as controlling and unnecessarily strict, and as smothering.

These stereotypes find their source in the lives of women who, having been uprooted from their communities and familiar customs and values, had to find ways to help their children succeed in an often hostile and discriminatory environment. Too rarely, though, is the struggle and sacrifice of immigrant women depicted. The losses they endure in hope for a better future for their children remain largely unheralded. Jasjit Sangha and Tahira Gonsalves' *South Asian Mothering: Negotiating Culture, Family and Selfhood* (2013) is one attempt to correct this image by presenting a counter-narrative to the stereotypes of immigrant mothers.

Motherhood and the Media. An ideology of motherhood is "sold" along with a variety of commercial products in mainstream media. Online and print advertising and television commercials blatantly convey an image of motherhood as "it ought to be." Most film and media representations of mothers in Canada, the US, and the UK are still created by men, and most are narrow and hegemonic (Abby 2003). In the last 30 years or so, the representation of the mother has undergone considerable change, but stereotypes persist. Until the 1970s the mother figure was usually depicted as a weak woman who had few significant anxieties or non-domestic functions and was always neat, well dressed, calm, eminently middle class, white, and suburban. She rarely was shown having a job, making major decisions, or having sexual desires. As the feminist movement became stronger, so did the image of the mother. Mothers from other classes and ethnicities began to appear in the media; some were "liberated," others divorced or otherwise independent. In recent years, representations of mothers on television have become more diverse.

Despite the growing involvement of fathers in raising children, mothers are the primary target for media about parenting and children. Magazines intended explicitly for parents speak almost exclusively to women. Motherhood is marketable; articles on the Web and magazine stories, like the advertisements that support them, create "needs" by spelling out the requisites of good mothering, and strike fear into mothers that not doing the "right" thing could permanently disadvantage their children. There is a proliferation of information offering a confusing array of choices and demands, and demonstrating that mothers are held to a very high standard. Meanwhile the media promote the so-called mommy wars that pit women who stay at home full-time or part-time with their children against those who work full-time outside the home. Rarely are there meaningful discussions of the diversity of women's feelings about combining mothering and paid work, whether those feelings are positive, negative, or ambivalent. Even breastfeeding has become a site of anxiety for women. Feminist advocacy for breastfeeding, which took on childcare "experts" and their corporate sponsors who argued that breastfeeding was unsanitary, has been transformed by the media and the marketplace into judgment against women who cannot or choose not to nurse. Expensive "breastfeeding kits" with all sorts of equipment are marketed as obligatory for women, even as nursing is represented as completely natural and self-evident, rather than a skill both mother and baby learn together.

In most cases the advertisements and advice that saturate the media foster women's feelings of personal inadequacy and dependence. The images of "celebrity moms" who have endless patience for their children while maintaining flawless figures implies that any mother who is less than emotionally and physically perfect has failed. The media largely serve the interests of commercial enterprises, whose goal is to sell products, and bolster the view of the professionals such as obstetricians and pediatricians who advise women on proper mothering and feeding. If the public image of motherhood reflects women's social position in general, it must be concluded, despite considerable changes in women's economic roles during the last 30 years, much less has changed than would be believed.

Mothers Speak Out. Feminists have long spoken out about the ways in which their experiences as mothers had been misrepresented or erased. Some of this self-expression has taken the form of autobiographical literature. Adrienne Rich's treatise on motherhood, *Of Woman Born* (1976), and Anne Lamott's diary of her first year of motherhood, *Operating Instructions: A Journal of My Son's First Year* (1993), combine autobiography with analysis of being a mother, exposing it to scrutiny to disrupt ideological assumptions. Rachel Cusk's *A Life's Work: On Becoming a Mother* (2002) and Ayelet Waldman's *Bad Mother* (2009) are part of a wave of "backlash" literature that confesses that negative feelings are part of mothering. More recently, blogs have emerged as an accessible space for women to talk about the contradictions of motherhood, especially for women of colour, working-class women, and lesbians. Blogs such as loveisntenough.com, latinamombloggers.com, and mombian.com are both intimate and public spaces for women to challenge social stereotypes about mothering.

Though historically some women have supported wars, other women have often used their status as mothers to advocate for peace. For example, in Aristophanes's fifth-century BCE comedy *Lysistrata*, the women of Greece (who were disenfranchised and could not hold political office or serve on juries) claim a right to engage in politics and make political decisions because they have produced the men who are dying in a long war. During the Latin American military dictatorships of the last century, women organized in their maternal roles to demand justice for the kidnapping/disappearances of their children. Recently in Liberia, Muslim and Christian women joined together to protest the ongoing violence of a civil war: they wore white and invoked their importance as mothers, many of whom had lost children in the war. This protest was instrumental in bringing the combatants to the negotiating table, ending the conflict, and eventually electing Liberia's first woman president, Ellen Johnson Sirleaf. In Canada, women have also led the peace movement: for years, beginning in 2004, grandmothers and other peace activists have showed their opposition to the wars in Afghanistan and Iraq (Haberman 2010).

Parental Behaviour: "Instinct" and Culture

As has been seen, media of all kinds provide a window into the society that produces and receives it; by investigating the constructions of motherhood and mothering in the media, much can be learned about cultural attitudes toward parenting. It is true, however, that being a mother is a biological process: mammals gestate the young, breastfeed them, and care for them. Most people are raised by mothers, and their relationships with their mothers are often the first intimate relationship they experience. At the same time, as the discussion above shows, motherhood is more than just biology: it is inextricable from the social, legal, cultural, religious, sexual, and economic roles women play in their societies and the power relations that structure those societies. How, if at all, the ideology be separated from the reality of motherhood? Perhaps working through the biological aspect of mothering can lead to at least partially separating it from the social and cultural components.

All organisms come from other organisms. In this sense, all organisms have "parents." Even when parents never see a child after birth, they are called its "mother" and "father" (biologically if not practically). For other animals, like birds or cats, parenting activities appear to be instinctive; that is, their nervous systems are so programmed by genetic inheritance that, as parents, they will automatically behave in certain ways. Feeding and protecting the offspring are two basic parental instincts. Among mammals, a classification named for the breast (in Latin, *mamma*) of its female members because they *lactate* (produce milk), there is considerable variability in parental roles.

Concerning more complex animals, particularly primates, genetically close to humans, is the applicability of the notion of "instinct" (Hrdy 1999, 2009). Studies show that for complex animals maternal behaviour must be learned and that its expression by females or males depends on their experience and social conditions, which calls the idea of "maternal instinct" into question. But these processes are not necessarily the same as the set of behaviours called "mothering": fulfilling the emotional and developmental needs of children. The desire to care for children is not universal, nor do all women feel instinctively protective or loving toward their own or other children.

Scientific studies of female hormonal changes during pregnancy and motherhood are contradictory. On the one hand, breastfeeding triggers the release of the hormone oxytocin (a hormone also released during orgasm), which can produce feelings of intimacy and nurturance. On the other hand, many women experience rapid hormonal shifts after childbirth, which can result in depression and anxiety and a feeling of alienation from the new baby. Feelings about motherhood are so strongly determined by social expectations that it is difficult to separate biological reactions from cultural expectations.

Humans have innate predispositions for complex and varied sorts of behaviour; genetic inheritance provides the general pattern, not the details, of such conduct. Of all primate species, humans are the most utterly helpless at birth and remain dependent on their caretakers for the longest time. When advanced apes, such as the chimpanzee, reach the age at which they can have their own babies, human infants are only beginning to venture away from their parents' arms. The dependent period of the human child lengthens in industrialized countries, where there is less urgency for the child to separate from the family in search of other means of support, be it a job or a spouse. This phenomenon of dependence on the part of the child causes a symbiotic relationship between it and its caretakers/parents in which the child demands and the parent gives. Because of the necessity even today in most societies for a woman to provide her child with breast milk, it is not uncommon for a woman to form emotional bonds with her baby from the moment of birth. Emotions and biological needs intermingle, and traditions in almost every society work to strengthen mother–child togetherness, to ensure the survival of the child, and to maintain the continuity of the human species.

The expectation that mothers be "selfless" is not far removed from the cultural belief that women's lives should be organized around others. In part, it is true that new babies need constant care: feeding, bathing, protecting from the dangers of the world. What nature starts, society soon takes over: biology creates women's capacity for reproduction, but society dictates the task of *mothering*, assigning a multitude of nurturing tasks to women. But the demands and rewards of caring for another person need not and should not be limited to women. Anyone can nurture and raise a child: anyone can "mother."

The Assignment of Motherhood: Whose Interest Does It Serve?

A woman's biological contributions to reproduction, though costly in time, energy, and risk, are of relatively short duration compared to the social role of motherhood, which lasts a lifetime. Rearing children is very hard work, and usually it is mothers who have borne the primary responsibility for this indispensable contribution to human society.

Why does a woman want to be a mother? Societal norms everywhere in the world expect a woman to bear children; there are few strong-willed and rebellious women who could resist such pressure (see Ratner 2000). Childless women have been burned as witches, persecuted as lesbians, and refused the right to adopt if unmarried. Because women are physically the primary progenitors and, by social convention, the primary caretakers of the human species, the female psyche has been conditioned and shaped to accept having children. Women are generally brought up to expect the role of motherhood. Once a baby is born, this helpless and needy new person can effortlessly dominate her love; she sees it as an extension of her body, of her self; the possibilities of enabling her baby to have a better life than hers seem endless. However, can mothers alone achieve these goals?

The assignment of long-term, daily childcare responsibilities to mothers rather than to fathers has left men free to acquire economic, political, and social power, which can, and too often has, been used against women (Treblicot 1984). More importantly, because mothering has been constructed as women's most important task, societies in which women care for their own children without any pay create a huge economic savings: imagine what would happen if every mother was paid a wage for her work. The fact that mothers and others see women's primary job as child-bearing helps to justify low levels of job training, high levels of unemployment, and lower pay for many women. Thus, women form a pool of cheap labour. Today in most industrialized societies the provision of paid maternity leave, day care, and family allowances has helped to mitigate some of the costs of motherhood to women, in theory to spread the sacrifice more evenly. Parental leave in Canada helps encourage fathers or male partners to share in the potential career sacrifices necessary in taking time from work, while also encouraging bonding and investment in the child. A notable exception is the United States where only 13 per cent have access to paid family leave; of new mothers who work, 33 per cent take no time off (Holohan 2015). As of this writing, a Congressional bill is planned to move forward that would provide paid parental leave for federal employees (Lunney 2015).

The Cultural Shaping of Biological Events Related to Motherhood

Attitudes about Pregnancy. A woman's emotional state, attitudes, and reactions to her social environment can influence the way she experiences the physiological process involved with motherhood. How women encounter pregnancy, for example, depends in part on whether the pregnancy is wanted or not. It also depends on the social support system she has, her perceptions of motherhood, perhaps her relationship with her own parents, and her relationship with the father of the expected child or with her partner. It also depends on whether it is her first pregnancy, the nature of her previous experiences, and her expectations.

The veneration of pregnant women ceased in societies with patriarchal monotheistic religions as the act of sexual intercourse came to be seen as "the fall of man," a reminder of a sinful event even within marriage, or the consequence of private conduct that should be properly covered up in public; hence, the billowing "maternity dress." In the middle and upper classes of European society, pregnant women were once secluded from public life. Early in the twentieth century, obstetricians advised pregnant women to avoid a variety of activities, including bathing, physical exercise, and sexual intercourse. Today, however, healthy pregnant women are encouraged to engage in all activities until they no longer physically can do so.

Will science soon have the capacity to eliminate pregnancy altogether? It is now possible to fertilize the ovum in a dish. Will it be long before a fetus can be brought to term in an artificial womb? Science fiction (like Marge Piercy's *Woman on the Edge of Time* [1976]) has long considered the possible implications of such a development. Would it help to equalize female–male relations by producing a more balanced parenthood? Much may depend on who would control the technology.

Childbirth: A Cultural or a Natural Event? For the first time since 1983, a worldwide decline in maternal deaths has been reported (Grady 2010). The reasons include more available health care, education for women, reduced rates of pregnancy in some countries, and higher incomes (resulting in better nutrition and working conditions).

Most women in North America give birth in hospitals, where the process is monitored and controlled by medical professionals. A significant subset of women have increasingly preferred to have their children in midwife-supervised birthing centres or at home, assisted by a midwife, believing that there is something "unnatural" about hospital births. In general, every society has customs that provide the basis for shaping the birthing event. It is the culture that informs women and other participants about what should be done, who should do it, and how.

Breastfeeding: Attitudes and Choices. Social and cultural factors, as well as the physical context of motherhood, affect breastfeeding practices. The biological aspects of lactation, like the treatment and welfare of babies, are shaped by a combination of physiology and society. Women who are supported by their social environment are more successful at breastfeeding; stress and distractions can interfere with a mother's production of milk. Physiology is on the side of the mother and her child when she breastfeeds. Mother's milk builds immunity in the newborn baby, which it needs vitally at this stage. Mother's milk also contains almost all the nutrients that larger amounts of prepared milk "formula" can provide. Breastfeeding often delays the resumption of women's fertility and can help space out pregnancies. In those societies where cultural factors place taboos on having sexual intercourse with a lactating mother, a mother is aided by not conceiving another child immediately. This natural contraception, though far from perfect, provides her with some respite from continuous pregnancy and ensures enough milk for the child until another one arrives and claims the breast. And as seen above, the release of the hormone oxytocin can make breastfeeding enjoyable and even relaxing.

In Canada 89 per cent of women breastfeed, at least for the first six months (Gionet 2015). Most women, in most parts of the world over history, have had no choice; breastfeeding has often been the only way to nourish infants. Mothers carry their infants with them wherever they go, to gather food (as do the dwellers of the Kalahari Desert in South Africa) or on their jobs (as do the domestic workers in South and Central America). For working- middle- or upper-class women, devices such as breast pumps were introduced so that they can store their milk to be fed to the child in their absence. In many countries there are cultural proscriptions against revealing the breast in public, even for feeding babies. In most professional workplaces, babies and children are still rarely welcome.

The development of prepared milk formula for babies has had mixed results for women. On the one hand, formula is essential for women who cannot breastfeed or produce enough milk for their babies. It allows women to return to work and men to share in baby care by outsourcing nutrition. But baby formula has become a huge business: until recently, all new mothers were given "gift bags" of formula in North American hospitals. In the 1950s and 1960s, when the Swiss company Nestlé pushed its "prepared or fortified" powdered milk in areas of South Asia and Africa, where the water to mix formula powder could not be sterilized or women would water the formula down to make it last longer, children died from water-borne diseases and malnutrition. In "The Politics of Breastfeeding: An Advocacy Update," anthropologist Penny Van Esterik (2013) provides a historical overview of the anti-formula campaign and presents a comprehensive refutation of arguments against "mother's milk." It was after a widespread outcry and international boycott that Nestlé and other companies agreed that "breast is best" for babies and mothers.

Baby formula was not the first replacement for mother's milk that some societies have found. Substitutes for breastfeeding (or at least for doing the feeding oneself) have a long history. In imperial Rome, as in seventeenth-century France and eighteenth-century England, wealthy women and working women had an option other than nursing: the use of "wet nurses" who were paid to breastfeed other women's infants. Likewise, during slavery, enslaved women were often wet nurses for the slavers' children.

Though some women find nursing their babies sensually and emotionally gratifying, others resent the idea of being tied down to a nursing schedule or feel that breastfeeding is uncomfortable and exhausting (Rosin 2009). There is also the issue of breastfeeding in public, and the social (and in some places, legal) stigma around it—there are ongoing demonstrations and legal battles in Canada attempting to improve the situation for these women. It should be possible for women to make informed choices concerning breastfeeding, as well as childbirth, not on the basis of stereotypes, corporate advertising, or cultural strictures in which they have had no say at all, but rather to suit their own personal beliefs, desires, and circumstances.

Women Other Than Birth Mothers Who Mother

Trans and Lesbian Co-mothers. One facet of the second wave of the feminist movement was increased attention to women's sexual self-determination. For some women, this led to a realization of or the ability to finally act upon sexual desires for other women and to come out as lesbian. Many of these women had children from marriages to men and brought these children into their new relationships. This was new territory for the non-biological mother of the children and for society as a whole. Sometimes the children's fathers fought to have their ex-wives declared "unfit mothers" because of their sexuality. This earlier group of women gave way to a generation of lesbians who grew up with the legacy of LGBTQ liberation campaigns and chose to raise children in the context of a lesbian relationship. While some couples adopt children, others choose to have one partner become pregnant and bear the child(ren). The legal status of non–birth mothers varies from country to country: in some they can "adopt" their children and become legal co-parents. In others lesbians and gay men are prevented from adopting children at all, and non–birth mothers have no legal relationship to the children they raise. After years of advocacy and protest, in 2016 new legislation gave Ontario same-sex parents who are not biologically related to their children the same legal rights as heterosexual parents.

Stepmothers. Any woman who substitutes for the "natural" mother does not fare well in the collective imagination. The story of Cinderella and her stepmother is told in many languages and versions; the stepmother is not only an ugly woman but also evil. The negative image of the stepmother in myth and fiction, the resentment a child may feel toward the woman who replaces the mother, the absence of an early bonding between the child and the stepmother, and the latter's possible preference for her own children over the stepchild are potential reasons to anticipate the difficult role that awaits the stepmother. In almost every country today, however, "blended families" made up of step-parents and stepchildren are becoming common, and the figure of the "wicked stepmother" seems to be fading in relevance.

Foster Mothers and Adoptive Mothers. In Canada, abandoned children are often placed in foster care. Foster mothers provide children with homes in exchange for wages. Although there is abuse in some foster homes, children can be reasonably well cared for, and intimacy and love can grow between foster mother and child, which in some cases may lead to adoption. Adoptive mothers are usually married women because most adoptions are governed by the state or by the biological mother. Professionally successful single women, however, sometimes find it possible to adopt and find they also can turn to international adoption.

Godmothers. Since human children mature over a very long period, they need to be entrusted to the supervision of some adult if the parents are unable to care for them. The designation of a godmother is made in good will by the parents of the child. Sometimes a baby is given the godparent's name to create a recognizable link between them. In North America, the tradition of asking trusted friends and especially influential people to serve as godparents is widespread. In Latin America, godmothers are elevated with the designation of *co-madres*. The practice of "othermothering," an effort to build up support networks in the black community, includes godmothers (Chase and Rogers 2001). One goal is to create substitute parents who, if needed, will look after the offspring.

Women Growing Older: The Double Standard of Aging

The experiences that shape the growing-up years for girls continue to resonate in the years that mark women reaching adulthood and growing older. Although men are viewed as retaining their redeeming qualities of autonomy and competence during the aging process, and even increasing in power and status, the process of aging for women in any society that emphasizes the value of youth and beauty is generally accompanied by a stigma and a devaluing of their worth. Women are viewed as losing their most desirable qualities as they age; they are seen as less physically attractive and thus less sexually desirable and, where women are viewed primarily for their reproductive function, less fertile and less capable of producing children (one notable exception is Suriname, where older women are valued and eroticized). This is referred to as the "double standard of aging" (Sontag 1979). Since women have been taught that their worth rests upon physical appearance and desirability, more older women than men are dissatisfied with their appearance (Halliwell and Dittmar 2003) (see Box 7.5).

This double standard can have a negative effect on women's attitudes, motivation, and feelings of self-worth. Women in general, and older women in particular, experience inequalities in terms of their access to care, treatment, assessment, and relevant research related to their well-being (Etaugh and Bridges 2006). Although women are typically in good health as they age, especially in comparison to men, they are more likely to live with chronic illnesses (Crimmins, Kim, and Hagedorn 2002) and often struggle more than men with both daily living, such as basic self-care skills, and instrumental activities, including money management, shopping, and meal preparation (U.S. Department of Health and Human Services 2004). Despite the health problems that may develop during the aging process, even older women living with disabilities do not always experience diminished life satisfaction; many express feelings of happiness and mastery (Unger and Seeman 2000). Although it is common for older women to experience negative emotions and a lowered sense of well-being, especially in comparison to men, their overall psychological health improves as they age (Etaugh 2008) (see Box 7.5). Though no single incident marks this transition, a number of life events and their accompanying role transitions signal that growing older has begun.

Life Events and Role Transitions

Mid-life to Later Adulthood

In societies where youth is revered, growing older is popularly depicted as fraught with identity crises and turmoil. It can be quite the opposite, particularly for women. This is a time for women to review their lives and begin to form an independent identity that is separate from their spouses and families. For many women, forging this new identity often involves paid employment; being a part of the workforce is associated with positive psychological well-being (Etaugh 2008). Many other women focus their full efforts on their home life or being students or volunteering. The exact role a woman pursues does not matter as long as it is a role she is happy with. These developments are among the many role transitions that a woman may confront in later adulthood.

When work, parenting, and household responsibilities diminish over a lifetime, many women find time to devote to their own projects. Some are able to use their energy in activist causes. One example of this in Canada is the active political group The Raging Grannies. The group was founded in Victoria, BC, in 1987 and has since become an international movement of "mature women" who work for social justice. Organized into local "Gaggles," the Grannies are committed to leaving a better world for future generations. Their concerns cover a wide range of issues from war and peace to environmental causes. They are famous for their songbook that takes familiar tunes and sets them to new lyrics.

Divorce

Divorce is a major transition that is occurring increasingly for older women. Divorce rates do vary by race, ethnicity, and class. Divorce is also more likely to occur among poorer women, those with disabilities, and those with lower levels of education (Etaugh and Bridges 2006).

Divorce can be a distressing experience, particularly for women if they have centred their life on their marriage and lack up-to-date skills for the workplace and have limited financial means. Consequently, divorced women are much more likely to be living in poverty than are divorced men. On the other hand, often divorce is initiated by women. They experience few long-term negative psychological effects, and many actually experience it in positive terms, including renewed feelings of liberation, competence, and independence (Hetherington and Kelly 2002). Many factors may influence the way a woman feels and functions after a divorce in late adulthood, including the kind of support she receives from those around her (Jenkins 2003).

Widowhood

In most countries, older women are much more likely to experience the death of a spouse than are older men; this is a reflection of women's longer life expectancy and the fact that they often marry individuals older than themselves (Kinsella and Velkoff 2001).

Deborah van den Hoonaard's research confirms "'Common Knowledge' in Canada that older women who are widowed are unlikely

Members of the Raging Grannies march in Vancouver in an anti-war protest.

to remarry while men are both more likely to marry and marry more quickly, too . . .'' (van den Hoonaard 2003, 105). In *By Himself: The Older Man's Experience of Widowhood* (2010) van den Hoonaard reconfirms her earlier data.

Why this discrepancy? There are many more unmarried older women than there are unmarried older men, and men typically marry women who are younger than themselves. This leaves a small group of available older men. Also, widowed older women may be less interested in beginning a new relationship and report a desire to enjoy their independence. A husband's death does not end a woman's life. As Japanese poet and fiction writer Tomioka Taeko writes in one of her stories: "When a man's left a widower the maggots start to crawl, but when a woman's left a widow flowers come out in bloom!" (Tanaka and Hanson 1982, 176).

Widowhood is undoubtedly a difficult life experience, particularly immediately following a spouse's death; this holds true for all individuals, whether trans, heterosexual, lesbian, or gay. While most women become adjusted to their new role within two to four years, up to 20 per cent of widows can experience significant and persistent problems, including depression and substance abuse (Etaugh 2008). A woman's age, her relationship with her deceased spouse or partner, and her personal and financial resources are influential factors in this transition (Bradsher 2001). Widows may experience a significant decrease in their financial resources, and elderly women who live alone are much more likely than elderly men to be living in poverty (Jenkins 2003). The loss of a partner may be particularly difficult for LGBTQ folks; not only do they experience bereavement and a significant loss, but they must contend with a society that did not necessarily recognize and honour their relationship and now does not recognize their loss (Shernoff 1997).

However, older widows have fewer instances of depression and physical illness and lower rates of suicide than older widowers (Canetto 2003). This major variation is often attributed to men and women's different support systems; women are more likely both to accept their need for social support during a difficult time and to have a larger social support network (Nagurney, Reich, and Newsom 2004). Such choices and supports, however, are not necessarily available to widows everywhere and may lead to situations in which they find themselves the targets of abuse.

Singlehood

Many women—heterosexual, trans, and lesbian—consciously choose not to marry or to live with a long-term partner. Though this is increasingly the norm, single women are still often perceived in a negative light and may be portrayed as such by various media sources. Lacking a husband or partner does not mean a lack of companions. Single persons often have rich social lives and many interpersonal relationships with family, friends, and romantic partners. In comparison to married or partnered women of the same age, older women who have never married or been in a sustained relationship are often better educated and in better physical and mental health (Gottlieb 1989). They also have more time to focus on self-development, their career, and autonomy.

Motherhood

While many women choose not to have children, it is still much more common for women to become mothers. Some women are choosing motherhood after the age of 40 (Etaugh 2008). Older motherhood is increasingly possible through better health, adoption, in vitro fertilization (IVF) treatments, or use of a surrogate as well as marrying a spouse or partner with children. Later motherhood is enriching the lives of many women; however, in many cases this role is available only to those with financial means. It can also be fraught with emotional and physical costs when a sought-for pregnancy does not occur.

Grandparenthood

Grandmothers are essential figures in the lives of families. The specific role of a grandmother within a family can vary greatly. Although grandmothers themselves may still be working and have many other responsibilities of their own, they are often highly involved in raising their grandchildren, and in some instances grandparents live within the same household as their grandchildren. There are many cases where there is not a parent present and grandparents become the primary caregivers. Raising a child again as a grandmother can be a difficult task. Those who take on this responsibility often experience more physical, psychological, and financial effects than grandparents who do not, including an overall decline in their perceived physical and emotional health (Gibbons and Jones 2003). Still, the experience affords the grandparent an opportunity to become especially close to their grandchild and to have a major influence on the child's life. Thus, overall, this new role can be satisfying and emotionally fulfilling.

Housing Transitions

When and if adult children support and take care of their elderly parents, generally it is daughters who assume the caregiving position (Katz, Kabeto, and Langa 2000). Often this position is assumed during women's middle or later adulthood, and it can become an added responsibility to their other roles, including as a mother, wife, employee, or student. Many women sacrifice aspects of their daily lives and often give up or cut back on paid work, which decreases their income and retirement benefits (MetLife 2011).

In some instances, elderly parents who are ill or unable to care for themselves may move in with their children or other family members. Multigenerational living can be a mixed blessing, with loss of independence balanced by increased supports for older women. Feminists argue that equality for women calls for eldercare to be recognized as a societal responsibility and not one left to individual women (Harrington 2000).

Workforce Changes

The number of employed older women reached an all-time high at the beginning of the twenty-first century (Rife 2001). As women have increased their workforce participation in recent years, they also are working until later adulthood. In contrast, older men are beginning to retire at an earlier age (Etaugh 2008). The reasons older and young women give for working are similar; it is often out of economic necessity. In addition, as previously mentioned, often women pursue work, including (unpaid) volunteer work, for self-satisfaction (see Chapter 11).

Across all ages, and particularly during later adulthood, working is related to women's physical and psychological well-being. It provides opportunities for renewal and social contacts and feelings of competency and accomplishment. Older women who are employed have higher levels of morale than do women who have retired. Women who have never pursued a career outside of their home experience the lowest levels of self-esteem (Etaugh 2008). Older women must deal with the stigma associated with aging across all contexts of their lives, and work is no exception. They experience age discrimination in terms of hiring, promotion, and wages; they also begin confronting this discrimination at a younger age than men (Rife 2001).

Retirement

Much past research has focused only on the effects of retirement in the lives of men. However, retirement is just as critical a life event for women, although it may function in their lives in different ways. For example, while men often retire for involuntary reasons, women are more likely to retire by choice; this is often due to family issues, including having sick relatives or a recently retired husband (Canetto 2003). In addition, newly retired men and women may face this experience with very different resources. Since women earn less than their male counterparts in similar positions, often experience discontinuity in their work throughout their careers, and frequently entered the paid workforce later in life, they generally have fewer resources in retirement. They are also much less likely to be covered by a pension plan; similarly, their old age benefits are typically lower (Bethell 2005).

Women may also be more hesitant about retiring; if they began working at a later age, they may not have accomplished all their career goals yet (Etaugh 2008). Other women who strongly identify with their career and their work may not want to retire, particularly women who are self-employed or professionals (Etaugh and Bridges 2006). In contrast, some women, especially widows, those divorced, and singles, may be unable to retire until much later in their lives, if at all, due to financial stressors (Duenwald and Stamler 2004). There are also a number of women who choose to retire early; some may be forced to retire due to poor health, while others may choose to do so to provide care to family members, including a spouse, elders, or grandchildren (Etaugh 2008). Still other older women (and men) have become unemployed and were forced into early retirement when their companies closed or downsized in the new global economy. Many older women struggle in part-time jobs, if they can find them, to make ends meet. Elizabeth Strout's 2008 novel *Olive Kitteridge* explores the complex feelings and experiences of a retired Maine schoolteacher as she ages.

Retirement not only affects older women as individuals, it also affects their marriages and other relationships. The first two years following retirement are reported as a time characterized by marital conflict. However, women and men who retire at the same time as their partners are happier and experience less conflict. Distress is highest when husbands retire before wives (Etaugh 2008). Although in the long term women adjust positively to retirement, they may experience a longer initial period of transitioning. Often women have higher levels of depression and reduced levels of morale immediately following retirement in comparison to men (Moen, Kim, and Hofmeister 2001). This may be because women strongly value and identify with their working role and, as a result, struggle more with the transition. Nevertheless, the time of retirement is generally associated with elevated levels of satisfaction, though this is more likely to happen when the retiree is in good health and good financial standing, and is highly active (Fitzpatrick and Vinick 2003).

The Sisterhood of Women

One of the challenges that gender and women's studies must meet in redefining women from the centre of their own experiences is to expose the power relationships that threaten to oppress them and then to reconstruct womanhood as a positive experience. Many feminists believe that the struggles that mark the relationships between daughters and mothers and between sisters are a consequence of inflexible family, sex, and gender roles and of the oppression of women, including heteronormativity. A woman's identity based on the rejection of mothers and sisters contributes to self-denigration and dependence. The early slogan of women's liberation, "sisterhood is powerful," sought to strengthen the bonds between women that male-oriented kinship and political structures have obscured. Reaching past the long and often difficult barriers of age and experience to see their mothers, in particular, and their sisters as full members in the sisterhood of women is a task that all women must undertake to fully appreciate their own selves.

Women must also reach out across the differences of culture, race, class, religion, and nationality without ignoring them and recognize the power relationships that operate within them. Global efforts in recent decades by women and supportive males to improve the lives of females, young, adult, and elderly, are evidence of the value of collaboration. Every woman is the daughter of another woman. Every mother is a daughter. All women are potential sisters if structures of difference are acknowledged and existing power relations subverted.

Summary

Girlhood is not all sweet and passive but complex and varies widely. Girls worldwide experience societal pressures to conform to gender roles and especially with the additional burden brought by globalization. Societies worldwide are seeking to promote policies, strategies, and programs to support girls' empowerment, often led by girls themselves.

Virtually no society expresses a preference for girl babies over boy babies. Female infanticide and neglect are ways of controlling the population on the basis of gender. The devaluation of daughters has its roots in the low value placed on women in society at large. Although sons are privileged, daughters have value as the reproducers of the next generation and in the services they provide to the family. The names given to daughters indicate their place in the social scheme. Most surnames perpetuate the male lineage.

Many Western feminist studies have emphasized conflict in mother–daughter relationships, especially when a daughter seeks an independent life and identity. Women of colour identify strong mother–daughter bonds as mothers help prepare their daughters to survive and thrive in unsupportive racist environments.

Certain personality characteristics go with one's birth order and often are long-lasting. Gender ranking may nullify age ranking, subordinating a girl's talents to those of her male relatives. Gender often determines legal inheritance rights. Most societies favour sons over daughters in the inheritance of property and position.

A double standard of aging exists in which older women are devalued. Life events, such as divorce, widowhood, grandparenthood, eldercare, and retirement affect an older woman's psychological and physical health, lifestyle, and financial resources, both positively and negatively. Work, in particular, enhances her well-being and sense of accomplishment. Too frequently, female retirees receive much lower pensions than their male counterparts.

Later adulthood overall can be a positive time in a woman's life. Older women continue to develop dynamic relationships and a rich sense of self.

Discussion Questions

1. Draw a chart illustrating naming patterns of all the members of your extended family. What conclusions can you draw?
2. Chart your home responsibilities for a week. Contrast this with that of a sibling or relative of another gender. Do they differ? If so, how?
3. Recall your favourite book from when you were younger. What did you like about it? What was its message?
4. How do women's responsibilities change as they grow older? What options open up for women? What additional tasks are relegated to women? In your opinion, do women gain or lose options in society as they age?
5. It has been shown that, on average, women live longer than men do. Why do you think this is? What are the positive and negative consequences of longevity?

Recommended Resources

Abrams, Abby. 2014. "Older Mothers Tend to Live Longer, Study Finds." *Time*, 25 June. http://time.com/2922235/mothers-birth-pregnancy-aging/. This article explores the implications of research that demonstrates women who give birth later in life, live to significantly later ages than women who become mothers when young.

Acker, Alison, and Betty Brightwell. 2010. *Off Our Rockers and into Trouble: The Raging Grannies*. Victoria, BC: TouchWood Editions. *Off Our Rockers* tells the story of the Grannies from their beginning in Victoria to the international growth of the movement. Written by two of the founders, it is filled with the same humour that characterizes their protests.

Catalyst. 2013. "Family Leave—U.S., Canada, and Global." www.catalyst.org/knowledge/family-leave-us-canada-and-global. A comparative study of family leave policy and practice in the United States, Canada, and Global examples.

CBC News. 2011. "Slavery in Canada: Do We Know Our History? An Interactive Timeline." www.cbc.ca/news2/interactives/slavery-canada/.

CBC News provides a look at Canada's history of slavery and the slave trade by means of a timeline from 1550 to 2008.

de Beauvoir, Simone. 1973. *The Coming of Age.* New York: Warner. Similar in scope and breadth to *The Second Sex*, this text covers wide geographical and historical areas to focus on how societies treat the elderly. She particularly scorns modern industrial societies that too often view old people as disposable.

Gonick, Marnina, and Susanne Gannon, eds. 2014. *Becoming Girl: Collective Biography and the Production of Girlhood.* Toronto: Women's Press. *Becoming Girl* engages critical narrative analysis to explore how girlhood is constituted and embodied.

Kollontai, Alexandra. 2005 (1923). *Love of the Worker Bees.* Chicago: Chicago Review Press. Russian feminist, revolutionary, and free love advocate Kollontai wrote *Worker Bees* in 1923 as a testament to changing sexual mores. She portrayed the past, present, and future of Russian women's lives represented by a grandmother, mother, and daughter as changing contexts allowed them more social options and personal sexual freedom.

North American Network in Aging Studies (NANAS). Readings. http://agingstudies.org/NANAS/?page_id=33. NANAS provides a comprehensive compilation of books, edited volumes, journal articles, journals, blogs, and other publications related to aging studies with particular attention to gender.

"Raging Grannies Songs." n.d. http://raginggrannies.net/. The Raging Grannies (see Acker resource above) invite readers to explore their musical webpage to find a song "to express outrage about all of those things that threaten our grandchildren's futures—pollution, militarism, greed, 'isms and more."

Rajiva, Mythili, and Sheila Batacharya, eds. 2010. *Reena Virk: Critical Perspectives on a Canadian Murder.* Toronto: Canadian Scholars Press. This book discusses the murder of Reena Virk in Saanich, BC, in 1997. Virk was a racialized 14-year-old girl beaten to death by her female friends in a swarming. The volume provides an analysis of how racism, colonialism, and hierarchies of gender, class, age, and sexuality are implicated beyond the concept of girl bullying.

Rich, Adrienne. 1976. *Of Woman Born: Motherhood as Experience and Institution.* New York: Norton. In this book, now a feminist classic, Rich examines motherhood as a social institution and the way that it has evolved from antiquity to the present. She shows how relationships between women and men are reflected in the institution of motherhood and how concepts related to this institution change with changes in women's status. Rich, a feminist and poet, draws from her own experience as well as scholarly literature.

Sangha, Jasjit K., and Tahira Gonsalves, eds. 2013. *South Asian Mothering: Negotiating Culture, Family and Selfhood.* Toronto: Demeter Press. This text examines how gender, race, class, caste, and sexuality influence the practice of mothering in South Asia and in the diaspora. It highlights how the social construction of families intersects with identity to produce particular complexities for families and communities.

University of New Brunswick Libraries. n.d. "The Ward Chipman Slavery Brief." www.lib.unb.ca/Texts/NBHistory/chipman/about.html. Ward Chipman was a prominent New Brunswick lawyer, judge, and Loyalist who in 1800, along with Samuel Denny Street, defended the right of an enslaved woman, Nancy, to obtain her freedom. There was no existing legislation in New Brunswick on slavery and Chipman and Street offered their services pro bono in an attempt to establish a precedent. Although they were not successful in their bid to free Nancy from her owner, Caleb Jones, their efforts are considered seminal in directing the course of New Brunswick law. The original manuscript is available here.

Woolf, Virginia. 1966 (1938). *The Three Guineas*. New York: Harcourt Brace. As the daughter of an "educated gentleman," Woolf presents a critique of the educated fathers and brothers who monopolize the ruling structures of the state, its government, educational establishments, and professions to the exclusion of daughters and sisters. Her footnotes present a feminist history of the English women of her class from the nineteenth century to her own day.

8 Women's Health

Chapter Outline

- The Women's Health Movement
- Uncovering the Gender Dynamics of Western Medicine
- The Medicalization of Life Processes
- Gendered Violence
- Impact of Social and Cultural Disparities on Women's Health
- Women and Physical Health: Some Specific Concerns
- Women and Mental Health
- Women as Special-Risk/Vulnerable Populations

This chapter will help you
- Learn about a comprehensive definition of health beyond the absence of disease
- Appreciate the intersectional elements that affect health
- Recognize the social determinants of health and how they affect gender and women
- Understand how the biological function of reproduction is impacted by social and cultural control
- Comprehend the role of women's agency in developing appropriate health policy and practice

Clayquet Indian healers were predominantly women and they sang songs to compel the spirits to relinquish control of the sick person. We must investigate how the women's healing songs were lost and displaced and learn how women have begun to reclaim their own songs. One such song cautioned:
Do not listen to the other singing.
Do not be ashamed to sing your own song.
—JASKOSKI (1981)

Health systems reflect the societies that create them. Thus they can either perpetuate or ameliorate the inequities that exist in that particular society.
—WORLD HEALTH ORGANIZATION (2009, 75)

The Women's Health Movement

This chapter examines why, in the twenty-first century, women's health matters and why different groups of women have widely differing health outcomes, which then affect the lives of all individuals and their families, regardless of gender. Health issues have galvanized political consciousness among women globally and relate to the most fundamental of political questions: Who is to control women's own bodies, their physical selves? Also, how do health-care policies reinforce and sustain power hierarchies within class, race, age, sexuality, and gender structures? Understanding the structures that affect women's health and prevent good health helps to identify an important impetus for women to organize to right the wrongs done to women in society.

The publication in 1971 of *Our Bodies, Ourselves* (OBOS) by the Boston Women's Health Book Collective marked the coming of age of second-wave feminism in North America. This volume analyzed the implications of patriarchal society for the total well-being of women and provided three critical routes to change: (1) empowerment through self-knowledge, (2) establishment of women's rights and obligation to choose what to do with their own bodies, and (3) reliance on mutual support among women. In 2011, OBOS celebrated the fortieth anniversary of the first printing. It has been published in more than 25 languages worldwide and additional volumes, such as *OBOS: Menopause* (2006), *OBOS: Pregnancy and Childbirth* (2008), *Nuestros Cuerpos, Nuestras Vidas* (2000), and *The New Our Selves Growing Older* (1994), are also available. In addition, there is now both a website and a blog (www.ourbodiesourblog.org/) available in English.

Such publications provide essential health information for women. Equally important, women have used this knowledge as a stepping stone to their empowerment. For example, Toyoko Nakanishi founded the Shokado Women's Bookstore in 1975 in Japan. There women found a space where free discussion could take place, for example, in the wake of the Fujimi Hospital scandal in 1981, when it came to light that more than 1000 unnecessary hysterectomies had been performed over many years. The women who had had surgery were informed that it was necessary due to a "rotten" uterus or their ovaries that were "a mess." Initially, many women were embarrassed to even voice the term *uterus* in discussions with other women. The bookstore meetings provided opportunities for discussions with less shame and created shifts in language. The term *shame hair* for genital hair became *sexual hair* and *menstruation* (linked in many cultures to pollution) was renamed *monthly occurrence* (Davis 2007).

In Canada many organizations such as Women's Health in Women's Hands, a Toronto community-based clinic that provides health care for racialized women, organize and educate around women's health issues, often focusing on immigrant and refugee women or particular health concerns. Eating Disorders Action Group in Halifax takes a community-based approach to promoting healthy body image and offers peer-support groups, workshops, and an eating disorders resource centre. The Women's Health Clinic in Winnipeg is a feminist, community-based health centre offering a range of services to women from teens to elders with a holistic approach that emphasizes prevention, education, and action. Advocates also address how racism, transphobia, and homophobia, both inadvertent and institutional, can affect an individual's health. The wording of medical history forms, for example, can be incomplete or misleading if it is assumed that every patient is a heterosexual cisbodied woman.

Most importantly, the women's health movement has been largely responsible for new approaches to health care. Health is viewed as not just the absence of disease, but an integral part of a woman's total life experience, inextricably linked to her place in society. This ecological or **social determinants of health** model analyzes the impact of social factors such as race, ethnicity, gender, sexuality, educational attainment, and socio-economic status on health. "The social determinants of health are the conditions in which people are born, grow, live, work and age. These circumstances are shaped by the distribution of money, power and resources at global, national and local levels" (WHO 2013). Each of these factors locates an individual or group in the structure of society, giving differential access to power, privilege, and desirable resources (Williams 2002). Women's movements underscore the importance of understanding the intersectional nature of health inequalities. Socially patterned characteristics and inequalities have great impact on health and illness, and can even govern whether access to care is available. Improving the health of Canadians requires thinking about health and its determinants in a more sophisticated manner than has been the case to date. *Social Determinants of Health: The Canadian Facts* (Mikkonen and Raphael 2010) considers 14 social determinants of health:

1. Income and income distribution
2. Education
3. Unemployment and job security
4. Employment and working conditions
5. Early childhood development
6. Food insecurity
7. Housing
8. Social exclusion
9. Social safety network
10. Health services
11. Indigeneity
12. Gender
13. Race
14. Disability

Redefining and Reframing Health

Definitions of health are culturally variable: what is considered *normal* and what an illness vary widely across societies and across time frames. Health is not a static state: how health is defined reflects a dynamic, shifting adaptation to the environment over the life cycle and is influenced by the values inherent in any specific culture. The reader should evaluate how different definitions (see below) fit (or not) into one's own life and in what ways the definition/s might be modified to be both more inclusive and reactive to the myriad influences on health.

In 1946, the World Health Organization (WHO) defined health as "a state of complete physical, mental, and social well-being and not merely the absence of disease and infirmity." Today, current Western attitudes have expanded the definition to include the physical, emotional, social, intellectual, and spiritual dimensions of a person's life. Health thus has both subjective and objective components that influence the way it is defined, the nature of the data collected in order to study health and disease, and the way different groups of people will be treated by the medical establishment.

Women's health has been defined as distinct from the WHO definition in a number of important ways. Employing the broader definition used at the Fourth World Conference of Women in Beijing, the Ontario Women's Health Council defined women's health as "a state of emotional, social, cultural, spiritual and physical well-being, determined by social, political and economic context of women's lives, as well as biology. In

The Broken Column (1944) by Frida Kahlo (1907–1954), oil on canvas. Kahlo was in a trolley accident as a teenager and had to wear a variety of corsets to support her spine for the rest of her life. In this painting, the scattered pins and her naked and corseted upper body display both her pain and her courage.

addition, the definition recognizes the validity of women's life experiences and women's own beliefs and experiences of health" (Phillips 1995).

Another definition, formulated for use in training physicians, states: "Women's health recognizes the importance of the study of gender differences . . . recognizes the diversity of women's health needs over a life cycle and how these needs reflect differences in race, class, ethnicity, culture, sexual preferences[1] and levels of education and access to medical care; includes the empowerment of all women, as for all patients, to be informed participants in their own health care" (Donoghue 1996).

Moreover, people with higher levels of education and higher income have lower rates of many chronic diseases compared to those with less education and lower-income levels. Even in Canada, a country with an ostensibly universal health-care system, studies have shown that education levels and income inequality adversely affect health (Armstrong and Pederson 2015; Alter et al., Health Matters 2011; Raphael, CJS Foundation 2002). Thus the definition of health is broader than the individual and must consider the multiplicity of factors in a woman's life.

Why "Women's" Health?

In the twenty-first century most women can expect to live longer and healthier lives than their grandmothers did. Though advances have been made, these developments are by no means universal or uniform. Health status, in terms of illness and death rates, varies according to gender and is influenced by life factors such as income level, ethnicity, race, human environment, geography, lifestyle, and access to health care. As a result, some groups of women benefit more from scientific and/or social advances, while other women fall behind.

Women's health has historically been focused on maternal health, ignoring the rest of the woman (Wenger 2004). Not all women give birth, and even those who do so have a life before and after childbirth. Because the totality of female life over a lifespan has not yet been adequately addressed, the study of women's health is a necessary corrective, both for theory and practice. Such a focus should not be seen to be exclusionary, as health has a profound influence on the ability to participate fully in life—whether one is cisbodied, transgender, or intersex.

New areas of study such as *epigenetics* (gene modifications induced by local changes in the environment brought on by stress, diet, behaviour, toxins, and other factors) and a life-course approach to **health** (beginning in utero) influence the manner in which health and health outcomes are now studied. These theories place increased importance on the ways that experiences both before birth and throughout one's lifetime affect one's health and the health of one's potential offspring. Studies of the offspring born to women living in the Netherlands during the post–World

War II famine years, for example, found that these children were more likely to be obese than those born before and after the famine (Francis 2011). It is believed that the fetus physiologically adapted to the uterine environment—in this case, one of starvation—even though born into a world of plenty. Thus, physiological adaptations that take place before birth are manifested over an individual's lifetime. Other studies of pregnant women following stressful events, such as hurricanes, provide additional evidence of long-lasting changes in the fetus (Paul 2010).

As women usually have different roles than men, mediated by social and cultural mores, they are exposed to different risks and experiences by virtue of their gender. The HIV/AIDS pandemic is a stark example of how the different paths of exposure, risk factors, disease pathways, and treatment manifest themselves according to gender. The primary routes of transmission of HIV also vary in different parts of the world. Women make up a growing proportion of people living with HIV/AIDS (50 per cent). However, in Canada, approximately 23 per cent of all new HIV infections are reported in women, with the majority of new infections still being diagnosed in men (Public Health Agency of Canada 2015). Health, therefore, is a central element in people's lives. Being healthy makes it possible for women to care for themselves and their families, to contribute to their community, to be a productive member of the workforce, and to build a base of economic stability (findings from the 2010 Kaiser Family Foundation Women's Health Survey).

Health, Gender, and Human Rights

As Eleanor Roosevelt presciently declared, "Where, after all, do human rights begin? In small places, close to home—so close and so small that they cannot be seen on any map of the world" (Roosevelt 1958). "The ability to attain the highest possible standard of health is not a privilege for the elite but a right that comes with being human" (Levison and Levison 2001). If only the wealthy and elite have access to the factors that enhance health and the prospect of engaging in life's challenges to the fullest from birth, health becomes a privilege and not a right. When male infants are provided with more nourishment than female infants, based on their greater perceived worth to a particular society, children have unequal access to health based on gender.

Based upon drafts written by Canadian John Humphrey in 1948, the United Nations issued a Universal Declaration of Human Rights, meant to "protect the integrity and dignity of human beings," which has had meaningful repercussions for the health of women globally (Agosin 2001). Together with the 1979 Convention for the Elimination of All Forms of Discrimination against Women (CEDAW), these UN instruments are potentially pivotal devices to ensure the implementation of human rights. Both professional and activist groups increasingly call attention to the inextricable link between health, gender, and human rights. The concept of health as a right is still not universally accepted or applied. Yet the link between health as a human right and the lives of the girls and women who do not yet live as equals with the males in their societies provides an important focus or rationale for women's health as a special area of concern. The lack of available and appropriate health care for transgender and intersex persons is a serious violation of rights in most places, including Canada.

One egregious human rights abuse in Canada that is gendered was the unwanted, unnecessary forced sterilization of the most vulnerable females (the poor, Indigenous, women of colour, immigrants, and the disabled) without their consent; a wrong that has only recently been addressed. In 1995, Leilani Muir became the first person to successfully sue the province of Alberta for wrongful sterilization (Dambrofsky 2016).

Health-Care Systems

Throughout the world, women encounter a wide variety of health-care systems. Many countries around the world offer some kind of public health-care plan, while in others, health-care remains in the hands of private insurance companies. In the context of reframing women's health as a human rights issue, the women's health movement has taken steps on multiple fronts to reform and improve health-care systems and make them more responsive to women's needs. Feminists have encouraged women to ask: What is a healthy woman? How do women become and remain healthy? How should women deal with illness or disease? These questions are essential because women's health has been perceived differently from men's and because women's bodies and biological processes are different from men's in some respects. The women's health movement has also called for changes in the services a society provides for women, based on its recognition that women have been discriminated against both as recipients and as providers of health-care services. As shall be examined in more detail in this chapter, women have been both ignored and exploited in research about medical conditions and medical devices. Medication and treatment for medical conditions not specific to women, such as heart disease, had long been investigated and norms established primarily on the basis of research on men (Sechzer, Rabinowitz, and Denmark 1994).

Canada's system of publicly funded universal health care is delivered provincially and was implemented throughout the country, province by province, in the mid-twentieth century. Each province has its own guidelines, and while coverage may vary between them, basic essential health care is available, if not always accessible or appropriately delivered, for citizens and permanent residents. Advocates have also struggled to promote culturally accessible health care and to reduce discrimination based on gender, race, sexuality, class, age, or citizenship. In particular, the federal government's 2012 elimination of the Interim Federal Health Care program for persons claiming refugee status or waiting for their status to be confirmed caused a serious breach in service. This decision was overturned in 2014 by Justice Anne Mactavish of the Federal Court who ruled that the cuts were "cruel and unusual treatment" by denying treatment to pregnant women, sick children, and persons with serious illnesses.

Canada's health care is often said to be a two-tiered system. While public funding accounts for approximately 70 per cent of health care, the remaining is supplied privately through insurance companies. Private clinics offer faster service and more types of treatments but at a cost not all can afford. The Council of Canadians cites evidence from studies in Canada and elsewhere that shows that two-tiered health care creates longer wait times for the "99 per cent" and less equality for everyone. Studies also show that private health care is expensive and often of inferior quality (Council of Canadians 2014). Even in Canada, the intersection of gender and class can result in slow, insufficient, unavailable, or even counter-productive care, as in the case of health research experimentation.

Experimentation and exploitation of the most vulnerable in health research has a long history in Canada and around the world. For example, documents obtained by the Truth and Reconciliation Commission revealed Canada's medical and pharmaceutical experimentation on Indigenous children in residential schools. Justice Murray Sinclair commented

> We do know that there were research initiatives that were conducted with regard to medicines that were used ultimately to treat the Canadian population. Some of those medicines were tested in aboriginal communities and residential schools before they were utilized publicly. . . . Some of those medicines which we know were able to work in the general population, we also have discovered were withheld from children in residential schools, and we're trying to find the documents which explain that too. (CBC News 2013)

The efforts of health-care movements in the Global South are somewhat different from those found in the North. In developing countries, a primary focus of health-care systems is on delivering

> **Box 8.1** Women in Media
>
> ### Henrietta Lacks
>
> Henrietta Lacks, a poor African American tobacco farmer, was treated at Johns Hopkins University Hospital for terminal cancer and, after her death, was buried in an unmarked grave. Without her knowledge or consent, her cancer cells were taken and became the first "immortal" human cells grown in a culture and hereafter referred to as HeLa cells (using the first two letters of Henrietta Lacks' name). Although Mrs. Lacks has been dead for more than 60 years, her cells are still living. This gave rise to a multi-million dollar industry which has been vital for development of the polio vaccine, gene mapping, and IVF, among other research areas. Mrs. Lacks' descendants (most of whom had no access to health care) only learned of this when Rebecca Skloot, investigating HeLa for a book she was writing, informed them of Mrs. Lacks' enormous contribution to science. Her family gained no financial compensation from the worldwide bio-tech industry that continues to profit from her cells. The intersection of her race, class, and gender allowed the Johns Hopkins scientists to take and use her cells without concern for her rights, and without considering them a contribution worth crediting. Only in 2013, after her family engaged a lawsuit, was Mrs. Lacks given proper acknowledgement for her contribution to medical breakthroughs.
>
> Source: Skloot (2011).

basic resources such as food, clean water, and shelter to people as well as provisions to alleviate the suffering of the vulnerable and the poor. Greater use of contraception, access to antiretroviral drugs for pregnant women, and more birth attendants, such as midwives, particularly in rural areas, has reduced maternal mortality worldwide in the past two decades. Still many countries struggle to meet these goals. New assisted reproductive techniques (ART) have created new areas of potential abuse and exploitation. For example, transnational surrogacy has become a lucrative market in which lower-income women in India and Central America are inseminated as surrogates for more affluent women in the Global North.

Uncovering the Gender Dynamics of Western Medicine

In most societies women have been the primary caretakers of human bodies from birth to death. It has been women's work to tend to birthing, to care for infants and children, and to teach basic habits of sanitation and nutrition to young people. Women care for the sick and wounded, the ailing and weak, and the elderly. Thus, when the caretaker herself requires assistance, especially in later years, in many industrialized nations there is often no one to help her. Although regular day-to-day caretaking has been, and continues to be, done largely by women, male authorities in many Western societies have taken control of the more prestigious forms of healing. For men, who do not menstruate, menstruation seemed unhealthy, abnormal, and dangerous. Pregnancy and childbirth were also mysterious, frightening, and threatening. If men are the authorities to whom women turn for information about these events, certainly men's subjective interpretations are conveyed to women, who learn to perceive the world through men's "expert" eyes. Men's ideals of women's health reflected not only gender bias but class, race, heterosexist, and transphobic biases as well and are deeply embedded in Western ideas of the female body as "other."

Woman as Deviant

The notion that a woman is an aberrant man has deep roots. Galen of Pergamon (c. 129–200 CE), a

Greek physician whose writings influenced Western medicine for centuries, taught that women were "inside-out men." Accordingly, women had insufficient body heat to force genitals outward. Thus, using man as his measure, Galen viewed women (as had Aristotle) as "defective" persons. Since women were "inferior," it followed that their diseases were caused, almost entirely, by their inferior genitalia (Dean-Jones 1994).

In later centuries, as the new promoters of "science" and "reason" began to overtake the dominant role of the religious leaders in Western societies, many moral and spiritual concerns became the domain of science.

Woman as "the Weaker Sex"

As the Industrial Revolution began to change the structure of modern Western society, women were placed in an illogical, dichotomous position. While their bodies continued to be considered pathological, women were considered the moral guardians of society (Martin 1987; Ehrenreich and English 2005). Upper- and middle-class women were perceived as physically weak, of delicate health, and vulnerable to a great variety of ailments arising from the fact that they had wombs. The uterus was believed to be the source of a vast array of illnesses of both the body and the mind. Excessive physical and mental challenges were thought to be damaging to women's most exalted function, procreation. By the middle of the nineteenth century, physicians claimed that women of the upper classes had little or no sex drive. If they did exhibit some libido, this was thought to be symptomatic of severe illness, to be treated surgically. Any form of rebellion to or deviance from gender prescriptions was met with severe medical measures (Barker-Benfield 1977). A refusal to be satisfied with housework, a tendency to masturbate, an overeagerness to be educated, or a desire for the vote might be deemed cause for surgical practices ranging from clitoridectomy (the removal of the clitoris) to hysterectomy (the removal of the uterus) (Marieskind 1977). These actions or their threat kept women of the more privileged classes more or less in line. Working-class women, poor women, and women of colour were less vulnerable to such strictures, for they were not thought to share all of the weakness of those of privilege.

The Gendered Profession of Medicine

By the end of the nineteenth century, the Western health-care system had begun to crystallize into the professionalized and gendered form it takes today. Men prevailed as leaders of the professional health-care system and propagated ideals about what was normal in woman's health. In turn, women health-care specialists, healers, and midwives were prohibited from practising even among low-income women (Petchesky and Judd 1998). This proscription had special repercussions for low-income women, who did not have the same access as wealthy women to professional medical practices.

Today the increase in women's goals to earn advanced degrees is reflected in the medical profession. In Canada in 2011, women represented nearly two-thirds of adults aged 25 to 34 with a medical degree compared to just over one-quarter among those aged 55 to 64 (Statistics Canada 2013b). How this phenomenon is changing the profession, such as the medicalization of women's health discussed below, is understudied at present. Women practise predominantly internal medicine, pediatrics, family medicine, and obstetrics and gynecology. Dr Noni MacDonald was the first woman to be named a dean of medicine in Canada, at Dalhousie University in 1999. She was followed by Dr Catharine Whiteside at the University of Toronto, and Dr Hélène Boisjoly at Université de Montréal. Of all physicians worldwide, 32 per cent are women (Catalyst 2012b). In many developing nations women are the primary health-care providers and caregivers, in both formal and informal settings. Yet here, too, women have still to gain substantial positions of power.

Box 8.2 In Her Own Words

National Aboriginal Council of Midwives

An Aboriginal midwife is a committed primary health care provider who has the skills to care for pregnant women, babies, and their families throughout pregnancy and for the first weeks in the postpartum. She is also a person who is knowledgeable in all aspects of women's medicine and she provides education that helps keep the family and the community healthy. Midwives promote breastfeeding, nutrition, and parenting skills. A midwife is the keeper of ceremonies for young people like puberty rites. She is a leader and mentor, someone who passes on important values about health to the next generation.

Aboriginal communities across Canada have always had midwives. It has only been in the last hundred years that this practice has been taken away from communities. This occurred for a number of reasons, including colonization and changes in the health care system in Canada. As a result of losing midwifery, many rural and remote Aboriginal communities are currently required to deliver their babies and access care outside of their communities. Despite these changes, there are still some Aboriginal midwives practising in a variety of settings across Canada. The vision of these midwives is to one day see "[a]n Aboriginal midwife working in every Aboriginal community."

Source: Reprinted from www.aboriginalmidwives.ca, by permission of the National Aboriginal Council of Midwives.

The Medicalization of Life Processes

The following subsections consider how the "normal" functions in women's life processes were medicalized and came to be dominated by a patriarchal medical system, leaving many women disempowered. Yet women have consistently organized, both formally and informally, and increasingly have challenged and resisted this encroachment on their bodily integrity with success.

Medicalization involves organizing a broad (and ever-expanding) range of behaviours and aspects of everyday life into categories of health and illness (Boston Women's Health Book Collective 2011). Western society has medicalized menstruation, childbirth, menopause, and sexuality, even though these are normal parts of the life cycle and experience of most women. Nevertheless, some women rarely, if ever, menstruate; some women never give birth; some women do not experience any symptoms, such as hot flashes, with the onset of menopause. Even among those who do experience these processes, there are wide variations in the experience.

Why, then, has women's health been the object of excessive medicalization? Is premenstrual syndrome (PMS) real? Why are there excessive numbers of hysterectomies in North America? How did small breasts become a *disease* known as micromastia (Ratcliff 2002)? Furthermore, the biomedical model, which has been predominant in the West since the seventeenth century, emphasizes identifying a pathology, seeking biological causes within the individual, and finding a "cure." A socio-cultural and social determinant of heath approach—one that includes the intra-personal, the personal, the community, and the government and its policies—provides more opportunity to examine the multiple causes of ill health, culturally defined. This shifts the emphasis to prevention from diagnosis and treatment, something the women's health movement advocates for both their families and their communities.

Menstruation to Menopause

Menarche (the onset of menstruation) can occur any time between the ages of 10 and 18. Menstruation also varies by individual: it may occur every 28 days or be less regular; it may last a whole week or only a couple of days; it may be accompanied by a blood flow that is heavy or light, with strong abdominal cramps or none at all; it may be preceded by a variety of changes in a woman's body or emotions or it may not.

It was once thought essential for women of the privileged classes—because they were "finer" in makeup—to take to bed while menstruating, during the latter phases of pregnancy (confinement), and for several weeks after childbirth. No such strictures applied to women of the working classes, racialized groups, or colonies, whose physical makeup was thought to be "coarser." Despite these class, racial, and imperial disparities, menstruation was persistently conceptualized as a form of illness. By the late nineteenth century, physicians began to define and treat menstruation, thus sharing with mothers the role of socializing adolescent girls about their bodies, a strategy that enlarged their influence (Brumberg 1997).

Menopause refers to what happens in a woman's body as she reaches the end of her child-bearing years. The increased lifespan for women means that more women now reach menopause and live long years thereafter. Most women cease menstruating between the ages of 45 and 55, experiencing in the process some irregularity in the timing and character of the menstrual cycle. Women may also experience sensations thought to relate in large part to the reduced production of estrogen, which marks the eventual cessation of the menstrual cycle. Symptoms (usually temporary) may include hot flashes, night sweats, sleep difficulties, psychological distress, and weight gain. In response, the medical profession has intervened with hormonal treatment and even surgical removal of the uterus. Although many women do suffer discomforts that might be relieved medically, today feminists question whether such measures are needed, whether they are worth the cost in terms of health risk, and whether alternative measures have been adequately considered. Lack of substantial

Box 8.3 Time to Reflect

DES in Canada

DES (diethylstilbestrol), developed in England in 1938, was the first synthetic version of estrogen. At its peak, DES was manufactured by over 200 different drug companies under as many names for the purpose of preventing miscarriages and as a "wonder drug" that would make "bigger and stronger babies." Despite scientific evidence that DES caused cancer in laboratory animals, DES continued to be marketed for use by pregnant women for over 30 years. In 1953, a randomized, controlled, double-blind study at the University of Chicago showed DES to be completely ineffective for its intended purpose of preventing miscarriage.

DES was prescribed to approximately 200,000–400,000 pregnant women in Canada from 1941 to 1971 leaving approximately 100,000 to 200,000 DES daughters and 100,000 to 200,000 DES sons. DES daughters face a 1-in-1000 risk for clear cell adenocarcinoma, a rare cancer of the vagina or cervix. They need special screening tests to detect this cancer. Pregnancy problems affect the greatest number of DES daughters. These problems include malformations of the reproductive organs and may lead to increased infertility. Women who took prescribed DES while pregnant face a 30–40 per cent increased risk for breast cancer.

Source: Adapted from "Brief History of Diethylstilbestrol." DES Action Canada Website.

funding (reflecting traditional [male] research priorities) has resulted in continuing gaps in the understanding of the mechanisms of menopause as they affect individual women. Globally, women authors have worked to dispel the notion of menopause as a disease or illness, including in the United States (Sheehy 1998), in Turkey (Cifcili et al. 2009), in Denmark (Hvas 2001), and in Iran (Khademi and Cooke 2003). In urban Iran, women consider menopause to be a natural and even positive stage of life, particularly for heterosexual women who can now enjoy sex without the fear of pregnancy.

Reproductive Rights

The 1994 Cairo Programme of Action defined reproductive rights at the International Conference on Population and Development. Subsequently, it was adopted by 184 United Nations member states. It states

> Reproductive health is a state of complete physical, mental and social well-being and not merely the absence of disease or infirmity, in all matters relating to the reproductive system and its functions and processes. Reproductive health therefore implies that people are able to have a satisfying and safe sex life and that they have the capability to reproduce and the freedom to decide if, when and how often to do so. Implicit in this last condition are the right of men and women to be informed [about] and to have access to safe, effective, affordable and acceptable methods of family planning of their choice, as well as other methods for regulation of fertility which are not against the law, and the right of access to appropriate health-care services that will enable women to go safely through pregnancy and childbirth and provide couples with the best chance of having a healthy infant. (United Nations 2014)

The ability to control pregnancy has been an important boon to women in many ways. In 1969, contraception was decriminalized in Canada. For the first time, a woman could have control over conception, even without a partner's awareness. In addition, sexual intercourse could be separated from conception, enabling women to explore their sexuality in new ways. However, it too has become increasingly medicalized, primarily through the exploitation of test subjects and concerns about safety and access.

Women in many societies, past and present, have been able to control pregnancy through the use of herbal remedies. However, their services gradually became illegal. In Canada the 1892 Criminal Code rendered birth control obscene, "tending to corrupt morals." Some birth control providers were able to prove that their advocacy had been "for the public good" and could thereby avoid jail time. In the 1960s, hormone pills and intrauterine devices were distributed freely among millions of women before adequate testing and other precautions were taken. Some of these devices were later found to be damaging to women's health (Rathus et al. 2011). New methods of contraception have recently become available or are being developed, including transdermal patches, vaginal rings, and injectables that protect against pregnancy for 12 weeks. At this stage of their development, such contraceptive methods must be supervised by a physician. Funding levels for research into new methods of contraception, however, remain minuscule relative to other health concerns. The testing of birth-control devices and medications, often required by Western nations, all too often is done on women from poorer nations, while research into male contraception, aimed at interrupting the production of sperm, is still in its very early stages.

Sterilization has a long history of use as a form of birth control, generally in the form of *tubal ligation*, a medical procedure that blocks the tubes carrying a woman's egg to her uterus so it cannot be fertilized, and also in the form of male vasectomy. Sterilization without informed consent continued well into the twentieth century. Alberta's 1928 Sexual Sterilization Act established a Eugenics Board that operated for more than 40 years and never once turned down an application for involuntary sterilization. Of its 4785 approved sterilization orders, 59 per cent underwent the procedure. The decisions were based on racialized criteria related to perceived mental and physical conditions and behaviour (Strohschein and Weitz 2014). British Columbia was the other Canadian province to enact a sterilization law, which was in effect from 1933 to 1973. Like Alberta, BC also established an Eugenics Board to approve the procedures and, like Alberta, the victims were disproportionally immigrants or Indigenous, including Métis. During the 1960s, Puerto Rican women in both the continental United States and Puerto Rico were sterilized in large numbers without informed consent. Where other birth control alternatives were lacking, sterilization became the only family-planning "choice," known as *la operacion* (Lopez 1987).

Abortion is often a last resort for women for whom birth control has failed. In 1869, abortions were declared illegal under Canada's first Criminal Code. One hundred years later, the federal government amended the criminal law to legalize abortion as long as a therapeutic abortion committee of three doctors affirmed that it was warranted to protect the woman's physical or mental well-being. There is a consensus within the women's health movement that the decision whether to have an abortion should be in the hands of the pregnant woman (Solinger 2007). Dr Henry Morgentaler challenged Canada's new ruling by performing abortions without committee approval, based solely on a woman's decision to have an abortion. He was supported by women who formed 1970's Abortion Caravan, which started in Vancouver and ended in a two-day protest in Ottawa. In 1974, the Canadian Alliance to Repeal the Abortion Law (CARAL) formed and continued the effort to make abortion accessible and available without medical committee approval. Fifteen years later, the Supreme Court of Canada declared the existing law unconstitutional. Today, while abortion is legal, access to the procedure is limited by disparities in provincial funding and remains completely unavailable in Prince Edward Island—though in January 2016, abortion activists sued the provincial government for the right to an abortion, and in March of the same year the province announced that it would move to provide surgical abortions in the province (Fraser and Sinclair 2016). But the abusive treatment of women seeking abortions (and violent threats against those women and men who have aided them) has escalated among abortion opponents, making abortion once again a highly politicized issue.

The shift in many parts of the world from medicalization to politicization provides an additional area of concern (WHO 1998). Worldwide, nearly half of all abortions are unsafe (56 per cent in the Global South, 6 per cent in the Global North) (Guttmacher Institute 2012). In the face of these challenges women continue to demand respectful reproductive choices and accurate information about their bodies.

Pharmaceutical or medical abortion, which does not require surgery, is used in many parts of the world. The limitations and failures of birth control make the availability of legal abortion vital to the health of women. In Bangladesh, for example, where the abortion law is rigidly restrictive, menstrual regulation services avert unsafe abortions, one of the leading causes of death there. It is legal, however to use "manual or electric vacuum aspiration to induce abortion, provided within 10 weeks of a woman's last period," and this serves as backup to difficult-to-acquire contraception (Johnston et al. 2010).

When hygienically and correctly induced, abortion is extremely safe. But when women must resort to clandestine and illegal means of terminating unwanted pregnancies, many of which are poorly performed abortions, at least 47,000–70,000 women die annually and hundreds of thousands more suffer serious complications. Women continue to suffer from a shortage of facilities that can provide safe, prompt, and affordable abortions and that can also safeguard their anonymity if they desire it (World Health Organization 2011; Guttmacher Institute 2012).

An anti-abortion backlash in Canada and the United States resulted in the murders and attempted murders of abortion providers, death threats, clinic bombings and arsons, and increasingly restrictive state mandates and continues today. Despite the fact that "13 per cent of global maternal mortality" is attributed to complications from unsafe, illegal abortions, the biggest problem facing women wanting or needing an abortion service is accessibility (Guttmacher Institute 2012). Worldwide, abortion statutes range from legal to illegal or severely restricted only to save a woman's life. Every year, 25 to 30 million legal abortions and 20 million unsafe abortions are performed worldwide (Seager 2009).

Childbirth

Pregnancy and childbirth are not diseases, but they do carry risks. As childbirth became the domain of medical specialists, it was experienced even more passively by women in hospital settings. New medicines, instruments, and procedures removed childbirth from the home traditional experience, although home births are once again slightly increasing. In addition, women have once again begun to rely on the medical expertise of nurse midwives as well as using doulas, who provide continuous, non-medical support through labour and delivery and after birth. Doulas have also begun to support women in miscarriage and abortion procedures.

In recent decades, delivery has also frequently meant Caesarean sections (surgical delivery of the fetus). Although this procedure is convenient and profitable for physicians and hospitals and extremely useful in medical emergencies, it is disabling for a large number of women (Martin 1987). The rate of Caesarean section (C-section) in childbirth in Canada was 26.9 per cent in 2010, up from 17.6 per cent in 1995. This tendency is similar to the worldwide increase in this procedure (Kelly et al. 2013). This rate is more than twice the WHO recommended range of 5–15 per cent (Amnesty International 2010).

In a 2010 report, WHO explains how the overuse of C-sections is actually a barrier to universal health coverage, noting that in 2008, 6.2 million unnecessary sections were performed, costing approximately US $2.32 billion (Gibbons et al. 2010). The paradox remains that women with access to such care have fewer deaths (of both mother and child) while also being subjected to unnecessary risks in some cases.

The acceptance of innovations, such as anesthetics during childbirth, hospital-based births,

---

Box 8.4 Women in Media

Lidia Casas

For her long-term work in legal advocacy to make abortion and contraception available in Chile, Lidia Casas received the International Planned Parenthood Federation Western Region Outstanding Contribution Award for the Defense of Family Planning in 2001. In "Women and Reproduction: From Control to Autonomy? The Case of Chile" (2011), Casas spells out both the barriers to legalizing abortion and the remedies. She poses the concept of the "double discourse" or "double morality" where society hypocritically speaks against women's right to choose while secretly engaging in the practices they maintain as illegal.

Lidia Casas has served in different years as a member of the Gender and Right Advisory Group of the Department of Human Reproduction of the World Health Organization, and is a law professor and member of the Human Rights Centre of the Diego Portales Law School in Santiago, Chile. Casas spent much of her youth in Canada, where her family found political refuge from the Pinochet dictatorship.

and use of fetal screening through amniocentesis and other testing, reveals that not all medicalization has been forced upon women. The use of new technologies also reflects a confluence of sociocultural attitudes and the availability of medical procedures. Many women today are grateful that such technologies exist. However, the potential for abuse through such innovations is not always sufficiently evaluated before widespread acceptance occurs; past experiences have made increasing numbers of women and health activists more wary.

Until the twentieth century, the risks of childbirth were grave for women everywhere; they remain serious for low-income women in the modern industrial world as well as in developing countries. Of the half-million women who die each year in childbirth, 99 per cent live in poor countries. Many more women worldwide contract serious illnesses, which result in approximately 62 million grave childbirth-related health problems annually (WHO 2007; Amnesty International 2010). This intersection between poverty and health risks due to childbirth can be found in Canada as well. One in four children on Canada's First Nations reserves lives in poverty. In 2010, an extensive study of infant mortality in Manitoba showed that the death rate for Indigenous babies was more than twice the Canadian average (CTV News 2014). The health risks for pregnant and child-bearing adolescents and their infants are also great, since teenage mothers are disproportionately found among groups with low income (WHO 2011).

Sexuality

Sexuality has also become medicalized and is closely tied to existing gender ideals and expectations. As sexuality is a "learned and deeply socialized phenomenon," using a medical model to study sexuality requires an examination of norms and may result in another mode of social control (Tiefer 2004). Moreover, as sexuality education is by no means comprehensive or accurate globally, it is difficult for girls and women to make educated decisions about their sexual health. In the twenty-first century, blogs (such as Spring Talks Sex on the Canadian Women's Health Network: www.cwhn.ca/en/node/45359) and 'zines (such as Shamelessmag.com) provide more accessible (and explicit) informal sexuality education to those with access to the Internet (see Box 8.5).

The double standard of sexual conduct remains firmly in place in many women's lives,

Box 8.5 Key Issues

Tips on Searching for Health Information on the Web

Searching for current, reliable information in health sites on the Internet is a useful skill but one that requires care. Look for recognizable educational organizations, particularly those not affiliated with or funded by governments. Commercial sites tend to be the most problematic, though there are exceptions. If you cannot tell by looking through the site information where the funding is coming from, that can be a red flag—you should be able to tell, by reading the "About Us" section, what the mission and funding resource of any informational website is. When assessing content, look for factual, sourced information rather than opinions (with sources that you can check and verify yourself). Check both the date that the information was uploaded and the date of the research on which the information is based—do not assume that just because you found the article today, it was written recently. Look also at whatever else the site links to; are their suggested resources reliable? If you're still having trouble, or if you want a safe place to start, check the Health on the Net Foundation (www.healthonnet.org) for accredited websites that have been verified as useful and reliable.

even as some young women explore their sexuality with greater ease and freedom. The medicalization of female sexuality, including discussions of *female sexual arousal disorder* as a diagnosis in the latest *Diagnostic and Statistical Manual of Mental Disorders* (American Psychiatric Association 2013), is cause for concern, as this may result in greater focus on medication and less emphasis on dealing with the cultural and emotional constraints in women's sexual lives.

The development of Viagra and other medications for erectile or sexual dysfunction in males is one example of the "politics of sexuality" (Vance 1984). Until 2015, no such drug had been produced for women. Women seeking enhanced sexual pleasure began using Viagra (both with and without a physician's prescription) and increasingly purchase untested over-the-counter drugs that claim to enhance arousal, even though no research has established their effectiveness and safety in women (Ellin 2012). In 2015 a drug billed as the "female Viagra" (a failed anti-depressant), was approved by the US Food and Drug Administration. Health Canada has, as of this writing, not yet approved the drug for sale in Canada.

Gendered Violence

Intimate-Partner Violence

A large proportion of women who show up in hospital emergency rooms for treatment of injuries are victims of intimate-partner abuse and sexual violence. Non-fatal violence between intimate partners compromises the health of millions of women worldwide. Studies in 48 countries reveal that 10–69 per cent of women report having been physically assaulted by an intimate partner during their lifetime. Countries and cultures vary in the extent of their domestic violence against women, but the phenomenon appears pervasive worldwide, with few minor exceptions in small societies (Seager 2009; UN Department of Economic and Social Affairs 2010). Some women face increased risks. A DisAbled Women's Network Canada study of disabled women found that, although one out of five of Canadian women live with a disability, 40 per cent of respondents had experienced some form of violence in their lives (Masuda and Ridington 1992).

Although some physicians do provide supportive care to victims of intimate-partner abuse, others do not. There is a continued need to educate less skilled physicians who may not recognize the cause of the injuries. Physicians can cause more physical and emotional harm to women who have been abused when they examine women roughly, minimize an injury or the abuse, accuse the patient of lying, or blame the patient for the abuse (Hamberger et al. 1998). Assault can result in not only chronic disabilities, both physical and mental, but also death. Between 2003 and 2013, Canadian police recorded 960 homicides against intimate partners. Of these, 747 involved a female victim (Beaupré 2015).

Intimate-partner violence is most often thought of as physical, but can also be emotional, financial, or verbal. Emotional, verbal, or financial abuse often escalates into physical violence, but even on their own these abuses cause "serious emotional, social, and economic consequences for victims, their family, and society, making this phenomenon a public health issue" (Beaupré 2015). Emotional and financial forms of violence are not typically considered crimes under the Canadian Criminal Code, so the recourse for these women can be limited (Sinha 2013).

Rape and Its Impact

Rape has obvious health consequences, both physical and psychological, including possibly exposing the victim to sexually transmitted diseases, such as human immunodeficiency virus/acquired immunodeficiency syndrome (HIV/AIDS). A further consequence in many cultures is the stigma attached to the loss of virginity by unmarried women. Women who have experienced rape may become unwanted, "unmarriageable" members of the household, further victimized. In some instances, female victims may even be murdered by their own male kin for their loss of "honour" (PLOS 2009). Rape victims are also at high risk for chronic re-experiencing of the traumatic event that involves detailed reliving of the experience, panic attacks, depression, nightmares, and sleep disorders (PLOS 2009). Both the likelihood and the effects of sexual assault are affected by the intersectional nature of racial, citizenship, sexuality, and gender expression–based inequalities. In Canada, 57 per cent of Indigenous women have been sexually assaulted, and immigrant and refugee women often fear losing their status in Canada if they report violence in the home. Egale reports increasing incidents of violence against LGBTQ members and explains that, while Statistics Canada reports on hate crimes motivated by sexual orientation, it does not report on hate crimes against trans and gender-variant people because gender identity and expression are not yet included within the hate crime provisions of the Criminal Code (Allen and Boyce 2013).

Understandably, many women are reluctant to come forward when they are raped because of the way they believe they may be perceived and/or treated by both legal and medical personnel. A "second rape" during post-assault interactions unnecessarily blames rape survivors and may exacerbate long-term health problems (Campbell et al. 2003). The experience of reporting to the police, and if the case is pursued, testifying in court, can also be retraumatizing and damaging to a woman's reputation, as was made clear during the Jian Ghomeshi trial of 2016. In 2014, Canadian women used the Twitter hashtag #BeenRapedNeverReported as a vehicle to break the silence around sexual assault and create a space to share experiences and highlight the lack of safe spaces for women in Canada to report these crimes and see them prosecuted. In Canada, 1397 sexual assaults occur every day, and 51 per cent of Canadian women have been victims of physical or sexual violence after the age of 16 (Fredericton Sexual Assault Centre, n.d.)

Bodies as Battlegrounds

The use of sexual violence during wartime is a historical and worldwide phenomenon. It would be difficult to name either an ancient or a modern war in which some form of sexual violence did not regularly occur. As part of governments' efforts to provide for male soldiers' presumably "natural" sexual needs, women have often been held as prisoners in war zones or other conflict-ridden arenas and compelled to provide sexual services. In one example, Japanese officials forced women in the many Asian countries under its imperial control to work as so-called comfort women, providing sexual services for Japanese soldiers during World War II. Women were commonly abducted from their homes or were fooled into leaving their homes voluntarily after being told that they would be working in Chinese factories. The government rationalized this program of sexual slavery by arguing that it prevented soldiers from raping local women (Tanaka 2002). The Nazi regime in Germany held women prisoner in work camps and death camps where they were routinely sexually assaulted and medically experimented upon. Near the end of World War II and during the subsequent occupation of Germany, Allied troops committed mass rapes of German girls and women with estimates ranging from hundreds of thousands to millions of victims.

Rape is so common a feature of armed conflict that it has been called a weapon of war (Card 1996). The Bosnian war of the 1990s is an important case study in the use of rape as an act of political aggression, one that fits Cynthia Enloe's description of "systematic mass rape" (Enloe 2000). During the war in the former Yugoslavia, Serbian men held Croatian women in "rape camps" for months on end, where the women were often victimized bodily and emotionally. Men, held in separate camps, were also sexually tortured. In some instances they were made to witness the rapes of women. It is estimated that at least 14,000 women were so brutalized. The profound shame associated with rape has led many victims, male and female, to remain silent (Olujic 1998).

One of the important features of wartime rape is that its victims are civilians and should hence, according to the Geneva Conventions, be spared from military aggression. Yet despite how commonplace rape and other forms of sexual violence are, these were not recognized as war crimes or crimes against humanity until 1993, when International Criminal Tribunals were established to prosecute the perpetrators of genocide in the former Yugoslavia and in Rwanda (Engle 2005). According to Article 7 of the Rome Statute of the International Criminal Court, crimes against humanity now include "rape, sexual slavery, enforced prostitution, forced pregnancy, enforced sterilization, or any other form of sexual violence of comparable gravity." So while no Japanese, Nazi, or Allied perpetrators of sexual slavery and rape were ever brought to justice for those specific crimes, there is hope that perpetrators will continue to be held accountable for acts of profound sexual violence against women and men since that time.

The Democratic Republic of Congo (DRC) has been declared the most dangerous place in the world to be a woman (War Child, n.d.). DRC has been engaged in armed internal conflict since 1998, when Rwandan and Ugandan militias aided Congolese rebels in the overthrow of the government. Afterward, foreign militias, including the main perpetrators in the Rwandan genocide, became mutual antagonists in a broad-based armed conflict in eastern DRC. With close to 6 million dead by 2008, it is the worst armed conflict since World War II (IRC 2008).

Since the start of the conflict, at least 10,000 women have been raped—sometimes gang-raped—every single year, not only by foreign militias but also by the Congolese army, rebel groups, and, increasingly, other civilians. The UN peacekeeping forces in DRC, the largest in the world, have been chastised for being ineffectual at either creating peace (much less "keeping" it) or protecting women.

Crucially, the conflict in DRC has its roots in the global demand for a common item: cellphones. Tin, tantalum, and tungsten are heat-resistant materials used in cellphones and other everyday electronic devices such as laptop computers, video game consoles, and DVD players. These materials derive from a mineral ore called columbite-tantalite, which is found in abundance in eastern DRC. The competition for control of mines is intense, and the lack of any kind of political order enables these various armed groups, from the government to various and sundry foreign and domestic militias, to fight for control. In this milieu, the most powerful militias profit financially. Together, these militias are estimated to reap $180 million (US) in profit each year (Prendergast and Cheadle 2010).

Sexual violence is not limited to actual rape, and women are not its only victims (in fact, women can also be perpetrators). It can also include sexually loaded acts of humiliation targeted at men, such as those committed by US soldiers in the infamous Abu Ghraib prison in Iraq in 2003 and the abuses of Afghan detainees carried out with the complicity of Canadian soldiers between 2001 and 2011 (Champ 2014). Again, the roots of these crimes are worth briefly laying out. It might begin by noting the deeply entrenched masculinization that US male soldiers undergo as an informal part of their basic training, in which recruits "aggressively practice . . . the unofficial rites handed down from man to man through the generations" (Burke 2004, xiv). These rites include singing banned songs celebrating rape. And of course, if masculinity has such a high value, that must mean that feminization can be wielded as a weapon in its own right (Enloe 2007). Through feminization, attributes normally ascribed to women are ascribed to men in order to humiliate and disempower them. The photographs taken at Abu Ghraib and subsequently shown around the world featured naked Iraqi male prisoners in denigrating poses as US female military officers looked on (Hersh 2004). This act of humiliation becomes sexualized through the nudity of the men and the presence of the women. Another deeply gendered cultural dynamic of this incident concerns the way it was processed in the United States. "Women . . . were conventionally expected by most editors and news watchers to appear in wartime as mothers and wives of soldiers, occasionally as military nurses and truck mechanics, and most often as victims of wartime violence. Women were not supposed to be the wielders of violence and certainly not the perpetrators of torture. When those deeply gendered presumptions were turned upside down, many people felt a sense of shock" (Enloe 2007, 100). Such shock should inspire "a feminist curiosity" about war (Enloe 2007). Or, even more critically, it should force the sober realization that "a uterus is not a substitute for a conscience" (Ehrenreich 2004).

The DRC case presents a different set of possibilities for understanding of women's agency. An important book, *The Enough Moment: Fighting to End Africa's Worst Human Rights Crimes*, details numerous activist efforts among Congolese women and men aimed at helping women survive economically and psychologically in the aftermath of rape (Prendergast and Cheadle 2010). Some local activists work through the transformative power of narratives, especially those that link local Congolese women to each other and to the larger world. For example, one Congolese journalist travels from one remote location to another, giving women radios so that they can hear her radio program in which she features interviews with other women affected by rape. The various stories that Congolese women relay to the Enough Project (enoughproject.org) and in *The Enough Moment* (Prendergast and Cheadle 2010), are meant to inform international readers about their experiences. If the local crisis in DRC has its roots in global consumerism, then perhaps local–global activism will bring about its demise (Cockburn 2010).

Female Genital Cutting

One of the more difficult challenges of developing a progressive transnational feminist politic, while avoiding the persistence of the colonial gaze, is to speak out against the forms of oppression that specifically target the bodies of women and girls while arguing against the representation of women—especially women in the Global South—as perpetual victims. This section develops this chapter's concern for how the dynamics of power and agency intersect with health, highlighting gendered inscriptions that originate not in mind/body, nature/culture, or male/female dualisms, but in power, complex social institutions and political antagonisms.

It is hard to imagine a more contentious issue relating to the broad question of embodiment than that surrounding what is variously called female circumcision, female genital mutilation (FGM), female genital cutting (FGC), or female genital surgery. One's choice of term announces one's position, with many international agencies and activists choosing the critical term *female genital mutilation* over the more value-neutral terms *female circumcision* and *female genital cutting*. WHO, in defining the practice, writes, "Female genital mutilation comprises all procedures involving partial or total removal of the external female genitalia or other injury to the female genital organs for non-medical reasons" (WHO, n.d.). Demographic and Health Surveys uses the term *female genital cutting*. This term is also adopted here less for neutrality than to acknowledge, in view of earlier sections of this chapter, that discourses *about* the body can affect the lived experience *of* the body. Indeed, some women who have undergone the surgery are offended by the implication that their bodies have been "mutilated."

FGC is commonly practised in 28 African countries and some in Asia, Latin America, and the Middle East (WHO 2011). Although popular perception in the West is that the practice predominates among Muslims, most Islamic societies do not practise it, while many non-Muslim groups within Ethiopia, Sudan, and Kenya do. An estimated 3 million girls undergo some form of the procedure per year, and between 130 and 140 million living women have done so (WHO 2011). Data collected between 2005 and 2008 comparing the prevalence of FGC among older and younger women in various countries show that the practice has been steadily declining.

Twenty-seven per cent of all women and girls who have undergone FGC live in Egypt, representing the highest proportion in the world (WHO 2011). (Ethiopia is in second place, at 17 per cent.) By the time the Egyptian government banned the practice in 1996, 97 per cent of women and girls had undergone FGC, with 82 per cent of mothers expressing continued support for it. Despite being illegal, the practice continues. In 2008, a major national demographic and health survey asked mothers about their intention to have their daughters circumcised. The data revealed that by 2023, 45 per cent of girls will have likely undergone FGC, a figure that represents a steady decline in yet continuing support for the practice (El-Zanaty and Way 2009). Even though there is no doctrinal injunction for the practice in either Islam or Christianity, people most commonly cite religion and tradition as the reasons for supporting the practice. In addition, there is widespread belief that young women are more marriageable and can attract men of higher economic and social status if they have been circumcised.

Efforts to abolish the practice largely centre on its negative health effects. These vary according to the exact kind of cutting performed, the quality and cleanliness of the instruments used, the skill of the person performing the procedure, and the health of the girl or woman. The most commonly cited health consequences include severe pain and bleeding, sometimes resulting in clinical shock and/or anemia; infections, including potentially fatal ones; urinary retention; abscesses, cysts, and keloids; infertility; and various childbirth complications (WHO 2011). In an inter-agency statement, several international human rights groups had this to say about FGC:

Seen from a human rights perspective, [female genital cutting] reflects deep-rooted inequality between the sexes, and constitutes an extreme form of discrimination against women. Female genital mutilation is nearly always carried out on minors and is therefore a violation of the rights of the child. The practice also violates the rights to health, security and physical integrity of the person, the right to be free from torture and cruel, inhuman or degrading treatment, and the right to life when the procedure results in death. (WHO 2008).

Although most anthropological studies are critical of FGC, they have been careful to emphasize the specific cultural values and imperatives deemed to make the surgeries necessary. The work of African anthropologist Fuambai Ahmadu is of interest not only because she voluntarily underwent FGC but because she provides a cultural analysis that highlights the importance of seeing beyond Western philosophical and cultural constructs about nature and the body. Ahmadu grew up in Washington, DC, but hails originally from Kono society in Sierra Leone. There, she says, bodies are not born complete; nor is sex a "natural" attribute, given at birth. Rather, a girl achieves those qualities by enduring a variety of rituals, including the painful experience of having one's genitals cut. In particular, part of the clitoris is removed because it is associated with masculinity and excessive sexuality—that is, superfluous to reproduction. Furthermore, "ritual officials and other Kono women adamantly maintain that if left untouched, the clitoris will continue to grow and become unsightly, like a penis ... and ... will categorically lead to incessant masturbation and sexual insatiability" (2000, 297). Ahmadu, for her own part, reports no noticeable decline in sensations from the nerves that lie beneath her own vaginal surface.

A common perception of FGC is that it supports patriarchy by attempting to control women's sexuality. Yet Ahmadu stresses that there is "no cultural obsession with feminine chastity, virginity, or women's sexual fidelity" because the Kono have a matrilineal kinship principle (2000, 285). That is, women are at the centre of many of the society's most crucial roles, and these pass through mothers. Biological fathers are marginal, and society is organized around a hierarchy of women: ritual leaders of female secret societies, elders, one's grandmother, and one's mother. What is at stake, she argues, is fertility and successful procreation, which can only be assured if one's genitals do not become masculine. What is more broadly at stake, though, is one's full membership as an adult woman in all the goings-on of the community. Despite having a physical body, one is not truly a person—in the most meaningful sense of the word—unless one has undergone this process. Hence, according to Ahmadu, "[it] is incumbent on mothers to initiate their daughters properly, according to ancestral customs, in order for the latter to become legally recognized as persons with rights and responsibility in society" (2000, 300). FGC, in this view, assures that one will become a woman, which is an achieved, and indeed, exalted status.

Even within countries in which FGC has been common, there is hardly a single, monolithic point of view about this issue. FGC is outlawed in 15 of the 28 African countries where it is practised. In many of these countries the issue has become an object of political machination. In Sierra Leone, from which the Kono case is drawn, women activists who condemn the practice charge that it is bolstered by corrupt campaign practices. Fearing for their political careers, politicians try to win the support of the same powerful, women-run secret societies described above. And to garner the support of Kono communities, they offer to pay for the cost of the surgeries, which can cost up to $200 per girl. Opposition to the practice can come both from the outside and from the grassroots. In 2007, one Sierra Leonean female gynecologist travelled among Kono villages carrying a doll to use as a model in explaining the dangers of FGC (Bowers 2007). The fact that she carried on her work in the face of death threats shows the deep and strong feelings on both sides of the issue.

Dr Olayinka Koso-Thomas lives in Sierra Leone and campaigns against female genital cutting.

The issue of FGC affects several thousand Canadian immigrants. While FGC is illegal for a doctor to perform in Canada, there is some evidence that it is practised here, and more evidence that families from communities that regularly practise FGC send their daughters to their countries of origin in order to have this procedure performed (Gutbi 1995).

Impact of Social and Cultural Disparities on Women's Health

Health Status and Risks

Women's and men's bodies are more alike than they are different from one another. They are largely subject to the same hazards to their health: illnesses, accidents, and disabilities. However, there are some significant differences, which can be identified by comparing men's and women's health status. Health status is typically depicted according to rates of morbidity (illness) and mortality (death). In the past, men on average had greater access to nutritional foods and lived longer than women. However, worldwide for every age group, women on average outlive men (United Nations 2010). The leading cause of death for both women and men is coronary heart disease, but each year more women die of it than men, especially in Europe (Gupta 2003; United Nations 2010). According to indicators such as disability days, hospitalization, and visits to physicians, women display greater rates of illness than men.

Disparities in health worldwide have been persistent over time. Some hazards are unique to women because they concern the female reproductive organs and female reproductive experiences. Other hazards are shared by women and men but experienced differently because of the different roles assigned to women (such as jobs resulting in different workplace hazards) or because society supports different behaviours that are potentially a threat to health. Behavioural differences that affect health risks, such as substance abuse and driving behaviour, also are gendered (Travis 1988). In addition to the biological component of health, the role of risk factors (see below) requires examination in addressing women's health.

Poverty

Poverty is probably the single greatest hazard to women's health; it is often lethal when combined with other serious hazards. Women worldwide are more likely than men to be poor. Vulnerable groups, such as women-headed households, the elderly, and those with disabilities lack assistance as countries of every economic level increasingly cut back on their "safety nets" of social services. At higher rates than others, these more vulnerable women experience such ailments as chronic anemia, malnutrition, severe fatigue, and increased susceptibility to infections of the respiratory and reproductive tracts. Premature death is a frequent outcome of poverty.

Poverty explains many of the health inequities found among different groups of humans. It is directly related to disease incidences and to avenues for cure. For example, low-income women are likely to have fewer years of formal education and may lack access to information to identify and avoid risks or to respond adequately to them (even if they had the means to do so). Low-income women are less likely to access health care because of child-care needs, transportation costs, or time lost from work. Poverty means inadequate housing for shelter and inadequate clothing and shoes for protection. It means inadequate sanitation due to insufficient or unclean water, food storage, and waste removal. It means exposure to risks of violence and it means dependence on others for survival. So "choosing" to avoid a potentially dangerous situation, be it environmental, behavioural, or occupational, as many women are warned to do, may not, in fact, be a choice for many women who live in poverty. For example, poverty is one reason why women sometimes stay in abusive relationships—women who leave a partner to raise children on their own are five times more likely to live in poverty than those who stay with their partner (Howard 2015).

Poverty is unequally distributed among groups within Canada. For example, 28 per cent of visible-minority women in Canada live in poverty; 21 per cent of single mothers live in poverty; 36 per cent of First Nations women (off reserve) and 23 per cent of Métis and Inuit women in the provinces and territories live in poverty (Howard 2015). And although over 70 per cent of transgender men and women in Ontario have at least some college or university education, about half make $15,000 or less per year (Bauer et al. 2011). Using the social determinants of health and an intersectional framework, the reasons underlying these inequities becomes clear. Poorer conditions of health are generated by racism (including environmental racism—e.g. racialized communities tending to live in highly polluted areas), unequal economic status, barriers to education and employment, homophobia, and transphobia.

Racial and Ethnic Discrimination

Race and ethnicity also affect the health risks of women. As researchers have shown that biological or genetic factors and wealth or lifestyle inadequately explain the persistence of racial differences in health, Dressler (1993) proposes a "social structural model" to explain the health risks faced by racialized groups. The stress of "race" as it plays out in daily life does affect physical disease (such as cardiovascular problems) as well as mental health (such as depression). This stress, combined with preconceptions and misconceptions within the health-care industry about the health needs and risks of various ethnic and racialized groups, conspires to maintain health inequalities even when controlling for heredity, income, and social class. Although all women face additional health risks because of gender, for women of colour poverty, discrimination, and racism combine to pose even greater health risks (Harrell et al. 2003). These intersectional inequalities create particularly difficult conditions for, as an example, transgender people who are also racialized: for instance, 31 per cent of both racialized and Indigenous transgender respondents in Ontario said that they had felt uncomfortable in transgender spaces because of their race or ethnicity (Longman Marcellin et al. 2013).

Occupational Health Risks

Women suffer from different occupational health risks compared to men. Although men are injured at work more often than women, women suffer illnesses related to work conditions that are harder to detect and less often reported (CDC 2012). Higher rates of illness among people of colour are often attributed to factors related to biology or culture, rather than being sought in their work roles. Racialized women work in riskier and lower-paying jobs compared to white women; consequently they experience more work-related injuries and illnesses. As part-time or temporary workers, they may not report safety concerns for fear of being fired. A large number of women of colour work in low-paid health-service jobs that have a high rate of occupational illness. Many immigrant women work in the garment industry, often in sweatshops where workers face health risks from overcrowding, lack of adequate ventilation, danger of fire due to inadequate escape routes and fire-prevention features, and other hazards that result in much higher injury rates (CDC 2012; Ng 1999).

Women and Physical Health: Some Specific Concerns

Heart Disease

According to Public Health Agency of Canada, heart disease is the number-one cause of death in Canada for women over the age of 55. Women are more likely to die from heart disease than from any other disease (Public Health Agency of Canada 2009) and cardiovascular mortality in women exceeds that in men (Miller and Best 2011). Women also have more severe first strokes at an older age than men, require longer hospitalization, and are more likely to remain disabled (World Heart Federation 2012). Women appear to be diagnosed with heart disease at later stages, to have their illness treated less aggressively by physicians, and to require different medical and surgical treatment than men. Even risk factors such as cholesterol and triglyceride levels appear to pose different risks according to gender. Clinical trials for cardiovascular disease focus on symptoms more typical of males than females and provide more information about men than women (Adler 2010). Awareness of the dangers of heart disease to women is underestimated by both professionals and women themselves. Women develop chronic diseases such as coronary artery disease well before menopause; hence, prevention of heart disease must begin young, and early detection and awareness is needed to more effectively manage women with cardiovascular disease (Raymond, Greenberg, and Leeder 2005).

Cancer

The most common type of cancer among women is breast cancer (which very rarely occurs in men), although its occurrence varies substantially among different racialized groups. As with most cancers, the risk of breast cancer increases with age. This may be due to the long-term effect of exposure to environmental and other toxins. Although scientists and activists have urged greater investigation of the role of environmental factors, a major shift in the focus of research has not yet occurred (Gray 2008). Nonetheless, more attention has been given to breast cancer, largely because of women's efforts to demand more funds for breast cancer awareness and research, especially related to prevention.

A variety of possible factors causing higher risk for cancer have been investigated. It is not clear whether, or to what extent, either dietary fat or obesity increases the risk of breast cancer. Alcohol consumption has been implicated, but questions remain about how the age at onset of drinking or amount of drinking is related to risk (Porzelius 2000). Guidelines for the use of hormone replacement therapy (HRT) have been modified to reduce their potential harm to women (Boston Women's Health Book Collective 2011).

The incidence of breast cancer has gone up dramatically in recent years. According to the Breast Cancer Society of Canada, in 2014 an estimated 24,400 Canadian women would be diagnosed with breast cancer and 5000 would die from it. If detected before it spreads through the body, it can often be treated effectively. Performing breast self-examinations, though no longer recommended, contributes to awareness of possible changes in a woman's body and can be important for this reason. Access to health-care practitioners is necessary as physicians or nurse practitioners may detect breast cancers through manual examination, which should be performed at regular gynecological examinations. Cancers of the ovaries, uterus, and cervix cannot be detected by self-examination. Early detection of cervical cancer is possible, however, through a Pap smear, which detects abnormalities in sampled cells. A vaccine now provides protection against the virus (human papillomavirus, or HPV) that cause most cervical cancers.

Sexually Transmitted Disease Infections, Including HIV/AIDS

For women of reproductive age (15–44 years) unsafe sex is the single greatest risk factor for disability and death, as it may result in contraction of HIV or other sexually transmitted diseases (STDs). STDs are quite prevalent in the world today. They are a major cause of infertility and can contribute to blindness and brain damage as well as to difficulties in child-bearing. Chlamydia infection is the most common sexually transmitted bacterial disease in Canada, with a 72 per cent increased incidence between 2001 and 2010 (Public Health Agency Canada 2013b). Untreated chlamydia, which is largely asymptomatic in women, can result in pelvic inflammatory disease, which in turn may cause infertility as well as ectopic pregnancy and chronic pelvic pain (CDC 2010).

The human immunodeficiency virus (HIV), the precursor of AIDS, is transmitted through genital secretions or through blood. At the end of 2015, an estimated 36.7 million people worldwide—including 1.8 million children younger than 15 years—were living with HIV/AIDS (UNAIDS 2016). Approximately 70 per cent of them (25.5 million) live in sub-Saharan Africa; another 14 per cent (5.1 million) live in Asia and the Pacific (ibid). Approximately 50 per cent of adults living with HIV/AIDS worldwide are women (UN Women 2016). Numbers continue to rise among adolescents. One particular consequence for women with this disease is that they can transfer it to their fetuses unless medication is available during pregnancy.

Since HIV reporting began in Canada in 1985, a cumulative total of 76,275 positive HIV test reports had been reported to Public Health Agency Canada as of 2012. In 2012, as in previous years, Ontario accounted for the highest number of cases (843) followed by Quebec (450), Alberta (239), British Columbia (238), and Saskatchewan (184). Both Ontario and British Columbia noted a decrease in their annual number of cases from 2011 to 2012—a 10.8 per cent decrease in Ontario and a 17.4 per cent decrease in British Columbia (Public Health Agency of Canada 2013a).

AIDS, like other sexually transmitted diseases, is avoidable for adults *who have control over their own bodies*. Protected sex (using a latex or a female condom) is the most common effective prevention method (although "safe sex" alternatives, such as using fantasy and masturbation, have also been recommended). Although condom use has consistently risen, some women do engage in sexual relations without using condoms. Their reasons include inconvenience, shame, and *refusal* by their male partners (Hinkle et al. 1992). Older heterosexual women are particularly at risk, as they may have recently begun having new sexual partners after many years of marriage and may be uncomfortable addressing safer sex concerns as well as believing it is not relevant to them. Older women living with HIV/AIDS are an often-overlooked population.

In sub-Saharan Africa, problems of HIV transmission are acute. There, poverty forces large numbers of women into sex work and extreme vulnerability to exposure to both HIV/AIDS and abuse. Women of lower status may lack the control to protect themselves from HIV transmission. Many young women in sub-Saharan African countries have stated that their first experience of sexual intercourse was forced (UNAIDS 1998). Issues such as lack of knowledge, inaccessibility, and disregard for one's own safety are some of the reasons for the lack of contraception use worldwide.

Women who engage in heterosexual intercourse with an HIV carrier are at greater risk of contracting HIV than are men who have sexual intercourse with an HIV-positive woman. Female condoms, sometimes referred to as "vaginal pouches" (because they are inserted in the vagina), can help women exert greater control in preventing HIV transmission. While these are available in some parts of the world, they require practice to use correctly and can be expensive. Microbicides

Box 8.6 Key Issues

Research on Equality and AIDS

"There's No AIDS Here Because Men and Women Are Equal"
Although infection with HIV/AIDS is widespread in southern Africa, it is virtually absent in the 3000 or so people of the Ju/'hoansi (or !Kung) society, who live near the northern borders of Botswana and Namibia. According to research by Canadian anthropologist Richard Lee, the reason is gender equality: when it comes to choosing sexual and marriage partners the women have a great deal of freedom:

> In the other societies around the region, the young men will say, "Oh no, a girl has to obey me if I want to have sex with her, and if I don't want to use a condom, that's it." With the Ju/'hoansi, their high status in the community gives women plenty of leverage in sexual negotiations.

> Before the age of AIDS the Ju/'hoansi were famous in anthropology for being among the last hunting and gathering people in the world. Hunter-gatherers typically granted women significant respect and status, Lee says.

Source: Joseph Hall. African tribe stays virtually AIDS free: Few infected because women have equality. *The Toronto Star*. Aug. 12, 2006: A23.

appear to provide a new means of female protection, and research into them continues.

Hysterectomy

More than 40,000 Canadian women lost their uteruses to the invasive procedure of hysterectomy in 2012–13, according to data released in 2014 by the Canadian Institute for Health Information. Sometimes the healthy ovaries of women over 45 are removed (oophorectomy) during a hysterectomy, which is inadvisable, as the ovaries will continue to produce some hormones after menopause (Parker et al. 2009).

In the nineteenth century, the uterus was thought to be the principal source of women's ailments; its removal was the obvious cure. Although modern medical science rejects this idea, hysterectomies continue to be performed on women with a healthy uterus. Physicians have offered to perform this "service" for women citing two primary reasons: it is an effective form of sterilization for those who no longer wish to bear children, and it is a preventive measure since the uterus may be the site of cancer at some future time. However, hysterectomies may have long-lasting negative physical, emotional, and sexual effects for women. Alternative procedures, such as localized treatments and surgery to remove only fibroids, are available but may not be made known to women (Boston Women's Health Book Collective 2011).

Osteoporosis

Osteoporosis, a process linked to estrogen changes, is associated with a decrease in bone density and occurs in all humans after the age of 35. Increased medicalization of osteoporosis may occur in the form of unnecessary or too frequent bone density screenings and subsequent treatment with medications prescribed for women who are not at risk of osteoporosis. Prevention, in the form of adequate calcium intake as a child and young woman and weight-bearing exercise throughout life, is too often ignored. Women and men alike begin to lose bone in their mid-thirties; as they approach menopause, women lose bone mass at a greater rate, from 2 to 3 per cent per year, resulting in bone ailments and a highly increased vulnerability to bone fractures. Osteoporosis is a major cause of physical disability in older women (twice as common as for older men) (Galsworthy 1994).

Alzheimer's Disease

Alzheimer's disease and related dementias afflict approximately half a million Canadians; close to 75 per cent of those with Alzheimer's are women. About 14 per cent are between 60 and 65, and 10 per cent under the age of 60. (*Prince George Citizen* 2014).

Women and Mental Health

Gendered Differences

In the realm of mental health, the interconnections between perceptions of health, diagnoses of the causes of illness, and women's place in society seem unavoidable. Phyllis Chesler's classic work *Women and Madness* (1972) pointed to the way ideas about "madness" in society were used to oppress and control women. While the interpretation of human behaviour as mentally healthy or mentally ill clearly contains a subjective element, it equally reflects the dominant social and cultural views. For example, until the mid-1970s homosexuality was listed as an illness in the *Diagnostic and Statistical Manual of Mental Disorders* of the American Psychiatric Association.

Gender differences in this phenomenon can be traced to two sources: patients and physicians. Women are more likely than men to go to a physician for help. This may be because they experience more problems, they more readily admit they have problems, they feel less able to cope with these problems without help, or they have readier access to physicians due to more flexible working hours. It may be a combination of some or all of these factors. Physicians, on the other hand, are more likely to attribute problems reported by women to psychic causes and to deal with these problems by prescribing psychotropic drugs (Hebald 2001). The focus on the individual as the source of the problem ignores the social conditions and processes affecting women that exist outside them and are beyond their direct control. Humans are extremely plastic, and most individuals in a society will tend to fit themselves into a pattern of behaviour they are taught is "normal." However, behaviour that is considered "normal" in one society might be interpreted as "insane" or "neurotic" in another.

Feminist researcher Karen Pugliesi (1992) depicts two basic positions regarding gender differences in mental health. One, which she terms the "social causation approach," looks at aspects of women's experience in society that affect their mental well-being. The social conditions mentioned earlier, such as greater likelihood of experiencing poverty, sexual abuse, and violence, and the compounded likelihood due to the intersectional inequalities of racialized, disabled, lesbian, bisexual, transgender, Indigenous, and immigrant women, produce stresses that endanger women's mental as well as physical well-being. Mental health advantages can also be attributed to social conditions that differentially affect women and men. For example, the fact that women are encouraged to express emotions while men are encouraged to repress them might have specific mental health repercussions favouring women (Klonoff and Landrine 1995).

The second position Pugliesi describes, the "social constructionist approach," focuses on different methods of the conception and diagnosis of mental health and illness. Phyllis Chesler's (1972) work falls squarely in this category. Certain behaviours by women are labelled as the product of mental disorders by sexist psychiatrists and psychologists (Lopez et al. 1993). While both approaches locate the source of difference in women's and men's mental health in patriarchal understandings, one takes the discovery of gender differences as "real," the product of different experiences in a gender-biased society, and the other treats this discovery as an artifact of biased diagnosis, a misinterpretation of what actually exists.

These approaches complement one another in possibilities for dealing with treatment.

Behavioural differences between women and men related to mental health also reflect social circumstances. Substance abuse is one area. Women are less likely than men to be abusers of alcohol and tobacco, but when their lifestyles more closely resemble those of men, so do their substance abuse patterns. As women entered the workforce, for example, they more frequently used alcohol and tobacco. On the other hand, women make greater use of prescription drugs and, with greater access to the drugs, are more likely to use and abuse them. Yet women, especially pregnant women and women with children, who seek treatment for substance abuse are more likely than men to be turned away from programs or to encounter problems with the legal system over child custody (Larrieu et al. 2008).

Homophobic and Transphobic Bias

Feminist therapists, to be effective, must recognize homophobia and transphobia experienced by women, along with gender, race, class, and sexual discrimination (Greene 1993). For example, the problems facing a lesbian or transgender woman seeking assistance through therapy must be understood in terms of the heterosexist and cis-sexist bias in the larger social environment and the struggles the woman may experience with negative self-image resulting from taught prejudice. If therapeutic practices are based on an assumption of cisgender heterosexuality, their impact can be devastating for non-gender conforming persons. (Glassgold and Iasenza 2000 [1995]).

Women as Special-Risk/Vulnerable Populations

Life situations may expose particular groups of women to greater levels of ill health and injury as well as more limited access to care. The focus is on four groups here.

Depression

Women are at about twice the risk for depression as men. This finding applies not only in North America but also globally. Depression is characterized by the persistence over a prolonged time (two weeks according to current diagnostic procedures) of a number of symptoms from a list. Typical symptoms include feeling sad, anxiety, decreased capacity to experience pleasure, diminished ability to think or concentrate, indifferent grooming, change in appetite, sleep disturbance, and many more. Yet the Institute of Medicine has noted that women are still under-represented in clinical trials, and in early stages of research in this area, "more than 55% of samples testing animal models of depressions and anxiety (disorders twice as common in women than men) failed to include any female animals" (Institute of Medicine 2010).

Psychiatrists and psychologists recognize a variety of types of depression. The report of the American Psychological Association's National Task Force on Women and Depression (McGrath et al. 1990) urges a "biopsychosocial" perspective on depression with regard to both diagnosis of causes and prescription for treatment. The biological component of this perspective includes a consideration of the biological and psychological consequences of reproduction-related events, including menstruation, pregnancy, childbirth, infertility, abortion, and menopause. The psychological component refers to characteristics of the female personality as constructed by society and the ways that women are oriented by this construction toward certain patterns of perception, social interaction, and coping with stress. The social component refers to the stresses produced by the roles to which women are assigned and to the risks to which women are subject, such as rape, sexual and gender discrimination, and poverty. Because women are subjected to particular gender expectations, the source of their depression may be misidentified. A woman might feel she needs to seek help because she feels "depressed," locating the source of the problem in herself but not recognizing that her social situation might be the major contributor to her feelings. Her consultant, psychiatrist, or psychologist might compound this by "blaming the victim," characterizing a perfectly normal reaction to a terrible situation as a symptom of mental illness.

If the risk for depression or diagnosis of depression is higher among women than among men, the risk for members of racialized groups is also high and higher still for women of these groups than for men. The conditions affecting rates of depression for racialized Canadians vary according to the situation of the groups in question; while racism and discrimination produce stress and depression at a greater rate than for the population of women in general, the ways in which they are experienced and expressed are specific to each group. Poverty and homelessness, especially among young mothers, also exacerbates the risk of depression (Grant et al 2011).

Age is another important and variable dimension. Adolescence and old age are considered high-risk categories for depression. These life stages are characterized by both biological changes accompanying changes in reproductive status and social changes resulting in much adjustment.

A final dimension of risk for depression is sexuality and gender identity and expression. Alcoholism and drug abuse continue to affect lesbians, gay men, and transgender persons at two to three times the rate of the general population. Programs are needed to address the special risks of LGBTQ populations who are at greater risk of experiences of violence and victimization that have long-lasting effects. Lesbians also report higher levels of stress than heterosexual women. Adolescents may be particularly vulnerable. Lack of family and social acceptance can place a significant burden on mental health (US Department of Health and Human Services 2010). Research results generally confirm that LGBTQ youth have much higher levels of suicidal thinking and attempts than their heterosexual peers—four to seven times more attempts. "Among lesbian, gay and bisexual youth, the risk of attempting suicide was 20% greater in unsupportive environments compared to supportive environments" (Parreñas 2005).

Addressing institutionalized racism and discrimination is an important factor in reducing the risk of negative health outcomes. Positive factors reducing the likelihood of depression for lesbians include group support from the lesbian community (among those who have come out and have a community to consult), LGBTQ health centres, and the sharing of housework and child care in lesbian households. Legislation supporting same-sex marriage, unions, and adoptions also is beneficial.

Women as Refugees

Approximately half of the world's refugee population are women. Although many refugees are homeless, impoverished, separated from other family members, and under threat, women refugees have special vulnerabilities that may include sexual violence and a lack of safe shelter and food. Sometimes the threats come from the purported protectors. United Nations staff members, including Canadian officers, have been accused of "sex for food" schemes in refugee camps and during peacekeeping missions, where they withhold provisions from women who do not accede to their sexual demands (Perkel 2016). When refugee women are finally resettled, many find themselves in a strange new land, without traditional means of social support, not knowing the language and customs, and consulting health-care workers (if they have access to health care), whose understanding of illness and disease might be very different from their own (Smyke 1991; Cohn 2013). Settlement in another country is often a lifelong negotiation with a different culture. How well people can resettle is most often affected by "the warmth of the welcome" (Beiser 1999).

Women with Disabilities

Women who are considered or identify as disabled tend to be stigmatized everywhere. Feminist disability studies aims to denaturalize disability. It thus "defines disability broadly from a social rather than a medical perspective, arguing that disability is a cultural interpretation of human variation. This shows that disability—similar to race and gender—is a system of representation that marks bodies as subordinate" (Garland-Thomson 2005). Traits thought of as a disability range from vision and hearing differences to various levels of mobility to intellectual functioning (Linton 2007; Hall 2011). As intersectional analyses have shown, poverty and isolation from a supportive family unit generally compound disability. Only recently have many high-income countries made accommodations to support the disabled to participate "in the mainstream" by providing means of access in public places; poorer countries lag far behind (Boylan 1991).

Women who are disabled enter a world of "sexism without the pedestal" (Fine and Asch 1988). In contrast to disabled men, who are thought of as weak but interested in sex, women who are disabled are often thought of as asexual. Nonetheless, women who are differently abled have claimed the right to sexual lives, to marry, and to bear children and have shown that they, their partners, and their children can thrive as families (Linton 1997).

Older Women

Much of what has been said of disabled women could also be (and has been) said of older women, who are often treated as disabled persons, with the entire stigma that goes with assumptions about disability. With improvements in health care, more women are living to advanced ages but frequently become disabled with chronic diseases. Isolation exacerbates their difficulties in coping with a disability as heterosexual women live longer than their male partners and, in urban areas, often live apart from their families (Fried et al. 2001; Gillick 2001). Membership in an ethnic or racialized group may exacerbate the problems women experience as aging persons who are female and poor. These intersectional inequalities can compound to make greater difficulties for these women. In other cases they also have coping strategies and support systems within their families and communities that counteract larger societal disadvantages (Padgett 1989). Often their families need their help, and they offer one another support.

Women Who Are Incarcerated

Women are being incarcerated in swiftly rising numbers. Their health needs include all the concomitant issues of poverty, violence, and racism that affect male prisoners; however, institutions must also focus on concerns specific to women, such as reproductive health, including pregnancy, and mental health needs (Braithwaite, Arriola, and Newkirk 2006).

Indigenous women make up only 3.8 per cent of the Canadian population, but represent some 41 per cent of the prison population (CTV News 2015). As well, a 2013 Justice Department study found the overall number of Indigenous women behind bars in federal institutions nearly doubled between 2002 and 2012, increasing by 97 per cent. (Rennie 2014). The legacy of colonialism, compounded by the intersectional inequalities of continued discrimination, racist policies, poverty, lack of access to care and resources, and systemic barriers to and discrimination within the criminal justice system, all work together to make this happen (Native Women's Association of Canada 2007).

Empowering women to be vigilant in addressing the ways that the medicalization of their life processes affects their health can change attitudes, medical practice, and even behaviours. Through the field of women's and gender studies, how the patriarchal lens has warped women's health and create a new vision for the future can be examined.

Summary

Around the globe, women's political consciousness has been galvanized around health issues.

The women's health movement has sought to empower women about their own bodies. It has also undertaken to reform and improve the health-care system and public policy by making them more responsive to all women's bodies and women's needs and by ensuring that the issues of all women are addressed as an integral aspect of human rights. Because women's bodies are often at the crux of politico-socio-cultural battles, constant vigilance and creative strategies are required.

Women's health has been perceived differently from men's because women's bodies and biological processes are different in some respects from men's. Feminists have uncovered biases in the gender dynamics of Western medicine. In the past women were considered to be physically defective; more recently women were viewed as the "weaker sex." With the professionalization of the Western health-care system in the nineteenth century, men displaced midwives, and male "experts" came to predominate in providing guidance and information previously offered by women kinfolk and other women.

Society has medicalized the normal parts of the life cycle and experiences of most women, such as menstruation, childbirth, and menopause. Male experts and policy-makers have enormous influence and control over women's access to health information and health care. Control over women's bodies is especially politicized around birth control and abortion and jeopardizes women's right to safe and legal abortions and other reproductive rights. Women who do not have cisgender "female" bodies are often not recognized by the medical system at all.

Childbirth has become the domain of medical specialists, with women as passive consumers of their expertise and medical procedures. In developing countries and among the poor everywhere, childbirth remains a risk to the health of the mother and her child. Male biases are also seen in the treatment of menopause and women's sexuality.

Poverty is probably the single greatest hazard to women's health, and poverty is exacerbated when it intersects with other inequalities such as race, sexuality, gender identity and expression, Indigeneity, disability, and age. The stress of racism contributes to physical disease as well as mental health, contributing to unequal treatment from the health-care system and its professionals. Women are frequently employed in low-paying and hazardous conditions that contribute to health risks that are harder to detect and less often reported than men's occupational health risks. Physical abuse and rape are forms of violence that women experience and that are very much under-reported—emotional and financial violence even more so because these actions are often not considered criminal.

Heart disease, cancer, sexually transmitted diseases, and osteoporosis should be of special concern to women everywhere. These aspects of physical health are too often under-diagnosed, under-researched, and under-treated in women. Hysterectomies, which occur at a very high rate, may have long-lasting negative physical, emotion, and sexual effects for women. Women also have mental health issues: they experience depression at a much higher rate than men, and drug therapy is also prescribed for women more frequently and for longer than for men.

Some groups of women, such as refugees, the disabled, the elderly, and the incarcerated, are especially vulnerable. They are at special risk for violent attacks and neglect and have limited access to good health care. Lesbian and transgender women are often at a disadvantage when seeking appropriate care.

The women's health movement has made great strides in bringing women's health issues to the public and to women's own agendas. Working to counter gender, racial, ethnic, sexuality, and class biases will address their issues and improve women's health.

Note

1. *Preference* is an outdated term; some even regard it as a slur.

Discussion Questions

1. What would be the consequences for women's health if women had greater control of reproduction? What factors affect their control; how might their control be increased? What concerns might arise in the future?
2. Select a group of women at special risk for health problems as a consequence of disability, age, political status, or other factors. Using an intersectional analysis, discuss these problems, their causes, how they are addressed in the present health-care system, and how health-care delivery might be improved.
3. Interview a woman *at least* 20 years older than you. Compare your health experiences—health care, family remedies, information shared about reproductive health matters, beliefs, etc. Who are her health-care practitioners? How does treatment differ from that with which you are familiar?
4. Questions continue to arise today concerning who has control over one's own biological materials (the tissue from a biopsy, the results of blood tests, etc.). How does power and context influence a person's own bodily integrity?
5. Identify a definition of health, either one from this chapter or one that you create yourself. Explain how and why it best fits your experience and understanding of women's health.

Recommended Resources

Anderson, Kim. 2011. *Life Stages and Native Women: Memory, Teachings and Story Medicine.* Winnipeg: University of Manitoba Press. Through a series of interviews with Métis, Cree, and Anishinaabe females, Anderson shares their experiences at different life stages. She explains how an understanding of how healthy communities worked in the past can assist to rebuild healthy Indigenous communities today.

Armstrong, Pat, and Ann Pederson, eds. 2015. *Women's Health: Intersections of Policy, Research, and Practice.* Toronto: Women's Press. This collection highlights the need for gender inclusion in all aspects of healthcare policy and delivery. New updates include sections on health-care providers in the neo-liberal workplace. Its gender-based analysis demonstrates how the new social, political, and economic context impacts the delivery of health care in Canada.

Mikkonen, Juha, and Dennis Raphael. 2010. *Social Determinants of Health: The Canadian Facts.* Toronto: York University School of Health Policy and Management. A clear depiction of how class, race, sexuality, ability, and age, each alone and in combination, determine health.

Seaman, Barbara, and Laura Eldridge, eds. 2012. *Voices of the Women's Health Movement,* vols. 1 and 2. New York: Seven Stories Press. This two-volume anthology includes writings by a broad range of feminists, from Elizabeth Cady Stanton to contemporary activists and authors. Topics range from history of the women's health movement to self-help, body image, and chronic illness.

Skloot, Rebecca. 2011. *The Immortal Life of Henrietta Lacks.* New York: Broadway Paperbacks. A poor woman's cancer cells fuel scientific advances, although she herself dies and her family remains poor, despite the multi-million dollar industry the cells generate. The role of race, gender, and poverty, as well as informed consent, the beginnings of bioethics, as each affects the members of the Lacks family, are examined.

Strohschein, Lisa, and Rose Weitz. 2014. *The Sociology of Health, Illness and Health Care in Canada: A Critical Approach.* Toronto: Nelson Education. A compendium of issues pertinent to women's health set within the foundation of the social determinants of health.

Part III

Women in Society

The earlier sections of this volume explored the various ways in which women have been defined by others—in society and culture, in the family—and the alternatives they have chosen for themselves. This final section deals with women's relationships to what has often been called the "public sphere."

Women have always participated in the world beyond the family circle, but all too often these contributions and efforts have been undervalued, ignored, or treated as invisible. For many people, the threat of feminism has been the growing claims by women to power in the public domain and the redefinition of women's roles in what has been misleadingly called the "private" domain.

How women shaped the fields of education, religion, work, and political power is explored in this section. Education stimulates questions and search for answers. Women's education can be a controversial issue. Will education provoke them to challenge the status quo? What is appropriate for women to learn? Access to certain fields often requires specific educational preparation. In the past, women were not permitted to obtain instruction in the male-dominated professions of the church ministry, law, and medicine. Women continue to challenge long-held beliefs about their lack of ability for scholarship. In doing gender-conscious research, feminist scholarly questions often differ from the traditional approaches of the past, and such research is adding to the knowledge base about both women and men.

Education is not the only way in which women lay claim to central social and cultural beliefs. Religion has been a continuing force in many women's lives. Varieties of religion prescribe human behaviour and provide models for human aspiration. Women have often been viewed as saints or sinners. Many women through history have chosen a "religious life" as an alternative to secular life and marriage. They have not only been involved as worshippers and followers but have also been venerated and taken leadership roles, ranging from curers to clergy.

Feminists involved in religions and religious life have reinterpreted doctrines, rituals, and practices and have questioned the sexist biases of the language and cultural practices in which these dogmas are framed.

The most dramatic shift of the past century in terms of women's place in the world outside the family and religious institutions has been the enormous increase in the numbers of women working for wages outside the home. Much of the work traditionally done by women has been interwoven with the traditional roles of housewife and mother. Within the context of the household, women have rarely, if ever, been paid or given credit for their daily work. With the advent of industrialization and modernization, much of the work formerly done by women in the home was transformed into activities performed outside the home for wages—for example, spinning, sewing, education of the young, and care of the sick. Some of the traditional areas of women's work were taken over by men in factories, schools, and hospitals. When done by men, the status of the work and the pay received for it rose. In the industrialized world, technology continues to change the nature of work, for better and for worse, and women as workers have been at the forefront of the globalization of industrial labour.

Since women's work lives cannot be separated from their personal and familial lives, the growing number of women and mothers in the workforce has led to demand for changes in the workplace and the family to accommodate women's needs. Child-care facilities, flexible working hours, and parental leave have begun to be implemented by employers and governments in response to the influx of women into the workforce. As will be seen, much more needs to be accomplished to reduce the "double day" of women's labour.

Even beyond the workplace, politics has been the final frontier for women's involvement in society. Politics and the power to change society are crucial to women's lives. Where there is power, there are means for exerting social control. In societies where power is accorded to certain groups of people by virtue of race, religion, ethnic origin, or gender, it has been difficult for oppressed groups to gain sufficient power to alter the status quo. This is no less true in women's struggles for their political rights.

Women's struggle for political power is international. In a variety of contexts, both formal and grassroots, women from different countries come together to share their common experiences and work together to improve women's lives. Acknowledging the differences that separate women enables the women's movement and feminism to become genuine global phenomena.

Should women strive to reform the existing social system, or will nothing less than a radical restructuring be necessary? Certainly, different women and different communities have different political objectives. Moreover, recently feminist political theorists have challenged some of the foundational ideas in Western political thought, such as human rights, the individual, and the meaning of equality, which are all products of a specific time (the Enlightenment) and a particular place (western Europe). However, although women do not make up a homogeneous group, they can and do support one another in realizing a variety of shared goals.

This book has travelled outward from the individual to interpersonal relationships to the larger world, but it is also understand understood that these distinctions are in many ways artificial. Individuals simultaneously exist in relation to each other and to communities—local, regional, national, and international. Feminist work recognizes the varieties and multiplicities of women's experiences, even as the ways in which patriarchal values have affected women *and* men over time and across geographic space are acknowledged. By knowing the past, and analyzing the present, old and new tools can construct a more equitable and more just future.

9 Women and Education

Chapter Outline

- Why Education Matters
- Education as a Contested Arena: What Should Be Taught?
- Education as a Contested Arena: Who Should Be Taught?
- Schools as Socializers of Gender Inequities
- Educational Barriers of Girls/Women in Diverse Communities in the Global North
- The Contemporary Struggle for Equal Access to Knowledge
- Empowering Women Learners

This chapter will help you
- Learn the background to gender inequity in education
- Appreciate the struggles women worldwide have engaged to access educational opportunities
- Recognize the complex and structural patterns that continue to limit learning possibilities
- Comprehend the role educational institutions have played in maintaining colonial and neo-colonial systems of oppression
- Learn how critical thinking and critical analyses can deconstruct dominant notions of gender, race, and class

> One study after another has shown that educating girls is one of the most effective ways to fight poverty. Schooling is also often a precondition for girls and women to stand up against injustice, and for women to be integrated into the economy.
>
> —NICHOLAS D. KRISTOF AND SHERYL WUDUNN, 2009

Why Education Matters

Are students in Canadian post secondary institutions members of a highly elite and privileged group? Consider the following facts. Only a small percentage of the world's population and an even smaller percentage of the world's women ever take post-secondary courses. Two-thirds of the adults in the world who cannot read or write are women (774 million in 2007), which means that millions of women are unable to read a book like this one (United Nations Department of Economic and Social Affairs 2010, 54). There is a need to understand why this is so it can be changed.

When girls do gain access to formal education, as the quote at the beginning of this chapter suggests, they actually achieve benefits for themselves, their families, their communities, and the world. For example, increased education for women of child-bearing ages (15–44 years) has been found to have a direct effect on infant mortality. Why? Because the more education that women get, the more they realize the importance of health services for themselves and their children (Gakidou et al. 2010). Where women achieve a higher level of education, they find opportunities to take on new roles and raise their status in society. Education provides a way to understand the world and helps to achieve goals.

A Matter of Life or Death

Education can also be a matter of life or death. The devaluation of girls by families and society, which is previously explored has helped create the problem of "missing daughters," the selective destruction by abortion and neglect of girl babies. When families believe boys are worth more than girls in the family, they make decisions about how to spend their scarce resources, like who should be vaccinated or taken to the hospital or sent to school, that have a serious impact on the health and education of girls.

The Politics of Knowledge

Knowledge is acquired from experiences, families, and schooling, and increasingly from many forms of media. What is considered knowledge reflects assumptions about what is valuable to know and how knowledge includes an understanding of the world. Women are not a homogeneous group; they differ from one another depending on such factors as their class, race, ethnicity, sexuality, ability, and religion. How individuals learn from experience is, as already discussed, affected by the particular mix of the identities individuals have, and their reactions to the world based on this mix and the way that are socialized by earliest experiences in families and communities. These include, from the beginning, experience of power relationships into which people are born. The "pecking order" of who has power over whom is learned and these power relations can tell them what to do (Wylie 2004a). This same power relationship applies to what is learned. This chapter will show how elite males in the past exercised their power to shape what was called "knowledge" and to create barriers to acquiring that knowledge for women and men over whom they had power. It will also show that acquiring that knowledge empowers learners not only to advance their own lives but to reshape knowledge to make it more inclusive of the experiences of all people. In that sense, knowledge itself becomes power, and power can be used in positive as well as negative ways.

Education as a Contested Arena: What Should Be Taught?

Women's Traditional Knowledge

The question of *what* should be taught is also basic to the contested arena of educational equity. Through the centuries and across cultures, women have taught themselves and their daughters the knowledge needed to survive. Women's traditional knowledge has played a crucial role in the survival of their families and communities in terms of providing food and clothing as well as healing, birthing, and mourning rituals. Among most nomadic peoples, women designed, built, and transported the tents that housed their families. Among settled villages, women bartered goods and, in some areas, organized long-distance trade. Women's productive role was constant but varied with societies and regions. In some instances, women were acknowledged as crucial to all aspects of village life, but what they contributed to the group's survival could remain relatively invisible to the men around them, subsumed under women's domestic roles.

Men as the Measure of Knowledge

Formal education in the past was largely in the hands of men of privilege in their societies worldwide. These men simply assumed that their experiences were "universal." Formal education developed on the basis of such assumptions ensured that these assumptions were accepted as the "truth." The politics of knowledge was based on the belief that non-elite women and men had inferior intellectual abilities and that their proper place in society did not warrant that they share the kind of education that would prepare them for the educated professions, the occupations monopolized by privileged men with formal training. It also included the conviction that knowledge is power not to be easily shared with those who could challenge elite positions.

As specific academic disciplines emerged in the context of universities, few scholars anywhere questioned the prevailing view that to understand any society and how it changed over time, it was necessary to study primarily the lives and actions of men, especially powerful men. Men's experiences were considered universal, while women's experiences, if considered at all, were thought to be of lesser importance, excluded as they were from the public domain. Scholars—and men as a group—might acknowledge that women had always had important reproductive and family roles, but they viewed these roles as functional and "natural" and part of the private domain.

The Rise of Feminist Scholarship

Women have too often accepted men's devaluation of women's knowledge and men's assertion that their knowledge was the standard of intellectual excellence. As a result, some women sought to gain access to men's formal education on the assumption that it would give them educational equality. When feminist historians in the 1970s tried to find out what women had been doing in the past, they found very little recorded about them in the histories written by men—unless the women were powerful queens. This led to a search for missing information—they asked such questions as: Did women have a Renaissance? What were women doing during the French Revolution? Feminist scholars soon learned that much information about women was available—if you looked for it. For example, there were those who became so-called learned ladies during the Renaissance, but they had to choose between marriage and scholarship, for only as unmarried women living in cloistered convents could they pursue their learning. During the French Revolution, as is now known, groups of women asserted political equality with men, but despite male revolutionary leaders' advocacy of equality, these men resisted treating women as political equals. They even sent to the guillotine Olympe de Gouges (1748–1793), the most outspoken of the women who made such claims (Kelly-Gadol 1977; Levy and Applewhite 1979; King 1980; Scott 1996).

Feminist scholars began to examine what questions a particular discipline, such as history, did not ask, since it was shaped earlier by elite men who believed, with rare exceptions, that women had made no significant contributions to history. Asking questions about women's lives reveals that the notion that women and men always led lives in completely separate spheres never accurately described past reality (Helly and Reverby 1992). Asking questions about women's activities in the past could begin in earnest only when it became visible that such information had been excluded and therefore not explained. Becoming visible meant they could no longer simply be ignored.

One of the achievements of the second wave of feminism in the twentieth century was to show that what privileged men had in the past defined as formal knowledge is only partial knowledge. This approach to knowledge had long excluded large portions of human experiences and achievements, including those for which women, and in particular racialized women, were largely responsible. To include this neglected portion necessarily changes the whole. Making women's lives visible is the work of increasing numbers of feminist scholars asking woman- and gender-centred questions. The creation of hundreds of women's studies programs reflects this scholarly revolution of intellectual discovery, where questions are asked about information that had been neglected and that should be included and taught so it will not again be lost (Boxer 1998). An ongoing trend in academia seeks to include more intersectional experiences, including those of poor women, racialized women, lesbian and bisexual women, transgender women, and differently abled women, in women's studies.

Contemporary Constraints

People grow up learning the lessons taught to them by their surroundings, but today there are more possibilities to make choices about who to be. Of course there are risks being labelled "deviant" by those who have different expectations. Education plays a role in this process, either confirming acceptance in the world or opening up new opportunities. Making changes is not easy, for cultural and structural barriers may limit and prevent, and certainly add to the cost of, making such choices. This chapter deals with some of these challenges.

Education as a Contested Arena: Who Should Be Taught?

Gender, Educational Participation, and Illiteracy Globally

There has been a long historical debate over *who* should be educated. Information about school enrolment shows the attention that states have begun to give to educating girls and women. More girls worldwide are attending primary school today than ever before, and in most countries they are at or near parity with boys. UNESCO reports that women and girls are also increasingly enrolled at the secondary and post-secondary levels, but that global educational parity has not been achieved:

> . . . Central and Eastern Europe is the top region in terms of achieving parity at both the primary and secondary level, with 18 of its 21 countries with data having done so. It is followed by two regions where a majority of countries have done so: Central Asia, and North America and Western Europe. With only one country in this category, South and West Asia ranks last in the number of countries reaching parity at both levels. Sub-Saharan Africa has the lowest proportion of such countries: two out of 35. (UNESCO 2012)

In 2007, women worldwide made up 51 per cent of higher education enrolment, but there are wide disparities by region. There are also large differences in the fields of study between male and female students and this too varies according to region.

Box 9.1 Time to Reflect

"Gender Parity and Equality in Education—What's the Difference?"

Gender parity and gender equality in education mean different things. The first is a purely numerical concept. Reaching gender parity in education implies that the same proportion of boys and girls—relative to their respective age groups—would enter the education system and participate in its different cycles. Gender equality, on the other hand, means that boys and girls would experience the same advantages or disadvantages in educational access, treatment, and outcomes. In so far as it goes beyond questions of numerical balance, equality is more difficult to define and measure than parity. The achievement of full gender equality in education would imply:

- Equality of opportunities, in the sense that girls and boys are offered the same chances to access school, i.e. parents, teachers and society at large have no gender-biased attitudes in this respect;
- Equality in the learning process, i.e. girls and boys receive the same treatment and attention, follow the same curricula, enjoy teaching methods and teaching tools free of stereotypes and gender bias, are offered academic orientation and counselling not affected by gender biases, and profit from the same quantity and quality of appropriate educational infrastructures;
- Equality of outcomes, i.e. learning achievements, length of school careers, academic qualifications and diplomas would not differ by gender;
- Equality of external results, i.e. job opportunities, the time needed to find a job after leaving full-time education, the earnings of men and women with similar qualifications and experience, etc., would all be equal.

The last condition, while not strictly part of a notion of educational equality, is nevertheless entailed by it: the persistence of gender discrimination in the labour market prevents the attainment of equality of access, treatment and outcomes in education by affecting the relative costs and perceived benefits of educating girls and boys. Accordingly, if full gender equality in education were to be achieved, it is probably the case that ending labour market discrimination, in all its gendered forms, would be required.

Source: United Nations (2010).

Being considered "different" contributes to fewer opportunities for schooling. Among those less likely to be formally educated are women (and men) from socially excluded or marginalized groups, including Indigenous peoples (such as the Aboriginals of Australia); those with physical or mental disabilities; immigrants; members of ethnic, language, and religious minorities; and those who reside in rural areas or in urban poverty (Lockheed 2008). But enrolment data is only a partial portrait of women's educational access. Who is *not* in school? Of primary school–age children worldwide in 2007, about 72 million were not enrolled, and most (41 million) of these were girls. As formal education is a primary road to literacy, many girls are in danger of remaining illiterate, like so many of the adult women in their communities. Nearly two-thirds of the people in the world today who cannot "read and write a short simple statement" are female, a proportion that has remained unchanged since 1990 (United Nations 2010, 54). Moreover, the United

Nations now advocates that in this age of advancing technology and information media everyone be "functionally literate" in oral expression, numeracy, and problem solving as well so that human beings in any culture can improve their lives and participate fully in economic and civic life (UNESCO 2005, 15–16).

Unequal access to education is gendered in large part because of continuing disagreements over who should be educated. The pattern of social subordination that women experience globally accounts for some of this disparity. In every society, female family members are still expected to be responsible for domestic duties, even when they work for pay outside the home. The idea that domestic skills should be the primary goal of any girl's education has a long history. Through the centuries daughters who have aspired to the kind of formal education considered appropriate for their brothers have had to struggle to achieve it (Sicherman 2010).

An extreme example in the contemporary world is the views promulgated by the Taliban regime of Afghanistan (1996–2001), absolutely prohibiting the schooling of girls outside their homes. Before this regime took power, a number of Afghani women had acquired a university education and held professional positions. The Taliban's objection to girls and women being educated was drawn from a conservative belief that school was not a "woman's place" (see Box 9.2). Throughout history, elite males of all religions have attempted some measure of control over women's access to reading and writing.

Nonetheless, it is important that in learning about the prohibition of girl's and women's access to education in other parts of the world, the analytical context needs to be considered so as to not fall into the trap of viewing the Global North as more advanced or superior to other places in the world. It is necessary to be aware of the efforts of women and male allies in facilitating social and cultural change; women everywhere act as agents of change. As transnational feminism (see Chapter 2) has alerted, such comparisons elicit a "rescue fantasy" among feminists in developed states that both emanates from and further encourages imperialism.

Womens Struggles for Formal Education in the Past

The West has long praised the ancient world of Greece, beginning in 800 BCE, as the cradle of liberty and political participation among its citizens. When looked at closely, however, it is shown that only males made up its small, privileged citizen class (perhaps 10 per cent of the population), who were educated in athletics, music, and reading. The sisters of elite male citizens were only occasionally taught to read and write. A few did study and practise poetry, music, philosophy, and even medicine (Pomeroy 1975, 1977). Formal education was not available to the rest of Greek society, made up of the merchant classes and enslaved women and men. In ancient Rome, propertied citizens similarly educated their sons, but unlike the Greeks they were more inclined to think it desirable that their daughters read Latin and Greek literature, play the lyre, and know how to dance (Pomeroy 1975; Snyder 1989).

Late in the ancient world, in Egypt, a truly exceptional woman named Hypatia (c. 370–415 CE), taught by her learned father, became a teacher of mathematics, astronomy, and philosophy at the school at Alexandria. In the next thousand years (c. 400–1400), formal education in medieval western Europe continued mainly within Christian monasteries and convents and among the Muslims and Jews who settled in Spain. Most European men of titled and propertied families were more concerned about swordsmanship and field sports than in learning to read. Formal education was left to male clergy, some of whom used their skills on behalf of their secular rulers, and to cloistered nuns (Lucas 1983; McNamara 1996).

There were a few notable learned women in medieval Europe, however. Their intellectual achievements include Latin plays by the German nun Hroswitha of Gandersheim (935–1001), the

Box 9.2 Women in Media

The Teenage Girl Who Wanted to Go to School

Malala Yousafzai was given honorary Canadian citizenship in 2014.

Malala Yousafzai, who campaigned for girls' right to an education, at the age of 15 was targeted and shot on her school bus by the Taliban in Pakistan on 9 October 2012. The following excerpt is from her speech on 12 July 2013 to the United Nations Youth Assembly.

Dear Friends, on the 9th of October 2012, the Taliban shot me on the left side of my forehead. They shot my friends too. They thought that the bullets would silence us. But they failed. And then, out of that silence came, thousands of voices. The terrorists thought that they would change our aims and stop our ambitions but nothing changed in my life except this: Weakness, fear and hopelessness died. Strength, power and courage was born. I am the same Malala. My ambitions are the same. My hopes are the same. My dreams are the same. . . . So let us wage a global struggle against illiteracy, poverty and terrorism and let us pick up our books and pens. They are our most powerful weapons. One child, one teacher, one pen and one book can change the world. (Yousafzai 2013)

---

mystical writings by the abbess Hildegard of Bingen (1098–1179), and song poems by women troubadours in southern France. One woman, Trotula (c. eleventh century), the wife and mother of physicians, taught at a medical school in Salerno, Italy, where both women and men were allowed to study and teach (Green 2001). By the thirteenth century, however, when European universities came to dominate formal learning, these institutions were devoted solely to training men in theology, law, and medicine.

Elsewhere in the world during the fifth to fifteenth centuries, some women of aristocratic or royal families could learn to read and write. Several at the Japanese emperor's court in the Heian period (794–1192) kept diaries and wrote letters to each other. One royal woman, Lady Murasaki Shikibu (c. 978–1030), produced the world's earliest epic novel, the *Tale of Genji*, about the love adventures of a prince at court (Jayawardena 1986). In Islamic Spain, Walladah Bint al-Mustakfi (c. 1001–1080), the daughter of the caliph (ruler) of Cordoba, composed love poetry in the flourishing intellectual climate established by her father. In the Middle East generally, Islam as a religion required both women and men to study the Quran, creating a measure of literacy for girls. A number of Muslim women from scholarly and noble households were highly educated, a few of them contributing to literary and theological writings (Nashat 1999).

From the 1400s to the 1700s in Europe, the developing government bureaucracies employed men with learning. An urban commercial class, whose trades required a high level of literacy, grew in importance. Knowledge enabled states to govern more efficiently and business enterprises to expand. However, men's assumptions about women's inferior "nature" and impaired mental capacities remained. A few educated women did dare to speak out against this dominant view. Christine de Pizan (c. 1364–1430), a young widow with children at the French court, supported herself by writing lyric poetry, courtly romances, and tracts on moral conduct as well as public matters. In *The Book of the City of Ladies* (1405), she wrote of the achievements of famous women of the past, chiding male writers who distorted women's abilities (Boxer and Quataert 2000). With the invention of movable type and the printed book in the late fifteenth century, literacy increasingly flourished among men, who benefited from new schools available to them in their villages and growing cities. These secular schools, reflecting prevailing views about women's inferior intellects, did not admit girls (Lee 1975).

Two women trained in their fathers' courts in sixteenth-century Europe to be humanist scholars became powerful rulers in their own right: Catherine de Medici (1519–1589) in France and Elizabeth I (1533–1603) in England. Though male Protestant reformers promoted reading the Bible as the proper education for both girls and boys, they soon restricted independent reading to higher-class women, while placing an increased emphasis on the use of education for women's moral training, not their intellectual development.

European Struggles for Women's Education

In Europe, conservatives and progressives vehemently debated the proper goals of women's education. One influential counsellor at the court of King Louis XIV of France heartily endorsed the idea that girls should be taught primarily "women's subjects," defined as the duties of a good (obedient) wife (Lougee 1976). While few contemporaries dared oppose this position, three Englishwomen did and founded schools for girls that provided the more rigorous academic education taught young men, including logic, Greek, Hebrew, math, and poetry. One of these women, Mary Astell (1666–1731) boldly asserted that it was solely custom and prejudice that limited women's educational development, while Hannah Woolley made her case in more crude and witty terms (see Box 9.3) (Hill 1986; Boxer and Quataert 2000).

In the late eighteenth century the French philosopher Jean-Jacques Rousseau set out his views about the ideal education for a young man in *Émile* (1966 [1762]). For Émile's wife, Sophie, he recommended an education to make her a charming companion, submissive to her husband's will and domestic needs (Keohane 1980). Rousseau's blatant prescription was challenged by Catharine Macaulay (1731–1791), author of the eight-volume *History of England* (1763–83), who called for women to learn alongside men, sharing the same curriculum and physical exercises (Boos 1976).

Mary Wollstonecraft opposed Rousseau's views with even more passion. Supporting herself from the age of 19 as a lady's companion, needleworker, governess, schoolmistress, journalist, and translator, the middle-class Wollstonecraft deplored the useless "accomplishments" society thought appropriate for young women. Her

Box 9.3 In Her Own Words

The Right Education of the Female Sex

Hannah Woolley (1622–c. 1675), whose mother was skilled in medical remedies, worked as a servant and then married a schoolmaster when she was 24. Together they ran a grammar school, first in the county of Essex in England and then in London. Widowed in 1661, Woolley wrote *The Ladies Directory* and *The Cook's Guide* and used them to advertise her skills. The excerpt is from her book *The Gentlewoman's Companion*, published in 1675, expressing her mature views about women's right to acquire knowledge.

> The right Education of the Female Sex, as it is in a manner everywhere neglected, so it ought to be generally lamented. Most in this depraved later Age think a Woman learned and wise enough if she can distinguish her Husbands Bed from another. Certainly Man's Soul cannot boast of a more sublime Original than ours, they had equally their efflux from the same eternal Immensity, and [are] therefore capable of the same improvement by good Education. Vain man is apt to think we were merely intended for the Worlds propagation, and to keep its humane inhabitants sweet and clean; but by their leaves, had we the same Literature, he would find our brains as fruitful as our bodies. Hence I am induced to believe, we are debar'd from the knowledge of humane learning lest our pregnant Wits should rival the towering conceits of our insulting Lords and Masters.

Source: From Hannah Wooley in Joan K. Kinnaird, "Mary Astell and the Conservative Contribution to English Feminism," *Journal of British Studies* 19 (1979): 53. Reprinted with the permission of the University of Chicago Press.

Vindication of the Rights of Woman (1792) scornfully points out that since Sophie's abilities were left uncultivated, she would make a poor mother for Émile's children. Young women must have the same education as men, she argues, to enable them to be rational, competent, and independent. She claimed not to be radical in her views, for she insisted that women could fulfill their domestic roles best if they learned first to respect themselves as individuals (Sapiro 1992).

This fierce debate was not limited to European societies. In China, for example, Confucian teachings sustained a deeply patriarchal system, its greatest rewards going to males who mastered the learning required to become scholar-officials. Here, too, a few independent-minded scholar-officials advocated some modified forms of education for women. One of these was Ch'en Hung-mou (1696–1771), who taught that all people were educable in some fashion and that women should not be neglected. Throughout the world, women of upper and middle ranks were more likely to lead somewhat less restricted lives than conventional prescriptions required, a few managing to become scholars, writers, artists, and poets (for India, see Tharu and Lalita 1993; for Africa, see Daymond et al. 2003; Sutherland-Addy and Diaw 2005; Lihamba et al. 2007; Sadigi et al. 2009).

European Colonization and Womens Education

After 1500 and until the second half of the twentieth century, Western countries acquired territories overseas through the use of force to control far-flung resources, trade, and wealth. In imposing European power, institutions, and practices on many parts of Asia, Africa, the Middle East, and the Americas, the issue of who should be educated became critical. The primary goal of the colonizers was to create an empire with an orderly and disciplined local labour force. For women, the consequences were mixed. Christian missionary schools for girls often provided colonized women with their first opportunity for formal education, but Western education introduced the concepts of European racial and cultural superiority. As the West increasingly viewed the education of women as a symbol of modernity, Indigenous elites who identified with their colonial masters sought to redefine their traditional concepts, including that of womanhood (Berger and White 1999; Edwards and Roces 2000). In new Latin American nations in the latter part of the nineteenth century, for example, enlightened local leaders expanded secular education for women in order to demonstrate the modern nature of their states (Sànchez Korrol 1999).

Multiracial British Caribbean colonies followed a pattern that held true elsewhere in imperial systems. Europeans in positions of power sought to replicate hierarchical European codes of conduct. After the abolition of slavery, working-class racialized girls and boys attended schools together but studied different subjects. Boys were expected to become skilled and unskilled labourers; girls were prepared to become domestic servants. Upper-class white males were educated for the professions and senior positions in the colonial administration, while middle-class males, many of whom were of mixed race, received training for the lower ranks of the civil service and commerce. Middle-class and upper-class European girls were groomed to be suitable wives for educated husbands, and while they received more years of schooling, the curriculum, with its emphasis on household subjects such as needlework, differed little from that provided to working-class black girls (Ellis 1986).

By the twentieth century, most European colonies had government-supported elementary schools for both girls and boys, increasing general literacy; but boys more than girls were encouraged to take advantage of it. A few private secondary schools and a very small number of universities were established to train local men as professionals and potential political leaders. A handful of women studied at secular and church-related schools in Europe or North America. Such opportunities enabled a select group of women in India, for example, to return home as teachers, midwives, doctors, and lawyers (Burton 1998) and a few women in Africa to train for vocations deemed suitable for women, such as teaching and nursing (Berger 1999).

Some colonial governments, either believing their subjects did not have the intellectual capacity to absorb Western learning or determined to prevent them from doing so, simply neglected to supply any educational services, as in the Portuguese territories of Angola, Guinea-Bissau, and Mozambique (Lindsay 1980). In the Belgian Congo, discrimination against women in schooling was a matter of colonial law, resulting in one of the lowest literacy rates for women in the world (Yates 1982). Where it existed, European-sponsored education mirrored patriarchal European gender values, which meant that secular schools for colonized peoples emphasized formal education for boys only. In conjunction with the elevation of Western learning, traditional languages and knowledge were denigrated in the colonies. In regions where local women in pre-colonial societies had wielded a measure of political and economic power, colonial regimes diminished their status.

The Debate in Canada

In colonial North America, formal education for women beyond their "letters" was considered inappropriate, dangerous, and unsettling to the performance of domestic duties:

> In the early 19th century, Canadian women taught children in private domestic settings, in so-called "dame" schools. Some pioneers ran their own schools; for example, Anne Langton (1804-93) ran a small informal school with her brother at Fenelon Falls. By midcentury, women began to be employed in public schools, and by 1900 elementary school teaching was done almost entirely by women. In 1872 the BC superintendent of education declared that a woman's mission was "predominantly that of an educator," specifically of infants and young children. The change occurred largely because women could be hired at lower wages than men at a

Teaching became one of the first "female professions" in Canada. In this famous painting, Robert Harris depicts PEI teacher Kate Henderson "laying down the law" to the more conservative school trustees who disliked her progressive teaching practices. Source: Robert Harris, *A Meeting of the School Trustees*, 1885. Oil on canvas, 102.2 x 126.5 cm, Purchased 1886, National Gallery of Canada, Ottawa. Photo © National Gallery of Canada.

time when the cost of an expanding school system weighed heavily on taxpayers. The change both caused and reflected an increasing acceptance of the participation of middle-class women in work outside the home and an ideology that emphasized women's special abilities to nurture and educate children. (Gaskell 2014)

Women's Struggles for Education in the World Today

Local reformers and feminist thinkers in the Global South have successfully challenged colonial and traditional views of women's education. After 1906, for example, literate Iranian women could obtain a weekly newspaper called *Danish* ("Knowledge"), published by one of several women's secret societies aimed at expanding educational opportunities for girls. By 1914, literate Egyptian women could choose from 15 journals in Arabic (Baron 2005). In 1919 in China, where revolution had removed the ruling dynasty, there were 400 new nationalist and feminist periodicals openly questioning Chinese women's subordination, including the practice of foot binding and traditional marriage customs (Jayawardena 1986).

Like women who took part in the "Arab Spring" uprisings in 2012, women in the decades after World War II actively supported the independence movements and wars of national liberation that ended Western colonialism, including fighting as soldiers. Consequently, they expected more inclusion in all sectors of their societies, such as schooling, than their male counterparts were prepared to give them (Disney 2008).

Poverty and the lack of schools only partially explain gender disparities in developing states. Violence, including rape, directed against girls and women in areas of armed conflict, for example in Rwanda and Sudan, regularly followed by displacement and refugee status, has contributed to a serious decline in their enrolment rates (UNESCO 2003). Whether because of wars, traditional or renewed religious fundamentalism, or the enormous costs of national reconstruction, social and economic choices are often made at the expense of women's access to formal education.

Efforts at economic development in poorer countries are sometimes accompanied by gender inequity. Development planning that upholds patriarchal values can deprive women of access to new resources, ignoring their historic and real but "invisible" contributions to economic growth (Fraser and Tinker 2004).

In the Global South, most states have focused on providing primary and secondary school access. Given the opportunity, however, women worldwide will pursue higher education. In the post-Taliban era at Kabul University in Afghanistan, for example, women numbered 1700 of the 7000 students. Yet, even among these one commented, "I was one of the very few girls in my town allowed to seek higher education. I was lucky that my parents allowed me to study" (Nemtsova 2010).

As the global community has come to accept access to formal education as a human right for all, feminists throughout the world have expanded the debate about women's education, calling for a curriculum that reflects the values, perspectives, and experiences of women, as well as their full and equal participation at all levels (Martin 2000).

Broadening Canadian Educational Participation

The struggles for educational access and equality for racialized students, are deeply embedded in history, as are political debates over who should be educated and how that could be best accomplished.

In Canada, racism constitutes a significant barrier to quality education. The 2000 Canadian Race Relations Foundation report, *Racism in Our Schools*, documented the historical basis for contemporary racial discrimination:

> We need to remind ourselves that racism is an intrinsic part of Canada's history: the attempts to annihilate Aboriginal cultures, slavery, the racist immigration policies that have excluded Chinese, South Asian, Jewish and Black immigration, the internment of Japanese Canadians during WWII, represent only a few examples of the various manifestations of institutional racism in Canada's past. Racism, once it becomes institutionalized, also becomes a part of a society's psyche that cannot be easily removed and has an impact on all areas of its public spheres. The Canadian educational sphere has not escaped from this affliction, even though that part of history, too often, remains silenced in the school curriculum. (Canadian Race Relations Foundation 2000)

LGBTQ students have often been isolated in educational institutions. Bullying and violence take their toll and can have devastating consequences. Egale Canada reports that "68% of trans students, 55% of LB students and 42% of GB students reported being verbally harassed about their perceived gender identity or sexual orientation with 20% of LGBTQ students reported being physically harassed or assaulted about their perceived gender identity or sexual orientation" (Egale 2013). Gay–straight alliances in schools can provide meaningful solidarity even though some Canadian schools do not allow them. Other initiatives, such as more inclusive curricula, can have important results when LGBTQ students see their lives represented in meaningful ways.

Students who have immigrated to Canada or are the children of immigrants often face barriers to educational equity and refugee claimants are often prevented from attending school. Programs devised in conjunction with immigrant communities have seen success. Heritage language programs and more inclusive cultural curricular initiatives create a more diverse and respectful learning environment.

Schools as Socializers of Gender Inequities

Schools help socialize girls to be obedient, nice, respectful, and quiet, in contrast to attempting to instill in boys a sense of competition and independence of thought. By replicating society's gender prescriptions, schools perpetuate the prevalent structures of sexism in the classroom. Schools do not consciously set out to discriminate in this way, but researchers find that insofar as teachers and administrators represent the values in which they themselves have been socialized, they propagate these structures in educational settings worldwide.

Elementary Schools

Reading materials prepared to guide children reflect a gendered world. During the 1970s, feminist scholars found a male world in much-admired children's picture books, including the works of Maurice Sendak, Dr Seuss, and Richard Scarry (Fisher 1974). School textbooks in this period reinforced the idea that girls would grow up to be passive and boys to be active. In "new math" texts, which arranged people in sets, groups of men appeared as doctors, firefighters, chefs, astronauts, and letter carriers, ignoring the presence of women in some of these occupations (Federbush 1974). Not until the 1980s and under pressure from feminist revelations of biases against girls and women did introductory social studies and history texts begin to use more gender-neutral terms, replacing terms such as *political man* and *industrial man* with *political behaviour* and *industrial life* (Smithson 1990).

Efforts to address gender stereotyping in textbooks continue. Worldwide, teachers' guides and primary school illustrations often reproduce traditional roles, featuring women in the home or as teachers, while men are shown in public spaces and at work in a variety of professional occupations (Lloyd 2005, 115).

Secondary Schools

Even today girls at the secondary level can be discouraged from intellectual achievement, especially in mathematics and science, where boys are

---

Box 9.4 Key Issues

Teaching Women

In the very first year of our century, the year 1801, there appeared in Paris a book entitled "Shall Woman Learn the Alphabet?" The book proposes a law prohibiting the alphabet to women, and quotes authorities weighty and various, to prove that the woman who knows the alphabet has already lost part of her womanliness. The author declares that women can use the alphabet only as Molière predicted they would, in spelling out the verb *amo*; . . . while Sappho, Aspasia, Madame de Maintenon, and Madame de Stael could read altogether too well for their good; finally if women were once permitted to read Sophocles and work with logarithms, or to nibble at any side of the apple of knowledge, there would be an end forever to their sewing on buttons and embroidering slippers.

. . . Now I claim that it is the prevalence of Higher Education among women, the making it a common everyday affair for women to reason and think and express their thoughts, the training and stimulus which enable and encourage women to administer to the world the bread it needs as well as the sugar it cries for . . . that has given symmetry and completeness to the world's agencies.

Source: Loewenberg and Bogin (1976, 318–19, 321).

expected to excel. Gender bias subtly influences the use of educational technology, a necessity in the twenty-first century, leaving many girls behind. The digital divide by gender, race, and class is even more pronounced in developing countries where Internet access is more limited (United Nations 2010).

The 1990s were a turning point in attention to girls' achievement. Feminist scholars considered how adolescent girls were being hurt psychologically by societal pressures to conform to the cultural construction of being female. They described how confident girls experience a loss of their authentic voice and develop low self-esteem and even depression in seeking to be conciliatory and nice (Gilligan 1993; Orenstein 1994; Pipher 1994). Although it has been supposed that adolescents are preoccupied with achieving independence, researchers found that this notion is not sufficient for young women. Finding that girls were conflicted about their desires to find an autonomous self and identity and to establish relationships (Gilligan et al. 1990)—that they sought both autonomy and connection (Stern 1990)—galvanized parents and educators to rethink how girls were being taught in and outside the home. One influential report, *How Schools Shortchange Girls* (American Association of University Women 1992), cited the unequal treatment girls experienced in curricula, testing, and teacher attention, problems identified decades ago. Another study found that girls are sexually harassed in public daily by male classmates and by teachers. It also showed how the high school curriculum continued to teach young women to accept this abuse and how young men continued unchallenged in their intimidating behaviour (Stein et al. 1993). This phenomenon is global. In Botswana, for example, where the female drop-out rate in secondary school is a national problem, pregnancy is a leading explanation. It is an outcome in part of gender inequity that allows male students, teachers, and other older males to sexually abuse young women (Makwinja-Morara 2009).

Bullying also reveals gender disparities and is exacerbated through texting and cyberbullying. Although widespread in schools globally, authorities have been slow to address it. Boys tend to be more physically violent and outwardly aggressive; girls often use more covert and emotional forms of taunting, such as spreading false stories about individuals and excluding them from activities. Educators are only just beginning to address how schools are unsafe for LGBTQ students, a situation that has caused some of them to abandon schooling rather than to be harassed (Biegel and Kuehl 2010). Homophobia creates a hostile environment in schools and in the larger society with the accompanying higher risk of attempting suicide (28 per cent for LGBTQ youth versus 4 per cent for heterosexual youth) (McCreary Centre Society 2008).

Media representations present a different portrait of high school life than research findings. In the widely syndicated American TV show *Glee*, high school youth regularly break into song and dance. The show suggests that both female and male youth, even those who might be different from mainstream youth in their race, ethnicity, gender, and sexuality, can find a place for themselves in high school and be supported by peers and teachers. The question is, does this unrealistic representation help the situation by setting a good example or does it cover up the problem by failing to address gender and other inequities that still prevail in schools?

In the Global South, advocating for a woman's right to be educated as a human right and the creation of "gender-friendly schools" where girls are physically safe to learn are part of the larger agenda of bringing and keeping them in schools (Mannathoko 2008).

Post-secondary Education

Early post-secondary education in Canada was strictly gendered. Consider the case of Dr Emily Stowe. Emily Howard Stowe was the first woman to practise medicine in Canada. She applied to medical schools in Canada multiple times, but was rejected because of her gender. She moved to the United States to obtain her medical degree; in 1867 she received her degree in homeopathic medicine and moved back to Canada to start a practice. The Canadian government required US-trained homeopathic doctors to take further courses in Canada, but again the University of Toronto would not allow her entry, so she continued practising without a licence. Finally in 1871 she and Jenny Trout were allowed special entry to the university, making them the first women to attend lectures at the Toronto School of Medicine. Both women were humiliated by both students and faculty; Dr Stowe either failed or refused to sit her exams in protest (Jenny Trout persevered and became the first licensed female medical practitioner in Canada), and practised without licence until the College of Physicians and Surgeons of Ontario granted her a license in 1880. Dr Stowe's struggles encouraged her to be active in the women's movement throughout her career. She helped found the Ontario Medical College for Women, the first of its kind in Canada, in 1883—the same year her daughter Augusta Stowe-Gullen became the first woman to graduate from a Canadian medical school. These types of struggles occurred in most post-secondary faculties throughout the nineteenth and twentieth centuries (Collections Canada 2006).

From the 1970s to the present, the post-secondary population in North America grew enormously, driven in large part by women of all racial/ethnic backgrounds making a concerted effort to be educated, further their career goals, and increase their earning potential. Gains in access have not eliminated other forms of gender, racial, ethnic, and class inequalities and biases.

Statistics Canada (2015e) reports: "Since the early 1990s, women have made up the majority of full-time students enrolled in undergraduate university programs. The proportion of women among students enrolled in undergraduate programs has never reached or exceeded 60%. However, their percentage among graduates has risen above this threshold since 2001. In 2008 for example, 62% of all university undergraduates were women" (see Figure 9.1).

The educational level of women has been on the rise in Quebec since the early 2000s, with Montreal having the most female university graduates. In 2012, 32 per cent of Quebec women had a university degree compared to 27 per cent

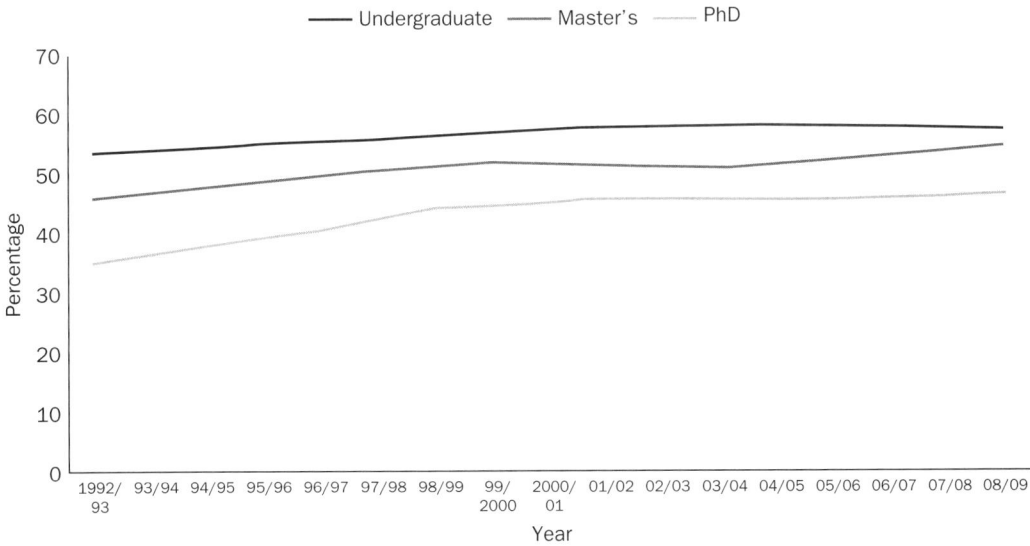

Figure 9.1 Percentage of Women among Full-Time University Enrolments, by Program Level, Canada, 1992/1993 to 2008/2009

Source: Statistics Canada, Post Secondary Student Information System, 1992/1993 to 2008/2009.

of men. In addition, women are less likely to be under-educated. Only 12 per cent of Quebec women have not graduated from high school, compared with 15 per cent of men (Institut de la statistique Québec 2014).

In the 1980s and 1990s, a number of studies described the unwelcoming cultural and structural environment that women students, faculty, and administrators experienced in academe as a "chilly climate." They documented how attitudes and actions that marginalized women's intellectual pursuits harmed their academic and career goals (Hall and Sandler 1982, 1984; Sandler and Hall 1986; Sandler, Silverberg, and Hall 1996). Women faculty of colour identified policies and practices that made them invisible and dismissed their scholarship, while women students of colour emphasized their absence in the curriculum and how intersections of race, gender, class, and anti-immigrant bias compounded their lack of support and respect from faculty, staff, and other students, contributing to everyday inequities in their learning experiences (Moses 1989; Hune 1998, 2006).

Studies in the 2000s find that post-secondary women earn better grades than their male counterparts but may experience lower self-esteem about their academic abilities. One cause lies in faculty interactions. If women students feel that faculty, most of whom remain white and male, do not take their scholarly interests and career aspirations seriously, or if they too readily internalize dismissive comments by faculty, they may lower their goals and even make themselves physically ill (Sax 2008). One consequence worldwide is that women continue to choose traditionally "feminine" fields—education, health, humanities, and social sciences—and remain under-represented in areas considered "masculine"—science, technology, engineering, mathematics (STEM), and related fields—where they would earn higher wages (United Nations 2010, 64–5).

New research on and by women of colour describes the strategies they adopt as students, faculty, and administrators to resist their marginalization in academe and being seen as having deficits because of their race, gender, class, sexuality, and culture. Women of colour emphasize how their family background and life experiences provide them with cultural strengths to achieve and that their perspectives, community-based knowledge, and leadership qualities need to be viewed as assets (Jean-Marie and Lloyd-Jones 2011a, 2011b).

Sexual harassment is another form of gender inequity. Female and male students are almost equally likely to experience sexual harassment and find it harder to pay attention in class, have trouble sleeping, and often change their behaviour, for example avoiding certain locations. LGBTQ students are deeply affected by sexual harassment, threats, and violence, becoming more insecure on campus and anxious about being able to complete their studies (Hill and Silva 2005). Rape culture is prevalent on Canadian university campuses. The "Slut-Walk" movement started in 2011 as a response to a police officer's speech to students at York University, in a campus safety information session, during which he told students to avoid sexual assault by "not dressing like a slut" (Kwan 2011). Dalhousie's dentistry school experienced significant backlash in 2014 when a sexist Facebook group condoning sexual violence against female students was brought to the media's attention. In 2015, the University of British Columbia came under fire for taking over a year to expel a graduate student who was accused of numerous sexual assaults. And in 2016, it was revealed that Brock University officials told a woman who came forward with a sexual assault complaint against her professor to "keep quiet" after the three-month investigation was concluded and found him guilty; over a month passed following the investigation before the professor stopped teaching and was removed from campus (Sawa 2016). Feminists have long advocated for safer campuses for women; some results of this advocacy are phones in parking lots, blue-light waiting areas, foot patrol services, and sexual assault centres on campuses. Still, CBC reports that sexual assaults are significantly under-reported on campuses (Sawa and Ward 2015); there is clearly significant work to be done to combat rape culture on campuses.

What would "women-friendly campuses" be like? Lisa Wolf-Wendel (2000) identifies high academic expectations for women; positive role models; a caring, supportive environment; strong student mentorship; leadership opportunities; and connecting students to their communities among the institutional practices that were "doing right" for women students. Strategies that successfully increase female participation in male-dominated fields include co-operative and hands-on teaching approaches, integration of computer technology into fields like politics and health, supportive mentors, and role models (National Council for Research on Women 2001).

Educational Institutions as Gendered Workplaces

At every level of formal learning, gender plays a distinctive role, including in the teaching profession. The "feminization" of teaching is a global phenomenon. In countries today where women have a low socio-economic status, becoming a teacher still offers new and socially accepted opportunities and a role that parents can support (United Nations 2010, 65). In industrialized nations in the nineteenth century, however, a gender hierarchy emerged. As the profession came to be dominated by women and pay was lowered, principals and supervisors remained more highly paid men. In high schools, women usually taught what men called the "softer" subjects of literature, languages, art, and music, while men were the better-paid specialists in physics, chemistry, mathematics, and social studies.

More women in the Global North now hold faculty positions, but they often occupy the lower-paid lower ranks. Women faculty, administrators, and staff, regardless of their race or ethnicity, continue to experience gender bias in being hired, evaluated, and promoted.

CAUT's 2011 report "The Persistent Gap: Understanding Male–Female Salary Differentials amongst Canadian Academic Staff" reveals that while the pay ". . . gap has narrowed over time, women's average hourly wages still remain about 16% lower than that earned by men. . . . Much of the research literature has suggested that discriminatory hiring decisions and pay structures may explain this persistent inequality in pay" (1).

Today, as colleges and universities move away from serving the public to serving the corporate world (a shift described as "academic capitalism"), women are being marginalized again despite their greater presence at all levels. Men are seeking out entrepreneurial sectors on campus, rich in rewards of copyrights, patents, and industrial and commercial partnerships, leaving women to do much of the service and teaching while coping in departments with scarce resources (Metcalfe and Slaughter 2008). Although more women have achieved the educational credentials traditionally associated with men, they receive disproportionately fewer rewards and less professional acceptance.

Historically, women have argued that equal access to formal education would give them gender equity. Why does gender discrimination in the academy remain subtle, all-encompassing, and persistent into the twenty-first century? Virginia Valian (1998) sought to explain why women do not advance professionally as far and as rapidly as men. In addition to overt discrimination against women, she concludes that in early childhood both women and men acquire the same unconscious hypotheses about gender differences that affect their expectations about women's and men's roles, including how their professional work should be evaluated. These "gender schemas" contribute to small differences in how women and men are treated, but over time they result in pronounced gender disparities in salary, rank, promotion, and prestige.

Women's professional advancement is slowed because women accumulate disadvantages while men accumulate advantages. Letters of recommendation illustrate these schemas. Male applicants are more likely to be described as doers and leaders, while women are characterized in social or emotive terms such as helpful and agreeable, characteristics ranked lower by employers, again to the disadvantage of women in their job search and promotion efforts (Madera, Hebl, and Martin 2009).

Faculty women's advancement is also made more difficult by the challenges of balancing their careers and personal lives, conflicts that male faculty experience to a lesser extent. Ladder-rank women faculty often forgo or delay childbirth to keep to the timeline for tenure, a system that was designed for faculty men with wives at home. Even after tenure, women report being enormously stressed because they bear the majority of household responsibilities, especially child care and eldercare, duties more daunting if they are the primary or sole breadwinner. Consequently, some female doctorates leave the professoriate, choose not to enter it at all, or seek part-time positions (Mason and Goulden 2004; Wolfinger, Mason, and Goulden 2009). Other research, however, finds that men have increased their time with chores and children in recent years but are not given credit for this. Moreover, men today too are feeling the pressure to be successful at work and involved as fathers (Konigsberg 2011).

The need for family-friendly workplaces and policies is universal. Despite the challenges of academia, professional women in other fields, such as law and medicine, point out that women faculty have advantages in balancing work and family because of their flexible work schedules. For women to break through the glass ceiling requires attention to stereotypes and gender biases, hidden and overt, held by both women and men. Despite the above, in Canada, incrementally, more women are becoming college and university presidents, deans, and provosts.

Box 9.5 Time to Reflect

Female University Presidents in Canada

As of August 2009, 15 out of 94 universities (roughly 16 per cent) that make up the Association of Universities and Colleges of Canada (AUCC) were headed by females. Table 9.1 is an updated list of these women and their universities and the length of each of their terms as president.

Table 9.1 Female University Presidents in Canada, 1998–Present

Indira Samarasekera	University of Alberta	2005–15
Celia Ross	Algoma University College	1998–2010
Deborah Poff	Brandon University	2009–14
Colleen Hanycz	Brescia University College	2008–13
Elizabeth Cannon	University of Calgary	2011–Present
Roseann Runte	Carleton University	2008–Present
Judith Woodsworth	Concordia University	2008–10
Ramona Lumpkin	Huron University College	2001–10
Heather Munroe-Blum	McGill University	2003–13
Suzanne Fortier	McGill University	2013–Present
Kathryn Laurin	Mount Saint Vincent University	2006–09
Ramona Lumpkin	Mount Saint Vincent University	2010–Present
Lesley Lovett-Doust	Nipissing University	2009–14
Sara Diamond	Ontario College of Art & Design	2005–Present
Johanne Jean	Université du Québec en Abitibi-Témiscamingue	2004–Present
Vianne Timmons	University of Regina	2008–Present
Luce Samoisette	Université de Sherbrooke	2009–Present
Anne Anderson	University of St. Michael's College	2009–15
Kathleen Scherf	Thompson Rivers University	2008–09

Source: Charbonneau (2009). Accessed August 10, 2014 and updated 2017.

Educational Barriers of Girls/Women in Diverse Communities in the Global North

Gender and Cultural Assimilation

To maintain power in multiracial/multicultural societies, dominant groups disempower and marginalize groups they deem different and inferior. One strategy is to deny or limit the access of Indigenous, working-class, and racial, ethnic minority groups to formal education. Another is to curtail their resistance by promoting the prevailing language, values, and institutions as superior and treating minority cultures as wanting rather than as an advantage. In North America, the dominant group has long called for the cultural assimilation of those different from them and used the education system to play a leading role in the process. The schools attended by working-class girls and girls of colour up have been generally inferior. Moreover, because domestic work, factory work, and entry-level service work were the major positions offered to immigrant women and women of colour, little effort was made to educate them beyond these areas. Women of colour and white working-class women have utilized an unequal education system to change their lives and those of their families and communities. Readers need to consider the role of intersectionality, namely how race, ethnicity, class, sexuality, language, immigration status, and other identities intersect with gender, in advancing and/or limiting one's educational possibilities.

Indigenous Experiences

Indigenous peoples have been forcibly incorporated into the dominant culture of many settler states and have had their traditional languages and cultures suppressed. In Canada this includes Indigenous people from coast to coast to coast. Indigenous children were forcibly taken from their communities by the government and placed in residential boarding schools (1876–1996) in order to accelerate their assimilation into European settler colonialist culture. Funded by the government, these schools were operated by Christian churches. Poor facilities and maltreatment resulted in at least 4000 students dying while attending these schools. Not only did the academically limited, gendered, racialized, and culturally alienating curriculum and pedagogy contribute to high dropout rates, some girls became disengaged from Indigenous gender roles and knowledge that once empowered women (Almeida 1997).

The lasting traumatic impact of residential schools on Indigenous peoples prompted the formation of a Truth and Reconciliation Commission with the mandate to assess the legacy of devastation. Among its significant recommendations are many concerning education, including that the government fund Indigenous schooling equally with other school systems and create new curriculum in consultation with Indigenous communities, and that post-secondary institutions create programs in Indigenous languages (Truth and Reconciliation Commission of Canada 2015).

Other Indigenous women in Canada use their "Western" training to benefit their people, promote Indigenous rights, and preserve and advance women's participation in band matters (Almeida 1997). Roberta Jamieson was the first Indigenous woman to earn a law degree in Canada; for 10 years she served as Ontario's first female ombudsman and is president of the National Aboriginal Achievement Foundation. In 2015, Prime Minister Justin Trudeau named former BC Crown prosecutor Jody Wilson-Raybould as federal justice minister, the first Indigenous person to hold this office.

Black Canadian Experiences

Racial segregation is not a long-ago fact of history in Canada: the last racially segregated school in Canada closed in 1983. While some larger hubs in Canada never established racially segregated schools, it took significant political action from the black community in Canada to remove segregated schools. One notable example of this activism is Mary Ann Shadd Cary. Mary Ann Shadd arrived in Canada West (Ontario) in 1851 fleeing the US Fugitive Slave Act. After Shadd crossed the border, she set about organizing abolition movements, settlement services for black freedom seekers and a newspaper thus making her the first woman newspaper editor and publisher in North America. Shadd fervently opposed racially segregated education and established an integrated school in the racially segregated area of Windsor, Ontario. Her newspaper published debates against segregation, which ultimately lost her funding for her school. She is notable for her dedication to a pedagogical practice that espoused self-reliance and freedom (Yari 2015).

After a history of racial segregation, black Canadian women sought to ensure that their children were schooled. They have pursued education as a tool of liberation: to empower their communities, uplift those in poverty, and become scholars in their own right (Collins 2001). Today, black Canadian women are attending college and university at higher rates than their male counterparts and have moved into many professional fields, including as university and college faculty.

Immigrant Experiences

Most immigrants leave their homelands reluctantly to escape hunger, war, and religious and cultural persecution and to improve their economic well-being. Recipient states are often ambivalent about immigrants, seeking their "cheap" labour in many cases, while contesting their difference and perceived social "costs." States also benefit from the skills and expertise of highly educated immigrants, such as scientists and medical personnel, in a "brain gain." Immigrant communities throughout Canada's history have relied on the educational system to provide new opportunities for their children, but they are not always welcomed (Suárez-Orozco, Suárez-Orozco, and Todorova 2008). Anti-immigrant politics in Europe and North America, expressed particularly through Islamophobia and hostility toward people of colour from Africa, Asia, the Middle East, Latin America, and the Caribbean, is waged in the education system as well.

Immigrant women often contend with the gender restrictions and conflicting expectations of the dominant society and their own communities. Work and family responsibilities often hinder their obtaining a formal education. Not all immigrant girls have been joyful about the new worlds opened to them. Memories of adapting, some painful for how they were ridiculed for their accents, dress, and food habits and for being treated as inferior during their school years, abound in the writings of celebrated ethnic authors from Europe, Asia, Africa, and elsewhere (Mendoza and Shankar 2003).

In the past, higher education for women was viewed globally as a detriment rather than an asset, since marriage was supposed to be the ultimate goal. Hence a woman's desire for more education could contribute to conflict in households, both immigrant and Canadian born. Women teachers were among the few role models for girls until the latter part of the twentieth century. Today, observing the job opportunities and income differences that an education can bring, immigrant parents are more encouraging of their daughters' educational goals. Their support and their daughters' aspirations contribute to the growth in post-secondary participation of women of colour (Hune 1998; Qin-Hilliard 2003).

Multicultural Education/Ethnic Studies as Resistance

Communities of colour have long resisted cultural assimilation and seek to retain their cultures while expressing pride in their contributions to Canadian society. In so doing they have forced educational changes. In the 1970s communities of colour initiated new pedagogical

"Children from other countries bring experiences and hopes to others in Canada. Our roles in schools and in the community is to form circles of support through which these children will learn, interact, and fulfill their potential in a protective and healing context. Refugee children are open to learn, they are interested and curious, and are able to cope with difficult and traumatic experiences when supported." —Dr Yaya de Andrade, pictured here (right) with some of her international students (left).

approaches and curricula at the K–12 level, often referred to as "multicultural education." On college and university campuses, scholars and activists of colour and their supporters demanded ethnic studies with women of colour, in particular arguing for courses on race and gender issues. Like the contemporaneous scholarly revolution in terms of gender, ethnic studies aims at greater inclusion of the knowledge from the various cultures of the country's diverse population and serves as a more democratic model than that of assimilation (Nieto 2009). The introduction of sexuality studies has advanced an even more comprehensive view of what constitutes knowledge.

The politics of cultural assimilation, multicultural and ethnic education, and sexuality studies are part of the historic debates of who is being educated and what should be taught, and as such are highly contested. Today, nations everywhere struggle to incorporate "minority" groups, while communities of difference push back and assert their cultural rights. In France, for example, aggressive assimilation efforts have come to focus on African-origin Muslim girls, as exemplified by a 2004 law forbidding the wearing of religious symbols that might be considered provocative or proselytizing. The demand that they remove their head scarves while in school, an impossible cultural choice for some, or be expelled is one example of how the politics of gender, race, ethnicity, and nationhood creates barriers to women's access to education (Keaton 2005).

The Contemporary Struggle for Equal Access to Knowledge

The second half of the twentieth century was marked by an extraordinary increase in access to higher education. For example, the Canadian "GI Bill" (the Servicemen's Readjustment Act) enabled thousands of returning World War II veterans, including a few ex–service women, to attend college or university by paying for their educational expenses. Post-secondary institutions also expanded in size and type. Women in particular took advantage of new opportunities made available in two-year community colleges.

Re-entry/Adult Women

By the 1960s, the number of *re-entry women*—adult women who had previously "dropped out" of college or university to marry and raise children as was expected of them—was on the rise in higher education. A growing women's movement led more adult women to "drop back in" to prepare themselves for employment or career transitions (Chamberlain 1988). At this time it was found that attending college or university even for only one semester helped strengthen a mature woman's concept of her abilities (Denmark and Guttentag 1967). This principle has been found true at all levels of education for women worldwide.

Adult women today are among the many students who are over 24 years of age, work part- or full-time, often are single parents, and are attending college or university for the first time. They are invisible and underserved because they are "non-traditional." Their ability to complete their diplomas or degrees is complicated by women's limited financial resources and multiple work and family responsibilities (Deutsch and Schmertz 2011). Consequently, many adult women have turned to and have been targeted for online education and distance learning programs (Kramarae 2001).

Women: The New Post-secondary Majority?

Women's strivings to obtain post-secondary degrees is a remarkable achievement occurring in higher education in Canada and several European states (OECD 2010). Today, the new global economy and changing family structures and gender roles leads more women to secure college and university credentials to attain economic security as they enter the paid workforce on a permanent basis—often as the main or sole breadwinner. Both adult women and men, finding their jobs eliminated in a time of severe economic recession, are returning to college and university to be retrained for new jobs, while older women continue to seek education not only for themselves but also as a role model for their families (King 2010; Deutsch and Schmertz 2011).

The fact that women form the statistical majority in higher education overall, however, oversimplifies the notion that gender equity has been achieved. *Full* educational participation requires an examination of different types of gender disparities that persist in higher education. Presently despite few, if any, restrictions on the choice of a college or university major, women remain heavily concentrated in fields identified with "women's work," namely, the "helping professions," such as teaching, health care, and social and retail service. These fields of study have long attracted women: they were among the few open to them until recently but generally are lower paying than male-dominated professions. Moreover, women are earning the majority of master's degrees—in absolute numbers—because they predominate in education and nursing, which graduate more students than do the male-dominated fields of engineering and business administration (King 2010). Why do women choose these fields? Is it to serve their own interests and goals, or are they being directed to these traditionally women-dominated professions? It raises the issue of how much the older debate about women and education and their "proper place" in society continues to affect choices

Is There a Male Crisis in Educational Access?

That women in several countries in the Global North now make up the majority of post-secondary undergraduates (OECD 2010) has led to considerable discussion as to why men are not enrolling at the same rates. Research on the academic achievements of girls and boys concludes that both groups need attention and have different academic and social problems. Boys are more likely to have issues with literacy, low grades, and being inattentive in class. Twice as many boys as girls are diagnosed with attention deficit hyperactivity disorder or a learning disability. Elementary school teachers, in particular, who are mostly female, are considered to be less supportive of boys' more active learning styles, perhaps contributing to their disengagement. Nonetheless, middle- and upper-class white males overall continue to perform well and attend college and university at high rates just as they have done in the past (Kleinfeld 2009b; College Board 2010). What has changed is the increased number of working-class women and men who attend or expect to attend post-secondary institutions today.

Incorporating an analysis of gender, race, class, sexuality, and other categories provides greater insight into how educational advantage and disadvantage works today. The educational gender gap lies primarily with low-income young men of colour. Many students of colour live in low-income households, attend low-performing schools, and are less proficient in English-language, basic-writing, and reading skills. However, many more low-income, immigrant, and racialized boys struggle in school and drop out than their female counterparts. More girls of all racial, ethnic and class backgrounds are excelling in their studies, scoring high on standardized tests, and are better prepared for college. Yet girls continue to lag behind boys in the sciences and mathematics, and experience high rates of depression, eating disorders, and suicide attempts (Corbett, Hill, and St. Rose 2010; Kleinfeld 2009b; College Board 2010).

If many young men are not in college or university, where are they? Historically, low-income youth have entered the workforce after high school. Presently, many working-class women are choosing post-secondary education over work or in conjunction with work to better secure their future, given that jobs offered to women without a post-secondary degree, such as retail and office work, are low paying. Men's options are different. Many men seek high-paying male-dominated jobs that do not require college or university, such as construction and manufacturing, and until recently could in this way support a family. But these opportunities are shrinking. Hence, educational access is a larger and more complex economic, social, and political issue that affects both women and men and influences their commitment to schooling or lack of it and, concomitantly, future career pathways in distinct ways (R. Wilson 2007; Kleinfeld 2009a; College Board 2010).

Transforming the Curriculum

Beginning in the late 1960s, feminist scholars began to question the nature of what was being taught. They discerned that what was labelled as "universal" knowledge had failed to include the activities and achievements of women. Among the efforts to transform this male-centred curriculum were programs undertaken to acquaint faculty in all disciplines with the advances in knowledge being achieved by studies that focused on women, gender, race, ethnicity, class, and sexuality (Luxton and Mossman 2012; Fiol-Matta and Chamberlain 1994). As a debate developed with those who saw their traditional core values being challenged, a backlash against the new curriculum took place—the so-called "culture wars" of the 1990s (Boxer 1998; Messer-Davidow 2002). Those unsympathetic to the goals of gender inclusiveness and diversity in education accused those who were instituting curriculum changes of watering down the traditional curriculum in terms of the "achievements of Western civilization." This catchphrase was used to refer to the long-honoured achievements of elite men in the West. It was also meant to denigrate those who favoured a more inclusive curriculum, and "political correctness," an ironic phrase used by inclusionists to gently jibe themselves, was taken over by those who opposed them to accuse them of introducing politics into the curriculum (Graff 1994; Levine 1997). Since the use of power to make policy is always "political," the argument was intense between the two groups, like all politics. The debate was complicated by the concern of some feminist scholars that multiculturalism could introduce a cultural relativity that might be used to justify patterns of oppression against women in other cultures (Okin 1999). The highly public debate aired some of the intellectual ferment stirred up by challenging the traditional European- and male-centred knowledge base and highlighted the importance of the questions of *who* should be taught and *what* should be taught.

Empowering Women Learners

Educational Achievements of Girls and Womens Schools Debated

Over the last several decades, female students' interest, participation, and achievement levels in STEM (science, technology, engineering, and mathematics) have been on the rise. However, there is still a significant gender gap in education. Pamela Kramer Estol's qualitative Toronto study of four all-girls schools in 2014 indicates that all-girls schools are more effective than coeducational schools in stimulating girls' interest, participation, and self-confidence in non-traditional fields of study. Findings from the study show that girls are more likely to participate, more willing to take risks, and less likely to be affected by the threat of stereotyping in all-girls learning environments compared to coeducational learning environments (Kramer Estol 2014).

The increased participation of women in higher education has been accompanied by a shift from single-gender education to coeducation. For many, coeducation is a sign of women achieving equality with men, suggesting that women's educational institutions are inferior and that women who attend them are ill prepared for competing in the larger society. However, these arguments assume that women and men are treated the same in coeducational institutions (Wolf-Wendel 2003). The research findings on the "chilly climate" for women students, faculty, and administrators, discussed above, document the persistence of gender disparities, as well as racist, ablest, homophobic and transphobic biases, in coeducational institutions.

Proponents of women's schools point to the impressive outcomes for women's academic, professional, and personal development. Women who attended US post-secondary institutions between 1910 and 1960 and who were listed in *Who's Who of American Women* were more often graduates of women's colleges than of coeducational institutions (Tidball 1973, 1980). Though they are less than 4 per cent of all college-graduate women, women's college graduates make up 20 per cent of women in Congress and 32 per cent of women board members of Fortune 1000 companies (Holmgren 2006). They also expressed having a more positive university experience, were more involved in philanthropy, held more advanced degrees, and tended to hold higher positions and earn higher salaries than women from coeducational institutions. Moreover, women's colleges and universities serve women of colour and non-traditional-aged women and produce women science graduates in greater proportions than do coeducational institutions. Institutional selectivity or admitting the most qualified female students and women's own self-selection are only partial explanations of these positive outcomes. Findings argue that it is women's colleges' and universities' consciously adopted mission to serve women, offer them female role models, and provide co-operative learning environments, which are infused in all aspects of classroom and campus life, that produces confident women leaders and intellectuals who excel. Coeducational institutions thus have much to learn from women's schools in achieving gender equity (Wolf-Wendel 2003; Wolf-Wendel and Eason 2011).

Womens Struggles to Become Scientists

Considering all the educational gains that women have made, why are there still so few women in science? Women's struggles to become scientists and to stay active in the field of science, as well as in technology, engineering, and mathematics, are a reminder that the issue of gender bias remains a many-headed dragon.

The career of Warsaw-born Marie Curie, née Maria Sklodowska (1897–1934), is often held up as a prime example of what a woman in science might achieve. She conducted research with her husband Pierre Curie in France and became the first

Box 9.6 Time to Reflect

The Montreal Massacre

The École Polytechnique Massacre, known as the Montreal Massacre, occurred on 6 December 1989 when an assassin entered a classroom and declared that he was "fighting feminists." After separating male and female engineering students, he started firing weapons, killing 14 women, and injuring 10 other women and 4 men before turning the gun on himself. The anniversary of the massacre is now the National Day of Remembrance and Action on Violence against Women, with campus commemorations taking place across Canada.

person to receive two Nobel Prizes, for her work in radioactivity: one in physics in 1903 and the other in chemistry in 1911. Widowed at a young age, she raised two daughters alone. The eldest, Irene Joliot-Curie, was awarded a Nobel Prize for chemistry in 1935. Marie Curie's professional achievements, combined with family responsibilities, set a very high standard for women scientists (Kohlstedt 2004; Des Jardins 2010).

Whether women possess the intellectual ability to do STEM fields continues to be debated. This is evident both in the way women's achievements remain invisible and in the way traditional assertions persist about women's "nature" and intellectual inferiority. To explain women's under-representation in STEM fields, feminists have focused on the unsupportive environment of their education, research, and employment. In describing how science became a profession in the United States, Julie Des Jardins (2010) identified its methods and practices as "masculine." In the first half of the twentieth century, the few women scientists were relegated to the roles of assistants, technicians, and helpers in men's laboratories and observatories, mainly to keep records and clean equipment. A few struck out on their own, such as Ellen Swallow Richards, who, able to work in her husband's laboratory at Massachusetts Institute of Technology, developed the new woman-identified field of home economics (Kohlstedt 2004). Although a woman scientist married to another scientist may gain some advantages for opening doors, there are also disadvantages of limited recognition and delayed advancement. Some women scientists chose not to marry, while others partnered with women (Kohlstedt 2004; Des Jardins 2010).

Until recently women with science degrees found few opportunities to carry out research and hold a full-time university position, except at women's educational institutions with few resources and less prestige. Ursula Franklin, physicist and metallurgist, immigrated to Canada after World War II and her internment in a Nazi forced-labour camp. In 1967, she became the first woman professor in University of Toronto's Faculty of Engineering. Franklin has claimed that she was often referred to simply as "she," since she long remained the only female faculty member in the department.

Physics and atomic science reigned in the United States between 1941 and 1962. A "cult of masculinity" glorified Albert Einstein, Robert Oppenheimer, and other men for building the first atomic bomb, while largely omitting the contributions of women scientists and engineers (Des Jardins 2010), many of whom gave up their positions to men returning from World War II (Ambrose et al. 1997). Engineering also became identified with machinery and was promoted as better suited for males (Kohlstedt 2004). Pressures placed upon women to stay at home and make children their priority (leading to Betty Friedan's analysis of the "Feminine Mystique") in the postwar 1950s also inhibited the ambitions of women in these fields. In short, women's scientific work and career decisions were restricted by the highly gendered world of science and society.

Feminist scholars have long critiqued the epistemology of science, its masculine and Eurocentric biases, and its patriarchal views of nature and society as social constructions by men (Harding 1991; Solomon 2009; Alcoff 2010). In contesting the traditional model of objectivity and the advisability of keeping distance from subjects, feminist scientists often seek to present new ideas about nature and the universe and to develop scientific practices that nurture others and the environment. Marine biologist Rachel Carson (1907–1964) was an early pioneer. Her book *Silent Spring* (1962), now praised as one of the leading science books of all time, brought attention to widespread pesticide use and launched a grassroots environmental movement, but Carson was denounced at the time for challenging established (male) scientific authorities.

Often feminist scholars challenge the concept of objectivity and question whether it is even possible to achieve, given that knowledge is constructed through the lens of experience and social location (Letherby 2003). Stephen Jay Gould in *Wonderful Life: The Burgess Shale and the Nature of History* (1989) claims that paleontologist Charles Doolittle Walcott's scientific discoveries were interpreted through his prominent and privileged social position and thus created a skewed view of evolution. Mary Hawkesworth's "Truth and Truths in Feminist Knowledge Production" (2012b) maintains that feminist scholars may achieve more "truthful" knowledge with "strong objectivity" that includes the experience and vision of marginalized groups.

Why do many competent women STEM graduates not persevere? Research points to persistent cultural biases of parents, teachers, and school counsellors (Hill, Corbett, and St. Rose 2010) and the continued "chilly climate" that privileges male students and allows only a few women students to advance as possible answers (Fox 2001; Bystydzienski and Bird 2006). International students of colour, such as African women in graduate science programs in Canada, Europe, and the United States, have identified racism, gender bias, and their perceived marginality as discouraging factors in their training (Beoku-Betts 2006). In sum, the overly masculine, authoritarian, and competitive academic and social interactions can alienate many women students (Herzig 2004; Colyar 2008; de Pillis and de Pillis 2008).

The public debate over women's underrepresentation in science escalated in January 2005 after Harvard University president Lawrence Summers, attending a diversity conference, commented that a more likely hypothesis than gender discrimination for explaining women's limited presence in mathematics and science lay in women's "innate limitations." His widely reported statement harked back to the centuries-old debate on the subject and eventually contributed to his resignation. A report of MIT senior women scientists (MIT Committee on Women Faculty 1999, 2011) also made visible wide institutional disparities that continued to disadvantage them in their careers.

Can a woman be a scientist, spouse or partner, and mother at the same time? Marie Curie juggled watching her daughter Irene in the crib placed in the lab while eyeing the test tube of glowing radium, expressing a common tension felt by women who work outside the home. The adult children of Nobel Prize winners and other women scientists have related how little time they had with their mother, given her long hours in the lab away from home and children, dinnertime conversations that centred around work, and often a lack of involvement in their children's lives (Des Jardins 2010). Does a double standard exist? Do adult children say the same things about their fathers and have the same expectations of them?

Social scientists ask whether it is or is not a socially learned preference for women to work with people rather than machines or abstractions. One study of mathematically gifted girls and boys found that as adults they chose different career paths. Math-precocious women tended to choose medicine, biological sciences, humanities, and the social sciences. Their male counterparts preferred engineering and the physical sciences (McArdle 2008). Psychologists also suggest that the pursuit of romantic or familial goals can diminish women's interests in advancing in STEM fields (Park et al. 2011).

Women's participation in STEM fields remains a complex issue, including the question of whether these fields should be given priority. In an era of DNA, stem cells, biotechnology, and global efforts to solve health and environmental dangers, the biological sciences have gained ground and prestige and have been favoured by women in recent decades. Women scientists are transforming the methods of detached, technological "masculine" science through their own methodology and research subjects. Examples include the work of the naturalist Rachel Carson (1907–1964), the geneticist Barbara McClintock (1902–1992), whose research on genes in maize increased crop production and earned her a Nobel Prize in 1983, and Jane Goodall (1934–), who in 1960, beginning without a science degree (later obtaining a Ph.D. in ethology), helped to change primate studies by living among chimpanzees in Tanzania. These women scientists carved new pathways for scientific discovery and the preservation of life and society. They and other women like them are innovators and serve as inspirations in the twenty-first century, just as Marie Curie did in the twentieth.

Women and Gender Studies

The Introduction to this textbook describes the development of women's studies, and later, women's and gender studies. The institutionalization of these fields on campuses is not monolithic, however, and involves healthy debate among feminists. Women students of all social classes, faculty of colour, and LGBTQ members, for example, continue to critique feminist theories and agendas that seem to universalize white middle-class cisbodied heterosexual women's lives or to exclude the significance, perspectives, and experiences of race, ethnicity, national origin, sexuality, class, and other differences among women and trans folk. In taking diverse positions, for example, some engage in writing and teaching feminist theory. Others criticize feminist theory and language as being elitist, like many male writers whose work reinforces traditional hierarchies in higher education and ignores the grounding democratic tendency of women's studies (Luxton and Mossman 2012; Messer-Davidow 2002).

In its focus on women's and gender realities and theories to explain them, the study of women and gender holds the possibility of restructuring knowledge to make it resonate with perceptions of the world and consciousness and thereby could bring forth a true intellectual revolution.

Summary

Knowledge is not objective but a social construct and part of a cultural and political system that has historically marginalized and continues to marginalize women's experiences. It can have the effect of teaching women to be passive. The rise of feminist scholarship worldwide challenges a specifically patriarchal perspective of knowledge and seeks to make women visible and to validate their perspectives. It enables scholarship to depart from a binary notion of gender and be open to more diverse understandings of how knowledge is produced and whose experience is valued. The intersectional understanding of knowledge furthers this; no longer are "women's" experiences considered universal for all women in the way that "men's" experiences were historically considered universal for all people.

Societies worldwide always have debated who should be educated. That women's proper place has traditionally been viewed as within the domestic sphere and men's within the public sphere explains in part why women make up two-thirds of illiterate persons worldwide today. In the ancient world, and through the medieval period, only a few exceptional women became accomplished in literary and scientific endeavours.

Religious requirements sometimes provided girls and women with opportunities to learn to read; however, the emphasis was on women's moral training, not their intellectual development. Across cultures and over time, women have struggled for access to formal education.

From the 1500s until the 1960s, European colonialism had varying consequences for colonized women's education. Western ideologies of race, colour, class, sexuality and gender roles, and models for economic development most often contributed to a decline in Indigenous women's status from their pre-colonial period. Today, women in the Global South have gained more schooling, but this varies greatly given the wide range of cultures, political ideologies, and economic resources among these states.

Societies of all cultures past and present have debated whether girls and women should have the same curriculum as boys and men to achieve equity or should be schooled in subjects to prepare them primarily to be traditional wives and mothers. Feminists who sought to provide a rigorous education for women often established their own schools. As more women, including adult "re-entry" women, and students of colour are earning degrees at all levels of higher education and efforts to diversify the curriculum have intensified since the 1970s, a backlash to defend "Western civilization" in the curriculum and to oppose diversity has occurred.

For the most part, the educational system at all levels—through textbooks, curricula, and teacher preparation—has socialized women to be quiet and submissive, to accept male authority rather than their own experiences, and to choose traditional women's careers. Schools can shortchange girls, and in higher education women experience a "chilly climate," which is even more unwelcoming for women of colour and LGBTQ students. That women and men are evaluated differently, resulting in women accumulating disadvantages and men accumulating advantages, contributes to gendered workplaces. Women college and university faculty are concentrated in the lower ranks and paid less at all ranks than their male counterparts.

Dominant men and groups maintain their influence in part by limiting access to formal education and by using the educational system as a tool of cultural assimilation. In North America, racialized and marginalized groups experience pressures to acculturate to the European North American values taught in schools and to suppress their own languages and cultures. Although girls and women of colour find new opportunities in schooling, educational systemic barriers remain. Multicultural ethno-specific education and sexuality studies hold the possibility to resist dominant group assimilation and promote inclusivity of communities of difference.

Changes in the global economy and employment, women's aspirations, and greater opportunities account in large part for women earning more college diplomas and university degrees than men in recent decades in the Global North. Greater access to higher education has not meant equality in treatment and representation in all disciplines and as faculty and administrators, however. Women remain under-represented in STEM fields but are making breakthroughs in some fields, such as the biological sciences. The challenges women experience, past and present, in becoming scientists and pursuing their careers underscore the persistence of gendered notions of who is to be educated and what is to be taught and appropriate career paths for women and men, while also seeking to fulfill family roles.

Feminist scholars also debate what kinds of educational experience benefit women's academic achievements. Since the 1970s, women's and gender studies programs, as a feminist critique of knowledge, have been established as a distinct field of study in higher education and have begun to be taught in traditional disciplines as well. The early feminist insistence on praxis, or the practice of theory, was a significant influence on the inclusion of experiential learning programs throughout post-secondary institutions. The growth of sexuality studies has further expanded opportunities for inclusive knowledge production. There is also a healthy debate among feminists about the nature and institutionalization of women and gender studies in the academy. Their future and substance as an intellectual revolution depends on the inclusion of diverse voices as students, faculty, and administrators. As Luxton and Mossman establish, the increasing corporatization of universities poses new and severe challenges to the independence and breadth of knowledge production.

Discussion Questions

1. Why did early feminists believe that education was important for women, and why was this idea resisted? How do the world figures for literacy and school enrolment reflect the position of women in various societies?
2. Investigate the statistics for women at your college or university. Compare the numbers of women and men enrolled, breaking this down by race and ethnicity if possible. How do majors break down? Are there women faculty members in all disciplines? If not, why do you think this is so?
3. On your campus, what institutional supports and resources, if any, are available to women of colour, low-income women, lesbian women, bisexual women, transgender women, women who are disabled, and adult re-entry women?
4. Trace the educational history of the women in your family as far back as you can go. How do their experiences compare with your own, and how do you account for the differences and similarities?
5. Why do you think differences in academic subject choice between male and female students persist? What do you think are the barriers to gender equity throughout your campus or university? How might these barriers be overcome?

Recommended Resources

Abdi, Ali, and Ratna Ghosh. 2004. *Education and the Politics of Difference: Select Canadian Perspectives*. Toronto: Canadian Scholars' Press. This book takes up the global debates about multiculturalism and politics of difference and engages notions of postcolonialism, post-modernity and cultural studies, drawing from the Canadian experience.

Frize, Monique. 2009. *The Bold and the Brave: A History of Women in Science and Engineering*. University of Ottawa Press. This text provides a rich rendering of key concepts and debates that contextualize the historic and contemporary barriers facing women in the fields of science and engineering. Frize also proposes meaningful ways to move gender equity into STEM fields.

Grant, Agnes. 2004. *Finding My Talk: How Fourteen Native Women Reclaimed Their Lives after Residential School*. Calgary: Fifth House. Fourteen Indigenous women who attended residential schools describe their experiences and how they faced the resulting trauma.

Letherby, Gayle. 2003. *Feminist Research in Theory and Practice*. Philadelphia: Open University Press. Letherby's text is an accessible distillation of feminist theory and scholarship. It takes up questions around the ethics of research, the patriarchal legacy in education, and feminist reconstructions of knowledge, and is especially useful for considerations of experiential learning/praxis.

Luxton, Meg, and Mary Jane Mossman. 2012. *Reconsidering Knowledge: Feminism and the Academy.* Halifax, NS: Fernwood. This collection charts the influence of feminist scholarship within post-secondary institutions and how it transformed teaching and learning. It examines how feminist theory and methodology changed the way knowledge is understood and practised and speaks to the challenges for feminism as corporatization redefines the role of universities in a global world.

Manicom, Linzi, and Shirley Walters, eds. 2012. *Feminist Popular Education in Transnational Debates: Building Pedagogies of Possibility.* New York: Palgrave Macmillan. This collection of reflective accounts provides pedagogical and theoretical insights from around the globe and across a variety of learning settings. A unique and valuable collection of lessons gleaned from feminist knowledge production for social transformation.

Rich, Adrienne. 2001. "Claiming an Education." In *Women's Voices, Feminist Visions: Classic and Contemporary Readings*, edited by Susan Shaw. Houston, TX: Mayfield. Rich's 1977 convocation speech urges students to *claim* an education not *receive* one. Watch a rendition of her message: www.youtube.com/watch?v=6xLPt2QTjQA

Tremonti, Anna Maria. 2013. "I Am Malala: The Girl Who Stood Up for Education and Was Shot by the Taliban." *CBC Radio: The Current.* www.cbc.ca/thecurrent/episode/2013/10/09/i-am-malala-the-girl-who-stood-up-for-education-and-was-shot-by-the-taliban/. Malala Yousafzai was just 15 years old when a would-be assassin shot her in the head as she headed home from school in Pakistan. On the first anniversary of that attack, Malala sits down with Anna Maria Tremonti for her only Canadian interview to speak about her fight for female education in Pakistan.

Woolf, Virginia. 1957 (1929). *A Room of One's Own.* New York: Harcourt, Brace. This classic work explores the ways women have been prevented from achieving higher education and what this has meant for their lives, independence, and creativity.

10 Women and Religion

Chapter Outline

- Religious Beliefs
- Religion and Social Controls
- Women as Religious Leaders
- Women's Impact on Religious Movements

This chapter will help you
- Learn how religion influences the law and culture of societies
- Understand the gender dimension of organized religions
- Recognize the multiple roles women play within faith communities
- Appreciate the difference among and between organized religions
- Distinguish the variety of spiritual beliefs that women hold globally

I think it must be lonely to be God.
— GWENDOLYN BROOKS, *SELECTED POEMS*. NEW YORK: HARPER AND ROW, 1963. REPRINTED BY CONSENT OF BROOKS PERMISSIONS.

Religious Beliefs

What Is Religion?

What is called "religion" is something about which people feel passionately. Wars have been fought, people have been maimed and tortured, and some have even sought martyrdom in the name of "religion." The subject has not lost its force in modern times by any means and remains a major element in world politics. Religion is among the most elusive of the concepts used to describe human societies. Some theorists distinguish religion in terms of its reliance upon a supernatural element, but it is possible to be an adherent to some religions without believing in any god. Furthermore, many religions that have a distinctive label, such as "Hinduism" or "Christianity," incorporate many distinct variants that are so different from one another, occasionally even hostile to one another, that they cannot be described as unitary in any sense and it would be mistaken to consider them essentially the same. In many societies, religious belief permeates, at least for some women and men, virtually all aspects of life. Planting a garden, eating a meal, having a baby, and burying the dead have both secular and religious aspects. This is so even in societies that have sought rigorously to establish and enforce a separation between religion and secular society; many societies have not sought to separate in this way but, rather, have combined a mutually reinforcing religious and political establishment.

While some have come to see religion as a relic of the past, representative of older traditions and a bastion of conservatism, it has long been a force for change and continues to be so in the present. Religious believers often seek reform rather than acceptance. They criticize what they see as injustice, oppression, and evil and try to change the behaviour both of individuals and of whole societies. At times they attempt to do this through established religious institutions—such as the churches and the clergy—and at times through new religious movements (in which women sometimes play leading roles) within or outside of established religions.

Varieties of religion can be spoken of just as varieties of society. On the one hand, there are the religious beliefs and practices of societies that have little social hierarchy or few or no specialized religious institutions. On the other hand, there are the major world religions, diverse in character but each claiming millions of adherents, in state-organized societies that have specialized ordained clergy and that play roles recognized and protected by state-level political institutions. These often contain sects that, though established, are extremely different from one another, some granting prominent roles to women and others being more patriarchal in character. Finally, there are religious movements, outside of the established large-scale religions, such as what are called "fundamentalist" religions and "new" religions.

Many religious traditions appeal to a "higher authority," something above human will or desire, for a formulation of right and wrong. For some women and men, this appeal strengthens the dicta about morality. Sometimes this authority involves sanctions, such as blessings for those who, according to that set of beliefs, do right and punishments for those who do wrong. However, the motivations of believers lie not only in sanctions but also in the wish to do and to see done what they believe is right. Some women and men resort to interpretations of texts for guidance into what is "right" and what is "wrong," while others look to the vision of charismatic leaders or even direct religious experience (though this itself is usually much influenced by leaders and customs). Generally, it is not a live-and-let-live world. Believers are not usually satisfied with following the right path only for themselves or even for themselves and their children. They want others to see and follow the right path and to avoid supporting systems that take the wrong path. The vehemence with which they insist on this in part determines whether outsiders label them as extremely conservative, "fundamentalists," or "fanatics."

Religion and Social Reform

Historically, women have been on the outskirts of religious movements. This is not to say that they have not played a major role, but that the role has not been one equal to that of men, or one that has come about as easily, since usually religious leaders have been wary of the power that women possess, individually and collectively. Therefore, in much of the history of women and religion, there has been a dichotomy. In some ways, religion has been an impetus for change where women are active, and in other ways the majority of the world's religions have adhered to and prompted patriarchal standards and mores. There is a paradox, therefore, in how women are viewed in religion. On the one hand, women have been repressed in ways that constrict access to birth control, limit the role they can play in leadership, and denounce women's sexuality. On the other hand, women sometimes are venerated as saints and can be looked upon as pious and worthy of reverence and respect.

Much feminist research and writing has been critical of religious institutions for their treatment and views of women, especially religion's exclusion of women from positions of leadership. Women in male-dominated religions have had to fight to be permitted to be educated in the text or the liturgy and are often banned from participation in central practices of worship. Women's value is connected to their roles as mothers and spouses, roles that support men and help propagate membership in the religion. Many of the world's religions adhere to beliefs and ideas that devalue women or assign them to a separate subordinated sphere. They are concerned about women as sexual tempters to men, advocating a mode of dress that covers their sexuality, reserving it only for their husbands. Carried to extremes, this attitude creates a cycle of repression and reinforces a power differential between men and women.

If they are devalued, why should women be attracted to religion? Why do so many remain members of their faiths? In confronting the difficulties of their daily lives, women may turn to religion for support and spiritual guidance. Religious belief is usually transmitted from older generations to younger ones, and both women and men grow up with the beliefs taught to them as important aspects of their lives. To leave their religions would be to walk away from an important part of themselves, for better or for worse. Also, women in particular can find a social network of support from other women in their congregations and places of worship. If they are unhappy, they may seek religion for help, seeing in religion a set of beliefs that represent a higher purpose in life, one that offers comfort in times of distress.

In addition to providing comfort and a purpose to life, religion offers individuals a moral code. Through time doctrines, teachings, and customs concerning right and wrong have been associated with religion. Religions not only set standards for good behaviour but also tell their adherents how to achieve a state of "goodness," whether this is defined as moral health or conduct that sets things right with the world. Religion is also often associated with healing, a matter that will be explored later in this chapter. Healing, or achieving a better state of being, can be directed toward the individual or society as a whole. When directed toward the individual, it can involve diagnosis (discovery of what is wrong, whether through divination, confession, or some other means) and repair (through penitence, atonement, or restoration—by sacrifice or making amends). The believer in a particular religion is encouraged to improve her life by correcting what is wrong and doing what is right. They may be sustained by their faith. Women also seek in religion solace for the problems they face or the ill treatment they experience.

As individuals they may be deeply unhappy and turn to religion for help. They may also seek change for themselves and others like them, calling upon their communities to establish justice, compassion, harmony, and whatever else their belief system teaches them is right and proper.

Feminists have explored the many ways used to control women and keep them in a secondary role, but they have also found the majority of the women around the world have found value in their faith and their religious communities, and that women have devised ways of changing society for the better through their religions. Thus, for example, although their churches may have told Christian women in the nineteenth century that their place was in the home, it was through their churches that many women fought slavery and spoke out in the name of equality for all under God. Women have used religious platforms to advocate for others and for themselves.

Women have sustained their religious beliefs despite the regulations adopted by all the major religions of the world to repress women's independence by mandating far stronger constraints on women than on men and excluding them from positions of leadership. In fact, even in these religions, some women have asserted their views, sometimes as venerated saints and holy women, sometimes as leaders in the spheres allocated to them. Today, feminist theologians continue to analyze patriarchy in major world religious traditions in order to reformulate received doctrines to meet feminist ideals (see Sharma and Young 1999).

World Religions

World religions are those that number their adherents in the millions. Some of these are more unitary in their beliefs. Confucianism, Buddhism, and Christianity, for example, trace their origins to their namesakes: Confucius, the Buddha (Siddhartha Gautama), and Jesus Christ. Islam traces its origins to its Prophet, Muhammad. Judaism traces a common ethnic history as well as a common set of scriptures. Taoism has a coherent set of beliefs. Hinduism, like Judaism, is grounded in an ethnic history, yet it contains immense diversity of belief and believers. Indeed, each of these, with a history of movement through conversion and migration, has been transformed through time into a multitude of different variants, often with different names and different beliefs and practices.

These world religions are frequently associated with political structures, particularly the state itself or an arm of the state. In the past, for example, Christian states recognized an official religion, a particular variant of Christianity, and designated practitioners served important roles in government; conversely, the ruler had to be legitimized by the Church. Today, there are a number of Islamic nations in which Muslim clerics rule (such as Iran) or have great influence (such as Saudi Arabia). While states have varied in their degree of tolerance of other religions, a close linkage between the state and the religious establishment has been the rule, rather than the exception, in the history of complex societies.

As with secular leadership, women have long been excluded from positions of authority in these world religions. Nevertheless, women are adherents of these faiths. If they have access to wealth, they may achieve positions of relative power by becoming patrons of their religious establishments, endowing religious institutions, supporting the construction of religious edifices, and patronizing sacred arts and artifacts. Regardless of the lower status to which they are assigned, millions of women have found spiritual gratification in the major established religions of the world. Further, they have found the rewards of sisterhood through these religions, gathering together in mutual support and for the purpose of nurturing their own religious communities.

Females in the Supernatural World

Most forms of religious belief include some conceptualization of a supernatural world that is inhabited by forces with superhuman qualities. These saints, ghosts, and spirits of various sorts are often considered more approachable and more interested in "ordinary" people than the great deities. Although the formal traditions of Judaism, Christianity, and Islam are **monotheistic** (believing in a single divinity), their "folk" or "popular" versions have always included belief in lesser supernatural forces.

Origin Stories. Most religions provide a creation story, of what are thought to be the first humans and how they came to be. The creation story to which Jews, Christians, and Muslims subscribe, the story of Adam and Eve, is, of course, much more than a tale of the first humans. Like other people's creation stories, it provides a "charter" and a "plan" for relations between people and the supernatural, between women and men, and between humans and nature. Some of the implications for women of the Adam and Eve story have already been discussed in Chapter 1. Another creation story, one that tells of the descent of the Iroquois nation from females, was recorded by Father Louis, a missionary working in New France (Quebec) in the seventeenth century (see Box 10.1).

Immortal Women: Souls, Saints, and Ghosts. The question of what happens to the soul after

Photo of the sculpture *Skywoman* (1954) by Shelley Niro, depicting the Haudenosaunee origin story of a pregnant woman falling from the sky to the earth, starting the life of the Haudenosaunee on the back of a turtle.

Box 10.1 Time to Reflect

The Varied Creation Stories of Indigenous North Americans

The Cherokee say they came from Corn Mother, or Selu, who cut open her breast so that corn could spring forth, giving life to the people. For the Tewa Pueblo people, the first mothers were known as Blue Corn Woman, the summer mother, and White Corn Maiden, the winter mother. Iroquois people believe that they were born into this world from the mud on the back of the Earth, known as Grandmother Turtle, [and they along with other Indigenous nations call North America Turtle Island in recognition]. The essentials of life—corn, beans, and squash—were given to them by the Three Sisters. The Iroquois refer to the Three Sisters when giving thanks for food in everyday prayers. The Apache believe that they are descendants of Child of the Water, who was kept safe by his mother, White-Painted Woman, so that he could slay all the monsters and make the world safe for the Apache people. . . . For the Sioux, White Buffalo Calf Woman gave the people the gift of the Pipe, and thus a gift of Truth.

Source: Native American History (2002).

death is a critical one. Many people believe that the soul persists, to occupy a place in the supernatural world or to return to life in another body. The latter, called reincarnation, as represented in Hinduism and Buddhism, involves belief in a scale of perfection that an individual can ascend or descend, through successive lifetimes, depending on how virtuously each life was lived. Individuals are destined to be reborn again and again, to endure the pain of existence, until they reach the pinnacle of perfection, after which they are released. In Hinduism and in some, but not all, Buddhist traditions, the most virtuous life is one devoted to study, meditation, and unconcern about worldly things (like marriage, children, wealth, and comfort, even eating and sleeping). However, women are very unlikely to have the opportunity to pursue a life of study and meditation in Hindu and Buddhist societies. In Hindu cosmology, women came to symbolize the eternal struggle that men must wage between materiality and spirit. Kali (the goddess) symbolizes the womb, connected with rebirth and consequent illusion and entanglement in the world (Caldwell 2000).

In Buddhism the goal is enlightenment—ultimate perfection of the soul—and texts exist for both men and women to study and practise for attaining this goal. *The Lotus Sutra*, a primary text in Buddhist scripture, has influence as a unifying law or truth in Buddhism throughout Asia, including China, Korea, and Japan. The gender imagery in this text provides an inconsistent portrayal of women. Although it states that all people possess a Buddha-nature, and that women, as well as men, are capable of enlightenment, there are also passages suggesting that women are dangerous sources of sexual temptation.

Christianity and Islam teach direct individual immortality, with the soul experiencing punishment or reward in accordance with the virtues and vices of a single lifetime. These religions strongly espouse the idea that souls are essentially without sex and that salvation is open to both women and men. Some souls, because of unusual virtue, become saints. They continue to provide blessings for the living who appeal to them. Fiorenza (1979, 140) argues that "the lives of the saints provide a variety of role models for Christian women. What is more important is that they teach that women, like men, have to follow their vocation from God even if this means that they have to go frontally against the ingrained cultural mores and images of women."

Goddesses. Some feminists feel that the social position of women can be enhanced by the worship of a goddess and that belief in a female deity would give religion more usefulness and meaning. Such leading theologians and feminists as Mary Daly (1973), Carol Christ (1979, 1987), Naomi Goldenberg (1979), Judith Plaskow (1990), Rosemary Radford Ruether (2007), and Maureen Fiedler (2010) have taken this position. They believe that the image of the deity people worship is important to their understanding and appreciation of themselves. In patriarchal religions, divinity is male; hence, men see an image of themselves in the divine, while women are denied this identification with divinity.

Many people believe that the supernatural world consists of elevated regions inhabited by deities of wider sway than spirits, saints, and ghosts. This cosmos is generally perceived to be inhabited by a number of divine persons. The goddess is sometimes envisaged as a threatening and terrible being. This is the case with the Inuit goddess Sedna. In Hinduism, the goddess is Kali, whose orgiastic dancing brings death and destruction on the world. However, when she submits to her husband, Shiva, the goddess becomes beneficent, and her energy is harnessed for good by the rational principle of maleness. In the countryside, peasants in the nineteenth century prayed to Kali alone as the good mother.

Tamed and controlled, a goddess may become a great and well-loved figure, worthy of the worship of men as well as women. Some goddesses, known only in a small geographical space, are respected by local inhabitants because of their protection of the local people and the land (Monaghan 2011). Goddesses and goddess-like figures are found in all cultures throughout the world.

Buddhism provides a focus for worshippers in figures of *bodhisattvas*, personages whose perfection has freed them from mortal life but who choose to remain in a personalized existence in order to be accessible to the appeals of the struggling faithful. The greatest and most popular of all is Avalokitesvara, the bodhisattva of compassion, who appears as a goddess in one manifestation. Avalokitesvara originated in India but is worshipped in Tibet as Chenresig, in China as Gaunyin, in Japan as Kannon, and by other names throughout Asia. Guanyin is the very quintessence of the compassion of the Buddha. Pregnant women turn to her for help.

In the great polytheistic religions of later antiquity, goddesses appear with a variety of powers and attributes. They are patronesses of cities (Athena), marriage (Hera), and sex (Aphrodite). They are in charge of agriculture (Demeter) and human fertility (Artemis). Isis was an amalgam of female deities of the Mediterranean world, gathering their attributes, powers, and myths into her own cult. She began as a local Egyptian goddess associated with the cult of Osiris, who was both her brother and husband. By Hellenistic times, when the Greeks ruled Egypt, her cult was one of the most popular in the ancient world, promising immortality to its adherents. Women were active participants in the cult of Isis as priestesses, members of religious societies, and donors. However, male participants far outnumbered females, and the chief priesthoods were held by men (Pomeroy 1975).

In the sixth century BCE, Jews returning to the Holy Land from their exile in Babylon enforced their belief in one male divinity, outlawing the worship of all other gods and goddesses. When European pagans became Christians, they turned their backs on the gods and goddesses of the Greek and Roman worlds, reducing them to hollow idols. Some second-century Christians favoured endowing the Holy Ghost with a feminine persona; this impulse was rejected by the dominant faction, and all three persons of the Christian Trinity became male or without gender. In the seventh century, Muslims in their turn rejected the goddesses of their ancient Arabian roots in favour of the one (male) god.

For most ordinary worshippers, however, monotheistic religions have not entirely excluded the older idea of a female deity. For example, Christians exalted the memory and attributes of Mary, "mother of God (Jesus)," in direct proportion as God himself became increasingly patriarchal (Fiorenza 1979, 1983).

Box 10.2 Key Issues

Feminist Goddess Worship Today

What often began as more "secular" consciousness-raising groups turned into ritual circles creating a spiritual practice unique to each group. The rites conducted within these ritual circles are usually focused on the everyday experiences of women. Often, reproductive activities are highlighted: celebrations of menarche, menstruation, birthing and menopause. But other events such as divorce, abortion, and recovery from rape are ritually recognized often through rites of healing and renewal. . . . Small, non-hierarchical groups are the ideal of these ritual circles so that all women can be intimately involved in the ritual procedure (as opposed to the model of priest and congregation). The non-hierarchical model also allows each woman to form her own belief system rather than be told what to believe; in Feminist Goddess Worship, every woman is her own priestess.

Source: From Chris Klassen, *Storied Selves: Shaping Identity in Feminist Witchcraft*. Lanham: Lexington Books, 2008, 17–18.

Modern-day feminist goddess worship focuses on femaleness, the female body, healing, nature, tolerance, and independence from any central authority. Feminist goddess worship promotes healing and empowerment free from the oppression and pain of male dominance. Rituals serve as a tool to contact the sacred and to align with nature. There is typically no appointed leader during the ritual, and all women are considered priestesses (see Box 10.2) (Stuckey 2010).

The position of women in **polytheistic** societies varies widely, as did the position of women in ancient Egypt, Athens, and Rome. Similarly, there is such wide variation in the position of women in monotheistic societies that it becomes difficult to generalize about the influence of women's roles on beliefs about the gender of God and vice versa. Not everyone is convinced, then, that a female deity is needed to improve the status and position of women in society or that belief in such a deity would support that goal. Some argue that it is necessary to recognize both "masculine" and "feminine" attributes in the objects of worship.

Beyond the Gender Binary in Religions

While God in the Abrahamic religions (Judaism, Christianity, and Islam) is generally depicted and referred to as male (e.g. "He"), earlier thought was that God was beyond gender, sometimes being seen as inhabiting both male and female forms, sometimes a mix of both in one form, and sometimes as being something entirely different. Jewish mystics, for example, saw God as androgynous. Similarly, several Christian saints did not conform to a gender binary. Some were ciswomen, such as Saint Eugene and Saint Marius, who lived as men, though whether this is because they were transgender or because of the societal limitations placed on being a women is unknown (see Box 10.4 on Saint Joan of Arc). Others are more ambiguous figures, such as Saint Wilgefortis, who was a bearded woman.

In several First Nations in Canada, as was discussed in Chapter 4, two-spirited people were recognized as a revered third gender. The term was first used in Winnipeg in 1990, and is a translation of an Ojibwa term *niizh manitoag*. They were believed to have the spirit of both man and woman in their bodies, and were often visionaries, healers, and conductors of mourning rites, or performed tasks outside of prescribed gender roles (for example, a woman who is two-spirited engaging in tribal warfare). There are depictions of two-spirited people having strong mystical powers. Today, many Indigenous groups in Canada use the term *two-spirited* to refer to their members who are lesbian, gay, bisexual, transgender, intersex, or other gendered (Rainbow Resource Centre 2008). While no longer a distinctly religious role, there is a level of spirituality in the term.

In the African diaspora, several religions include gods and goddesses with more genders beyond the binary. As one example, Olokun is an androgynous ocean deity of the Yoruba people. Examples could continue indefinitely from religions around the world; religion is not a gender-binary space.

The Non-religious

While many women acknowledge religion or spirituality as important, there are many women who identify as non-religious. Why do some women and men choose not to believe in or practise a religion? In the eighteenth century, the intellectual movement known as the Enlightenment offered a critique of the abuse of church and state, as well as the intolerance prevalent throughout Europe. Instead, the Age of Enlightenment advocated the application of reason and science to solving society's problems. The Enlightenment movement gained many adherents, who played important roles in the profound changes that shaped how people in Europe and in the North American colonies organized their social and political systems. The growth and advancement of science and technology increased economic development and growth, which provided individuals with higher standards of living and well-being. As economic growth expanded, people's lives improved materially, and they became less reliant on religion. In general, people tend to be less religious in societies in which daily survival is not a problem, and these states gave rise to secularism. Secularism advocates the separation of church and state, the right to be free of a government-imposed religion, the right to be free from religious rules and teachings, and political decision making free of religious influence. The non-religious incorporates a broad spectrum of beliefs concerning the existence of a supreme being and attitudes toward religious practice. It also includes the anti-religious or anti-clerical (those who are hostile to religion or religious authorities), agnostics (those who remain skeptical about the existence of God and the importance of religion), and atheists or secular humanists (those who reject religion and the belief in the existence of deities). In Canada the 2011 census reported that 23.9 per cent of Canadians described themselves as secular, an increase from 16.2 per cent in 2001. The highest number of self-described secularists live in Yukon (49.9 per cent) and British Columbia (44.1 per cent), and the smallest number in Newfoundland and Labrador (6.2 per cent) (Statistics Canada 2012a).

Religion and Social Controls

Religion provides more than the imagery by which people can conceptualize the supernatural world. It provides a basis for a code of ethics to govern human conduct. In highly organized religions, clergy and other specialists interpret and sometimes enforce a code of ethics grounded in religious belief. However, all religious systems have some means for exerting control over human conduct.

Religion and the Family

Laws concerning family matters, particularly marriage, child rearing, and sexual relations, nearly always refer to religious beliefs. In most large-scale societies, such laws have supported patriarchal structures. Some nations bow to the more conservative rights of religious minorities to adhere to "tradition" (usually to the detriment of women's rights), while others override these group rights to protect women (Foblets 1999; Anantnarayan 2010; Htun and Weldon 2011; see Howland 1999 for many international examples of family law and religion).

Sexual Controls. At puberty in most cultures, the freedom girls might have enjoyed when they were little is sharply curtailed. Adolescent girls may be told that they are unclean and must learn to control the possible ill effects of their "polluted nature." At the same time, they may be schooled in the hard facts of their vulnerability to both public censure and physical attack. The leaders of every major literate religion in the world have produced literature against the sexuality of women. Representatives of the major religious hierarchies have continually urged women to contain themselves within the narrow limits of their homes and the narrower limits of female modesty and decorum, threatening them with both earthly and eternal punishments for the sins of their "nature."

The most effective method of controlling the dangers represented by women's sexuality is to ensure that they are kept under the authority of their male kin. At puberty, men are proclaimed mature and ready to undertake public responsibilities. Some societies begin a process of weakening the control of the father over his son at this point, to free the son for service in the greater community. Women, however, are not released from their fathers' power; rather, fathers (or other male kin) are given the right to hand them over to the power of a husband. In Christian societies that defended the individual's right of consent to marriage, the economic dependence of daughters still usually made them subject to paternal authority.

Religious laws in patriarchal societies often protect men from the "dangers" of pollution inherent in close proximity to women during their menstrual periods. In the Quran, the sacred book of Islam, men are ordered to separate themselves from their wives until the women have taken the ritual bath (Box 10.3) at the end of the menstrual period (Delaney et al. 1976). The same religious proscription on sexual relations between husband and wife applies to Orthodox Jews. Some feminists argue that such laws reinforce women's own fears about menstruation and undermine their self-esteem by labelling them as periodically "unclean." However, some adherents to these religions feel quite differently about them. These women feel that the ritual bath enhances their self-regard, the sanctity of their marriages, and even the warmth of their relationships with their husbands.

The codes of most religions urge husbands to use their authority prudently. They warn of the damage that may be caused to a family by the despair of unhappy women. They remind men of the blessings of a home cared for by a contented wife. However, while men are subjected to moral suasion, women are subjected to physical coercion. Nearly every written religious code is based on double-standard morality. Christianity, whose rhetoric consistently states that what is not allowed to women is not allowed to men either, has never made wide practical application of the rule.

Control over women's sexuality and reproduction is a high priority for what are called "conservative religious" groups (Brown 1994). Conservative religions consist of groups of people who challenge the authority of governments, oppose specific laws or reforms, or impose ideas

Box 10.3 In Her Own Words

The Ritual Bath: Positive and Negative

Rachel's experience [with the Jewish observance of mikveh, the ritual bath taken after menstruation] has been one of relative ease. Still even for Rachel, a New York City professional in her 40s, mikveh has always been a "mixed bag . . ."

Rachel says "I don't resent having to go." She finds something powerful about total immersion in water, a substance connected to the flood of Jewish history and the miracle of the parting sea.

When she emerges from her seventh dunk, she recites personal prayers. Concerning the label, "impuro," which defines women during niddah, Rachel says: "I really don't think about it at all. It's not on my radar screen."

When Rachel was younger, in child-bearing mode, she says, "every menstrual cycle became a missed opportunity for life as opposed to seeing myself as impure."

Asked if the observance strengthens her marriage, Rachel closes her eyes to the din of the Upper West Side Starbucks. She thinks.

"Yes, I do," she answers. "There is an element of longing. I liken it to a business trip. When I'm away I miss my husband."

During the days of niddah, before Rachel goes to the mikveh, when physical intimacy with her husband isn't possible, she senses a different dynamic in her marriage. "It makes it easier to talk because you know that's all you are going to do."

[On the negative side], she complains of the long wait at her local mikveh. . . . Often Rachel spends three hours there.

"Even if you have a miraculous experience, even if the spiritual mikveh lady is there, you leave praying your husband hasn't fallen asleep. What kind of date is that?"

Source: ©Elicia Brown. By Permission. Excerpted from "Immersed in a Dilemma," *The Jewish Week* Nov. 14, 2003, 62.

derived from their interpretations of established religions on others who do not share their beliefs. Women represent holy motherhood, their virtue reflecting the purity of the group and their subservience, the source of strength and dignity of men.

Protection of Women. While religious laws can justify authority and preach obedience, they also restrain human authority in the name of a higher power and teach the limits on an insubordinate will.

In this spirit, Jewish, Christian, and Islamic laws are concerned with the economic responsibilities of men toward their wives and daughters. The rights of women to dowries, inheritance, and other economic protections are spelled out carefully. Arbitrary divorce is discouraged, and polygyny is regulated to ensure the rights of co-wives. Catholic canon law sanctifies the consensual basis of marriage and protects wives from repudiation by husbands while discouraging divorce. It defines rape as a crime of violence against women and denies men the right to kill their wives. All the "peoples of the Book" are urged to protect and support widows and orphans and to treat moral and observant women with respect and kindness.

Within that framework, religion acts to establish and enforce the norms of family life. Sexual relationships between wife and husband resulting in the birth of children are universally viewed as divinely ordained. Deviation from that pattern is sometimes considered immoral and sometimes violently punished. While many religious constraints on women were rationalized as being for their protection, this notion has been challenged by feminist critics and sometimes rethought. An Algerian Muslim scholar's analysis has concluded that the function of the veil at the time of Muhammad was to protect women, and thus the veil's most appropriate modern equivalent is education and schooling, which in modern times give the most protection to a woman (Helie-Lucas 1999, 24).

Beyond the Family

Outside the religious activities of the family, most societies engage in a wider set of ceremonies, celebrations, and rituals devoted to the deities worshipped in the community. These require the services of a professional and trained clergy who enjoy the accoutrements of public art and architecture, conduct time-consuming and often occult rituals (sometimes in a language unknown to the laity), and make use of an extensive tradition of myth and law to enforce their social authority.

Women as Worshippers. Nearly all religions encourage, indeed command, the active participation of women as worshippers. Even as worshippers, though, women are subjected to a variety of restrictions. Lay participation in the performance of rituals is often restricted to men.

Yet underneath the restrictive and apparently prohibitive structure of the major world religions is the elusive, often undocumented world of women. From earliest times, for example, Christian moralists complained about women's habit of using the church as a social centre. Similarly, the shrines of Sufi saints are centres where Islamic women meet daily for rest and relaxation and to confide in the sympathetic saint (Fernea and Fernea 1972).

Religious Movements and Their Impact on Women. Religion often becomes a vehicle for social change. In some cases this involves the formation of a new religious movement or the joining of an existing one. Today, unlike in the past, such movements are not necessarily labelled "heretical" and might not risk their members' lives and freedom, but they are often called by pejorative terms, such as *cult*, and feared by mainstream religious groups and secular people alike. Religious movements, whether conservative or not, tend to protest and challenge contemporary social conditions, critiquing family and society as well as established religious institutions (Palmer 1994; Puttick 1997; Anderson and Young 2010).

Some such movements, known as "new religious movements," may offer women the means to escape traditional family and community constraints and provide alternatives to these structures. In the West, new religious movements are often inspired by Eastern religions, while in the East, (but not always) they are sometimes inspired by Western ones. Others, more conservative or even reactionary in character, seek to establish or re-establish traditional structures and roles, placing women in subordinate positions and confining them to the roles of homemaker, wife, and mother. Generally, these latter identify themselves with mainstream religions such as Christianity or Islam yet criticize them for their liberalism and acceptance of "modernism."

At the end of the twentieth century, the world witnessed a resurgence of political activism motivated by religious beliefs. Western discourse has tended to label such ideas and actions as "fundamentalism" and applied the term primarily to events, actors, and movements in the Global South, especially in the context of Islam and Middle Eastern countries. Western discourse has erroneously labelled Islam as fundamentalist and highlighted only the extreme forms. The tendency in the West has been to point out the Taliban refusal to let girls go to school or to work, the imposition of the burka on Afghan females, and laws prohibiting women from driving in Saudi Arabia as evidence of the lack of human rights for women in Islamic countries and their second-class status in their societies. But these examples are not representative of all Muslim countries. As a counter-example, in terms of the record in North America for electing women presidents or prime ministers, compared to some predominantly Muslim countries North America comes off looking far more prohibitive for women. Examples of female government leaders in Muslim countries are Sheikh Hasina, prime minister of Bangladesh, and Atifete Jahjaga, former president of Kosovo (Queiro 2014).

The word *fundamentalism* was originally a term certain US conservative Christians applied to themselves (Hawley 1994); it has now come to be applied to other religious movements. At the root of conservative or fundamentalist movements is a disappointment with modernity and a fear that modernity, with its emphasis on secularism, has pushed religion to the sidelines of modern society (K. Armstrong 2001). In the Global South, modernity, often imposed through the expansion of imperialism, colonialism, and globalization, denigrated and undermined Indigenous traditions and cultures. In the Global North, the rise of conservatism also results from a fear of modernity as well as fear of losing social, political, and economic power and control, and therefore being unable to influence social and economic forces (Boden 2007). In response, conservative religious groups and individuals have challenged secularist ideals and practices such as the separation of church and state and the belief in the right of people to be free of state religion. Rather than being a relic of some historical past, fundamentalism represents the flipside of modernity (K. Armstrong 2001). The conservatively religious reject some, if not all, aspects of feminist theories and emphasize conventional roles for women. In the Global North, conservative religious groups oppose abortion and contraceptive rights for women, same-sex marriage, and female sexual autonomy (Wald and Calhoun-Brown 2007). In the United States in the 1970s, Christian conservative groups spearheaded a movement against and eventually defeated the Equal Rights Amendment that would have enshrined equal rights for women in the US Constitution (Young 2008).

Transnationally, conservative organizations in the Global North have joined forces with their conservative counterparts in the Global South to develop a transnational conservative counter-network to undermine transnational feminist efforts to improve women's rights globally. In a number of United Nations conferences pertaining to women, population, and human rights, a transnational conservative network coordinated their efforts to weaken women's rights on issues involving sexuality, equality, and gender. This transnational conservative network comprised organizations such as the Organization of the Islamic Conference, the Catholic Family and Rights Institute, and the National Right to Life Committee, along with the Vatican, and was supported by conservative governments (e.g. Morocco, Nicaragua, and Iran) (Chappell 2006).

Fundamentalist or conservative values are not found only among the religious. Conservativism or fundamentalism exists among secularists. While secular societies often portray themselves as liberal, tolerant, and upholding the human rights of women and men, recently the rise of secular conservatism in Western societies has been accompanied by ideas, policies, and actions that can be considered illiberal, intolerant, and a violation of women's human rights. In 2004 the French Parliament passed a law prohibiting the wearing of headscarves to schools, a law primarily affecting Muslim girls. A few years later, France's lower house of Parliament overwhelmingly approved a bill that would ban wearing the full Islamic veil in public (Fraser 2010). This was a significant vote as it identified the religious dress (burka and/or niqab) as an outward sign of religious persecution against women. On the other hand, such bans deny women the right to make their own decisions about their lives, force women to choose between their religious beliefs and whether they can work or go to school, and deny women their right to self-expression and religious freedom (Najmabadi 2006; Sunderland 2012). Scott opines that the headscarf ban gives the appearance of gender equality in France but masks and ignores the continued denial of formal equality to women in the areas of jobs, wage discrimination, and preventing domestic violence (2007, 172). Similar attempts have been made in Quebec to follow France's example, with more divided results.

Efforts to overturn the "oppression" of Muslim women were woven into the justifications for the overthrow of the Taliban in Afghanistan in 2001 and of the Iraqi government in 2003, as well as motions put forward in Canada to prevent women in burka or niqab from swearing the citizenship oath. Such efforts replicate past interventions and the continuation of "the colonial gaze." Abu-Lughod explores the issue of the salvation rhetoric (saving Muslim women from their culture and religion) and how it is used to justify intervention, the war on terrorism, and the installation of regimes more sympathetic to the West, and asks whether "Muslim women really need saving" (Abu-Lughod 2002). Political efforts to use Islam as a hammer to engage in interventionist and imperialist practices have been questioned by Toor, who argues that often Western discourse on Islam essentializes Islamic societies (Toor 2011; Akbar and Oza 2013). Citing examples from Pakistan, Toor's research demonstrates the fluidity of Islamic practice and how the political and social elites ignore Islamic law when it is inconvenient or deploy it when it is useful for their social and political goals. Religion and culture are merely toolboxes used when they are convenient for societies and communities to uphold the moral, cultural, social, and political order (Toor 2011).

The issue of human rights, specifically women's human rights, lies at the centre of the debate about conservative religious movements (Howland 1999; Boden 2007). On the one hand, it seems obvious that certain international agreements concerning the rights of all people to a basic education, control over their bodies, and freedom to choose a mate, a job, or a form of religious expression are violated by a denial of these rights to women. On the other hand, multiculturalist societies often advocate respect for religious diversity and tolerance of religious practices which differ from one's own, and especially from those of the majority, but they have not always supported female religious minorities' rights to self-expression. As Boden argues, the choice between "authentic religion or human rights" is a false one. Religion and human rights address the human desire for justice, and the task remains to determine how communities of women can learn from each other (Boden 2007).

Political Persecution of Women. The late medieval period in Europe was a time of great social upheaval. From the fifteenth century on, women were perceived to behave in a variety of eccentric and unconventional ways. An example from the early fifteenth century (c. 1412–31) is Joan of Arc, who led troops of French soldiers against the invading English armies. The English burned her at the stake as a heretic and witch; however, the French honoured her memory as a martyr, and she was finally canonized by the Catholic Church (see Box 10.4).

Historians have recently been reinterpreting the great witch hunt (c. 1450–1750) in western Europe in light of the work of anthropologists on witchcraft in other cultures. The accused witches in eastern England, southwestern Germany, and Switzerland, for example, seem to have been the same sort of women accused in Africa and elsewhere outside Europe: elderly women, deprived of the protection of husbands or sons, living on the risky margins of society. These were the women who irritated and angered neighbours with efforts to gain assistance and ill-tempered cursing of the ungenerous.

During the medieval era, Europe, alongside the church, was a world of popular religion (Simpson 1994). Wise women devoted to healing and prophesying flourished, not unlike the female curers found in Roman Catholic countries in Latin America today. Medieval popular religion was full of vestiges of paganism, rituals, incantations, herbalism, and magic, both beneficial and malevolent. The medieval church systematically and successfully dealt with that religion. The harmless and beneficial practices of the country people were "Christianized"; for example, incantations to old goddesses were retained, with the names of Christian saints substituted. The demons of hell were reduced to mischief makers of limited intelligence and minimal power.

Another set of theories associates witchcraft with heresy. In this view, the sixteenth-century belief in demon worshippers and witch churches with covens, sabbaths, "black masses," and other paraphernalia of witchcraft developed as a result of the mentality of the Catholic Inquisition and the fear of women that the Protestant Reformation awoke.

Box 10.4 Women in Media

The Trial of Joan of Arc

Joan of Arc, at the instigation of "voices" sent by God, took up arms against the English occupation of France in 1428. Her military victories against the English began the process of ultimate French victory in the Hundred Years' War (1337–1453). She was captured by the English and tried. Her prosecutors dwelt particularly on her insistence on wearing male clothing:

> You have said that, by God's command, you have continually worn man's dress . . . that you have also worn your hair short, cut en rond [a "bowl" cut] above your ears, with nothing left that could show you to be a woman; and that on many occasions you received the Body of our Lord dressed in this fashion, although you have been frequently admonished to leave it off, which you have refused to do, saying that you would rather die than leave it off, save by God's command. And you said further that if you were still so dressed and with the king and those of his party, it would be one of the greatest blessings for the kingdom of France; and you have said that not for anything would you take an oath not to wear this dress or carry arms; and concerning all these matters you have said that you did well, and obediently to God's command.

Source: From W.S. Scott, editor and translator. *Trial of Joan of Arc*. London: Folio Society, 1968, 156. © The Folio Society, 1956. Reprinted by permission of the Folio Society.

There may indeed have been witch cults. One or two such groups have been uncovered. The women may have been religious visionaries or sexual nonconformists, rebels of one sort or another. These witches may have been women who had seized upon the illusion of religious and moral freedom that the Reformation seemed to offer, only to learn that the leaders of the new churches were no more welcoming than had been those of the old.

Women as Religious Leaders

Today, disparity continues in the practice of male-centred religious leadership. The most highly organized religions welcome women clergy the least. Thus, in Catholicism, the clergy has been restricted to not only men, but celibate men, since the eleventh century. Eastern Christianity (the Greek and Russian Orthodox churches) allows women to marry priests but not to be ordained. In some of the larger, institutionalized Protestant churches a growing number of women have been ordained: among the first were Shirley Jeffery (Presbyterian, 1968), Mary Mills (Anglican, 1969), and Lois Wilson (ordained in 1965, and the first woman Moderator of the United Church, 1980). In 2010, the Church of England's ruling body, after recognizing women deacons and priests for several years, decided to allow women to be ordained as bishops, a decision accompanied by controversy (BBC News 2010). In the twenty-first century, more women are breaking through the "stained glass ceiling," but they typically are found in associate positions and earn less pay and benefits than male religious leaders.

In the Roman Catholic Church, priests, bishops, archbishops—and of course the pope himself—are all males, and females are strictly prohibited from receiving the sacrament of Holy Orders, which confirms the person into life of holy service. Women can become nuns or sisters, but the true power in the Catholic Church lies in the priesthood. Although the reasons for this are said to date back to the apostles, the 12 male followers of Jesus Christ, little factual information regarding the prohibition of women into the priesthood is offered. In 2006, Fr. Roy Bourgeois, a Maryknoll priest, participated in the ordination of a woman priest, Janice Sevre-Duszynska. The Vatican told Fr. Bourgeois to recant his support of women priests, and this ordination was never officially recognized. The Vatican Congregation for the Doctrine of Faith issued a penalty of excommunication. Fr. Roy Bourgeois still advocates for the rights of women, stating that he believes the dismissal of women priests is committing a sexist act, which is a sin (Bourgeois 2011). Despite the Vatican's stance, Sevre-Duszynska is among 100 female priests and 11 female bishops to claim ordination from increasingly vocal priests and groups supporting the ordination of women.

Women tend to emerge as ministers in sects that do not control their clergy and that depend on genuine spontaneous religious

Toronto-based author Raheel Raza is the first Muslim woman in Canada to lead mixed gender prayers.

emotion, as opposed to a historically weighty establishment supported by endowments and state co-operation. Thus, women frequently minister in the more loosely organized Pentecostal or evangelical sects.

Since Jewish girls are not required by religious law to study the scriptures and sacred texts as boys are, in the past it was only the exceptional Jewish woman who qualified for the specialized learning of the rabbi. However, Judaism, like Protestant Christianity, lacks a single central hierarchy, so it allows for a proliferation of congregations of varying opinions on matters of administration and discipline. In Conservative and Reform Judaism, the predominant forms in North America, female rabbis are now ordained. Joan Friedman became the first woman to serve as rabbi in Canada (1980).

Islam, like Judaism, has no formal clergy and no institutional hierarchy. Mullahs and ayatollahs in the Shiite branch along with other teachers and prayer leaders serve many of the functions of clergy. The conventions of *purdah* (segregation of women) and *hijab* restrict Muslim women from participating in services and prayers with men. These same conventions have in some places given rise to a class of female mullahs whose job is to minister to women, to teach the rudiments of the Quran, and to conduct rituals with women at home. A few female adherents of Islam have led prayers to mixed-sex congregations in the United States, Canada, South Africa, and Great Britain, but such acts remain highly controversial and opposed by most Muslims, both male and female (Fiedler 2010).

In Hinduism, both women and men can be gurus, mystics, or sages—Gargi Vachaknavi, for example, was one of the first women known to be considered a sage, and is thought to be one of the authors of the Upanishads (the first of the three canonical texts of Hindu philosophy). Both women and men can also be appointed as either type of Hindu's main priests, *purohits* and *pujaris*. Despite it never being prohibited, it is rare for women to be appointed as a Hindu priest or named as a guru (Lobo 2014).

Healers

In folk traditions around the world, both in cities and in the countryside, women have served their communities as healers and midwives. These traditional arts are generally thought to have a supernatural or spiritual component as well as a practical one. Both illness and childbirth are widely viewed as spiritually dangerous states. Curers, sometimes termed shamans, are active in societies where it is believed that illness—or certain types of illness—is caused by supernatural agency. Both curers and midwives are thought to have esoteric knowledge about how to fend off or appease threatening supernatural beings. Traditional curers of this sort need not be exclusively female but often are, and midwifery almost everywhere is a women's profession.

Among the First Nations, women healers perform cures, lead hunting ceremonies, and create artifacts such as baskets, ornaments, and talismans. They officiate at burials, births, child namings, and menstrual and pregnancy rituals. The healers perform these rites through dancing and chanting as well as songs and stories. Indigenous women writers reflect in fiction and poetry the woman healer's connection to the spirit world (Allen 1988). One such work is the novel *The Woman Who Owned the Shadows* by Paula Gunn Allen (1983), and another is *Ceremony* by Leslie Marmon Silko (1977).

Missionaries and Martyrs

The large-scale religions of the world reflect the institutionalized worlds of men. However, they started as popular religions, often as sects of rebels against a greater system, as the Christians within the Roman Empire or the Buddhists in India. All have known periods of danger and persecution; all have entered into periods of struggle to win recognition for themselves. During these times, women often played significant roles.

While the role of a missionary is contentious, women have found favourable conditions for the expression of their zeal and spirit of adventure. Women were welcomed into the original Buddhist fellowships for their missionary contributions but later restricted as the religion became established and more secure (Carmody 1979). Likewise, women have enjoyed a long and honourable history in Christian missions. The Samaritan woman Jesus sent to spread news of his coming among her people might be called the first of all Christian missionaries (McNamara 1996). In the conversion of Europe, Christian queens opened the way for priests and monks by marrying pagan kings and converting them; the most famous of these was Clotilda, wife of Clovis, king of the Franks at the beginning of the sixth century CE (McNamara 1996). During colonialism missionaries often fulfilled a pacification role in subverting Indigenous cultures and religions and serving along with imperialist governors. Later, missionaries sometimes allied themselves with resistance movements, most notably in China and Central America.

Women's Impact on Religious Movements

A formal separation between church and state has not prevented special forms of dialogue between religious organizations and governments. Religious groups committed to major social reforms have spearheaded important political and legal changes; other religious groups, more conservative in orientation, have provided focal points for resistance and reaction. It was largely through their participation in religious groups, rather than in government itself, that women had a strong voice in political processes. In particular, feminism, with its call for women's rights and its role in other legislative reforms (most notably abolition of slavery and for suffrage), had a significant impact on the history of religion.

Protestant Denominations

Women emerged as religious leaders and reformers early in history in the notoriously intolerant

The Very Reverend Lois Wilson was ordained a United Church minister in 1965 and became the first woman moderator of the Church in 1980. She later served as co-president of the World Council of Churches, co-director of the Ecumenical Forum of Canada and chancellor of Lakehead University. In 1998 she was appointed to the Canadian Senate, where she served until 2002.

context of colonial North America. Anne Hutchinson, a Puritan woman from the Massachusetts Bay Colony, was banished for her refusal to stop preaching to mixed-sex groups. In 1638, she was driven out of Massachusetts with her husband and children and excommunicated from the Puritan community in Boston. She led her followers to Rhode Island, where she helped to establish a new colony and pursued her evangelical ministry. Her friend Mary Dyer, who supported her throughout her trials in Massachusetts, died on the gallows in 1660 for defending the Quakers who had begun to preach in the colony and for refusing to accept banishment (Dunn 1979).

The Quakers, or Society of Friends, believed in the equality of all people, including women and men. They opposed settlement on lands claimed by Indigenous peoples and particularly opposed the institution of slavery. Despite the hostility of the colonies to Quakerism, the movement spread. Nearly half the Quaker missionaries were women, mostly travelling without husbands and often with other women. They continued to travel and do missionary work through the seventeenth century. In these early years, while numbers of women's "meetings" (congregations) were established, there was some difference of opinion on how strong they should be or even how legitimate they were. Some women's meetings deferred to men; others were quite assertive of their autonomy and conducted their own affairs (Dunn 1979).

The Religious Society of Friends (Quakers) women's experience in the organization of religious meetings provided training in the public arena that few women of colonial or post-colonial times had an opportunity to gain. Friends became accustomed to public speaking, to creating organizational structures, and to feeling equal to others. Quakers were disproportionately represented among North American women abolitionists, feminists, and suffragists (Dunn 1979). Sarah Grimké (1792–1873), Angelina Grimké Weld (1805–1879), Lucretia Coffin Mott 1793–1880), and Dr Emily Stowe (1831–1903) were among the most famous of these women in the nineteenth century.

Christian Science, a late nineteenth-century sectarian religion, also supported women's rights. Its founder, Mary Baker Eddy (1821–1910), believed and preached that God is both masculine and feminine (Mary Baker Eddy Library 2011). She frequently referred to God in her writings as "Father–Mother God." Christian Science has a very successful and extensive establishment today, including its widely read newspaper, the *Christian Science Monitor*, published in Boston, and free reading rooms in towns and cities in Canada and throughout the world.

Many other women, black and white, rose to prominence and leadership in evangelical and revivalist movements in the nineteenth and twentieth centuries (Gilkes 1985; Blackwell 2001). Today, Holiness denominations are still working to keep women in clerical positions, drawing motivation from strong women leaders in their history (Teegarden 2011). Like Quakerism, the evangelical and revivalist movements have been a training ground for women activists, providing them with unique opportunities for public speaking and group organizing. Religious activity was practically the only important extrafamilial activity permitted to most women in the nineteenth and much of the twentieth centuries. Today there are societal

Box 10.5 In Her Own Words

Phillis Wheatley: "Thoughts on the Works of Providence"

Arise, my soul, on wings enraptur'd, rise

To praise the monarch of the earth and skies . . .

Creation smiles in various beauty gay,

While day to night, and night succeeds to day:

That *Wisdom*, which attends *Jehovah*'s ways,

Shines most conspicuous in the solar rays:

Without them, destitute of heat and light,

This world would be the reign of endless night:

In their excess how would our race complain,

Abhorring life! how hate its length'ned chain!

From air adust what num'rous ills would rise?

What dire contagion taint the burning skies?

What pestilential vapours, fraught with death,

Would rise, and overspread the lands beneath?

Hail, smiling morn, that from the orient main

Ascending dost adorn the heav'nly plain!

So rich, so various are thy beauteous dies,

That spread through all the circuit of the skies,

That, full of thee, my soul in rapture soars,

And thy great God, the cause of all adores . . .

Infinite *Love* where'er we turn our eyes

Appears: this ev'ry creature's wants supplies;

This most is heard in *Nature's* constant voice,

This makes the morn, and this the eve rejoice;

This bids the fost'ring rains and dews descend

To nourish all, to serve one gen'ral end,

The good of man: yet man ungrateful pays

But little homage, and but little praise.

To him, whose works array'd with mercy shine.

What songs should rise, how constant, how divine!

Source: From John C. Shields, editor, *The Collected Works of Phillis Wheatley*, 43–50. The Schomburg Library of Nineteenth-Century Black Women Writers, Henry Louis Gates, Jr., editor. New York: Oxford University Press, 1988.

forces that continue to encourage women to keep their main focus on religion, but women have been accepted as teachers in evangelical schools even in some more orthodox communities. Nevertheless, controversy and resistance still exist when a woman is thought to speak or teach with a certain amount of "authority" (Creegan and Pohl 2005).

Jewish Denominations

Jewish women contribute to religious life as professionals and through domestic activities. The heart of Judaism since the diaspora (exile from the Holy Land) has been the ritual of hearth and home. Of major importance to Jewish self-definition is *kashrut*, or purity, particularly of diet. It is the responsibility of religious Jewish women to keep kitchens *kosher*, to see that meat and milk are not mixed and that the family consumes no "unclean" foods such as pork or shellfish or improperly butchered meats. Women prepare the festive foods for holidays and most particularly for the celebration each week of the Sabbath. The conduct of traditional Jewish life is completely dependent on women's perpetuation of religious traditions in the home.

In 1988, Conservative Judaism moved women to the focal point by declaring that the home was the centre of Jewish religious life. Various Jewish women's groups, particularly charity organizations, provide an arena for major public activities. The National Council of Jewish Women of Canada was formed in 1897 to foster the rights of women and other disenfranchised groups. Hadassah, founded in 1912 in the US and in Canada in 1917, became a prominent charity. These organizations and others like them provide vehicles for women to learn how to organize, how to manage money, and how to raise funds; they raise and distribute millions of dollars in the causes they espouse.

Some women have turned to Kabbalah, a mystical offshoot of Rabbinic Judaism, to find a woman-centred approach to spirituality. Traditional kabbalistic beliefs posit that God has both male and female aspects and that the female divine element, the *shekhina*, plays a crucial role. While the prevalent understanding of God is synonymous with "male" and "power," the Torah includes descriptions of God as a mother caring for *his* children, and Isaiah describes God as a "midwife," "nurse," and "protective mother eagle." This Jewish feminist notion of God, which centres on women's power to create a strong sense of self, to destroy feelings of inferiority, and to transform the self attempts to address the conflicts of contemporary Jewish women through a more balanced spiritual practice (Besserman 2005).

Roman Catholicism

Roman Catholic women have had the option of following a "vocation" in religion by becoming nuns. As nuns, women have played a number of influential roles in their countries' life, particularly in education and nursing. Today, nuns may be women in street clothes, who may or may not wear symbolic head coverings and crosses. They are found no longer only in the shadows of a cloister but also in public places. Since medieval times, nuns have held professional responsibilities in education and attending the sick and elderly, but today they are also found in executive positions, managing self-supporting philanthropic or educational institutions and projects.

The decision to join a convent and become a nun may be prompted by expectations for the future that have nothing to do with religion. For a poor Catholic girl, convent life has long meant moving to another class with privileges that she would not have if she remained in secular life. She might be seeking an orderly and secure life where education is offered, friendship of sisters is promised, and marriage and children are prohibited. Organized religions do offer spiritual security and, above all, ethical and moral codes that are time tested. Catholic women have choices to make and require the freedom to follow their sincere beliefs.

Collectively, nuns in North America have challenged the male hierarchical model of leadership within the Roman Catholic Church. The Leadership Conference of Women Religious (LCWR), an organization comprising more than three-quarters of all US Catholic nuns, has called on the Church to engage in dialogue on issues such as artificial birth control and the ordination of females. This group has worked in partnership with its Canadian counterpart, the Catholic Network for Women's Equality, to gain the ear of the Vatican and the general public across North America (Catholic Network for Women's Equality n.d.). Their desire to make Catholicism more inclusive of secular and religious women has placed them in conflict with the Church. In response to the LCWR's request for dialogue on these matters, the Vatican accused the nuns of taking positions different from those of the Church (Birnbaum 2012) and took oversight of the nuns' organization until 2015.

In following Christian beliefs, Indigenous women often find themselves in conflict: some of their ancestral traditions are at the opposite pole from the monotheistic/patriarchal scriptures of Judeo-Christianity. The Native American (Laguna Pueblo) scholar Paula Gunn Allen (1939–2008) asserted that "traditional tribal lifestyles are more often gynocratic than not, and they are never patriarchal" (Allen 1988, 2). One can begin to judge the basic conflicts that arose when Native Americans were gradually converted to Christianity by missionaries and conquerors. The work of Mary TallMountain (1918–1994, Athabascan) demonstrates the "difficult and uneasy alliance between the pagan awareness that characterized tribal thought and the less earthy, more judgmental view of medieval Christianity" (Allen 1988, 172). TallMountain was a devout Roman Catholic, and her poetry reveals the conflict between her faith and her tribal awareness (TallMountain 1981).

Hinduism

One of the older and more successful movements in Hinduism was the *bhakti* movement, which took place between the sixth and seventeenth centuries CE in India. The *bhakti* movement sought to liberalize the process of religious worship, claiming that a personal relationship with the divine was more spiritual than the following of particular rules, regulations, or social ordering. For this reason, the *bhakti* movement went against the strict caste systems of Hinduism. The period is characterized by writings of poet-saints, many of whom were women (Women in World History, n.d.). One example is Mirabai, or Mira, from the sixteenth century, whose story is known mostly from her own poetry. As a child, Mira had a vision of the god Krishna and vowed that she would forever be his wife. Despite her wishes, her family arranged her marriage at a young age. Mira refused to accept her legal husband, insisting that Krishna was her true husband. There are numerous legends around Mira's struggles with her and her husband's families, in which she is depicted as truly pious and devoted. She eventually went on a pilgrimage to Brindaban, where Krishna was worshipped. Initially spiritual leaders there would not accept her presence, because she was a woman, but her piety eventually won them over and she was included within the community of saints of Brindaban (Biography Online, n.d.).

Islam: Piety Movement

The women's Mosque Movement, or Piety Movement, emerged in Egypt in the 1970s in response to the modernization and secularization of society. A group of middle-class, educated women formed a revivalist movement that returns to Islamic traditions of piety. In this movement, women learn that they cannot separate morality and piety from the ways in which they dress and comport themselves physically; simply believing and practising Islam is not enough. Although religious instruction is very important, it is through the body and the ritual repetition of particular behaviours that women ultimately achieve piety. For example, weeping during prayer expresses the pious virtue of fear of God and at the same time produces that fear. In an echo of Judith Butler's observations about gender, women in the mosque movement believe that continual and precise repetition of physical acts creates emotional and spiritual engagement with faith, so that over time virtuous practice becomes unconscious and inevitable (Mahmood 2005, 139). This phenomenon challenges Western ideas about what it means to be a woman with agency.

Modesty is one of the virtues that Muslim women seek to cultivate, and veiling is the practice that not only expresses modesty but produces it. As anthropologist Saba Mahmood writes of participants in the mosque movement:

> While wearing the veil serves at first as a means to tutor oneself in the attribute of shyness, it is also simultaneously integral to the practice of shyness: one cannot simply discard the veil once a modest deportment has been acquired, because the veil itself is part of what defines that deportment. This is a crucial aspect of the disciplinary program pursued by the participants of the mosque movement, the significance of which is elided when the veil is understood solely in terms of its symbolic value as a marker of women's subordination or Islamic identity. (Mahmood 2005, 158)

By advocating for piety in dress and comportment, Egyptian women seek to retain Islamic values throughout all sectors of their society (Mahmood 2005).

Feminist Contributions to Religious Change

While women exhibit diversity in their beliefs and practices, it is important to recognize that women in new religious movements represent an expression of dissatisfaction with the status quo in society and an attempt to repair its ills through religion.

Religious change comes from many different sources and in many different forms. For example, the Woman's Christian Temperance Union brought significant support to the fight for enfranchisement in Canada (see Chapter 12).

Rabbi Lisa Grushcow became Canada's first female rabbi appointed to a "senior" position (her synagogue has over 1000 members) when she was appointed in 2012 to lead Temple Emanu-El-Beth Sholom in Montreal. She also was Canada's first openly gay congregational rabbi.

In addition to changing the language of devotion, feminists developed new versions of traditional rituals. They took out the sexist bases of general rituals and added new rituals for women to complement those specifically intended for men. For example, some Jewish women wrote a complement to the boy's *brit milah* to bring their daughters into the covenant (Plaskow 1979). Aviva Cantor (1979) composed a woman's *Haggadah*, a version of the Jewish Passover text that traditionally celebrates freedom from slavery and oppression, while others developed Sabbath prayers for women (Janowitz and Wenig 1979).

Feminist theologians and philosophers address the deeper issues of belief and practice in all the world religions, including Buddhism (Gross 1999; Peach 2002), Confucianism (Woo 1999; Heisook 2009), and Islam (Hassan 1999; Helie-Lucas 1999; Badawi 2003). For some religious feminists, the old traditions are insufficient, even when revised. Some feminists continue to dismiss spirituality as irrevocably flawed in its patriarchal ideology. There are feminist sects within Judaism, Christianity, and Islam trying to bring about change, although this pursuit is often met with contention and hostility. Some feminists have chosen to blaze their own trail, cultivating a history and practices of feminist goddess worship (Stuckey 2010). Others, while looking for spiritual growth and healing, and finding the established religions outmoded, look to mysticism, paganism, and other sources to create new religions. They believe that "the margin may also be the leading edge, whose experiments create the future" (Puttick 1997, 2). They may, in fact, have had an impact in some areas, most discernibly in the incorporation of respect for the environment into religious doctrines as well as the promotion of alternative medicine and health approaches.

Summary

Religion and society affect each other. As societies become more complex and hierarchical, so do their religious institutions. In societies that deny leadership roles to women, religious institutions do so too. Religious beliefs about what is "good behaviour" influence societies.

Despite their devalued status in religion, women have been active participants in religions throughout history. Many women focus on certain aspects of religion that appeal to their concerns and evolve from their beliefs and practices. "Popular" versions of traditional religions often provide scope for women's activities.

Some ancient religions included goddess worship and gave priestesses status. The origin myths of many of the major religions support the dominant religious and social roles of men. Most religions have conceptions of supernatural beings, and females are featured among them. These beings may be souls, saints, ghosts, and goddesses. The goddess is often envisaged as a threatening being who is tamed and controlled by being linked to a male god. Some feminists believe that worship of a female God would enhance women's social position.

Religious codes govern human conduct and exert social controls. Life-cycle rituals for men enhance their power and status in the community, but the wedding ceremony, the most important ritual for women in patrilineal societies, serves to shift control over women from father to husband.

Religious leaders in many societies attempt to control female sexuality by urging women to stay within the home and to be modest and decorous. Many religious laws require women and men to be separate during the menstrual period. Religious codes also protect women and promote family life and procreation.

In public worship, women are subject to a number of controls. They are frequently prohibited from lay participation in rituals and sometimes segregated from men. Even so, it is women who spend the most hours of devotion in organized religion.

The most highly organized religions are the least welcoming to women as clergy. Many women find that they can play far more active roles in the religions that are on the fringes of or in conflict with "established" religion. Often, women emerge as preachers or leaders of these sects. Women have also served the various religions as missionaries and martyrs.

Women have also been active as rebels in religious movements, probably because they have often seen rebellion as the only means of winning more liberation for themselves. During the Reformation in Europe and North America, women heretics were frequently accused of being witches. Some women have found fulfillment in religions through an idiosyncratic approach. Mysticism and possession by spirits are both highly personal expressions of religion.

Women, especially Quakers, were among the early religious leaders and reformers. In nineteenth century North America, women had important parts to play in the founding and organization of the Shakers, Christian Scientists, Seventh-Day Adventists, and a number of evangelical movements. Jewish women and Muslim women have been responsible for maintaining religious traditions in the home and are active in the public arena by means of various religious women's groups. Canadian nuns have played influential roles in education and nursing, especially in the early history of Quebec.

Feminists have contributed to religious change and today are developing new versions of traditional rituals while adding new rituals for women.

Discussion Questions

1. Nearly everyone receives some religious education—in the home, in school, in church or other formal religious institution, in the community at large—on both a conscious and an unconscious level. If this includes you, what do you think you learned about relations between women and men from this background? What were the sources of what you learned (sacred texts, ritual, prayer, your parents)?
2. How do you see religion represented in popular culture or in the media? Do you find a particular religion ascribed to individuals?
3. What have been the arguments concerning the gender of God? Do you have an opinion? If so, what is your view and why?
4. When you read the descriptions in Boxes 10.2 and 10.5, what seems to you to be the different conceptions of deity described by Klassen and Wheatley?

Recommended Resources

Anderson, Leona, and Pamela Dickey Young, eds. 2015. *Women and Religious Traditions*. New York: Oxford University Press. A critical inquiry into the study of women in religion from historical, psychological, political, and sociological perspectives. It includes studies of major world religions as well as newer ones that focus on the notion of the Goddess.

Beaman, Lori G., ed. 2012. *Religion and Canadian Society: Contexts, Identities, and Strategies*. Toronto: Canadian Scholars Press. The text offers a historical overview of the role of religion in Canada and discusses three central themes: contexts, identities, and strategies. Notions of cultural diversity, gendered aspects of religion and sexuality, definitions, and challenges are explored throughout.

Dickey Young, Pamela, Heather Shipley, and Tracy J. Trothen, eds. 2015. *Religion and Sexuality: Diversity and the Limits of Tolerance*. Vancouver: University of British Columbia Press. This text challenges the commonly held assumption that religion's relationship to sexuality is solely bound up with regulation. In this provocative examination of both sexual and religious diversity, chapters go beyond the familiar debates over tolerance and accommodation to explore the ways in which various forms of religious affiliation and sexual identity do, in fact, coexist.

Hamdan, Amani. 2011. *Muslim Women Speak: A Tapestry of Lives and Dreams*. Toronto: Women's Press. This volume challenges essentialist notions of Muslim women and their roles in family, faith, and community within a Canadian and transnational context. Testimonies reveal the diverse lives of Muslim women and the complexities of their lived experience

Lee, Becky R., and Terry Tak-ling, eds. 2015. *Canadian Women Shaping Diasporic Religious Identities*. Waterloo, ON: Wilfred Laurier Press. This collection of essays explores how women from a variety of religious and cultural communities have preserved and transformed their cultures in contemporary Canada. Each essay explores the ways in which the religiosities of women serve as locations for both the assertion and the refashioning of individual and communal identity in transcultural contexts.

Marcos, Sylvia, et al., eds. 2010. *Women and Indigenous Religions*. Santa Barbara, CA: Praeger. Taking a global view of the theme, the book addresses the complex tensions between Indigenous traditions and gender and female authority in religion or spiritual matters. Includes examples from India, Korea, Mexico, and Turtle Island (Canada).

Stuckey, Johanna H. 2010. *Women's Spirituality: Contemporary Feminist Approaches to Judaism, Christianity, Islam and Goddess Worship*. Toronto: Inanna Publications and Education. Examines the religious traditions around the world and sheds light on the role of women's spirituality within these religions. It also speaks to the history and experiences of the marginalization of women in the context of mainstream religion and feminists' role in overcoming these forces.

"Tour of Bill Reid's Raven and the First Men Museum of Anthropology, Vancouver, BC." www.youtube.com/watch?v=aaRcj_BfbNA. An overview of Bill Reid's sculpture, Raven and the First Men at University of British Colombia Museum depicting the Haida Nation's story of human creation.

11 Women and Work

Chapter Outline

- The Labour of Women
- The Domestic Mode of Production
- The Capitalist Mode of Production
- The Politics of Work: Barriers and Strategies
- The Impact of Feminist Activism

This chapter will help you

- Learn how labour is gendered and how women's work is often rendered invisible
- Comprehend how different economic systems construct wage labour and engage or resist exploitation
- Appreciate how the processes of globalization impact labour across borders and understand the gendered impact of structural adjustment programs
- Recognize the roles of race, ethnicity, age, class, and so on in creating gendered workplaces
- Learn about the enduring gender wage gap and some of the key strategies that are used to close it

Women are 50 per cent of the world's population, perform 66 per cent of the world's work, produce 50 per cent of the food, but earn 10 per cent of the income and own 1 per cent of the property.
—NOELEEN HEYZER, PLENARY ADDRESS TO THE 1995 UN WORLD CONFERENCE ON WOMEN IN BEIJING, 1995

Human societies generally organize the work needed for survival by dividing tasks among their members. Individual work assignments are decided in a variety of ways. Strength and skill are obvious and basic determinants. Status and value also influence work patterns, and some tasks are thought to merit higher rewards than others. All known societies have used gender as a criterion for work assignments; these are largely arbitrary, however, because the content of roles varies from culture to culture and time to time. Yet a gendered division of labour exists.

Gender affects who is assigned which tasks, but class, race, and ethnicity further intervene so that women of colour and poor women are usually found in the most undervalued work. These class, caste, racial, and ethnic divisions among women are reinforced by *globalization*, an economic, social, political, and cultural process in which industries operate on a worldwide scale to take advantage of cheap labour costs to enhance their profits. Many societies judge the value of work in terms of economic rewards. "Do you work?" means, for many people, "Do you earn money?" That is why the idea that a homemaker does not "work" is so common. Although housekeeping services can be bought and sold, when this labour is performed for "free" it is not considered "work."

Many feminists have challenged the basic assumptions that most people hold about the nature and definition of "work" itself. Unpaid labour often contributes enormously to the goods and services that keep a society well and functioning. Masking the economic value of women's unpaid labour serves the interests of those who have property and power. Statistics indicate that women complete more than two-thirds of the world's unpaid work, and this labour is estimated to be worth 50 per cent of the world GDP, or almost $11 trillion (United Nations Development Fund for Women 2007). Failing to acknowledge the value of such work in economic terms distorts the assessment of a country's gross national product and keeps in place a system that undervalues both the producers of this labour—women—and their work.

Many theories hold that relationships between people are fundamentally based on economic power. The economic inequality between women and men has contributed to a widely held stereotype of women as dependent. A vicious cycle develops in which women's dependence is cited as the reason for their economic inequality. Hence, social inequalities between women and men are often the result of economic inequalities. This chapter examines some of these ideas in order to understand women's roles in reproduction and production and the impact of economic change on women's roles within and outside the family. It considers various types of work that women perform and the obstacles they face as workers. Finally, the chapter examines the roles played by support groups, government, and the women's movement in influencing women's opportunities for paid work.

Box 11.1 Key Issues

Equal Pay

Equal Pay Day illustrates how far into the next year a woman, on average, must work to earn the same amount a man made in the previous year. It is observed around the world. In Ontario, Equal Pay Day in 2016 was 19 April. It takes a woman in Ontario 15.5 months to earn what a man does in 12.

The Labour of Women

Division of Labour by Gender

Every known society has had some sort of division of labour by gender, but the work done by women and men has varied by geographical region, by historical era, and from society to society. While clerical work is typical for women in developed Western countries and in many developing countries in the Asia/Pacific region, employed women in the Middle East/North Africa are found predominantly in the professional/technical occupations. Women in other developing countries are concentrated in agriculture or the service sector (Ernst and Kapos 2012). The Asia/Pacific region has the lowest concentration of occupational sex segregation; the Middle East/North Africa region has the highest level. Table 11.1 indicates the extent to which occupational sex segregation (defined as an occupation in which one gender accounts for 80 per cent of the workforce) is an enduring feature within societies. In the past three decades there have been changes in the gender division of labour. Women have entered some occupations previously held by men—architects, engineers, legislative and government officials, managers, and buyers—as Table 11.1 illustrates. However, the other four predominantly male occupations—protective services such as police and firefighters; production supervisors; blacksmiths and toolmakers; and bricklayers, carpenters, and construction workers—remain strongly male identified. Women who have entered traditionally male occupations find that advancement is very difficult, and they typically remain at the lowest levels. Men, on the other hand, have always found work in "female" occupations, such as nursing, education, or social work, and they continue to do so. Once employed in a typically female occupation, men also move quickly into higher-level administrative or supervisory positions in these occupations (Kimmel 2000).

The division of labour by gender has often been related to the differences in the reproductive roles assigned to women and men. Since women necessarily bear and until recent times have necessarily nursed infants, they have always been assigned the additional social role of child care, even though this assignment is not necessitated by either function. Yet women's physical burdens while pregnant and nursing are often assumed to limit their ability to participate fully in the productive economy. An examination of women's roles in a variety of pre-industrial and developing societies, however, shows that they do engage in fairly strenuous economic activities even while pregnant and nursing.

Table 11.1 The Eight Most Typical Occupations for Women and Men Globally and the Percentage of the Dominant Sex in the Occupation

Eight Typical Female Occupations	%	Eight Typical Male Occupations	%
Maids, housekeepers, domestics	85	Protective services	96
Typists	85	Bricklayers, carpenters, construction	95
Nurses	82	Production supervisors, foremen	95
Tailors, dressmakers	64	Blacksmiths, toolmakers	95
Hairdressers, beauticians	60	Managers	86
Cashiers, bookkeepers	52	Legislators, government officials	84
Teachers	50	Sales supervisors, buyers	83
Salespersons, shop assistants	50	Architects, engineers	79

Source: Richard Anker, *Gender and Jobs: Sex Segregation of Occupations in the World*, p. 265. Geneva: ILO, 1998. Copyright © 1998 International Labour Organization.

The labour involved in reproduction itself is essential for any society. With the exception of those employed to care for the young, most women receive no economic compensation for mothering, even though societies could not exist without the work involved. In 2006, the long-form census revealed that two-thirds of unpaid work in Canada was being performed by women, and this work was valued (depending on the method of attributing value) at between 30 and 45 per cent of the $1.5 trillion GDP for the year (Zerbisias 2010).

Maintenance of the Domestic Unit

To the extent that women are involved in child care—and this extent varies historically and cross-culturally—the other work they do must be carried out at the same time. "Housework," such as cooking and cleaning, generally falls into this category. As with reproduction, this work serves an important function: it "services" the male worker so that he can return, fed and refreshed, to the workplace the next day. However, for this work too, female family members are not compensated (Eichler et al. 2010).

In most parts of the world for most of human history, virtually all women's productive labour was domestic, performed without compensation for the benefit of family members. Under these conditions, the labour done by women and men, although often differentiated, was viewed as making equivalent contributions. *Social labour*, labour done for the good of the larger community beyond the family, did have value, earning esteem for the labourer beyond family rewards. As the social labour sector grew with increasing urbanization and capitalism, it became a larger component of the whole economy. With this change, women began to lose ground. That women's domestic work was essential to the total economy but deemed lacking in economic or social value also diminished women's opportunities to participate in valued social labour outside the home (Dalla Costa and James 1975).

Feminists have challenged such traditional conceptions of the separate "private" and "domestic" spheres of life as misleading and damaging to women. Women combine many sorts of work with child care. Work such as weaving and making pottery and running businesses such as beauty parlours and family grocery stores can be carried out in or near the home. Alternatively, societies may take responsibility for making child-care facilities available so that both parents can work at other jobs. The separation of these spheres, as well as the under-valuing of women's domestic labour, can contribute to a woman's enforced helplessness in dangerous domestic situations.

Women's Work in the Marketplace

Despite women's assigned responsibilities in the domestic sphere, many have managed to sell some of their labour, and larger numbers continue to do so. Women find more restrictions in their job choices than men, men rarely take the jobs largely filled by women, and women's jobs are stereotyped in the workplace just as they are in the home. An activity that is highly regarded in one society when done by men may be considered unimportant in another society when done by women. A more insidious pattern of integrating women into the labour market is illustrated by an early twentieth-century example. This pattern encouraged women's entry into bookkeeping, which had been formerly occupied by men. Compensation was then lowered and office management, the traditional authority associated with the position, was eliminated. A new office position, accountant, was established, with higher prestige and pay, and became a male-identified occupation (Machung 1988). When work is divided along gender lines, it is not the work itself that determines its value but the gender of the person doing it.

The Contribution of Women to Economic Development

As long as women are expected to be the primary caretakers of their children, they will be forced to choose between child care, wage labour, or, as a compromise, part-time work. In Western societies, part-time work as a solution to problems associated with the lack of daycare penalizes the female wage earner. While universal daycare is an ongoing struggle in Canada, it is still far from reality, and the availability and accessibility of daycare varies greatly province by province. In 2011, 46 per cent of parents in Canada reported using some type of daycare for children aged 14 or younger (Sinha 2014; Quebec is the only province to have a subsidized universal child daycare program, and so unsurprisingly the numbers are higher in that province [closer to 60 per cent]).

Employers typically pay part-time workers lower hourly wages and provide few, if any, benefits compared to full-time workers in the same job. For those who must work for wages or who choose to do so, the problems of arranging for adequate child care may be severe, especially if fathers continue to maintain that these are the mothers' problems. Even in dual-career households, women, whether employed full-time or part-time, often have a "second shift": they assume the major share of household and childcare responsibilities after a "work day." This inequality strains familial relations and women's health and life satisfaction (Hochschild and Machung 2003) The further emotional work of managing the back-and-forth struggle between the first and second shift (the tension between being a good worker and being a good mother or housewife) is described as a "third shift" (Bolton 2000).

Many strides have been made in fathers' participation in domestic responsibilities. Couples with egalitarian gender views report the highest rates of familial satisfaction. Men now contribute more to housework than ever before (Coontz 2009), and Canadian law stipulates that parental leave be available to both mother and father.

However, there are still barriers to overcome and mindsets that continue to contribute to inequality. One has been termed the **masculine mystique**. This is some men's belief that women's work commitments and earning successes threaten them and their consequent resistance to sharing in household chores. Another, the **career mystique**, is the belief that a successful career requires all one's time and energy and that child care and household tasks should be delegated to others. Such an extreme attitude toward career responsibilities does not acknowledge the possibility of the creative integration of work and family responsibilities by both partners (Coontz 2009).

The lack of government policy for affordable child care severely limits options for working parents and directly influences the percentage of women in full-time employment. While Quebec has an established universal low-fee child-care policy (as low as $7.55 per day), affordability in the rest of Canada's provinces varies widely (see Table 11.2).

Table 11.2 How Much of a Woman's Income Goes to Child Care?

City	%	City	%
1. Gatineau, QC	4	11. Vancouver	29
2. Laval, QC	5	12. Kitchener, ON	30
3. Quebec City	6	13. Hamilton, ON	31
4. Montreal	6	14. Mississauga, ON	32
5. Winnipeg	15	15. St. John's	32
6. Saskatoon	23	16. Windsor, ON	32
7. Edmonton	24	17. Toronto	34
8. Ottawa	26	18. London, ON	34
9. Calgary	26	19. Surrey, BC	35
10. Halifax	28	20. Brampton, ON	36

Source: Macdonald and Friendly (2014).

In contemporary developing countries, models of economic growth and change tend to follow patterns set by Western industrialism. Where women were once heavily involved in small-scale agriculture based on intensive labour and simple technology, there is now a tendency to consolidate land holdings, to use industrial machinery, and to emphasize production for the market rather than for the home. It is consistently men who are taught to use the new machinery (such as tractors) and given the means to acquire it. As a result of being excluded from modernized agricultural production, women in developing countries have lost much of their influence over the deployment of resources, even within the home.

When men lose their jobs through the shift from labour-intensive to capital-intensive production, they are viewed as unemployed. Because what women do outside the home has been considered by societies to be economically negligible, women similarly "unemployed" often are not considered an economic casualty; since women's uncompensated work is not figured into the GDP, their lack of employment outside the home is not factored into unemployment numbers. Feminists question this standard interpretation of economic "development" and women's invisibility in it (Boserup 1970; Acosta-Belén and Bose 1990).

Shifting economies propel more women in to the workforce. Statistics Canada reports that in 2009, 58.3 per cent of women, representing 8.1 million women, were employed, more than doubling the number of women employed in 1976 (Statistics Canada 2010). In their households, women are now making more money management decisions and the majority of the buying decisions, substantially affecting global economies. Since money management has shifted to women to such a great extent, many companies have begun specifically targeting women clientele with their marketing campaigns and service delivery (Luscombe 2010). This phenomenon has been termed the **sheconomy**. Although most women still earn less than men, childless single women living in urban areas can actually out-earn men. This shift has a lot to do with women's increased education. There are now more women than men in their late twenties holding a bachelor's degree. But Status of Women Canada reports that university-educated women still earn only 68 per cent of what their male university-educated peers do (Status of Women Canada 2013).

The Domestic Mode of Production

Anthropologists use the phrase *domestic mode of production* to describe the organization of economic systems such as small-scale, hunting–gathering, frontier, and peasant economies. In such systems, the economic roles of women and men are integrated into other domestic roles within the household, which serves as the basic unit of both production and consumption. The division of labour is by age and gender, with relatively little specialization within these two categories. Women's contributions in these economies vary in type and extent.

Food Production

Although women's roles in food production (subsistence) are quite variable, some general patterns can be found. In hunting–gathering societies, women are primarily responsible for collecting and processing plant foods; in some cases, they also fish. Men are responsible for hunting large animals, an important but much less reliable form of protein. In horticultural societies that depend on cultivated plants, women tend to be mostly responsible for planting, cultivating, and harvesting; men are often assigned the more sporadic tasks of clearing the forest for new gardens and the like. In pastoral societies that depend on herding large animals (sheep, goats, cattle, yak, horses, llamas, alpacas, reindeer, camels), women are often associated with milking, preparing butter and cheese, and caring for young herd animals, while men are protect the herd from raiders and predators. Yet, in certain societies herding is women's work, and in others farming is men's work.

Increased technology curtails to some extent the participation of women in those traditional activities. For example, women in herding societies are rarely directly involved in ranching operations, which are oriented toward markets rather than household consumption. When agricultural production is intensified by the use of plow and oxen, men assume the tasks of cultivation. Women are generally credited with inventing most of the techniques of agriculture and storage (pottery and baskets). Further, women were likely the inventors of spinning (and later of the spinning wheel), weaving, and other techniques of cloth production. However, as with so many of the genuinely creative people in world history, women's names and records have been forgotten while the records of military adventures and the activity of men and their inventions survive.

Maintenance

Simply producing food by gathering, cultivating, fishing, or herding is not enough to provide for family needs. Researchers who attempt to find a relationship between subsistence activities (food production) and women's status often overlook this point. Food processing, for example, may be a critical task in subsistence. While Mexican peasant men are primarily responsible for growing their food staple, corn, Mexican peasant women spend considerable amounts of time and energy turning corn into food—husking and shelling it, grinding it, and forming and cooking tortillas. Food preservation and storage are critical tasks. Fish and meat may be dried or smoked or preserved in oil. Such tasks often are assigned to women.

Women farmers in low-income countries have begun to get more recognition and patronage internationally. Since food prices increased around the world in 2007 and 2008, the United Nations World Food Program has turned to locally grown agriculture to feed the hungry. Women produce 60–80 per cent of the food in poorer countries, but usually through small-scale agricultural businesses. The United Nations commitment to working with women farmers led them to gather data about gender disparities in agriculture, which can influence policy-makers and provide material help for women. Helping female farmers is beginning to be seen as an investment in a country's future, supporting both their capacity for production as well as their ability to provide for their families (Harshbarger 2010).

Women also tend to take on the tasks of making clothing. The Inuit men who hunt for sea mammals and caribou could not do so unless provided with warm parkas, leggings, and boots made by women. In societies that use plant or animal fibres for clothing, women generally do the spinning, weaving, and sewing. Women also construct tents and houses in many societies. They also have considerable responsibility for the care and health of their families. In many societies, women play important roles as healers of the sick, midwives, and "morticians" (laying out the dead).

Exchange and Marketing

Although economies based on the domestic mode of production are geared toward production for household use, some wares become commodities, exchanged to obtain goods and services not produced in the household. In some societies, like those in West Africa and the Caribbean, women play a significant role as traders, merchants, and brokers. Their participation in the market has tended (though not invariably) to be limited to short-distance trade in necessities, such as food and utensils, rather than long-distance "luxury" items, such as precious metals, gems, and ivory. Where women do engage in mercantile activities, they tend to retain considerable control over their income, enhancing their autonomy and status.

The Capitalist Mode of Production

Urbanization and Class Distinctions

The development of *social stratification*, socially constructed layers of classes that commanded vastly different shares of the economic resources of the community, was one of the by-products of the development of civilization. Urbanization and capitalism accelerated that process. Cities provide a wide range of socio-economic and cultural opportunities and depend on migrants for population growth and maintenance. Younger daughters and sons of the rural population come to the city with the hope of finding employment and social mobility.

Until relatively recently, women migrating to a city rarely found a dazzling array of choices open to them. Previously, they could enter into the class structure as the appendages of fathers or husbands. Or, if totally on their own, they probably most readily could find work as servants or enter the ranks of "unskilled" labourers. Such women were paid little, transient, and, through the discrimination of most societies against working women, sometimes obliged to supplement their meagre incomes with sex work. For women who lack skills, education, and social networks, this situation has not changed dramatically.

Working for Wages: Its Organizational Prerequisites

In order to "free" labour from the household, which requires work to sustain itself, certain basic arrangements must be made. One kind of arrangement involves a division of labour in the social sphere whereby some workers provide, on a regular basis, goods and services once produced only in the home for family consumption.

Labour directed strictly to household use, for example, the weaving of cloth for clothing, benefits only the family. When the same labour is sold in specialized production, the owner of the resources, tools, and products takes part of the value (after costs) produced by labour and allows the worker to take only a small share back to the family in the form of wages. The profit taken by the owner is accumulated and reinvested in more materials, tools, and products to increase future profits and personal wealth.

Women's Work

Enslavement, Serfdom, and Human Trafficking.

In some economic systems, people who were enslaved were not paid at all for working. Prior to the 1833 abolition of slavery in the British Empire, including Canada, enslaved people were worked to obtain the maximum amount of labour possible, generally by means of violence and coercion. In addition to the work performed for their masters, women who were enslaved cooked and cared for their own families and produced more children who would be enslaved by their owners. Unlike other women in this era, enslaved women were defined first as workers (Jones 1985; White 1985; Branch 2011). Enslaved women experienced much loss in their mothering as they and their children were often sold away from each other.

In Europe, after the slave-based economic system of the Roman Empire was overturned in the fifth century and replaced by small-scale economies of free and slave labour, there developed a system of serfdom which existed for centuries that bound female and male workers to the soil. One of the longest-lasting systems of entrenched servitude was in Russia, where it was only abolished in 1861. Serfdom gradually gave way to economic systems based on "free" wage labour. "Free" labour has been the most effective source of work in western European economies since the fourteenth century. The broad base of most contemporary economies is the "working class." With the development of industrial capitalism, the vast majorities of workers outside the home sell their labour for wages and cannot exist without doing so. They are "free" to accept what work they can find but are not free to withhold selling their labour for wages if they are to survive economically.

Although few people in the general public are aware, human trafficking is the fastest-growing criminal enterprise in the world. The United Nations Office on Drugs and Crime (2012) reports that internationally "2.4 million people are victims of human trafficking at any given time, and

80 percent of them are being exploited as sexual slaves." An estimated $32 billion is earned annually through these crimes (Humantrafficking.org 2012). It is not uncommon for poor people across the globe to be trapped in international sexual slavery rings, lured by false promises of good wages. They are vulnerable to crime and diseases, are brutalized, and often do not control or receive remuneration for their services.

Canada has seen people who have been trafficked forced into labour in private businesses, domestic service, and the construction industry. Public Safety Canada calculates that over 90 per cent of human trafficking cases before the courts involve domestic human trafficking while fewer than 10 per cent involve people brought into Canada from another country (Public Safety Canada 2012).

Sex Work. Sex work is defined as the sale of sexual services. Feminists have long been divided on the contentious issue of sex work. Historically, sex work has primarily been organized into relationships of economic dependence, very often with third parties as the employers or "bosses," as in the case of procurers, pimps, or madams. Men, but also women (parents, spouses, lovers, employers, brothel owners), can play these intermediary roles, and both gain by the dependent relationship involved (Hirata 1979; Rosen 1982; Butler 1985). Many people, though not all, do not intend or aspire to become sex workers; rather, in certain circumstances, sex work may provide the only means of generating an income. Poor females, LGBTQ people, and children, are among the most vulnerable groups (Bertone 2000; Brennan 2002).

On the other hand, sex work is many times the only opportunity available to earn a livelihood, especially for those marginalized by a heteropatriarchal culture. Laws and social stigma can isolate and render the worker vulnerable to violence and abuse. Thanks to the pioneering work of sex workers and advocates, the Supreme Court of Canada recently required the Canadian government to better protect its citizens who are also sex workers. Canadian Bill C-36, passed in 2014, criminalizes "customers," bans advertising, and forbids any material gain from sex work. The community of sex workers feared that the new law would isolate them and expose them to danger rather than help to protect them. They plan constitutional challenges to Bill C-36 due to the risk to their health and safety.

Working-Class Women: Skilled Labour. Production was generally a household enterprise until the development of the factory system and workplaces designed to fit the industrial model. In small-scale craft enterprises, it was commonplace for a man to work at the craft, producing goods, while his wife ran the shop, sold the goods, and kept the books. In Europe, where this division of labour was most pronounced, the more elite, urban professions and crafts had organized themselves into guilds by the thirteenth century. However, women were barred as members (except, in some cases, as widows) from the most skilled and lucrative occupations, and the knowledge of crafts was a "mystery" to them, opened for the most part only to licensed male apprentices.

In some guilds, women did participate as independent and active working members. Out of several hundred crafts registered in thirteenth-century Paris, six were composed exclusively of women: silk spinners, wool spinners, silk weavers, silk-train makers, milliners of gold-braided caps, and makers of alms purses. In England, fourteenth-century guilds listed women as brewers, bakers, corders, and spinners and as working in wool, linen, and silk. It is likely that these guilds were organized by employers or civil authorities for the purpose of placing women under surveillance to prevent them from pilfering materials (Shahar 1983).

Working-Class Women: Domestic Wage Labour. A vast proportion of wage-earning women have worked as domestic labourers: maids, cooks, and nursemaids. They have contributed to the maintenance of a distinctive standard of living for women and men of the middle and upper classes, enabling them to occupy large, sometimes luxurious residences, and to enjoy elaborate lifestyles.

Today, in industrially developed nations, many of the former tasks of female domestics are provided by service industries such as hospitals, daycare centres, hotels, and restaurants or by machinery in the home, such as washing machines. However, were it not for the availability of relatively cheap domestic labour, filled largely by immigrant women, many middle-class professional women would be obliged to stay at home to care for their families since women still are assigned primary responsibility for domestic caretaking work. Many women acknowledge their dependence on child-care workers, but the lack of affordable, flexible, high-quality, and well-paying child-care centres reduces all women's options in combining paid work and care for their children. In Canada, the government-run Live-in Caregiver Program enabled workers from outside Canada to provide elder and child care for individual families. Fraught with potential for exploitation by requiring the mostly female workers to live in the family home, the program requirement to "live-in" has been abolished. INTERCEDE for the Rights of Domestic Workers, Caregivers and Newcomers was established in 1979 to promote and advocate for the rights of those in the Live-in Caregiver Program as well as providing support services including orientation, information, and counselling.

Working-Class Women: Factory Workers. The proportion of women in the Canadian labour force has increased steadily, beginning in 1900 with a major influx of European immigrants, many with previous experience in the needle trade and garment factories. In the early twentieth century, Montreal and Toronto became centres of clothing manufacturing and thousands of young, single women entered the industry, composing 70–80 per cent of needle-trade workers. Female factory workers were not new in North America. In the 1820s and 1830s, single women were employed in textile mills throughout New England. They laboured 12–13 hours a day, 6 days a week, and were paid half or less than half the pay of men. Most were young daughters of farmers who worked for a short period before marriage to help support their families and themselves. At the new model factory in Lowell, Massachusetts, they lived in company housing and their lives were closely supervised.

In China, the female children of poor rural families helped their families survive by working in silk factories. Gail Tsukiyama's novel *Women of the Silk* describes the life of such a young girl, who leaves her rural home to work in the Chinese silk industry in the 1920s (Tsukiyama 1991). Like their sisters in North American mills, these young girls are depicted in Tsukiyama's novel as working long hours for very little pay.

From time to time, when able to do so, the women workers resisted their situation. However, their efforts to improve working conditions through protest, strikes, organizations, and alliances with men's groups met with little success until the organization of industry-wide trade unions such as the International Ladies Garment Worker Union. While 80 per cent of the garment workers were women, the ILGWU was dominated by male leadership.

Immigrant women worked in a wide variety of industries but were predominant in the garment industry—and still are. It was in this industry that their union activities had the greatest impact. Working conditions in the industry were notoriously substandard without any government requirements for health and safety. One of the worst tragedies in labour history was the Triangle Shirtwaist Factory fire in 1911 in New York City, which caused the deaths of 146 workers—123 women and 23 men—mostly young Jewish and Italian immigrants. They died when they were unable to escape the fire, since all the exit doors were locked; many jumped to their deaths to avoid the flames and smoke. The aftermath of the fire saw new legislation enacted, regulating working conditions and implementing some of the first health and safety regulations in North America.

Table 11.3 Labour Force Characteristics by Sex and Age Group

	2010	2011	2012	2013	2014
			thousands		
Labour Force	18,450.5	18,619.6	18,809.5	19,037.8	19,124.5
Males	9,704.9	9,803.1	9,885.6	9,996.5	10,071.8
Females	8,745.6	8,816.5	8,923.9	9,041.3	9,052.7
			%		
15 years and older	66.9	66.7	66.5	66.5	66.0
Males	71.6	71.4	71.0	70.9	70.6
Females	62.4	62.2	62.1	62.2	61.6
15 to 24 years	64.5	64.5	63.5	63.8	64.2
Males	64.2	64.6	63.3	63.8	63.8
Females	64.8	64.5	63.7	63.8	64.6
25 to 44 years	86.8	86.6	87.1	87.1	86.6
Males	91.3	91.3	91.9	91.5	91.2
Females	82.3	82.0	82.3	82.7	82.0
45 years and older	54.8	54.7	54.4	54.3	53.7
Males	60.8	60.6	60.0	59.9	59.5
Females	49.2	49.1	49.3	49.2	48.3
65 years and older	11.3	11.8	12.4	13.0	13.4
Males	16.0	16.4	16.9	17.6	18.2
Females	7.5	8.0	8.7	9.1	9.4

Source: Statistics Canada, CANSIM, table 282–0002.

In 1919, the Winnipeg General Strike served as a catalyst for labour organizing in Canada. Called for a "living wage" and safe working conditions, the six-week strike saw tens of thousands of workers walk off the job and is thought to be the largest such strike in North America. Women participated as strikers and supporters to such an extent that their involvement spurred the movement for women's right to vote.

Sweatshop conditions continued to predominate in the garment industry. In 1931, women garment workers in Toronto called a general strike for union recognition that ultimately ended in failure after nearly three months on the picket line. Working women have had to contend with society's view of the proper role of females. During the Great Depression of the 1930s, employed women were told they were taking jobs from men. This propaganda ignored the fact that most of the jobs women held were low-paid, traditionally female ones, which men had not previously performed. After World War II, they were told that to work away from home was unfeminine and harmful to their families. Women who had worked in heavy industry during both world wars to help the country and support their families were unwelcome there when the men came home. Women lacked the power to fight for their interests, to resist layoffs, and to hold on to their high wages. *Rosie the Riveter*, a documentary film, depicts the history of women's incorporation into and removal from manufacturing work in the 1940s.

Beginning in the 1970s, the garment sweatshop was revitalized in North America utilizing a new immigrant force—women from Asia, Latin America, and the Caribbean. Part of a global workforce in the apparel industry, immigrant women's exploitation and their resistance to it has remained largely unchanged over the decades (Maquila Solidarity Network n.d.; Louie 2001; Ng 1999); recall the 2013 garment factory collapse in Bangladesh that killed over 1300 workers (see Box 11.2), some of whom were making clothing for Loblaws, a Canadian company.

In the 1970s, a few women began to obtain high-paying heavy industrial jobs at twice the

---

Box 11.2 Women in Media

"Flowers and Threads": The FAST Campaign

Who makes our clothes? What is the real human cost of that cute $12 t-shirt? The "race to the bottom" has gutted garment manufacturing in North America and led to sweatshops in the developing world. In Bangladesh garment workers are routinely spat on, yelled at, hit, sworn at and not allowed bathroom breaks. For a monthly wage of about $90, they work punishing hours and are often not paid on time, or at all, for overtime. Over 800 workers have died in factory fires, and 1,138 were killed in the collapse of the Rana Plaza factory in Dhaka, April 24, 2013.

What role can art play in supporting these workers? How can we use art to build relationships between garment workers in Bangladesh and people in Canada?

In the fall of 2014, Robin Pacific, community artist Leah Houston, and portrait photographer Clare Samuel, travelled to Dhaka and conducted community art workshops with 100 garment workers. They made drawings on petals which will be constructed as "shaplas," the national flower of Bangladesh. Clare made 65 photographic portraits, and Robin held taped conversations with 36 workers. The three artists also worked with a group of Rana Plaza survivors.

Back in Toronto, Robin continued the shapla workshops with various groups including Canadian garment workers. The shaplas will be an embodiment of the support of groups in Canada for garment workers in Bangladesh.

Shapla workshop with garment workers in Toronto, run by the FAST Campaign. (See more at www.robinpacific.ca/projects/flowers-and-threads-the-fast-campaign/#sthash.MLtfeBLD.dpuf.)

Source: Pacific (n.d.).

wages they could earn as secretaries. Many women have fought for legal reforms to ban gender discrimination in hiring and promotion but remain rare in technical, industrial, and "skilled" trades. Several Canadian provinces have implemented programs to address this imbalance that are funded by federal–provincial labour market agreements. British Columbia's Women in Trades Training Initiative is one such program that promotes women's training in carpentry, milling, plumbing, and other trades requiring apprentice programs.

The Service Sector Worker. In North America women today predominate in clerical work, sales, and services. Although both women and men work as salespeople, they sell different things. Men generally sell cars and insurance; women sell cosmetics and women's clothing. In North America most women who work do so in the service sector, which involves the sale and distribution of goods and services themselves. In the past these exclusively female jobs were called *pink-collar* work to distinguish them from male *blue-collar* work.

"Office worker" is the largest occupational category for women today. Women occupy administrative support positions, while men primarily hold the management positions (Bravo 2003). In part, the gender segregation of office workers is something of an illusion, a product of labelling the things done by women and men differently. For example, men might be hired as administrative "analysts" and women as administrative "assistants," though they end up doing the same job. By giving the same job two different titles, one for men and one for women, companies can classify the title used for women at a lower wage rate.

Clerical and secretarial work became available to women late in the nineteenth century, especially with the introduction of the typewriter. Computers and other new technologies have further changed the nature and conditions of office work. The lowest-level clerical jobs, which have served as entry points for women, are disappearing. New technology with electronic surveillance capabilities—for example, the timing of customer-service calls—has enabled employers and supervisors to more closely monitor a woman's work, contributing to a loss of her sense of security and control. In other cases, jobs are being "outsourced" to "cheaper" labour markets overseas as corporations compete globally, drawing women in other parts of the world into automated office work. Although the new technologies do provide new opportunities for women, they also reinforce gender and economic inequalities worldwide (Bravo 2003; Scott-Dixon 2004).

Many women have also begun to work in the hospitality services, although getting a management position as a woman is rare. In Turkey, women working in hotel services generally enjoy working in tourism and tend to have formal training and education in this area. However, maintaining a work–life balance is difficult, wages are low, and promotions are hard to come by (Okumus et al. 2010). Only 7 per cent of the general managers in Middle Eastern hotels are women, and those reaching higher positions have had to work much harder and longer for it than their male counterparts (Warnock 2009). Blayney and Blotnicky researched the Canadian aspect of the phenomenon and found that by revising their personnel policies, hotel corporations could attract and maintain more women in executive positions (Blayney and Blotnicky 2010).

Thanks to historical and systemic discrimination, Canadian women working full-time and year-round earn about 70 per cent of what men earn. The main reasons for this include women taking more part-time work and taking time off in order to have children and accommodate their children's needs; women choosing (and being culturally encouraged to choose) occupations that pay less than men; and society under-valuing women's labour by paying jobs that are dominated by women less (for an example, consider the drop in pay for administrative assistants when the class of job became dominated by women rather than by men), and not paying women for labour at home. The differential has improved only slightly in some 30 years, although women are entering the workforce in increased numbers and are working in jobs formerly held only by men. In some countries, the pay differential between women and men is even greater. The International Labour Organization reports that the highest wage gaps between women and men are found in Korea, Thailand, Lithuania, and Kazakhstan (ILO 2010). One argument made to explain this discrepancy is that the pay differential results from women having less experience than men, which ignores the impact of gender discrimination. To test this argument, economists have held constant the variables of age, experience, and duration of the job and have found that women still get paid less than men and are still promoted more slowly (Rotella 1980; ILO 2010).

The Canadian Centre for Policy Alternatives produced a report in 2014 that revealed the persistence of the gender wage gap. *Narrowing the Gap: The Difference That Public Sector Wages Make* found intersectionally that in a comparison between workers in public- and private-sector employment, "significant gaps in the wages of women, aboriginal workers, and visible minority workers—and that those gaps are bigger in the private sector in every instance" (McInturff and Tulloch 2014). Table 11.4 illustrates the intersectional nature of the wage gap.

The Precarious Worker. Precarious workers include part-time, temporary, and freelance workers. They make up a "flexible" workforce and are increasingly prevalent. Employers are more and more relying on these workers when they perceive a need and release them when there is no present or future need.

Home workers and independent contractors are another part of the flexible workforce. Most home-based white-collar workers are self-employed (75 per cent) and married women (75 per cent). Home workers list four major reasons to work at home: (1) family responsibilities; (2) control over work hours and setting; (3) elimination of the expense of travelling and of office politics; and (4) the need to earn extra money (Christensen 1988). Women performing home work report stress in trying to balance work at home with household responsibilities (Ng 1999).

Precarious work raises disturbing issues concerning the development of a new workforce of women dependent on the capricious demands of employers. Precarious workers rarely receive the benefits and security associated with full-time employment. Employers feel less need to provide training and occupational advancement. On average, home workers receive lower wages than on-site employees. Yet, for many women, a precarious job with a weak attachment to an

Table 11.4 Average Public- and Private-Sector Worker Wages, Full-Time, Full-Year Work, for Workers Aged 40–54, Various Demographics

Group (gender, self-identified "race") 40–54 (the largest of any one age group)	Average Public-Sector Worker Wage (full-time, full-year) ($)	Average Private-Sector Worker Wage (full-time, full-year) ($)
Women	56,776	54,328
Men	72,209	74,619
Indigenous women	50,919	47,131
Indigenous men	58,123	55,529
Visible-minority women	54,837	49,776
Visible-minority men	70,165	68,630
Non-Indigenous, non-visible-minority women	57,481	54,965
Non-Indigenous, non-visible-minority men	73,214	76,189

Source: Adapted from McInturff and Tulloch (2014). © 2014 Canadian Centre for Policy Alternatives. This work is protected by copyright and the making of this copy was with permission of Access Copyright. Any alteration of its content or further copying in any form whatsoever is strictly prohibited unless otherwise permitted by law.

employer is the only solution to the problems of inadequate child care, partial retirement, and continuing education.

Approximately one-third of European women work part-time, which allows them to combine earning an income and keeping up their family responsibilities. Part-time female European workers also earn lower pay, have few benefits, and lack representation and voice in the workplace (ILO 2010). To overcome these disadvantages, the Netherlands provides part-time employees the same benefits (pensions, vacation, and sick pay) as full-time workers.

The Military. Women are increasingly serving active duty in the military; some 10,000 serve in diverse capacities in the Canadian Armed Forces. Many of these women also balance the responsibilities of a family and child care. While women in the military with and without children do not always show significant discrepancies between their levels of stress, role strain, health, and military career aspirations (Hopkins-Chadwick 2009), there are specific challenges for some mothers, particularly those who serve outside their country and have special-needs children.

The Professions. The professions include the arts, law, medicine, engineering, teaching, and management. They often require more training and education than other kinds of work. Most of the professions set their own standards for qualifications and performance and generally the pay is higher than for blue- and pink-collar work. Work in the professions is highly segregated by gender. Most fall into one of two categories: those that society deems "female" and those deemed "male." For example, in North America, nursing, elementary and secondary teaching, social work, and library work are considered women's professions, and women outnumber men in them. While women are increasingly represented in the medical profession, they are under-represented in others, especially in sciences, engineering, higher management, and stockbroking. Statistics Canada reveals that while more than half of university graduates are female, they are under-represented in the STEM fields: science, technology, engineering, and mathematics (Hango 2013; see Chapter 9).

Within the "women's professions" there is gender segregation that places men at the highest levels. More men than women, for example, are superintendents, chief officers, and faculty and administrators of professional schools. For the most part, these female-dominated professions offer limited career mobility to women; they are the lowest-paying and least prestigious of the professions. Yet, they are enormously important to society. They provide large numbers of women with the opportunity to pursue gratifying careers, although society has not elected to reward them with high pay or status.

Some governments have made the connection between women's low pay and high child poverty rates and have attempted to make changes for this reason. The United Kingdom planned to halve child poverty by 2010 and proposed an Equality Bill to improve maternity pay and allow for affordable child care, among other assistance. It was found that half the poor children in the United Kingdom lived in working households, but the mothers were stuck in part-time, low-paid jobs (BBC News 2008). Bridget Bodman found that when she switched jobs, the man who took her old job was paid significantly more, so she took legal action and won the case. She says, "I just wanted to equalize things. I wanted to get the money that the man after me and the man before me had got. I wasn't a hell raiser and it wasn't just about principle. . . . I did equal work" (Sugden 2009).

Although many women have been trained and are active in the arts, few have held top-ranking positions in architecture or design or as producers or directors in theatre or film. Women have also experienced systematic discrimination as artists, so it is harder for them than for men to gain recognition and to make a living in the arts. In recent years, thanks in part to the women's movement and in part to anti-discrimination laws, increasing numbers of women have entered and achieved success in professions formerly reserved for men. Today, more women gain employment in professions such as accounting, informational technology, sciences, and financial management (Rosin 2010).

Women in "male professions" often encounter serious obstacles. Not only will they be in the minority among their peers, but their employees, whether female or male, may have difficulty relating to them and vice versa. Research on perceptions of women in the workplace indicates that female candidates are often subject to prejudice, except when they are applying within an industry that is congruent with female gender roles (Garcia-Retamero and Lopez-Zafra 2006). Beyond prejudice, women in male-dominated professions often encounter harassment and unwelcoming attitudes that can prevent or discourage women from staying or feeling comfortable in the workplace. In the past few years, stories have come out about harassment of women in the information technology industry and in dentistry, and specifically in the RCMP, Canada's Parliament, and the CBC. It is very likely that more is occurring, since workplace harassment is often unreported. See more on this in the section "The Politics of Work: Barriers and Strategies" on page 291.

Gender segregation between and within the professions is in part the result of gender discrimination in education. For female professionals who pursue both career and family, there are many role conflicts since both jobs and families make demands on a woman's time and energy. The male model of professional development is especially problematic for women who are raising a family. Many professions and employers within the professions, especially male-dominated ones, assume that individuals dedicate most of their time and energies to work. Some women choose not to follow the male model of professional development. In India, professional women in the information technology sector may forgo promotions and advancement in their companies so as not to neglect their family responsibilities (Radhakrishnan 2009). In North America some professional women now in their thirties and forties are "choosing" to leave careers that had been closed to their mother's generation and previous generations of women, albeit perhaps only temporarily. Having experienced the fast track to a law partnership or corporate management, for example, they have found the male-defined work conditions enormously dissatisfying. Although this option is open primarily to the wealthy or those with high-income-earning spouses, their decision to "opt out" goes beyond the issue of balancing work and family to questioning the place and satisfaction of work itself in life (Belkin 2003).

Women in academia would benefit from more generous family policies, as the turnover rate is high. Family policies become a significant factor in advancement and retention, and women need better representation (Mayer and Tikka 2008). Family-friendly policies could be helpful to faculty with caregiving responsibilities; however, the structure and culture of academia often make it hard for women to balance work and family. In order to achieve tenure (a permanent faculty appointment), professors undergo a rigorous evaluation by a committee that examines research, publishing, and teaching. The way the tenure system is set up makes is hard on women because the six or seven years necessary to focus on tenure early in one's career often coincide with the optimal years for having children. It is found that men receiving tenure are more likely to be married with children than women receiving tenure. Women often feel they have to choose between work and family life. Certain policies, such as parental leave, have been implemented by individual universities that would make it easier for a woman to attain that balance. The University of California, Berkeley, has proposed a right to a one-semester relief from teaching duty for parents with young children, a right to one year of pausing the tenure clock for child- or adult-dependent care responsibilities, a right to request unpaid leave for the care of a sick family member, high-quality child and infant-care availability, spousal employment assistance, and more part-time options for faculty with family caregiving responsibilities (Cockrell 2003).

Other universities, finding that faculty want more balanced lives, have put in their own family-friendly and flexible workplace policies. Some schools have tried flexible work schedules, lactation stations, parenting seminars, eldercare, and "new mom" support groups to achieve more work–life balance. Universities must also make an effort to reduce the stigma involved in requesting utilization of these policies. Universities benefit from creating a balanced environment as much as the faculty do because employees work better when they have more flexible, supportive working conditions (Novotney 2010).

Women who attempt to balance both professional careers and family life face obstacles to success that vary by occupation, although there are some common barriers. For example, in the United Kingdom, civil engineering, with its dominant male culture, prioritizes work and long hours as the norm, with personal interests and family life taking the back seat. Such professions value **presenteeism**, so even when there is no significant work to be done, one shows commitment by staying late and working long hours (Watts 2009). Women engineers have developed various strategies to maintain a work–life balance, such as creating firm boundaries between work and personal life, cutting back on extracurricular work activities, or employing cleaners to free up some of their personal time. Unfortunately, these women engineers are often inhibited from speaking out against the practices of being overworked as they are culturally implicit within the occupation's practices (Watts 2007).

The manner in which men and women view and navigate life–work balance differs by gender across the life span. A study of mid-life men and women in Scotland between the ages of 50 and 52 found gender to have a large impact on how home and work life was handled. Men tended to view the struggle of life–work balance as a conflict of the past, when their children were younger (most of their children were now adolescents). Women, on the other hand, were still struggling with this conflict in the form of balancing paid work, adolescent/adult children, and aging parent responsibilities. Women also tended to have weaker boundaries between home and work responsibilities, which was often more acceptable in predominantly female careers that also placed value on caring. Men's careers that valued pragmatic qualities in their workers often fostered stronger boundaries between work and home life (Emslie and Hunt 2009).

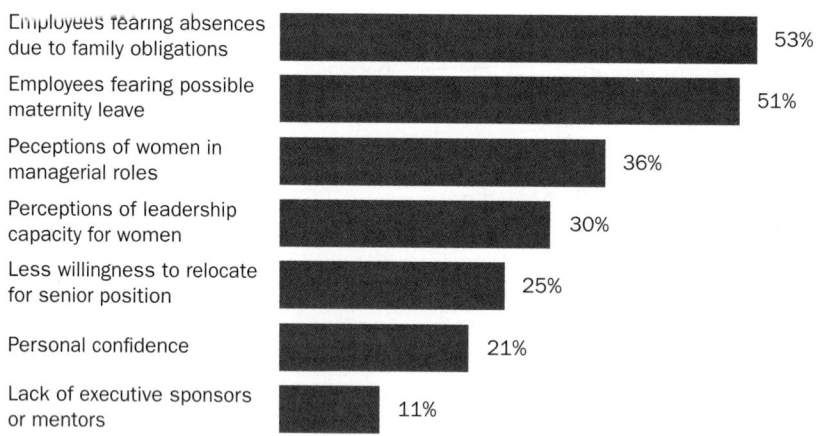

Figure 11.1 Gender Job Divide: Perceived Factors That Can Prevent Women from Advancing to Senior Roles, 2014

Source: Yew (2014). © Ranstad Canada

Some conceptualize the care of others as being a matter of ethical responsibility. A comprehensive approach views everyday decisions of caring for oneself and others as integral to the idea of "ethics." This restores the original essence of the word *ethics*, knowledge about how to live a good life (Tronto 2001). This is certainly applicable to women, in the extensive time they spend on household responsibilities and child and eldercare.

Corporate Management at the Highest Levels. More women are reaching middle-management ranks, but few are senior managers, being skipped over while male peers or juniors are chosen for these positions. Not surprisingly, women executives continue to be compensated at a lower rate than male executives. In 2011, only 3.6 per cent of Fortune 500 companies had female CEOs, and in 2009 women held only 15.2 per cent of Fortune 500 board seats (Catalyst 2012a)—very low percentages indeed. Yet one study found that gender diversity in business is associated with increased sales revenue, increased profits, and a greater market share (Herring 2009; Kay 2010).

Women who have achieved leadership positions have developed tactics to excel in both their home and work responsibilities. An interview with some of the top women leaders around the globe found similarities among the women who contributed to their success both at work and at home. These women were able to combine work and family as a result of flexible working conditions and family support. They also prioritized integrating different life domains. These women tended to display transformational leadership qualities at work, including an emphasis on interconnectedness, which gave them social support, contributing to their ability to balance their personal and professional lives. They excelled at optimization strategies, such as scheduling time and multitasking, and compensation strategies, such as outsourcing basic duties when resources were limited. These tactics contributed to their ability to successfully balance their lives (Cheung and Halpern 2010).

In the twenty-first century, some businesses are beginning to value those management styles, often identified with female leadership styles, which stress teamwork, flexibility, and collaboration in problem solving to better adapt to the current global economic environment characterized by uncertainty and the need to constantly evolve. Increasingly companies in both the Global North and Global South are choosing women to lead their businesses (Box 11.3). Corporations can commit to increasing the percentage of women on their boards of directors to 25 per cent by 2017 by signing the Catalyst Accord (catalyst.org). Twenty-eight Canadian corporations have signed the pledge, including Air Canada, Desjardins, RBC, Telus, and WestJet.

Whether women earn high salaries as professionals or low wages as caregivers, sales clerks, or sex workers, discrimination against them is found at all levels and categories of work. Women experience the "glass ceiling," which keeps them from reaching the highest levels of corporate and public responsibility; the "sticky floor" keeps the vast majority of the world's women stuck in low-paid jobs, the "glass wall" concentrates women in female-dominated jobs, and the "glass cliff" refers to the tenuous nature of women's leadership positions (Albeda and Tilly 1997; Kimmel 2000; Barreto, Ryan, and Schmitt 2009).

Unpaid Work. Capitalist society depends on women working in domestic and caregiving roles, unpaid, in order to support and enable the workers to continue working for corporations. It is vital to the capitalist structure that homemaking is not valued in terms of finances/labour, because otherwise workers may realize that their pay is not commensurate to their work and time. Despite strides made toward equality, and despite the increase of women in paid labour, these unpaid jobs are still overwhelmingly done by women. This creates what is known as the "double day" or "second shift," the shift of at-home work that women do after their shift at work. This work includes cleaning, cooking, organizing, and shopping (the general running and maintenance of the home); taking care of children; and taking care of seniors.

Box 11.3 Time to Reflect

Women at the Top

Around the world women are breaking the glass ceiling and taking positions at the head of companies.
   Sheryl Sandberg (US), COO of Facebook (technology)
   Indra Nooyi (US), Chair and CEO of PepsiCo (food)
   Maria das Graças Silva Foster (Brazil), CEO of Petrobas (oil)
   Ursula Burns (US), Chair and CEO of Xerox (technology)
   Marissa Mayer (US), CEO of Yahoo (technology)
   Zhang Xin (China), Co-founder and CEO, Soho China, Ltd. (real estate)
   Safra Catz (US), President and CFO of Oracle (technology)
   Cher Wang (Taiwan), Co-founder and Chair of HTC (technology)
   Chanda Kochhar (India), Managing Director and CEO of ICICI Bank (financial)
   Chua Sock Koong (Singapore), CEO of SingTel (technology)
   Shaikha Al-Bahar (Kuwait), CEO of National Bank of Kuwait (financial)
   Guler Sabanci (Turkey), Chair and Managing Director, Sabanci Holding (diversified)

Source: Forbes (2012).

Approximately 6 in 10 caregivers for seniors in Canada are women (57 per cent) and this proportion was higher than the proportion of women aged 45 and over who were not caregivers (51 per cent) (Cranswick and Dosman 2008). Lesbians and gay men also provide more eldercare than those in heterosexual households (National Alliance for Caregiving 2009). Many women sacrifice aspects of their daily lives and often give up or cut back on paid work, which decreases their income and retirement benefits (MetLife 2011).

Globalization and the Transformation of Work

Today, globalizing forces have profoundly altered national economies and the workplace. Globalization entails "the internationalization of the capitalist economy in which states, markets, and civil society are restructured to facilitate the spread of global capital" (Peterson and Runyan 2010, 193). Since the conclusion of World War II, capitalism has integrated the world's countries into a single global economy, a process that accelerated with the end of colonialism and the collapse of communism in Russia and Eastern Europe in the late 1980s. This led to the migration of jobs from industrial centres in Europe and North America to countries in which manufacturers could pay lower wages to non-unionized workers, reorganizing the global economy and powerfully affecting former industrial workers (Box 11.4).

Globalization deeply touches the lives of women and men in developing countries. As manufacturing industries have relocated to low-wage countries in search of cheap, docile labour, many women in developing countries have joined the global assembly line in industries as diverse as clothing, food production, and electronics. Governments in the Caribbean and Latin America, Eastern Europe, and many countries in Asia advertise the availability of a large supply of female labour, especially young female labour. Work in multinational corporation factories compromises workers' health and life expectancy; women perform repetitious tasks and are exposed to dangerous chemicals. However, the women in these countries face extreme poverty and need even the lowest wages for survival; despite this they do whatever they can to resist exploitation.

Many of these factories are located in Export Development Zones, where poorer countries grant tax exemptions to multinationals and often exempt them from labour laws. These are called maquiladoras, now found around the world, although they originated in Mexico. In these factories, workers are often forced into overtime, face regular pregnancy tests, and are subject to sexual exploitation. Despite the obstacles, women continue to work to improve working conditions in maquiladoras and sweatshops.

As economic conditions in developing countries worsened over the past four decades, governments were forced to implement specific policies of international financial institutions like the International Monetary Fund, the World Bank, and the World Trade Organization. These policies benefited the global economy as determined by the advanced industrialized countries. In exchange for loans and aid, developing countries have to agree to cut government spending on health, education, and welfare; reduce the number of government

Box 11.4 In Her Own Words

Maquila Leaders: Yannick Etienne, October 2012

A major problem we're facing right now is getting the employers to pay the legal minimum wage. For example, on October 1 the minimum wage for eight hours work was adjusted from 250 to 300 gourdes (~US$6.00–$7.00).

The law says that production quotas have to be set at a level that allows workers to earn at least 300 gourdes for eight hours work, but some employers set the quota at a level that a worker can never make more than 300, and others set the quotas so high that it would take you two days to reach them.

As a result, workers go to work early and work late or they spend less time in the break period in order to reach the quota. So, they are working more than eight hours for eight hours pay.

Yannick Etienne, organizer for the May First Union Federation, Haiti.

In different factories workers are raising their voices about this abuse; we've had work stoppages in a number of workplaces. So the owners of course reacted; they have fired the workers who protested or suspended them for up to 10 days. Can you imagine? The salaries are already low and the workers are already in debt, so missing five or 10 days pay is impossible.

The coming of [a new union in Port-au-Prince—Sendika Ouvriye Takstilak Abiman (SOTA)] was a breakthrough for freedom of association in Haiti. In the first two or three Better Work reports, they said there were no violations of freedom of association because there was no union. Our response was, "No, it's just the opposite—we don't have unions because freedom of association is not respected."

So, when SOTA arrived and its leaders were fired there was proof that there was no freedom of association. SOTA opened up the issue. And now we have a table of social dialogue convened every month by Better Work in which the factory owners and the worker representative organizations come together to discuss issues.

This is a breakthrough, and if we didn't have SOTA, we wouldn't have come so far.

Source: Maquila Solidarity Network (2012).

jobs; sell off businesses owned and operated by the government; and open their economies to foreign investors. These **structural adjustment programs (SAPs)** cause enormous hardships (Wichterich 2000; Dickinson and Schaeffer 2001).

Migration becomes an economic strategy for family survival in developing countries; women often lead the way. Those women who cannot find work in their own country migrate to developed countries or wealthier developing countries. They find jobs performing traditional women's tasks. They often work as nannies, maids, or sex workers and send remittances back home to feed, clothe, house, and educate their families there. Some become part of the "mail-order bride" phenomenon where websites advertise women's profiles and match them to prospective Western husbands. In a groundbreaking 2000 study, *Canada: the New Frontier for Filipino Mail-Order Brides*, the Philippine Women Centre of B.C. interviewed 40 such women in five provinces. They concluded that women who came to Canada as mail-order brides shared the situation of many trafficked women and were, in the main, racialized, economically and sexually exploited, and often physically and emotionally violated (Philippine Women Centre of B.C. 2000).

As part of the globalized labour force, Sri Lankan women are recruited to the Middle East and Filipinas to Hong Kong and Korea to work in households (Constable 2007). They make it possible for women in industrialized countries to go out and work with the knowledge that their children will be looked after, their homes cleaned, and their elderly relatives attended. These immigrant workers are poorly paid, have few or no rights in the host country, are often subject to emotional and physical abuse, and, in the case of sex workers, run the risk of contracting HIV/AIDS and other sexually transmitted diseases. Educated and skilled women from developing countries who seek to continue their professions in the developed countries generally experience downward mobility due to **de-skilling**, that is, starting over again (for example, by taking licensing exams) and getting little or no credit for their skills and years of experience.

Self-Employment

Historically, few women have been self-employed due, in part, to the different socialization of girls and boys. Girls tend not to be taught to take the initiative or to be assertive or independent. When girls do show these qualities, which underlie successful self-employment, they often receive fewer rewards than boys or even are negatively sanctioned. The Women's Enterprise Centre reports that over one-third of small businesses in BC and the rest of Canada are owned by women and that female-led small business continues to be a growing sector. The centre recognizes that these businesses face all the same difficulties that any start-up would, but that women face special challenges in terms of self-confidence, financial literacy, and access to capital. Experienced-based training that takes into account women's identified needs is a first step to overcoming these gendered barriers (Women's Enterprise Centre 2014).

Financial institutions globally have long maintained discriminatory practices, denying loans and credit that could enable women to start or run a business simply on the basis of gender. As women in the industrialized countries campaign to legislate against such discrimination, it is not easy to end traditional attitudes translated into business practices.

Despite the obstacles, quite a few ambitious women have managed to overcome many of the financial barriers to self-employment. Madame C.J. Walker (born Sarah Breedlove, 1867–1919), for example, was an early African-American inventor and entrepreneur who in 1905 developed and sold hair products for black women. With her wealth, she became an activist against lynching and a philanthropist (Bundles 2001). In the twentieth and twenty-first centuries, highly successful women can be found in the entertainment, cosmetics, and clothing industries: they include Lady Gaga, k.d. lang, Beyoncé, Beverly Mascoll, Linda Lundstrom, Shania Twain, and Sandra Oh.

The factors that propel women to become self-employed vary. In the Global North, self-employed women include those who previously worked in major corporations but left to start their own enterprises because of dissatisfaction over gender inequities in pay, power, and promotion (Wirth 2001). However, the vast majority of self-employed women in the world choose self-employment for other reasons. For many women who must combine work and family responsibilities, self-employment allows them to earn needed income and to take care of their families at the same time. Some female entrepreneurs in Africa have started their own businesses in non-traditional fields such as construction and information technology (Kigozi 2007).

Globally, self-employed women have some commonalities: they tend to work out of their homes; they are found in enterprises at the lower end of economic productive activities, particularly those with few barriers to entry (food preparation, child care, and craft production); and they start enterprises that allow them to use their traditional skills and knowledge.

Unemployment

Most countries recognize the responsibility to provide jobs to those who cannot find them, even though many governments may fail to avoid high levels of unemployment. The United States is almost alone in denying this obligation. Governmental attempts to encourage or stimulate private-sector employment are often unsuccessful, especially for women, the working class, and racialized groups, who are routinely "last hired and first fired." It has been argued that the right of an individual to employment, provided by the government if not available otherwise, should be recognized as a human right (Nickel 1978–79; Sen 2001).

Unemployment rates have almost always been higher for women than for men, and young women experience more unemployment and longer periods of unemployment than young men (United Nations Department of Economic and Social Affairs 2000). With the high unemployment rates and outsourcing of jobs in the North America today, there are more jobs available in the service sector but fewer available in manufacturing. For this reason, the job market has opened up for women. If women are to be able to lead decent, productive lives, among the first priorities must be the assurance that when they seek employment, jobs will be available. To be able to compete on equal terms with men for an inadequate number of actual jobs will not be enough.

The Politics of Work: Barriers and Strategies

Sexual and Gender Harassment

Sexual and gender harassment has only recently come under legal scrutiny. This pervasive problem for women workers is very much underreported. The experience of intersectional differences such as being lesbian, bisexual, transgender, a racialized minority, an immigrant, a refugee, or Indigenous also increases the frequency, severity, and likelihood of negative consequences for women who report being harassed in the workplace. While few studies have been able to untangle the effect of intersectional inequalities on harassment, it can be extrapolated from both general victimization reporting in Canadian society and reported experiences of women.

In the workplace, sexual harassment occurs when an employer or supervisor demands sexual favours from an employee under threat of dismissal or other reprisal, often not made explicit, or when an employee is subjected to persistent unwelcome sexual advances or innuendoes (see Box 11.5). It includes not only the harassment of females by males but also the harassment by customers of women whose job requires that they wear sexually provocative clothing, harassment of male employees by female supervisors, and same-sex advances (Christensen 1988). Studies have found that many men view certain sexual behaviours (sexual advances or solicitation of sex in exchange for a reward) as flattering to women. These behaviours contribute to a hostile work environment and may inflict great harm upon a victim. Sexual harassment is costly to both the private and public sectors. A 2009 Statistics Canada study showed that the estimated cost to society for the harassment and sexual assault of women in one year is roughly $3.9 billion (Hoddenbagh, Zhang, and McDonald 2014). The consequences of sexual harassment on the job include loss of productivity, turnover in the workforce, increased health-care costs, and great distress to those who are victimized.

For women, gender harassment usually has a sexual element. Examples include "GamerGate" and the Dalhousie University dentistry school scandal, where women in both instances, among other verbal and physical harassments, were threatened with rape for being in "male spaces," as well as the stories of women officers in the RCMP being presented with pornography, threatened with assault, and verbally assaulted in a sexualized manner.

In the past, women who were victimized by sexual harassment were unlikely to complain. They felt that speaking up or confronting a harasser would make no difference. Too often, they were not believed (or feared they would not be) when they lodged complaints against those with power and prestige. However, as more workplaces establish and implement codes of conduct to regulate such offensive behaviours (Box 11.5), women are increasingly seeking redress at their workplace and in the courts. Countries as diverse as Argentina, Canada, Costa Rica, Japan, New Zealand, the Philippines, South Africa, the United States, and the members of the European Union have defined sexual harassment as a legal wrong that merits sanctions and remedies.

Box 11.5 Key Issues

Levels of Sexual Harassment

What Is the Law on Sexual Harassment?

The BC Human Rights Code forbids sex discrimination, which includes sexual harassment in public services and in rental housing and employment circumstances. This means everyone has the right to be free from sexual harassment in their employment and in rental housing situations and services provided to the public generally. If sexual harassment is serious, it may be a crime under the Criminal Code of Canada, called "Stalking, criminal harassment and cyberbullying." A victim may also be able to sue the person doing the harassment for damages.

What Are Some Examples of Sexual Harassment?

Sexual harassment can include the following conduct:
- sexual behaviour that you feel you must accept to keep your job, get a promotion, get a good mark, keep your apartment, or get repairs done.
- unwanted touching, patting, or grabbing (which may also be a crime under the Criminal Code).
- the unwanted display of sexual pictures such as pin-ups; employers may be responsible for harassment if they allow some employees to harass others, instead of stopping the behaviour.
- sexual leering, teasing, or telling obscene jokes.
- an invitation to dinner or a movie, or to some other social activity, from a supervisor, teacher, or landlord who implies that you must accept it or risk negative effects on your job, your mark in school or your apartment.
- an unwanted invitation from a supervisor, co-worker, teacher, or landlord that is continually repeated.

Source: Canadian Bar Association, BC Branch (2014).

Social Support for Working Women

Trade Unions. The labour union is the principal organized support group for working people outside the family. It is noteworthy that many primary fields of women's employment, whether blue-collar, pink-collar, or professional, are not unionized. It is also noteworthy that in this current age of globalized labour, the obstacles to recognition of unions remain. When a union organized in Walmart's Jonquiere Quebec store in 2004 (the first Walmart in North America to do so), the company abruptly closed its doors, throwing 190 employees out of work. After a decade of legal challenges, in 2014 the Supreme Court of Canada ruled in favour of the employees and ordered damages to be paid.

Grace Hartman, CUPE president, is the first woman to lead a national union.

The conditions militating against women's participation in trade union activity today are much the same as they were over a century ago. Women are seen as dependents, whose primary role is in the home. The demands of domestic responsibility often leave women little time to devote to trade union activities. Women traditionally lack training and experience in public speaking and self-assertion, important aspects of union activity. Often the least skilled and lowest-paid workers, they have had little bargaining leverage with employers.

Unionization has proven beneficial to working women, and existing unions are becoming more aware of women's issues. The Canadian Labour Congress, for example, has endorsed pay equity, women's access to trades, and improved child care. It is on record as opposing racism, homophobia, transphobia, and violence against women. Despite unions' growing awareness of the importance of organizing for working women's rights, barriers still exist to women joining unions. During the past decade, a number of significant efforts have been made to organize clerical women workers, hotel and hospitality workers, and cleaners and to negotiate contracts that would address their interests.

One model for a trade union association sensitive to the productive and reproductive needs of women is the Self-Employed Women's Association (SEWA) in India. Formed in 1972, SEWA is a trade union of women who work as petty vendors and home-based producers. The union establishes savings and credit co-operatives to provide working capital to its members. Its producer co-operatives help women secure higher prices for their goods, enhancing their income. Through SEWA, members have been able to learn about plumbing, carpentry, radio repair, accounting, and management, thereby upgrading their skills. SEWA also provides legal services, which assist members in obtaining the benefits of Indian labour legislation, and welfare services, such as maternal protection schemes, widows' benefits, child care, and training of midwives (Self-Employed Women's Association 2008).

Professional Organizations. Since women have not been well represented in the professions in the past, they have not been prominent in the leadership of professional organizations. Beginning in the 1960s, groups of professional women began to take responsibility for raising the consciousness of the members of professional organizations about the problems and rights of women and the need to include women in leadership positions. One of the authors of the US editions of this text, Florence Denmark, helped develop a section on the psychology of women for the American Psychological Association and became its president (1980–81). In many other professional organizations, women's caucuses have been formed. As a result, women are playing a greater role than in the past in leadership positions and in keeping these groups alert to the problems of women professionals and to the need to include gender in the curriculum of these disciplines.

Networks. The family, the trade union, and the professional association are formal organizations that have a legal standing. Networks are loose connections among individuals who know one another (or of one another) and support one another; they are informal and have no legal standing. They are, for many, the most significant support group in the workplace. Networks are at once powerful and "invisible," operating to influence career opportunities and the workings of the business and professional worlds but not legally liable or open to attack.

Men in power have always relied on networks. The "old-boys' network" often begins in school, especially private schools, or at universities, where young men get to know others who share their interests. These acquaintances are often kept up through a lifetime and broadened and shaped through other associations: clubs, civic groups, and special membership organizations. Networks provide their members with access to important information and resources.

Women who share experiences and interests have developed their own groups and relationships for mutual aid, sometimes on a formal but more often on an informal basis (Hunt et al. 2009). The women's movement has created a supportive climate for the formation of women's networks by keeping women aware of their need for one another and by encouraging women's mutual support. Women use professional caucuses, newsletters, and regular meetings as more or less formal networking instruments.

Laws against Sexist Job Discrimination

The 1985 Canadian Human Rights Act (CHRA) prohibits discrimination on the basis of gender, race, ethnicity, age, and a number of other grounds. The Employment Equity Act (EEA) protects the rights of four "designated groups" in particular: women, people with disabilities, Indigenous people, and visible minorities. Employment equity requires that employers who have discriminated against women and other designated groups set goals for reducing or ending such discrimination. The Act states that "employment equity means more than treating persons the same way but also requires special measures and the accommodation of differences."

Rather than the term *employment equity*, the United States and some other countries use the term *affirmative action* for promoting employment for historically disadvantaged persons, including women and racialized groups. The European Court of Justice has ordered member states of the European Union to end discriminatory treatment of women in the workplace. As a result, national laws that discriminate against women in the workplace have been overturned. The Court has also ruled favourably on affirmative action cases for women. Its rulings in the 1990s require employers, when weighing the experience of women and men for a job, to take into consideration the time that women have taken off from their careers in order to meet their family responsibilities. The development of European law with respect to women, work, and equality has led to the advancement of women's rights on issues related to pay, pensions, part-time work, night work, and work in the armed services. Throughout Latin America, the majority of countries have constitutional guarantees or laws requiring equal pay for equal work. Chile has strengthened this right by allowing women the right to submit formal complaints or file court cases if they are the victims of wage discrimination (Berger 2012).

Many women experience job discrimination due to pregnancy and maternity leave. In Canada, Employment Insurance (EI) provides maternity and parental benefits to individuals who are pregnant, have recently given birth, are adopting a child, or are caring for a newborn. The basic rate for calculating EI benefits is 55 per cent of the average insurable weekly earnings. As of 1 January 2015, the maximum yearly insurable earnings amount is $49,500, making the maximum benefit $524 per week. The United States does not require that private employers provide any paid maternity leave, although many companies are required to give up to three months of unpaid leave. Europe tends to be more generous with maternity leave. Britain offers the longest maternity leave, providing 52 weeks leave with a partial salary. Germany, France, and Belgium offer closer to four months leave. Currently in the works in Europe is a proposal requiring fully paid maternity leave for five months and paternity leave for two weeks. The proposal was passed by the European Union Parliament and will go before the European Union states for review. Some governments feel that if passed, this will hurt the economy and deter employers from hiring women (Lieberman 2010). On the other hand, several studies have found that family-friendly policies may benefit companies in the long run because employees' productivity, commitment, and job satisfaction increase as a result (Sabattini and Crosby 2009).

Equal Pay–Comparable Worth

Those who have enforced laws against discrimination in the past have applied them only to persons doing the same work. It was illegal for an employer to pay a man more than a woman for the same job with the same job specifications. This interpretation may be in the process of changing. Only if it does will a real attack on the inequities faced by women in the labour force be possible, for few women do the same work as men. "Women's work" is generally compensated at rates substantially lower than what men get for work of comparable value. Discrimination against women begins with initial gender segregation of tasks and persists into the sphere of remuneration.

The Impact of Feminist Activism

Many feminist organizations have demanded recognition of a woman's right to engage in useful, meaningful, and rewarding work. Feminist activism has also stood for equal pay and respect for women in the workplace, equal opportunity in job and career advancement, and improvement in opportunity, pay, and recognition for women of colour.

Practical arrangements to relieve the burdens of women who work outside the home have been few and far between. The number of day care centres has increased but not nearly enough to accommodate all working mothers, and they are still too costly. A few work organizations have experimented with **flextime**, instituting a system of flexible work hours so that women and men can carry out home and family responsibilities during the day and work as well. However, such arrangements are still unusual, and not always actually flexible: ever-present mobile devices, laptop computers, and the expectation of constant availability pressure women and men at home with children to keep working even on their off-hours.

One of the most important developments in recent years is the growing recognition that deeper and more fundamental changes than these are needed in the economy. Women cannot achieve feminist objectives without a substantial breakdown of the class differences that pit the interests of advantaged women against those of disadvantaged women. An equal opportunity to exploit the weak is not the aim of the women's movement. More humane and less hierarchical organizations of work are needed, along with a concern on the part of society with what work is for, what investments shall be made, and what products shall be made. Work that serves human needs and interests while respecting the environment is better for both women and men than work for increased profits. Progress toward these objectives will require fundamental changes in the way the work of both women and men is organized and conducted.

Summary

Every known society has assigned work by gender, and the work done by women has traditionally been valued less than that done by men. Women's reproductive functions have been used as an excuse for the division of labour by gender. Although the labour involved in reproduction and child rearing is essential for any society, often it is not recognized, and it is almost always unpaid.

Maintaining the domestic unit is essential to the functioning of society and the economy, but it has been given neither economic nor social value. Women who sell their labour in the marketplace find their jobs devalued; they are restricted in their job choices and paid less than men.

When a society's economy is based on a simple domestic mode of production, economic and domestic roles tend to be integrated for both women and men. As a society modernizes and work becomes capital intensive rather than labour intensive, women tend to be phased out of the economy and confined to the domestic sphere. Women "subsidize" capitalist enterprises by servicing workers for free, producing and caring for the next generation of workers, and providing a cheap pool of labour when needed.

As slavery and serfdom gave way to "free" wage labour, a working class evolved. Within this class, women have been barred from most trades of skilled labour by guilds and craft organizations. Most working-class women have been employed as domestic wage labour. In past centuries, increasing numbers of women, particularly immigrants, have found work in factories. Today's immigrants, pushed by the forces of globalization, often can only find work in the service sector as nannies, maids, and sex workers. Most other women today are employed as pink-collar workers in clerical work, sales, and services, jobs considered "female." A growing economic trend is the use of precarious workers, who do not receive the benefits, security, or earnings of full-time workers.

The professions are also segregated by gender. Within the "female professions," men hold most top-level jobs. Women sometimes find it difficult to enter a "male profession," much less to rise within it, but some gains are evident. A few professional women are choosing to "opt out" of their careers, questioning the male-defined conditions of the work itself.

Economic competition between companies and countries has intensified as a result of globalization. Multinational corporations move their operations to regions where the labour costs are cheaper. Some women in developing countries migrate to developed countries or wealthier developing countries, where their labour often benefits middle-class and upper-class households, including allowing many professional women to advance their careers.

Women find it difficult to compete with men for jobs because their interests are not entirely separate from those of the men to whom they are in some way related. Some men do not support women's attempt to gain economic equality because they believe this would threaten their traditionally superior status in the job market and at home.

Women on the job may be subject to sexual or gender harassment, particularly those who experience intersectional inequalities. Women who work can find social support in formal organizations, such as trade unions and professional organizations. Women's informal networks are especially important for mutual aid and information and resource sharing.

More countries are passing laws to lessen job discrimination. Employment equity programs attempt to improve the opportunities of those who have suffered from discrimination. Many women around the globe are calling for laws that will require equal pay for work of comparable value.

The women's movement has raised women's aspirations and brought about some changes in attitude. However, it appears that feminist objectives will not be achieved without structural changes in the economy and society.

Discussion Questions

1. How might you deal with the tensions between managing unpaid work and your paid work? How will your answer change if you enter into a domestic partnership, if you are not in one already?
2. Select a place of work—a hospital, a business firm, a school—to which you have access. List all the positions and who holds them by gender. Are particular types of work done mainly or exclusively by women? Are women found mainly at some levels and not at others?
3. Many women feel that family obligations pose special problems for them as they pursue careers. In what ways does society provide "relief" for women who work or study outside the home? To what extent are these services satisfactory or unsatisfactory? What are some alternative means for alleviating this problem?
4. Research the experiences of working women in another country or region of the world. What kinds of work do these women do? What child-care options do they have? How do they balance family and work responsibilities? What are the similarities and differences between women in your society and the one you chose to study?
5. If you have a particular career goal, study the roles of women in that career or profession in the past and at present. What proportion of people in the field are female? If there are obstacles to women's success in this field, might they be overcome?

Recommended Resources

Ehrenreich, Barbara, and Arlie Russell Hochschild, eds. 2002. *Global Woman: Nannies, Maids, and Sex Workers in the New Economy*. New York: Henry Holt. This book examines the impact and consequences of globalization on women around the world. The lives of women migrants from the Dominican Republic, Taiwan, Vietnam, Mexico, Thailand, Sri Lanka, and the Philippines are analyzed.

Logan McCallum, Mary Jane. 2014. *Indigenous Women, Work, and History, 1940–1980*. Winnipeg: University of Manitoba Press. Historian Mary Jane Logan McCallum presents multiple case studies of Indigenous women in a variety of occupations and shows how they maintained links to social and cultural responsibilities of community building and state resistance.

Man, Guida, and Rina Cohen, eds. 2015. *Studies in Family, Work, and Identity: Engendering Transnational Voices*. Waterloo, ON: Wilfrid Laurier University Press. The contributors examine the transnational practices and identities of immigrant women, youth, and children in an era of global migration and neo-liberalism. It focuses on individual experiences and human agency as well as the social, economic, political, and cultural processes that affect them.

Sangster, Joan. 2010. *Transforming Labour: Women and Work in Postwar Canada*. Toronto: University of Toronto Press. Using case studies from across Canada, Sangster explores a range of themes, including women's experiences within trade unions, Indigenous women's changing patterns of work, and the challenges faced by immigrant women. She explores how women overcame the gender barriers to the workplace and advocated for their rights once they were on the job.

Vincent, Carole. 2013. *Why Do Women Earn Less Than Men?* Canadian Research Data Centre Network. www.rdc-cdr.ca/sites/default/files/carole_vincent_synthesis_final_2.pdf. This report unravels the gender wage gap and proposes policy recommendations to close it.

Vosko, Leah. 2010. *Managing the Margins: Gender, Citizenship and the International Regulation of Precarious Employment*. Oxford: Oxford University Press. Vosko analyzes the interplay of employment, gender, and citizenship boundaries using extensive original quantitative and qualitative material and research on the evolution of international labour regulations, demonstrating how these norms work to create a marginalized workforce.

Werner, Marion, et al. *Conceptual Guide to the Unpaid Work Module*. Gender and Work Data Base. www.genderwork.ca/gwd/?page_id=31. This module is an important resource as it evaluates how unpaid work like caregiving, domestic work, and volunteering are defined, socially valued, organized, and gendered. It provides statistical data on how unpaid work is measured in Canada and how it is shaped by gender relations as they intersect with race, ethnicity, (dis)ability, age, and sexuality.

12 Women and Politics

Chapter Outline

- Political Power
- Women as Political Leaders
- Women as Citizens
- Women's Political Participation

This chapter will help you
- Comprehend the nature of the public role that women have performed throughout history
- Understand the complex analysis of power, context, and agency
- Recognize the structural barriers that prevent women's political participation
- Appreciate how women have engaged in social transformation through non-governmental movements
- Learn about the strategies employed to promote and establish equality beyond gender

> *The very act of being an advocate for justice is ... fueled by a belief in political and social change, a belief in the idea that we can make a better world. As an activist, you have got to believe. This belief in the possibility of social change not only fuels people's willingness to engage in activism, but it is, in itself, the first lesson for social activists of any kind.*
>
> —URVASHI VAID, 2012

> *What is the moral meaning of who we are? What do we take personally? How do perceived issues propel or diffuse our political commitments? I think these questions can only be answered again and again with difficulty.*
>
> —JUNE JORDAN, 1998

Politics encompasses more than just voting and running for office—the public sphere. Politics is also that which influences the choices made and the lives lived in most intimate moments—the private sphere. Consider the following response by then prime minister Stephen Harper who answered calls for a federal inquiry into cases of missing and murdered Indigenous women by saying "... it isn't really high on our radar to be honest" (Kappo 2014). See Chapter 3 for more on the missing and murdered Indigenous women in Canada.

Todd Akin, was a US Congress Representative from Missouri and a contender in 2012 for a US Senate seat. Responding to a question about whether he would support a woman's right to an abortion in the event of rape, he answered: "It seems to me, from what I understand from doctors, that's really rare. If it's a legitimate rape, the female body has ways to shut that whole thing down." Implicit in Akin's statement is the idea that if a rape results in pregnancy, then it is the woman's fault and therefore her choices about what to do about that pregnancy must be circumscribed by law and policy. In reality, more than 32,000 women who are raped each year will become pregnant (Geiger 2012).

Now consider another view, that of Nobel Peace Prize laureate Leymah Gbowee. In her Nobel lecture, she argues that "rape and abuse is the result of a larger problem, and that problem is the absence of women in the decision-making space. If more women were part of decision-making in most societies, there would be less exclusive policies and laws that are blind to abuses women endure" (Gbowee 2011). Gbowee, who experienced the horrors of war in her country, Liberia, and its devastating impact on women, points out that rape and abuse under any circumstance reflect the gendered hierarchies and dichotomies pervasive in all societies (Peterson and Runyan 2010).

These two contrary views demonstrate that violence against women and members of the LGBTQ community, whether in the form of active

In 2013, six of Canada's premiers were women. From left to right: Eva Aariak (Nunavut), Bob McLeod (Northwest Territories), Alison Redford (Alberta), Robert Ghiz (Prince Edward Island), Greg Selinger (Manitoba), Darrell Dexter (Nova Scotia), Kathleen Wynne (Ontario), Pauline Marois (Quebec), David Alward (New Brunswick), Christy Clark (British Columbia), Brad Wall (Saskatchewan), Kathy Dunderdale (Newfoundland and Labrador), and Darrell Pasloski (Yukon).

violence (rape, sexual assault, domestic abuse, enforced sterilization, coerced heterosexuality, honour killings, homophobia, and transphobia) or structural violence (women's unpaid, precarious, and low-paid work; poverty; lack of access to capital and credit; employment discrimination; lack of reproductive rights; and lack of educational opportunities) all involve political and legal choices and decisions made by (mostly) men in both the private and public spheres. As the 1976s feminist phrase put it: "The personal is political." Gender hierarchies and structural inequalities shape realities daily and affect what choices can be made: at home, at work, and in the public square. This chapter examines these hierarchies and inequalities by focusing on the gender politics through which public laws and policies are created. Just as importantly, it examines how feminist scholars and activists—past and present, nationally and globally—have participated in the political process, often seeking to redress asymmetries of power. In this sense, politics is about ideas, morals, commitments, and, indeed, the desire and ability to effect social change.

Public laws, made and enforced largely by men, have determined women's sexual and reproductive rights by defining marriage, when sexual relations are or are not legal, and whether a woman must continue a pregnancy. Until recently violence against women was largely ignored by law enforcement and the seriousness of rape minimized, except when it was the rape of "our" women by men belonging to a subordinate minority or by the enemy under conditions of war. Also, the rights of women were not understood to be human rights, to be included on the agendas of those working to promote the international recognition of human rights (Tickner 2001).

Public policy determines the effective rights and obligations of women to their children and their ability to carry out their wishes with regard to their children's care, education, and safety. Public policy also restricts and shapes women's rights and capacities to select ways to support themselves and determines the conditions under which they work. Public policy intersects with women's lives as it structurally constructs and maintains patterns of oppression for racialized, disabled, impoverished, and LGBTQ persons.

Some groups of feminists have advocated that women increase their formal political participation, in part to change the male-centred and male-dominated construction of politics, policies, and laws. At the same time, they have argued that political and social life ought to better reflect women's particular concerns and values of caring and concern for others (Tronto 1993; Harrington 2000; Held 2006).

Feminist social scientists have explored the roles women play in formal and grassroots or community-level organizations; their leadership styles, intra-party roles, and power; and how they organize on issues they consider important (Bookman and Morgen 1988; Hawkesworth 2012a). In recent years, women have often voted quite differently from men, forcing candidates and political parties to pay attention to the "women's vote." Also, women have been gaining political power in Canada and around the world (Canadian Press 2013). Feminist political scientists have studied the rise of women to elective legislative and executive offices and ask whether having more women in positions of political power leads to more progressive policies and laws.

Political Power

What Is Power?

Power is the capacity to get something done, whether directly or indirectly. Women may exercise power in the domestic sphere in terms of their influence within their families. Men's power, in contrast, is "more co-ordinated and structured within an institutionalized framework" (Ridd and Callaway 1987, 3). Political power is usually exercised by means of institutionalized structures, including the military, the government, the economy, and religious, educational, and legal systems. Such structures protect those who wield power and enable them to disperse their power more widely (Hartsock 1983; Ridd and Callaway 1987).

The power that individuals or groups possess involves "a social relationship between groups that determines access to, use of, and control over the basic material and ideological resources in society" (Bookman and Morgen 1988, 4). Except in smaller societies (Sanday 1981, 2002), men generally have greater access to and control over resources. Power over others fosters relationships of social distance and subordination.

Power is also the capacity to not do something—to not marry, not bear or be responsible for a child, not engage in physical labour, and not have sexual intercourse when another demands it. Only those who have sufficient power to protect themselves from the aggression of others can ensure they will not be coerced to the will of others.

Feminists have pointed out that power need not imply dominance. Power to get things done can be shared and distributed evenly. This is the notion behind the organizations of most feminist utopias where the sharing of power is the chosen mode of governance. This has been attempted on a limited basis in communes and small societal groupings throughout the world. In a complex industrial society, the sharing of power has been difficult even to imagine. Feminists seek, at the very least, to reduce the extent to which society is organized hierarchically, with vast disparities of power between those who command and those who must obey.

Power is a social relationship. Power works within a particular context and is influenced by individual and collective agency (the ability of individuals and groups to act in particular situations). **Agency** can be, and is, exercised by both those in power and those who seek to influence them. Power can be wielded by the "powerless" despite the fact that they possess fewer resources and must often organize in larger numbers to offset their "powerlessness." As long as the analysis of power and politics is confined to the study of institutions in which fewer female faces are present—courts, bureaucracies, legislatures, and executive levels—women will be perceived as more powerless than they are. A more fruitful approach to a better understanding of women and politics would be to look at arenas where more women can be found—neighbourhoods, schools, voluntary associations, and organizations (Moser and Peake 1987; Bookman and Morgen 1988; Dalley 1988; Cott 1990).

Power and Authority

There is an important distinction between *power* and *authority*. Those with authority are accepted as being justified in having and using power. People who seize power need eventually to find a way of legitimizing it in order to command obedience to decisions without resorting to the continued use or threat of force. Economic power and authority are the ability and accepted right to control the production and distribution of resources; political power and authority are the ability and accepted right to control or influence decisions about war and peace, legal protection and punishment, and group decision making in general, including the assignment of leadership roles. In complex societies, political power usually includes a great deal of economic power, but political and economic power can and do operate separately. Sometimes they function in a complementary way; at other times, they are at odds.

Although power, influence, and authority are often exercised by the same person, they are distinct, and each may be exercised without the other. Women have from time to time exercised power (the ability to accomplish something or have others do so) but often have not held authority, due to cultural beliefs that women do not possess a legitimate right to power (O'Barr 1984). Women exercising power are sometimes accused of using their domestic or familial influence to "manipulate" others because they are not acknowledged as rightfully powerful.

History provides many examples of women who held power by virtue of their relationships with powerful men. Royal mistresses in the courts of European kings even had official status. In some countries in the twentieth and twenty-first centuries, women married to leaders have occasionally exercised notable political power. In the United States, Eleanor Roosevelt was able to undertake major humanitarian programs because of her influence with her husband, President Franklin Delano Roosevelt, and his associates. When some of her ideas were not endorsed by the president, she pursued them through women's

Box 12.1 Key Issues

Women Do Not Belong in the Public Sphere: "Nice Women Don't Want to Vote"

On 27 January 1914, a large delegation of both men and women appeared before the Legislative Assembly of Manitoba, once again to present the case for granting women the right to vote in provincial elections. Included in the group were representatives of the Political Equality League, the Grain Growers' Association, the Young Women's Christian Association, the Trades and Labor Council, the Icelandic Women's Suffrage Association, the Canadian Women's Press Club, and the Women's Christian Temperance Union. Dr. Mary Crawford, the President of the University Women's Club and of the Political Equality League, introduced the five speakers, two women and three men, and the last to address the lawmakers was Mrs. Nellie McClung. Then rivalling Ralph Connor as Manitoba's most popular writer, Mrs. McClung made her point with sharp lucidity. The delegation had come, she said, not to beg for a favour but to obtain simple justice. "Have we not the brains to think? Hands to work? Hearts to feel? And lives to live?" she demanded. "Do we not bear our part in citizenship? Do we not help build the Empire? Give us our due!"

The Conservative premier, Sir Rodmond Roblin, rejected Mrs. McClung's demand absolutely. "Most women," he told the petitioners, "don't want the vote." In Colorado, he informed them, where women could vote, "they shrank from the polls as from a pestilence." Woman suffrage, he said, "would be a retrograde movement . . . it will break up the home . . . it will throw the children into the arms of servant girls." Then he added, gallantly, that there was "nothing wrong with a society that produced such attractive, pure, and noble ladies" as these now before him, but "the mother that is worthy of the name and of the good affection of a good man has a hundredfold more influence in shaping public opinion around her dinner table than she would have in the market place, hurling her eloquent phrases to the multitude."

Roblin's flowery courtesies expressed the received attitude of his time and his social group towards the tender sex, simultaneously idealized and subjugated. He loved his mother, he said, and for her sweet sake he revered all women. "Gentle women," he described the ladies, "queen of the home, set apart by your great function of motherhood. . . . Women are superior to men, now and always." Nice women did not want to vote, the common argument ran, and since women exercised so important an influence for good, they must be sheltered from the world and its corruption.

Source: Gutkin and Gutkin (1996).

---

networks (Cook 1992). In Argentina, Eva Perón, wife of President Juan Perón, wielded significant power and her influence was portrayed in the musical play *Evita*. In China, Chairman Mao Zedong's wife, Jiang Qing, was a major force in that country's Cultural Revolution and was part of the "Group of Four." After Mao's death, she fell out with the new leadership and was sentenced to prison for counter-revolutionary activity. She later committed suicide. In Canada, the more gender-neutral "spouse of the prime minister" is not the equivalent of official titles such as the US "First Lady"; there is no official term at all for this role. In Canada, there is no expectation of a public role for the prime minister's spouse, but some have been influential advisers behind the scenes. The role of the partner of political leaders may be shaped differently as more heterosexual

Box 12.2 Time to Reflect

"Sultana's Dream" (1905)

I became very curious to know where the men were. I met more than a hundred women while walking there, but not a single man.

"Where are the men?" I asked her.

"In their proper places, where they ought to be."

"Pray let me know what you mean by 'their proper places.'"

"Oh, I see my mistake, you cannot know our customs, as you were never here before. We shut our men indoors."

"Just as we are kept in the *zenana*?"*

"Exactly so."

"How funny." I burst into a laugh. Sister Sara laughed too.

"But, dear Sultana, how unfair it is to shut in the harmless women and let loose the men."

"Why? It is not safe for us to come out of the *zenana*, as we are naturally weak."

"Yes, it is not safe so long as there are men about the streets, nor is it so when a wild animal enters a marketplace."

"Of course not."

"Suppose some lunatics escape from the asylum and begin to do all sorts of mischief to men, horses, and other creatures: in that case what will your countrymen do?"

"They will try to capture them and put them back into their asylum."

"Thank you! And you do not think it wise to keep sane people inside an asylum and let loose the insane?"

"Of course not!" said I, laughing lightly.

"As a matter of fact, in your country this very thing is done! Men, who do or at least are capable of doing no end of mischief, are let loose and the innocent women shut up in the *zenana*! How can you trust those untrained men out of doors?"

"We have no hand or management of our social affairs. In India man is lord and master. He has taken to himself all powers and privileges and shut up women in the *zenana*."

"Why do you allow yourselves to be shut up?"

"Because it cannot be helped as they are stronger than women."

"A lion is stronger than a man, but it does not enable him to dominate the human race. You have neglected the duty you owe yourselves, and you have lost your natural rights by shutting your eyes to your own interests."

"But my dear Sister Sara, if we do everything by ourselves, what will the men do then?"

"They should not do anything, excuse men; they are fit for nothing. Only catch them and put them into the *zenana*."

"But it would be very easy to catch and put them inside the four walls?" said I. "And even if this were done, would all their business—political and commercial—also go with them into the *zenana*?"

Sister Sara made no reply. She only smiled sweetly. Perhaps she thought it was useless to argue with one who was no better than a frog in a well.

*The *zenana* is the women's living quarters in a household.

Source: From Rokeya Sakhawat Hossain, *Sultana's Dream and Selections from the Secluded Ones*, edited and translated by Roushan Jahan. New York: The Feminist Press at The City University of New York, 1988. Translation copyright © Roushan Jahan, 1988. Reprinted with the permission of the publishers, www.feministpress.org. All Rights Reserved.

women, lesbian, gays, and bisexuals are elected to public office.

The exercise of power based on unofficial influence is difficult to establish or assess. Reference to the power of the "women behind the throne" has often been used by those who wish to justify a status quo in which women have little direct power—or authority—of their own. More than ever women are challenging traditional notions that women lack power and authority. As women fought to gain political power throughout the twentieth and twenty-first centuries, more women have become president, prime minister, or queen regnant of their countries, commanding considerable power and authority.

Types of Government

As societies have become larger and more complex, forms of government have become more specialized and exclusionary. Full participation occurs only in the smallest, more transparent societies, such as hunting-and-gathering bands, where political decisions are made by public discussion and consensus. There are no government specialists, and leaders arise in particular situations according to need and skills. An older woman with experience and skill might organize and direct others in food gathering. A good public speaker might assume responsibility for expressing the will of the community.

Similar principles apply in slightly larger and more complex societies but on a more restricted basis. Some persons hold positions of authority as "chief" or "war leader" or "council member." In these societies, women tend to be more segregated as a group. If women do play a role in political processes, they tend to do so as "women," not as ordinary and equal group members. Among the Iroquois in North America, certain women, and not men, were entitled to select male group leaders. Men, on the other hand, were entitled to hold the leadership positions; women were not (Sanday 1981). Some Indigenous nations were matrilineal, with clanmothers holding both power and authority.

The most complex forms of government are heteropatriarchal states, based on male heterosexual privilege, which exclude most members of society from direct participation in making governmental decisions, though to be considered democratic they must have periodic elections. At the higher levels of a hierarchical structure, few can participate; but on the local level, small communities can conduct much of their business themselves. Here, participatory democracy may be possible even in a large, complex state. It is at the local level that women's voices are most likely to be heard. For example, more women are found in China on public councils in rural communities and in Canada on school boards and town councils and in greater numbers in provincial legislatures than at the federal level.

Women's Political Power in the Past

Women have occasionally exercised authority and political power in the past, both in dynastic states and in some pre-industrial societies (Schiff 2010). Such power often derived from their kinship positions as daughters, sisters, wives, and mothers. In the early Middle Ages in Europe, when a ruler's officials were actually royal household servants (and the head of the household governed the domestic affairs of the royal estate, which was the kingdom), it was considered perfectly natural to place the ruler's wife, or queen, at the head of these servants. When Henry II of England went to war (which was a great deal of the time) he left his queen, Eleanor of Aquitaine (c. 1122–1204), in charge of his kingdom. All his officials were ordered to report to her whenever he was away. As regents for their husbands or sons, queens could wield significant political power. Only when Henry II began to suspect that his queen favoured their sons over him did he stop making her England's ruler in his absence (Kelly 1957).

Historically, the rules of **primogeniture** decreed that inheritance go to the first-born male heir, and thus limited the power wielded by royal women. In Great Britain such laws of primogeniture date back to the seventeenth century and gave male children the right to succession to the throne before their sisters. In an effort to modernize the British monarchy, this law was finally repealed in 2011, and as a result the new rules allow a first-born daughter to precede a son to the throne.

As governments became more bureaucratically organized, women were less likely to share in political power. The recognized offices that might have been delegated to the queen gradually shifted to ministers, judges, councillors, and other functionaries, who were never women. Even in the reign of Queen Elizabeth I (1558–1603), who governed by virtue of inherited right, not a single woman was ever appointed to a ministerial post (Neale 1957).

Similarly, European colonial rule precipitated erosion of women's power where it had existed. In colonial settler states such as Canada, the United States, Australia, and much of Latin America, power was usurped from Indigenous nations, and the governments that developed structured continued dominance into policy and practice. Among the Iroquois of North America, for example, both women and men participated in village decision making. Women appointed men to official positions in the League of the Iroquois and could veto their decisions, although men controlled league deliberations. Iroquois women and men exercised separate but equal political power during the height of the Iroquois confederacy (Sanday 1981; Mann 2000). After a steady encroachment on their power by British and French colonizers, the Iroquois became unable to sustain themselves economically. Christian missionaries, some of whom intended to preserve the Iroquoian culture, suggested solutions that fundamentally restructured Iroquois gender relationships. The missionaries insisted on patriarchal husband–wife nuclear family relationships, which shut out the traditional power of the wife's mother in the family. In imposing their own cultural assumptions, the missionaries helped develop a new pattern of male dominance where it had not existed before (Sanday 1981). Domination of Indigenous culture forced colonial patriarchal culture and law onto First Nations.

Another example of the erosion of women's political power under colonial rule is that of the Igbo of southern Nigeria, where pre-colonial social arrangements included women's councils. By tradition, these councils exercised peacekeeping powers, including the corporal punishment and public humiliation of an offender and the destruction of the offender's property (Sanday 1981). British colonial rule in the late nineteenth century disrupted these cultural practices, which had afforded women real power. British authorities created new "warrant" chiefs where none had existed before, giving the position to local men (Falola and Aderinto 2010).

Patterns of Patriarchy

Anthropologist Ernestine Friedl has defined *male dominance* as a pattern in which men have better access, if not exclusive rights, to those activities to which society accords the greatest value and by which control and influence are exercised over others (Sanday 1981). Thus, male dominance means excluding women from political and economic decision making and includes aggression against women to enforce oppression.

Male dominance occurs in various kinds of social relationships. It may consist of gendered cultural assumptions about natural male aggressiveness, about being "tough" and "brave." It may involve designating specific places where only males may congregate, like men's clubs and bars, street corners, legislative chambers, courts, or boardrooms. It may involve violence against women and wife battering (Gordon 1988). Another form of male control of women was seen during and after the 2011 "Arab Spring" in Egypt. Many female activists took to the streets and slept in Tahrir Square, encouraged by men to support the uprising that removed Hosni Mubarak from power. While many Egyptian women admit to being sexually harassed when they are in Cairo's public spaces, they noted that they were not sexually harassed in Tahrir Square. But outside of the square security forces punished women activists by forcing them to endure sexual assaults and virginity tests. Female activists continue to experience these tactics at the hands of the Egyptian security forces. Repulsed by such treatment and the everyday sexual harassment they experience, thousands of Egyptian women marched in December 2011 to demonstrate against state security forces caught on video in the act of attacking, beating, and stripping female demonstrators in Tahrir Square. Other men provided solidarity security so women could carry out the march (Kirkpatrick 2012).

Women as Political Leaders

History provides several examples of women political leaders. In contemporary times, powerful female political figures have included Margaret Thatcher (United Kingdom), Indira Gandhi (India), Corazon Aquino (Philippines), Golda Meir (Israel), Benazir Bhutto (Pakistan), Megawati Sukarnoputri (Indonesia), Isabel Perón and Cristina Fernández (Argentina), Vigdís Finnbogadóttir and Jóhanna Sigurðardóttir (Iceland), Angela Merkel (Germany), Michelle Bachelet (Chile), Dilma Rousseff (Brazil), and Ellen Johnson Sirleaf (Liberia). Sirimavo Bandaranaike (Sri Lanka) became the world's first female head of government in 1960, served as prime minister three times, and was the mother of Sri Lanka's fourth executive president, Chandrika Kumaratunga. Canada's one female prime minister was Kim Campbell, who served for six months in 1993. Iceland's Jóhanna Sigurðardóttir became the world's first self-disclosed lesbian to become head of government. In 2012, women functioned at the highest levels of political power in 22 countries, including Argentina, Brazil, Germany, India, Liberia, Slovakia, and Thailand. Today, more women serve as presidents and prime ministers, but even more women are winning political office as parliamentarians, state legislators, and local councillors. Most of these women would not have identified as "feminist" and often continued to act in the interests of heteropatriarchy. They have also experienced misogyny and heteropatriarchial backlash, sometimes in violent ways—Benazir Bhutto, for example, was assassinated in 2007.

Generally, there is an inverse relationship between higher political offices and the presence of women in them. Universally, there are many more women in local and provincial political offices than in federal ones. On average, in 2012 women made up 19 per cent of federal legislators and 7 per cent of executive cabinet ministers worldwide. Socialist states have made great efforts to recruit women into federal legislatures, but in most of the states of the former Soviet bloc, the number of women in political office declined when tradition and capitalism became more influential than communism. Since China's transition to state capitalism, the government has lifted gender quotas for women at the local governmental and administrative levels. Consequently, fewer women occupy seats in the National People's Congress and the Communist Party Committee (Edwards 2007). In Latin America many women are winning elections to provincial and federal legislatures (Schwindt-Bayer 2011). In 2008, Rwanda became the country with the highest number of elected women in the world when the majority of members of the Chamber of Deputies elected were female; 60 per cent were female in 2013.

In Canada, although more women are being elected, women of colour, poor women, and Indigenous women are nearly invisible in government. Efforts continue to overcome this historic imbalance including a December 2015 open letter to Prime Minister Justin Trudeau from the Colour of Poverty Coalition:

> Indigenous peoples and racialized people account for approximately 25% of Canada's population. They are under-represented in virtually every level of leadership in Canada,

Rosemary Brown (1930–2003). When Rosemary Brown was elected to the British Columbia Legislative Assembly in 1972, she was the first black Canadian woman to become a member of any Canadian provincial legislature. She was also the first woman to run for leadership for a political party (NDP). After she left politics she taught women's studies at Simon Fraser University and was later appointed Chief Commissioner of the Ontario Human Rights Commission. She was a strong advocate for women's rights beyond Canadian borders and served as long-time CEO of MATCH International Women's Fund.

In the past women who held cabinet-level positions often found themselves appointed to ministries reserved for women—health and welfare, education, culture, the family, and consumer affairs (Randall 1987). But today throughout the world, more women serve in high cabinet positions in areas once considered exclusively male, such as defence, treasury, and foreign affairs.

In 1957 Ellen Fairclough became Canada's first female federal cabinet minister when she was appointed secretary of state by Progressive Conservative prime minister John Diefenbaker as the result of his campaign promise. Later serving as minister of Citizenship and Immigration, in 1960, Fairclough extended the franchise to Indigenous Canadians designated by the government as Status Indians. While Inuit could vote starting in the 1950s, previously First Nations could only vote if they gave up their treaty rights. In 1962, she introduced reforms to the immigration system that eliminated the "colour bar"—policy and language that racialized immigrants and prevented them from entering Canada. In its place she initiated "the points system" which she intended to be a bias-free assessment of potential immigrants.

Political Gains of Women in Office around the Globe

The forty-second Canadian Parliament includes a record number of female members of Parliament, with 88 women elected to the House of Commons in the 2015 election. This represents a gain of 12 seats over the previous record of 76 women in the forty-first Parliament. Gender equity in cabinet appointments fulfilled a campaign promise by Prime Minister Justin Trudeau. When asked by a journalist why this was important, Trudeau replied, "Because it's 2015."

How can countries elect more women to national legislative bodies? In many countries, gender quotas help more women get elected to office. In India, a 1993 constitutional amendment created the Panchayat Raj Act, which allocates 33 per cent of seats at the village and

but particularly so in the Senate. They are over-represented among those living in poverty in Canada, but their experiences and voices are often absent in governing and policy decisions made by Parliament and the Senate. We are encouraged that your Senate nominees selection criteria names priority consideration of those who represent Aboriginal peoples and linguistic, minority and ethnic communities, in addition to other factors. We ask that these considerations are foremost in the final selection and future appointments to the Senate. With your leadership, Canada can achieve racial as well as gender balance in the governance of the country. (OCASI 2015)

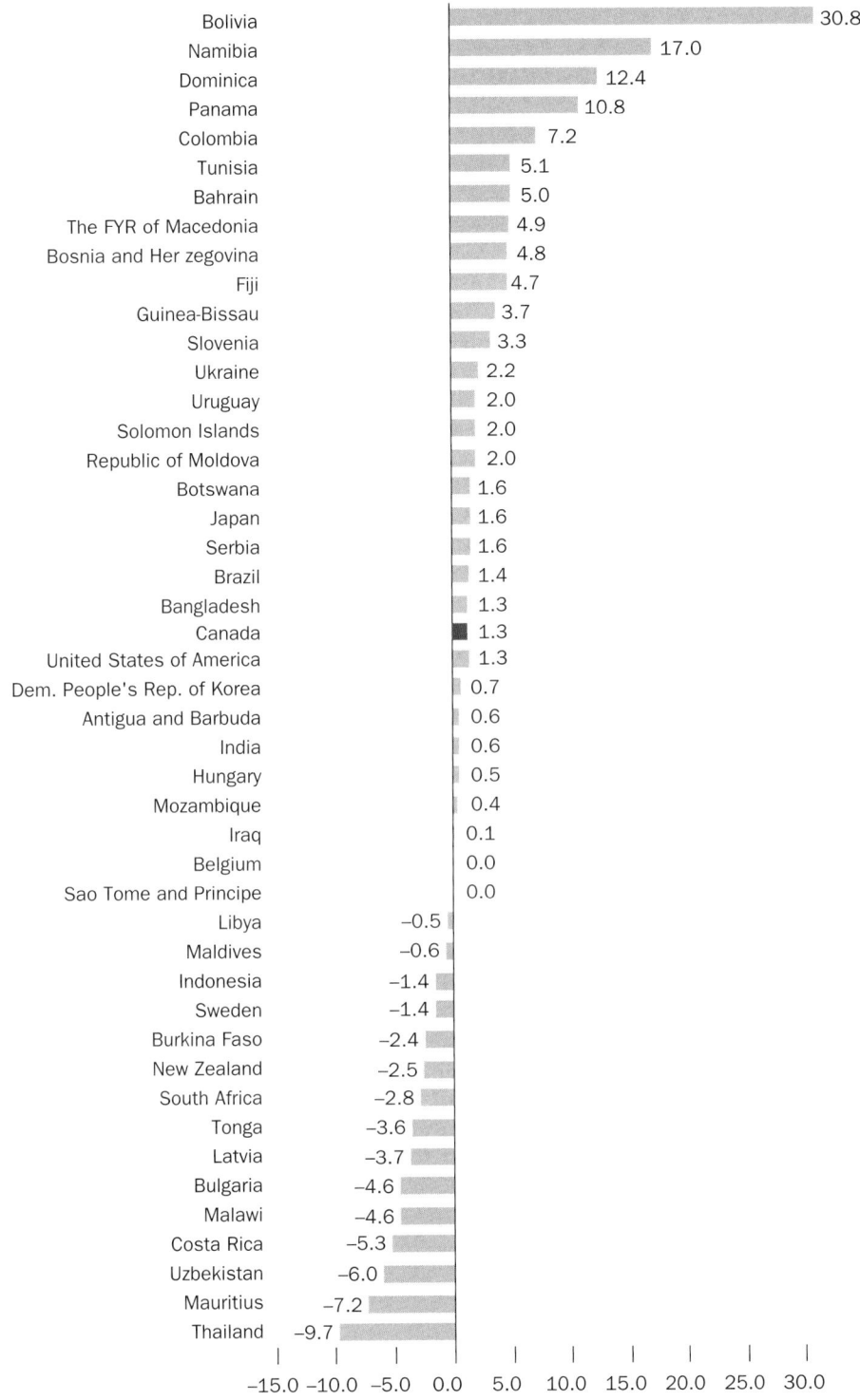

Figure 12.1 Progress and Setbacks of Women in Upper Houses of Parliament, 2015

Note: The figures show the percentage point difference between renewals in 2014 compared with the previous legislature.

Source: Adapted from "Figure 2. Parliamentary renewals in 2014." Women in Parliament: 20 years in review, Copyright © Inter-Parliamentary Union (IPU), 2015. http://www.ipu.org/pdf/publications/WIP20Y-en.pdf

district levels to women. As a result of this act, close to 6 million women have been elected to village- and district-level office. In South Africa, the post-apartheid African National Congress government adopted a law to require a 30 per cent quota for women candidates. Today, women hold 44.5 per cent of the lower legislative seats in South Africa. The Nordic countries have made tremendous gains in getting women elected to higher office. Women in Sweden and Norway respectively occupy 45 per cent and 39.6 per cent of parliamentary seats. There are 26 countries in which women account for 30 per cent or more of their national Parliaments. Although more and more women are gaining political office in some countries, Belize, Oman, Qatar, and Saudi Arabia have no women sitting in Parliament as representatives (Inter-Parliamentary Union 2012).

Do Women in Office Make a Difference?

If women in political office make a difference, what kind of difference do they make? What is the link between women's participation in political office and the advancement of public policy supportive of women's needs? Indeed, women heads of state can make a difference by appointing more women to cabinet positions, establishing policies that support working women and women's reproductive rights, and criminalizing practices harmful to women's integrity as Jóhanna Sigurðardóttir of Iceland, Michele Bachelet of Chile, and Dilma Rousseff of Brazil have done (Hawkesworth 2012a). But it takes more than having a female head of government to achieve policies and programs that address the needs and interests of women.

Some scholars have noted a critical threshold of 30 per cent; that is, when women make up 30 per cent of representation in political institutions, they are able to influence policy outcomes. In the Nordic countries, where women account for at least 30 per cent of the parliamentary seats, public policy has addressed women's needs. In Norway, the government provides opportunities for women to combine their child-care and employment demands. Women- and family-centred public policies include expanding child-care services, offering flexible work hours, improving pension rights for unpaid care work, and increasing child benefits for families that do not use public child-care services. In South Africa, where government quotas reserve 30 per cent of parliamentary and 50 per cent of local government candidacies for women, the impact has made a difference in women's lives. In 1995, the South African Parliament passed the Convention on the Elimination of All Forms of Discrimination against Women without reservations, and it has introduced "the women's budget process," which analyzes the gender impact of the government's budget (Women's Environment and Development Organization 2001). Studies of village female representatives in India document that they possessed a better understanding of their constituents' needs than did their male counterparts (Lindgren, Inkinen, and Widmalm 2009).

Even in countries that have not attained the 30 per cent threshold, women office-holders generally, regardless of political party or label, take more women-friendly positions on women's issues than their male colleagues. Studies conducted of women parliamentarians in Europe support this view (Randall 1987; Leyenaar 2008). In Malaysia, though females only make up 10 per cent of the national Parliament, they successfully pushed through legislation that concerned child care, crimes related to children, and improving the lives of disabled children (Zakuan 2010). There is also sufficient evidence that in the US Congress "in addition to advocating for their districts, female legislators do exhibit a profound commitment to the pursuit of policies for women, children, and families" (Swers 2002, 132). Women office-holders are often more open and inclusive than their male counterparts. In place of carrying out business behind closed doors, women often favour involving the general public in the political process and providing increased access to constituent groups often left out of policy-making (Center for the American Woman and Politics 1991; Kathlene 1992; Dolan

2001; Women's Environment and Development Organization 2001). Women legislators also more willingly work collectively across party lines to accomplish specific goals (Waylen 2010).

Other scholars question the "critical mass" argument and point out that not all women elected to office can be counted on to represent women's interests (Chowdhury 2008; Childs and Krook 2009). Women do not constitute a monolithic group; they are divided by political ideology, sexuality, class background, race, and religious beliefs, which influence their attitudes and beliefs about women's place in society. Even women who are very supportive of women's rights differ over what strategies and policies can best improve women's lives. Molyneux argues that women divide between those who argue for practical gender interests and others who support strategic gender interests (Molyneux 1998). In other words, some women in office are more concerned about meeting the short-term basic needs of women such as providing equality in the areas of education and employment; others are concerned with transformational politics and seek to implement policies that tackle structural oppression, the division of labour, and reproductive issues. The former accept gender inequality and male authority as a given; the latter want to undermine or transform gender inequalities and the structures that render women subordinate to men (Molyneux 1998). Conflicts over which policies and laws best improve the lives of women often drive a wedge in the unity of women.

Perhaps an indication of the importance and success of women in the political arena has been the emergence of the ultra-conservative right and its anti-feminist platform. The values of cultural and religious ultra-conservatives (fundamentalist Christians, Jewish, and Islamic groups and individuals as well as non-governmental organizations such as REAL Women of Canada) are often shaped by a belief that women are subordinate to men. Strongly committed to traditional family values, they believe that women should confine themselves to the private sphere of the home and men should be the breadwinners and active in the public sphere. Such beliefs lead ultra-conservative groups and individuals to oppose gender equality, LGBTQ rights, sexual reproductive rights, and sexual equality rights for women and men who challenge conventional norms (Chappell 2006). The rise of female conservative politicians challenges the notion that a critical mass of female politicians will deliver the appropriate gender "goods" to their female constituents. Childs and Krook (2009) argue against excessive reliance on a critical mass of women in public office; rather, it is more effective to find "critical actors"—women and men willing to propose and support legislation that addresses women's human rights and needs. Other scholars have added that it is not enough to have men and women politicians actively promoting women's rights. Without an effective and strong women's movement outside of government helping to promote a feminist legislative agenda and pushing to hold politicians accountable, gender-friendly legislation and policies will not result (Gouws 2008; Leyenaar 2008).

Right-Wing Women

Backlash against women's rights has come not only from governments and corporate interests, but also from right-wing women and transnational conservative activists and organizations (Chappell 2006). Throughout history, women not only have organized in support of equality and justice, but have been part of fascist movements. Claudia Koonz (1987), for instance, has written about the history of women's involvement in Nazi Germany. Kathleen Blee (1991, 58) has written about women in the Ku Klux Klan. She writes that "one of the largest and most influential right-wing women's organizations of the immediate post-suffrage period was the Women of the Ku Klux Klan (WKKK). From 1923 to 1930, women poured into the Klan movement to oppose immigration, racial equality, Jewish-owned businesses, parochial schools, and 'moral decay.'" Women's involvement in right-wing movements has a long history and is in evidence from around the world. For instance, women participated in the destruction of the Babri Masjid (a sixteenth-century mosque destroyed by Hindu mobs in 1992 in India) and the systematic violence against Muslims in Gujarat in 2002. Women were part of Italian fascist movements and also actively participated in Latin American dictatorships. Women's participation in racist and fascist movements underscores that women's political organizing, while overwhelmingly marked by a quest for justice and equality, is not an "essential" calling; that is, women are not innately more prone to justice and, as their participation in right-wing movements demonstrates, can be just as racist and homophobic as their male counterparts.

Yet history shows that women have come together to elect representatives and influence governmental decisions supportive of social justice and equality for all and can promote policies and practices that attend to women's issues. Increasingly, women realize that they have to become the change they wish to see, and they often do this by running for office and seeking appointments themselves. Can women build together significant political forces to oppose further incursions on the gains made and make further progress? Have women developed the networks, the organizations, the ways of offering support to one another to marshal their forces, get their opinions heard, and make their presence felt in political processes? The answer depends on women and their allies.

Obstacles Facing Women in Politics

Scholars identify three theoretical explanations for why more women are not elected to public office. The sociological theory attributes the low level of women office-holders to culture. Patriarchal cultures socialize their citizens to think in terms of a public/private dichotomy that locates women in the domestic sphere (Hang 2012). Women are not expected to hold political decision-making positions. The question raised about female, but not male, candidates is: Who is taking care of the family? As a result, social norms and expectations about women's proper roles act as a brake to recruitment into politics and to political advancement. Even when women are as qualified as men to run for office, they are more likely to believe that they are not as qualified and also less likely to believe that they can actually win office. Men, on the other hand, are more likely to overestimate their qualifications for running for office and winning (Krook 2010). In addition, when women have the education and the occupational experience for holding higher political office, their fellow citizens must be willing to vote for them. Opinion polls taken of voters in countries such as Japan and Nigeria find that voters remain unfavourably disposed to electing a female to political office. And, a majority of Nigerian men indicated they would not let their wives participate in politics (Arowolo and Aluko 2010; Eto 2010).

A second explanation for the low rates of women in elected office points to their involvement in non-political activities. The "double day" or "second shift" means that household, childcare, and work responsibilities are still disproportionately done by women, leaving them little time to engage in the political process (Conway 2001; Peterson and Runyan 2010). This more greatly works against working-class and poorer women, who do not have the financial means to hire domestic help.

A third explanation has to do with institutional impediments. Gatekeepers such as party leaders, interest group leaders, and campaign fundraisers often discourage women from running for office (Conway 2001; Krook 2010; Hawkesworth 2012a). Many political parties, dominated by men, tend to recruit men, whom they view as more likely to win elections. In many countries, male candidates are recruited in male-dominated clubs and meeting (Arowolo and Aluko 2010), or political activities take place in the evenings and until late at night when women are expected to be home taking care of their families (Krook 2010). Voters often judge more negatively a woman who sacrifices her family to run for political office. Traditionally, male politicians have sought campaign funds from business and community leaders who are interested in backing candidates as a way of establishing future access to them. Women candidates often face difficulties in finding backers, raising funds, and creating large-scale organizations of devoted followers who see possible benefits in their election. This is beginning to change as more women are seen as successful viable candidates.

Another institutional impediment to the selection of women to run for office concerns the election procedure. Studies document that gatekeepers are more willing to endorse

Box 12.3 In Her Own Words

Donna Dasko: Getting Women Elected in Canada

I have been active in getting more women elected in Canada since 1987, when I joined a group of women called The Committee for 94. This multi-partisan "ginger group" had the ambitious goal of electing half the House of Commons female by 1994! But the strains of a multi-partisan effort tore apart, and the economic recession of 1990 and deflated political environment drained our energy. With only 13 per cent of Parliament female in 1991, we were just three years away from our deadline but light years away from achieving equality. So we threw in the towel.

Donna Dasko

Flash forward ten years to 2001. Several of us from the old Committee found ourselves sitting together at a LEAF (Women's Legal Education and Action Fund) breakfast lamenting the fact that progress in electing women had been slow. Although we had made gains early in the previous decade, the recent federal election of 2000 showed no increase: women made up 20 per cent of Parliament, the same as in 1997. If female equality was not progressing as a "natural" development, then something was clearly wrong. What if anything, could be done?

Soon after that breakfast, lawyer Libby Burnham and journalist Rosemary Speirs invited a small group of about ten of us to Libby's house for dinner to talk about whether a new initiative along the lines of the old committee was possible. Opinions were decidedly mixed. A prominent political scientist argued that non-elected politics was more important than trying to get women elected to an antiquated institution. Others at the meeting thought the goal was important but doubted that there was an appetite "out there" for collective action. Others, including me, thought that we could indeed light the fires of a new social movement. So we decided to test it out by inviting a multi-partisan group of about 100 feminist women (and some men) to a party. At the event, we handed out position papers to take away. We conducted a survey of those who came, collecting contact information and opinions as to what we should do. Equal Voice was born.

continued

We went away pumped up and got to work to figure out what this new organization would do. After about a year of endless meetings around kitchen tables, a broad strategy was agreed to: Equal Voice would focus on convincing the political parties to nominate more women, it would be multi-partisan, and it would seek out media opportunities to get the message out that more women are needed in politics.

Within a few years the organization set up chapters in four provinces, and we incorporated as a not-for-profit organization in 2005. By 2012 we had nine chapters across the country, mainly focusing on provincial politics.

Over the years the initiatives of Equal Voice have evolved even as the goal of electing more women has remained the same. We set up outreach programs to encourage young women to consider politics as a career and developed a web-based campaign school, including a section for First Nations and Indigenous women. We developed events to celebrate women in politics, most prominently, the EVE Award. But mainly, we focused on lobbying the political parties to get more women nominated.

From the beginning Equal Voice made real efforts to press party officials to take the issue of women seriously. For example, in 2006, a "rainbow" multi-partisan group of three prominent political women met with the party leaders to seek their pledge to "do more." After much negotiation, the three leaders agreed to make statements in Queen's Park (the seat of Ontario's government) in June 2006 promising to run more women in the 2007 election. After receiving these promises, Equal Voice followed up with research and media releases tracking the numbers nominated through the campaign and the numbers of women running in "winnable" ridings, followed by a final media release on election day. The 2007 and 2011 Ontario elections resulted in modest increases in the number of women running and elected, but the 2014 election resulted in a substantial improvement—from 130 nominated in 2011 to 145 women in 2014, and from 30 to 38 women elected to Queen's Park on June 12. The election of Ontario's first female premier was an added bonus. Finally, we had lots to celebrate.

In spite of our successes, this strategy has generally produced incremental changes. To preserve multi-partisan buy-in, we do not ask for or receive promises to achieve a target or minimum number. We simply ask each party to do better than last time in their nominations. We encourage and press them rather than harangue them and criticize. The approach is oriented to the "carrot" and not the "stick." And none of the electoral gains are guaranteed: witness the six female premiers whose number has gone down to only three. Still, I believe that we have to keep pressing the parties and the system because I am convinced that progress would disappear if we were to disappear. Activism is vital and we have to keep working at it.

The real question for me is whether we should pursue other strategies that would be more effective. Without question, there are more effective ways to increase female representation. These include:

1. Electoral reform: There is no doubt that Canada's first-past-the-post electoral system is not helpful for electing women. Around the world, systems based on proportional representation have been much better at this.

    It is difficult to assess the prospects for achieving such electoral reforms in this country. Canadians seem reluctant to embrace proportional representation.

2. Quotas: Quotas involve setting specific numbers of women who must be chosen for various positions. An analysis of the top countries in the world in terms of female representation in parliaments shows that almost all of them have some combination of proportional representation and quotas.

    Canada has no quotas for women in politics, and we always sense resistance to this when we raise it.

3. Dedicated outreach: Dedicated outreach involves political parties making a dedicated effort to find, encourage, support, and run more women as candidates. This is the general approach that Equal Voice has promoted.

    It would be stronger to build dedicated outreach formally into party processes. In Canada, for example, the New Democratic Party federally and in many provinces requires their riding associations to search for a female or minority candidate when they have an open nominations process (they usually protect incumbents). This requirement has resulted in a significantly higher percentage of female candidates than the other parties, and a resulting higher percentage of women in their caucuses. For example, in Ontario in the 2014 election, 41 per cent of NDP candidates were women and 52 per cent of their new caucus was female.

    Suffice to say that progress is possible even in this country with its unfavourable electoral system, if political parties build such processes into their operations.

    Why does this matter? Women make up over half the Canadian population, but women's voices are vastly under-represented in our Parliament and legislatures. Women's views differ from those of men in some extremely important areas related to public policy; that means that these policy perspectives are under-represented as well. Canada currently ranks forty-eighth in the world in terms of female representation in Parliament. Surely we can do better than that.

Source: Donna Dasko; used with permission.

and promote women candidates running in multi-member, rather than single-member, electoral districts. Electoral systems that use some form of proportional representation (with more than one candidate representing an electoral district) have had greater success in getting women to run for and win elections. Proportional representation electoral systems exist in the Nordic countries and elsewhere, but yet not in Canada, where it is under debate. The 2015 Liberal majority government under Prime Minister Trudeau included electoral reform in its platform and promised to convene a parliamentary committee to change Canada's **first-past-the-post** voting system. In first-past-the-post, the candidate with the most votes in a riding wins the seat, and the party with the most elected seats becomes the new government; this system often results in winning candidates and ruling governments with far less than 50 per cent of the vote. One suggested reform is a ranked ballot system, in which voters rank their choices; if no candidate reaches 50 per cent of the first-choice votes, the second- and third-choice votes are taken into account in determining the winner. Another option is mixed-member proportional representation, in which voters cast two votes: one for an individual candidate and one for a party. It is as yet unclear which electoral reform will be pursued by the Trudeau government.

Women as Citizens

Women's relationship to their country has always been contentious. This section explores, how both women and men are important to the state, but in different ways. In order to understand how women and men's relationship to their country differs, first the country itself is looked at closely and how "nation" and "state" differ. Neither states nor nations are pregiven or "natural" formations. That is, all nations and states were created or invented at particular moments in history. "Invented" is meant not that they are fictitious but that they are constantly being created. From the smallest and the most mundane actions, such as buying postage stamps depicting a flag, to spectacular performances such as celebrating national holidays such as Canada Day, people are constantly generating a sense of common identity through notions of a common past and collective destiny. Most nations depend on a sense of territorial integrity; a shared history, language, and religion; and a belief that everyone in the country is—or should be—part of the "imagined community" that possesses a common culture (Anderson 1993). Such a belief is called nationalism, a dynamic and highly ideological phenomenon—one that changes over time and is often highly contested. Nations in this sense are created as an embodiment of a particular ethnicity, and some nations do not have a state (e.g. Uyghurs, Kurds, Roma, and Sinti). The state is the system of government, the machinery of governance, which rules a particular geographic territory. European empires partitioned Poland in the eighteenth and nineteenth centuries, and its territory was absorbed into other lands. Yet, the Polish people did not disappear and were able to re-establish their state following World War I. In Canada, Quebec and the rest of Canada come under the jurisdiction of the federal government. Quebec's auto licence plates read "Je me souviens" ("I remember"), referring to a time before British rule, and its provincial parliament is termed the National Legislature, the only such province to have that designation.

Ann McClintock famously stated, "All nationalisms are gendered, all are invented, and all are dangerous" (McClintock 1996, 104). So what does it mean to say that nations are profoundly gendered entities? Consider, for instance, the way nation-states are called "fatherland" or "motherland," two terms that evoke distinct sentiments. "The motherland provides a passive, receptive, and vulnerable image in contrast to the active image of the fatherland, which is the force behind government and military action—invasion, conquest, and defense" (Ivekovic and Mostov 2006, 11). During war and invasion, the occupied nation is described in feminized terms while the invading army is masculinized. In addition to being gendered, nations are also "raced." That is, nations are imagined as a collective of particular races. The racialized construction of nations is most acutely evidenced during conflict, when women from one nation or community are raped by another in order to emasculate its men, shame the community, and impregnate its women by the "seed of the enemy." Much of the literature on nations and nationalism does not examine gender closely (Yuval-Davis 1997). Nira Yuval-Davis and Flora Anthias (1989) suggest five different ways in which to understand this relationship:

1. Women are thought to be biological reproducers of the nation. That is, they give birth to the nation-state's citizens, to its heroes and martyrs.
2. Women are symbolic signifiers of the nation. They represent the female nation such as "mother India" that needs to be protected even while being a source of fierce power. Symbolically they are cherished for the sacrifices they make for their children as well as for the nation. Since women are a source of both pleasure and sacrifice, they are also potential enemies and traitors to the nation.
3. Women are considered the boundaries of the nation. Women's bodies serve as territorial markers of the nation. Being symbolic of nation and community, women's bodies invite both protection and violation, facilitating both

nation-building endeavours and acts of war. Thus an enemy's "rape and violation of individual women becomes symbolically significant in nationalist discourse and the politics of national identity as a violation of the nation and an act against the collective men of the enemy nation" (Ivekovic and Mostov 2006, 11).
4. Women are made into repositories of national culture. Women are responsible for transmitting "appropriate and correct culture" to children and for safeguarding cultural boundaries intergenerationally. Women are often ascribed the role of moral arbiters who embody the national honour.
5. Women actively participate in the political, economic, and militaristic enterprises of the nation. Women are part of formal and informal governance of the nation; they contribute to its economy through both waged and unwaged labour; and they are also part of the nation's military apparatus. While historically women were not admitted into combat units, since the 1970s many countries have begun to allow women to engage in active combat. Yet women's participation in a country's military is not limited to their direct participation. Rather, as Cynthia Enloe explains, people need to understand the militarization as "a step-by-step process by which a person or a thing gradually comes to be controlled by the military *or* comes to depend for its well-being on militaristic ideas" (Enloe 2000, 3).

The dominant model of "citizen" is often based on the image of the male warrior-hero (Hartsock 1983). Consequently, even though the concept of citizenship implies an equality of rights and obligations of all members within the nation-state, it is

Box 12.4 Women in Media

The Struggle for the Vote

Women in Canada organized to gain the right to vote. The Dominion Women's Enfranchisement Association was incorporated in 1889 as one such effort to obtain women's suffrage; the Women's Political Equality League was another. Nellie McClung (1873–1951) was a prominent suffragette with a great deal of talent for cultural parody. McClung with others in the league organized a theatrical mock parliament in 1914 to turn on its head the notion that men were the dominant gender. In this portrayal, women were the "natural" politicians playing members of Parliament considering a petition for the right to vote by a delegation of men. McClung played the premier; her satirical speech to the mock parliament, "Should Men Vote?", echoed the language that men would use in talking about women and the vote, including its opening remarks that praised the men's appearance, just as men tended to do when speaking to women. Below is a sample of "the speech's tongue-in-cheek approach" (Graveline 2011):

> Oh, no, man is made for something higher and better than voting. . . . The trouble is that if men start to vote, they will vote too much. Politics unsettle men and unsettled men means unsettled bills, broken furniture, broken vows, and divorce. Men's place is on the farm . . . if men were to get the vote, who knows what would happen? It's hard enough to keep them home now!

The women's mock parliament proved to be so popular that it was replicated in many other venues. Some people even credited it as the final push to women gaining the vote.

Source: Historica Canada (n.d.).

rarely so. In fact there are tremendous disparities in the privileges and penalties of citizens among different races, classes, sexualities, and genders. In Canada, cisbodied heterosexual, white, upper-class elite men are "ideal" citizens while women have had to inhabit correspondingly circumscribed positions. Niral Yuval-Davis writes that "in Britain women lost their citizenship during Victorian times, when they got married; they continued to lose it if they got married to 'foreigners' until 1948, and it was not until 1981 that they got independent right to transfer their citizenship to their children" (Yuval-Davis 1997, 12). While voting alone does not encapsulate the rights conferred through citizenship, it is one of its most visible markers. One of the ways in which women demanded that the state acknowledge their citizenship was through the right to vote.

By the time women gained the right to vote in Canada, they could already do so in other countries. The first country to grant women's suffrage was New Zealand, in 1893. Women's suffrage was achieved in England after an equally long but far more militant struggle: women aged 30 and over were allowed to vote in 1918, and women under 30 were given the vote in 1928. Women gained the right to vote in Ecuador in 1929 and in Turkey in 1930, while in France they had to wait until 1944. After World War II, women in South Korea, Japan, Greece, and Italy were allowed to vote, but it was not until 1971 that most women in Switzerland won this right (only in 1990 did all cantons permit it).

Although many women in Canada did gain the vote federally in 1918 (see Chapter 3), they found that they were still prohibited from appointment to the Senate because they were not designated as *persons* in the 1867 British North American Act, the law of the land. Five women, Emily Murphy, Irene Marryat Parlby, Nellie Mooney McClung, Louise Crummy McKinney, and Henrietta Muir Edwards, began a petition to overturn this part of the law. It was filed in 1927 but in 1928, Canada's Supreme Court decided unanimously that women were not "persons" under the law. Since Canada was still part of the British Empire, it took an appeal to the British Privy Council on 18 October 1929 to make women persons in law. The "Famous Five" are renowned in Canadian history and in feminist movements for this success. They even are represented by a group of statues on Parliament Hill in Ottawa, the only women so honoured.

However, the legacy of some of the Five is marred by their support for eugenics and opposition to immigration by racialized groups. Emily Murphy, in particular, lobbied for forced sterilization of those she considered inferior and prone to social disease. Nellie McClung succeeded in establishing eugenics legislation in Alberta that led to the forced sterilization of thousands of immigrant, racialized, and Indigenous women.

Royal Commission on the Status of Women

Canadian women continued to work for full equality. A coalition of 32 women's groups launched a campaign to urge the full equality of women across society. Prime Minister Lester Pearson acceded to their demands and established a Royal Commission to investigate where the gaps to full equality were. In 1968 the commission held public hearings across Canada for six months.

> It heard 468 briefs, receiving 1,000 letters of opinion and additional testimony, which confirmed widespread problems experienced by women across Canadian society. The RCSW produced a 488-page report containing 167 recommendations to the federal government on such matters as equal pay for work of equal value, maternity leave, day car, birth control, family law, the Indian Act, educational opportunities, access of women to managerial positions, part-time work and pensions (Morris 2006).

Women and the Law

Women's attempts to get legal equality and recognition have a long history and a contentious relationship with the law. Laws are the governing rules of the state and therefore society. They develop from several sources: ancient custom, legislative bodies, judicial decisions, and administrative agencies. Feminists, however, pose critical questions about the gendering of law in society. Feminist legal theorists note "ostensibly 'objective' legal rules rest on the perspectives of 'the reasonable man'" (Martin and Jurik 2007, 154). Moreover, "the law sees and treats women the way men treat women" (MacKinnon 1991, 186). Critical race theorists take these understandings a step further, arguing that it is not simply men who are the subject of law but specifically cisbodied heterosexual white men. Such theorists seek a jurisprudential method that would incorporate a "multiple consciousness" to give voice to those historically rendered silent and invisible in the law because of race, sex, class, sexual orientation, or physical abilities (Matsuda 1989). As historian Linda Kerber (1998, 309) puts it, "whether one is male or female, racially marked in a system that treats Caucasians as 'normal,' married or single, heterosexual or homosexual, continues to have implications for how we experience the equal obligations of citizenship."

In its regulation of the family, the law's concern has traditionally been to create a space in which the male head of the household can exercise power and authority (O'Donovan 1981). By viewing women as belonging to the "private" domestic sphere, the men who make and interpret laws, like the men who theorize about political power, act on assumptions that make women less than full legal citizens and political beings. These assumptions about women's rightful place are intimately linked to the patriarchal political philosophies that underpin democratic societies (Okin 1979). For example, laws have explicitly commanded husbands and fathers to control their families. Colonial Americans used ducking stools, stocks, and other instruments of humiliation and torture to correct women found guilty of scolding, nagging, or disturbing the peace. When women are thus classified as a group and subjected to gender-based social policies, their social roles are often reinforced by political and legal sanctions whose legacies continue to influence contemporary society.

Traditional moral codes are based on a sexual double standard for women and men that affects criminal law and a large amount of civil law, especially family law. Moreover, a society's laws, moral code, and popular conceptions of social norms reinforce each other. Lawmakers and those who enforce the law start from an idea of what the "normal" family is. They act on the basis of their notions of what women are like and ought to do and their unexamined assumptions about what women need and want. Anyone who does not conform to their assumptions is either treated as invisible (as victims of violence and incest, and working female heads of households have tended to be) or sought out and made the object of pressure to conform (as are lesbians, trans, and poor women).

In studying the lives of young working-class and poor black women, sociologist Joyce Ladner (1972) pointed out that their lives were in large part governed by laws, customs, and restrictions

Box 12.5 In Her Own Words

Why Organize?

I'm not an elected representative of black people in Toronto, and neither is anyone in my group. We are a group of people who were frustrated and enraged and facilitated a method for people to express their anger in an organized and mobilized fashion.—Sandy Hudson, co-founder of Black Lives Matter Toronto

Source: Turgeon (2016).

based on a white middle-class male perception of what is "normal" and what is "deviant." For example, until recently, white middle-class male norms associated "working mothers" with deviance, though it was very common for racialized mothers to hold jobs. Women of colour, then, face "intersecting" sets of subordination. That is, they have to deal with their racial and gender subordination simultaneously within structures that assume white and male as normative. These intersectional inequalities are still a serious issue, and it is no coincidence that the Black Lives Matter movement in North America, particularly the movement in Toronto, is run predominantly by black women (both cis- and transgender).

Feminist scholars have also pointed to the conflict within legal cases between equality and difference (Scott 1988). The conflict arises in anti-discrimination law that recognizes that women must get equal pay for equal work. At the same time feminist scholars and others have argued for recognizing that there are important differences among women. Yet the law does not have the capacity to simultaneously deal with women as a "class" while recognizing the differences between them.

Other contexts of legal bias include a double standard of sexual morality. For instance, laws have customarily treated adultery as a serious crime when committed by women, while often disregarding it when committed by men. The prejudice in favour of the "unwritten law" that excuses husbands who murder adulterous wives is still not entirely eradicated from society's practice of law.

Although many more women are entering the legal profession, and media images suggest that women are often judges, attorneys, and police officers, the law still treats women unfairly in many ways. Lawmakers determine governmental budgets and the respective priorities of health services, daycare centres, education, job creation, and expenditures on weapons and defence. The government shapes social program regulations that determine the legal obligations of mothers and that fail to recognize unpaid caring for children or others as work.

Women's Political Participation

Even though women's role in the state, law, and citizenship has been curtailed, diminished, or denied because of institutional structural bias, women have historically challenged these practices and priorities of the state and its laws by formally and informally organizing. Prior to achieving the vote for women, women's primary form of political participation was the voluntary association. Women had, in fact, little choice if they wanted to effect change in political and social arenas. Women's organizations lobbied the government and other institutions, effectively innovating the strategy of lobbying politics, now a commonly recognized political practice (Cott 1990; Lebsock 1990; Scott 1991). Women continue to initiate and participate in voluntary associations in large numbers.

In previous centuries, middle- and upper-class women organized societies to assist the poor. In the nineteenth and early twentieth centuries, women organized against alcohol consumption, the most notable organization being the Woman's Christian Temperance Union. Women called for the abolition of slavery, educational opportunities for women, better working conditions, and help for "fallen" women. Women developed the club movement, culminating in such national organizations as the National Council of Women in Canada (1893), and the Canadian Women's Press Club (1904). Local clubs on topics ranging from literary interests to public affairs sprang up across Canada, and many took up the social welfare issues of the day.

In the twentieth century, led by Emma Goldman (1869–1940), Elizabeth Gurley Flynn (1890–1964), and Margaret Haile (no dates available; politically active in 1902) many radical women became pacifists and socialists. They supported Margaret Sanger (1879–1966) in her campaign for legalizing birth control. Women organized to reform cities, alleviate the evils of industrialization, and prevent the exploitation of children, working women, and immigrants. In this way they helped lay the foundation for the modern

For over 30 years, Justice Rosalie Abella has engaged the law in areas of equity and human rights. In 1976, when appointed to the Ontario Family Court, she was the youngest judge in Canada and the first to become pregnant. As commissioner for the 1984 Royal Commission on Equality in Employment she created the term *employment equity*. This fundamental concept was upheld by the Supreme Court of Canada and thus the idea of equality was embedded in law, policy, and practice. She later served on the Ontario Human Rights Commission and as chair of the study *Access to Legal Services by the Disabled*. In 2004, she was the first Jewish woman appointed to the Supreme Court of Canada.

welfare state (Lebsock 1990), which has been steadily dismantled through neo-liberal policy over the last 20 years.

Women and Peace Movements

A significant proportion of women's movements have expressed their political disagreement with many men about the excessive use of force, the priority given to militarism versus social agendas, and the effects of nuclear weapons on societies. This is not to suggest that there is something "essential" or innate about women in their call for peace; indeed, many women have also participated in armed struggles. Rather, because women disproportionately suffer the political, economic, and social consequences of militarism, it is in that context that women have agitated against armed conflict. Women have historically worked for peace through voluntary associations.

In the last two centuries, women have organized a number of local, countrywide, and international peace societies. In the late nineteenth century, international socialist leaders Clara Zetkin (1857–1933) and Rosa Luxemburg (1870–1919) were committed to breaking down national borders and ending military competition, positions that were not always taken by their male colleagues. An Austrian woman, Bertha von Suttner (1843–1914), wrote a major book about disarmament, *Lay Down Your Arms* (1889), and suggested the creation of the Nobel Peace Prize. She received it herself in 1905 (Boulding 1977). Other significant women recipients have been Alva Myrdal in 1982 for her work to further disarmament and peace in international organizations (Bok 1991) and Rigoberta Menchú Tum in 1992 for her opposition to the cultural genocide of the Indigenous peoples of Guatemala (Burgos-Debray 1984). Shirin Ebadi, an Iranian human rights lawyer, received the Nobel Peace Prize in 2003 for her work in promoting women's human rights in Iran. The following year Wangari Muta Maathai from Kenya was awarded the Nobel Peace Prize for her work in "sustainable development, democracy, and peace." And in 2011 Ellen Johnson Sirleaf of President of Liberia, received the Nobel Peace Prize along with Leymah Gbowee of Liberia and Tawakkol Karman of Yemen for their efforts in promoting peace and democracy in their countries.

The First World War (1914–1918) galvanized women into forming peace organizations. The International Woman Suffrage Alliance (IWSA) wanted to continue to work together even though their countries were at war with each other. In 1915, 1300 members met in The Hague, Netherlands, and drafted resolutions that they hoped would bring the warring sides to peace. After the war ended, the women tried to present their resolutions at Versailles, France where the peace treaty was being negotiated. But they were forbidden to do so because their delegation included women from the losing side of the war; only the victors were permitted hearing. Subsequently, the women held a second conference, this time in Zurich, Switzerland, and formed the Women's International League for Peace and Freedom (WILPF) to continue to press for peace and justice.

During the 1960s, Canada's Voice of Women for Peace (VOW Peace) was founded in response to threats to the world's atmosphere from nuclear testing and to protest the US pursuit of the war in Vietnam. It had chapters across the country. One of its most effective campaigns was collecting baby teeth in North America; renowned scientist Ursula Franklin used her metallurgical expertise to analyze the teeth and demonstrated that they contained high levels of Strontium-90, a radioactive isotope produced by nuclear fission. VOW pressured the Canadian government to promote a treaty banning nuclear testing and urged the United Nations to do the same. In 1963, a treaty was signed by the United States, the Soviet Union, and Great Britain that banned nuclear testing in the atmosphere, in outer space and under water.

The peace movement is global. In the early twentieth century, peace was a concern of women's suffrage and internationalist socialist movements worldwide, including the Pan Pacific and Southeast Asia Women's Association and, after World War II, the All African Women's Conference and the Federation of Asian Women's Associations (Boulding 1977). And women's peace organizations were active in the United Nations Decade for Women (1976–85).

In 1981, British women organized the first peace encampment at Greenham Common to protest the placement of US cruise missiles in England (Snitow 1985); Nordic women sponsored a peace march across Europe; and women of the Pacific Islands campaigned against the nuclear testing in the Pacific that contributes to the high incidence of birth defects and miscarriages among women in the region. Code Pink, a women's peace and social justice organization formed in 2002 to oppose war and militarism in all its forms. Its name is an ironic take on US Homeland Security's colour-coded alert system, choosing pink as a colour associated with girls and women.

Around the world and across historical time, women have always organized; they have organized against colonialism, formed trade unions, and protested against socially destructive practices within their own communities, such as in the pervasiveness of alcoholism. The latter can be seen in the anti-arrack movement in the southern state of Andhra Pradesh, India (arrack is an alcoholic drink common in South Asia). Political organizing by women is not limited to urban educated arenas but is also evident among women from rural and peasant classes. For, contrary to the dominant way in which such histories are narrated, feminist historians highlight the ways in which peasant men and women organized collectively during Chile's agrarian reform. Women's involvement in these struggles helped shape both agrarian as well as national politics (Tinsman 2002). Formal histories have also tended to ignore the importance of grassroots activism and of women's place within it. Elise Boulding's (1976) *The Underside of History: A View of Women Through Time* is an early contribution to filling in the gaps of the traditional historic record.

Global Feminism and Human Rights

Today, networks of global feminist organizations engaged in grassroots activism challenge and influence governments and their policies through the World Wide Web, the Internet, Twitter, fax machines, and other telecommunications media (Hawkesworth 2012a). Lori Wallach, director of Public Citizen's Global Trade Watch, organized successful protests against the World Trade Organization (WTO) at its meeting in Seattle in 1999. Effectively protesting the potential consequences of globalization on women and the poor, grassroots activism contributed to the collapse of the WTO meeting. Women's grassroots activism has been critical in promoting educational opportunities for girls in school, has led to the passage of equal pay legislation, and has mobilized women to ensure their continued access to reproductive health care (Palley 2001).

In the 2010–11 uprisings across North Africa that came to be known as the "Arab Spring," their women leaders were able to effectively use telecommunications media to spread word about their protests. In Tunisia, for instance, where the uprisings first began to oust President Zine El-Abidine Ben Ali, it was Lina Ben Mhenni who would broadcast information about the street protests unfolding throughout Tunisia via her blog and her Facebook and Twitter accounts. And she took the courageous step of using her real name. The Egyptian protests in Tahrir Square inspired many other protests around the world. Analogous protests in Yemen were sparked by the arrest of Tawakkol Karman, the head of Women Journalists Without Chains. She was award the Nobel Peace Prize for her efforts in 2011 along with Liberians Leymah Gbowee and Ellen Johnson Sirleaf. In other countries, women have been central in sparking, coordinating, and generating uprisings. The extent to which the participation of thousands of women across these movements has necessarily advanced a feminist agenda—whatever might be meant by that term—is still a matter of debate. It is important to acknowledge, though, that feminism looks different in different places, and it would be a fallacy to judge the movements in other parts of the world on the basis of the feminist movements in North America.

The movements in North Africa generated solidarity from around the world, including from women's movements around the world. These began in the 1970s with the development of feminist consciousness and women's increased participation in nation building, which led individuals and groups to pressure the United Nations to take up a year of intensive discussion on the position of women worldwide. Delegates agreed, and the first UN-sponsored world conference on women took place in 1975 in Mexico City. The themes of the UN women's conference as well as those of the second (held in Copenhagen in 1980) and the third (in Nairobi in 1985) were equality, peace, and development. The Fourth World Conference on Women, in Beijing in 1995, assessed global progress toward improving the lives of women and girls, as well as identifying the factors that hinder such progress. A special session of the UN General Assembly, designated Beijing+5, was held in 2000 to consider how the platform for action resulting from the Beijing conference had been implemented.

An important outcome of the first UN conference on women was the creation of a major international treaty concerned with women's rights—the Convention on the Elimination of All Forms of Discrimination against Women (CEDAW) that became effective in 1979. To date, 188 countries have ratified CEDAW, though many have attached reservations that weaken it. While most of the world's governments have ratified it, the United States has yet to do so.

These four UN-sponsored world conferences enabled women from all over the globe to share experiences and views. The official UN conferences brought together government representatives (some of whom were men) and the members of many non-governmental groups, which met in unofficial sessions. At the end of these conferences, global blueprints of action were approved by the UN General Assembly, calling upon governments and communities to eliminate all forms of discrimination against women and to work to improve the lives of women worldwide. At the Fourth World Conference on Women, governments agreed that women's rights are human rights; recognized the right of women to have control over and to decide on matters relating to their sexuality; adopted language that recognized the family "in its various forms"; and agreed to end female genital cutting and prenatal sex selection, to eradicate violence against women and girls, to secure girls' education free of discrimination in schools, and to promote international feminism (Indigenous Peoples' Council on Biocolonialism, n.d.). Even so, the Indigenous women attending the Beijing conference issued a declaration describing their own perspective, which was not represented by the nation-state membership base of the United Nations.

In addition to the UN-sponsored world conferences on women, other major UN conferences have benefited from the contributions of feminist thinkers and activists working throughout the 1980s and 1990s. The 1992 UN Earth Summit in Rio de Janeiro successfully incorporated women's issues related to the environment and sustainable development. The 1993 World Conference on Human Rights in Vienna accepted the principle that "women's rights are human rights." The Vienna Plan of Action called for the eradication of violence against women in both the public and private spheres. The 1994 Conference on Population and Development in Cairo acknowledged that the empowerment and education of women are means of improving women's health and that these are the best methods to reduce population growth rates.

Global feminist organizing is very effective at highlighting the issue of violence against women, which affects women globally and cuts across lines of class, race, sexuality, educational attainment, ethnicity, region, religion, and language. Women experience violence in various forms: in the home, in refugee camps, in prisons, during armed conflict and civil war, in international sex trafficking operations, and on university campuses. The most far-reaching international treaty to work toward the eradication of violence against women is the Inter-American Convention on the Prevention, Punishment and Eradication of Violence against Women (ICVW), which went into effect in 1995. The convention defines violence against women as "any act or conduct, based on gender, which causes death or physical, sexual or psychological harm or suffering to women." The ICVW requires states to take immediate action "to prevent, investigate and impose penalties for violence against women" as well as to "modify legal or customary practices that sustain violence" (Meyer 1999; O'Hare 1999).

Violence against women remains an enormous problem, and women are far from actually attaining equal rights. However, internationally, women have made great progress in gaining recognition of these problems and have had an impact on global issues affecting them. Conferences and meetings have raised consciousness as women from around the world have gained new insights on the varieties of patriarchal oppression and have developed a healthy respect for the differences among themselves. In the process, women have changed how gender is understood and lived worldwide.

More progress toward feminist goals has been made in the past 30 years than in any other period of modern history. Such success, though, has set off a strong reaction to these gains and they remain fragile.

Summary

Women have been far less visible than men in formal political activity. The women's movement challenges women's exclusion from the "public" sphere. Power is distinct from authority and is different from influence. Women have seldom exercised either power or authority, although they exert influence from time to time.

As societies become more complex, governmental power tends to be exercised by the few on behalf of the many. Women tend to be segregated as a group and excluded from political power, along with subordinated racialized, LGBTQ, and religious groups. Women who do participate in government tend to do so on the local level.

In the past, some women exercised political power in their own right in dynastic states, in Indigenous lands, and in pre-colonial African societies. As government became more bureaucratic and as colonial powers altered these societies, the power of these women leaders was eroded.

Male dominance is associated with the increasing complexity of societies and societal responses to stress and change. It is manifested in the exclusion of women from economic and political decision making and in violence against women and LGBTQ communities and racialized persons.

The women's movement encourages increasing numbers of women to seek public office. Studies show that regardless of party label or level of office, women office-holders tend to take more feminist positions on women's issues than do men. Nonetheless, women still face opposition, which they attempt to overcome through such methods as raising their own funds to support candidates with feminist viewpoints. In various other countries, women have won political office in greater percentages than in Canada.

Laws tend to have a gender bias because they are based on patriarchal norms. Many laws and moral codes are based on a double standard. Family law often coerces women into confining roles. Laws designed to "protect" women often have the effect of restricting women's choices and activities.

Marginalized from "politics" as men define it, women have sought to achieve their objectives through a wide range of voluntary and community associations.

Women's involvement in peace movements testifies to their political opposition to many wars. While women may seem to be more "pacific" than men, this does not mean that they cannot be motivated to fight. Nor does it mean that women leaders cannot support and instigate war.

Women at the beginning of the twentieth century mobilized to obtain the right to gain political and legal rights, including the right to vote. The more contemporary feminist movement developed from two sources: organizations formed to work for women's equality within existing systems and more radical groups involved in anti-colonial struggles, and civil rights and peace movements working to change or replace existing systems of governance.

In the 1980s, a global feminism emerged with the aid of the United Nations conferences on women, human rights, the environment, and sustainable development. These global conferences brought together women worldwide to share experiences and to develop strategies to eliminate global forms of patriarchy and improve the lives of women and other subordinated persons.

Feminist unity is complicated by the fact that women are constituted differently. They have different ethnic, national, religious, class, and racial backgrounds, as well as different sexualities, and thus have different priorities. Some women carry multiple oppressions in having to deal with sexism, ableism, homophobia, transphobia, and/or racism. The need for all women to engage in political processes, formal and informal, and to focus clearly on necessary goals is paramount if they are to ensure that recent gains will not be lost and that new gains will be won. Women's unity will only be accomplished with understanding difference and recognizing the differential power relations among women.

Women have demonstrated their power to mobilize themselves and others to elect legislators and promote policies supportive of women's issues. Other initiatives have been successful through grassroots political action. Future progress in all areas of women's rights and equality depends largely on women themselves.

Discussion Questions

1. Document the life of a woman political leader of your choice. How did she manage to succeed, given the obstacles to women's political leadership?
2. In 2008, Rwanda became the nation with the highest percentage of elected female representatives. Do some research to explain the obstacles this nation faced (historically, politically) and how this goal of electing women was achieved. How might Canada learn from the Rwandan experience?
3. Do an oral-history interview with women in your own family on their role in and views on key aspects of the women's movement in your country of origin (whether it be Canada or elsewhere). Were members of your family

activists? Did any participate in social movements? How many have been involved in voluntary organizations? Which ones? Have any participated in politics? If not, why not?
4. What kinds of organizations exist in your locality to deal with issues concerning women, violence, and the law (such as a rape crisis centre, a women's shelter, a group concerned with women in prison or women living in poverty)?
5. How do women from different racialized groups or economic classes differ in their perceptions and attitudes on feminist issues? Select one issue as a problem and suggest solutions. How might women from two groups argue from the perspectives of their different backgrounds? How might an intersectional analysis assist?

Recommended Resources

Bannerji, Himani. 2000. *Dark Side of the Nation: Essays on Multiculturalism, Nationalism, and Gender.* Toronto: Canadian Scholars Press. Delineating the experiences of racialized people living in Canada, Bannerji provides a critical theoretical perspective of difference including and extending beyond the cultural—and multicultural—into political economy, state, and ideology.

Bashevkin, Sylvia. 2009. *Women, Power, Politics: The Hidden Story of Canada's Unfinished Democracy.* Toronto: Oxford University Press. Bashevkin argues that Canadians have a profound unease with women in positions of political authority—what she calls the "women plus power equals discomfort" equation. She explores the specific reasons why this discomfort is particularly severe in Canada. Bashevkin also evaluates a range of barriers faced by women who enter politics, including the media's role in assessing the leadership styles, personal appearances, and private lives of female politicians.

Boulding, Elise. 1976, 1992. *The Underside of History: A View of Women Through through Time.* Boulder: Westview Press. The feminist classic that explores the representation of civilization's development by offering a comprehensive inventory of women's contributions to history and social transformation.

Equal Voice. www.equalvoice.ca/mission.cfm. "Equal Voice is a national, bilingual, multi-partisan organization dedicated to electing more women to all levels of political office in Canada. Equal Voice regards the equal representation of women in Canada's Parliament, in our provincial/territorial legislatures, and on municipal and band councils, as a fundamental question of fairness for women in terms of their access to Canada's democratic institutions."

Irving, Dan, and Rupert Raj, eds. 2015. *TransActivism in Canada: A Reader.* Toronto: Canadian Scholar's Press. This anthology brings together activists and allies to examine the various strategies and forms of resistance needed to transform oppression into opportunity for change. Reflecting upon the challenges trans communities face and offering insight into achieving institutional reform, the themes addressed range from poverty and isolation to health care and best practices. By drawing on feminist, anti-racist, and social justice frameworks, the contributors approach oppression and activism as inseparable from heteropatriarchal, colonialist, and capitalist power relations.

Mitchell, Penni. 2015. *About Canada: Women's Rights.* Halifax, NS: Fernwood Mitchell traces the origin of gender inequality in Canada to the arrival of colonialism. She explores the more powerful roles of women in Indigenous societies and how they later became subordinated to the settler state. The book explores the history and strategies that women engaged to win (back) freedoms and reveal the little-told stories of women's individual and collective agency.

Neigh, Scott. 2012. *Gender and Sexuality: Canadian History Through the Stories of Activists.* Halifax, NS: Fernwood. Neigh offers a compendium of histories of the grassroots movements to overcome racism, sexism, and poverty in Canada and their intersectional challenges to the state.

Glossary

agency refers to the intentional exertion of power by an individual, group, or system, as well as the ability of an individual, group, or system to exert power or achieve a particular desired outcome.

androcentric relates to the placing of men, male bodies, and male-identified characteristics at the centre of ideas and society.

androgyny is gender ambiguity that precludes a determination of gender. It may refer to a combination of masculine and feminine assumed traits or to an undetermined gender identity.

anti-women sentiment is part of a patriarchal system of thinking where women are viewed as lesser than the dominant male gender. The sentiment pervades all aspects of life. Simone de Beauvoir coined the phrase "women as the other" as a metaphor for the term.

apartheid was the state system of institutional racial segregation violently enforced in South Africa from 1948 to 1991. The term now refers to any systemic, violently enforced segregation.

blacklist refers to a practice where persons are placed on a secret list that marks those listed for punishment, to be barred from employment or other opportunities, or otherwise excluded due to suspected controversial political opinion. The blacklist as practiced in 1950s USA was part of the Cold War when Communists or suspected Communists were persecuted by being blacklisted (placed on a blacklist).

career mystique describes the prevalent belief that hard work will result in professional, economic, and social success, and that the only legitimate choice for individuals in North American society is to devote all possible time, attention, and energy toward one's career. It is critiqued because it fails to appreciate the contemporary context of the precarious nature of work, and perpetuates the undervaluation of homemaking, caretaking, and childcare (among others).

cisgender applies to persons who identify with the gender identity that matches the biological sex they were assigned at birth.

cisgender language is terminology that assumes all persons have a gender identity that matches the sex they were assigned at birth.

co-constitutive refers to a sociological process where more than one element influences the construction and meaning-making of one another.

colonialism is a system of domination by one country or empire over another territory and people. It enriches the dominant country through exploitation of resources from the dominated country, most often imposed through violent means.

colonial settler state see *settler state*.

culture refers to the ideas, attitudes, behaviour, customs, art, and organizations of a particular group, people, or society.

cybernetics is the study of information or communication systems and interacting automatic systems of power and control in both machines and living things.

de-skilling occurs when formerly skilled workers lose their jobs and their skills are no longer valued or needed, and opportunities for alternate skilled labour are eliminated, typically due to technological changes or changes in demand.

diaspora literally means a scattering of seeds (Greek) but today describes a population whose members exist outside of their original homeland. It refers to people who relate to each other across geographic boundaries.

embodiment is the tangible or physical aspect of an idea, quality, or feeling, or the representation of an idea, quality, or feeling (or any aspect of the human experience) in a physical form.

essentialism refers to the concept that a person, culture, or object can be reduced to a set of fixed unchanging attributes or essences.

epigenetics is a term that refers to factors outside DNA that affect the development of an organism.

eugenics is the belief that the human species can be improved by the regimented social regulation of reproduction. Inherent in eugenics is the belief that not everyone can contribute positively to society, and therefore some human beings should be prevented from procreating due to their presumed "inferior" status.

extended family refers to the wider network of familial relations beyond parent and child.

first-past-the-post generally refers to a method of judging a race by whichever contestant passes the finish line first; in political contexts, it refers to a specific voting system in which the candidate in a particular constituency with the most votes wins. Additionally, in Canada, candidates represent different parties, and the party that has the most candidates occupying elected seats then becomes the ruling government.

flextime is a flexible hour schedule that allows workers to alter their workday beyond the standard nine-to-five set schedule.

gaze in general usage means an attentive or persistent look. In feminist theory gaze is used to describe a particular process of seeing that involves power relationships. It creates an asymmetrical relationship between the viewer and objectifies the viewed. See also *male gaze*.

gender expression is the external way in which persons publicly represent their gender identity, through appearance, behaviour, and dress.

gender non-conformity is the characterization of individual behaviour that does not follow male/female binary stereotypes.

gender identity is an individual's internal experience and understanding of their own gender and may not match the gender they were assigned at birth.

health is the state of a person's physical, mental, and social well-being taken as a whole. It does not only refer to being free from illness, injury, or infirmity.

heteronationalism is the concept of a state structure based on a nationalism embedded with heteronormativity. See also *heteronormativity*.

heteronormativity is the belief that male and female are the only two genders with both incorporating fixed characteristics. It maintains that heterosexuality is the only "normal" sexual orientation and denies existence of LGBTQ sexuality.

heteropatriarchy is the social, political, and cultural domination of heterosexual males.

heterosexism is the discriminatory assumption that heterosexuality is superior to other sexual identities.

intersex is a term used for a person whose primary sex organs do not correspond to either of the socially constructed binary categories of male or female.

lesbophobia is the hatred of lesbians. It is related to homophobia, the hatred of LGBTQ persons, but it is a term specifically employed against women.

male gaze refers specifically to a dominant male heterosexual viewpoint that assumes the standard audience are all heterosexual men. This framed relationship objectifies and commodifies who or what is viewed in terms of their value to the presumed heterosexual male audience.

masculine mystique is the perception that stereotypically masculine behaviour is ideal or necessary for men to follow, and that embodying these stereotypes constitutes a legitimate rationale for systemic inequality and sexism.

matrilocal refers to the practice of making the marital home in the wife's community or family dwelling.

miscegenation is the term applied when differently racialized individuals marry, cohabit, or have sexual relations.

misogyny is the hatred of women and girls (both cis- and transgender) based solely upon their gender.

monotheistic describes a religion that is based on the belief in one deity.

norm is an expected pattern of behaviour based on dominant social and cultural beliefs. A norm is assumed to be part of a natural order.

normalization is the process that creates an expected pattern of behaviour based on dominant social and cultural beliefs, and the assumption (informing everyday behaviours, as well as public policy) that this pattern of behaviour will apply to everyone.

nuclear family is a term applied to the 1950s ideal of a core family unit, consisting of a mother, a father, and their children.

polyandry is the practice in which an individual may be married to or partnered with more than one man at the same time. See also *polygamy*.

polygamy is the practice in which an individual may have more than one spouse or life partner at the same time. See also *polyandry*; *polygyny*.

polygyny is the practice in which an individual may be married to or partnered with more than one woman at the same time. See also *polygamy*.

polytheistic describes a religion that is based on the belief in more than one deity.

presenteeism describes the behaviour in which an employee is present at work for longer hours than is required, including while sick or even when there is no work to be done, often in order to display commitment in the face of job insecurity or when competing for promotion.

primogeniture describes the state of being born first of the children by the same parents, and the exclusive inheritance rights related to being first-born.

scientific socialism was first advanced by Friedrich Engels and refers to the Marxist theories espoused by the former Soviet Union and other communist states. It maintains that its ideas are historically proven and therefore objectively "scientific."

settler states or **colonial settler states** are those states that have built a self-sustaining society and complex political infrastructure on territory already occupied by another society or groups of people. The pre-existing population is subordinated to, and governed by, the occupying settlers of the settler-state.

sexuality is an individual's capacity for desire, erotic, sexual, and romantic feelings, as well as the individual's preferences regarding (a) partner(s).

sexualization is the process of instilling something or someone with sexual characteristics and, through this process, assigning them the status of a sexual object (with no other utility, identity, or personhood).

sheconomy refers to the rising role women play in the economy both as producers and consumers, and the attempts made to capitalize on these women.

social determinants of health are the intersectional social, cultural, and economic factors that affect a person's well-being. They include gender, race, sexuality, (dis)ability, class, educational attainment, housing, food security, indigeneity, and social exclusion, among others.

structural adjustment programs (SAPs) are the economic conditions stipulated by global bodies, in particular the International Monetary Fund and the World Bank, to grant loans to countries that are in need of capital. SAPs are imposed in ways that reduce social spending to pay for the incurred debt, creating or exacerbating poor social conditions in those countries.

suffrage laws are those that govern all aspects of voting in public elections.

transgender is a person who identifies as and/or expresses a different gender from the one that was assigned at birth. See also *gender expression*.

Underground Railroad was the secret network of pathways to freedom for African Americans under the US system of slavery. Because slavery was legal, the Underground Railroad operated clandestinely as a form of resistance to the institution.

References

Abby, S.M. 2003. "Deconstructing Images of Mothering in Media and Film: Possibilities and Trends." *Future Journal of the Association for Research on Mothering* 5 (1): 7–23.

Abu-Lughod, Lila. 2002. "Do Muslim Women Really Need Saving? Anthropological Reflections on Cultural Relativism and Its Others." *American Anthropologist* 104: 783–90.

Acosta-Belén, Edna, and Christine Bose. 1990. "From Structural Subordination to Empowerment: Women and Development in Third World Contexts." *Gender and Society* 4 (3): 299–320.

Adler, Nancy E. 2010. "Commentary: When Separate Is More Equal." *Journal of the American Medical Association* 304: 2738–9.

Agosin, Marjorie, ed. 2001. *Women, Gender, and Human Rights: A Global Perspective*. New Brunswick, NJ: Rutgers University Press.

Ahmadu, Fuambai. 2000. "Rites and Wrongs: An Insider/Outsider Reflects on Power and Excision." In *Female "Circumcision" in Africa: Culture, Controversy, and Change*, edited by Bettina Shell-Duncan and Ylva Hernlund. London: Lynne Rienner.

Ahmed, Leila. 1992. *Women and Gender in Islam: Historical Roots of a Modern Debate*. New Haven, CT: Yale University Press.

———. 1999. *A Border Passage*. New York: Farrar, Straus and Giroux.

Akbar, Amna, and Rupal Oza. 2013. "'Muslim Fundamentalism' and Human Rights in the Age of Terror and Empire." In *Gender, National Security and Counter-Terrorism: Human Rights Perspectives*, edited by Margaret Satterthwaite and Jayne Huckerby. New York: Routledge.

Albeda, Rany, and Chris Tilly. 1997. *Glass Ceilings and Bottomless Pits: Women's Work, Women's Poverty*. Boston: South End Press.

Alcoff, Linda. 1988. "Cultural Feminism versus Post-structuralism: The Identity Crisis in Feminist Theory." *Signs* 13 (3): 405–36.

———. 1997. "The Politics of Postmodern Feminism, Revisited." *Cultural Critique* 36 (Spring): 5–27.

———. 2006. *Visible Identities: Race, Gender and the Self*. New York: Oxford University Press.

———. 2010. "Epistemic Identities." *Episteme* 7 (2): 128–137.

——— and Elizabeth Potter, eds. 1993. *Feminist Epistemologies*. New York: Routledge.

Alcott, Louisa M. 1873. *Little Women*. New York: Western.

Alexander, M. Jacqui. 2006. *Pedagogies of Crossing: Meditations on Feminism, Sexual Politics, Memory, and the Sacred*. Durham, NC: Duke University Press.

Ali, Ayaan Hirsi. 2007. *Infidel*. New York: Simon & Schuster.

Allen, Mary, and Jillian Boyce. 2013. "Police-Reported Hate Crime in Canada 2011." *Juristat*, 11 July. www.statcan.gc.ca/pub/85-002-x/2013001/article/11822-eng.htm

Allen, Paula Gunn. 1983. *The Woman Who Owned the Shadows*. San Francisco: Spinsters Ink.

———. 1988. *The Sacred Hoop: Recovering the Feminine in American Indian Traditions*. Boston: Beacon Press.

Allen, Richard. 2006. "Social Gospel." Historica Canada. www.thecanadianencyclopedia.ca/en/article/social-gospel/

Almeida, Deidre A. 1997. "The Hidden Half: A History of Native American Women's Education." *Harvard Education Review* 67: 757–71.

Amato, Paul R. 2010. "Research on Divorce: Continuing Trends and New Developments." *Journal of Marriage and Family* 72: 650–66.

Ambrose, Susan A., Kristin L. Dunkle, Barbara L. Lazarus, et al. 1997. "Women, Science, Engineering, and Technology through the Ages." In *Journeys of Women in Science and Engineering: No Universal Constants*, edited by Susan A. Ambrose, Kristin L. Dunkle, Barbara L. Lazarus, et al. Philadelphia: Temple University Press.

American Association of University Women. 1992. AAUW *Report: How Schools Shortchange Girls*. Washington, DC: American Association of University Women.

American Psychiatric Association. 2013. *Diagnostic and Statistical Manual of Mental Disorders*, 5th edn. Washington, DC: American Psychiatric Association.

American Psychological Association. 2007. *Report of the* APA *Task Force on the Sexualization of Girls*. Washington, DC: APA.

Amnesty International. 2010. *Deadly Delivery: The Maternal Health Care Crisis in the USA*. Amnesty International USA.

Amt, Emilie, ed. 1993. *Women's Lives in Medieval Europe: A Sourcebook*. London: Routledge.

Anantnarayan, Lakshmi. 2010. "Why Are US Doctors Allowing Female Genital Mutilation?" *The Guardian*, 11 May. www.guardian.co.uk/commentisfree/2010/may/11/female-genital-mutilation-us-nicking

Anderson, Benedict. 1993. *Imagined Communities: Reflections on the Origin and Spread of Nationalism*. New York: Verso.

Anderson, Elizabeth. 2004. "Uses of Value Judgments in Feminist Social Science: A Case Study of Research on Divorce." *Hypatia* 19: 1–24.

Anderson, Leona M., and Pamela Dickey Young, eds. 2010. *Women and Religious Traditions*, 2nd edn. Toronto: Oxford University Press.

Anderson/Sankofa, David A. 1991. *The Origin of Life on Earth: An African Creation Myth*. Mt. Airy, MA: Sights Productions.

Anker, Richard. 1998. *Gender and Jobs: Sex Segregation of Occupations in the World*. Geneva: International Labour Office.

Anzaldúa, Gloria, ed. 1990. *Making Face, Making Soul—Haciendo Caras: Creative and Critical Perspectives by Women of Color*. San Francisco: Aunt Lute Books.

Arat-Kroc, Sedef, and Fely Villasin. 2001. "Caregivers Break the Silence." Toronto: Intercede.

Aristotle. 1943. *The Generation of Animals*, vols. 1 and 4, translated by A.L. Peck. Cambridge, MA: Harvard University Press.

Armstrong, Karen. 2001. *Islam: A Short History*. New York: Modern Library.

Armstrong, Laura. 2014. "What's In an Abbreviation? WorldPride 2014 Organizers Go Long." *Toronto Star*, 24 June. www.thestar.com/news/pridetoronto/2014/06/24/whats_in_an_abbreviation_worldpride_2014_organizers_go_long.html

Armstrong, Pat, and Ann Pederson, eds. 2015. *Women's Health: Intersections of Policy, Research, and Practice*. Toronto: Women's Press.

Arowolo, Dare, and Folorunso Aluko. 2010. "Women and Political Participation in Nigeria." *European Journal of Social Sciences* 144: 581–93.

Atwood, Margaret. 1986. *The Handmaid's Tale*. Boston: Houghton Mifflin.

Austen, Jane. 1959. *Pride and Prejudice*. New York: Dell.

Backhouse, C. 1986. "Pure Patriarchy: Nineteenth-Century Canadian Marriage." *McGill Law Journal* 31: 264–312.

Badawi, Jamal. 2003. *Gender Equity in Islam: Basic Principles*. Plainfield, IL: American Trust Publications.

Bandura, Albert. 1965. "Influence of Models' Reinforcement Contingencies on the Acquisition of Imitative Responses." *Journal of Personality and Social Psychology* 1: 589–95.

Barreto, Manuela, Michelle K. Ryan, and Michael T. Schmitt, eds. 2009. *The Glass Ceiling in the 21st Century*. Washington, DC: American Psychological Association.

Barjatya, Sooraj, dir. 1994. *Hum aapke hain koun!* (film). Rajshri Productions.

Barker-Benfield, G.J. 1977. "Sexual Surgery in Late Nineteenth-Century America." In *Seizing Our Bodies: The Politics of Women's Health*, edited by Claudia Dreifus. New York: Vintage.

Baron, Beth. 2005. *Egypt as a Woman: Nationalism, Gender, and Politics*. Berkeley: University of California Press.

Baron-Cohen, Simon. 2003. *The Essential Difference: Men, Women and the Extreme Male Brain*. London: Allen Lane.

Bauer, G., N. Nussbaum, R. Travers, L. Munro, J. Pyne, and N. Redman. 2011. "We've Got Work to Do: Workplace Discrimination and Employment Challenges for Trans People in Ontario." *Trans PULSE e-Bulletin* 2(1, 30 May).

Bauer, Nancy. 2010. "Lady Power." *Opinionator* (blog), *New York Times* online, 20 June. http://opinionator.blogs.nytimes.com/2010/06/20/lady-power/

Baumgardner, Jennifer, and Amy Richards. 2000. *ManifestA: Young Women, Feminism, and the Future*. New York: Farrar, Straus and Giroux.

BBC News. 2008. "Women's Low Pay 'Behind Poverty.'" 20 June. http://news.bbc.co.uk/go/pr/fr/-/2/hi/business/7465136.stm

———. 2010. "Women Bishops Should Be Allowed, General Synod Rules." 12 July. www.bbc.co.uk/news/10603968

Beaupre, Pascale. 2015. "Intimate Partner Violence." In *Family Violence in Canada: A Statistical Profile, 2013*. Statistics Canada. www.statcan.gc.ca/pub/85-002-x/2014001/article/14114/section02-eng.htm

Bechdel, Alison. 1998. *The Indelible Alison Bechdel: Confessions, Comix, and Miscellaneous Dykes to Watch Out For*. Ithaca, NY: Firebrand Books.

———. 2006. *Fun Home: A Family Tragicomic*. New York: Houghton Mifflin.

———. 2012. *Are You My Mother? A Comic Drama*. New York: Houghton Mifflin.

Beiser, Morton. 1999. *Strangers at the Gate: The "Boat People's" First Ten Years in Canada*. Toronto: University of Toronto Press.

Belkin, Lisa. 2003. "The Opt-out Revolution." *New York Times Magazine*, 26 October, 42–7, 58, 85–6.

Bell, Linda, ed. 1983. *Visions of Women*. Clifton, NJ: Humana Press.

Bem, Sandra L. 1981. "Gender Schema Theory: A Cognitive Account of Sex Typing." *Psychological Review* 88: 354–64.

———. 1983. "Gender Schema Theory and its Implications for Child Development: Raising Gender-Aschematic Children in a Gender-Schematic Society." *Signs* 8: 598–616.

———. 1985. "Androgyny and Gender Schema Theory: A Conceptual and Empirical Integration." In *Nebraska Symposium on Motivation, 1984: Psychology and Gender*, edited by T.B. Sonderegger. Lincoln: University of Nebraska Press.

Beoku-Betts, Josephine. 2006. "African Women Pursuing Graduate Studies in the Sciences: Racism, Gender Bias, and Third World Marginality." In *Removing Barriers: Women in Academic Science, Technology, Engineering, and Mathematics*, edited by Jill M. Bystydzienski and Sharon R. Bird. Bloomington: Indiana University Press.

Berger, Iris. 1999. "Women in East and Southern Africa." In *Women in Sub-Saharan Africa: Restoring Women to History*, edited by Iris Berger and E. Frances White. Bloomington: Indiana University Press.

———. and E. Frances White, eds. 1999. *Women in Sub-Saharan Africa: Restoring Women to History*. Bloomington: Indiana University Press.

Berger, Maurice, Brian Wallis, and Simon Watson. 2012. *Constructing Masculinity*. New York: Routledge.

Berger, Ryan. 2012. "Equal Access/Equal Pay." *Americas Quarterly* 6 (3): 77.

Bertone, Andrea Marie. 2000. "Sexual Trafficking in Women: International Political Economy and the Politics of Sex." *Gender Issues* 18 (1): 4–22.

Besserman, Perle. 2005. *A New Kabbalah for Women*. New York: Palgrave MacMillan.

Bethell, T.N. 2005. *The Gender Gap*. Washington, DC: AARP.

Bhattacharya, Priyanka. 2008. Indian Men Seeking Male-Specific Skin Care." *GCI Magazine*, 5 September. www.gcimagazine.com/marketstrends/regions/bric/27921834.html

Biegel, Stuart, and Sheila James Kuehl. 2010. *Safe at School: Addressing the School Environment and LGBT Safety through Policy and Legislation*. Los Angeles: Great Lakes Center for Education Research and Practice, National Education Policy Center and the Williams Institute in the UCLA Law School.

Biography Online. n.d. "Mirabai Biography." www.biographyonline.net/spiritual/mirabai.html

Bird, Christopher. 2008. "*Loving v. Virginia* and Its Impact on Canadian Jurisprudence." *The Court*. www.thecourt.ca/2008/05/14/loving-v-virginia-and-its-impact-on-canadian-jurisprudence/

Birnbaum, Norman. 2012. "The Vatican's Latest Target in the War on Women: Nuns." *The Nation*, 24 April.

Bishop, Sharon, and Marjorie Weinzweig, eds. 1979. "Preferential Treatment." In *Philosophy and Women*. Belmont, CA: Wadsworth.

Blackwell, Marilyn S. 2001. "Surrogate Ministers: Women, Revivalism and Maternal Associations in Vermont." *Vermont History*, 69 (suppl.): 66–78.

Blackwood, Evelyn. 2006. "Mothers to Daughters: Social Change and Matrilineal Kinship in a Minangkabau Village." In *Globalization and Change in Fifteen Cultures: Born in One World, Living in Another*, edited by George Dearborn Spindler and Janice E. Stockard. Belmont, CA: Wadsworth.

———. 2010. *Falling into the Lesbi World: Desire and Difference in Indonesia*. Honolulu: University of Hawaii Press.

Blayney, Candace, and Karen Blotnicky. 2010. "The Impact of Gender on Career Paths and Management Capability in the Hotel Industry in Canada." *Journal of Human Resources in Hospitality & Tourism* 9 (3): 233–55.

Blee, Kathleen M. 1991. "Women in the 1920s Ku Klux Klan Movement." *Feminist Studies* 17 (1): 57–77.

Blount, Marcellus, and George P. Cunningham, eds. 1989. *Representing Black Men*. New York: Routledge.

Blum, Linda M. 1991. *Between Feminism and Labor: The Significance of the Comparable Worth Debate*. Berkeley: University of California Press.

Boden, Alison. 2007. *Women's Rights and Religious Practice: Claims in Conflict*. Basingstoke, UK: Palgrave Macmillan.

Bok, Sissela. 1991. *Alva Myrdal*. Reading, MA: Addison Wesley.

Bolton, Michele K. 2000. *The Third Shift: Managing Hard Choices in Our Careers, Homes, and Lives as Women*. San Francisco: Jossey-Bass.

Bonomi, Patricia U. 2000. *The Lord Cornbury Scandal: The Politics of Reputation in British America*. Chapel Hill: University of North Carolina Press.

Bookman, Ann, and Sandra Morgen, eds. 1988. *Women and the Politics of Empowerment*. Philadelphia, PA: Temple University Press.

Boos, Florence S. 1976. "Catherine Macaulay's *Letters on Education* 1790: An Early Feminist Polemic."

University of Michigan Papers in Women's Studies 2: 64–78.

Bordo, Susan. 1993. *Unbearable Weight: Feminism, Western Culture, and the Body*. Berkeley: University of California Press.

Bornstein, Kate. 1994. *Gender Outlaw: On Men, Women and the Rest of Us*. New York: Routledge Press.

———. 2012. *A Queer and Pleasant Danger*. Boston: Beacon Press.

Boroditsky. Lera. 2009. "How Does Our Language Shape the Way We Think?" *Edge*, 6 November. http://edge.org/conversation/how-does-our-language-shape-the-way-we-think

Boserup, Esther. 1970. *Women's Role in Economic Development*. New York: St Martin's Press.

Boston Women's Health Book Collective. 2011 (1971). *Our Bodies, Ourselves*. New York: Simon & Schuster.

Botelho-Urbanski, Jessica. 2016. "Baby Storm Five Years Later: Preschooler on Top of the World." *Toronto Star*, 11 July. www.thestar.com/news/gta/2016/07/11/baby-storm-five-years-later-preschooler-on-top-of-the-world.html

Boulding, Elise. 1976. *The Underside of History: A View of Women through Time*. Boulder, CO: Westview Press.

———. 1977. *Women in the Twentieth Century World*. New York: Wiley.

Bourgeois, Fr Roy. 2011. "Father Roy Bourgeois Responds to Second Canonical Warning." Letter from Father Bourgeois to the Maryknoll Community and Superior General Rev. Edward Dougherty. 8 August. www.womensordination.org/contnt/view/366/42/

Bowers, Emily, 2007. "FGM Practitioners Sway Elections in Sierra Leone." *We News*, 7 September. http://womensenews.org/2007/09/fgm-practitioners-sway-elections-in-sierra-leone/

Boxer, Marilyn. 1998. *When Women Asked the Questions: Creating Women's Studies in America*. Baltimore: Johns Hopkins University Press.

———, and Jean H. Quataert. 2000. "Women in the Early Modern Era: Religious Upheaval, Political Centralization, and Colonial Conquest." In *Connecting Spheres: Women in the Western World, 1500 to the Present*, edited by Marilyn J. Boxer and Jean H. Quataert. New York: Oxford University Press.

Boylan, Esther. 1991. *Women and Disability*. Atlantic Highlands, NJ: Zed Books.

Bradsher, J.E. 2001. "Older Women and Widowhood." In *Handbook on Women and Aging*, edited by J.M. Coyle. Westport, CT: Greenwood.

Braithwaite, Ronald L., Kimberly Jacob Arriola, and Cassandra Newkirk, eds. 2006. *Health Issues among Incarcerated Women*. New Brunswick, NJ: Rutgers University Press.

Branch, Enobong Hannah. 2011. *Opportunity Denied: Limiting Black Women to Devalued Work*. New Brunswick, NJ: Rutgers University Press.

Bravo, Ellen. 2003. "The Clerical Proletariat." In *Sisterhood Is Forever*, edited by Robin Morgan. New York: Washington Square Press.

Brennan, Denise. 2002. "Selling Sex for Visas: Sex Tourism as a Stepping-Stone to International Migration." In *Global Women: Nannies, Maids, and Sex Workers in the New Economy*, edited by Barbara Ehrenreich and Arlie Russell Hochschild. New York: Metropolitan Books.

Bright, Susie. 1992. *Susie Bright's Sexual Reality: A Virtual Sex Reader*. Seattle, WA: Cleis Press.

British Columbia Law Institute. 2014. "Uniform Vital Statistics Act Project Backgrounder." www.bcli.org/wordpress/wp-content/uploads/2014/07/ULC-Vital-Statistics-Act-Project-Backgrounder.pdf

Brizendine, Louanne. 2006. *The Female Brain*. New York: Morgan Road Books.

Bronstein, Phyllis. 2006. "The Family Environment: Where Gender Role Socialization Begins." In *Handbook of Girls' and Women's Psychological Health*, edited by Judith Worell and Carol D. Goodheart. New York: Oxford University Press.

Brooks, Gwendolyn. 1963. *Selected Poems*. New York: Harper & Row.

Brooks, Rosa. 2006. "No Escaping Sexualization of Young Girls." *Los Angeles Times*, 25 August. www.commondreams.org/views06/0825-33.htm

Brown, Karen McCarthy. 1994. "Fundamentalism and the Control of Women." In *Fundamentalism and Gender*, edited by John Stratton Hawley. Oxford: Oxford University Press.

Brown, Lyn Mikel. 2008. "The 'Girls' in Girls' Studies." *Girlhood Studies* 1 (1): 1–12.

———, and Carol Gilligan. 1992. *Meeting at the Crossroads: Women's Psychology and Girls' Development*. Cambridge, MA: Harvard University Press.

Brumberg, Joan J. 1997. *The Body Project: An Intimate History of American Girls*. New York: Random House.

Brydon, Anne, and Sandra Niessen. 1998. *Consuming Fashion: Adorning the Transnational Body*. Oxford, Berg.

Buirski, Nancy, dir. 2011. *The Loving Story*. New York: HBO Documentary.

Bunch, Charlotte. 1975. "Lesbians in Revolt." In *Lesbianism and the Women's Movement*, edited by Nancy Myron and Charlotte Bunch. Baltimore: Diana Press.

Bundles, A'Lelia Perry. 2001. *On Her Own Ground: The Life and Times of Madame C.J. Walker.* New York: Scribner.

Burgos-Debray, Elizabeth, ed. 1984. *I, Rigoberta Menchu.* London: Verso.

Burke, Carole. 2004. *Camp All-American, Hanoi Jane, and the High-and-Tight: Gender, Folklore, and Changing Military Culture.* Boston: Beacon Press.

Burstyn, Varda, ed. 1985. *Women against Censorship.* Vancouver: Douglas and McIntyre.

Burton, Antoinette. 1998. *At the Heart of the Empire: Indians and the Colonial Encounter in Later Victorian England.* Berkeley: University of California Press.

Butler, Anne M. 1985. *Daughters of Joy, Sisters of Misery: Prostitutes in the American West, 1865–90.* Urbana: University of Illinois Press.

Butler, Judith. 1990. *Gender Trouble: Feminism and the Subversion of Identity.* New York: Routledge.

———. 1993. *Bodies That Matter: On the Discursive Limits of "Sex."* New York: Routledge.

———. 2004. *Undoing Gender.* New York: Routledge.

Bystydzienski, Jill M., and Sharon R. Bird. 2006. Introduction. In *Removing Barriers: Women in Academic Science, Technology, Engineering, and Mathematics,* edited by Jill M. Bystydzienski and Sharon R. Bird. Bloomington: Indiana University Press.

Calder, Gillian, and Lori G. Beaman, eds. 2014. *Polygamy's Rights and Wrongs: Perspectives on Harm, Family and Law.* Vancouver: University of British Columbia Press.

Caldwell, Sarah. 2000. *Oh Terrifying Mother: Sexuality, Violence and Worship of the Goddess Kali.* New York: Oxford University Press.

Califia, Pat. 1988. *Sapphistry: The Book of Lesbian Sexuality.* Tallahassee, FL: Naiad Press.

Callan, Hilary, and Shirley Ardener, eds. 1984. *The Incorporated Wife.* London: Croom Helm.

Campbell, Rebecca, Tracy Sefl, and Courtney E. Ahrens. 2003. "The Physical Health Consequences of Rape: Assessing Survivors' Somatic Symptoms in a Racially Diverse Population." *Women's Studies Quarterly* 31: 90–7.

Canadian Association of University Teachers. 2011. "The Persistent Gap: Understanding Male–Female Salary Differentials amongst Canadian Academic Staff." CAUT *Equity Review* 5. www.caut.ca/docs/equity-review/the-persistent-gap-mdash-understanding-male-female-salary-differentials-amongst-canadian-academic-staff-%28mar-2011%29.pdf?sfvrsn=12

Canadian Bar Association, BC Branch. 2014. "Sexual Harassment." www.cbabc.org

Canadian Press. 2013. "Woman Politicians Canada: Will Ontario Add a Sixth Female Premier?" *Huffington Post,* 23 January. www.huffingtonpost.ca/2013/01/23/woman-female-premiers-politicians-canada_n_2535302.html

Canadian Human Rights Commission. n.d. "Voting Rights." *Human Rights in Canada: A Historical Perspective.* www.chrc-ccdp.ca/historical-perspective/en/browseSubjects/votingRights.asp

Canadian Race Relations Foundation. 2000. *Racism in Our Schools: What to Know about It; How to Fight It.* www.crrf-fcrr.ca/images/Clearinghouse/ePubFaShRacScho.pdf

Canetto, S.S. 2003. "Older Adulthood." In *The Complete Guide to Mental Health for Women,* edited by L. Slater, J.H. Daniel, and A.E. Banks. Boston: Beacon Press.

Cantor, Aviva. 1979. "Jewish Women's Haggadah." In *Womanspirit Rising: A Feminist Reader in Religion,* edited by Carol P. Christ and Judith Plaskow. San Francisco: Harper & Row.

Carby, Hazel. 1987. *Reconstructing Womanhood: The Emergence of the Afro-American Woman Novelist.* New York: Oxford University Press.

Card, Claudia. 1995. *Lesbian Choices.* New York: Columbia University Press.

———. 1996. "Rape as a Weapon of War." *Hypatia* 11 (4): 5–18.

Carmody, Denise. 1979. *Women and World Religions.* Nashville, TN: Abingdon.

Carr, E. 1946. *Growing Pains: An Autobiography.* Toronto: Irwin.

Carson, Rachel. 2002 (1962). *Silent Spring.* Boston: Houghton Mifflin Harcourt.

Carty, Linda, and Chandra Talpade Mohanty. 2014. "Mapping Transnational Feminist Engagements: Neoliberalism and the Politics of Solidarity." In *The Oxford Handbook of Transnational Feminist Movements,* edited by Rawwida Baksh and Wendy Harcourt. DOI: 10.1093/oxfordhb/9780199943494.013.010

Casas, Lidia. 2011. "Women and Reproduction: from Control to Autonomy? The Case of Chile." *Journal of Gender, Social Policy and the Law* 12 (3): 427–51.

Catalyst. 2012a. *Women CEOs of the Fortune 1000.* www.catalyst.org/publication/271/women-ceos-of-the-fortune-1000

———. 2012b. "Women in Medicine: Quick Takes." April. www.catalyst.org/publication/208/women-in-medicine

———. 2016. "Working Parents." www.catalyst.org/knowledge/working-parents

Catholic Network for Women's Equality. n.d. "The History of Canadian Catholics for Women's Ordination

(CCWO) and the Catholic Network for Women's Equality (CNWE): The First Twenty Years 1981–2001." www.cnwe.org/wp-content/uploads/2011/10/CNWE-History-1981-2001.pdf

CBC News. 2013. "Aboriginal Children Used in Medical Tests, Commissioner Says." 31 July. www.cbc.ca/news/politics/aboriginal-children-used-in-medical-tests-commissioner-says-1.1318150

———. 2015. "Hydro One Employee Fired after FHRITP Heckling of CityNews Reporter Shauna Hunt." www.cbc.ca/beta/hydro-one-employee-fired-after-fhritp-heckling-of-citynews-reporter-shauna-hunt-1.3070948

Center for the American Woman and Politics. 1991. *The Impact of Women in Public Office: An Overview.* New Brunswick, NJ: Eagleton Institute of Politics, Rutgers University.

Centers for Disease Control and Prevention (CDC). 2010. "Chlamydia." Atlanta, GA: CDC. www.cdc.gov/std/stats10/chlamydia.htm

———. 2012. "Women's Safety and Health Issues at Work." Atlanta, GA: CDC. www.cdc.gov/niosh/topics/women

Chadha, Gurinder, dir. 2004. *Bride and Prejudice* (film). Miramax Films.

Chadwick, Whitney. 1990. *Women, Art, and Society.* London: Thames and Hudson.

Chakravarty, Sumita. 1993. *National Identity and Indian Popular Cinema, 1947–1987.* Austin: University of Texas Press.

Chamberlain, Mariam K., ed. 1988. *Women in Academe: Progress and Prospects.* New York: Russell Sage Foundation.

Champ, Paul. 2014. "Alleged Afghan Prison Torture Controversy Slips Quietly into the History Books." CBC News, 10 March. www.cbc.ca/beta/news/politics/

Chappell, Louise. 2006. "Contesting Women's Rights: Charting the Emergence of a Transnational Conservative Counter-Network." *Global Society* 20: 491–520.

Charbonneau, Leo. 2009. "Female University Presidents." *University Affairs*, 5 March. www.universityaffairs.ca/margin-notes/female-university-presidents/

Chase, Susan E., and Mary F. Rogers, eds. 2001. *Mothers and Children: Feminist Analyses and Personal Narratives.* New Brunswick, NJ: Rutgers University Press.

Chatterjee, Partha. 1993. *The Nation and Its Fragments: Colonial and Postcolonial Histories.* Princeton, NJ: Princeton University Press.

Cherlin, Andrew J. 2005. "American Marriage in the Early Twenty-First Century." *The Future of Children* 15 (2): 33–55.

———. 2010. "Demographic Trends in the United States: A Review of Research in the 2000s." *Journal of Marriage and Family* 72 (3): 403–19.

Chesler, Phyllis. 1972. *Women and Madness.* Garden City: Doubleday.

Cheung, Fanny M., and Diane F. Halpern. 2010. "Women at the Top: Powerful Leaders Define Success as Work + Family in a Culture of Gender." *American Psychologist* 65 (3): 182–93.

Childs, Sarah, and Mona Lena Krook. 2009. "Analysing Women's Substantive Representation: From Critical Mass to Critical Actors." *Government and Opposition* 44 (2): 125–45.

Chodorow, Nancy. 1978. *The Reproduction of Mothering: Psychoanalysis and the Sociology of Gender.* Berkeley: University of California Press.

Chowdhury, Najma. 2008. "Lessons on Women's Political Leadership from Bangladesh." *Signs* 34 (1): 8–15.

Christ, Carol P. 1979. "Why Women Need the Goddess: Phenomenological, Psychological, and Political Reflections." In *Womanspirit Rising: A Feminist Reader in Religion*, edited by Carol P. Christ and Judith Plaskow. San Francisco: Harper & Row.

———. 1987. *Laughter of Aphrodite: Reflections on a Journey to the Goddess.* New York: Harper & Row.

Christensen, A.S. 1988. "Sex Discrimination and the Law." In *Women Working: Theories and Facts in Perspective*, edited by Ann H. Stromberg and Shirley Harkness. Mountain View, CA: Mayfield.

Cifcili S.Y., M. Akman, A. Demirkol, et al. 2009. "'I Should Live and Finish It': A Qualitative Inquiry into Turkish Women's Menopause Experience." *BMC Family Practice* 10: 2.

Cixous, Hélène. 1981. "The Laugh of the Medusa." In *New French Feminisms*, edited by Elaine Marks and Isabelle de Courtivron, translated by Keith Cohen and Paula Cohen. New York: Schocken. (Originally published [1976] as "Le rire de la meduse," *Signs* 1: 875–93.)

Clarke, Cheryl. 1983. "The Failure to Transform: Homophobia in the Black Community." In *Home Girls: A Black Feminist Anthology*, edited by Barbara Smith. New York: Kitchen Table Women of Color Press.

Clifton, Donna, and Charlotte Feldman-Jacobs. 2011. *Current Status of the World's Women and Girls.* Washington, DC: Population Reference Bureau.

Clifton, Lucille. 1991. "Wishes for Sons." In *Quilting: Poems 1987–1990.* Rochester, NY: BOA Editions.

Cockburn, Cynthia. 2010. "Gender Relations as Casual in Militarization and War." *International Feminist Journal of Politics* (10 May).

Cockrell, C. 2003. "Making Academia More Family-Friendly." *Berkeleyan*. April. http://Berkeley.edu/news/berkeleyan/2003/04/30_facfam.shtml

Cohn, Carol. 2013. *Women and Wars*. Cambridge, UK: Polity Press.

Coleman, Emily. 1976. "Infanticide in the Early Middle Ages." In *Women in Medieval Society*, edited by Susan Mosher Stuard. Philadelphia: University of Pennsylvania Press.

Colette, Sidonie-Gabrielle. 1953 (1930). *My Mother's House, and Sido*, translated by Una Vincenzo and Enid McLead. New York: Farrar, Straus and Giroux.

Collections Canada 2006. "Dr. Emily Howard Stowe." *Library and Archives Canada*. www.collectionscanada.gc.ca/physicians/030002-2500-e.html

College Board, The. 2010. *The Educational Crisis Facing Young Men of Color*. New York: The College Board.

Collins, Alicia C. 2001. "Black Women in the Academy." In *Sisters of the Academy*, edited by Reitumetse Obakeng Mabokela and Ann L. Green. Sterling, VA: Stylus.

Collins, Gail. 2009. *When Everything Changed: The Amazing Journey of American Women from 1960 to the Present*. Boston: Little, Brown.

Collins, Patricia Hill. 1990. *Black Feminist Thought: Knowledge, Consciousness, and the Politics of Empowerment*. New York: Routledge, Chapman, and Hall.

———. 1998. "It's All in the Family: Intersections of Gender, Race, and Nation." *Hypatia* 13 (3): 62–82.

———. 2000a. *Black Feminist Thought: Knowledge, Consciousness, and the Politics of Empowerment*, 2nd edn. New York: Routledge.

———. 2000b. "The Meaning of Motherhood in Black Culture and Black Mother–Daughter Relationships." In *Double Stitch: Black Women Write about Mothers & Daughters*, edited by Patricia Bell-Scott, Beverly Guy-Sheftall, Jacqueline Jones Royster, et al. Boston: Beacon Press.

Collins, Suzanne. 2008. *The Hunger Games*. New York: Scholastic Press.

Colyar, Julia. 2008. "Communities of Exclusion: Women Student Experiences in Information Technology Classrooms." *Journal about Women in Higher Education* 1 (1): 123–42.

Conboy, Katie, Nadia Median, and Sarah Stanbury, eds. 1997. *Writing on the Body*. New York: Columbia University Press.

Constable, Nicole. 2005. *Cross-Border Marriages: Gender and Mobility in Transnational Asia*. Philadelphia: University of Pennsylvania Press.

———. 2007. *Maid to Order in Hong Kong: Stories of Migrant Workers*. Ithaca, NY: Cornell University Press.

Conway, M. Margaret. 2001. "Women and Political Participation." *PS: Political Science and Politics* 25 (2): 231–3.

Cook, Blanche Wiesen. 1992. *Eleanor Roosevelt*, vol. 1. New York: Penguin.

Cook, Daniel Thomas, and Susan B. Kaiser. 2004. "Betwixt and Between: Age Ambiguity and the Sexualization of the Female Consuming Subject." *Journal of Consumer Culture* 4: 203–27.

Cooke, Lynn Prince, and Janeen Baxter. 2010. "'Families' in International Context: Comparing Institutional Effects across Western Societies." *Journal of Marriage and Family* 71: 516–36.

Cookson, Shari, dir. 2001. "Living Dolls: The Making of a Child Beauty Queen." In *American Undercover* (documentary), produced by L. Otto. New York: HBO DOCUMENTARY.

Coontz, Stephanie. 2009. "Sharing the Load: Quality Marriages Today Depend on Couples Sharing Domestic Work." In *The Shriver Report: A Woman's Nation Changes Everything*. Washington, DC: Center for American Progress.

Cooper, Anna Julia. 1998 [1892]. *A Voice from the South*. New York: Oxford University Press.

Corbett, Christianne, Catherine Hill, and Andresse St. Rose. 2010. *Why So Few? Women in Science, Technology, Engineering and Mathematics*. Washington, DC: AAUW.

Cott, Nancy F. 1990. "Across the Great Divide: Women in Politics before and after 1920." In *Women, Politics and Change*, edited by Louise A. Tilly and Patricia Gurin. New York: Russell Sage Foundation.

Council of Canadians. 2014. "Why We're Fighting against Two-Tiered Health Care." 27 June. http://canadians.org/blog/why-were-fighting-against-two-tiered-health-care

Cranswick, Kelly, and Donna Dosman. 2008. "Eldercare: What We Know Today." Statistics Canada. www.statcan.gc.ca/pub/11-008-x/2008002/article/10689-eng.htm#a2

Creegan, Nicola Hoggard, and Christine D. Pohl. 2005. *Living on the Boundaries: Evangelical Women, Feminism, and the Theological Academy*. Downers Grove, IL: InterVarsity Press.

Crenshaw, Kimberlé. 1989. "Demarginalizing the Intersection of Race and Sex: A Black Feminist Critique of

Antidiscrimination Doctrine, Feminist Theory, and Antiracist Politics." *The University of Chicago Legal Forum*, 139–67.

———. 1991. "Mapping the Margins: Intersectionality, Identity Politics, and Violence against Women of Color." *Stanford Law Review* 43 (6): 1241–99.

Crimmins, Eileen, Jung Ki Kim, and Aaron Hagedorn. 2002. "Life with and without Disease: Women Experience More of Both." *Journal of Women & Aging* 14 (1–2): 47–59.

Cross, Philip, and Peter Jon Mitchell. 2014. *The Marriage Gap Between Rich and Poor Canadians.* Institute of Marriage and Family Canada. www.imfcanada.org/sites/default/files/Canadian_Marriage_Gap_FINAL_0.pdf

CTV News. 2014. "Maternal Health: Should Harper Focus on First Nations First?" 27 May. www.ctvnews.ca/health/maternal-health-should-harper-focus-on-first-nations-first-1.1841239

———. 2015. "Female Inmates Need Specialized Treatment for Physical, Sexual Trauma: Report." 6 January. www.ctvnews.ca/health/female-inmates-need-specialized-treatment-for-physical-sexual-trauma-report-1.2175939#ixzz3O7DXq6ud

Currah, Paisley, Richard M. Juang, and Shannon Price Minter. 2006. "Introduction." In *Transgender Rights.* Minneapolis: University of Minnesota Press.

Cusk, Rachel. 2002. *A Life's Work: On Becoming a Mother.* New York: Picador.

Dalla Costa, Mariarosa, and Selma James. 1975. *The Power of Women and Subversion of the Community.* Bristol, CT: Falling Wall Press.

Dalley, Gillian. 1988. *Ideologies of Caring: Rethinking Community and Collectivism.* London: Macmillan Education.

Daly, Mary. 1973. *Beyond God the Father: Toward a Philosophy of Women's Liberation.* Boston: Beacon.

———. 1978. *Gyn-ecology: The Metaethics of Radical Feminism.* Boston: Beacon Press.

Dambrofsky, Gwen. 2016. "Woman Who Made History with Lawsuit against Alberta Government Dies." *National Newswatch,* 16 March. www.nationalnewswatch.com/2016/03/16/woman-who-made-history-with-lawsuit-against-alberta-government-dies-2/#.WA5vWiSrGg8

Dames Making Games. n.d. "About." https://dmg.to/about

Das Gupta, Monica. 2009. "Family Systems, Political Systems, and Asia's 'Missing Girls': The Construction of Son Preference and Its Unraveling." Washington, DC: The World Bank. DOI: http://dx.doi.org/10.1596/1813-9450-5148

Davis, Angela. 1971. "Reflections on the Black Woman's Role in the Community of Slaves." *Black Scholar* 3: 2–15.

———. 1983. *Women, Race, and Class.* New York: Random House.

———. 1998. *The Angela Davis Reader,* edited by Joy James. Malden, MA: Blackwell.

Davis, Flora. 1991. *Moving the Mountain: The Women's Movement in America since 1960.* New York: Simon & Shuster.

Davis, Kathy. 2007. *The Making of Our Bodies, Ourselves. How Feminism Travels across Borders.* Durham, NC: Duke University Press.

Dawkins, Richard. 1976. *The Selfish Gene.* New York: Oxford University Press.

Daymond, M.J., Dorothy Driver, Sheila Meintjes, et al., eds. 2003. *Women Writing Africa I: The Southern Region.* New York: Feminist Press.

Dean-Jones, L. 1994. *Women's Bodies in Classical Greek Science.* Oxford: Clarendon.

Deaux, Kay, and Brenda Major. 1987. "Putting Gender into Context: An Interactive Model of Gender-Related Behavior." *Psychological Review* 94: 369–89.

de Beauvoir, Simone. 1964. *Force of Circumstance,* translated by Richard Howard. New York: Putnam.

———. 2011 (1949). *The Second Sex,* translated by Constance Borde and Sheila Malovany-Chevallier. New York: Vintage.

Delaney, Janice, Mary J. Lupton, and Emily Toth, eds. 1976. *The Curse: A Cultural History of Menstruation.* New York: New American Library.

Delany, Samuel R. 1993. *The Tales of Nevèrÿon.* Hanover, NH: University Press of New England/Wesleyan University Press.

DeMello, Margo. 2000. *Bodies of Inscription: A Cultural History of the Tattoo.* Durham, NC: Duke University Press.

Demerson, Velma. 2003. *Incorrigible.* Waterloo, ON: Wilfrid Laurier Press.

D'Emilio, John. 1983. *Sexual Politics, Sexual Communities: The Making of a Homosexual Minority in the United States, 1940–1970.* Chicago: University of Chicago Press.

DeNavas-Walt, Carmen, Bernadette D. Proctor, and Jessica C. Smith. 2011. *Income, Poverty, and Health Insurance Coverage in the United States: 2010.* US Census Bureau, Current Population Reports, P60–239. Washington, DC: US Government Printing Office.

Denmark, Florence L. 1977. "What Sigmund Freud Didn't Know about Women." Convocation address, St Olaf's College, Northfield, MN. January.

———. 2002. "The Myths of Aging." *Eye on Psi Chi* 7 (1): 14–21.

——— and Marcia Guttentag. 1967. "Dissonance in the Self-Concepts and Educational Concepts of College and Non-College-Oriented Women." *Journal of Counseling Psychology* 14: 113–15.

———. V.C. Rabinowitz, and J.A. Sechzer. 2005. *Engendering Psychology: Women and Gender Revisited*, 2nd edn. Boston: Pearson Education.

Den Tandt, Michael. 2012. "Census: Stephen Harper Has More to Consider Than the Traditional Nuclear Family." *Canada.com*, 19 September. www.canada.com/Census+Stephen+Harper+more+consider+than+traditional+nuclear+family/7265373/story.html

de Pillis, Emmeline, and Lisette de Pillis. 2008. "Are Engineering Schools Masculine and Authoritarian? The Mission Statements Say Yes." *Journal of Diversity in Higher Education* 1 (1): 33–44.

Derrida, Jacques. 1978. *Writing and Difference*, translated by Alan Bass. London: Routlege.

DES Action Canada. 2005. "Our Organization." www.descanada.ca/anglais/anglais.html

Des Jardins, Julie. 2010. *The Madame Curie Complex: The Hidden History of Women in Science*. New York: Feminist Press.

Deutsch, Nancy L., and Barbara Schmertz. 2011. "'Starting from Ground Zero': Constraints and Experiences of Adult Women Returning to College." *The Review of Higher Education* 34 (3): 477–504.

De Veaux, Alexis. 2006. *Warrior Poet: A Biography of Audre Lorde*. New York: W.W. Norton.

Dickie, Margaret, and Thomas Travisano, eds. 1996. *Gendered Modernisms: American Women Poets and their Readers*. Philadelphia: University of Pennsylvania Press.

Dickinson, Torry D., and Robert K. Schaeffer. 2001. *Fast Forward: Work, Gender, and Protest in a Changing World*. Lanham, MD: Rowman & Littlefield.

Didion, Joan. 2006. *The Year of Magical Thinking*. New York: Vintage.

Dinnerstein, Dorothy. 1977. *The Mermaid and the Minotaur: Sexual Arrangements and Human Malaise*. New York: HarperCollins.

DisAbled Women's Network Canada. 2015. "Executive Summary: Legislation, Policy and Service Responses to Violence against Women with Disabilities and Deaf Women in Canada." www.dawncanada.net/main/wp-content/uploads/2015/11/LPS-executive-summary_Eng.docx

Disney, Jennifer. 2008. *Women's Activism and Feminist Agency in Mozambique and Nicaragua*. Philadelphia, PA: Temple University Press.

Divale, William Tulio, and Marvin Harris. 1976. "Population, Warfare, and the Male Supremacist Complex." *American Anthropologist* 78 (3): 521–38.

Dolan, Julie. 2001. "Political Appointees in the United States: Does Gender Make a Difference?" *PS: Political Science and Politics* 25 (2): 213–16.

Donoghue, Glenda D., ed. 1996. *Women's Health in the Curriculum: A Resource Guide for Faculty*. Philadelphia: National Academy on Women's Health Medical Education.

Dreby, Joanna. 2009. "Negotiating Work and Parenting over the Life Course: Mexican Family Dynamics in a Binational Context." In *Across Generations: Immigrant Families in America*, edited by Nancy Foner. New York: New York University Press.

Dressler, William W. Health in the African American community: Accounting for health inquiries. *Medical Anthropology Quarterly*, 7:4, 325–45, 1993.

Driscoll, Catherine. 2008. "Girls Today, Girls, Girl Culture and Girl Studies." *Girlhood Studies* 1 (1): 13–32.

Dua, Enakshi. 1999. "Beyond Diversity: Exploring the Ways in Which the Discourse of Race Has Shaped the Institution of the Nuclear Family." In Enakshi Dua and Angela Robertson, eds, *Scratching the Surface*. Toronto: Women's Press.

Duenwald, M., and B. Stamler. 2004. "On Their Own, in the Same Boat." *New York Times*, 13 April, E1, E13.

Duggan, Lisa, and Nan Hunter. 1995. *Sex Wars: Sexual Dissent and Political Culture*. New York: Routledge.

Duncan, Carol. 1973. "Happy Mothers and Other New Ideas in French Art." *Art Bulletin* 55: 570–83.

Dunn, Mary Maples. 1979. "Woman of Light." In *Women of America: A History*, edited by Carol Ruth Berkin and Mary Beth Norton. Boston: Houghton Mifflin.

Durham, Meenakshi Gigi. 2007. "Sex in the Transnational City: Discourses of Gender, Body and Nation in the 'New Bollywood.'" In *Cinema, Law and the State in Asia*, edited by Corey Creekmur and Mark Sidel. New York: Palgrave Macmillan.

Dworkin, Andrea. 1979. *Pornography: Men Possessing Women*. New York: G.P. Putnam.

Dyck, Erika. 2013. *Facing Eugenics, Reproduction, Sterilization, and the Politics of Choice*. Toronto: University of Toronto Press.

Eagly, Alice H. 1987. *Sex Differences in Social Behavior: A Social-Role Interpretation*. Hillsdale, NJ: Erlbaum.

Edwards, Louise. 2007. "Strategizing for Politics: Chinese Women's Participation the One-Party State." *Women's Studies International Forum* 30 (5): 380–390.

——— and Mina Roces, eds. 2000. *Women in Asia*. Ann Arbor: University of Michigan Press.

Egale. 2013. "What You Should Know about LGBTQ Youth Suicide in Canada." http://egale.ca/backgrounder-lgbtq-youth-suicide/

Ehrenreich, Barbara. 2004. "Feminism's Assumptions Upended." *Los Angeles Times*, 16 May.

——— and Deirdre English. 1977. "Complaints and Disorders: The Sexual Politics of Sickness." In *Seizing Our Bodies: The Politics of Women's Health*, edited by Claudia Dreifus. New York: Vintage.

——— and Deirdre English. 2010. *Witches, Midwives, and Nurses: A History of Women Healers*, 2nd edn. New York: Feminist Press.

——— and Arlie Russell Hochschild, eds. 2002. *Global Women: Nannies, Maids and Sex Workers in the New Economy*. New York: Metropolitan.

Eichler, Margrit. 2012. "Marriage and Divorce." *Canadian Encyclopedia*. www.thecanadianencyclopedia.ca/en/article/marriage-and-divorce/

———. Patrizia Albanese, Susan Ferguson, et al., eds. 2010. *More Than It Seems: Household Work and Lifelong Learning*. Toronto: Canadian Scholars Press.

Eisenstein, Zillah. 1981. *The Radical Future of Liberal Feminism*. New York: Longman.

———. 2004. *Against Empire: Feminisms, Racism and the West*. London: Zed Books.

Eisler, Benita, ed. 1977. *The Lowell Offering: Writings by New England Mill Women*. New York: Harper & Row.

El-Zanaty, Fatma, and Ann Way. 2009. *Egypt Demographic and Health Survey 2008*. Cairo, Egypt: Ministry of Health.

Ellin, Abby. 2012. "More Women Look over the Counter for a Libido Fix." *New York Times*. www.nytimes.com/2012/07/03/health/more-women-seek-over-the-counter-sexual-reme dies.html?pagewanted=all&_r=0

Ellis, Kate, Nan D. Hunter, Beth Jaker, et al., eds. 1986. *Caught Looking: Feminism, Pornography and Censorship*. New York: Caught Looking.

Ellis, Pat, ed. 1986. *Women of the Caribbean*. London: Zed Books.

Employment and Social Development Canada. 2016. "Family Life: Divorce." http://well-being.esdc.gc.ca/misme-iowb/.3ndic.1t.4r@-eng.jsp?iid=76

Emslie, C., and K. Hunt. 2009. "'Live to Work' or 'Work to Live'? A Qualitative Study of Gender and Work–Life Balance among Men and Women in Midlife." *Gender, Work and Organization* 16 (1): 151–72.

Engels, Friedrich. 1972 (1884). *The Origin of the Family, Private Property and the State*, translated by Alec West and Eleanor Burke Leacock. New York: International Publishers.

Engle, Karen. 2005. "Feminism and its (Dis)Contents: Criminalizing Wartime Rape in Bosnia and Herzegovina." *American Journal of International Law* 99 (4): 778–816.

Enloe, Cynthia. 2000. *Maneuvers: The International Politics of Militarizing Women's Lives*. Berkeley: University of California Press.

———. 2007. *Globalization and Militarism: Feminists Make the Link*. New York: Rowman & Littlefield.

Ernst, E., and S. Kapos. 2012. *Global Employment Trends 2012: Preventing a Deeper Job Crisis*. Geneva: International Labour Office.

Etaugh, Claire. 2008. "Women in the Middle and Later Years." In *Psychology of Women: A Handbook of Issues and Theories*, edited by Florence Denmark and Michele Antoinette Paludi. Westport, CT: Greenwood Press.

———and Judith S. Bridges. 2006. *Women's Lives: A Topical Approach*. Boston: Pearson Allyn and Bacon.

Eto, Makiko. 2010. "Women and Representation in Japan: The Causes of Political Inequality." *International Feminist Journal of Politics* 12 (2): 177–201.

Fabian, Ann. 2010. *The Skull Collectors: Race, Science, and America's Unburied Dead*. Chicago: University of Chicago Press.

Fah, Breanne. 2010. "Radical Refusals: On the Anarchist Politics of Women Choosing Asexuality." *Sexualities* 13: 445.

Falk, Nancy Auer. 1980. *Unspoken Worlds: Women's Religious Lives in Non-Western Cultures*. New York: HarperCollins.

Falola, Toyin, and Saheed Aderinto. 2010. *Nigeria, Nationalism, and Writing History*. Rochester, NY: University of Rochester Press.

Fausto-Sterling, Anne. 2000. *Sexing the Body: Gender Politics and the Construction of Sexuality*. New York: Basic Books.

Federbush, Marsha. 1974. "The Sex Problems of School Math Books." In *And Jill Came Tumbling After: Sexism in American Education*, edited by Judith Stacey, Susan Béreaud, and Joan Daniels. New York: Dell.

Feeney, J., dir. 1963. *Eskimo Artist: Kenojuak* (film). NFB. www.nfb.ca/film/eskimo-artist-kenojuak

Ferguson, Rob. 2016. "Ontario Same-Sex Couples No Longer Have to Adopt Their Own Children."

Toronto Star, 29 September. www.thestar.com/news/queenspark/2016/09/29/ontario-same-sex-couples-no-longer-have-to-adopt-their-own-children.html

Fernea, Robert A., and Elizabeth W. Fernea. 1972. "Variation in Religious Observance among Islamic Women." In *Scholars, Saints, and Sufis: Muslim Religious Institutions since 1500*, edited by Nikki R. Keddie. Berkeley: University of California Press.

Fiedler, Maureen E., ed. 2010. *Breaking through the Stained Glass Ceiling: Women Religious Leaders in Their Own Words*. New York: Seabury Books.

Field, Connie, dir. 1980. *The Life and Times of Rosie the Riveter* (film). Clarity Films.

Fine, Cordelia. 2010. *Delusions of Gender: How Our Minds, Society, and Neurosexism Create Difference*. New York: W.W. Norton.

Fine, M., and A. Asch, editors. *Women with Disabilities: Essays in Psychology, Culture and Politics*. Philadelphia: Temple University Press, 1988.

Fiol-Matta, Lisa, and Mariam K. Chamberlain. 1994. *Women of Color and the Multicultural Curriculum: Transforming the College Classroom*. New York: Feminist Press.

Fiorenza, Elisabeth Schussler. 1979. "Word, Spirit, and Power: Women in Early Christian Communities." In *Women of Spirit: Female Leadership in the Jewish and Christian Traditions*, edited by Rosemary Ruether and Eleanor McLaughlin. New York: Simon & Schuster.

———. 1983. *In Memory of Her: A Feminist Theological Reconstruction of Christian Origins*. New York: Crossroad.

Firestone, Shulamith. 2003 (1970). *The Dialectic of Sex: The Case for Feminist Revolution*. New York: Farrar, Straus and Giroux.

Fisher, Elizabeth. 1974. "Children's Books: The Second Sex, Junior Division." In *And Jill Came Tumbling After: Sexism in American Education*, edited by Judith Stacey, Susan Béreaud, and Joan Daniels. New York: Dell.

Fitzpatrick, Tanya R., and Barbara Vinick. 2003. "The Impact of Husbands' Retirement on Wives' Marital Quality." *Journal of Family Social Work* 7 (1): 83–100.

Flaubert, Gustave. 2003 (1857). *Madam Bovary*, translated by Geoffrey Wall. London: Penguin.

Fliegel, Zenia. 1980. "Half a Century Later: Current Status of Freud's Controversial Views of Women." Paper presented at the American Psychological Association Conference, Montreal.

Foblets, Marie Claire S.F.G. 1999. "Family Disputes Involving Muslim Women in Contemporary Europe: Immigrant Women Caught between Islamic Family Law and Women's Rights." In *Religious Fundamentalisms and the Human Rights of Women*, edited by Courtney W. Howland. New York: St Martin's Press.

Folbre, Nancy. 2001. *The Invisible Heart: Economics and Family Values*. New York: New Press.

Forbes. 2012. "The World's 100 Most Powerful Women." www.forbes.com/power-women/list/

Forman-Brunell, Miriam. 2001. *Girlhood in America: An Encyclopedia*. Santa Barbara, CA: ABC-CLIO.

Foucault, Michel. 1978. *The History of Sexuality. An Introduction*, vol. 1, translated by Robert Hurley. New York: Pantheon.

———. 1980. *The History of Sexuality*. New York: Vintage.

Fox, Mary Frank. 2001. "Women, Science, and Academia: Graduate Education and Careers." *Gender & Society* 15 (5): 654–66.

Francis, Richard C. 2011. *Epigenetics: The Ultimate Mystery of Inheritance*. New York: W.W. Norton.

Fraser, Arvonne S., and Irene Tinker, eds. 2004. *Developing Power: How Women Transformed International Development*. New York: Feminist Press.

Fraser, C. 2010. "French MPs Vote to Ban Islamic Full Veil in Public." BBC News, 13 July. http://www.bbc.com/news/10611398

Fraser, Sara, and Jessica Sinclair. 2016. "Abortion Services Coming to PEI." CBC News, 1 April. www.cbc.ca/beta/news/reproductive/rights/

Fredericton Sexual Assault Centre. n.d. fsacc.ca.

Freud, Sigmund. 1925. "Some Psychological Consequences of the Anatomical Distinction between the Sexes." *International Journal of Psychoanalysis* 8: 133–43.

Fried, L.P., C.M. Tangen, J. Walston, et al. 2001. "Frailty in Older Adults: Evidence for a Phenotype." *Journal of Gerontology* 56A (3): M146–56.

Friedan, Betty. 1963. *The Feminine Mystique*. New York: Dell.

Gakidou, E., Cowling, K., Lozano, R., et al. 2010. "Increased Educational Attainment and Its Effect on Child Mortality in 175 Countries between 1970 and 2009: A Systematic Analysis." *Lancet* 376: 959–74.

Gallagher, Catherine, and Thomas Laqueur, eds. 1987. *The Making of the Modern Body: Sexuality and Society in the Nineteenth Century*. Berkeley: University of California Press.

Galsworthy, Theresa D. 1994. "Osteoporosis: Statistics, Intervention, and Prevention." *Annals of the New York Academy of Sciences* 736: 158–64.

Gangoli, Geetanjali. 2005. "Sexuality, Sensuality and Belonging: Representations of the 'Anglo-Indian' and the 'Western' Woman in Hindi Cinema." In *Bollyworld: Popular Indian Cinema through a Transnational Lens*, edited by Raminder Kaur and A.J. Sinha. Thousand Oaks, CA: SAGE.

Garcia-Retamero, R., and E. Lopez-Zafra. 2006. "Prejudice against Women in Male-Congenial Environments: Perceptions of Gender Role Congruity in Leadership." *Sex Roles* 55 (1–2): 51–61.

Garland-Thomson, Rosemarie. 2005. "Feminist Disability Studies." *Signs* 30 (2): 1557–87.

Garry, Ann. 2011. "Intersectionality, Metaphors, and the Multiplicity of Gender." *Hypatia* 26 (4): 826–50.

Gaskell, Elizabeth. 2008 (1855). *North and South*, edited by Angus Easson. New York: Oxford World's Classics.

Gaskell, Jane. 2014. "Women and Education." *The Canadian Encyclopedia*. www.thecanadianencyclopedia.ca/en/article/women-and-education/

Geiger, Kim. 2012. "Statistics on Rape and Pregnancy Are Complicated." *Los Angeles Times*, 23 August. http://articles.latimes.com/2012/aug/23/news/la-pn-statistics-on-rape-and-pregnancy-are-complicated-20120822

Germon, Jennifer. 2009. *Gender: A Genealogy of an Idea*. New York: Palgrave Macmillan.

Gibbons, C., and T.C. Jones. 2003. "Kinship Care: Health Profiles of Grandparents Raising Their Grandchildren." *Journal of Family Social Work* 7 (1): 1–14.

Gibbons, Luz, José M. Belizán, Jeremy A. Lauer, et al. 2010. "The Global Numbers and Costs of Additionally Needed and Unnecessary Caesarean Sections Performed per Year: Overuse as a Barrier to Universal Coverage." World Health Report Background Paper, 30, Geneva: WHO.

Gilchrist, Roberta. 1994. *Gender and Material Culture: The Archaeology of Religious Women*. London and New York: Routledge.

Gilkes, Cheryl Townsend. 1985. "'Together and in Harness': Women's Traditions in the Sanctified Church." *Signs* 10: 687–99.

Gillick, M. 2001. "Pinning Down Frailty." *Journal of Gerontology* 56A (3): M134–5.

Gilligan, Carol. 1993. *In a Different Voice*. Cambridge, MA: Harvard University Press.

———. Nona P. Lyons, and Trudy J. Hanmer, eds. 1990. *Making Connections: The Relational Worlds of Adolescent Girls at Emma Willard School*. Cambridge, MA: Harvard University Press.

Gilman, Charlotte Perkins. 1979 (1915). *Herland*. New York: Pantheon.

Gilman, Sander. 1985. *Difference and Pathology: Stereotypes of Sexuality, Race, and Madness*. Ithaca, NY: Cornell University Press.

Gines, Kathryn T. 2011. "Black Feminism and Intersectional Analyses: A Defense of Intersectionality." *Philosophy Today*, SPEP Supplement 36, 275–84.

Gionet, Linda. 2015. "Breastfeeding Trends in Canada." *Health at a Glance*. Statistics Canada. Catalogue no. 82-624-X. www.statcan.gc.ca/pub/82-624-x/2013001/article/11879-eng.htm

Girls, Women + Media Project. n.d. www.mediaandwomen.us/

Glassgold, Judith M., and Suzanne Iasenza, eds. 2000 (1995). *Lesbians and Psychoanalysis: Revolution in Theory and Practice*. New York: Free Press.

Glickman, Rose L. 1993. *Daughters of Feminists*. New York: St Martin's Press.

Gokulsing, K. Moti, and Wimal Dissanayake. 2004. *Indian Popular Cinema: A Narrative of Cultural Change*. Stoke-on-Trent, UK: Trentham Books.

Goldenberg, Naomi. 1979. *Changing of the Gods: Feminism and the End of Traditional Religions*. Boston: Beacon.

Goldman, Emma. 1996 (1911). "The Traffic in Women; Marriage and Love." In *Red Emma Speaks: An Emma Goldman Reader*, 3rd edn, edited by Alix Kates Shulman. New York: Humanity Books.

Goody, Jack. 1976. *Production and Reproduction: A Comparative Study of the Domestic Domain*. Cambridge: Cambridge University Press.

Gopinath, Gayatri. 2005a. "Bollywood Spectacles: Queer Diasporic Critique in the Aftermath of 9/11." *Social Text* 23 (3–4): 157–69.

———. 2005b. *Impossible Desires: Queer Diasporas and South Asian Cultures*. Durham, NC: Duke University Press.

Gordon, Linda. 1988. *Heroes of Their Own Lives*. New York: Penguin.

Gottlieb, N. 1989. "Families, Work and the Lives of Older Women." In *Women as They Age: Challenge, Opportunity, and Triumph*, edited by J. Dianne Garner and Susan O. Mercer. New York: Haworth.

Gould, Stephen Jay. 1980. *The Panda's Thumb: More Reflections in Natural History*. New York: W.W. Norton.

———. 1989. *Wonderful Life: The Burgess Shale and the Nature of History*. New York: W.W. Norton.

Gouws, Amanda. 2008. "Obstacles for Women in Leadership Positions: The Case of South Africa." *Signs* 34 (1): 21–7.

Govindan, Padma P., and Bisakha Dutta. 2008. "'From Villain to Traditional Housewife!' The Politics of Globalization and Women's Sexuality in the 'New' Indian Media." In *Global Bollywood*, edited by Anandam P. Kavoori and Aswin Punathambekar. New York: New York University Press.

Grady, Denise. 2010. "Maternal Deaths in Sharp Decline across the Globe." *New York Times*, 14 April, A1, 11.

Graff, Gerald. 1994. *Curriculum Reform and the Culture Wars*. New York: Garland.

Grant, Therese M., Dana C. Jack, and Annette L. Fitzpatrick. 2011. "Carrying the Burdens of Poverty, Parenting, and Addiction: Depression Symptoms and Self-Silencing among Ethnically Diverse Women." *Community Mental Health Journal* 47, 1: 90–8.

Graveline, Denise. 2011. "Famous Speech Friday: Nellie McClung's 'Should Men Vote?' Speech." 23 September. http://eloquentwoman.blogspot.ca/2011/09/famous-speech-friday-nellie-mcclungs.html

Gray, Janet. 2008. *State of the Evidence: The Connection between Breast Cancer and the Environment*, 5th edn. San Francisco: Breast Cancer Fund.

Green, Monica H., ed. and trans. 2001. *The "Trotula": A Medieval Compendium of Women's Medicine*. Philadelphia: University of Pennsylvania Press.

Greenberg, Julie A. 2006. "The Roads Less Traveled: The Problem with Binary Sex Characteristics." In *Transgender Rights*, edited by Paisley Currah et al. Minneapolis: University of Minnesota Press.

Greene, Beverly. 1993. "Psychotherapy with African-American Women: Integrating Feminist and Psychodynamic Models." *Journal of Training and Practice in Professional Psychology* 7 (1): 49–66.

Gross, Rita. 1999. "Strategies for a Feminist Revalorization of Buddhism." In *Feminism and World Religions*, edited by Courtney W. Howland. Albany, NY: SUNY Press.

Grosz, Elisabeth. 1994. *Volatile Bodies: Toward a Corporeal Feminism*. Bloomington: Indiana University Press.

Grubow, Liz. 2010. "The Mystique of Mainstream Middle Eastern Beauty." *GCI Magazine*, 5 November.

Gupta, Sanjay. 2003. "Those Fragile Hearts." *Time*. 10 February, 84.

Gutbi, Omayama. 1995. "Preliminary Report on Female Genital Mutilation in Ontario." Ontario Human Rights Commission. www.ohrc.on.ca/en/policy/femalegenitalmutilation/

Gutgold, Nichola. 2008. *Seen and Heard: The Women of Television News*. Plymouth, UK: Lexington Books.

Gutkin, Harry, and Mildred Gutkin. 1996. "Mantoba History: 'Give Us Our Due!' How Manitoba Women Won the Vote." Manitoba Historical Society. www.mhs.mb.ca/docs/mb_history/32/womenwonthevote.shtml

Guttmacher Institute. 2012. *Making Abortion Services Accessible in the Wake of Legal Reforms*. New York: Guttmacher Institute.

Guy-Sheftall, Beverley, ed. 1995. *Words of Fire: An Anthology of African American Feminist Thought*. New York: New Press.

Gwobee, Leymah. Nobel lecture, delivered December 10, 2011. http://www.nobelprize.org/nobel_prizes/peace/laureates/2011/gbowee-lecture_en.html. Accessed December 19, 2012.

Haberman, Clyde. 2010. "On 5th Ave., a Grandmothers' Protest as Endless as the Wars." *New York Times*, 7 May, A20.

Haewood, Sophie. 2016. "Ellen Page: Being Out Became More Important Than Any Movie." *The Guardian*, 10 Feb. www.theguardian.com/film/2016/jan/30/ellen-page-being-out-became-more-important-than-any-movie

Halberstam, J. Jack. 2012. *Gaga Feminism: Sex, Gender, and the End of Normal*. Boston: Beacon Press.

Hall, Joseph. 2006. "African Tribe Stays Virtually AIDS-Free." *Toronto Star*, 12 August.

Hall, Kim. 2011. *Feminist Disability Studies*. Bloomington: Indiana University Press.

Hall, Roberta M., and Bernice R. Sandler. 1982. *The Classroom Climate: A Chilly One for Women?* Washington, DC: Association of American Colleges.

Hall, Stuart. 1990. "Cultural Identity and Diaspora." In *Identity: Community, Culture, Difference*, edited by Jonathan Rutherford. London: Lawrence and Wishart.

Halliwell, Emma, and Helga Dittmar. 2003. "A Qualitative Investigation of Women's and Men's Body Image Concerns and Their Attitudes toward Aging." *Sex Roles* 49 (11–12): 675–84.

Hamberger, L.K., B. Ambuel, A. Marbella, et al. 1998. "Physician Interaction with Battered Women." *Journal of the American Medical Association* 7: 575–82.

Hang, Truong Thi Thuy. 2008. "Women's Leadership in Vietnam: Opportunities and Challenges." *Signs* 34 (1): 16–21.

Hango, Darcy. 2013. "Gender Differences in Science, Technology, Engineering, Mathematics and Computer Science (STEM) Programs at University." *Insights on Canadian Society*. Statistics Canada. www.statcan.gc.ca/pub/75-006-x/2013001/article/11874-eng.htm#wb-tphp

Haraway, Donna. 1989. *Primate Visions: Gender, Race, and Nature in the World of Modern Science*. New York: Routledge.

Harding, Sandra, ed. 1987. *Feminism and Methodology: Social Science Issues*. Bloomington: Indiana University Press.

———. 1991. *Whose Science? Whose Knowledge? Thinking from Women's Lives.* Ithaca, NY: Cornell University Press.

———. 2004. *The Feminist Standpoint Theory Reader.* New York: Routledge.

Harrell, Jules P., Sadiki Hall, and James Taliaferro. 2003. "Physiological Responses to Racism and Discrimination: An Assessment of the Evidence." *American Journal of Public Health* 93 (2): 243–8.

Harrington, Mona. 2000. *Care and Equality: Inventing a New Family Politics.* New York: Routledge.

Harris, Ann Sutherland, and Linda Nochlin. 1977. *Women Artists 1550–1950.* New York: Knopf.

Harshbarger, Rebecca. 2010. Status of Female Farmers Rises during Food Crisis. *Women's eNews*, 11 August. www.womensenews.org

Hartmann, Heidi. 1981. "The Unhappy Marriage of Marxism and Feminism." In *Women and Revolution*, edited by Lydia Sargent. Boston: South End Press.

Hartog, Hendrik. 2000. *Man and Wife in America: A History.* Cambridge, MA: Harvard University Press.

Hartsock, Nancy C.M. 1983. *Money, Sex, and Power.* New York: Longman.

———. 1998. *The Feminist Standpoint Revisited and Other Essays.* Boulder, CO: Westview Press.

Hassan, Riffat. 1999. "Feminism in Islam." In *Feminism and World Religions*, edited by Courtney W. Howland. Albany, NY: SUNY Press.

Hawkesworth, Mary. 2012a. *Political Worlds of Women.* Boulder, CO: Westview Press.

———. 2012b. "Truth and Truths in Feminist Knowledge Production." In *Handbook of Feminist Research: Theory and Praxis*, edited by S. Hesse-Biber. Thousand Oaks, CA: SAGE.

Hawley, John Stratton, ed. 1994. *Fundamentalism and Gender.* Oxford: Oxford University Press.

Hebald, Carol. 2001. *The Heart Too Long Suppressed: A Chronicle of Mental Illness.* Boston: Northeastern University Press.

Heisook, Kim. 2009. "Feminist Philosophy in Korea: Subjectivity of Korean Women." *Signs* 34: 247–51.

Held, Virginia. 1979. "The Equal Obligations of Mothers and Fathers." In *Having Children: Philosophical and Legal Reflections on Parenthood*, edited by Onora O'Neill and William Ruddick. New York: Oxford University Press.

———. 2006. *The Ethics of Care: Personal, Political, and Global.* New York: Oxford University Press.

Helie-Lucas, Marie-Aimee. 1999. "What Is Your Tribe?: Women's Struggles and the Construction of Muslimness." In *Religious Fundamentalisms and the Human Rights of Women*, edited by Courtney W. Howland. New York: St Martin's Press.

Heller, Nancy G., Susan Fisher Sterling, Jordana Pomeroy, et al. 1980. *Women Artists: Works from the National Museum of Women in the Arts.* Washington, DC: National Museum of Women in the Arts.

Helly, Dorothy O., and Susan M. Reverby, eds. 1992. *Gendered Domains: Rethinking Public and Private in Women's History* (*Essays from the Seventh Berkshire Conference on the History of Women*). Ithaca, NY: Cornell University Press.

Henley, N. M. 1977. *Body Politics: Power, Sex, and Nonverbal Communication.* Englewood Cliffs, NJ: Prentice-Hall.

Herman, Rebecca, and Kay Wallen. 2007. "Cognitive Performance in Rhesus Monkeys Varies by Sex and Prenatal Androgen Exposure." *Hormones and Behavior* 51 (4): 496–507.

Herring, C. 2009. "Does Diversity Pay? Race, Gender, and the Business Case for Diversity." *American Sociological Review* 74: 208–24.

Hersh, Seymour M. 2004. *The Road to Abu Ghraib.* New York: HarperCollins.

Herzig, Abbe H. 2004. "Becoming Mathematicians: Women and Students of Color Choosing and Leaving Doctoral Mathematics." *Review of Education Research* 74 (2): 171–214.

Hetherington, E. Mavis, and John Kelly. 2002. *For Better or for Worse: Divorce Reconsidered.* New York: W.W. Norton.

Highway, Tomson. 1998. *Kiss of the Fur Queen.* Toronto: Doubleday.

Hill, Bridget, ed. 1986. *The First English Feminist: Reflections upon Marriage and Other Writings by Mary Astell.* Aldershot, UK: Gower/Maurice Temple Smith.

Hill, Catherine, and Elena Silva. 2005. *Drawing the Line: Sexual Harassment on Campus.* Washington, DC: American Association of University Women Educational Foundation.

Hinkle, Yvonne, Ernest Johnson, Douglas Gilbert, et al. 1992. "African-American Women Who Always Use Condoms: Attitudes, Knowledge about AIDS, and Sexual Behavior." *Journal of American Medical Women's Association* 47 (6): 230–7.

Hirata, Lucie Cheng. 1979. "Free, Enslaved, and Indentured Workers in Nineteenth-Century Chinese Prostitution." *Signs* 5: 3–29.

Hirji, Faiza. 2011. "Ranis Making Rotis: Dreams of the Good South Asian Girl." *Topia* 26 (Fall): 145–63.

Historica Canada, n.d. "Heritage Minutes: Nellie McClung." www.historicacanada.ca/content/heritage-minutes/nellie-mcclung

Historical Boys' Clothing. 1999. http://histclo.com/gender/col/col-pink.html

Hochschild, Arlie Russell, with Anne Machung. 2003. *The Second Shift*. New York: Penguin.

Hoddenbagh, Josh, Ting Zhang, and Susan McDonald. 2014. "An Estimation of the Economic Impact of Violent Victimization in Canada." Department of Justice. www.justice.gc.ca/eng/rp-pr/cj-jp/victim/rr14_01/index.html

Hoebel, E. Adamson. 1960. *The Cheyennes: Indians of the Great Plains*. New York: Holt, Rinehart and Winston.

Hoffman, Walter James. 1890. *Mythology of the Menomoni Indians*. Washington, DC: Judd and Detweiler.

Holmgren, Janet L. 2006. "The Compelling Case for Women's Colleges." *San Jose Mercury News*, 11 October.

Holmstrom, Nancy, ed. 2002. *The Socialist Feminist Project*. New York: Monthly Review.

Holohan, Megan. 2015. "The Problem with Parental Leave in the US and How Other Policies Compare." *Today*. 20 November. www.today.com/health/problem-parental-leave-u-s-t38701

hooks, bell. 1981. *Ain't I a Woman? Black Women and Feminism*. New York: South End Press.

———. 1984. *Feminist Theory: From Margin to Center*. Boston: South End Press.

Hopkins-Chadwick, D.L. 2009. "Stress in Junior Enlisted Air Force Women with and without Children." *Western Journal of Nursing Research* 31 (3): 409–27.

Horney, Karen. 1973. "On the Genesis of Castration Complex in Women." In *Psychoanalysis and Women*, edited by Jean Baker Miller. New York: Brunner/Mazei.

Hossain, Rokeya Sakhawat. 1988. *Sultana's Dream and Selections from the Secluded Ones*, edited and translated by Roushan Jahan. New York: Feminist Press.

Hou, Feng, and John Myles. 2007. "The Changing Role of Education in the Marriage Market: Assortative Marriage in Canada and the United States Since the 1970s." Statistics Canada. www.statcan.gc.ca/pub/11f0019m/11f0019m2007299-eng.htm

Howard, Jessica. 2015. "Women's Poverty Is Everyone's Business." Canadian Women's Foundation. 2 July. www.canadianwomen.org/blog/oh-canada

Howland, Courtney W., ed. 1999. *Religious Fundamentalisms and the Human Rights of Women*. New York: St Martin's Press.

Hrdy, Sarah Blaffer. 1999. *Mother Nature: A History of Mothers, Infants and Natural Selection*. New York: Pantheon.

———. 2009. *Mothers and Others: The Evolutionary Origins of Mutual Understanding*. Cambridge, MA: Belknap Press.

Htun, Mala, and S. Laurel Weldon. 2011. "State Power, Religion, and Women's Rights: A Comparative Analysis of Family Law." *Indiana Journal of Global Legal Studies* 18 (1): 145–65.

Humantrafficking.org. 2012. "News and Updates." 4 April. www.humantrafficking.org/updates/893

Hune, Shirley. 1998. *Asian Pacific American Women in Higher Education: Claiming Visibility and Voice*. Washington, DC: Association of American Colleges and Universities.

———. 2006. "Asian Pacific American Women and Men in Higher Education: The Contested Spaces of Their Participation, Persistence, and Challenges as Students, Faculty, and Administrators." In *"Strangers" of the Academy: Asian Women Scholars in Higher Education*, edited by Guofang Li and Gulbahar H. Beckett. Sterling, VA: Stylus Publishing.

Hunt, Arthur S., and C.C. Edgar. 1932. *Select Papyri. 1, Non-Literary Papyri, Private Affairs*, in Greek text with English parallel translation, introduction, and notes. London: Heinemann; Cambridge, MA: Harvard University Press.

Hunt, Laurie, Gina LaRoche, Stacy Blake-Beard, et al. 2009. "Cross-Cultural Connections: Leveraging Social Networks for Women's Advancement." In *The Glass Ceiling in the 21st Century*, edited by Manuela Barreto, Michelle K. Ryan, and Michael T. Schmitt. Washington, DC: American Psychological Association.

Hunter, Erica. 2011. "Change and Continuity in American Marriage." In *Introducing the New Sexuality Studies*, 2nd edn, edited by S. Seidman, N. Fischer, and C. Meeks. London: Routledge.

Hunter College Women's and Gender Studies Collective. 2015. *Women's Realities, Women's Choices: An Introduction to Women's and Gender Studies*, 4th edn. New York: Oxford University Press.

Huston, Perdita. 2001. *Families as We Are: Conversations from Around the World*. New York: Feminist Press.

Hvas, L. 2001. "Positive Aspects of Menopause: A Qualitative Study." *Maturitas* 39 (1): 11–17.

Indigenous Peoples' Council on Biocolonialism. n.d. "Beijing Declaration of Indigenous Women." www.ipcb.org/resolutions/htmls/dec_beijing.html

Institut de la statistique Québec. 2014. "Educational Level of Women on the Rise in Québec in University and Professional Levels." www.stat.gouv.qc.ca/salle-presse/communique/communique-presse-2014/fevrier/fev1412_an.html

Institute for Intersectionality Research and Policy (IIRP). n.d. "About Us." www.sfu.ca/iirp/aboutus.html

Institute of Medicine. 2010. *Women's Health Research: Progress Pitfalls, and Promise.* Washington, DC: National Academies Press.

International Labour Organization (ILO). 2010. *Women in Labour Markets: Measuring Progress and Identifying Challenges.* Geneva: ILO.

Inter-Parliamentary Union. 2012. *Women in National Parliaments.* www.ipu.org/wmn-e/classif.htm

———. 2015. *Women in Parliament: 20 Years in Review.* www.ipu.org/pdf/publications/WIP20Y-en.pdf

International Rescue Committee (IRC). 2008. *Mortality in the Democratic Republic of Congo: An Ongoing Crisis.* New York: International Rescue Committee.

Intersex Society of North America. n.d. "What Is Intersex?" www.isna.org/faq/what_is_intersex

Ions, Virginia. 1991. *Egyptian Mythology.* New York: Peter Bedrick Books.

Irigaray, Luce. 1985 (1974). *Speculum of the Other Woman*, translated by Gillian C. Gill. Ithaca, NY: Cornell University Press.

Ivekovic, Rada, and Julie Mostov, eds. 2006. *From Gender to Nation.* New Delhi: Zubaan.

Iverson, Torben, and Frances Rosenbluth. 2010. *Women, Work, and Politics.* New Haven, CT: Yale University Press.

Jackel, Susan. 2013. "Women's Suffrage." *Canadian Encyclopedia.* www.thecanadianencyclopedia.ca/en/article/womens-suffrage/

Jackson, Stevi. 2006. "Gender, Sexuality and Heterosexuality: the Complexity (and Limits) of Heteronormativity." *Feminist Theory* 7 (1): 105–121.

———. Jane Prince, and Pauline Young. 1993 "Introduction to Science, Medicine and Reproductive Technology." In *Women's Studies: Essential Readings*, edited by Stevi Jackson. New York: New York University Press.

Jacobs, Sue-Ellen, Wesley Thomas, and Sabine Lang, eds. 1997. *Two-Spirit People: Native American Gender Identity, Sexuality, and Spirituality.* Urbana: University of Illinois Press.

Jaggar, Alison. 1983. *Feminist Politics and Human Nature.* Totowa, NJ: Rowman & Allanheld.

Janowitz, Naomi, and Maggie Wenig. 1979. "Sabbath Prayers for Women." In *Womanspirit Rising: A Feminist Reader in Religion*, edited by Carol P. Christ and Judith Plaskow. San Francisco: Harper & Row.

Jardanova, Ludmilla. 1993. "Natural Facts: An Historical Perspective on Science and Sexuality." In *Women's Studies: Essential Readings*, edited by Stevi Jackson. New York: New York University Press.

Jaskoski, Helen. 1981. "'My Heart Will Go Out': Healing Songs of Native American Women." *International Journal of Women's Studies* 4: 2:118–34.

Jay, Karla, and Allen Young. 1992. *Out of the Closets: Voices of Gay Liberation*, 20th anniversary edition. New York: New York University Press.

Jayawardena, Kumari. 1986. *Feminism and Nationalism in the Third World.* London: Zed Books.

Jean-Marie, Gaetane, and Brenda Lloyd-Jones. 2011a. *Women of Color in Higher Education: Changing Directions and New Perspectives.* Bingley, UK: Emerald Group.

———. 2011b. *Women of Color in Higher Education: Turbulent Past, Promising Future.* Bingley, UK: Emerald Group.

Jenkins, C.L. 2003. "Introduction: Widows and Divorcees in Later Life." *Journal of Women & Aging* 15: 2–3: 1–6.

Johnson, Merri Lisa. 2002. *Jane Sexes It Up: True Confessions of Feminist Desire.* New York: Seal Press.

Johnston, Heidi Bart, Elizabeth Oliveras, Shamima Akhter, et al. 2010. "Health System Costs of Menstrual Regulation and Care for Abortion Complications in Bangladesh." *International Perspectives on Sexual & Reproductive Health* 36 (4): 196–200.

Jones, Geoffrey. 2010. *Beauty Imagined: A History of the Global Beauty Industry.* Oxford: Oxford University Press.

Jones, Jacqueline. 1985. *Labor of Love, Labor of Sorrow: Black Women, Work, and the Family from Slavery to the Present.* New York: Basic Books.

Jordan-Young, Rebecca. 2010. *Brainstorm: The Flaws in the Science of Sex Differences.* Cambridge, MA: Harvard University Press.

Jordan, June. 1998. *Affirmative Acts: Political Essays.* New York: Anchor Books.

Joseph, Gloria. 1981. "Black Mothers and Daughters: Their Roles and Functions in American Society." In *Common Differences: Conflicts in Black and White Feminist Perspectives*, edited by Gloria I. Joseph and Jill Lewis. New York: Anchor Press/Doubleday.

———. 1991. "Black Mothers and Daughters: Traditional and New Perspectives." In *Double Stitch: Black Women Write About Mothers & Daughters*, edited by Patricia Bell-Scott et al. Boston: Beacon Press.

Kappo, Tanya. 2014. "Stephen Harper's Comments on Missing, Murdered Aboriginal Women Show 'Lack of Respect.'" CBC News, 19 December. www.cbc.ca/news/aboriginal/stephen-harper-s-comments-on-missing-murdered-aboriginal-women-show-lack-of-respect-1.2879154

Karkazais, Katrina. 2008. *Fixing Sex: Intersex, Medical Authority, and Lived Experience*. Durham, NC: Duke University Press.

Kathlene, Lyn. 1992. "Studying the New Voice of Women in Politics." *Chronicle of Higher Education*, 18 November, B1–2.

Katz, S.J., M. Kabeto, and K.M. Langa. 2000. "Gender Disparities in the Receipt of Home Care for Elderly People with Disability in the United States." *Journal of the American Medical Association* 284 (23): 3022–7.

Kay, Kathy. 2010. "She-Power: The Impact of Women in Society." *Foreign Policy* 181 (special section): 12–13.

Keaton, Trica. 2005. "Arrogant Assimilationism: National Identity Politics and African-Origin Muslim Girls in the Other France." *Anthropology and Education Quarterly* 36 (4): 405–23.

Kehily, Mary Jane. 2008. "Taking Centre Stage? Girlhood and the Contradictions of Femininity across Three Generations." *Girlhood Studies* 1 (2): 51–71.

Keller, Evelyn Fox. 1985. *Reflections on Gender and Science*. New Haven, CT: Yale University Press.

———. 2010. *The Mirage of a Space between Nature and Nurture*. Durham, NC: Duke University Press.

Kelly, Amy. 1957. *Eleanor of Aquitaine and the Four Kings*. New York: Vintage.

Kelly, Sherrie, Ann Sprague, Deshayne B. Fell, et al. 2013. "Examining Caesarean Section Rates in Canada Using the Robson Classification System." *Journal of Obstetrics and Gynaecology Canada* 35: 206–14.

Kelly-Gadol, Joan. 1977. "Did Women Have a Renaissance?" In *Becoming Visible: Women in European History*, edited by Renate Bridenthal and Claudia Koonz. Boston: Houghton Mifflin.

Kennedy, Elizabeth Lapovsky, and Madeline D. Davis. 1993. *Boots of Leather, Slippers of Gold: The History of a Lesbian Community*. New York: Penguin Books.

Keohane, Nannerl O. 1980. "'But for Her Sex...': The Domestication of Sophie." *University of Ottawa Quarterly* 49: 390–400.

Kerber, Linda K. 1998. *No Constitutional Right to Be Ladies: Women and the Obligations of Citizenship*. New York: Hill & Wang.

Khademi, S., and M.S. Cooke. 2003. "Comparing the Attitudes of Urban and Rural Iranian Women toward Menopause." *Maturitas* 46: 113–21.

Khan, Mehboob, dir. 1940. *Aurat* (film). National Studios.

———. dir. 1957. *Mother India* (film). Mehboob Productions.

Kigozi, Margaret. 2007. "Women as Wealth Creators and Managers in Uganda." In *Unpacking Globalization: Markets, Gender, and Work*, edited by Linda C. Lucas. Lanham, MD: Lexington Books.

Kilbourne, Jean, prod. and dir. 2010. *Killing Us Softly 4: Advertising's Image of Women* (film). The Media Education Foundation.

Kimmel, Michael S. 2000. *The Gendered Society*. New York: Oxford University Press.

King, Jacqueline E. 2010. *Equity in Higher Education, 2010*. Washington, DC: American Council on Education.

King, Margaret L. 1980. "Book-Lined Cells: Women and Humanism in the Early Italian Renaissance." In *Beyond Their Sex*, edited by Patricia H. Labalme. New York: New York University Press.

King, Ynestra. 1995. "Engendering a Peaceful Planet: Ecology, Economy, and Eco-feminism in Contemporary Context." *Women's Studies Quarterly* 23 (3): 15.

Kingston, Anne. 2015. "Sophie Grégoire-What? It May Be 2015, but Not for Political Wives." *Maclean's*, 27 November. www.macleans.ca/society/life/sophie-gregoire-what-it-may-be-2015-but-not-for-political-wives/

Kinnaird, Joan K. 1979. "Mary Astell and the Conservative Contribution to English Feminism." *Journal of British Studies* 19: 53–75.

Kinsella, K., and V. Velkoff. 2001. *An Aging World*. US Cenus Bureau. Series P95/01–1. Washington, DC: GPO.

Kinsey, Alfred C. 1953. *Sexual Behavior in the Human Female*. Philadelphia: W.B. Saunders; Bloomington: Indiana University Press.

——— et al. 1948. *Sexual Behavior in the Human Male*. Philadelphia: W.B. Saunders; Bloomington: Indiana University Press.

Kirkpatrick, David D. 2012. "Egypt's Women Find Power Still Hinges on Men." *New York Times*, 10 January. http://www.nytimes.com/2012/01/10/world/middleeast/egyptian-women-confront-restrictions-of-patriarchy.html

Klein, Naomi. 1999. *No Logo*. Toronto: Random House.

———. 2007. *The Shock Doctrine: The Rise of Disaster Capitalism*. Toronto: Knopf.

———. 2014. *This Changes Everything: Capitalism vs. the Environment*. Toronto: Knopf.

Kleinfeld, Judith. 2009a. "No Map to Manhood: Male and Female Mindsets Behind the College Gender Gap." *Gender Issues* 26: 171–82.

———. 2009b. "The State of American Boyhood." *Gender Issues* 26: 113–29.

Klinenberg, Eric. 2012. *Going Solo*. New York: Penguin Press.

Klonoff, E.A., and H. Landrine. 1995. "The Schedule of Sexist Events: A Measure of Lifetime and Recent Sexist Discrimination in Women's Lives." *Psychology of Women Quarterly* 19: 439–72.

Kohlberg, Lawrence. 1966. "A Cognitive-Developmental Analysis of Children's Sex-Role Concepts and Attitudes." In *The Development of Sex Differences*, edited by E.E. Maccoby. Stanford, CA: Stanford University Press.

——— and Dora Z. Ullian. 1974. "Stages in the Development of Psychosexual Concepts and Attitudes." In *Sex Differences in Behavior*, edited by R.C. Friedman, R.M. Richard, and R.L. Vande Wiele. New York: Wiley.

——— and Edward Zigler. 1967. "The Impact of Cognitive Maturity on the Development of Sex-Role Attitudes in the Years 4–8." *Genetic Psychology Monographs* 75: 89–165.

Kohlstedt, Sally Gregory. 2004. "Sustaining Gains: Reflections on Women in Science and Technology in 20th-Century United States." *National Women's Studies Association Journal* 16 (1): 1–26.

Kollontai, Alexandra. 1972 [1911]. *Sexual Relations and Class Struggle: Love and the New Morality*, translated and introduced by Alix Holt. Bristol, UK: The Falling Wall Press.

Komarovksy, Mirra. 1962. *Blue-Collar Marriage*. New Haven, CT: Vintage.

Konigsberg, Ruth Davis. 2011. "Chore Wars." *Time*, 8 August, 45–9.

Koonz, Claudia. 1987. *Mothers in the Fatherland: Women, the Family, and Nazi Politics*. New York: St Martin's Press.

Koshan, Jennifer. 2010. "Sentencing for Spousal Sexual Violence: Different but Equal." University of Calgary Faculty of Law. ABlawg.ca. http://ablawg.ca/2010/08/20/sentencing-for-spousal-sexual-violence-different-but-equal/

Kramarae, Cheris. 2001. *The Third Shift: Women Learning Online*. Washington, DC: American Association of University Women Educational Foundation.

Kramer Estol, Pamela N. 2014. *Combating the Chilly Climate of the Sciences: Examining the Efficacy of All-Girls Schools in Increasing Female Participation in STEM*. Unpublished master's thesis. Ontario Institute for Studies in Education, University of Toronto.

Kristeva, Julia. 1980. *Desire in Language: A Semiotic Approach to Literature and Art*, edited by Leon Roudiez, translated by Thomas Gora, Alice Jardine, and Leon Roudiez. New York: Columbia University Press.

Kristof, Nicholas D., and Sheryl WuDunn. 2009. *Half the Sky: Turning Oppression into Opportunity for Women Worldwide*. New York: Alfred A. Knopf.

Krook, Mona Lena. 2010. "Why Are Fewer Women Than Men Elected? Gender and the Dynamics of Candidate Selection." *Political Studies Review* 8 (2): 155–68.

Kulick, Don. 1998. *Travesti: Sex, Gender, and Culture among Brazilian Transgendered Prostitutes*. Chicago: University of Chicago Press.

Kwan, Raymond. 2011. "Don't Dress Like a Slut: Toronto Cop." *Excalibur*, 16 February. www.excal.on.ca/dont-dress-like-a-slut-toronto-cop/

Ladner, Joyce A. 1972. *Tomorrow's Tomorrow: The Black Woman*. Garden City, NY: Doubleday.

La Ferla, Ruth. 2003. "Underdressed and Hot: Dolls Moms Don't Love." *New York Times*. 26 October. www.nytimes.com/2003/10/26/style/noticed-underdressed-and-hot-dolls-moms-don-t-love.html?pagewanted=all&src=pm

Lamb, Sharon. 2001. *The Secret Lives of Girls: What Good Girls Really Do—Sex Play, Aggression, and Their Guilt*. New York: Free Press.

Lamott, Anne. 1993. *Operating Instructions: A Journal of My Son's First Year*. New York: Pantheon.

Larrieu, Julie A., Sherryl S. Heller, Anna T. Smyke, et al. 2008. "Predictors of Permanent Loss of Custody for Mothers of Infants and Toddlers in Foster Care." *Infant Mental Health Journal* 29 (1): 48–60.

Larsen, Nella. 1928. *Quicksand*. New York: Knopf.

———. 1929. *Passing*. New York: Knopf.

Leach, Fiona. 2010. "Negotiating, Constructing and Reconstructing Girlhoods." *Girlhood Studies* 3 (1): 3–8.

Leboucher, G. 1989. "Maternal Behavior in Normal and Androgenized Female Rates: Effect of Age and Experience." *Physiology and Behavior* 45 (2): 313–19.

Lebsock, Suzanne. 1990. "Women and American Politics, 1880–1920." In *Women, Politics and Change*, edited by Louise A. Tilly and Patricia Gurin. New York: Russell Sage Foundation.

Lee, Vera. 1975. *The Reign of Women in Eighteenth-Century France*. Cambridge, MA: Schenckman.

Lees, Susan. 1984. "Motherhood in Feminist Utopias." In *Women in Search of Utopia*, edited by Elaine Baruch and Ruby Rohrlich-Levy. New York: Schocken Books.

Leonhardt, David. 2003. "It's a Girl! (Will the Economy Suffer?)." *New York Times*. 26 October, 1, 11.

Lerner, Gerda. 1992. *The Female Experience: An American Documentary*. New York: Oxford University Press.

Letherby, Gayle. 2003. *Feminist Research in Theory and Practice.* Philadelphia: Open University Press.

LeVay, Simon. 1991. "A Difference in Hypothalamic Structure between Heterosexual and Homosexual Men." *Science* 253 (5023): 1034–7. DOI: 10.1126/science.1887219

Levine, Ann D., and Naomi Neft. 1997. *Where Women Stand: An International Report on the Status of Women in Over 140 Countries, 1997–1998.* New York: Random House.

Levine, Lawrence. 1997. *The Opening of the American Mind: Canons, Culture, and History.* Boston: Beacon.

Levine, Nancy E., and Joan B. Silk. 1997. "Why Polyandry Fails: Sources of Instability in Polyandrous Marriages." *Current Anthropology* 38: 375–98.

Levison, Julie H., and Sandra P. Levison. 2001. "Women's Health and Human Rights." In *Women, Gender and Human Rights,* edited by Marjorie Agosin. New Brunswick, NJ: Rutgers University Press.

Lévi-Strauss, Claude. 1963 (1958). *Tristes tropiques,* translated by J. Russell. New York: Basic Books.

Levy, Ariel. 2005. "Raunchiness Is Powerful? C'mon, Girls." *Washington Post.* 8 September, B5.

Levy, Darline Gay, and Harriet Branson Applewhite, eds. 1979. *Women in Revolutionary Paris, 1789–1795.* Urbana: University of Illinois.

Leyenaar, Monique. 2008. "Challenges to Women's Political Representation in Europe." *Signs: Journal of Women in Culture and Society* 34 (1): 1–7.

Lieberman, A. 2010. "EU Okays Moms Paid Leave; Women Not at Peace Tables." *WomensENews.* www.womensenews.org

Liera, Talyaa (Karen Murphy). 2007. "Public Says Children Better Off When Unhappy Parents Divorce, and Single Moms Suck." www.babble.com/CS/blogs/strollerderby/archive/2007/09/20/public-says-children-better-off-when-unhappy-parents-divorce.aspx

Lihamba, Amandina, Fulata L. Moyo, Mugaybuso M. Mulokozi, et al. 2007. *Women Writing Africa III: The Eastern Region.* New York: Feminist Press.

Lindgren, Karl-Oskar, Magdalena Inkinen, and Sten Widmalm. 2009. "Who Knows Best What the People Want: Women or Men? A Study of Political Representation in India." *Comparative Political Studies* 42 (1): 31–55.

Lindsay, Beverly, ed. 1980. *Comparative Perspectives of Third World Women: The Impact of Race, Sex, and Class.* New York: Praeger.

Linton, Simi. 1997. *Claiming Disability: Knowledge and Identity.* New York: New York University Press.

———. 2007. *My Body Politic: A Memoir.* Ann Arbor: University of Michigan Press.

Littleton, Christine. 1987. "Reconstructing Sexual Equality." *California Law Review* 25: 1279–337.

Livingston, Jennie. 2012 (1991). *Paris Is Burning* (film). Lionsgate.

Lloyd, Cynthia B., ed. 2005. *Growing Up Global: The Changing Transitions to Adulthood in Developing Countries.* Washington, DC: The National Academies Press.

Lobo, Feelix. 2014. "India's Female Hindu Priests Challenge Age-Old Tradition." UCAnews.com. 8 August. www.ucanews.com/news/indias-female-hindu-priests-challenge-age-old-tradition/71626

Lockheed, Marlaine E. 2008. "The Double Disadvantage of Gender and Social Exclusion in Education." In *Girls' Education in the 21st Century,* edited by Mercy Tembon and Lucia Fort. Washington, DC: The International Bank for Reconstruction and Development/The World Bank.

Loewenberg, Bert James, and Ruth Bogin, eds. 1976. *Black Women in Nineteenth-Century Life: Their Words, Their Thoughts, Their Feelings.* University Park: Pennsylvania State University Press.

Longino, Helen. 1990. *Science as Social Knowledge: Values and Objectivity in Scientific Inquiry.* Princeton, NJ: Princeton University Press.

———, and R. Doell. 1987. "Body, Bias and Behavior: A Comparative Analysis of Reasoning in Two Areas of Biological Science." In *Sex and Scientific Inquiry,* edited by S. Harding and J.F. O'Barr. Chicago: University of Chicago Press.

Longman Marcellin, R., A. Scheim, G. Bauer, and N. Redman. 2013. "Experiences of Racism among Trans People in Ontario." *Trans PULSE e-Bulletin* 3 (1, 7 March).

Lopez, Iris. 1987. "Sterilization among Puerto Rican Women in New York City: Public Policy and Social Constraints." In *Cities of the United States,* edited by Leith Mullings. New York: Columbia University Press.

Lopez, S., A. Smith, B. Wolkenstein, et al. 1993. "Gender Bias in Clinical Judgment: An Assessment of the Analogue Method's Transparency and Social Desirability." *Sex Roles* 28: 35–45.

Lorber, Judith. 2001. *Gender Inequality: Feminist Theories and Politics,* 2nd edn. Los Angeles: Roxbury Publishing.

Lorde, Audre. 1983. "The Master's Tools Will Never Dismantle the Master's House." In *This Bridge Called My Back: Writings by Radical Women of Color,* edited by

Cherrie Moraga and Gloria Anzaldúa. New York: Kitchen Table Press.

———. 1984. *Sister Outsider*. Trumansberg, NY: Crossing Press.

Lougee, Carolyn C. 1976. *Le Paradis des Femmes: Women, Salons, and Social Stratification in Seventeenth-Century France*. Princeton, NJ: Princeton University Press.

Louie, Miriam Ching Yoon. 2001. *Sweatshop Warriors: Immigrant Women Workers Take on the Global Factory*. Cambridge, MA: South End Press.

Lucas, Angela M. 1983. *Women in the Middle Ages: Religion, Marriage and Letters*. Brighton, UK: Harvester Press.

Lugones, Maria. 2003. *Pilgrimages/Peregrinajes: Theorizing Coalition against Multiple Oppressions*. Lanham, MD: Rowman & Littlefield.

———. 2007. "Heterosexualism and the Colonial/Modern Gender System." *Hypatia* 22 (1): 186–209.

Lunney, Kellie. 2015. "Feds Would Get Six Weeks of Paid Parental Leave under Bill." *Government Executive*. 15 September. www.govexec.com/pay-benefits/2015/09/feds-would-get-six-weeks-paid-parental-leave-under-bill/121025/

Luscombe, B. 2010. "The Rise of the Sheconomy: How Women Are Using Their Rapidly Increasing Spending Power to Impel Changes in the Way Companies Operate." *Time*. 22 November, 58–61.

Luxton, Meg, and Mary Jane Mossman. 2012. *Reconsidering Knowledge: Feminism and the Academy*. Halifax, NS: Fernwood.

Lynch, Caitrin. 2007. *Juki Girls, Good Girls: Gender and Cultural Politics in Sri Lanka's Global Garment Industry*. Ithaca, NY: Cornell University Press.

McArdle, Elaine. 2008. "The Freedom to Say 'No.' Why Aren't There More Women in Science and Engineering? Controversial New Research Suggests: They Just Aren't Interested." *Boston Globe*, 18 May.

Macdonald, David, and Martha Friendly. 2014. *The Parent Trap: Child Care Fees in Canada's Big Cities*. Canadian Centre for Policy Alternatives. November. www.policyalternatives.ca/publications/reports/parent-trap

McClintock, Ann. 1996. "'No Longer in a Future Heaven': Gender, Race and Nationalism." In *Becoming National: A Reader*, edited by Geoff Eley and Ronald Suny. New York: Oxford University Press.

McCreary Centre Society. 2008. Newsletter. Fall/Winter. www.mcs.bc.ca/pdf/winter2008.pdf

McGrath, Ellen, Gwendolyn Keita, Bonnie R. Strickland, et al., eds. 1990. "Women and Depression: Risk Factors and Treatment Issues." In *Final Report of the American Psychological Association's Task Force on Women and Depression*. Washington, DC: American Psychological Association.

Machung, Anne. 1988. *The Politics of Office Work*. Philadelphia, PA: Temple University Press.

McInturff, Kate, and Paul Tulloch. 2014. *Narrowing the Gap: The Difference That Public Sector Wages Make*. Canadian Centre for Policy Alternatives. https://policyalternatives.ca/wage-gap#sthash.NwhUPgCR.R7dxRyM2.dpuf

MacKinnon, Catharine A. 1987. *Feminism Unmodified: Discourses on Life and Law*. Cambridge, MA: Harvard University Press.

———. 1991. "Feminism, Marxism, Method and the State: Toward Feminist Jurisprudence." In *Feminist Legal Theory*, edited by Katharine T. Bartlett and Rosanne Kennedy. Boulder, CO: Westview Press.

———. 1993. *Only Words*. Cambridge, MA: Harvard University Press.

McNamara, Jo Ann Kay. 1996. *Sisters in Arms: Catholic Nuns through Two Millennia*. Cambridge, MA: Harvard University Press.

McWhorter, Ladelle. 2009. *Racism and Sexual Oppression in Anglo-America: A Genealogy*. Bloomington: Indiana University Press.

Madera, Juan M., Michelle R. Hebl, and Randi C. Martin. 2009. "Gender and Letters of Recommendation for Academia: Agentic and Communal Differences." *Journal of Applied Psychology* 94 (6): 1591–9.

Mahmood, Saba. 2005. *Politics of Piety: The Islamic Revival and the Feminist Subject*. Princeton, NJ: Princeton University Press.

Maimonides. 1972. *The Code of Maimonides. Book 4: The Book of Women*, translated by Isaac Klein. New Haven, CT: Yale University Press.

Mairs, Nancy. 1997. "Carnal Acts." In *Writing on the Body*, edited by Katie Conboy, Nadia Median, and Sarah Stanbury. New York: Columbia University Press.

Makwinja-Morara, Veronica. 2009. "Female Dropouts in Botswana Junior Secondary Schools." *Educational Studies*, 45: 440–62.

Mankekar, Purnima. 1999. "Brides Who Travel: Gender, Transnationalism, and Nationalism in Hindi Film." *Positions* 7 (3): 731–61.

Mann, Barbara Alice. 2000. *Iroquoian Women: The Gantowisas*. New York: Lang Press.

Mannathoko, Changu. 2008. "Promoting Education Quality through Gender-Friendly Schools." In *Girls' Education in the 21st Century*, edited by Mercy Tembon and Lucia Fort. Washington, DC: The International Bank for Reconstruction and Development/The World Bank.

Maquila Solidarity Network. n.d. http://en.maquilasolidarity.org/

———. 2012. "We Had to Build a Workers' Movement: An Interview with Yannick Etienne." 14 November. http://en.archive.maquilasolidarity.org/node/1107

Maracle, Lee. 1996. *I Am Woman: A Native Perspective on Sociology and Feminism*. Vancouver: Raincoast.

Marchetti, Gina. 1993. *Romance and the "Yellow Peril": Race, Sex, and Discursive Strategies in Hollywood Fiction*. Berkeley: University of California Press.

Marieskind, Helen. 1977. "The Women's Health Movement: Past Roots." In *Seizing Our Bodies: The Politics of Women's Health*, edited by Claudia Dreifus. New York: Vintage Books.

Marlane, Judith. 1999. *Women in Television News Revisited: Into the Twenty-First Century*. Austin: University of Texas Press.

Martin, Emily. 1987. *The Woman in the Body: A Cultural Analysis of Reproduction*. Boston: Beacon Press.

———. 1994. *Flexible Bodies: Tracking Immunity in American Culture from the Days of Polio to the Age of* AIDS. Boston: Beacon Press.

Martin, Jane Roland. 2000. *Coming of Age in Academe: Rekindling Women's Hopes and Reforming the Academy*. New York: Routledge.

Martin, Susan Ehrlich, and Nancy C. Jurik. 2007. *Doing Justice, Doing Gender*, 2nd edn. Thousand Oaks, CA: SAGE.

Mary Baker Eddy Library. 2011. *Science & Health with Key to the Scriptures*. Boston: The Mary Baker Eddy Library for the Betterment of Humanity. www.marybakereddylibrary.org/mary-baker-eddy/writings/science-and-health

Marx, K., and F. Engels. 1848. *Communist Manifesto*.

Mascia-Lees, Frances E., and Nancy Johnson Black. 1999. *Gender and Anthropology*. Prospect Heights, IL: Waveland Press.

——— and Patricia Sharpe. 1994. "The Anthropological Unconscious." *American Anthropologist* 96: 649–60.

———. Patricia Sharpe, and Colleen B. Cohen. 1990. "The Female Body in Postmodern Consumer Culture: A Study of Subjection and Agency." *Phoebe: An Interdisciplinary Journal of Feminist Scholarship, Theory and Aesthetics* 2: 29–50.

Mason, Mary Ann, and Marc Goulden. 2004. "Marriage and Baby Blues: Redefining Gender Equity in the Academy." *Annals,* AAPSS 596: 86–101.

Masters, William H., and Virginia E. Johnson. 1966. *Human Sexual Response*. Boston: Little, Brown

Masuda, S., and J. Ridington. 1992. "Meeting Our Needs: An Access Manual for Transition Houses." Vancouver: DAWN Canada.

Matsuda, Mari J. 1989. "When the First Quail Calls: Multiple Consciousness as Jurisprudential Method." *Women's Rights Law Reporter* 7: 9.

Matsui, Yayori. 1989. *Women's Asia*. London and Atlantic Highlands, NJ: Zed Books.

Matthews, Gareth. 1986. "Gender and Essence in Aristotle." *Australasian Journal of Philosophy* 64 (suppl.): 17–25.

May, Vivian. 2007. *Anna Julia Cooper, Visionary Black Feminist: A Critical Introduction*. New York: Routledge.

Mayer, A.L., and Tikka, P.M. 2008. "Family-Friendly Policies and Gender Bias in Academia." *Journal of Higher Education Policy and Management* 30, 4: 363–74.

Mayo, Katherine. 2000 (1927). *Mother India: Selections from the Controversial 1927 Text* Mrinalini Sinha. Ann Arbor: University of Michigan Press.

Mead, Margaret. 1935. *Sex and Temperament in Three Primitive Societies*. New York: Morrow.

———. 1949. *Male and Female: A Study of the Sexes in a Changing World*. New York: Dell.

Meadows, Susannah, and Mary Carmichael. 2002. "Meet the Gamma Girls." *Newsweek*. 3 June.

Mendoza, Louis, and S. Shankar, eds. 2003. *Crossing into America: The New Literature of Immigration*. New York: The New Press.

Merchant, Carolyn. 1980. *The Death of Nature: Women, Ecology, and the Scientific Revolution*. San Francisco: Harper & Row.

Messer-Davidow, Ellen. 2002. *Disciplining Feminism: From Social Activism to Academic Discourse*. Durham, NC: Duke University Press.

Metcalfe, Amy Scott, and Sheila Slaughter. 2008. "The Differential Effects of Academic Capitalism on Women in the Academy." In *Unfinished Agendas: New and Continuing Gender Challenges in Higher Education*, edited by Judith Glazer-Raymo. Baltimore: Johns Hopkins University Press.

MetLife. 2011. *The MetLife Study of Caregiving Costs to Working Caregivers: Double Jeopardy for Baby Boomers Caring for Their Parents*. Westport, CT: MetLife Mature Market Institute. www.metlife.com/assets/cao/mmi/publications/studies/2011/mmi-caregiving-costs-working-caregivers.pdf

Meyer, Mary K. 1999. "Negotiating International Norms: The Inter-American Commission of Women and the Convention on Violence against Women." In *Gender Politics* in *Global Governance*, edited by Mary K. Meyer and Elisabeth Prügl. Lanham, MD: Rowman & Littlefield.

Mikkonen, Juha, and Dennis Raphael. 2010. *Social Determinants of Health: The Canadian Facts*. Toronto: York University School of Health Policy and Management.

Mill, John Stuart. 1970 [1896]. "On the Subjection of Women." In *John Stuart Mill and Harriet Taylor Mill, Essays on Sex Equality*, edited by Alice S. Rossi. Chicago: University of Chicago Press.

Miller, Virginia M., and Patricia J.M. Best. 2011. "Implications for Reproductive Medicine Sex Differences in Cardiovascular Disease." *Sexuality, Reproduction and Menopause* 9 (3): 21–8.

Millett, Kate. 1970. *Sexual Politics*. Garden City, NY: Doubleday.

Mishra, Vijay. 2002. *Bollywood Cinema: Temples of Desire*. New York: Routledge.

MIT Committee on Women Faculty. 1999. *A Study on the Status of Women Faculty in Science at MIT*. Cambridge, MA: MIT Press.

———. 2011. *A Report on the Status of Women Faculty in the Schools of Science and Engineering at MIT*. Cambridge, MA: MIT Press.

Mitchell, Juliet. 1973. *Woman's Estate*. New York: Vintage.

Moen, Phyllis, Jungmeen E. Kim, and Heather Hofmeister. 2001. "Couples' Work/Retirement Transitions, Gender, and Marital Quality." *Social Psychology Quarterly* 64 (1): 55.

Mohanty, Chandra Talpade. 2003. *Feminism without Borders: Decolonizing Theory, Practicing Solidarity*. Durham, NC: Duke University Press.

Molyneux, Maxine. 1998. "Analysing Women's Movements." *Development and Change* 29 (2): 219–45.

Monaghan, Patricia, ed. 2011. *Goddesses in World Culture*. 3 vols. Santa Barbara, CA: ABC-CLIO.

Monem, Nadine. 2007. *Riot Grrrl: Revolution Style Girl Now!* London: Black Dog.

Money, John, and Anke Ehrhardt. 1972. *A Man and Woman, Boy and Girl*. Baltimore: Johns Hopkins University Press.

Moore, Holly. 2014. "Family Support Arrears across Canada: Deadbeats Owe $3.7 Billion across the Country." CBC News. 1 October. www.cbc.ca/beta/news/family-support-arrears-across-canada-1.2782421

Morello, Carole. 2011. "Old Terms for Blended Families Out of 'Step.'" *Seattle Times*. 20 January.

Morris, Cerise. 2006. "Royal Commission on the Status of Women in Canada." *Canadian Encyclopedia*. www.thecanadianencyclopedia.ca/en/article/royal-commission-on-the-status-of-women-in-canada/

Moser, Caroline O.N., and Peake, Linda. 1987. *Women, Human Settlements, and Housing*. London: Tavistock.

Moses, Yolanda T. 1989. *Black Women in Academe: Issues and Strategies*. Washington, DC: Association of American Colleges.

Muncy, Raymond L. 1973. *Sex and Marriage in Utopian Communities in 19th Century America*. Bloomington: Indiana University Press.

Mungin, Lateef. 2014. "Actress Ellen Page: 'I Am Gay.'" CNN. 17 February. www.cnn.com/2014/02/15/showbiz/page-comes-out/

Murdock, George P. 1950. "Family Stability in Non-European Cultures." *Annals of the American Academy of Political and Social Science* 272: 175–201.

Murphy, Karen (now Talyaa Liera). 2007. "Public Says Children Better Off When Unhappy Parents Divorce, and Single Moms Suck." *Babble Blog*, 20 September. www.babble.com/CS/blogs/strollerderby/archive/2007/09/20/public-says-children-better-off-when-unhappy-parents-divorce.aspx

Murphy, Peter F., ed. 2004. *Feminism and Masculinities*. New York: Oxford University Press.

Nagurney, Alexander J., John W. Reich, and Jason Newsom. 2004. "Gender Moderates the Effects of Independence and Dependence Desires during the Social Support Process." *Psychology and Aging* 19 (1): 215–18.

Najmabadi, Afsaneh. 2006. "Gender and Secularism of Modernity: How Can a Muslim Woman Be French?" *Feminist Studies* 32: 239–55.

Nanda, Serena. 1986. "The Hijras of India: Cultural and Individual Dimensions of an Institutionalized Third Gender Role." *Journal of Homosexuality* 11: 35–54.

Narayan, Uma. 1997. *Dis-locating Cultures: Identities, Traditions, and Third-World Feminism*. New York: Routledge.

Nash, Jennifer. 2008. "Re-thinking Intersectionality." *Feminist Review* 89: 1–15.

Nashat, Guity. 1999. "Women in the Middle East, 8,000 B.C.E.–C.E. 1800." In *Women in the Middle East and North Africa*, edited by Guity Nashat and Judith E. Tucker. Bloomington: Indiana University Press.

National Aboriginal Council of Midwives. n.d. "Aboriginal Midwifery in Canada." www.aboriginalmidwives.ca/aboriginal-midwifery-in-canada

National Alliance for Caregiving, AARP, and Foundation Metropolitan Life. 2009. "Caregiving in the U.S." National Alliance for Caregiving, AARP. http://assets.aarp.org/rgcenter/il/caregiving_09_fr.pdf

National Council for Research on Women. 2001. *Balancing the Equation: Where Are Women and Girls in Science, Engineering and Technology?* New York: National Council for Research on Women.

National Eating Disorders Association. 2005. "Eating Disorders in Women of Color: Explanations and Implications." www.nationaleatingdisorders.org/nedaDir/files/documents/handouts/WomenCol.pdf

Native American History. 2002. "Native American Women: Foundations of the People." www.snowwowl.com/histswritnawomen.html

Native Women's Association of Canada. 2007. "Federally Sentenced Aboriginal Women Offenders." Paper prepared for the National Aboriginal Women's Summit, 20–22 June, in Corner Brook, NL. www.laa.gov.nl.ca/laa/naws/pdf/nwac-federally.pdf

Neale, John E. 1957 [1934]. *Queen Elizabeth I: A Biography*. Garden City, NY: Doubleday.

Neel, Carol. 1989. "The Origins of the Beguines." *Signs* 14 (2): 321–41.

Nemtsova, Anna. 2010. "Women and Higher Education Make Steady Progress in Afghanistan." *The Chronicle of Higher Education*, 28 March. New York: Amnesty International USA.

Newbeck, Phyl. 2012. "Loving v. Virginia." In *Encyclopedia Virginia*, edited by Brendan Wolfe. Virginia Foundation for the Humanities. www.encyclopediavirginia.org/Loving_v_Virginia_1967

Newton, J. 1995. *The Feminist Challenge to the Canadian Left, 1900–1918*. Montreal: McGill–Queen's University Press.

Ng, Roxana. 1999. "Homeworking: Dream Realized or Freedom Constrained?" *Canadian Woman's Studies* 18 (1): 110–14.

Nickel, James W. 1978–9. "Is There a Human Right to Employment?" *Philosophical Forum* 10: 149–70.

Nieto, Sonia. 2009. "Multicultural Education in the United States." In *The Routledge International Companion to Multicultural Education*, edited by James A. Banks. New York: Routledge.

Ninian, Alex. 2003. "Bollywood." *Contemporary Review* 283 (1653): 235–40.

Nordberg, Jenny. 2010. "Afghan Boys Are Prized, So Girls Live the Part." *New York Times*. 20 September, A1, A10–11.

Novotney, A. 2010. "A More Family-Friendly Ivory Tower?" APA *Monitor* 41 (1): 54.

NPD Group. 2014. "Canadian Consumers Spending Big on Beauty." 12 November. www.npdgroup.ca/wps/portal/npd/ca/news/press-releases/canadian-consumers-spending-big-on-beauty/

O'Barr, Jean. 1984. "African Women in Politics." In *African Women South of the Sahara*, edited by Margaret Jean Hay and Sharon Stichter. New York: Longman.

O'Brien, Margaret. 2009. "Fathers, Parental Leave Policies, and Infant Quality of Life: International Perspectives and Policy Impact." *The Annals of the American Academy of Political and Social Science* 624 (1): 190–213. DOI: 10.1177/0002716209334349

O'Donovan, Katherine. 1981. "Before and After: The Impact of Feminism on the Academic Discipline of Law." In *Men's Studies Modified: The Impact of Feminism on the Academic Disciplines*, edited by Dale Spender. New York: Pergamon.

OECD. 2010. *Education at a Glance 2010:* OECD *Indicators*. Organisation for Economic Co-operation and Development.

O'Hare, Ursula A. 1999. "Realizing Human Rights for Women." *Human Rights Quarterly* 21 (2): 364–402.

Ontario Council of Agencies Serving Immigrants (OCASI). 2015. "Open Letter to Prime Minister on Racial and Gender Equality in the Senate of Canada." www.ocasi.org/open-letter-prime-minister-racial-and-gender-equality-senate-canada

Okin, Susan Moller. 1979. *Women in Western Political Thought*. Princeton, NJ: Princeton University Press.

———. 1989. *Justice, Gender, and the Family*. New York: Basic Books.

———. 1999. *Is Multiculturalism Bad for Women?* Princeton, NJ: Princeton University Press.

Okumus, F., M. Sariisik, and S. Naipaul. 2010. "Understanding Why Women Work in Five-Star Hotels in a Developing Country and Their Work-Related Problems." *International Journal of Hospitality & Tourism Administration* 11 (1): 76–105.

Olujic, Maria B. 1998. "Embodiment of Terror: Gendered Violence in Peacetime and Wartime in Croatia and Bosnia-Herzegovina." *Medical Anthropology Quarterly* 12 (1): 31–50.

Orenstein, Peggy. 1994. *School Girls: Young Women, Self-Esteem, and the Confidence Gap*. New York: Anchor Books.

———. 2011. *Cinderella Ate My Daughter: Dispatches from the Front Lines of the New Girlie-Girl Culture*. New York: HarperCollins.

Overall, Christine. 2013. *Why Have Children: The Ethical Debate*. Cambridge, MA: MIT Press.

Oxford Latin Dictionary: Fascicle III. 1971. Oxford: Oxford University Press.

Pacific, Robin. n.d. "'Flowers and Threads'—The FAST Campaign." www.robinpacific.ca/projects/flowers-and-threads-the-fast-campaign/#sthash.MLtfeBLD.dpuf

Padgett, Deborah. 1989. "Aging Minority Women: Issues in Research and Health Policy." In *Women in the Later Years: Health, Social and Cultural Perspectives*, edited by Lois Grau and Ida Susser. New York: Harrington Park Press.

Palley, Marian Lief. 2001. "Women's Policy Leadership in the United States." *PS: Political Science and Politics* 25 (2): 247–50.

Palmer, Susan Jean. 1994. *Moon Sisters, Krishna Mothers, Rajneesh Lovers: Women's Roles in New Religions*. Syracuse, NY: Syracuse University Press.

Palmieri, Patricia. 1987. "From Republican Motherhood to Race Suicide: Arguments on the Higher Education of Women in the United States, 1820–1920." In *Educating Men and Women Together: Co-education in a Changing World*, edited by Carol Lasser. Urbana: University of Illinois Press.

Park, Lora E., Ariana F. Young, Jordan D. Troisi, et al. 2011. "Effects of Everyday Romantic Goal Pursuit on Women's Attitudes toward Math and Science." *Personality and Social Psychology Bulletin* 37 (9): 1259–73.

Parker, W.H., M.S. Broder, E. Chang, et al. 2009. "Ovarian Conservation at the Time of Hysterectomy and Long-Term Health Outcomes in the Nurses' Health Study." *Obstetric Gynecology* 113 (5): 1027–39.

Parker-Pope, Tara. 2011. "In a Married World, Singles Struggle for Attention." *Well (blog). New York Times.* 19 September. http://well.blogs.nytimes.com/2011/09/19/the-plight-of-american-singles/?_r=0

Parreñas, Rhacel Salazar. 2005. *Children of Global Migration: Transnational Families and Gendered Woes*. Stanford, CA: Stanford University Press.

Paul, Annie Murphy. 2010. *Origins: How the Nine Months before Birth Shape the Rest of Our Lives*. New York: Free Press.

Peach, Lucinda Joy. 2002. "Social Responsibility, Sex Change, and Salvation: Gender Justice in the Lotus Sutra." *Philosophy East & West* 52: 50–74.

Peiss, Kathy. 1999. *Hope in a Jar: The Making of America's Beauty Culture*. New York: Holt.

Pelley, Lauren. 2015. "Gender-Neutral Clothing Goes Mainstream with New Department Store Campaign." *Toronto Star.* 3 March. www.thestar.com/business/2015/03/03/gender-neutral-clothing-goes-mainstream-with-new-department-store-campaign.html

Peres, Judy. 1998. "In 50 Years, Kibbutz Movement Has Undergone Many Changes." *Chicago Tribune.* 9 May.

Perkel, Colin. 2016. "Two Canadian Officers Accused of Sex Abuse during UN Peace Missions." *Globe and Mail.* 4 March.

Petchesky, Rosalind P. 2002. "Human Rights, Reproductive Health, and Economic Justice: Why They Are Indivisible." In *The Socialist Feminist Project: A Contemporary Reader in Theory and Politics*, edited by Nancy Holmstrom. New York: Monthly Review Press.

——— and Karen Judd. 1998. *Negotiating Reproductive Rights: Women's Perspectives across Countries and Cultures*. New York: Zed Books.

Petersen, Alan. 2007. *The Body in Question: A Sociocultural Approach*. New York: Routledge.

Peterson, V. Spike, and Anne Sisson Runyan. 2010. *Global Gender Issues in the New Millennium,* 3rd edn. Boulder, CO: Westview Press.

Pharr, Suzanne. 1997. *Homophobia: A Weapon of Sexism*. Oakland, CA: Chardon Press.

Phelan, Shane. 1994. *Getting Specific: Postmodern Lesbian Politics*. Minneapolis: University of Minnesota Press.

Philippine Women Centre of BC 2000. *Canada: the New Frontier for Filipino Mail-Order Brides*. Status of Women Canada. http://publications.gc.ca/collections/Collection/SW21-62-2000E.pdf

Phillips, Susan. 1995. "The Social Context of Women's Health: Goals and Objectives for Medical Education." *Canadian Medical Association Journal* 152 (4): 507–11.

Piercy, Marge. 1976. *Woman on the Edge of Time.* New York: Knopf.

Pipher, Mary. 1994. *Reviving Ophelia: Saving the Selves of Adolescent Girls*. New York: Grosset/Putnam.

Plaskow, Judith. 1979. "Bringing a Daughter into the Covenant." In *Womanspirit Rising: A Feminist Reader in Religion*, edited by Carol P. Christ and Judith Plaskow. San Francisco: Harper & Row.

———. 1990. *Standing Again at Sinai: Judaism from a Feminist Perspective*. New York: HarperCollins.

Plato. 1998. *The Republic*, translated by Robin Waterfield. Oxford: Oxford University Press.

———. 2005. *The Collected Dialogues of Plato, Including the Letters*, translated by Edith Hamilton, Huntington Cairns, and Lane Cooper. Princeton, NJ: Princeton University Press.

PLOS Medicine Editors. 2009. "Rape in War Is Common, Devastating, and Too Often Ignored." *PLOS Med* 6 (1): e1000021. DOI:10.1371/journal/pmed.1000021

Pollet, Alison, and Page Hurwitz. 2004. "Strip Til You Drop." *The Nation*. 12 January, 20–1, 24–5.

Pomeroy, Sarah B. 1975. *Goddesses, Whores, Wives, and Slaves: Women in Classical Antiquity*. New York: Schocken.

——. 1977. "Technicai Kai Mousikai: The Education of Women in the Fourth Century and in the Hellenistic Period." *American Journal of Ancient History* 2: 51–68.

Porzelius, Linda Krug. 2000. "Physical Health Issues for Women." In *Issues in the Psychology of Women*, edited by Maryka Biaggio and Michel Hersen. New York: Kluwer Academic/ Plenum.

Potash, Betty, ed. 1986. *Widows in African Societies: Choices and Constraints*. Stanford, CA: Stanford University Press.

Prasad, Madhava M. 1998. *Ideology of the Hindi Film: A Historical Construction*. Delhi, India: Oxford University Press.

Prendergast, John, and Don Cheadle. 2010. *The Enough Moment: Fighting to End Africa's Worst Human Rights Crimes*. New York: Three Rivers Press.

Pride Toronto. n.d. "About Us." www.pridetoronto.com/about-us/

Prince George Citizen. 2014. "What the Numbers Say about Dementia." 21 May. www.princegeorgecitizen.com/news/local-news/what-the-numbers-say-about-dementia-1.1069444

Puar, Jasbir. 2007. *Terrorist Assemblages: Homo-nationalism in Queer Times*. Durham, NC: Duke University Press.

Public Health Agency of Canada. 2009. "Are Women at Risk for Heart Disease?" www.phac-aspc.gc.ca/cd-mc/cvd-mcv/women-femmes_01-eng.php

——. 2013a. "HIV and AIDS in Canada: Surveillance Report to December 31st, 2012." www.phac-aspc.gc.ca/aids-sida/publication/survreport/2012/dec/index-eng.php

——. 2013b. "Sexually Transmitted Infections—A Continued Public Health Concern." www.phac-aspc.gc.ca/cphorsphc-respcacsp/2013/sti-its-eng.php

——. 2015. "Summary: Estimates of HIV Incidence Prevalence and Proportion Undiagnosed in Canada, 2014." http://healthycanadians.gc.ca/publications/diseases-conditions-maladies-affections/hiv-aids-estimates-2014-vih-sida-estimations/index-eng.php

Public Safety Canada. 2012. "Human Trafficking in Canada." *National Action Plan to Combat Human Trafficking*. www.publicsafety.gc.ca/cnt/rsrcs/pblctns/ntnl-ctn-pln-cmbt/index-eng.aspx#toc-01.2

Pudasaini, Surabhi. 2009. "Filmi Feminism v Fraternity." *Himal: Southasian*. www.himalmag.com/component/content/article/598-filmi-feminism-v-fraternity-women-in-indian-film-1-10-edited-by-nasreen-munni-kabir.html

Pugliesi, Karen. 1992. "Women and Mental Health: Two Traditions of Feminist Research." *Women and Health* 19 (2–3): 43–68.

Puttick, Elizabeth. 1997. *Women in New Religions: In Search of Community, Sexuality and Spiritual Power*. New York: St Martin's Press.

Qin-Hilliard, Desirée Baolian. 2003. "Gendered Expectations and Gendered Experiences: Immigrant Students' Adaptation in Schools." *New Directions for Youth Development* 100: 91–109.

Queiro, Alicia. 2014. "Who Belongs to the Worldwide Club of Women Leaders?" 19 November. BBC News Scotland. www.bbc.com/news/uk-scotland-scotland-politics-30087358

Radhakrishnan, Smitha. 2009. "Profession Women, Good Families: Respectable Feminisms and the Cultural Politics of a 'New' India." *Qualitative Sociology* 32: 195–212.

Rainbow Resource Centre. 2008. "Two Spirit People of the First Nations." www.rainbowresourcecentre.org/wp-content/uploads/2011/09/TwoSpirit.pdf

Rakow, Lana F., ed. 1992. *Women Making Meaning: New Feminist Directions in Communication*. New York: Routledge.

Randall, Vicky. 1987. *Women and Politics*, 2nd edn. Chicago: University of Chicago Press.

Ratcliff, Kathryn Strother. 2002. *Women and Health: Power, Technology, Inequality, and Conflict in a Gendered World*. Boston: Allyn & Bacon.

Rathus, Spencer A., Jeffery S. Nevid, and Lois Fincher-Rathus. 2011. *Human Sexuality in a World of Diversity*, 8th edn. Boston: Pearson College.

Ratner, Rochelle, ed. 2000. *Bearing Life: Women's Writings on Childlessness*. New York: Feminist Press.

Ray, Nicholas. 2006. *Lesbian, Gay, Bisexual, and Transgender Youth: An Epidemic of Homelessness*. Washington, DC: National Lesbian and Gay Task Force.

Raymond, Susan U., Henry M. Greenberg, and Stephen R. Leeder. 2005. "Beyond Reproduction: Women's Health in Today's Developing World." *International Journal of Epidemiology* 34 (5): 1144–8.

Rayor, Diane. 1991. *Sappho's Lyre. Archaic Lyric and Women Poets of Ancient Greece*. Berkeley: University of California Press.

Reisenwitz, Cathy. 2013. "Christina Hoff Sommers, Maternal Feminism: Same Old Sexism, New Packaging." *Sex and State* (blog). http://cathyreisenwitz.com/christina-hoff-sommers-maternal-feminism-same-old-sexism-new-packaging/

Rennie, Steve. 2014. "Huge Increase in Number of Aboriginal Women in Canadian Prisons." *Toronto Star*, 3 December. www.thestar.com/news/canada/2014/12/02/huge_increase_in_number_of_aboriginal_women_in_canadian_prisons.html

Rice, Carla. 2014. *Becoming Women: The Embodied Self in Image Culture*. Toronto: University of Toronto Press.

Rich, Adrienne. 1976. *Of Woman Born: Motherhood as Experience and Institution*. New York: Norton.

———. 1980. "Compulsory Heterosexuality and Lesbian Existence." *Signs* 5 (4): 631–60.

Ridd, Rosemary, and Helen Callaway. 1987. *Women and Political Conflict*. New York: New York University Press.

Rife, J. 2001. C. "Middle-Aged and Older Women in the Work Force." In *Handbook on Women and Aging*, edited by Jean M. Coyle. Westport, CT: Greenwood Press.

Rivera, Raquel Z. 2012. "Butta Pecan Mamis: Tropicalized Mamis: Chocolate Caliente." In *That's the Joint: The Hip-Hop Studies Reader*, 2nd edn, edited by Murray Forman and Mark Anthony Neal. New York: Routledge.

Robbins, Wendy. 2010. "'The Work Is Far from Done': Women, Feminism, Intersectionality." *Equity Matters*. Federation for the Humanities and Social Sciences. www.ideas-idees.ca/blog/work-far-done-women-feminism-intersectionality

Roberts, Monica. 2016. *TransGriot* (blog). http://transgriot.blogspot.ca/

Roosevelt, Eleanor. 1958. "Where, after All, Do Universal Human Rights Begin?" *Commission on Human Rights*. New York: United Nations, 27 March.

Rosen, Ruth. 1982. *The Lost Sisterhood: Prostitution in America, 1900–1918*. Baltimore: Johns Hopkins Press.

Rosenberg, Tina. 2009. "The Daughter Deficit." *New York Times Magazine*. 19 August. www.nytimes.com/2009/08/23/magazine/23FOB-idealab-t.html

Rosenblatt, Roger, ed. 1999. *Consuming Desires: Consumption, Culture, and the Pursuit of Happiness*. Washington, DC: Shearwater.

Rosin, Hanna. 2009. "The Case against Breast-Feeding." *The Atlantic*. April. www.theatlantic.com/magazine/archive/2009/04/the-case-against-breast-feeding/ (7311/)

———. 2010. "The End of Men." *The Atlantic* (July–August): 56–72.

Rotella, Elyce J. 1980. "Women's Roles in Economic Life." In *Issues and Feminism: A First Course in Women's Studies*, edited by Sheila Ruth. Boston: Houghton Mifflin.

Rothwell, E. 1999. "Knitting up the World: L.M. Montgomery and Maternal Feminism in Canada." In *L.M. Montgomery and Canadian Culture*, edited by I. Gammel and E. Epperly. Toronto: University of Toronto Press.

Rousseau, Jean-Jacques. 1966 [1762]. *Émile*, translated by Barbara Foxley. New York: Dutton.

Roy, Arundhati. 1997. *The God of Small Things*. New York: Harper.

Rubin, Alissa J. 2010. "For Afghan Wives, a Desperate, Fiery Way Out." *The New York Times*, 8 November.

Rubin, Gayle. 1975. "The Traffic in Women: Notes on the 'Political Economy' of Sex." In *Toward an Anthropology of Women*, edited by Rayna Reiter. New York: Monthly Review Press.

———. 1993. "Thinking Sex: Notes for a Radical Theory of the Politics of Sexuality." In *The Lesbian and Gay Studies Reader*, edited by Henry Abelove, Michele Aina Barale, and David M. Halperin. New York: Routledge.

Ruble, Thomas L. 1983. "Sex Stereotypes: Issues of Change in the 1970s." *Sex Roles* 9: 397–402.

Ruether, Rosemary Radford, ed. 2007. *Feminist Theologies: Legacy and Prospect*. Philadelphia, PA: Westminster Press.

Rushdie, Salman. 1995. *The Moor's Last Sigh*. New York: Random House.

Russ, Joanna. 1975. *The Female Man*. New York: Bantam Books.

Russell, Diana E., ed. 1993. *Making Violence Sexy: Feminist Views on Pornography*. New York: Teacher's College Press.

Russo, Francine. 2016. "Transgender Kids: What Does It Take to Help Them Thrive?" *Scientific American*, 1 January. www.scientificamerican.com/article/transgender-kids-what-does-it-take-to-help-them-thrive/

Sabattini, Laura, and Faye J. Crosby. 2009. "Ceilings and Walls: Work-Life and 'Family-Friendly' Policies." In *The Glass Ceiling in the 21st Century*, edited by Manuela Barreto, Michelle K. Ryan, and Michael T. Schmitt. Washington, DC: American Psychological Association.

Sadigi, Fatima, Amira Nowira, Azza El Kholy, et al., eds. 2009. *Women Writing Africa IV: The Northern Region*. New York: Feminist Press.

Saldivar-Hull, Sonia. 1998. *Feminism on the Border: Contemporary Chicana Writers*. Berkeley: University of California Press.

Sànchez Korrol, Virgina. 1999. "Women in Nineteenth- and Twentieth-Century Latin America and the Caribbean." In *Women in Latin America and the*

Caribbean, edited by Marysa Navarro and Virginia Sànchez Korrol. Bloomington: Indiana University Press.

Sanday, Peggy Reeves. 1981. *Female Power and Male Dominance: On the Origins of Sexual Inequality.* Cambridge: Cambridge University Press.

———. 2002. *Women at the Center: Life in a Modern Matriarchy.* Ithaca, NY: Cornell University Press.

Sandler, Bernice R., and Roberta M. Hall. 1986. *The Campus Climate Revisited: Chilly for Women Faculty, Administrators, and Graduate Students.* Washington, DC: Association of American Colleges.

———. Lisa A. Silverberg, and Roberta M. Hall. 1996. *The Chilly Classroom Climate: A Guide to Improve the Education of Women.* Washington, DC: National Association for Women in Education.

Sangha, Jasjit, and Tahira Gonsalves. 2013. *South Asian Mothering: Negotiating Culture, Family and Selfhood.* Toronto: Demeter Press.

Sapiro, Virginia. 1992. *A Vindication of Political Virtue: The Political Theory of Mary Wollstonecraft.* Chicago: University of Chicago Press.

Satz, Debra. 2011. "Feminist Perspectives on Reproduction and the Family." In *The Stanford Encyclopedia of Philosophy*, edited by Edward N. Zalta. http://plato.stanford.edu/archives/sum2011/entries/feminism-family

Sawa, Timothy. 2016. "Brock University Tells Student to Keep Quiet about Sexual Harassment Finding." CBC News, 11 March. www.cbc.ca/news/canada/brock-university-sexual-harrassment-1.3485814

Sawa, Timothy, and Lori Ward. 2015. "Sex Assault Reporting on Canadian Campuses Worryingly Low, Say Experts." CBC News, 6 February. www.cbc.ca/news/canada/sex-assault-reporting-on-canadian-campuses-worryingly-low-say-experts-1.2948321

Sax, Linda J. 2008. *The Gender Gap in College.* San Francisco: Jossey-Bass.

Schiff, Stacy. 2010. *Cleopatra: A Life.* New York: Little, Brown.

Schulman, Sarah. 2009. *The Ties That Bind: Familial Homophobia and Its Consequences.* New York: The New Press.

Schwartz, Pepper. 2011. "Long-Distance Love." AARP The Magazine. November.

Schwender, Martha. 2002. "A Life of Marital Bliss (Segregation Laws Aside)." *New York Times.* 26 January. www.nytimes.com/2012/01/27/arts/design/the-loving-story-at-international-center-of-photography.html

Schwindt-Bayer, Leslie A. 2011. "Women Who Win: Social Backgrounds, Paths to Power, and Political Ambition in Latin American Legislatures." *Politics & Gender* 7 (1): 1–33.

Scott, Anne Firor. 1991. *Natural Allies: Women's Associations in American History.* Urbana: University of Illinois Press.

Scott, Joan Wallach. 1988. "Deconstructing Equality-versus-Difference: Or, the Uses of Poststructuralist Theory for Feminism." *Feminist Studies* 14 (Spring): 33–50.

———. 1992. "Experience." In *Feminists Theorize the Political*, edited by Joan Scott and Judith Butler. New York: Routledge.

———. 1996. *Only Paradoxes to Offer: French Feminists and the Rights of Man.* Cambridge, MA: Harvard University Press.

———. 2007. *The Politics of the Veil.* Princeton, NJ: Princeton University Press.

Scott, W. S., trans. and ed. 1968. *Trial of Joan of Arc.* London: Folio Society.

Scott-Dixon, Krista. 2004. *Doing IT: Women Working in Information Technology.* Toronto: Sumach Press.

Seager, Joni. 2009. *The Penguin Atlas of Women in the World*, 4th edn. New York: Penguin.

Seaman, Barbara, and Laura Eldridge, eds. 2012. *Voices of the Women's Health Movement*, vol. 1. New York: Seven Stories Press.

Sechzer, J., V.C. Rabinowitz, and F.L. Denmark. 1994. "Sex and Gender Bias in Animal and Human Research." In *Forging a Women's Health Research Agenda*, edited by J.A. Sechzer, A. Griffin, and S. Pfafflin. New York: New York Academy of Sciences.

Self-Employed Women's Association. 2008. *Annual Report 2008.* www.sewa.org/Annual_Report_2008-English.pdf

Sen, Amartya. 2001. "Work and Rights." In *Women, Gender, and Work*, edited by Martha Fetherolf Loutfi. Geneva: International Labour Office.

Shahar, Shulamith. 1983. *The Fourth Estate: A History of Women in the Middle Ages*, translated by Chaya Galai. London: Methuen.

Sharma, Arvind, and Katherine K. Young, eds. 1999. *Feminism and World Religions.* Albany, NY: SUNY Press.

Sheehy, Gail. 1998. *The Silent Passage: Menopause.* New York: Pocket Books.

Shernoff, M. 1997. "Gay Marriage and Gay Widowhood." *The Harvard Gay & Lesbian Review* 4: 4.

Shiva, Vandana. 1988. *Staying Alive: Women, Ecology, and Development in India.* London: Zed Books.

Sicherman, Barbara. 2010. *Well-Read Lives: How Books Inspired a Generation of American Women.* Chapel Hill: University of North Carolina Press.

Silko, Leslie Marmon. 1977. *Ceremony.* New York: Penguin.

Simmons, Christina. 2009. *Making Marriage Modern*. New York: Oxford University Press.

Simmons, Rachel. 2002. *Odd Girl Out: The Hidden Culture of Aggression in Girls*. New York: Harcourt.

Simpson, George E. 1978. *Black Religions in the New World*. New York: Columbia University Press.

Simpson, Jaqueline. 1994. "Margaret Murray: Who Believed Her and Why?" *Folklore* 105.

Sinclair, Raven. 2007. "Identity Lost and Found: Lessons from The Sixties Scoop." *First Peoples Child and Family Review* 3 (1): 66.

Sinha, Maire. 2012. "Portrait of Caregivers, 2012." Statistics Canada. www.statcan.gc.ca/pub/89-652-x/89-652-x2013001-eng.htm

———. ed. 2013. "Measuring Violence against Women: Statistical Trends." Statistics Canada. www.statcan.gc.ca/pub/85-002-x/2013001/article/11766-eng.pdf

———. 2014. "Child Care in Canada." Statistics Canada. www.statcan.gc.ca/pub/89-652-x/89-652-x2014005-eng.htm

Sinha, Mrinalina. 2004. "Gender and Nation." In *Women's History in Global Perspective*, vol. 1, edited by Bonnie Smith. Urbana: University of Illinois Press.

Sinnott, Megan J. 2004. *Toms and Dees: Transgender Identity and Female Same-Sex Relationships in Thailand*. Honolulu: University of Hawaii Press.

Skloot, Rebecca. 2011. *The Immortal Life of Henrietta Lacks*. New York: Broadway.

Smith, Barbara, ed. 1983. *Home Girls: A Black Feminist Anthology*. New York: Kitchen Table Women of Color Press.

Smith, Dorothy. 1989. *The Everyday World as Problematic: A Feminist Sociology*. Boston: Northeast University Press.

Smith, Patricia, ed. 1993. *Feminist Jurisprudence*. New York: Oxford University Press.

Smith, Valerie. 1998. *Not Just Race, Not Just Gender: Black Feminist Readings*. New York: Routledge.

Smith, Zadie. 2000. *White Teeth*. New York: Random House.

Smithson, Isaiah. 1990. "Introduction: Investigating Gender, Power, and Pedagogy." In *Gender in the Classroom: Power and Pedagogy*, edited by Susan L. Gabriel and Isaiah Smthson. Urbana: University of Illinois Press.

Smyke, Patricia. *Women and Health*. London: Zed Books, 1991.

Snitow, Ann. 1985. "Holding the Line at Greenham Common: Being Joyously Political in Dangerous Times." *Mother Jones* (February/March): 30–47.

Snyder, Jane McIntosh. 1989. *The Woman and the Lyre: Women Writers in Classical Greece and Rome*. Carbondale: Southern Illinois University Press.

Solinger, Rickie. 2007. *Pregnancy and Power: A Short History of Reproductive Politics in America*. New York: New York University.

Solomon, Miriam. 2009. "Standpoint and Creativity." *Hypatia* 24 (4): 226–37.

Sontag, S. 1979. "The Double Standard of Aging." In *Psychology of Women: Selected Readings*, edited by Juanita H. Williams. New York: Norton.

Spelman, Elizabeth V. 1988. *Inessential Woman: Problems of Exclusion in Feminist Thought*. Boston: Beacon Press.

Spivak, Gayatri Chakravorty. 1988. "Can the Subaltern Speak?" In *Marxism and the Interpretation of Culture*, edited by Cary Nelson and Lawrence Grossberg. Urbana: University of Illinois Press.

Sprinkle, Annie. 2005. *Dr. Sprinkle's Spectacular Sex: Make over Your Love Life with One of the World's Greatest Sex Experts*. New York: Penguin.

Stanton, Elizabeth Cady. 1871. "On Marriage and Divorce." Speech in San Francisco, 18 August. http://gos.sbc.edu/s/stantoncady3.html

———. 1971 (1898). *Eighty Years and More: Reminiscences 1815–1897*. New York: Schocken Books.

———. 1972. *The Woman's Bible* (1895–8): parts I, II, and appendix. New York: Arno.

Stastna, Kazi. 2012. "Canada's Working Moms Still Earning Less, Doing More Than Dads." CBC News, 10 May. www.cbc.ca/news/canada/canada-s-working-moms-still-earning-less-doing-more-than-dads-1.1184685

Statistics Canada. 2010. "Paid Work." In *Women in Canada: A Gender-Based Statistical Report*. www.statcan.gc.ca/pub/89-503-x/2010001/article/11387-eng.htm

———. 2012a. "2011 Census of Population: Families, Households, Marital Status, Structural Type of Dwelling, Collectives." *The Daily*. 19 September. www.statcan.gc.ca/daily-quotidien/120919/dq120919a-eng.htm

———. 2012b. "Average Total Income by Family Type, Select Years, 1976 to 2008." www.statcan.gc.ca/pub/89-503-x/2010001/article/11388/tbl/tbl003-eng.htm CANSIM 202-0410

———. 2013a. "Births and Total Fertility Rate, by Province and Territory." Statistics Canada. CANSIM, table 102-4505. www.statcan.gc.ca/tables-tableaux/sum-som/l01/cst01/hlth85b-eng.htm

———. 2013b. "Education in Canada: Attainment, Field of Study and Location of Study." www12.statcan.gc.ca/

nhs-enm/2011/as-sa/99-012-x/99-012-x2011001-eng.cfm

———. 2015a. "Canadian Households in 2011: Type and Growth, Figure 1 Distribution (in Percentage) of Private Households by Household Type, 2001 to 2011." www12.statcan.gc.ca/census-recensement/2011/as-sa/98-312-x/2011003/fig/fig3_2-1-eng.cfm

———. 2015b. "Conjugal Status and Opposite/Same-Sex Status, Sex and Age Groups for Persons Living in Couples in Private Households of Canada, Provinces, Territories and Census Metropolitan Areas, 2011 Census." www12.statcan.gc.ca/census-recensement/2011/dp-pd/tbt-tt/Rp-eng.cfm?LANG=E&APATH=7&DETAIL=0&DIM=0&FL=C&FREE=0&GC=0&GID=0&GK=0&GRP=1&PID=102574&PRID=0&PTYPE=101955&S=0&SHOWALL=0&SUB=0&Temporal=2011&THEME=0&VID=0&VNAMEE=Conjugal%20status%20and%20oppos

———. 2015c. "Fertility: Fewer Children, Older Moms." *Canadian Megatrends*, www.statcan.gc.ca/pub/11-630-x/11-630-x2014002-eng.htm

———. 2015d. "Labour Force Characteristics by Sex and Age Group." 28 January. www.statcan.gc.ca/tables-tableaux/sum-som/l01/cst01/labor05-eng.htm

———. 2015e. "Percentage of Women among Full-Time University Enrolments, by Program Level, Canada, 1992/1993 to 2008/2009." www.statcan.gc.ca/pub/89-503-x/2010001/article/11542/c-g/c-g007-eng.htm

———. 2015f. "Portrait of Families and Living Arrangements in Canada." www12.statcan.gc.ca/census-recensement/2011/as-sa/98-312-x/98-312-x2011001-eng.cfm

Status of Women Canada. 2013. "Women in Canada at a Glance Statistical Highlights: Economic Well-Being." www.swc-cfc.gc.ca/rc-cr/stat/wic-fac-2012/sec8-eng.html

Stein, Nan, Nancy L. Marshall, and Linda R. Tropp. 1993. *Secrets in Public: Sexual Harassment in Our Schools*. Center for Research on Women, Wellesley College and NOW Legal Defense and Education Fund. Wellesley, MA: Wellesley Centers for Women.

Steinem, Gloria. 1978. "Far from the Opposite Shore, or How to Survive Though a Feminist." *Ms* 7: 65–7, 90–4, 105.

Stern, Lori. 1990. "Conceptions of Separation and Connection in Female Adolescence." In *Making Connections: The Relational Worlds of Adolescent Girls at Emma Willard School*, edited by Carol Gilligan, Nona P. Lyons, and Trudy J. Hanmer. Cambridge, MA: Harvard University Press.

Strohschein, Lisa, and Rose Weitz. 2014. *The Sociology of Health, Illness and Health Care in Canada: A Critical Approach*. Toronto: Nelson Education.

Strong, Bryan, Christine DeVault, and Theodore F. Cohen. 2011. *The Marriage and Family Experience*. Belmont, CA: Wadsworth.

Strout, Elizabeth. 2008. *Olive Kitteridge*. New York: Random House.

Stuckey, Johanna H. 2010. *Women's Spirituality: Contemporary Feminist Approaches to Judaism, Christianity, Islam and Goddess Worship*. Toronto: Inanna.

Suárez-Orozco, Carola, Marcelo M. Suárez-Orozco, and Irina Todorova. 2008. *Learning a New Land: Immigrant Students in American Society*. Cambridge, MA: Harvard University Press.

Sugden, J. 2009. "Women Get Annoyed by Low Pay and Leave to Have Children." *The Times*. http://business.timesonline.co.uk/tol/business/law/article6157782

Sunderland, Judith. 2012. "Damned If You Do, Damned If You Don't: Religious Dress and Women's Rights." In *The Unfinished Revolution: Voices from the Global Fight for Women's Rights*, edited by Minky Worden. New York: Seven Stories Press.

Sutherland-Addy, Esi, and Aminata Diaw, eds. 2005. *Women Writing Africa II: West Africa and the Sahel*. New York: Feminist Press.

Swers, Michele L. 2002. *The Difference Women Make: The Policy Impact of Women in Congress*. Chicago: University of Chicago Press.

TallMountain, Mary. 1981. "There Is No Word for Goodbye." *Blue Cloud Quarterly* 27 (1).

Tanaka, Yukiko. 2002. *Japan's Comfort Women: Sexual Slavery and Prostitution during World War II and the US Occupation*. London: Routledge.

——— and Elizabeth Hanson, trans and eds. 1982. *This Kind of Woman: Ten Stories by Japanese Women Writers, 1960–1976*. New York: Pedigree Books.

Tattoo Rant. 2004. 28 September. www.wiccan-refuge.com/tattoorant.html.

Tavakoli-Targhi, Mohamad. 2015. Personal communication.

Taylor Mill, Harriet. 1970 (1851). "The Enfranchisement of Women." In *John Stuart Mill and Harriet Taylor Mill, Essays on Sex Equality*, edited by Alice S. Rossi. Chicago: University of Chicago Press.

Teegarden, Jessica. 2011. "'Come to the Water' Inspires Holiness Movement in Women." Indianapolis, IN:

Wesleyan Church Department of Communications. www.wesleyan.org/doc/news_article?id=1456

Tharu, Susi, and K. Lalita. 1993. *Women Writing in India*, 2 vols. New York: Feminist Press.

Thompson, Clara. 1942. "Cultural Pressures in the Psychology of Women." *Psychiatry* 5: 331–9.

———. 1943. "Penis Envy in Women." *Psychiatry* 6: 123–5.

Thornton Dill, Bonnie, and Marla Kohlman. 2012. "Intersectionality: A Transformative Paradigm in Feminist Theory and Social Justice." In *Handbook of Feminist Research, Theory and Practice*, edited by Sharlene Nagy Hesse-Biber. Los Angeles: SAGE.

Tickner, J. Ann. 2001. *Gendering World Politics*. New York: Columbia University Press.

Tidball, M. Elizabeth. 1973. "Perspective on Academic Women and Affirmative Action." *Educational Record* 54: 130–5.

———. 1980. "Women's Colleges and Women Achievers Revisited." *Signs* 5: 504–17.

Tiefer, Lenore. 2004. *Sex Is Not a Natural Act & Other Essays*. Boulder, CO: Westview Press.

Tinsman, Heidi. 2002. *Partners in Conflict: The Politics of Gender, Sexuality and Labor in the Chilean Agrarian Reform, 1950–1973*. Durham, NC: Duke University Press.

Tolman, Deborah L. 2002. *Dilemmas of Desire: Teenage Girls Talk about Sexuality*. Cambridge, MA: Harvard University Press.

Tolstoy, Leo. 2000 (1873–77). *Anna Karenina*, translated by Richard Pevear and Larissa Volokhonsky. New York: Penguin.

Tomasello, Michael. 1999. "The Human Adaptation for Culture." *Annual Review of Anthropology* 28: 510.

Toor, Saadia. 2011. "Gender, Sexuality, and Islam under the Shadow of Empire." *The Scholar and Feminist Online* 9. http://sfonline.barnard.edu/religion/print_toor.htm

Travis, C. B. 1988. *Women and Health Psychology: Mental Health Issues*. Hillsdale, NJ: Erlbaum.

Treblicot, Joyce, ed. 1984. *Mothering: Essays in Feminist Theory*. Totowa, NJ: Rowman & Allanheld.

Trexler, Richard C. 1973. "The Foundlings of Florence, 1395–1455." *History of Childhood Quarterly: The Journal of Psychohistory* 1 (2): 259–84.

Tronto, Joan C. 1993. *Moral Boundaries: A Political Argument for an Ethics of Care*. New York: Routledge.

———. 2001. "An Ethics of Care." In *Ethics in Community-Based Elder Care*, edited by Martha Holstein and Phyllis Mitzen. New York: Springer.

Truth and Reconciliation Commission of Canada. 2015. *Truth and Reconciliation Commission of Canada: Calls to Action*. www.trc.ca/websites/trcinstitution/File/2015/Findings/Calls_to_Action_English2.pdf

Tsukiyama, Gail. 1991. *Women of the Silk*. New York: St Martin's Press.

Turgeon, Carolyn. 2016. "Q&A with Sandy Hudson, co-founder of Black Lives Matter Toronto." 8 April. https://ca.news.yahoo.com/qa-with-sandy-hudson-co-founder-of-black-lives-185115767.html

US Department of Health and Human Services. 2004. *Women's Health in the U.S.: Research on Health Issues Affecting Women*. NIH Publication No. 04–4697.

———. 2010. *Healthy People 2020. Lesbian, Gay, Bisexual, and Transgender Health*. Washington, DC: US Government Printing Office.

Uchendu, Victor. 1965. *The Igbo of South East Nigeria*. New York: Holt, Rinehart & Winston.

Udry, Richard. 2000. "The Biological Limits of Gender Construction." *American Sociological Review* 65 (3): 443–57.

Umeå Center for Gender Studies. 2011. "Arena for Reflection and Theoretical Development." www.ucgs.umu.se/english/research/previous-research-projects/challenging-gender/arena/

UNAIDS. 2016. *Fact Sheet November 2016*. http://www.unaids.org/en/resources/fact-sheet

———. 1998. "Force for Change: World AIDS Campaign with Young People." In *World AIDS Campaign Briefing Paper*. Geneva: UNAIDS.

UNESCO. 2003. *EFA Global Monitoring Report 2003/4*. http://unstats.un.org/unsd/demographic/products/Worldswomen/WW_full%20report_color.pdf

———. 2005. *Education for All. Literacy for Life*. Paris: UNESCO.

———. 2012. *World Atlas of Gender Equality in Education*. www.uis.unesco.org/Education/Documents/unesco-world-atlas-gender-education-2012.pdf

Unger, J. B., and T.E. Seeman. 2000. "Successful Aging." In *Women and Health*, edited by Marlene B. Goldman and Maureen Hatch. San Diego, CA: Academic Press.

United Nations. 2014. "Guidelines on Reproductive Health." UN.org/popin/unfpa/taskforce/guide/iatfreph.gdl.html

United Nations Department of Economic and Social Affairs. 2000. *The World's Women 2000: Trends and Statistics*. New York: United Nations.

———. 2010. *The World's Women 2010: Trends and Statistics*. New York: United Nations Statistics Division.

United Nations Development Fund for Women. 2007. *World Poverty Day 2007: Investing in Women; Solving the Poverty Puzzle*. New York: United Nations.

United Nations Office on Drugs and Crime. 2012. "People for Sale." www.unodc.org/toc/factsheets/

University of New Brunswick Libraries. n.d. "The Ward Chipman Slavery Brief." www.lib.unb.ca/Texts/NBHistory/chipman/about.html

UN Women. 2016. *Facts and Figures: HIV and AIDS*. http://www.unwomen.org/en/what-we-do/hiv-and-aids/facts-and-figures

Vaid, Urvashi. 2012. *Irresistible Revolution: Confronting Race, Class and the Assumptions of LGBT Politics*. New York: Magnum Books.

Valentine, David. 2007. *Imagining Transgender: An Ethnography of a Category*. Durham, NC: Duke University Press.

Valian, Virginia. 1998. *Why So Slow? The Advancement of Women*. Cambridge, MA: MIT Press.

Vance, Carol S. 1990. "Negotiating Sex and Gender in the Attorney General's Commission on Pornography." In *Uncertain Terms: Negotiating Gender in American Culture*, edited by Faye Ginsburg and Anna Lowenhaupt Tsing. Boston: Beacon.

Van den Hoonaard, Deborah. 2003. "Attitudes of Older Widows and Widowers in New Brunswick, Canada toward New Partnerships." In *Intimacy in Later Life*, edited by Kate Davidson and Graham Fennell. Transaction Press.

van den Hoonaard, Deborah. 2010. *By Himself: The Older Man's Experience of Widowhood*. University of Toronto Press.

Van Esterik, Penny. 2006. "Texts and Contexts in Canadian Anthropology." In *Historicizing Canadian Anthropology*, edited by Julia Harrison and Regna Darnell. Vancouver: University of British Columbia Press.

———. 2013. "The Politics of Breastfeeding: An Advocacy Update." In *Food and Culture: A Reader*, 3rd edn, edited by Carole Counihan and Penny Van Esterik. New York: Routledge.

Vetterling-Braggin, Mary. 1981. *Sexist Language*. Totowa, NJ: Littlefield, Adams.

Waite, Linda, and Maggie Gallagher. 2000. *A Case for Marriage: Why Married People Are Happier, Healthier, and Better Off Financially*. New York: Doubleday.

Wald, Kenneth D., and Allison Calhoun-Brown. 2007. *Religion and Politics in the United States*, 5th edn. Lanham, MD: Rowman & Littlefield.

Waldman, Ayelet. 2009. *Bad Mother: A Chronicle of Maternal Crimes, Minor Calamities, and Occasional Moments of Grace*. New York: Doubleday.

Wallace, Michele. 1978. *Black Macho and the Myth of the Superwoman*. New York: Dial Press.

Wallerstein, Judith, Julia Lewis, and Sandra Blakeslee, eds. 2000. *An Unexpected Legacy of Divorce*. Boulder, CO: Hyperion.

War Child. n.d. "The World's Worst Place to Be a Woman?" www.warchild.org.uk/features/worlds-worst-place-be-woman

Warner, Marina. 1981. *Joan of Arc: The Image of Female Heroism*. New York: Knopf.

Warnock, M. 2009. "Glass Ceiling for Women in Middle East Hotels." *Hotelier Middle East*. September. www.hoteliermiddleeast.com/5537-glass-ceiling-for-women-in-middle-east-hotels/

Watts, J.H. 2009. "'Allowed into a Man's World' Meanings of Work-Life Balance: Perspectives of Women Civil Engineers as 'Minority' Workers in Construction." *Gender, Work and Organization* 16 (1): 37–57.

Waylen, Georgina. 2010. "A Comparative Politics of Gender: Limits and Possibilities." *Perspectives on Politics* 8 (1): 223–31.

Welchman, Lynn, and Sara Hossain. 2005. "Introduction: 'Honour,' Rights and Wrongs." In *"Honour": Crimes, Paradigms, and Violence against Women*, edited by Lynn Welchman and Sara Hossain. London: Zed Books.

Welter, Barbara. 1966. "The Cult of True Womanhood: 1820–1860." *American Quarterly* 18: 151–74.

Wenger, Nanette K. 2004. "You've Come a Long Way, Baby: Cardiovascular Health and Disease in Women: Problems and Prospects." *Circulation* 109: 558–60.

West, Candace, and Don H. Zimmerman. 1987. "Doing Gender." *Gender and Society* 1: 125–51.

Weston, Kath. 1991. *Families We Choose: Lesbians, Gays, Kinship*. New York: Columbia University Press.

White, Deborah Gray. 1985. *Ain't I a Woman: Female Slaves in the Plantation South*. New York: Norton.

Wichterich, Christa. 2000. *The Globalized Woman: Reports from a Future of Inequality*, translated by Patrick Camiller. London: Zed Books.

Williams, Cara. 2004. "The Sandwich Generation." Statistics Canada, *Perspectives on Labour and Income* 5 (9). www.statcan.gc.ca/pub/75-001-x/10904/7033-eng.htm

———. 2013. "Economic Well-being." Statistics Canada. www.statcan.gc.ca/pub/89-503-x/2010001/article/11388-eng.htm

Williams, D. 2002. "Racial/Ethnic Variations in Women's Health: The Social Embeddedness of Health." *American Journal of Public Health* 92: 588–97.

Williams, Patricia J. 1991. *The Alchemy of Race and Rights*. Cambridge, MA: Harvard University Press.

Wilson, E.O. 1975. *On Human Nature*. Cambridge, MA: Harvard University Press.

Wilson, Robin. 2007. "The New Gender Divide." *The Chronicle of Higher Education*, January 26.

Wirth, Linda. 2001. "Women in Management: Closer to Breaking through the Glass Ceiling?" In *Women, Gender, and Work*, edited by Martha Fetherolf Loutfi. Geneva: International Labour Office.

Wolfinger, Nicholas H., Mary Ann Mason, and Marc Goulden. 2009. "Stay in the Game: Gender, Family Formation and Alternative Trajectories in the Academic Life Course." *Social Forces* 87 (3): 1591–621.

Wolf-Wendel, Lisa E. 2000. "Women-Friendly Campuses: What Five Institutions Are Doing Right." *The Review of Higher Education* 23 (3): 319–45.

———. 2003. "Gender and Higher Education: What Should We Learn from Women's Colleges?" In *Gendered Futures in Higher Education: Critical Perspectives for Change*, edited by B. Ropers-Huilman. Albany, NY: State University of New York Press.

——— and Becky Eason. 2011. "Women's Colleges and Universities." In *Gender and Higher Education*, edited by Barbara J. Bank. Baltimore: Johns Hopkins University Press.

Wollstonecraft, Mary. 2012 (1792). *A Vindication of the Rights of Woman*. New York: Norton.

Women in World History. n.d. "Bhakti Poets." http://chnm.gmu.edu/wwh/modules/lesson1/lesson1.php?s=0

Women's Enterprise Centre. 2014. *Women's Entrepreneurship in BC & Canada*. http://weoc.ca/wp-content/uploads/2015/11/Womens-Entrepreneurship-in-BC-and-Canada_2014_09_05-final.pdf

Women's Environment and Development Organization. 2001. www.wedo.org/factsheet1.htm

Woo, Terry. 1999. "Confucianism and Feminism." In *Feminism and World Religions*, edited by Courtney W. Howland. Albany, NY: SUNY Press.

World Health Organization (WHO). n.d. "Female Genital Mutilation." www.who.int/topics/female_genital_mutilation/en/

———. 2008. "Eliminating Female Genital Mutilation: An Interagency Statement UNAIDS, UNDP, UNECA, UNESCO, UNFPA, UNHCHR, UNHCR, UNICEF, UNIFEM, WHO." Geneva. www.un.org/womenwatch/daw/csw/csw52/statements_missions/Interagency_Statement_on_Eliminating_FGM.pdf

———. 2009. *Women and Health: Today's Evidence Tomorrow's Agenda*. Geneva: WHO.

———. 2011. *An Update on WHO's Work on Female Genital Mutilation (FGM): Progress Report*. http://whqlib doc.who.int/hq/2011/WHO_RHR_11.18_eng.pdf

———. 2013. "The Social Determinants of Health." www.who.int/social_determinants/sdh_definition/en/

———. World health day/safe motherhood, 7 April 1998: Address unsafe abortion. WHD 98.10, http://www.who.int/archives/whday/en/pages1998/whd98_10.html (accessed April 7, 1998).

World Health Organization, UNICEF, UNFPA and The World Bank. 2012. *Trends in Maternal Mortality: 1990 to 2010*. Geneva. www.who.int/reproductivehealth/publications/monitoring/9789241503631/en/

World Heart Federation. 2012. *Women and Cardiovascular Disease*. www.world-heart-federation-org/press/fact-sheets-women-and-cardiovascular-disease/

Wright, Elizabeth. 2000. *Lacan and Postfeminism*. Cambridge, UK: Icon Books.

Wylie, Alison. 2004a. "Feminist Science Studies." *Hypatia* (special issue co-edited with Lynn Hankinson Nelson) 1 (2).

———. 2004b. "Why Standpoint Matters." In *The Feminist Standpoint Theory Reader: Intellectual and Political Controversies*, edited by Sandra Harding. New York: Routledge.

Yanagisako, Sylvia Junko. 1985. *Transforming the Past: Tradition and Kinship among Japanese Americans*. Stanford, CA: Stanford University Press.

Yari, Eli. 2015. "Mary Ann Shadd." *The Canadian Encyclopedia*. www.thecanadianencyclopedia.ca/en/article/mary-ann-shadd/

Yates, Barbara A. 1982. "Church, State and Education in Belgian Africa: Implications for Contemporary Third World Women." In *Women's Education in the Third World: Comparative Perspectives*, edited by Gail P. Kelly and Carolyn M. Elliott. Albany, NY: SUNY Press.

Yew, Madhavi Acharya-Tom. 2014. "Canadian Women Still Hesitant to Climb Corporate Ladder, Study Says." *Toronto Star*, 17 November. www.thestar.com/business/2014/11/17/canadian_women_believe_salary_gap_is_closing_survey_finds.html

Yezierska, Anzia. 2003 (1925). *Bread Givers: A Novel*. New York: Persea Books.

Young, Neil. 2008. "'The ERA Is a Moral Issue': The Mormon Church, LDS Women, and the Defeat of the Equal Rights Amendment." In *Religion and Politics in the Contemporary United States*, edited by R. Marie Griffith and Melani McAlister. Baltimore: Johns Hopkins University Press.

Young, Rebecca M., and Evan Balaban. 2006. "Psychoneuroindoctrinology." *Nature* 443: 12.

Yousafzai, Malala. 2013. Speech to United Nations Youth Assembly, 12 July 2013. https://secure.aworldatschool.org/page/content/the-text-of-malala-yousafzais-speech-at-the-united-nations/

Yuval-Davis, Nira. 1997. *Gender and Nation*. Thousand Oaks, CA: SAGE.

——— and Flora Anthis, eds. 1989. *Woman-Nation-State*. New York: St Martin Press.

Zakaria, Rafia. 2015. *The Upstairs Wife: An Intimate History of Pakistan*. Boston: Beacon Press.

Zakuan, Umma Atiyah Ahmad. 2010. "Women in the Malaysian Parliament: Do They Matter?" *Intellectual Discourse* 18 (2): 283–322.

Zalk, Sue Rosenberg. 1980. "The Re-emergence of Psychosexual Conflicts in Expectant Fathers." In *Pregnancy, Birthing and Bonding*, edited by Barbara Blum. New York: Human Science Press.

———. 1987. "Women's Dilemma: Both Envied and Subjugated." Paper presented at the Third International Interdisciplinary Congress on Women, Trinity College, Dublin, Ireland. June.

——— and Janice Gordon-Kelter, eds. 1992. *Revolutions in Knowledge: Feminism in the Social Sciences*. Boulder, CO: Westview Press.

Zerbisias, Antonia. 2010. "Census Change Devalues Women's Unpaid Work." *Toronto Star*. 6 August. www.thestar.com/news/canada/2010/08/06/census_change_devalues_womens_unpaid_work.html

Zetkin, Clara. 1984. *Clara Zetkin: Selected Writings*. Foreword by Angela Y. Davis. New York: International Publishers.

Zuger, Abigail. 2007. "The Brain: Malleable, Capable, Vulnerable." *New York Times*, 29 May. www.nytimes.com/2007/05/29/health/29book.html

Index

Abdi, Ali, and Ratna Ghosh, 243
Abdullah (Saudi king), 132
Abella, Rosalie, 321
abortion, 69, 140, 193–4, 300; pharmaceutical/medical, 193
Abortion Caravan, 193
Abrams, Abby, 179
Abu Ghraib prison, 198–9
Abu-Lughod, Lila, 257
academia: women in, 231–2, 285–6
Achilles Effect, The, 29
Acker, Alison, and Betty Brightwell, 179
activism: grassroots, 322–4; intersectionality and, 68–71; writing as, 23
Act to amend the Canadian Human Rights Act and Criminal Code, 104
Adam and Eve story, 9–10
adoption, 69, 172, 173; of Indigenous children, 162
adultery, 131, 141, 320
advancement: women in academia and, 231–2
"affirmative action," 40, 294
Afghanistan: education in, 220, 226; girls in, 159
age: marriage and, 152; mental health and, 208
agency, 302
aging: women and, 173–4
agriculture: gender and, 274–5; local, 276
Aguirre, Carmen, 23
Ahmadu, Fuambai, 200–1
Ahmed, Leila, 154
Akin, Todd, 300
Alberta: sterilization in, 192–3
Alcoff, Linda, 121
alcohol: cancer and, 204
Alexander, M. Jacqui, 64, 74, 105
Allen, Paula Gunn, 260, 265
Allende, Isabel, 23
Alzheimer's disease, 206

American Psychological Association, 11, 15, 294
Amnesty International, 60
anarchism, 43
anatomy: gender and, 84–6
"anatomy is destiny," 87, 91
Anderson, Elizabeth, 53
Anderson, Kim, 212
Anderson, Leona, and Pamela Dickey Young, 268
androgen, 89
androgyny, 45–6
anorexia, 17
anthropology, 34, 53, 120
anti-sexism, 53
anti-women sentiment, 14–15
Aquino, Corazon, 307
"Arab Spring," 306–7, 323
Arapesh people, 87
Archer Mann, Susan, and Ashley Suzanne Patterson, 57
Aristophanes, 168
Aristotle, 36, 85
Armstrong, Pat, and Ann Pederson, 212
art: images of mothers in, 166; Inuit, 19; women and, 9, 19–29
Ashevak, Kenojuak, 19
assimilation: cultural, 233, 235; gender, 233
assisted reproductive techniques (ART), 188
Astell, Mary, 222
athleticism: women and, 17–18
Atlantis, 57
atomic science, 239
Atwood, Margaret, 23
Augustine, 36
Austen, Jane, 22
authority: power and, 302–3, 305
Avalokitesvara, 251

Baartman, Saartjie, 110
Babri Masjid, 312
"baby-boomers," 139
Bachelet, Michelle, 307, 310

Bain, Beverly, 71
Bakan, Abigail B., and Enakshi Dua, 57
Bandaranaike, Sirimavo, 307
Bandura, Albert, 94
Bangladesh factory collapse, 281
Bannerji, Himani, 29, 62, 326
Baron-Cohen, Simon, 88, 112
Bashevkin, Sylvia, 326
Basran, Gurjinder, 23
bath, ritual, 254
Bauer, Nancy, 13
Beaman, Lori G., et al., 268
beauty industry, 15–16, 17, 108
beauty pageants, child, 15
Bechdel, Alison, 23
"Bechdel test," 94
beguinages, 142
Behn, Aphra, 22
Bem, Sandra, 95, 99
Berger, Maurice, et al., 81
Berkman, Alexander, 43
Beyoncé, 18
bhakti movement, 265
Bhutto, Benazir, 307
bible, 10
Bill C-36, 278
Bin Al-Mustakfi, Walladah, 222
biology, evolutionary, 92–3
biopsychosocial approach, 208
Bird-Wilson, Lisa, 23
birth control, 192
blacklist, 13
Black Lives Matter, 319, 320
black people: education and, 233–4; feminism and, 48, 56, 72, 76; marriage and, 139; *see also* people of colour; women of colour
Blayney, Candace, and Karen Blotnicky, 282
Blee, Kathleen, 311
blogs: feminist, 24; mothering, 168
Boden, Alison, 257
bodhisattvas, 251

bodies: of colour, 110–11; feminism and, 108–11, 118–21; gender and, 107–23; idealized, 7; images of, 15–18; modifications to, 118
Bodman, Bridget, 284
Boisjoly, Hélène, 189
Bollywood cinema, 24–8
Book of the City of Ladies, The, 222
Bordo, Susan, 109, 115, 122
Bornstein, Kate, 103, 108
Bosnian War, 197–8
Boston Women's Health Collective, 11
Botswana: girls' education in, 228
Boulding, Elise, 322, 326
Bourgeois, Roy, 259
boys: bullying and, 228
brain: gender and, 88–90, 92–3, 111–13
"brain gain," 234
Brand, Dionne, 23, 46, 62
Breast Cancer Society of Canada, 204
breastfeeding, 168, 169, 171–2
brideprice/bridewealth, 130
British Columbia: sterilization in, 193; vote in, 59
British Columbia Human Rights Code, 292
Brizendine, Louann, 112
Brock University, 230
Bromley, Victoria L., 57
Brooks, David, 17
Brooks, Gwendolyn, 246
Brown, Rosemary, 308
Buddhism, 35, 142, 248, 251; feminist, 266; missionaries of, 261; reincarnation and, 250
bulimia, 17
bullying, 228
Bunch, Charlotte, 47
burka, 257
Burnham, Libby, 313
butch, 84
Butler, Judith, 100–1, 105, 119–20, 265
Butler, Octavia, 95

Caesarean section, 194
Calder, Gillian, and Lori G. Beaman, 154
Campbell, Kim, 307

Canada: families in, 146, 148, 149; health-care system in, 187; HIV/AIDS in, 204–5; non-religious in, 253; women in politics in, 307–8; women's vote in, 37, 59
Canadian Alliance to Repeal the Abortion Law, 193
Canadian Armed Forces, 284
Canadian Broadcasting Corporation (CBC), 179–80
Canadian Centre for Policy Alternatives, 283
Canadian Human Rights Act, 294
Canadian Institute for Health Information, 206
Canadian Labour Congress, 293
Canadian Race Relations Foundation, 226
Canadian Research Institute for the Advancement of Women, 78
Canadian Socialist League, 42
Canadian Women Artists History Initiative, 29
Canadian Women in Trades, 65
Canadian Women's Press Club, 320
Canadian Women's Studies, 57
cancer, 191, 204; breast, 204; cervical, 204
Cannon, M., and L. Sunseri, 57
Cantor, Aviva, 266
capitalism, 43; ecofeminism and, 51; feminism and, 40, 41; globalization and, 288; social labour and, 273; unpaid work and, 287–8; work and, 276–91
capitalist mode of production, 276–91
career mystique, 274
Caregiver Program, 128
caregiving, 128, 137–8, 176–7, 287–8; gender and, 188; paid, 278–9
Carr, Emily, 20
Carson, Rachel, 240, 241
Cartesian dualism, 109
Carty, Linda, and Chandra Mohanty, 71, 78
Casa, Lidia, 194
caste system, 265
"castration anxiety," 88

Catalyst Accord, 179, 287
categories, co-constitutive, 60, 63, 73
Catholic Family and Rights Institute, 257
Catholic Network for Women's Equality, 265
celibacy, 144
CEOs: women as, 287, 288
Cheal, David, and Patrizia Albanese, 154
Ch'en Hung-mou, 223
Chenresig, 251
Chesler, Phyllis, 206, 207
childbirth, 169, 171; death in, 39, 171; medicalization of, 190, 191, 194–5
child care, 273–4; women in politics and, 312
"child-free by choice," 151
children: families and, 135–7; Indigenous, 130, 162, 233; marriage and, 130–1; sexualization of, 15
child support, 142
Childs, Sarah, and Lena Krook, 311
China: factory work in, 279; families in, 136; women in politics in, 307; women's education in, 223
Chipman, Ward, 180–1
chlamydia, 204
Chodorow, Nancy, 50
Christ, Carol, 250
Christianity, 142, 248, 249, 251; education and, 222–3; feminist, 267; fundamentalist, 256–7; god in, 252; immortality and, 250; Indigenous culture and, 265, 306; missionaries and, 261; protection of women and, 255; sexuality and, 36; socialism and, 42; women leaders in, 259
Christian Science, 262
chromosomes, 113–14
Church of England, 259
cisgender, 8–9
Cixous, Hélène, 21, 50, 118
Clark, Joe, 134
Clarke, Cheryl, 48
Clarke, Edward, 86

class: bourgeois, 41; intersectionality and, 60–3; marriage and, 138, 140; motherhood and, 166–7; paid domestic labour and, 279; pay and, 69; work and, 276–7; *see also* working class
clothing: gender and, 7; gender-neutral, 95; production of, 276
Clotilda, 261
co-constitutive categories, 60, 63, 73
Code Pink, 322
coeducation, 238
cognitive-developmental theory, 93–4
cohabitation, 147–8
Colette, Sidonie-Gabrielle, 161
collectives, women's, 142–3
Collins, Patricia Hill, 48, 72, 162; and Sirma Bilge, 78
Collins, Suzanne, 160
colonialism, 64; families and, 129–30; missionaries and, 261; women and, 148; women's education and, 223–4
colonial settler states, 59, 129
Colour of Poverty Coalition, 307–8
colours: gender and, 7
columbite-tantalite, 198
communities: alternative, 142–5; experimental, 143–5; factory, 143; laboring, 142–3; religious, 142; utopian, 143–5
community colleges, 235; *see also* universities
Comte, Auguste, 39
"Concubinage Circular," 148
condoms, 205–6
Conference on Population and Development, 324
Confucianism, 248; feminist, 266
Confucius, 35
Congress of Black Women of Canada, 60
consensual unions, 147–8
conservatism: political, 311–12; religious, 254–5, 257
consumption: women and, 15–18
contraception, 192
Convention for the Elimination of All Forms of Discrimination against Women (CEDAW), 186, 310, 323
Cooper, Anna Julia, 65, 66, 67, 77
corporations: women executives in, 287, 288
corpus callosum, 89, 112
Council of Canadians, 187
Couric, Katie, 19
coverture, 164
Coyote, 84
Crawford, Mary, 303
Crenshaw, Kimberlé, 48, 61, 75, 78; feminist organizations and, 70–1
crime: hate, 104, 197; sex, 197; war, 148
Criminal Code, 192, 193
critical race theory, 319
"Cult of True Womanhood," 85–6
cults, 255; witch, 259
culture: definition of, 6; gender representation and, 5–30; language and, 8–9; popular, 12–15; women's/men's, 46; women's sexuality in, 12–15
"culture wars," 237
curers, 260
Curie, Marie, 238–9, 240
curriculum: gender and, 237–8
Cusk, Rachel, 168
cybernetics, 47

Dalhousie University, 230, 292
Daly, Mary, 46, 250
Dames Making Games, 24
Dasko, Donna, 313–15
Davis, Angela, 48, 57, 66–7, 78
Dawkins, Richard, 86
daycare, 279, 295; cost of, 274
de Beauvoir, Simone, 44–5, 46, 57, 81, 105, 180; bodies and, 109–10; wave metaphor and, 35
Declaration of Sentiments, 139
de Gouges, Olympe, 39, 217
D'Eon, Charles, 102
Delany, Samuel R., 91
dementia, 206
Demerson, Velma, 148
Democratic Republic of Congo (DRC), 198, 199
Denmark, Florence, 294
de Pizan, Christine, 222
depression, 208–9
Derrida, Jacques, 49
DES (diethystilbestrol), 191
Des Jardins, Julie, 239
de-skilling, 290
development: ideology of, 51
Diagnostic and Statistical Manual of Mental Disorders, 196, 206
diaspora, South Asian, 25–6, 27
Dickey Young, Pamela, et al., 268
Diderot, Denis, 37
Diefenbaker, John, 308
difference: bodies and, 111–14; intersectionality and, 60, 68
Dinnerstein, Dorothy, 51
disabilities: women with, 63, 196, 209
DisAbled Women's Network Canada, 60, 63, 196
"discourse," 49; bodies and, 114–15; sexuality and, 115–17
discrimination: in education, 285; in employment, 294–5
division of labour, gendered, 139, 271, 272–3
divorce, 132, 141–2, 174; children and, 135, 136; religion and, 255; settlements and, 135
Dixon, Marlene, 60
Doctor, Farzana, 23
domestic mode of production, 275–6
domestic partners, 147–8
dominance: intersectionality and, 60; male, 306; power and, 302
domination: "matrix of," 72
Dominion Women's Enfranchisement Association, 317
Doolittle, Hilda, 22
"double day," 135, 287, 312
doulas, 194
Dove Campaign for Real Beauty, 16
dowry, 130, 255
drag shows, 120
Dressler, William W., 203
Dryden, OmiSoore H., and Suzanne Lenon, 105–6

Dua, Enakshi, 127, 154; and Angela Robertson, 78–9
dualism, mind/body, 109
Dworkin, Andrea, 11
Dyer, Mary, 261
dystopias, 144

Eagly, Alice, 99
Earth Summit, 324
eating disorders, 16; men and, 17
Eating Disorders Action Group, 183
Ebadi, Shirin, 321
ecofeminism, 50–1, 56
École Polytechnique Massacre, 239
Eddy, Mary Baker, 262
education, 215–44; access to, 220, 235–8; barriers to, 233–5; gender discrimination in, 285; gender disparities in, 226, 227–32; knowledge and, 217–18; marriage and, 146; multicultural, 234–5; parity in, 218, 219; post-secondary, 226, 228–31, 231–2, 236; primary, 226, 227; secondary, 227; sexuality, 195; women's, 38, 39, 86; women's achievements in, 238–41; women's history of, 220–5
Edwards, Henrietta Muir, 318
Egale Canada, 197, 226
Egypt: ancient, 220; Arab Spring in, 306–7, 323; female genital cutting in, 200
Ehrenrich, Barbara, and Arlie Russell Hochschild, 197
Einstein, Albert, 239
Eisenstein, Zillah, 70
elders: care of, 176–7, 287; families and, 137–8; health of, 209–10
Eleanor of Aquitaine, 305
electoral systems, 313, 315
Eliot, George, 22
Elizabeth I, 222, 306
Elliot, Missy, 14
embodiment, 108
Émile, 222–3
employment: self-, 290–1; women's, 137, 146, 177; *see also* work
Employment Equity Act, 294

Employment Insurance (EI), 294–5
Engels, Friedrich, 41, 133
Enlightenment, 37, 252
Enloe, Cynthia, 197–8, 317
Enough Project/Moment, 199
entail, 164
environment: feminism and, 50–1; gender and, 92–3
epigenetics, 92–3, 185–6
equality: education and, 218, 219; legal, 318–20
Equal Pay Coalition, 65
Equal Pay Day, 271
Equal Rights Amendment, 256
Equal Voice, 313–15, 326
equity, employment, 69, 294, 295
erotic, 118
essentialism, strategic, 60
Estol, Pamela Kramer, 238
estrogen, 89, 191
Eternia, 15
Ethiopia: female genital cutting in, 200
ethnic studies, 234–5
ethnicity: health and, 203; motherhood and, 166–7; suffrage laws and, 59
Etienne, Yannick, 289
eugenics, 86
Eugenics Board, 193
European Court of Justice, 294
European Union: employment equity in, 294, 295
Eve and Adam story, 9–10
evolution: gender and, 84–6, 92–3
exchange: domestic mode of production and, 276
experimentation, medical, 187
Export Development Zones, 289
e-zines, feminist, 24

factory work, 143, 279–82
Fahs, Breanne, 144
Fairclough, Ellen, 308
false consciousness, 49
Falubert, Gustave, 141
families, 126–54; black feminism and, 48; blended, 146, 173; daughters in, 162–3; dual-earner, 146, 274; in early twenty-first century, 145–6; extended, 127, 129–42, 145; female lone-parent, 141; liberal feminism and, 37–8; lone-parent, 141, 146–7; multigenerational, 145; multiracial, 148–9; "new," 146–52; nuclear, 127, 129–42, 145; recent changes in, 129; religion and, 253–5; same-sex, 149; step-, 146; transnational, 150–1; trends in, 145–6
"Famous Five," 318
fascism: women and, 312
fashion, 16–17
FAST Campaign, 281
"fatherland," 316
"father-right," 45
Fausto-Sterling, Anne, 89, 122
feet, deformed, 16
Female Brain, The, 112, 113
female genital cutting (FGC), 199–201
female sexual arousal disorder, 196
femininity: language and, 9
feminism: black, 48, 56, 72, 76; body and, 108–11, 118–21; classical liberal, 37–40; contemporary, 45–56; contemporary debates in, 45–52; contemporary liberal, 40–1, 55; contemporary socialist, 43–4; corporeal, 119; cultural, 45–8, 50–1, 55; definition of, 38; development of, 65–8; family and, 48, 127; gender and, 90–3; global, 322–4; goddess worship and, 251–2; history of, 31, 34–45; intersectionality and, 60–3, 68–71; labels and, 54; Marxist, 41–4; maternal, 42–3, 50–1; pornography and, 11–12; post-modern, 48; psychoanalytic, 49–50; radical, 45–8, 55; religion and, 248, 266–7; scholarship and, 72–5, 217–18; socialist, 40–4, 55; transnational, 51–2, 56, 71; twenty-first century, 35; types of, 35, 37–56; "waves" of, 34–5; workplace issues and, 295

Feministe website, 12
Feminist Frequency, 24
"feminist standpoint epistemology," 54
feminization: teaching and, 231
femme, 84
Fern, Fanny, 22
Fernández, Cristina, 307
fibre arts, 19
Fiedler, Maureen, 250
film: gender in, 94; Indian, 24–8
Finnbogadóttir, Vigdís, 307
Fiorenza, Elisabeth Schussler, 250
Firestone, Shulamith, 46–7
first-past-the-post system, 315
Fitzgerald, Maureen, and Scott Rayter, 106
Fleras, Augie, 29
flextime, 295
Fliegel, Zenia, 90–1
Flynn, Elizabeth Gurley, 320
food: processing of, 276; production of, 275–6
formula, baby, 172
foster parents, 173
Foucault, Michel, 49, 115, 121
fourth wave, 34
France: assimilation in, 235; secularism in, 257
Franklin, Ursula, 239, 322
"free" labour, 277
French Revolution, 39, 217
Freud, Sigmund, 49–50, 86–8, 90, 92, 116
Friedan, Betty, 140, 239
Friedl, Ernestine, 306
Friedman, Joan, 260
Frize, Monique, 243
fundamentalism, 256–7, 311–12
Furtado, Nellie, 13

Galen, 85, 188–9
"GamerGate," 24, 292
gaming, 24
Gandhi, Indira, 307
Gargi Vachaknavi, 260
Garry, Ann, 76
Gaskell, Elizabeth, 143
Gaunyin, 251
Gay Liberation movement, 83, 84
gay men, 119–20; eating disorders and, 17; gender and, 103; hormones and, 89; *see also* LGBTQ people
gaze, male, 16
Gbowee, Leymah, 300, 321, 323
gender, 80–106; alternative arrangements of, 101–4; ancient and early modern ideas on, 33, 35–7; bodies and, 107–23; construction of, 6–7; cultural representation and, 5–10; defining, 3–4; doing, 90, 99; enforcement of, 101; explanations for differences in, 84–90; health care and, 188–90; intersectionality and, 60–3; language and, 8–9; learning of, 93–101; mental health and, 206–7; sex and, 82–3, 100–1; sexuality and, 84, 117; social interactions and, 99–100; terms for, 117; third, 104; values and, 53; violence and, 196–201; as voluntary, 103–4; work division and, 271, 272–3; *see also* boys; girls; men; women
gender conformity, 101
gender expression, 83–4, 117
"gender frames," 73–4
gender identity, 82–3, 117
gender non-conformity, 82, 84, 101
gender roles, 99–100
gender schemas, 94
gender schema theory, 95, 99
gender studies, 1, 3, 4, 241; intersectionality and, 59, 60–3, 71; research and, 73–5
Geneva Conventions, 198
genitalia, 113–14
genocide, 198
Germany: *see* Nazi Germany
Ghomeshi, Jian, 197
ghosts, 249–50
"GI Bill," 235
Gilman, Charlotte Perkins, 144
Gines, Kathryn, 76
"girl power," 18, 156–7
girls, 156–64; education of, 227–8; "missing," 216; names of, 160; sexualization of, 15; value of, 158–60; work of, 160–1
Girls, Women + Media Project, 24
"glass ceiling/wall/cliff," 287
globalization: families and, 145, 150–1, 162–3; work and, 271, 288–90
Global North, 51–2; abortion in, 193; families in, 145–6
Global South, 51–2; abortion in, 193; families in, 145; health-care movement in, 187–8; women's education in, 225–6, 228
Global Trade Watch, 322
goddesses, 250–2; feminist, 251–2
godmothers, 173
Goldenberg, Naomi, 250
Goldman, Emma, 12, 43, 320
Gonish, Marnina, and Susanne Gannon, 180
Good for Her Feminist Porn Awards, 12
Goodall, Jane, 241
Gordimer, Nadine, 23
Gould, Stephen Jay, 88–9, 240
government: families and, 127–8; gender registration and, 104; heterosexism and, 64; religion and, 248; types of, 305
grandparenthood, 176
Grant, Agnes, 243
grassroots activism, 322–4
Great Depression, 280
Greece, ancient, 220
Greenham Common, 322
Grimké, Angelina Weld, 22
Grimké, Sarah, 262
gross domestic product (GDP), 271
Grosz, Elizabeth, 119, 121
guilds, 278

Hadassah, 264
Haile, Margaret, 42, 320
Haiti: factory work in, 289
Halberstam, J. Jack, 13–14
Hall, Stuart, 6
Hamdan, Amani, 268

harassment: levels of, 292; sexual, 230; workplace, 285, 291–2
"hard-wired," 113
Harding, Sandra, 54, 66
Harper, Laureen, 134
Harper, Stephen, 300
Hartmann, Heidi, 43
Hasina, Sheikh, 256
hate crimes, 104, 197
healing, 247, 260
health, 182–212; aging and, 173–4; definition of, 184–5; definition of women's, 184–6; disparities in, 201–3; human rights and, 186; maternal, 185; mental, 203, 206–7; reproductive, 192
Health on the Net Foundation, 195
health-care movements, 187–8
health-care systems, 186–8; gender and, 188–90; two-tiered, 187
health status, 201–2
heart disease, 202, 203–4
Hegel, G.W.F., 33
Henley, N.M., 99–100
Herland, 144
heroism: gender and, 21–2
heternormativity, 63–5, 84
heteronationalism, 64
heteropatriarchy, 64, 305
heterosexism, 63–5
heterosexuality, compulsory, 64
Heyzer, Noeleen, 271
Highway, Tomson, 10
hijras, 84
Hildegard of Bingen, 221
Hinduism, 248, 265; goddesses in, 250; reincarnation and, 250; women leaders in, 260
Hingis, Martina, 18
HIV/AIDS, 186, 196, 204–6; gender and, 104
Hochschild, Arlie, and Anne Machung, 135
Holy Ghost, 251
homicides, intimate-partner, 196
homophobia, 48, 70, 207; education and, 228
homosexuality, 206; black people and, 48; as term, 116; *see also* gay men; lesbians; LGBTQ people

"honour killing," 197
hooks, bell, 48, 61, 65, 66, 71; families and, 127; wave metaphor and, 35
hormone replacement therapy, 191, 204
hormones, 113–14; childbirth and, 169; gender and, 88–90
Horney, Karen, 91
hospitality sector, 282
Hossain, Rokeya Sakhawat, 143–4, 304
"Hottentot Venus," 110
households: types of, 128, 129
housework, 135, 273, 287–8; paid, 278–9, 290
housing: transitions in, 176–7
Houston, Leah, 281
How Schools Shortchange Girls, 228
Hroswitha of Gandersheim, 220
Hudson, Sandy, 319
Hudson's Bay Company, 148
human papillomavirus (HPV), 204
human trafficking, 277–8, 290
Hume, David, 37
Humphrey, John, 186
Hunt, Shauna, 19
Hurston, Zora Neale, 62
Huston, Perdita, 154
Hutchinson, Anne, 261
Hwang, David, 111
Hyde, Edward, 102
Hypatia, 36, 220
hypothalamus, 89
hysterectomies, 183, 206

ideas: ancient and early modern, 33, 35–7; importance of, 32–4
identity: dominant, 74; gender, 82–3, 117; intersectionality and, 59, 60, 72–3; sexual, 115–16
Igbo people, 306
illiteracy, 216, 218–20
images: "body beautiful" and, 15–18; contemporary feminist, 20; gender and, 9–10; reality and, 18–20
immigrants: education and, 234; factory work and, 279; families and, 127–8, 150–1, 167;

heteronormativity and, 64; *see also* migration
immortality, 250
incest, 130
income: families and, 141, 146; *see also* pay; wages
India: education in, 224; film in, 24–8; politics in, 308, 310; women's trade union in, 293
Indian Act, 59, 129–30, 148
Indian Rights for Indian Women, 60
Indigenous people: education and, 233; gender and, 84; government of, 305; incarceration of, 210; infant mortality and, 195; legends of, 10, 249; religion and, 252; residential schools and, 187, 233; "60s scoop" and, 162; vote and, 59, 308; *see also* specific groups
Indigenous women, 68; Christianity and, 265, 306; as elders, 137; healing and, 260; marriage and, 129–30, 139, 141, 148; as midwives, 190; missing and murdered, 60, 300; poverty and, 202; rights of, 129–30; sexual assault and, 197; vote and, 59; as writers, 22–3; *see also* specific groups
indivisibility: principle of, 70
Industrial Revolution, 41
inequalities, economic, 271, 275
infanticide, 157–8
influence: power and, 302–3, 305
inheritance, 163–4
Inquisition, 258
instinct, maternal, 169–70
Institute for Critical Studies in Gender and Health, 61
Institute for Intersectionality Research and Policy, 61
Institute of Medicine, 208
insults, gendered, 9
Inter-American Convention on the Prevention, Punishment and Eradiation of Violence against Women, 324
INTERCEDE, 279
Interim Federal Health Care program, 187

International Criminal Tribunals, 198
International Labour Organization, 283
International Ladies Garment Worker Union, 279
International Monetary Fund, 289
International Woman Suffrage Alliances, 321–2
International Women's Day, 42
Internet: activism and, 322; health information and, 195; women's representation and, 23–4
intersectionality, 1, 35, 58–79; black feminism and, 48; debates over, 75–7; global, 70–1; historical foundations of, 65–8; policy and, 69–70; as term, 75; weak/strong, 74
intersex people, 82, 83, 103; language and, 8
intimate-partner violence, 196
Inuit: art of, 19; vote and, 308
Irigaray, Luce, 50, 118
Iroquois people: decision making by, 306; origin story of, 249
Irving, Dan, and Rupert Raj, 326
Isis (goddess), 251
Islam, 248, 249, 257; feminist, 266, 267; fundamentalist, 256; god in, 252; immorality and, 250; marriage and, 132; menstruation and, 253–4; women in, 222, 255, 265–6
Islamophobia, 70
Israel: kibbutz movement in, 144–5

Jackson, Janet, 12
Jackson, Laura (Riding), 22
Jackson, Stevi, 64
Jaffer, Fatima, 62
Jahjaga, Atifete, 256
Jamieson, Roberta, 233
Japan: families in, 146; wartime sex crimes and, 197
Jaskoski, Helen, 183
Jeffrey, Shirley, 259
Jepsen, Carly Rae, 13
Jews, 111; *see also* Judaism
Jiang Qing, 303

Joan of Arc, 102, 258
Joe, Rita, 23
Johnson, Samuel, 33
Joliot-Curie, Irene, 239
Jordan, June, 300
Joseph, Gloria, 162
Ju/'hoansi people, 205
Judaism, 248, 249, 251; feminist, 266, 267; god in, 252; inheritance and, 163; menstruation and, 254; protection of women and, 255; women and, 264; women leaders in, 260
Julien, Pauline, 12

Kabbalah, 264
Kabul University, 226
Kali, 250
Kannon, 251
Kant, Immanuel, 37
Karman, Tawakkol, 321, 323
Keller, Evelyn Fox, 92–3
Kerber, Linda, 319
kibbutz movement, 144–5
Kilbourne, Jean, 16
Kimmel, Michael, et al., 122
King, Larry, 19
King, Ynestra, 51
Kinsey, Alfred, 11, 116
Klein, Bonnie Sherr, 161
Klein, Naomi, 161
knowledge: bodies and, 114–15; politics of, 216; theories of, 52, 53–5, 56; women's traditional, 217
Kollontai, Alexandra, 42, 180
Komarovsky, Mirra, 140
Kono people, 200–1
Koonz, Claudia, 311
Krishna, 265
Kristeva, Julia, 50
Kristof, Nicholas D., and Sheryl WuDunn, 216
Ku Klux Klan, 311
Kumaratunga, Chandrika, 307

labour: "free," 277; gendered division of, 139, 271, 272–3; social, 273; *see also* employment; work
Lacan, Jacques, 92

Lacks, Henrietta, 188
Ladies Home Journal, 7
Ladner, Joyce, 319–20
Lady Gaga, 13–14
"Ladyland," 143–4
Lamott, Anne, 168
Langton, Anne, 224
language: bodies and, 114–15; cisgender, 8–9; culture and, 8–9; feminism and, 50; gender and, 81–2; gender-neutral, 227; ideas and, 32, 34; Indigenous, 8
Laqueur, Thomas, 106
Larsen, Nella, 22
lateralization, brain, 112
Latin America: women in politics in, 307
Lavigne, Avril, 13
law: women and, 318–20
Leadership Conference of Women Religious, 264–5
Lee, Ann, 144
Lee, Becky R., and Terry Tak-ling, 268–9
Lee, Jen Sookfong, 23
Lee, Richard, 205
lesbianism, 47–8
lesbians: adoption and, 69; feminism and, 63–4; gender and, 103; hormones and, 89; as mothers, 172; *see also* LGBTQ people
lesbophobia, 48
Letherby, Gayle, 243
LeVay, Simon, 89
Lévi-Strauss, Claude, 48
LGBTQ people: children and, 172; education and, 226; families and, 149; gender and, 103; music and, 13; sexual harassment and, 230; violence against, 197; widowhood and, 175–6; *see also* gay men; lesbians; transgender people
liberalism: classical, 37–40; contemporary, 40–1, 55
life-course approach, 185–6
life-work balance, 286
L'il Kim, 14
literature: women and, 20–3
Live-in Caregiver Program, 128, 279

"living apart together," 150
Livingston, Jennie, 119–20
Loblaws, 281
Logan McCallum, Mary Jane, 297
Longino, Helen, 53
Lopez, Jennifer, 17, 18
Lorde, Audre, 34, 59, 61, 63, 66, 67–8, 73; erotic and, 118; homophobia and, 48; *Sister Outsider*, 106
Lotus Sutra, The, 250
love: marriage and, 141
Lovelace, Sandra, 129
Loving (film), 150
Loving v. Virginia, 149, 150
Lowell, MA, 143
Lugones, Maria, 75
Lumb, Jean, 148
Luxemburg, Rosa, 321
Luxton, Meg, and Mary Jane Mossman, 244

Maathai, Wangari Muta, 321
Macaulay, Catharine, 222
McClintock, Ann, 316
McClintock, Barbara, 241
McClung, Nellie, 303, 317, 318
MacDonald, Noni, 189
McKinney, Louise, 318
MacKinnon, Catharine, 11, 100
Mactavish, Anne, 187
McTeer, Maureen, 134
Maddow, Rachel, 19
Mad Men, 139
Madonna, 165
Madonna (performer), 12
Mahmood, Saba, 266
Maicom, Linzi, and Shirley Walters, 244
"mail-order bride," 290
Maimonides, 36–7
maintenance: households and, 276
Malacrida, Claudia, and Jacqueline Low, 122–3
"male-bodied," 120
male gaze, 16
Man, Guida, and Rina Cohen, 297
management: women in, 287, 288
Mandell, Nancy, and Ann Duffy, 154

Manitoba: women's vote in, 303
maquiladoras, 289
Maracle, Lee, 22–3, 68
Marcos, Sylvia, et al., 269
marriage, 127, 129–35; age at, 152; alternatives to 142–5; arranged, 130, 131; common-law, 138; companionate, 139; "complex," 144; cross-cousin, 131; history of, 138–41; individualized, 141; interracial, 139, 150; levirate, 131; multiracial, 148–9, 150; partners in, 131–2; reasons for, 130–1; same-sex, 147, 149; types of, 132–3; "women,"151
"marriage gap," 146
martyrs, 260–1
Marx, Karl, 41, 49
Marxism, 43; feminism and, 41–4
Mary, 251
Mascia-Lees, Frances, and Patricia Sharpe, 118
masculine mystique, 274
masculinity, 74; language and, 9
Masters, William, and Virginia E. Johnson, 11, 116–17
matchmakers, 131
maternity leave, 294–5
mathematics, 240–1
matrilocal society, 141
"matrix of domination," 72
May, Vivian M., 79
Mayo, Katherine, 25
M. Butterfly, 111
MC Lyte, 14
Mead, Margaret, 86, 87, 156
media: motherhood and, 167–8
Media Smarts, 29
medicalization, 190–6
medical profession, 189; women in, 228–9
Medici, Catherine de, 222
Mehta, Deepa, 27
Meir, Golda, 307
men: aging and, 173; beauty industry and, 15–16; domestic mode of production and, 275–6; eating disorders and, 17; educational access and, 236–7; education of, 220; health of, 201–2, 203; as

"ideal," 3; knowledge and, 217, 218; language and, 8; as medical experts, 188, 189; paternity leave and, 138; religion and, 254, 255; remarriage and, 175; retirement and, 177, 178; science and, 239; in service sector, 282; sexual assault of, 197–8, 198–9; unpaid work and, 274; wage gap and, 282–3; work and, 271, 272–3; *see also* gay men
Menchú, Rigoberta, 321
menopause, 190, 191–2
menstruation, 190, 191; religion and, 253–4
mental health, 203, 206–7
Merchant, Carolyn, 50
Merkel, Angela, 307
Métis people, 148
Mhenni, Lina Ben, 323
Michie Mee, 14–15
midwives, 190, 194, 260
migration: families and, 150–1; globalization and, 290; *see also* immigrants
Mikkonen, Juha, and Dennis Raphael, 212
mikveh, 254
military: women in, 284
Mill, John Stuart, 39–40
Millett, Kate, 45–6
Mills, Mary, 259
Minaj, Nicki, 14, 18
Mira/Mirabai, 265
misogyny: music business and, 14–15; post-modern feminism and, 49; radical feminism and, 45
"missing daughters," 216
missionaries: women as, 260–1
Mitchell, Juliet, 50
Mitchell, Penni, 326–7
modes of production: capitalist, 276–91; domestic, 275–6
Mohanty, Chandra, 2; colonialism and, 148; transnational feminism and, 51, 52, 76–7
Mojab, Shahrzad, 62
Molyneux, Maxine, 311
Money, John, 82; and Anke Ehrhardt, 82

monogamy, 133
monotheism, 249, 252
Monroe, Alice, 22
Montgomery, Lucy Maud, 43
Montreal Massacre, 239
Monture, Patricia, 62
Moore, Holly, 154
More, Thomas, 143
Morgentaler, Henry, 193
Morissette, Alanis, 13
Mormons: marriage and, 132, 133
mortality: infant, 195, 216; maternal, 39, 171, 188, 194
Mosque Movement, 265–6
motherhood, 109–11, 164–73, 176; feminism, and, 42–3, 50–1; girls and, 161–2; images of, 164–8
Mother India, 25, 27
"motherland," 316
Mothers against Nuclear Disarmament, 50–1
Mott, Lucretia Coffin, 138–9, 262
Muir, Leilani, 186
Mukherjee, Arun, 62
Mundugumor people, 87
Murphy, Emily, 318
music: gay role models in, 13; images of women and, 12–15
Myradal, Alva, 321
myths: gender and, 84–5; Greek, 10; images of women in, 9–10; Indigenous, 10, 249

Nakanishi, Toyoko, 183
Namaste, Vivien, 123
names, female, 160
Napoleon Bonaparte, 33
Narayan, Uma, 52
Nargis, 27
National Aboriginal Council of Midwives, 190
National Action Committee, 47
National Council of Jewish Women of Canada, 264
National Council of Women in Canada, 320
National Day of Remembrance and Action on Violence against Women, 239

National Right to Life Committee, 257
National Task Force on Women and Depression, 208
nationalism, 316
nations, gendered, 316
Native Women's Association of Canada, 60, 129
nature: bodies and, 109–11
Naugler, Diane, 106
Nazi Germany, 111, 197, 311
Neigh, Scott, 327
Nemat, Marina, 23
Nestle, Joan, 84
Nestlé (company), 172
networks, women's, 294
Newfoundland: vote in, 59
"new religious movements," 256
New Zealand, 37, 318
Nicholas, Jane, 29
niqab, 257
Nobel Prize, 22, 321
Noel, Jan, 2
non-religious people, 252–3
Nordberg, Jenny, 159
normalization: heterosexuality and, 64
norms, 7
North America: marriage in, 138–41
North American Network in Aging Studies, 180
Norway: women in politics in, 310
"not-men," 120
nuclear test ban, 322
nuns, 142, 264–5
Nzinga, "King," 102

Obama, Michelle, 17
objectification: bodies and, 108
occupational health risks, 203
Oedipal complex, 88
"office worker," 282
Okin, Susan Moller, 38
Olokun, 252
Ontario Medical College for Women, 229
Ontario Women's Health Council, 184–5
Oppenheimer, Robert, 239

oppression: intersectionality and, 60–3; privilege and, 59–60
Organization of the Islamic Conference, 257
organizations: feminist, 60, 70–1, 295; professional, 293–4; women's, 320
Organized Working Women Ontario, 65
orgasm, 11, 50, 116–17
origin stories, 249
osteoporosis, 206
"othermothering," 173
Our Bodies, Ourselves, 11, 183
outsourcing, 282
Overall, Christine, 151

Pacific, Robin, 281
Page, Ellen, 115
"palimony," 135
Panchayat Raj Act, 308, 310
Pandora, 10
Pankhurst, Emmeline, 161–2
parental leave, 138, 170, 294–5
parenting, 168–70
Paris Is Burning, 119–20
parity: education and, 218, 219
Parlby, Irene, 318
parthenogenesis, 144
paternity leave, 138
patriarchy, 43; patterns of, 306–7; radical feminism and, 45–6, 47; religion and, 267
patronymics, 160
Pauktuutit, 60
pay: equal, 271, 295; women's, 69; *see also* income; wages
peace: women and, 168, 321–2
Pearson, Lester, 318
"penis envy," 49, 87–8, 91
people of colour: education and, 234–5; health and, 203; immigrant, 234; representation of, 7; *see also* race; women of colour
"Perfectionists," 144
performance: bodies and, 119–20
performativity theory, 100–1
Perón, Eva, 303
Perón, Isabel, 307

"personal is political," 46, 301
Persons case, 318
Petchesky, Rosalind P., 69–70, 77
phallus, 92
"phat," 18
Philip, M. NourbeSe, 21
Philippine Women Centre of B.C., 290
philosophies, contemporary feminist, 52–6
physics, 239
Piercy, Marge, 23, 143
Piety Movement, 265–6
Planned Parenthood, 71
Plaskow, Judith, 250
Plato, 35–6, 143
policy: intersectionality and, 69–70; public, 301
"political correctness," 237
politicians: marriage and, 134
politics: local v. federal, 307; power and, 301–7; threshold of women in, 310; women and, 299–327
polyandry, 132
polygamy, 132
polygyny, 131, 132–3
polytheism, 252
pornography, 11–12; "feminist," 12
positionality, 54
post-modernism, 48
post-structuralism, 48, 54, 55, 56
poverty: child, 284; childbirth and, 195; divorce and, 141–2; health and, 202; mental health and, 208; women's education and, 226
power: definition of, 301–2; dominance and, 302; intersectionality and, 60; political, 301–7
precarious worker, 283–4
pregnancy, 170–1, 191; control of, 192–3
pregnancy leave, 294–5
presenteeism, 286
Pride Toronto, 117
prime minister: spouse of, 303
primogeniture, 164, 305–6
Prince Edward Island: abortion in, 69, 193

prison: women in, 210
privilege: oppression and, 59–60
professions: legal, 320; "male," 285; medical, 189, 228–9; organizations of, 293–4; women in, 284–7; "women's," 284
pronouns, 8–9, 81–2
proportional representation, 315
Protestantism: women and, 261–4; women leaders in, 259
Protestant Reformation, 258–9
provinces: cohabitation in, 148; health-care system in, 187; HIV/AIDS in, 205; vote in, 59
psychoanalysis, 49–50, 56; feminist, 90–2; gender and, 86–8
psychology, evolutionary, 86
"psychosexual development," 86–8
Puar, Jasbir, 70, 76
puberty, 253
Public Health Agency of Canada, 203, 204
Public Safety Canada, 278
Puerto Rico, 193
Pugliesi, Karen, 207
Purim, 102

Quakers, 261–2
Quebec: daycare in, 274; families in, 138, 148; marriage in, 160; as nation, 316; sovereignty in, 60; vote in, 59; women's education in, 229–30
Queen Latifah, 14
Quran, 10, 222

race: brain and, 112; education and, 233–4; families and, 127–8, 148–9; health and, 202, 203; intersectionality and, 60–3; mental health and, 208; motherhood and, 166–7; *see also* ethnicity; people of colour; women of colour
racism: education and, 226; Marxism and, 43
Rafaat, Azita, 159
Raging Grannies, 174, 180
Rajiva, Mythili, and Sheila Batacharya, 180

Rana Plaza factory collapse, 281
rape, 196–7; colonialism and, 148; in marriage, 127; pregnancy and, 300; "systematic mass," 197–8; wartime, 197–9
rape culture, 230
Raphael, 36
rationality, women's, 37, 52
reality: construction of, 6, 7; images and, 18–20
Redstockings collective, 46
refugees: health care and, 187; women as, 209
Reid, Bill, 269
Reik, Theodor, 33
reincarnation, 250
religion, 222–3, 245–69; as alternative to family, 142; conservative, 254–5, 257; definition of, 246–7; education and, 220, 220; female genital cutting and, 199–200; human rights and, 257; images of women in, 9–10; marriage and, 144; social controls and, 253–9; social reform and, 247–8; women leaders in, 247; world, 248
religious movements: women and, 255–7, 261–7
Renaissance, 217
representation: culture and gender and, 5–10; proportional, 315
reproduction, 121; liberation from, 47; as work, 272–3
reproductive rights, 69, 192–4
Republic, 143
research: intersectionality and, 73–5
Researchers and Academics of Colour for Equality (RACE), 47
residential schools, 130, 233; medical experimentation in, 187
retirement, 177–8
Rice, Carla, 16, 29–30, 123
Rich, Adrienne, 244; lesbianism and, 48, 64; motherhood and, 168, 180; patriarchy and, 46
Richards, Ellen Swallow, 239
rights: civil, 34; economic, 41; human, 186, 257, 322–4; legal,

41, 318–20; LGBTQ, 70; married women's, 133, 139; reproductive, 69, 192–4
Riot Grrrl movement, 18
risks: childbirth, 195; health, 186, 201–2, 203; occupational health, 203
ritual bath, 254
Robbins, Wendy, 60, 61–2
Robinson, Eden, 23
Roblin, Rodmond, 303
Roman Catholicism: women and, 264–5; *see also* Christianity
Rome, ancient, 220
Roosevelt, Eleanor, 186, 302–3
Rosie the Riveter, 280
Rousseau, Jean-Jacques, 37, 38, 222–3
Rousseff, Dilma, 307, 310
Roy, Arundhati, 23
Royal Canadian Mounted Police, 60, 285, 292
Royal Commission on the Status of Women, 318
Rubin, Gayle, 12, 83, 84, 100
Ruether, Rosemary Radford, 250
Rushdie, Salman, 27
Russ, Joanna, 95, 143, 160
Rwanda: education in, 226; genocide in, 148, 198; women in politics in, 307

El Saadawi, Nawal, 23
St Lewis, Joanne, 62
Sainte-Marie, Buffy, 12–13
saints, 249–50, 252
Salt-N-Pepa, 14
"salvation rhetoric," 257
Samuel, Clare, 281
"sandwich generation," 137
Sanger, Margaret, 320
Sangha, Jasjit, and Tahira Gonsalves, 167, 180
Sangster, Joan, 297
Sappho, 20–1, 165
Sarkeesian, Anita, 24
Saudi Arabia, 256
scholarship: feminist, 111, 114–15, 217–18; intersectionality and, 4, 60, 61, 72–5

schools: all-girl, 238; "gender-friendly," 228; residential, 130, 187, 233
Schopenhauer, Arthur, 33
science: as exclusionary, 53; sex differences and, 111–14; sexuality and, 115–17; women and, 238–41; *see also* STEM
Scott, Joan Wallach, 257
Seaman, Barbara, and Laura Eldridge, 212
Second Sex, The, 44, 46, 57
"second shift," 135, 274, 287, 312
sector: division of work by, 272
secularism, 253, 257
Sedna, 250
segregation: occupational, 272; professional, 284; racial, 233-4
Self-Employed Women's Association (SEWA), 293
self-employment, 290–1
self-esteem: girls' education and, 228
self-image, 16, 18
Selfridges, 95
Sendika Ouvriye Takstilak Abiman (SOTA), 289
separatism, gender, 47
septicemia, 39
serfdom, 277–8
Service Employees International Union, 71
service sector, 279, 282–3
settler states, 59, 129
Sevre-Duszynska, Janice, 259
sex: gender and, 82–3, 100–1; politics of, 114; premarital/extramarital, 131, 141
"sex/gender system," 83, 100
sexism, 43; intersectionality and, 62–3; post-modern feminism and, 48
sexual assault, 196–7, 230; *see also* sexual violence
sexuality: cultural representations of, 11–15; discourses of, 115–17; gender and, 84, 117; intersectionality and, 63–5; lesbian, 116; marriage and, 130, 131; medicalization of, 190, 195–6; mental health and, 208–9; terms for, 117; values and, 53; women's, 11–15, 36–7
sexualization, 11, 15
sexual liberation: Goldman and, 43
sexually transmitted diseases (STDs), 196, 204–6
sexual revolution, 10–12
Sexual Sterilization Act, 192–3
sexual violence: post-modern feminism and, 48; war and, 52, 148, 226; *see also* sexual assault
sex work, 205, 278
Shadd, Mary Ann, 234
Shakers, 144
shamans, 260
"sheconomy," 275
Shikibu, Murasaki, 221–2
Shiva, 250
Shiva, Vandana, 51
Shokado Women's Bookstore, 183
siblings, 163
Sierra Leone, 200–1
Sigurðardóttir, Jóhanna, 307, 310
Silko, Leslie Marmon, 260
Simard, Monique, 60
Simon Fraser University, 61
Simpson, Leanne, 23
Sinclair, Murray, 187
singlehood, 151–2, 176
Sirleaf, Ellen Johnson, 169, 307, 321, 323
sisterhood, 178
"Sisterhood is Universal," 69
Sister Wives, 133
"60s Scoop," 162
Skloot, Rebecca, 212
slavery, 139, 277–8; families and, 163, 167; sexual, 197, 198, 278
"Slut-Walk," 230
Smith, Barbara, 48
Smith, Dorothy, 54, 55
Smith, Malinda S., 62; and Fatima Jaffer, 79
Smith, Valerie, 73, 77
Smith, Zadie, 23
social causation approach, 207
social constructionist approach, 207
social determinants of health, 184
Social Gospel, 42–3

socialism: feminism and, 40–4, 55; scientific, 42; utopian, 42–3
socialization: gender and, 84–5; girls' education and, 227–8
social labour, 273
social learning theory, 94–5
social stratification, 276–7
Society of Friends, 261–2
socio-biology, 86
solidarity: intersectionality and, 62, 71, 76–7
soul(s), 109, 249–50
sovereignty: feminism, and, 60
Soviet Union, 42
Speirs, Rosemary, 313
Spelman, Elizabeth, 61, 73
"spirit," 109
Spivak, Gayatri Chakravorty, 60
Spoon, Rae, 84
Sprinkle, Annie, 12
standpoint theory, 54, 55, 56
Stanton, Elizabeth Cady, 138–9
state: families and, 127–8; gender registration and, 104; heterosexism and, 64; religion and, 248; settler, 59, 129; types of, 305
Statistics Canada: gender data and, 104; hate crimes and, 197; women in university and, 229; workforce and, 275, 284
Status of Women Canada, 275
Stein, Gertrude, 22
Steinem, Gloria, 54
STEM (science, technology, engineering, mathematics), 230, 238–41, 284
stepmothers, 173
stereotypes, gender, 9–10
sterilization, sexual, 69, 186, 192–3, 206
"sticky floor," 287
Stienstra, Deborah, 123
Stocker, David, 97–9
Stolen Sisters report, 60
Stoller, Rober, 82–3
Storm, 97–9
Stowe, Emily, 228–9, 262
Stowe, Harriet Beecher, 22
Stowe-Gullen, Augusta, 229

stratification, social, 276–7
Strohschein, Lisa, and Rose Weitz, 212
Strout, Elizabeth, 177–8
structural adjustment programs, 290
structuralism, 49
Stuckey, Johanna H., 269
substance abuse, 207, 208
Sudan: education in, 226
suffrage laws, 59; *see also* vote
suicide, 208–9
Sukarnoputri, Megawati, 307
"Sultana's Dream," 304
Summers, Lawrence, 114, 240
supernatural: females in, 248–52
Supreme Court of Canada: abortion and, 193; *Persons* case and, 318; sex work and, 278; Walmart and, 293
Supreme Court (US), 139, 149, 150
surgery, genital, 103
surrogacy, transnational, 188
surveillance, work, 282
sustainability, ecofeminism and, 51
Suttner, Bertha von, 321
sweatshops, 280–1
Sweden: families in, 146; women in politics in, 310
Swedish Academy, 8
Switzerland, 37

Taeko, Tomioka, 175
Taliban, 220, 221, 256, 257
TallMountain, Mary, 265
Taoism, 248
tattoos, 118
Tavakoli-Targhi, Mohamad, 35
Taylor, Harriet, 39–40
Tchambuli people, 87
teaching: feminization of, 231
Tegan and Sara, 13
television: "reality," 19; women and, 18–19
temperance movement, 42–3
tenure, 232, 285
testosterone, 89
Thatcher, Margaret, 134, 307
theatre: gender and, 102
theories: importance of, 32–4

Thobani, Sunera, 47, 62
Thompson, Clara, 91
Thornton Dill, Bonnie, and Marla Kohlman, 75
Toby's Law, 97–8
Tolstoy, Leo, 33, 141, 160
"tombois," 120
Toms, 84
Toor, Saadia, 257
total fertility rate (TFR), 136, 137
"trailing spouse," 134
Trans Murder Monitoring Project, 104
Transgender Archive, University of Victoria, 123
transgender people, 101, 103–4, 120; language and, 8; as mothers, 172; poverty and, 202; race and, 203
transphobia, 207
Tremblay, Diane-Gabrielle, 138
Tremonti, Anna Maria, 244
Triangle Shirtwaist Factory fire, 279
"trickster," 10
Trotula, 221
Trout, Jenny, 229
Trudeau, Justin, 307, 308, 315
Trudeau, Sophie Grégoire, 134
Truth, Sojourner, 35, 65, 66, 77
Truth and Reconciliation Commission, 130, 187, 233
Tsukiyama, Gail, 279
tubal ligation, 192
Tubman, Harriet, 21
Tunisia: Arab Spring in, 323
two-spirit people, 84, 151, 252

Udry, Richard, 88
Underground Railroad, 21
unemployment, 275, 291
unionization, 69
unions, 279, 280, 293
United Arab Emirates, 37
United Kingdom: child poverty in, 284; maternity leave in, 295; monarchy in, 306
United Nations, 186, 192; education and, 219–20; women's conferences and, 323–4; women's rights and, 256

United Nations Human Rights Committee, 129
United Nations Office on Drugs and Crime, 277
United Nations World Food Program, 276
United States: affirmative action in, 294; families in, 146–7, 149, 150; fundamentalism in, 256; marriage in, 139; maternity leave in, 295; sterilization in, 193; unemployment in, 291
Universal Declaration of Human Rights, 186
universities: faculty in, 285–6; female presidents of, 232; women employed by, 231–2, 285–6; women's, 238; women's enrolment in, 229–30
University of British Columbia, 230
University of New Brunswick, 180–1
University of Umeå, 104
urbanization: capitalism and, 276–7
uterus, 191, 206
Utopia, 143

Vaid, Urvashi, 300
Valian, Virginia, 231
values: reasoning and, 52, 53–5, 56
van den Hoonaard, Deborah, 174–5
Van Esterik, Penny, 2, 172
Vatican, 257, 259
veil, 255, 257, 266
Viagra, 196
videos, music, 12
Vienna Plan of Action, 324
Vietnam: war in, 322
Vincent, Carole, 297–8
violence: gendered, 196–201; intimate-partner, 196; sexual, 48, 52, 148; against women, 196–7, 226, 230, 300–1, 324; against women with disabilities, 63
"visiting unions," 150
Voice of Women for Peace, 322
voluntary associations, 6, 302, 320, 321
Vosko, Leah, 298
vote: in Canada, 37, 59; women's, 34, 37, 303, 317, 318

wage gap, 137, 275, 282–3
wages: academic, 231; capitalism and, 277; "living," 280; *see also* income; pay
Waite, Linda, and Maggie Gallagher, 135
Walcott, Charles Doolittle, 240
Walcott, Rinaldo, 30
Waldman, Ayelet, 168
Walker, Madame C.J., 16, 290
Wallach, Lori, 322
Walmart, 293
war: "culture," 237; ecofeminism and, 52; rape and, 148; sexual assault and, 148, 197–9; "on terror," 257; women's education and, 226; women's employment and, 139
war crime, 148
waves: as metaphor, 34–5
Weber, Andrew Lloyd, 27
Welchman, Lynn, and Sara Hossain, 75
Weld, Angelina Grimké, 262
Wells-Barnett, Ida, 65
Welter, Barbara, 85
Werner, Marion, 298
West, Candace, and Don H. Zimmerman, 90, 99
Weston, Kath, 149
"wet nurses," 172
Wheatley, Phillis, 262–3
Whiteside, Catharine, 189
white supremacy, 43
widowhood, 174–6
Williams, Venus and Serena, 18
Wilson, E.O., 86
Wilson, Lois, 259
Wilson, Margo, and Martin Daly, 75
Wilson-Raybould, Jody, 233
Winnipeg General Strike, 280
witch hunt, 50, 258–9
Witterick, Kathy, 97–9
Wittgenstein, Ludwig, 76
Wittig, Monique, 73
Wolf-Wendel, Lisa, 230–1
Wollstonecraft, Mary, 38–9; beauty and, 15; education and, 55, 138, 222–3
Woman's Christian Temperance Union, 42, 43, 266, 320

women: African American, 65–8; ancient and early modern ideas on, 33, 35–7; Asian, 110–11; black, 14–15, 17, 110, 139; as citizens, 316–20; cultural representation of, 5–10; Deaf, 63; definition of, 3–4, 32–7, 55; as deviant, 188–9; with disabilities, 63, 196, 209; education and, 215–44; "fragility" of, 85–6; health and, 182–212; heterosexual, 63–4; ideas about, 31–57; images of, 9–10; immortal, 249–50; incarcerated, 210; Indian, 24–8; language and, 8–9; law and, 318–20; life course of, 155–81; married, 133–5; music and, 12–15; number in workforce, 275; as "object," 44; obstacles to political office and, 312–13, 315; older, 209–10; as "other," 3–4, 44–5; political gains of, 308–10; political history of, 305–6; as political leaders, 307–15; political participation by, 320–4; political persecution of, 258–9; politics and, 299–327; racialized, 16, 18; re-entry, 236; religion and, 245–69; as religious leaders, 259–61; religious movements and, 255–7, 261–7; religious protection of, 255; right-wing, 311–12; role transitions of, 174–8; single, 151–2, 176; social support for, 293–5; as vulnerable, 207–10; as "weaker sex," 189; work and, 270–98; as worshippers, 255; *see also* Indigenous women; women of colour
Women in Trades Training Initiative, 282
Women Journalists Without Chains, 323
women of colour: education and, 230, 234–5; families and, 127–8; feminism and, 48; health and, 203; immigrant, 234; intersectionality and, 61–2, 65–8; representation of, 7; *see also* people of colour

Women's Enterprise Centre, 290
Women's Health Clinic, 183–4
Women's Health in Women's Hands, 183
women's health movement, 183–8, 187
women's liberation movement, 34, 140
Women's Political Equality League, 317
women's studies, 1, 81, 178, 218, 241
Woolf, Virginia, 22, 181, 244
Woolley, Hannah, 222, 223
work, 270–98; barriers to, 291–5; blue-collar, 282; educational, 231–2; emotional, 274; factory, 143, 279–82; families and, 137, 139; gender equity in, 69; girls', 160–1; health and, 203; married women and, 133–5; men and, 237; paid, 273, 277, 278–9, 290; paid domestic, 145, 278–9, 290; part-time, 274, 284; pink-collar, 282; politics of, 291–5; precarious, 283–4; sectors and, 272; service sector, 282–3; unpaid, 135, 271, 272, 273, 287–8; women's, 40, 41, 177, 277–88; *see also* employment; housework; labour
working class, 41, 277; factory, 279–82; paid domestic work, 278–9; skilled, 278
World Bank, 289
World Conference on Human Rights, 324
World Health Organization, 183, 194; definition of health and, 184; female genital cutting and, 199

World Trade Organization, 289, 322
World War II: gender and, 102; sex crimes in, 197
Wrigley, Edith, 43
writers: women, 22–3; Indigenous, 22–3

Young, Rebecca M., and Evan Balaban, 112
Yousafzai, Malala, 221
youth: gender-non-conforming, 101; *see also* boys; girls
Yugoslavia, 148, 198
Yuval-Davis, Nira, 52, 318; and Flora Anthias, 316

Zack, Naomi, 75–6
Zakaria, Rafia, 133, 154
Zetkin, Clara, 41–2, 321